THE PSYCHOLOGY OF INDIVIDUAL
AND GROUP DIFFERENCES

A Series of Books in Psychology

Editors:

Richard C. Atkinson
Jonathan Freedman
Gardner Lindzey
Richard F. Thompson

THE PSYCHOLOGY OF INDIVIDUAL AND GROUP DIFFERENCES

Lee Willerman
The University of Texas at Austin

W. H. Freeman and Company
San Francisco

Library of Congress Cataloging in Publication Data

Willerman, Lee, 1939–
    The psychology of individual and group differences.

    (A series of books in psychology)
    Bibliography: p.
    Includes index.
    1. Differences (Psychology)   2. Individuality.
3. Social groups.   4. Nature and nurture.   5. Intellect.
6. Personality. I. Title.
BF697.W494   155.2'2   78-9865
ISBN 0-7167-0292-4

Printed in the United States of America

1 2 3 4 5 6 7 8 9

This book is dedicated to the memory of

Ben

Contents

III   GROUP DIFFERENCES

Preface

Historically, the debate concerning the roles of nature and nurture in producing psychological differences among individuals and groups has assumed the character of a soap opera, continuing endlessly with little sign that a denouement is forthcoming. For many years battles between environmentalists and hereditarians have been little more than readings or misreadings of ambiguous or insufficient evidence combined with the prejudicial expression of political ideology. Today there are indications that the wider application of more powerful research methodologies may accelerate the resolution of these issues. In general, these approaches try to hold either genetic or environmental factors fairly constant while systematically permitting the other to vary. One of the main purposes of this book is to review both the methodology and the findings of these designs, especially as they apply to individual differences in intelligence, personality, education, and psychopathology, and to group differences according to sex, age, and ethnicity. A second purpose is to describe the scope of individual and group differences, with the intention of providing accurate information on what we know about differences among people.

During the past forty years three authors have published textbooks covering much the same territory as this one. The books by Anne Anastasi and Leona Tyler have gone through three editions each; Anastasi's last was published in 1958 and Tyler's in 1965. Both books can be regarded as classics in the field and can still be read profitably. The third book, by Raymond B. Cattell, which was published in 1971, bears the unmistakable imprint of his inventiveness and erudition but requires a relatively sophisticated background in many statistical matters to be properly understood.

The present volume attempts to update the field at a technical level appropriate to undergraduate students with little background other than introductory psychology and some statistics. The book should also be useful to graduate students in psychology, education, and human genetics who may never have obtained an overview of the field of differential psychology.

I have tried to provide comprehensive coverage of the topics in this book, but the subject is so vast that much justifiably relevant material had to be left out. I have undoubtedly erred on more than one occasion but hope the reader will find sufficient compensation so as not to judge too harshly the final product.

Although I must bear final responsibility for this book, the contributions of colleagues and students through discussion and argument have had an important influence on the ideas expressed herein. I want to thank the entire group in behavior genetics at the University of Texas at Austin for trying to keep me on the right path. I particularly want to single out John C. Loehlin for helping me to draw the proper inferences from much of the data, Jan Bruell for correcting some misunderstandings about genetics, David B. Cohen for continually challenging me to go beyond the information given, and Joseph M. Horn, whose extensive experience in teaching differential psychology has helped me to sift out some of the wheat from the chaff. Others who have made helpful contributions to this volume include Arnold H. Buss, Martin Manosevitz, Robert Plomin, Janet T. Spence, Delbert D. Thiessen, and Robert G. Turner.

I am also grateful to W. Hayward Rogers of W. H. Freeman and Company, who provided advice and encouragement during the preparation of the manuscript. Nancy Flight, project editor at Freeman, immensely improved the grammar and readability of the original manuscript. I also thank three outside reviewers who read earlier versions of all or portions of the manuscript: Arthur R. Jensen, K. Warner Schaie, and Richard Rose.

Finally, I want to express my gratitude to my wife Benné, who maintained good spirits during the strain of my preoccupation with the book, and to my children Raquel and Amiel, who good-naturedly endured my frequent evening absences from the family.

September 1978   Lee Willerman

THE PSYCHOLOGY OF INDIVIDUAL
AND GROUP DIFFERENCES

I

BACKGROUND

1

Introduction

Adaptation and diversity are facts of life. Those who cannot adapt biologically are destined for misfortune, because nature plays for keeps. Those who cannot adapt behaviorally may find themselves miserable because they cannot keep pace with their environment. But adaptation implies more than coping; it also means arriving at better solutions than those which previously existed. The historical collection of these solutions account for much of the diversity we observe among creatures of the same and of different species.

The dual themes of adaptation and diversity were the essence of Charles Darwin's monumental work on evolution, *On the Origin of the Species by Means of Natural Selection or the Preservation of Favoured Races in the Struggle for Life* (1859). He argued that many more individuals of a species are born than survive to reproduce offspring. Superior adaptability of some species members can account for differential survival, and this increased fitness often has a hereditary basis. If the adaptability has a hereditary component, those favored will tend to transmit their genetic advantage to their offspring, consequently making the offspring genetically more fit than those of the previous generation. The gradual accumulation of genetically based fitness is a major process in evolution; it leads to genetic differences among the members of a species as well as to the genetic differences between the species.

Adaptation and fitness values are specific to particular environments and to different components of those environments. Changes in environments or components thereof can affect adaptations, and what might have been adaptive once may be maladaptive at another time. All genetic adaptation, however, begins with genetic variation among the species members. Without that original variation, no hereditary changes can be transmitted to successive generations. If the observed variation were not due to genetic factors, then each new generation would have to start afresh in selecting out those who are to survive to produce offspring and no selective advantage would accrue to successive generations.

The house sparrow provides a good example of how adaptive selection responds to the environmental background. This bird is especially instructive because its date of introduction (1852) from Germany and England into America is known, and thus, since it breeds only once yearly, the number of generations in America is known precisely. Johnston and Selander (1964) have shown that the house sparrow has become differentiated throughout America according to many factors, including climate. Northern and Pacific Coast sparrows are more darkly pigmented, larger, and smaller billed than those from warmer and sunnier climates. Gradations in the physical characteristics occur fairly regularly as one moves through gradations in climate. Figure 1.1 gives the body weights of sparrows trapped in seventeen different cities and areas in Mexico, the United States, and Canada, according to isophanes. Isophanes are lines plotted through maps that represent similar climates after longitude, latitude, and altitude have been taken into account.

You can see that in general house sparrows from warmer climates weigh less than those from the colder climates. Climate is only one factor influencing body weight, however, and a fuller picture emerges if other regional factors are also taken into account. The assumption is that much of the genetic variation was already present among the first members of the species to enter America. Species members that happened to have the traits suitable to a particular environment were at a selective advantage and, consequently, were more likely to leave offspring than ones deficient in those characteristics. The offspring of the genetically superior species members in turn were more likely to have the appropriate characteristics, and so on.

Darwin's theory of evolution sent rumblings of earthquake proportions through Western scientific and religious circles. It directly countered religious antievolution arguments, which stated that the variety and superb fitness of creatures were due to special creation and

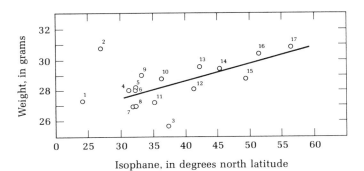

Figure 1.1

Mean body weights of adult house sparrows plotted against isophanes (see text for explanation). Localities: 1. Oaxaca City, Mexico; 2. Progreso, Texas; 3. Mexico City, Mexico; 4. Houston, Texas; 5. Los Angeles, California; 6. Austin, Texas; 7. Death Valley, California; 11. Oakland, California; 12. Las Cruces, New Mexico; 13. Lawrence, Kansas; 14. Vancouver, B.C.; 15. Salt Lake City, Utah; 16. Montreal, Quebec; 17. Edmonton, Alberta. (From R. F. Johnston and R. K. Selander, "House Sparrows: Rapid Evolution of Races in North America," *Science* 144 [May 1964]: 548–550. Copyright © 1964 by the American Association for the Advancement of Science.)

the beauty of God's design. Acrimonious debates between opposing factions followed, but independent evidence generally began to accumulate on the side of Darwin. The fossil record was particularly instructive in this regard, because it showed that the vast majority of species that had ever existed were now extinct. If the Biblical account of creation were correct, then there should have been no biological "mistakes" or dead ends in the fossil record.

Darwin did not invent the concept of evolution, as it had been bruited about in conversation and written about for many years preceding the publication of his book. *The Origin of the Species* was in fact hastily published in response to a preprint of a shorter enunciation of the evolutionary thesis by A. R. Wallace, the two pieces appearing simultaneously.

Landmark Developments in Individual Differences

FRANCIS GALTON

A half-cousin of Darwin, Francis Galton, was overwhelmed by the force of Darwin's evolutionary argument. For him the book had driven away "the constraint of my old superstition as if it had been a nightmare" (in

Forrest 1974, p. 84). Galton went on to become the acknowledged father of individual differences with the publication of his own book, *Hereditary Genius: An Inquiry into Its Laws and Consequences*, in 1869. It should be noted, however, that the paternity could be attributed to Darwin himself, for his book included a section entitled "Individual Differences," in which he said:

> No one supposes that all individuals of the same species are cast in the same actual mould. These individual differences are of the highest importance for us, for they are often inherited, as must be familiar to everyone; and they thus afford materials for natural selection to act on and accumulate [1958 edition, p. 59].

Galton, however, went on to extend this remark both theoretically and empirically, assiduously applying the results of his observations and methods to the question of individual differences among humans.

Hereditary Genius was only one of many books that Galton published during his long life. We shall take up some of his findings in detail in Chapter 4, but the essential argument of that book is that genius seems to follow hereditary lines; some families have much more than their fair share of geniuses. Galton did not have much respect for the environment as a promoter of genius. His cursory studies of individuals reared by unrelated or distantly related people of high social status failed to find frequent eminence among those individuals. Thus, he argued, the advantage of high social status was not responsible for outstanding achievements.

The actual details of these studies are not given in his book, but the strategy of using individuals reared by those unrelated to them has formed the basis of the adoption design, one of the most effective techniques for untangling genetic and environmental influences on behavior traits. More shall be said about this design in Chapter 5.

ALFRED BINET

One of the most significant figures in the history of individual differences is Alfred Binet, who is best known for authoring, with T. Simon in 1905 in France, the first recognized intelligence scale. This accomplishment was by no means his only important one; he investigated many different problems of relevance to contemporary psychology, including mental abnormality, imageless thought, creativity, hypnosis, graphology, and other topics. Wolf's (1973) recently published biography of Binet nicely illustrates his prodigious inventiveness and perspicacity.

Binet's intelligence scale was predicated on the notion that in intelligence elementary sensory processes were less important than judgment. Thus, he included items that increased in complexity with age, were relatively unrelated to formal schooling, and required good judgment and reasoning for successful performance. The value of this test, which was translated into English in 1908 by Goddard and revised by Terman at Stanford in 1916, is that it provided quantitative estimates of intelligence rather than unvalidated judgments. Testing procedures were standardized so that the results would be "affected neither by the bad humor nor bad digestion of the examiner" (in DuBois 1970).

THE EQUALITY ASSUMPTION AND THE EUGENICS MOVEMENT

The assumption that individuals are born with equal capacities and potential was challenged by much of Darwin's and Galton's work. Their perspective was regarded with apprehension and fear, because it could serve as a justification for the status quo and preserve existing inequalities. Philosophers such as Herbert Spencer could maintain that *laissez faire* governmental policies were the most righteous ones to follow on the ground that they would ensure the continued evolution of the human species by eliminating those least fit. These social Darwinists, as they came to be called, founded the eugenics movement, which was the attempt to improve the human race by scientific means through selective breeding.

The eugenics movement, which was also fathered by Galton, included a curious mélange, among whom could be counted distinguished philosophers and scientists, humanistic social workers, racists and scoundrels, those who supported hereditary doctrines and those who did not (Haller 1963). Custodians of institutions for the retarded and insane were among the most vociferous advocates of the eugenics movement. They saw widespread illegitimacy and faulty care of children and wanted to reduce illegitimacy rates, first by castration and later by sterilization. These leaders did not necessarily believe that heredity was responsible for the generations of social dependents but recognized that, if such individuals were prevented from reproducing, much misery, regardless of cause, would be averted.

Incendiary stories about families such as the Jukes (Dugdale 1877) and the Kallikaks (Goddard 1912), who presumably produced hundreds of criminals, paupers, feebleminded, alcoholics, and insane over the five or six generations they could be traced, raised fears in the minds of many. Goddard (1912) summarized his findings this way:

> The Kallikak family presents a natural experiment in heredity. A young man of good family becomes through two different women the ancestor of two lines of descendants,—the one characterized by thoroughly good, respectable, normal citizenship, with almost no exceptions; the other

being equally characterized by mental defect in every generation.... In later generations, more defect was brought in from other families through marriage....

We find on the good side of the family prominent people in all walks of life and nearly all of the 496 descendants owners of land or proprietors. On the bad side we find paupers, criminals, prostitutes, drunkards, and examples of all forms of social pest with which modern society is burdened [p. 116].

Goddard relied extensively on a fieldworker named Elizabeth S. Kite for information on the current status of the descendants. Kite's enthusiasm for the project was commendable, but the precision of her inferences left much to be desired. For example, this is an account of a home visit:

... the girl of twelve should have been at school, according to the law, but when one saw her face, one realized it made no difference. She was pretty, with olive complexion and dark languid eyes, but there was no mind there.... Benumbed by this display of human degeneracy, the field worker went out into the icy street [Goddard 1912, p. 73].

Kite's diagnosis was unacceptable by current standards. Furthermore, could one ever reasonably conclude that such impairment, even if supported by objective evidence, could be due to heredity and not to the impoverished environment? Even from a genetic perspective, only one-half of the genetic complement is transmitted from each parent to each child. Six generations after the feebleminded mate of Kallikak, Sr., bore a child, the degree of genetic overlap between this unnamed woman and the comtemporaneous Kallikaks would only be $(0.5)^6$, or one sixty-fourth. Of course other deviants marrying into the family after Kallikak, Sr., could help to maintain the disastrous status of the line.

What is needed to untangle the genetic and environmental arguments are designs that can trace directly the genes themselves or adoption studies of children reared in environments unlike the environments of their biological parents. It is important to note, however, that from one eugenic perspective it was not urgent to distinguish between hereditary and environmental factors as causes of the generations of deficients. The most important thing was to prevent such tainted individuals from reproducing, regardless of cause of the taint.

With the development of the intelligence test by Binet in 1905, many quantitative reports followed showing that a great proportion of those in public institutions were feebleminded, and arguments appeared to assume an even more scientific patina. During World War I, the federal government commissioned a group of American psychologists to devise a group-administered intelligence test, the purposes of which were to identify the feebleminded so that they could be excluded from service and to select those most fit to be officers (Yerkes 1921). One conclusion drawn from this eight-hundred-page report was that nearly half of the potential inductees had mental ages from seven to twelve years, so that the population seemed to be overrun by morons.

These workers failed to recognize fully that there was a large element of arbitrariness to the assignment of mental ages. More importantly, the argument could be hoisted by its own petard, since the potential inductees were individuals in the generality, presumably functioning adequately, and not in institutions. It was one thing to say that most inmates of institutions were retarded; it was another to say that morons made up a large proportion of the general population.

Some eugenic activists tried to persuade state governments to pass laws promoting sterilization of various classes of unfortunates. There was also considerable eugenic effort directed at stemming the wave of immigration to the United States for fear that the good American stock would become degenerate by breeding with inferior elements or be swamped by the greater fecundity of those immigrant populations. Accounts of this period can be found in Haller (1963) and Kamin (1974). The latter account provides a view that is occasionally very penetrating but is often unnecessarily litigious and one-sided. For example, Kamin claims that the mental testers had a powerful influence on immigration policies in the United States. Samelson (1975), after a careful reading of congressional hearings as well as the literature of that time, points out that this view is erroneous. Mental testers appear to have had no discernible influence on immigration policies. Unfortunately, biased accounts of that era often fail to point out that the eugenics movement had both scoundrels and saints.

Almost all eugenic arguments lacked a historical perspective. Great civilizations had come and gone. Greeks, Italians, Spanish, Chinese, Egyptians, and Persians had at various times represented the apotheosis of civilization. Less than four hundred years before eugenicists decried the influx of Italian immigrants into America, the Renaissance had its center in Italy and those of "good American stock" might have been regarded as nearly feral. While we do not have good answers for why civilizations rise and fall, it seems clear that abrupt changes in the successes of civilization cannot be traced to hereditary factors alone.

The extreme social Darwinist view was essentially that those who performed below some arbitrary social norm did so because of genetic inferiority. This view is, of course, unscientific and pernicious. Nevertheless, individuals do differ in their genetic makeup and some do possess genetic traits that are unappreciated by the society in which they live. It is almost impossible to state with certainty (except for clear-cut disorders such as Downs syndrome) that the deficient performance of a particular individual is due to his genes, but the theoretical picture clearly indicates that hereditary influences have important behavioral consequences for specific individuals and families.

There was certainly no justification, give the state of knowledge in 1930, for Watson's famous utterance:

> Give me a dozen healthy infants, well-formed, and my own specified world to bring them up in and I'll guarantee to take any one at random and train him to become any type of specialist I might select—doctor, lawyer, artist, merchant-chief and, yes, even beggar-man and thief, regardless of his talents, penchants, tendencies, abilities and vocation, and race of his ancestors [Watson 1930, p. 104].

From the foregoing review it should be clear that the study of the origin of individual differences as a science had its roots in biology, although much of the research has been done with behavior rather than with genetic or physiological elements directly. In general, the effort has been focused on inferring underlying physiological and genetic processes from the observed behavior. The picture is now changing somewhat as the development of new techniques permits more direct identification of the underlying physiological and genetic mechanisms.

GREGOR MENDEL

In 1865 Gregor Mendel first reported the results of his experiments with garden peas. These experiments paved the way for the understanding of many genetic mechanisms and represented an achievement of extraordinary proportions. The garden pea is particularly useful for genetic experiments because it can be grown and crossed readily. In addition, each plant contains both the male and female sexual apparatus, so it can be "selfed" when desired. In his 1866 paper Mendel described genetic studies on seven different traits for these peas, among which was height. Previously selfed plants were divided into tall and dwarf peas, and, when each plant was permitted to pollinate itself, tall peas produced only tall offspring (about six feet high) and dwarf peas produced only dwarf offspring (about one foot high).

When the tall plants were crossed with the dwarfs to produce the F_1 generation, only tall plants resulted. When the tall plants from the F_1 generation were then selfed to yield the F_2 generation, however, they produced offspring in a $3:1$ ratio of tall to dwarf.

An important conclusion drawn from these observations was that genes could account for differences as well as similarities between parents and offspring. Thus, tall parents produce not only tall offspring but dwarf offspring as well. The fact that each individual contains both types of parented genes and that the two types independently segregate in the offspring became known as Mendel's *principle of segregation*.

The second major principle discovered by Mendel was the *law of independent assortment.* When plants had two or more different characters, each behaving like height, the various combinations of the two characters in the offspring followed the laws of probability. The occurrence of each particular combination could be predicted by multiplying the probability of one type's occurrence by the probability of the other type's occurrence. Thus, if tall peas occurred .75 of the time and yellow peas occurred .25 of the time, then the probability of the occurrence of a tall yellow pea would be .75 $\times$ .25 = .1875.

The significance of Mendel's discoveries was not appreciated for thirty-five years, although they were occasionally cited by some investigators working in plant hybridization. It was only in 1900 that the full importance of Mendel's work was understood.

In 1909 Johannsen made the distinction between *phenotype,* which refers to the visible or measurable characteristics of the organism, and *genotype,* which refers to the genetic composition of the organism. Strictly speaking, one never sees the genes themselves but only their consequences in the phenotype. The important point of Johannsen's distinction is that there is not always a perfect correspondence between genotype and phenotype. He also pointed out that the phenotype could be affected by a variety of environmental influences but the genotype would remain unchanged.

The laws of Mendel were of undoubted importance, but there awaited an approach that would deal adequately with the inheritance of continuously graded characters rather than characters that could take only two or three values. Mendel's principles as first enunciated applied only to traits showing dominance and recessivity. It was later learned that, even for traits affected by single genetic locations, intermediate types could also be distinguished. Further, it appeared that some traits were affected by multiple genes, and the relatively simple rules derived from Mendel had to be extrapolated by quantitative analyses to these continuously graded characteristics. Some of the developments in statistical methodology relevant to these problems are given in Chapters 2, 3, and 5 and will not be discussed here.

BEHAVIOR GENETICS

Much of this early work suggested that observed differences between individuals often had biological underpinnings. The eugenics movement had suggested this relationship with respect to human behavior traits, but the evidence was often seriously flawed or questionable. A series of studies initiated by Tolman and his students in the 1920s attempted to show under more rigorous experimental conditions that "intelligence" as measured in animals seemed to follow genetic laws as well.

In 1924 Edward Tolman began to select rats that were either bright or dull, according to their performance in a learning maze. The best of the bright rats were mated to other brights and the poorest learners to other sibling dulls. From the beginning the results indicated appreciable differences in learning ability between the offspring of these two types of rats, but successive generations of inbreeding the brights with the brights and the dulls with the dulls produced no further increases in differences in learning ability among the offspring. One suggestion was that the successive matings of brothers and sisters had deleterious consequences itself, a hypothesis that turned out to be correct.

Tryon continued the work of Tolman, still using brother-sister matings. Over twenty-two generations the offspring of dull rats made more errors than the offspring of bright rats, but by the seventh generation the differences were about as large as they would ever be. McClearn and DeFries (1973) provide a review of this early work, pointing out that generalizations from the observed results might be affected by inbreeding or lack of an unselected control group that might correct for long-term environmental changes that could have influenced the learning scores over successive generations. They further suggest that selected lines should be replicated in separate experiments, since the results might be unstable from one group of rats to the next.

McClearn and DeFries (1973) report an experiment in which these problems were corrected for a trait of open field activity level in mice, the results of which are shown in Figure 1.2. The results show considerable responsiveness to selection for high or low open field activity over the generations; the two groups selected for high open field activity are somewhat more active than the controls and substantially more active than the groups selected for low activity. These findings, in conjunction with those of Tryon, support the view that genetic influences can play a considerable role in behavior.

We must hasten to add, however, that Searle (1949) showed that the performance of the maze-bright animals was relatively specific to the particular apparatus that Tryon employed. Searle found that maze-dull animals either equaled or outperformed maze-bright animals on three of five different mazes. Thus, the generalization to the breeding of human intelligence appears unwarranted. Human intellectual performance as measured by traditional ability tests can be generalized across situations, and this was not the case for the Tryon animals. It is possible, however, that animals can be bred for optimal performance over a variety of mazes; this situation would more closely approximate the generalizability of intellectual functioning in humans.

Those who ignore genetic differences in their studies may be treading on perilous grounds. One example of this danger is especially interesting because the researchers involved should have known better. Edward Tolman, in addition to initiating some important work in behavior

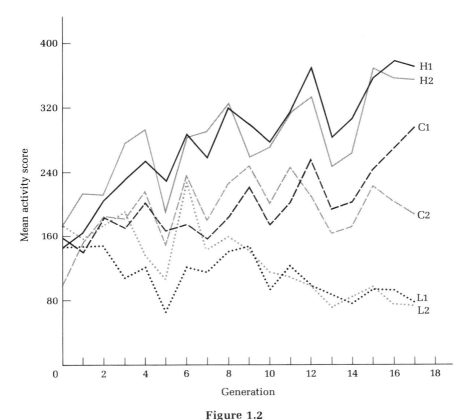

Figure 1.2

Response to selection for open field activity in mice. (From G. E. McClearn and J. C. DeFries, *Introduction to Behavioral Genetics.* San Francisco: W. H. Freeman and Company. Copyright © 1973.)

genetics, was an influential learning theorist who developed a cognitive theory of learning that emphasized concepts like "cognitive maps," "purposive behavior," and "expectancies." These cognitive labels were meant to apply to animals as well as to humans. Another school of learning theorists, led by Clark Hull and Kenneth Spence, emphasized "stimulus-response connections" and could be considered noncognitive in comparison with Tolman's orientation (Hilgard and Bower 1966). A feud in the professional literature between these two schools went on for years. Jones and Fennell (1965) noted, however, that the rats used by these two schools had different genetic backgrounds; one group had been bred in California, the other in Iowa. Jones and Fennell brought representatives of both strains to their laboratory in Florida. The animals were then put in a runway maze under conditions of either thirst or hunger, and the speed with which they ran down the runway to the reward was measured.

Figure 1.3 gives the results from that study. The upper curve gives the times it took the "Tolman" rats to run down the alley to a reward, and the lower curve gives the times it took the "Spence" rats to run down the alley. In both cases the rats were timed over a period of ten days. You can see that the Tolman rats took considerably more time traveling down the runway than the Spence rats. Jones and Fennell (1965) had this to say about the two strains of animals:

> The ... [Tolman] animals spent long periods of time in exploratory behaviors, sniffing along the walls, in the air, along the runway. Even toward the end of testing, they would stop, seemingly without reason, and renew their explorations.... Retracing was frequent. The Spence animals behaved differently. After the first two days, the animals popped out of the start box, ambled down the runway.... [p. 294]

The behaviors of these two strains of animals agree almost perfectly with the types of theories developed by the two orientations. The Tolman rats appeared very cognitive and thoughtful, the Spence rats very stimulus-response oriented. Had the two schools of thought compared the strains of animals they were using earlier, the controversy might have been averted. Which strain of animals is more useful for studies of

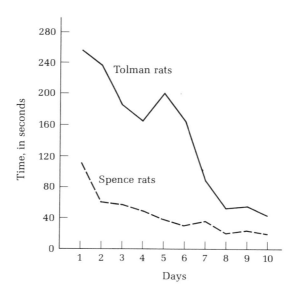

Figure 1.3

Averaged runway times under hunger or thirst in Spence and Tolman rats. (Adapted from Jones and Fennell 1965.)

learning becomes an empirical question, but it does seem apparent that the theories developed were considerably influenced by the strain of animal that happened to be employed.

Some of the simplest relations between genotypes and environments are shown in Figure 1.4. The vertical axis grades some hypothetical response, such as error, weight, or degree of pigmentation. The horizontal axis grades some hypothetical environmental factor, such as degree of environmental stimulation, nutrition, or temperature. The different lines represent the responses of different genotypes to these environmental changes. The graphs illustrate the kinds of insights that can be drawn from consideration of genotypic differences in responses to various kinds of environments.

Graph A in the figure shows two different genotypes and their responses to some environmental factor. Both show similar increases in response to changes in the environment, but the starting levels of the two genotypes differ. This circumstance is referred to as a difference in

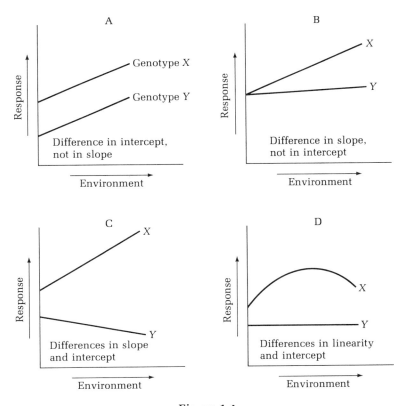

Figure 1.4

A sampler of relationships between genotypes and environments.

intercept but not in slope. Graph B illustrates two genotypes that start out similarly but differ in their response to the environment; they differ in slope but not in intercept. Graph C shows differences in slope and intercept as a function of genotype. Both genotypes start out at different levels and respond to environmental changes differently. These are all examples of linear changes, but relationships can also be nonlinear. In Graph D one genotype does not respond at all to changes in the environment, while the other one shows a curvilinear relationship to changes in the environment. Empirical examples of such interactions between genotypes and environments can be found in Vale and Vale (1969). The foregoing is only meant to acquaint you with the variety of responses that different genotypes may have to different environments.

These examples imply that environments can be graded on some dimension of interest. This implication has proved to be one of the biggest stumbling blocks in many of the studies to be cited. With lower animals it is possible to vary the environment systematically, but with humans it is difficult to decide which environment is "high" and which is "low." Take the example of high social class. Many aspire to reach the higher social echelons, but being a member of the higher social class does not indicate superiority on all relevant dimensions. One can imagine that high social class may foster intellectual achievements, but it may not encourage independence. It should be clear that the assessment of environments deserves as much attention as the assessment of genotypes. Fine-grained analyses of environments will probably be required before strong inferences can be made about the relationship of different genotypes to different environments. Thus, there is a need for those primarily interested in the genotype to join with those focusing on the environment. One hopes that this merger is what the new discipline of behavior genetics will accomplish.

The beginning of a distinct discipline called behavior genetics began with the publication of a book entitled *Behavior Genetics,* by Fuller and Thompson, in 1960. They reviewed the literature relevant to the topic and showed how attention to genetic factors could lead to powerful insights about behavior. Since then the field has burgeoned. Some investigators primarily interested in environmental influences have also gone into behavior genetics because they see that controlling for genetic factors can give a more sensitive index of how the environment operates. Investigators in behavior genetics have to learn both the principles of psychology and genetics in order to do their work.

The Discipline of Individual Differences

Psychologists can be classified broadly into two disciplines. One has its roots in experimental psychology, the other in correlational psychology or individual differences. In the model of experimental psychology, the experimenter creates two or more conditions by assigning different treatments to different conditions—the control group may represent the assignment of "no treatment" to a condition. Differences that emerge among the treatment conditions are then presumed to be under control of the variable or variables manipulated by the experimenter. The experimentalist assigns subjects randomly to each treatment to ensure that subjects in the different treatment conditions will not differ initially on the average for the variables of interest. Indeed, any relevant variations in the subjects' responses to a particular treatment condition are often undesired and regarded as error variance. The experimentalist's Valhalla would be a situation in which all subjects within a particular treatment responded exactly alike.

The differential or correlational psychologist is mainly interested in how things go together in nature rather than in creating differences by means of experimental manipulations (Cronbach 1957). For example, the correlational psychologist might look for relationships between intelligence and longevity. The investigator would not try to manipulate either one of the variables but would simply try to see whether they are related in any way in the natural world. Since the historical traditions of correlational psychologists are rooted in biology, they are naturally more concerned with the variations that nature produces than with those that can be achieved in the laboratory.

For many years these two disciplines acted in opposition or ignored each other. They neither read the same journals nor traveled in the same circles. For the differential psychologist, description was usually followed by theory; for the experimentalist, theory often preceded description. As Cronbach put it, the origin of differential psychology lay in asking how much people varied, while the experimental psychologists were concerned with estimating central tendencies.

The rift between the two disciplines was unnecessary. Often variations in nature needed to be brought into the laboratory for dissection and greater control. Conversely, propositions derived from laboratory experimentation needed to be tested outside the laboratory. Cronbach called for greater unification between the two disciplines, and there are strong signs that the rapprochement is now beginning to occur.

One such example comes from the area of high-speed information processing, largely developed by experimental psychologists. Experimentalists in this area were mainly concerned with the component stages of storing and retrieving information. Their search was for general principles that characterized all beings, and individual differences were often ignored. Recently, workers such as Hunt, Lunneborg, and Lewis (1975) have begun to apply concepts and methods derived from this body of research to the issue of individual differences in intelligence. They found, for example, that highly intelligent individuals could process relatively simple items of information more rapidly than people of average intelligence. The stimuli used in these researches are usually overlearned and do not call for tasks that are "difficult" for subjects to perform successfully.

At the theoretical level these two disciplines differ as to how science should best proceed. The experimentalists argue that we must first work out the basic mechanisms, and individual differences will be explained later by the interaction of these mechanisms. The differential psychologists emphasize the statistical properties of the problems they investigate. Statistics and genetics are their tools for the analysis of descriptive information.

At a practical level the two disciplines seem to be distinguished by major differences in attitudes and personal interests (Pastore 1949). The differential psychologist finds laboratory work remote and uninteresting and prefers natural phenomena that are more closely tied to "real life." The experimentalist finds the complexities of dissecting phenomena outside the control of the laboratory too unwieldy for investment.

Plan of the Book

The plan for this book is to take each trait of interest for human individual differences and try to specify its frequency and distribution in the population. Then, available data permitting, each of the traits will be examined from the perspective both of genetic and of environmental influences. I have not tried to be exhaustive in the recitation of study after study. Rather I have tried to provide examples of studies that have been most important in arriving at empirical and theoretical inferences about the traits discussed.

The author's bias should be made explicit in a book that presents only a small proportion of a vast literature. This is especially so when other psychologists could plausibly focus on a different set of approaches and incorporate research and theoretical findings not mentioned here. Many psychologists working in individual differences are primarily interested in statistical methodology and psychological measurement; these areas, however, do not strongly represent my own interests and talents. I do think such areas important, but a text that focuses on them has little room for much else. Furthermore, good current texts are already available in these areas.

One of my biases is to emphasize psychological traits that have some promise of being linked to biological phenomena. This preference is not meant to be a retreat from trying to understand psychological traits in their own terms, that is, from having recourse to antecedent psychological phenomena as explanation, but comes from a feeling that we have already been too quick to use one psychological variable as an explanation for another. Consider, for example, a child who has been mistreated by his parents and grows up to be a criminal. Common sense suggests that it is no wonder the child turned out that way, given the parental mistreatment. Such an explanation may be true, but, on the other hand, the child may have been hyperactive and relatively invulnerable to parental discipline, the mistreatment following rather than preceding the obstreperous behavior of the child. It may not have been psychological factors alone, but those factors in concert with biological dispositions, that increased the likelihood that the child would become deviant. Such a view explicitly acknowledges the value of an interdisciplinary approach and recognizes that, by connecting ourselves with the biological sciences, we may be in a better position to exploit variables that have already been well studied in other disciplines.

This book has a distinctly behavior genetic bias. My justification for this bias is that it helps to evaluate a large, and often competing, set of explanations for many traits of psychological interest. If, for example, no genetic (or other biological) evidence could be adduced to account for differences in a trait of psychological interest, then one might be justified in focusing exclusively on antecedent psychological variables to explain the trait under study. On the other hand, if it were shown that genetic (or other biological) factors play a large role in the expression of the trait, then a different set of investigative strategies might be undertaken.

The focus will not be exclusively on the genetics, however; we will also look at environmental influences when genetic factors are held constant or statistically controlled. Furthermore, the focus will be almost entirely on human behavior traits, with only occasional examples from studies on lower animals.

Much of experimental design and statistics can be appreciated from a logical or intuitive point of view rather than from a rigorous statistical one, and I have given preference to the logical and intuitive wherever possible. Unfortunately, I could often see no way to avoid statistical issues without considerable loss of expository efficiency.

Some areas of individual differences are more advanced than others, and this is undoubtedly reflected in the precision of the inferences that can be drawn. Some topics in individual differences are currently being reexamined because there has not been much progress over the years, and it is quite possible that much of what we believe now will have to be discarded in favor of radically new conceptual orientations. One could optimistically assume that the best has already been said, but a more probable eventuality is that almost a complete revamping of the field will be necessary for substantial signs of progress. One should not despair at this possibility, because the excitement of discovery awaits those who are to follow.

2

Some Statistics
and Measurement

Whenever we look for individual differences we usually find them. Such differences are usually those of degree, although even small differences in degree can lead to very substantial differences in consequence. Consider, for example, the difference in speed of a first-class runner and a world champion. For the 100-meter dash, this difference is probably less than half a second; yet a first-class sprinter garners little fame and fortune, while the world champion is feted and admired by millions. Thus, small differences are often magnified by cultures and may lead to qualitatively different consequences.

Why the "best" are so revered is a deep question, but this reverence is certainly present in animals below man, as can be seen in dominance hierarchies and other recognitions of superiority. Perhaps such reverence lies in a primordial recognition that the "best" are the most likely to enhance the survival of the group in times of difficulty. This chapter will document the extent of differences between individuals as well as show how we measure differences in ways that permit us to describe them in summary form and make inferences about them.

Extent of Individual Differences

Let us start with an animal common in Texas—the nine-banded armadillo. This creature routinely produces four monozygous (genetically identical) quadruplets. Consequently, within an armadillo litter genetic differences are eliminated and the influence of other biological and environmental factors can be checked.

Storrs and Williams (1968) sacrificed the offspring of sixteen armadillo mothers at birth and obtained measures of twenty different biological parameters for the offspring. Since all the offspring were killed at birth, none of the observed differences can be due to variations in postnatal experiences. Table 2.1 gives some values for eight of the twenty parameters presented in the original article.

The first column gives the maximal differences across all the animals born to the sixteen mothers. The median difference between the largest and smallest animal was 4.5-fold. The median was chosen to represent the average instead of the mean because it is not influenced by very extreme scores. For example, the 86-fold difference for brain epinephrine (a substance involved in neural transmission), if averaged with the others to obtain a mean, would produce almost a 4.5-fold difference alone. The median, which represents the middlemost score of the twenty parameters, is unaffected by such extreme scores.

The second column gives the values for the litter that showed the greatest differences among its members for that particular measure. These differences are also substantial, averaging 2.4-fold.

Table 2.1

A sampler of differences within and between
quadruplet nine-banded armadillo offspring sets

	Relative difference across all individuals	Maximum difference within a set
Birth weight	4.0-fold	2.5-fold
Brain weight	2.4-fold	63%
Heart weight	2.9-fold	92%
Kidney weight	2.1-fold	68%
Liver weight	2.6-fold	49%
Small intestine length	2.3-fold	70%
Brain epinephrine	86.0-fold	6.6-fold
Glycine in brain	5.6-fold	3.4-fold
Median for all 20 traits	4.5-fold	2.4-fold

Source: From Storrs and Williams 1968.

Storrs and Williams (1968) suggest that there are factors involved in the unequal splitting of extranuclear cell material that affect how much tissue of a particular kind will be produced. Even if each cell in an organ is programmed to produce a specified amount of product that is identical at the cell level for each genetically identical member of a litter, the number of cells in the organ varies from one member of the litter to another, thus producing vastly different amounts of the substance in each. If this theory is correct, we can no longer be sure that even genetically identical twins are really identical in terms of their characteristic biological functions.

One could quarrel with the use of the highest and lowest scores to form these ratios. The most extreme scores probably contain more measurement error, and the arithmetic ratios need not imply that the functional relationships are in similar proportion to these ratios. For example, compensatory factors may be present that reduce the efficiency of larger organs in relation to smaller ones (e.g., too large a structure might mean insufficient nutrient to the internal mass). Finally, "abnormal" individuals are more likely to be found at the extremes than in the middle.

At the outset we must acknowledge that there is no simple solution to this problem of determining the range of individual differences. Wechsler (1952) suggests that, instead of the most extreme scores, the second lowest per thousand and the second highest per thousand be used to construct these ratios. His "range ratio" would presumably exclude the rare abnormal cases and lead to more reliable estimates. Wechsler has compiled a large catalog of such differences in physiological and behavioral functions, after various statistical controls had been applied. Some of these differences are shown in Table 2.2.

Because so many of the values are less than a 3 : 1 ratio, Wechsler proposes that there might be a natural constant akin to such constants found in other areas of science and mathematics. The ratios of most interest to us are those associated with perceptual and intellectual abilities, and these are all above the 2 : 1 ratio. Wechsler suggests that psychological and perceptual functions have a larger range ratio because more components enter into the ultimate product. The psychological ratios are also those which are determined by arbitrary scaling units, and variations in the unit or the method of measurement could lead to very different outcomes.

In general, the measurements from Storrs and Williams show a greater range than those of Wechsler. Perhaps this is due to a species difference; other selective differences, such as newborns versus young adults (if aged individuals had been included, the range of scores would have been much greater); or the different ways for determining the ratios.

Table 2.2

Distribution of total range ratios

Trait or ability	Range ratio	Trait or ability	Range ratio
Body temperature	1.03 : 1	Respiratory rate	1.88 : 1
Calcium in spinal fluid	1.16 : 1	Platelets in blood	1.90 : 1
Urea in urine	1.21 : 1	Uric acid in blood	1.91 : 1
Length of head	1.22 : 1		
Breadth of head	1.23 : 1	High jump	2.01 : 1
Stature at birth	1.23 : 1	Rotation of eyeball	2.05 : 1
Hemoglobin in blood	1.25 : 1	Pulse rate (adult)	2.03 : 1
Calcium in blood	1.26 : 1	Blood pressure	2.03 : 1
Length of leg	1.26 : 1	Broad jump	2.07 : 1
Adult stature	1.27 : 1	Speed of inserting bolts	2.09 : 1
Acidity of blood	1.29 : 1	Upper limit of audibility	2.09 : 1
Cephalic index	1.27 : 1		
		Stringing discs	2.12 : 1
Length of femur	1.31 : 1	Weight of healthy heart	2.14 : 1
Sitting height	1.31 : 1	Vital capacity (age and height	
Height of sternal notch	1.31 : 1	constant)	2.13 : 1
Heat of body (per surface		Flexion of wrist	2.18 : 1
area	1.32 : 1		
Length of foot	1.32 : 1	Tapping	2.20 : 1
Span of arms	1.33 : 1	Simple reaction time	2.24 : 1
Duration of pregnancy	1.37 : 1	General intelligence (Binet	
Length of middle finger	1.39 : 1	M.A.)	2.30 : 1
Interpupillary distance	1.40 : 1	Weight of body at birth	2.32 : 1
Sugar in blood	1.40 : 1	Weight of healthy kidney	2.37 : 1
Phosphorus acid in urine	1.40 : 1		
Circumference of calf	1.43 : 1	Weight of hair	2.40 : 1
Length of arms	1.44 : 1	Weight of body (adult)	2.44 : 1
		Simple learning	2.42 : 1
Heat of body (per kg. wt.)	1.50 : 1	Weight of placenta	2.48 : 1
Red corpuscles in blood	1.53 : 1		
Patellar circumference	1.51 : 1	Memory span	2.50 : 1
Chest circumference	1.53 : 1	Card sorting	2.50 : 1
O_2 consumption per minute	1.53 : 1	Latent reflex time	2.50 : 1
CO_2 consumption per minute ...	1.54 : 1		
Neck circumference	1.56 : 1	Weight of healthy liver	2.64 : 1
Thigh circumference	1.57 : 1	Vital capacity (only age	
		constant)	2.75 : 1
Weight of brain	1.60 : 1	Intelligence quotients (Terman-	
Cranial capacity	1.63 : 1	Merrill)	2.86 : 1
Extension of wrist	1.65 : 1	Swiftness of blow	2.93 : 1
Running 60 meters	1.67 : 1		
Pulse rate (at birth)	1.66 : 1	Hard learning	3.87 : 1
Weight of cerebrum	1.78 : 1	Weight of suprarenals	3.63 : 1

Source: From D. Weschler, *Range of Human Capacities,* 2d edition. Copyright © 1952 by The Williams & Wilkins Co., Baltimore. Reprinted by permission.

To get an idea of the arbitrary nature of such psychological measurement, consider a contest between a professional mathematician and a student whose knowledge ends with college algebra. A set of very sophisticated problems could be given that would result in a "number correct" for each competitor, and a ratio of number correct for the two competitors that approached infinity could be formed. Conversely, we could construct a rather easy test so that the ratio of number correct for the two competitors would be very low. Without knowing a true zero point for most of our psychological measures, we can never be sure about the range of true differences in abilities. With measures such as height and weight we do have true zero points, and this problem does not arise.

Some psychophysical measurements appear to have a true zero point but are complicated by the fact that the psychophysical units may not have the same meaning at different points on the scale. For example, one might easily improve one's speed for the 100-yard dash from 15 to 14 seconds. Going from 10 to 9 seconds, however, might be virtually impossible, although an interval of only 1 second separates the two sets of time scores.

An especially important problem for psychologists is deciding what units shall be employed in making measurements. Most psychological measurements are multifactorial—many components enter into the final product, and each of these components may have different units of measurement and combine in unusual ways. For anthropometric measurements, the multifactorial nature is usually more evident. Thus, cranial capacity is related to at least the three components of volume (breadth, length, and depth); hence, one can expect more variability in cranial capacity than in each of the three linear components taken separately.

Like the search for the snark, the search for the single underlying unit of measurement for each psychological process may turn out to be fruitless. It may not exist. Instead, one must search for units that yield "meaningful" results, units that relate to other measurements in ways that produce new knowledge or insights. The established measurements may have no firmer foundation than the new measurements. Nevertheless, taken in combination, the new measurements and the old may be worthwhile.

Sometimes it is possible to "enhance" the quality of measurement for one variable by relating it to another that does have a firmer foundation. IQ scores, for example, are derived or transformed values from the number correct on a particular test. These statistical transformations involve assumptions that we will consider later, but it is illegitimate to say that an individual with an IQ of 120 is twice as bright as one with an IQ of 60. We might say that the 120 IQ person is smarter, but just how much smarter is debatable. If, however, we can relate the IQ scores to a more solid measure in a way that yields a functional relationship, it might be possible to say how much brighter one is with an IQ score twice as high as the next.

It has been shown, for example, that adolescents with IQs averaging 127 can process elements of information at the rate of 25 items per second on a particularly easy information-processing task (McCauley et al. 1976). Those averaging 105 IQ process information at about 23.7 units per second; those averaging 86 IQ process at 17 units per second; and those averaging 72 IQ process at the rate of 11 units per second. Since these time measurements are somewhat sturdier than the IQ scores, in the sense that 26 units per second is actually twice as fast as 13 units per second, and since the IQ rates of information processing are orderly (at least for the averaged speeds in each IQ group), the results suggest that IQ scores are measuring some more fundamental capacities than previously believed and that it would be possible to construct useful functional relationships between the two types of measures.

It is another thing to prove that the speed measure is any more fundamental than the IQ score, since the speed measure merely incorporates the notion that cognitive processes must take place in time. It would be helpful if the speed measure were an index of some aspect of neural function and thus were tied to yet another variable, but at this stage there is no strong evidence for that proposition.

Psychologists have spent a good deal of time investigating the nature of measurements, because it is widely believed that only certain types of arithmetical and statistical operations can be performed within each level of measurement (Stevens 1951). There are also a number of psychometric techniques that can be employed to raise the level of measurement so that a greater range of statistical manipulations can be performed (Guilford 1954). Others believe that such procedures are not always necessary, and, when higher levels of measurement have been developed, they have not been utilized (cf. Prytulak 1975). We will not discuss the different levels of measurement, except to say that most psychological measures have arbitrary origins or zero points. (What would zero intelligence mean, since one could always construct an easier test?) The more important problem is to see whether one set of measurements relates meaningfully to others.

Descriptive Statistics

Many traits of psychological and biological interest can be described as approximating a normal bell-shaped curve. This curve, when applicable, has a number of properties that make it especially amenable to a wide variety of statistical manipulations. The perfectly normal curve is achieved about as often as is perfection, but small departures from

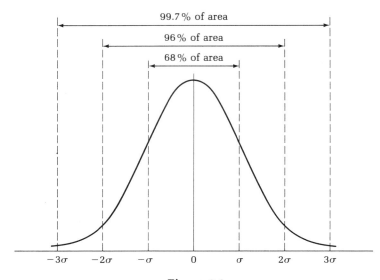

Figure 2.1

The normal distribution curve. (From G. E. McClearn
and J. C. DeFries, *Introduction to Behavioral Genetics*.
San Francisco: W. H. Freeman and Company. Copyright
© 1973.)

normality do not radically change most of the relevant statistical interpretations that might result.

Figure 2.1 shows a normal curve where scores for some measure are
given on the horizontal axis and the relative frequency with which
individuals have those scores is given on the vertical axis. You will note
that the curve is bilaterally symmetrical—the right half of the curve is a
mirror image of the left.

Because the curve is so regular, it becomes susceptible to a set of
descriptive statistics that helps to summarize and lend order to the
data. The critical pieces of summarizing information to know are the
mean and the standard deviation (SD, or σ). The mean is simply
the arithmetic average of the scores of all the individuals divided by
the number of individuals. It can be summarized symbolically in the
formula

$$\text{Mean} = \frac{\Sigma x}{N}$$

where

x = the score for an individual

N = the number of individuals

Σ = notation denoting "the sum of"

The standard deviation is simply the square root of the average of the squared deviations from the mean. An example of its computation is given in Table 2.3. The five scores listed in the table are not normally distributed and are used merely to illustrate the computation of the SD. First the mean is obtained, and then the deviation of each individual score from the mean is computed. Each of these deviations is then squared and summed. This sum is then divided by the number of cases to obtain the average of the squared deviations. This value is also called the variance (s^2) and is necessary itself for some statistical calculations to be shown. Finally, the square root of the variance is taken to obtain the standard deviation.

Let us now return to Figure 2.1, where the standard deviations from the mean are given along the horizontal axis. Because the normal curve is so regular, the standard deviation tells us that about 68 percent of individuals will fall ±1 SD from the mean and about 96 percent will fall ±2 SD from the mean. After the mean and SD are computed, it is possible to take the score of a single individual and determine the number of SD units from the mean at which that subject falls. Thus, if a test has a mean of 10 with an SD of 2, a subject with a score of 12 is 1 SD above the mean. A table of the normal distribution, which can be found in any statistics text, will tell where the individual falls in relation to the total population. It turns out that a value of 1 SD above the mean is equivalent to about the 84th percentile. Thus, this subject scores higher than 84 out of 100 representative individuals.

The beauty of the SD is that it is possible to obtain many different measures, even for different purposes, all in different units, and then convert the individual's scores to standard deviation units and deter-

Table 2.3

Computation of the variance and the standard deviation

Score	Deviation from mean (x)	x^2
5	2	4
4	1	1
3	0	0
2	−1	1
1	−2	4
$15 = \Sigma X$	0	$\sigma x^2 = 10$
Mean = 3		Variance = $s^2 = \frac{10}{5} = 2.0^*$
		SD = $\sqrt{2.0} = 1.41$

* For some statistical purposes a divisor of $N - 1$, called degrees of freedom, is used in calculating the standard deviation. In most practical cases, where reasonably large samples of individuals are involved, the two versions of calculating the standard deviation will differ only trivially in numerical value.

mine the individual's relative ranking on each of the measures, independent of the actual score values obtained. Thus, we can say that an individual is 1 SD above the mean of some defined population for IQ, 1.5 SD above the mean for height, and 2 SDs below the mean for weight. (This would be a bright, tall, but very skinny individual.) It would make no difference whether height was measured in inches or centimeters, or whether weight was measured in pounds or kilograms. The raw score values would differ, but the SD units above or below the mean would be perfectly and equally interpretable.

When scores are converted to standard deviation units they are called standardized scores. It is possible to standardize scores to any specific mean or standard deviation. Thus, scores on a measure can be set to any mean and any standard deviation. IQ scores are standard scores with a mean of 100 and a standard deviation of 15 for most tests. The raw score number correct for a particular age group is called 100, and the standard deviation of the raw scores has been arbitrarily set to equal 15. For example, if ten-year-olds averaged 83 items correct with a standard deviation of 19 items, 83 correct is called 100 IQ and someone with 102 items correct is given a score of 115 IQ, because his or her raw score is 1 standard deviation above the mean of the raw scores.

NONNORMAL CURVES

Unfortunately, many psychological measures are not normally distributed (i.e., in a bell-shaped curve), and departures from normality may prevent the interpretation of an SD in terms of proportions derived from the normal curve.

Examples of two nonnormal distributions commonly found in psychology are shown in Figure 2.2. The top curve is one that has a positive skew (pointing toward the right) and often occurs when a test or measure is too hard for the vast majority of subjects. The second curve is negatively skewed (pointing toward the left) and can occur when a test is so easy for the subjects that virtually everybody obtains near-maximum scores. The numbers to the side of each curve illustrate in abbreviated terms why the SD becomes less meaningful when there are distributions of this sort. For the top curve, imagine that five individuals take a test, four obtain scores between 1 and 5, and one obtains a score of 15. Here the SD equals 5.75 and the mean is only 5. Thus, there can be no individuals scoring even 1 SD below the mean. For the lower curve, four individuals obtain scores very close to one another and the fifth obtains a very low score. The SD of 4.53 will find nobody at 1 SD above the mean.

There are statistical procedures by which to determine whether or not and how far an obtained curve deviates from the normal curve (cf.

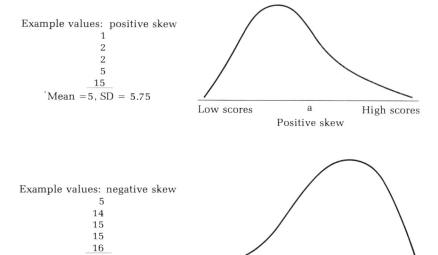

Figure 2.2
Two common departures from the normal distribution.

McNemar 1962). These techniques are probably not employed as often as they should be, but another way to examine for normality is to construct a curve from the raw data and see what it looks like. Small departures from the normal curve do not dramatically affect many statistical tests. Consequently, failure of normality assumptions to hold does not usually mean that the study need be terminated, because there are other statistical tests that do not require normality for their application (Siegal 1956). One way to correct distributions of the sort described in Figure 2.2 is to make transformations of the original data that would tend to reduce the influence of the extreme scores. For example, one could take square roots or logs of each of the scores on the variable before compiling them into a distribution. This would tend to make the distribution more nearly normal.

CORRELATION COEFFICIENT

Throughout this book we will have occasion to employ the *correlation coefficient* as a measure of the degree of linear association between two variables. Correlations range between −1.00 and 1.00. A value of −1.00 means that there is a perfect negative relationship between the two

variables—the higher the score on one measure, the lower the score on
the other. The correlation between the number of right and wrong
answers on a test is an example of a perfect negative correlation. A correlation of 0.00 means that there is absolutely no linear relationship between the score on one variable and the score on the other. One might
expect a 0.00 relationship between spelling test scores and the number
of hairs in the nose. A perfect positive correlation means that high
scores on the first variable perfectly predict high scores on the other. For
example, the heights of people measured in inches would correlate
perfectly with their heights measured in centimeters. For variables of
psychological interest, perfect correlations are rarely if ever to be
found. Since the correlation coefficient can take intermediate values, it
is nevertheless of substantial utility. An example of the computation of
the correlation coefficient is shown in Table 2.4, and sample scatter
plots for some correlation coefficients are shown in Figure 2.3.

The first column in Table 2.4 gives the data for the first variable
(conventionally called the X variable) and the fourth column gives the
scores on the second variable (called the Y variable). Thus, the first
subject obtained a score of 1 on the first variable and a score of 110 on
the second. Similarly, the subject with a 2 on the first variable obtained
a score of 115 on the second variable, and so on.

First the means for the X and Y variables are computed and then
deviations from each mean are taken and squared, just as in the computation of the variance shown in Table 2.3. The only addition is that the
deviation of a subject's score on the X variable is also multiplied by his

Table 2.4
Computing the Pearson product-moment correlation coefficient (r)

X	x	x^2	Y	y	y^2	$(x)(y)$
1	-2	4	110	-10	100	20
2	-1	1	115	-5	25	5
3	0	0	125	$+5$	25	0
4	$+1$	1	120	0	0	0
5	$+2$	4	130	$+10$	100	20
15	0	10	600	0	250	45

$$S_x^2 = \frac{10}{5^*} = 2 \qquad S_y^2 = \frac{250}{5^*} = 50 \qquad \text{Cov} = \frac{45}{5^*} = 9$$

$$r = \frac{\text{Cov}}{\sqrt{(S_x^2)(S_y^2)}} = \frac{9}{\sqrt{(2)(50)}} = .90$$

* To be technically correct with a sample of only five individuals, one should divide by $N - 1$, or
four rather than five.

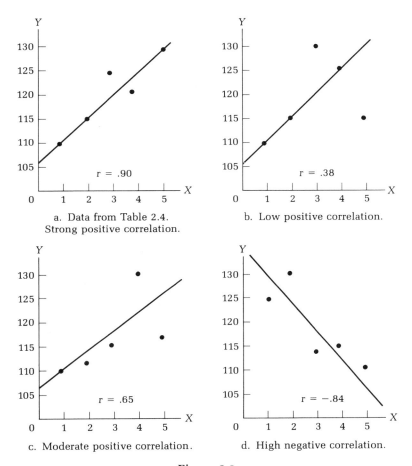

Figure 2.3

Scatterplots for correlation coefficients. For each scatterplot to yield a perfect negative or positive correlation, each data point must fall exactly on the straight line.

deviation on the Y variable. The average of these (x · y) deviations is then computed and is called the *covariance*. The covariance is analogous to the variance of the X or the Y variable. Thus, in a positive correlation, individuals with high scores on the X variable will also have high scores on the Y variable. Conversely, low scores on the X will be associated with low scores on the Y. Note that when there is no, or a low, relationship of X to Y, plus signs will be associated with minus signs about as often as plus signs with plus and minus signs with minus. Consequently, the covariance term will be near zero. The coefficient of correlation, symbolized as r, is computed as follows:

$$r = \frac{\text{Covariance}}{\sqrt{(S_x^2)(S_y^2)}} \quad \text{or} \quad \frac{\text{Covariance}}{(S_x)(S_y)}$$

An important thing to note is that the correlation coefficient is independent of the units of measurement for the X and Y variables. You can correlate height with weight, weight with IQ, weight with height, and so on. The covariance term in the numerator as well as the variances and standard deviations in the denominator are not independent of the units of measurement, however.

One way to see what a correlation coefficient means is to compare various levels of correlation coefficients with chance or zero relationship. If there were no relationship between two variables, knowledge of the subject's score on the first would be of no utility in predicting the subject's score on the second. Table 2.5 provides some examples of "hit rates" for various correlation coefficients.

Table 2.5 is read in the following way. Suppose there were two events, each of which had a fifty-fifty probability of occurring, and you had a test that could predict (with various levels of success) which of the two events would occur. If the level of success were .00, you would be correct 50 percent of the time and thus have a chance success rate. If the correlation between the test and the outcome were .60, you would be correct 70 percent of the time. The difference between the chance success rate and the rate obtained from a test that correlated with the

Table 2.5

Hit rates of various correlations for "50-50" events

Correlation	% Correct	Correlation	% Correct
.00	50	.55	69
.05	52	.60	70
.10	53	.65	73
.15	55	.70	75
.20	56	.75	77
.25	58	.80	80
.30	60	.85	82
.35	61	.90	86
.40	63	.95	90
.45	65	1.00	100
.50	67		

Source: From H. C. Taylor and J. T. Russell, "The Relationship of Validity Coefficients to the Practical Effectiveness of Tests in Selection," *Journal of Applied Psychology* 23 (1939): 565–578. Copyright © 1939 by the American Psychological Association. Reprinted by permission.

criterion in various degrees is called the *incremental validity* of the test. Many events of psychological interest occur much more rarely than 50 percent of the time. When one is trying to predict such rare events, the correlations must be higher than those shown to yield the same percentage of success. The article by Taylor and Russell (1939) offers a more expanded treatment of this problem as well as other tables giving incremental validities associated with various correlation coefficients as a function of the base rate chances of success.

We have pointed out that an advantage of the correlation coefficient is that it is insensitive to mean differences between the variables entering into the correlation. The correlation coefficient is instead mainly responsive to the relative rank orderings of subjects on the two variables.* Correlations are fine when one is interested primarily in individual differences and not in absolute levels of performance. One psychologist might try an early intervention program with children of mothers having IQs averaging 75 and find that, after exposure to the enrichment program, the children of these mothers average 95 IQ. A reasonable conclusion is that the intervention program was very effective. A correlational psychologist might add, however, that the relative rank orderings of the mothers among themselves in IQ was related to the rank orderings in IQ of their children, reasonably concluding that the parental individual differences component was the most important factor in accounting for the differential responsiveness of the children to the enrichment program. Thus, the correlational psychologist could point out that the effects of enrichment do not operate on an infinitely malleable organism that is simply molded by the environment. Both investigators are right. The problem is that they are speaking of different aspects of the data. Readers need to be alert to the fact that two sets of interpretations can be given to the same set of data.

VARIANCE

The concept of variance is often poorly understood, although it is widely used and is important in differential psychology. *Variance* is defined as the average of the squared deviations from the mean. Even if

---

* In actuality, the correlation coefficient can be slightly affected by the intervals between scores and not simply by the rank ordering of subjects. To take an extreme example, suppose each of the numbers from 1 to 20 is correlated with its respective square. Thus, 1 would be correlated with 1, 2 would be correlated with 4, and so on up to 20, which would be correlated with 400. Here the rank orderings of the two sets of numbers remain identical, but the intervals between the numbers are not comparable. The resulting interclass correlation would be .971 instead of 1.00. When the distributions of the two variables entering into the correlation are approximately normal, the effect of unequal intervals will usually be fairly negligible.

the causes of the variance values are genuine, from the point of view of the investigator, the variance can be regarded as an index of *uncertainty*. If every score on a measure is at the mean, there is no variance and no uncertainty. The greater the dispersal about the mean, the greater the uncertainty and the greater the variance. Much of what psychologists do is try to describe that uncertainty and then reduce it by understanding the mechanisms leading to variance or uncertainty, or by considering other predictor variables that help to reduce uncertainty (even if these predictors are not well understood).

There is another method of reducing variance. Another variable that can reduce or account for some of the variance around some mean of interest can be entered into an equation. For example, IQ scores predict grades in school about r = .50. We can therefore reduce the variance in grades of a particular group by including IQ scores as part of the predictor. As it happens, one must square the correlation coefficient between the predictor (e.g., IQ) and the grades to obtain the variance accounted for. Thus, in this example, individual differences in IQ can account for 25 percent of the variance in grades.

This knowledge says nothing about cause. Knowledge of rank in class will correlate nearly perfectly with grades, yet adding knowledge of class rank to a predictor (as a postdictor) is obviously not useful in understanding the causes of grade differences. Psychologists must use their ingenuity in constructing measures that not only correlate with the outcomes of interest but also can serve as explanatory constructs to account for that outcome.

REGRESSION

Closely related to the correlation coefficient is the *regression coefficient*, symbolized by the Greek letter beta, β. Only when the variances of the X and Y variables are identical is the regression coefficient equal to the correlation coefficient; most of the time the two are different. There are many formulas for calculating the regression coefficient; among the most convenient are the following two:

$$\beta = (r) \frac{SD_y}{SD_x} \quad \text{or} \quad \beta = \frac{Cov}{S_x^2}$$

The regression coefficient is used when the intent is to predict the *actual* amount of change in the Y variable as a function of the amount of change in the X variable. Unlike the correlation coefficient, the regression coefficient tells how many units of change to expect in Y for every unit change in X. (This is often expressed as the regression of Y on X.) For the example in Table 2.4,

$$\beta = (.9)\,\frac{7.07}{1.41} = 4.5 \qquad \text{or} \qquad \beta = \frac{9}{2} = 4.5$$

This means that for every unit change on the X variable a change of 4.5 points on the Y variable is predicted. The regression coefficient is very useful for predicting changes in actual scores on some outcome variable as a function of some change in an input variable. For example, one might want to know how much improvement in grade point to expect for every one-point increase on a pretest. The correlation coefficient would only give the degree of relationship between the pretest and grade point; the regression coefficient would give the expected improvement in actual grade point units. The reverse could also be done—the score on X could be predicted from the score on Y. In this case $\beta = (.9)1.41/7.07 = .18$. This means that for every point increase on the original Y variable there is a .18 increase on the original X variable. You can see that the regression of Y on X is not the same as the regression of X on Y.

REGRESSION TOWARD THE MEAN

There is another form of regression that has been confused with the regression coefficient described above. This form is called *regression toward the mean*. For example, whenever any imperfectly reliable measure is taken on a sample of individuals and extreme scorers on that measure are then selected to be either retested on the same instrument or given another measure, the second testing of the selected subjects will yield a group mean that is closer to the original unselected mean.

Galton described another example of this phenomenon in the 1892 preface to his book *Hereditary Genius*, originally published in 1869. He pointed out that

> ... the distribution of faculties in a population cannot possibly remain constant, if, on the average, the children resemble their parents. If they did so, the giants (in any mental or physical particular) would become more gigantic, and the dwarfs more dwarfish, in each successive generation. This counteracting tendency is what I call "regression" [p. 33].

What usually happens is that the offspring of exceptionally tall people tend to be taller than average but smaller than their parents. Similarly, the offspring of very short people tend to be larger than their parents but smaller than the population mean for height.

Another concrete example may be useful in understanding the phenomenon of regression toward the mean. Suppose children with average IQs of 70 are selected for a treatment program. Since IQ measures are not perfectly reliable, a retesting later will usually show the group to improve in average IQ, regardless of whether or not the treatment program was effective.

The theory behind this phenomenon is that every observed score contains both a "true" component and an "error" component. Presumably the error component is not correlated with the true component in the total sample. One may have just had an opportunity to learn about a particular item on a test; one may be feeling ill on the occasion of testing; or the examiner may make some scoring errors against the subject. In order to do poorly on the test, however, one must have poor ability as well as be unlucky. On the occasion of retesting, the chances are that things associated with error are unlikely to be as bad as on the first occasion, and, consequently one's score will improve. Whenever extreme scorers are selected for retesting, regression is likely to occur; the more extreme the selection, the greater the actual amount of expected regression. In the case of the 70 IQ group selected for a treatment program, it would be wise to have a control group of equally low IQ that is not given the treatment. Both groups should be retested and then the amount of improvement of the treatment group compared to the improvement of the control group. Only when the treatment group improves significantly more than the control group can the treatment program be said to work.

Regression toward the mean need not occur only because of unreliability in the measures, that is, the error component in the test. Two measures can be perfectly reliable, but, if they share only a portion of common factors, regression on the second measure will occur if selection has been on the first. Even if IQ scores and grades were each perfectly reliable and there were a positive correlation between the two, selecting subjects with very high IQs would not find them to be proportionately as high on grades as they were on IQ. This is because other factors enter into grades, such as motivation, teachers' attitudes, and good work habits. The IQ test probably does not tap these factors to the same extent that grades do, and, consequently, there will be regression toward the mean for the grades.

RELIABILITY

It should be clear that when measurements lack reliability (have a large component of random error) it is impossible for them to relate to other measurements. Thus, much time is spent in psychological research to develop instruments that have high levels of reliability. There are many ways to obtain quantitative measures of reliability. The most common way is to give a test on one occasion and then give it again at a later date and correlate the scores (*test-retest reliability*). Another way is to devise an alternative form of the test that is as similar in content as possible to the original (short of repeating the identical items) and then to look at the correlation between the two measures. Another way is to divide the test into halves—into odd-numbered items and even-numbered items, for example—and then correlate the scores on the two halves (*split-half reliability*). Each technique has distinctive advantages and disadvantages, so that it is often necessary to obtain more than one estimate of reliability to get the full picture. For example, the odd-even method of reliability should not be used with a highly speeded test. Since slower subjects will not be able to complete the test, perforce their scores on the later odd items will correlate perfectly with their scores on the later even-numbered items (they will fail them all). Thus, the apparent reliability of the test will be inflated.

It should be noted that the optimal level of reliability may not be that level which yields a perfect reliability correlation. Some measures should show only moderate test-retest reliability or they will not be susceptible to influences that might change the scores. For example, a scale of mood should not be perfectly reliable from one testing to the next, since perfect reliability would mean that no subjects change their relative rank orderings on the measure over the two occasions. Mood, by definition, is variable, and, consequently, one would not want a measure that was not susceptible to change. A more appropriate measure of the reliability of a mood questionnaire would be obtained by getting an index of internal consistency, that is, the degree to which items administered on one occasion intercorrelate with one another. Similarly, height in adults is very reliable, but, if one wanted to study the effects of different nutritional programs on adults, it would be a poor measure to use since it is unlikely to respond to changes in nutritional status. Obviously, a measure like weight would be much more useful, because it does not show the consistency from time to time that height does.

We have spoken of reliability in only the grossest sense. Tests can be unreliable because of measurement error (inadequacies of the test or examiner) or because the trait being measured is unstable from time to time. These two sources of error always need to be distinguished, and there are many techniques for identifying the individual sources of error (e.g., Nunnally 1967). Unreliability in the measuring instrument itself should always be kept at a minimum, but lowered reliability of measurement due to instability of the underlying trait can often be tolerated.

INTRACLASS CORRELATION

The correlation described previously is one way to measure reliability. There are other techniques, however, that often are preferable. The most important alternative is the *intraclass* correlation (the previously described correlation, in contrast, is sometimes called the *interclass* correlation).

We pointed out earlier that one of the beautiful features of the correlation coefficient is that it permits one to correlate variables having different metrics (e.g., height and weight). It is relatively insensitive to the means and variances of the X and Y variables and is mainly sensitive to the rank order of subjects on the two measures, regardless of their means and variances. Thus, a high correlation is obtained when the subject scoring highest on the first variable scores highest on the second, the second highest on the first scores second highest on the second, and so on. If an IQ test were administered on two occasions and the relative positions of the subjects remained the same, although the mean IQ of the group on the second occasion were 10 points higher than on the first, the interclass correlation would still be 1.00.

But what if it were important to know how well subjects' scores on the same test agreed over two or more occasions? In this case we would not be interested in the interclass correlation of just two measures, possibly with different metrics, but with agreement of scores over time for the same measure. The intraclass correlation would be the choice of method, for it checks agreement of actual scores on the same measurement instrument over occasions.

The intraclass correlation is used not only when the same test is given over two or more occasions to the same subject but also when a single test is given to genetically related family members believed to be samples having equal means and standard deviations drawn from the same underlying distribution.

The formula for the intraclass correlation is generally derived from the analysis of variance, but that requires too much exposition to consider in detail here. For those with a background in analysis of variance, the intraclass correlation is

$$r_i = \frac{S_b^2 - S_w^2}{S_b^2 + (n - 1)S_w^2}$$

where

S_b^2 = the variance between groups or families,

S_w^2 = the variance within groups or families, and

n = the average number of individuals per family, or the average number of occasions

The intraclass correlation has special utility in behavior genetics. When twin or sibling studies are done, one often wants to see how similar the twins or siblings are to one another. Using the interclass correlation, however, one would need to assign one observation to the X variable and the other observation to the Y variable. With twins or siblings there is often no rational basis for assigning one to be X and the other to be Y. In essence, one is really not trying to predict the score of the second twin or sibling from the score of the first. Instead, one is interested in seeing how similar twins within a set are relative to the difference between sets of twins or siblings. Here is where the intraclass correlation becomes especially valuable. We need not take up more space here describing its computation, since many good sources are already available (Haggard 1958; Nunnally 1967; Cronbach 1970). For much research in individual differences, the intraclass is more appropriate than the interclass correlation.

PEARSON DOUBLE-ENTRY CORRELATION

A shortcut computational procedure for getting a close approximation of the intraclass correlation when there are just two samples to be correlated is the Pearson double-entry method. Since there is no rational basis for assigning a particular twin or sibling to the X or Y column, each individual is simply entered twice, once as a score in the X column and once as a score in the Y column. In the case of twins, for example, twin A is entered in the X column and twin B in the Y column. Then twin B is entered in the X column and twin A is entered in the Y column. This double entering ensures that the X and Y columns will be equated for their means and variances or standard deviations. After all the pairs have been entered twice, the correlation is computed in the usual fashion. When N is large, the double-entry and the intraclass correlation will yield virtually identical values.

HETEROGENEITY

It is important to recognize that the amount of variability within a group will affect the correlations obtained, whether interclass or intraclass. When students are highly selected on a particular variable, it usually means that the variance or SD of the scores is considerably less than in the unrestricted population from which they were drawn. If the selected students differ less from one another on the average than do the students in the unrestricted population, the likelihood that one will find strong relationships with other variables is reduced. Suppose, for example, one selects graduate students in physics and correlates their aptitude test scores with their grades in graduate school. Since the group is already considerably restricted in range of ability, it is unlikely that strong relationships will be observed.

Consider an attempt to predict which of two children with IQ scores of 100 and 105, respectively, will do better in school. Since these IQ scores contain both true and error components, the difference between the two may well be completely due to error, and, consequently, one will find little predictability. On the other hand, the difference between a 90 IQ and a 130 IQ probably represents a true difference in ability, and the error component may be small relative to this true difference. Hence, predictions according to an academic criterion will probably be much better. One always must keep in mind the variability of the group under investigation. Diminished variability will always reduce correlational predictability, all other things being equal.

Statistical procedures are available for correcting for restriction in range and reliability. These techniques essentially make generalizations from the obtained correlations about what the correlations would be in the unrestricted population or if the test were perfectly reliable. A discussion of statistical corrections of this sort can be found in Guilford (1954).

MODERATOR VARIABLES

In recent years attention has been directed toward improving predictions by identifying other factors that might not be correlated with either the X or Y variable but nevertheless affect relationships between the two variables. One such factor might be sex. In a group of males there might be a correlation between two variables that would be absent in a group of females. Thus, the males might be predictable and the females not, and sex would be then regarded as a *moderator* variable. A thoughtful review of moderator variables can be found in Wiggins (1973), but perhaps an example will be instructive here.

Turner (1978) was interested in examining the correlation between different paper and pencil methods of assessing dominance and different laboratory criteria for dominance in fifty college students. He correlated the scores between the tests and the laboratory criteria, finding moderate relationships between the two. At the same time that the subjects completed the paper and pencil tests of dominance, they also completed a questionnaire to assess their private and public self-consciousness (Fenigstein, Scheier, and Buss 1975). This questionnaire was designed to identify people who were either high or low on habitual self-reflection and on habitual concern about what others thought of them. Scores on this scale did not correlate with either the paper and pencil measures or the laboratory measures of dominance. Turner then divided his subjects according to whether they obtained high or low scores on each of these self-consciousness measures and correlated the paper and pencil tests with the laboratory outcome measures with each self-consciousness combination separately. For those high on private self-consciousness, correlations between the better paper and pencil test and the outcome criteria averaged about .62. For those low on private self-consciousness, the correlations between the comparable predictor and outcomes were only .33. Similarly, for those high on public self-consciousness, correlations for the comparable predictor and outcomes were only .30; for those low on public self-consciousness, the correlations were .69.

The results were interpreted as indicating that some people cannot report accurately about themselves because they are not routinely self-reflective while others are so concerned about what others think of them that they cannot be expected to behave in ways that are consistent with what their own private intentions might be. Those who are high on private self-consciousness and low on public self-consciousness then ought to be the most predictable types. Those low on private and high on public self-consciousness should be least predictable. Internal analyses of the data obtained by Turner strongly confirmed these notions.

Other moderator variables are under study (Ghiselli 1963), and this may be a very fruitful approach to investigate in the future. It must be acknowledged, however, that in the past the success of moderator variables in improving prediction has not been great. With the emergence of newer moderator variables from a more solid theoretical framework, it may be possible to predict in advance which individuals are predictable.

THE TWISTED PEAR

Often when we try to predict outcomes, we find that prediction is better at some levels than others. Thus, on ability measures we can often predict with reasonable precision that an individual with a low IQ will do poorly in college, but we cannot be equally confident that someone with a high IQ will do well. This discrepancy is certainly due to the fact that minimal levels of intellectual adequacy are required for high-level performance and that those who don't even reach those levels will not be able to perform well, regardless of other factors. Those with high ability, however, might not perform well in school because of factors unrelated to intellectual ability; thus, predictions are less accurate for such individuals.

When one is examining correlations or regressions between a predictor and an outcome, it is often useful to see how well the predictor does at different levels. A schematic illustration of this phenomenon is seen in Figure 2.4.

42

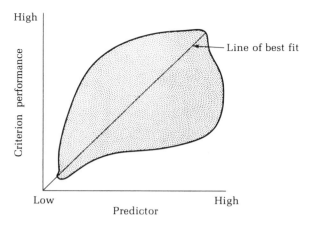

Figure 2.4

The twisted pear. Deviations from perfect prediction as a function of score on the predictor. (After J. Fisher, "The Twisted Pear and the Prediction of Behavior," *Journal of Consulting Psychology* 23 [1959]: 400–405. Copyright © 1959 by the American Psychological Association. Reprinted by permission.)

The figure gives the scores on some predictor (e.g., IQ) and some criterion (e.g., grades) for many subjects. Each dot represents an individual's location at an intersection of the predictor and the outcome. The straight line bisecting the figure is the line of perfect prediction. If a score falls on that line, it is perfectly predicted. Deviations from that line mean less accuracy in prediction—the further the deviation, the more inadequate the prediction.

At low scores on the predictor variable, the deviations from the line of perfect prediction are small. At higher levels the deviations become larger. The visual appearance of this scatter diagram assumes the shape of a twisted pear—hence the name (Fisher 1959). It is a good rule to construct scatter diagrams when you are doing research, since they can often tell you at a glance where predictability on the scale is more or less accurate.

VALIDITY

At the heart of all measurement is validity, namely, whether or not the measure does what it is intended to do. If a test is designed to predict school grades, does it, in fact, predict those grades? In this case, the measure of validity is the correlation between the test and the school grades. This correlation is called *predictive* or *concurrent validity*. The test is the predictor and the grades are the criterion. When the criterion is already available, such as current grade point average, the correlation is one of concurrent validity. If the criterion measure is to be obtained after the administration of the predictor, then the correlation is one of predictive validity. Sometimes a criterion in one instance becomes a predictor in another. The criterion of school grades, for example, may predict achievement in later life.

Another measure of validity is *content validity*. In essence, content validity measures whether the test items are sampling the domain of information they are meant to be sampling. One would not give a sociology test as a final exam in psychology, for example. Usually content validity can be ensured when representative items from the criterion itself are used in the construction of the test.

CONSTRUCT VALIDITY

Most of the business of science concerns the investigation of constructs or concepts. The measures we use are only convenient ways to index those constructs. For example, we are not really interested in the number of revolutions of a rat's running wheel, but we use that number as an index of the general activity level of that rat. If running-wheel activity were not related to some other measures of activity, we would probably want to cease using it. In psychological science, constructs are often not directly observable or precisely defined; consequently, tests must be validated by their correlations with other measures that presumably tap the same construct. No one of the measures alone is a perfect index of the construct. Most likely, running-wheel activity only correlates moderately with other measures of activity level, such as the number of square feet traversed by an animal in a box. This measure too could be regarded as only an index of activity level, and who is to say which index is better? If, however, a third activity test predicted running-wheel activity but not movement in a box, we would need to refine our construct of what we meant by activity level. If we validate new measures against other imprecisely defined criteria, we are employing methods of *construct validity*.

Although anxiety does not have a precise definition, any new test designed to tap anxiety should correlate positively with other already existing tests that are supposed to tap that construct. The new test need not correlate perfectly with existing tests, for then there would be little reason to construct the new test (unless it were more economical or had other practical advantages). Construct validity coefficients need not be extremely high to still be worthwhile indicants that a test measures some aspect of the trait of interest.

FACTOR ANALYSIS

Factor analysis is one approach to constructs and their components. In essence, all factor analyses (and there are many different techniques) begin with a matrix of intercorrelations between many variables. The idea behind factor analysis is to reduce the number of variables to a smaller number of factors that can account for the intercorrelations observed. Each cluster of related variables is said to "load" on a particular factor, and, when the factor analysis is ideally simple, clusters of variables that load on one factor do not load on any other factors.

Because the psychological meaning of each factor does not emerge from a factor analysis, it is up to the professional to label the factor appropriately. This task often requires a good deal of insight and thoughtfulness. It means that the professional must identify which tests or variables load on the factor and which others do not. Like the intercorrelations themselves, selection characteristics of the population from which subjects are drawn may affect the types of intercorrelations that emerge and, consequently, the factors that result after factor analysis. For example, the factor analysis that led to the construct of "primary mental abilities" by Thurstone (1938), which will be discussed later, was performed on a highly selected sample of college students, who averaged much above the national norm for IQ in college students. It is quite possible that in a more representative group of subjects the independent factors that emerged originally would not reappear upon retesting, and it is almost certain that the correlations among the obtained factors would be different.

Factor analysis can be useful in establishing construct validity when a number of different measures are included within an intercorrelation matrix and those measures are meant to be indices of the factor or construct under investigation. If these measures do not load together on the factor, then the construct needs to be reexamined.

Factor analysis is becoming more widely used in differential psychology. As it happens, however, the studies and interpretations described in this book do not depend upon the factor analytic literature to any great extent. Consequently, we will not spend much time explicating the technical aspects of factor analyses and their applications. When factor analytic materials emerge in the course of the text, however, the information necessary for conceptual understanding shall be provided.

MULTITRAIT-MULTIMETHOD MATRIX

A particularly useful way of obtaining validity and reliability estimates simultaneously is to apply the multitrait-multimethod matrix (Campbell and Fiske 1959). This procedure requires the assessment of at least two constructs or traits, each by at least two different methods. The idea is that, if a construct or trait is worthy of consideration, then retesting for the traits using the same method or a different method should still yield high test-retest correlations. If retesting by the same method yields high test-retest correlations but test-retest correlations are low when a different method is used to assess the trait the second time, the robustness of the construct or the methods used in its assessment is placed in doubt.

Another consideration is that a common method applied to two different, presumably nonoverlapping constructs should show little correlation between the two constructs. A correlation between two theoretically independent traits when both are measured by the same method suggests that the method itself is contributing to the correlation.

An example may clarify the notions behind the multitrait-multimethod matrix. Table 2.6 gives a fictional example of two traits that are each assessed by two different methods. Let's say that one method is by questionnaire and the second method involves ratings derived from naturalistic observations of the subjects. One of the traits might be extroversion and the second might be impulsiveness. The entries in the table are correlations. The upper left quadrant contains the correlations within and between each trait as assessed by the first method; the enclosed portion gives the test-retest reliabilities for each of the traits when they are assessed by the same method. These appear to be satisfactorily high by conventional standards. The .40 correlation in that quadrant refers to the assessment of the two different traits by the same questionnaire method and yields a moderate correlation. This correlation would place in doubt an argument that extroversion and impulsiveness are independent traits, but one cannot be sure from this correlation alone. It is possible that the questionnaire approach involves endorsement biases (e.g., some subjects may tend to see themselves in a favorable or an unfavorable light, regardless of the traits under consideration). Consequently, there will be correlations between any two traits simply be-

Table 2.6

A fictional multitrait-multimethod matrix

Traits		Method 1		Method 2	
		A	B	A	B
Method 1	A	.90			
	B	.40	.90		
Method 2	A	.75		.90	
	B	.00	.75	.20	.90

cause there is a tendency for subjects to endorse items in systematic ways, regardless of their content.

The quadrant on the lower right refers to the assessment of the two traits by naturalistic observation. The enclosed portion indicates that ratings from naturalistic observations on two occasions yield high test-retest correlations like those in the first method. The cross-trait correlation of .20 here is also lower than the cross-trait correlation of .40 shown in the upper left quadrant for the questionnaire method and suggests that the naturalistic method has less influence on the ratings of each trait.

The lower left quadrant gives the cross-method assessment of the same traits as well as the cross-method assessment of the two different traits. Two different methods for assessing the same trait yield lower correlations, enclosed in the dotted ellipse (.75), than the .90s found elsewhere on the matrix. This suggests that the two different methods themselves have an effect on the results. They may, for example, measure slightly different aspects of the trait. Note also that there is no correlation between the two different traits when they are each assessed by different methods.

What conclusions are we to draw from this example? First, we can see that the method used to assess the traits contributes to the degree to which they are apparently different or similar to one another. Thus, with the questionnaire method, we find the traits to be moderately correlated (.40), despite the fact that the cross-method correlation shows them to be independent. The naturalistic method shows less correspondence between the two traits.

Second, only when we assess the two traits by two different methods does it appear that the two traits are independent from one another. Note also, however, that when we assess the same trait by two different methods the correlation is lower than when we assess the same trait twice using the same method. If the cross-method reliabilities are low, regardless of high within-method reliabilities, the option of discarding the trait entirely can be considered.

The lesson to be learned from this example is that many traits or constructs can be shown to be similar to dissimilar depending on the methods used to assess them. Traits that are not robust because they depend exclusively on one method of assessment are generally less worthy of consideration than those which display robustness independent of the method used for assessment. Furthermore, when some methods of assessment are less reliable than others, measurement of the same trait by these different methods will lead to lower correlations than otherwise. Thus, it is usually a good idea to obtain reliability assessments of the same trait using the same method and show that these reliabilities are satisfactorily high before discarding any trait because of low cross-method correlations.

In this context, a reliability estimate can be regarded as the agreement between two attempts to measure the trait using maximally similar methods. A validity estimate can be seen as the agreement between two attempts to measure the same trait using maximally dissimilar methods (Campbell and Fiske 1959). We have shown here a rather simplified diagram, keeping traits and methods to a minimum. As you might imagine, adding more traits and more methods for assessing those traits makes things more complicated (and often more interesting). The article by Campbell and Fiske should be consulted for elaborations of the possible interpretations.

INFERENTIAL STATISTICS

Typically, researchers in individual differences are not content merely to describe distributions of scores for variables or even to describe relationships between variables. Researchers also try to draw inferences from the observations. The procedures by which this is accomplished are collectively called *inferential statistics*. Essentially, a statistical test is applied to see whether the relationships observed could have been obtained by chance alone. Thus, research conclusions are almost always couched in the following terms: if chance alone were operating, a difference (or a relationship) of the magnitude observed would be obtained only 5 times in 100 or 1 time in 100.

Whether chance alone could explain the findings observed depends not only on the degree of relationship or difference observed but also on the number of subjects in the study. If we asked 1024 individuals to guess whether heads or tails would turn up after each flip of ten flips of a coin, we would expect that on the average 1 of the 1024 subjects would guess correctly on all ten occasions (another one would guess incorrectly on all ten occasions). These expectations follow from the expansion of the binomial and would be consistent with empirical observations of the tossing of coins, rolling of dice, and so on. If someone who claimed to have special prognostic powers averred that he could guess the outcome and in fact was able to guess correctly on all ten trials, we could say that, if chance alone were operating, this phenomenon would occur only once in 1024 times. We would probably reject the hypothesis that chance alone was operating for this individual, although in fact the subject may just have been lucky. Perhaps a better decision would be to have the subject predict the coin tosses many more times, to increase our confidence in his ability.

Many of the findings in the chapters that follow will be based on inferential statistics. It will often be reported that a particular difference had a .05, .01, or .001 level of significance. These figures mean that the relationship observed could have been obtained by chance alone only 5 times in 100, 1 time in 100, or 1 time in 1000. There is nothing magical about these specific levels of statistical significance; they have simply become conventionally accepted and widely applied.

When groups are compared to see whether they differ from each other, it is necessary to know three things: (1) the difference in means between the groups, (2) the variability around each of those means, and (3) the number of subjects composing each group.

Groups can differ in mean scores, but because the variability of the scores in both groups is great, there is considerable overlap in the score distributions; consequently, the difference between the means of both groups may not reach statistical significance. Groups can also differ in their mean scores, but if the numbers of subjects in each group are not sufficient, the mean differences may not reach statistical significance. In general there is a trade-off between the magnitude of the mean difference required to reach statistical significance and the number of subjects entering into the groups. If a mean difference is large and there is little overlap between the groups, only small numbers of subjects are required in each group to reach statistical significance. If there are many subjects in each group, smaller mean differences will still yield statistical significance.

Sometimes one sees a study in which a particular mean difference reaches statistical significance but a replication of the original study fails to reach statistical significance. One must always notice whether the number of subjects in each of the studies was similar. The second study may have failed to find a statistically significant relationship simply because there were fewer subjects in that study.

Conclusion

The statistical techniques described in this chapter are only a small representation of those which are available. Since this book presupposes a background in introductory statistics, the material in this chapter is meant to serve as a refresher. If, however, you really understand the logic of the statistical techniques presented here, you ought to be able to read articles in professional journals with at least a moderate level of understanding.

The chapter that follows is on genetic methodology. It too will cover only the barest essentials of genetics. Nevertheless, appreciation of the logic and methods of genetics in that chapter will permit an intelligent reading of most professional articles in the area of behavior genetics.

3

Genetic Concepts

Basic Principles

In order to appreciate a number of the arguments and data presented in this book, it is necessary to understand some principles of genetics. Most of these principles are easy to follow, at least intuitively, and the ensuing review remains at the intuitive level wherever possible. Additional genetic concepts are presented in succeeding chapters where relevant to the data.

ZYGOTE

The entire genetic blueprint for the construction of an individual is contained in the *zygote*, the structure that results when a sperm penetrates an egg in the process of fertilization. The sperm and egg are both called *gametes*. Each zygote is composed of half the nuclear genetic material from the mother and half from the father. Note that the zygote does not contain all the nuclear genetic material from each parent. If this were to occur, the quantity of genetic material would double with each successive generation—in just 10 generations there would be 1024 times the genetic material contained in the first generation, and we would eventually become very heavy.

CHROMOSOMES AND GENES

Each cell contains structures called *chromosomes*. There are many *genes* arrayed in linear order along each chromosome. The genes are of fundamental importance, for they are the blueprints for the construction of the organism. Each gene is a brief section of a long macromolecule called deoxyribonucleic acid (DNA). The DNA in turn is composed of a long chain of smaller molecules, each link of which contains (1) a pentose sugar, (2) a phosphate, and (3) an organic base. The organic bases are of most interest because it is in the sequencing of these bases that the specific information for making a particular biochemical product is encoded.

The four organic bases are adenine, cytosine, guanine, and thymine. If each of these bases is treated as a letter of the alphabet and if one makes the sequence of letters as long as necessary, then with just these four letters one can make codes for very complicated substances. Actually, three-letter sequences are used to code for each of the twenty amino acids that serve as the building blocks for the organism. Since there are sixty-four possible three-letter sequences of the four bases and there are only twenty amino acids to code for, several three-letter sequences may code for one amino acid and others may serve as punctuation to terminate the coding. The full process is more complicated than this description indicates. The DNA actually serves as a template for ribonucleic acid (RNA), which interprets the DNA code and then goes into the cytoplasm of the cell to find the appropriate amino acids and order them into specified sequences.

MUTATIONS

Errors in the transcription or the translation of the DNA code cause *mutations*. These mutations can arise from many different causes and are the source of all genetically based differences both within and between species. The majority of mutations are deleterious, but some are either neutral or positive.

When mutations are deleterious they often impair the organism's potential to reproduce, usually because of premature death. Under these circumstances the mutation will not be transmitted to the next generation. Favorable mutations, on the other hand, may enhance the organism's reproductive capacity. In that case the mutant will transmit to the next generation disproportionate numbers of offspring carrying the mutation. Should this selective advantage continue, the mutation will become increasingly frequent in successive generations.

CHROMOSOME NUMBER

Each human cell, except for gametes, contains 46 chromosomes, 23 from each parent. Two of them are *sex chromosomes* and the others are *autosomes*. The sex chromosomes are called X and Y; females have two X's and males have an X and a Y. The number of chromosomes varies with the species; for example, the rhesus monkey has 42, while the chimpanzee and the potato have 48. For normal organisms of a particular animal species, however, the number is constant. A convenient way of expressing chromosome numbers for humans is 46XX for females and 46XY for males. Sometimes the chromosome number deviates from normal during the duplication process, producing individuals with chromosome constitutions that differ from the usual.

MITOSIS AND MEIOSIS

There are two forms of cell division, mitosis and meiosis. *Mitosis* is simply a doubling of cells along with a doubling of chromosomes. If each parent were to transmit his or her full complement of chromosomes to an offspring, however, the offspring would contain the sum of both parental chromosome numbers and over generations the number of chromosomes would become astronomical. The development of *meiosis* was the solution to this problem. It takes place only in gametic cells, where the number of chromosomes is exactly half of the total chromosomal complement. When a sex cell from one parent unites with that of the other, the total then equals the number of chromosomes originally present in each of the parents alone. In mitotic division, which takes place in all other cells of the body, the ratio of cells to chromosomes remains constant and there is no need for a reduction division in which only half the genetic complement of a parent cell is transmitted.

Figure 3.1 provides a simple illustration of cell division. In this figure each individual has only two chromosomes, one from each parent, although the actual number of chromosomes is 46 in humans.

In mitosis, each chromosome within a cell doubles and then the homologous chromosomes derived from each parent (e.g., a chromosome number 1 from the father and a chromosome number 1 from the mother) move to the same side of the cell. The other two chromosomes

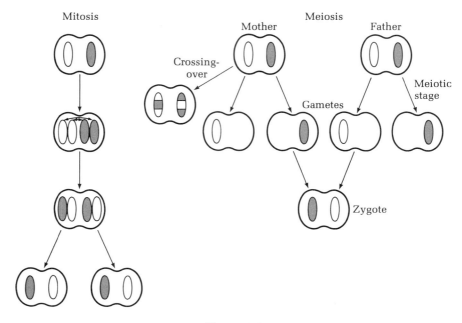

Figure 3.1

A schematic comparison of mitosis and meiosis. The open ellipse represents a chromosome from one parent; the darkened one represents a chromosome from the other parent.

go to the other side of the cell. Finally, the cell divides into two cells, each having the same chromosome complement as the original. Note that at one point during the duplication process there are actually 92 chromosomes in one cell, but after the cell divides there are again only 46 chromosomes per cell.

The essential difference between meiosis and mitosis is that, in the meiotic division process, only 23 chromosomes enter the gametic cell instead of 46. When these 23 chromosomes from one parental gamete unite with the 23 from the other parental gamete in the zygote, the number of chromosomes is again 46. Another difference between meiosis and mitosis is that *crossing-over* can occur in meiosis. At about the stage illustrated in the figure, chromosomal material can be exchanged between homologous chromosomes from each parent. When the chromosome number is then halved, 23 going into each gamete, one really cannot speak of *the* maternal or paternal chromosome anymore, since each whole chromosome may be a mixture of both.

Sometimes the duplication process is not carried out faultlessly. For example, during the division process both chromosomes from the same pair may enter the newly formed cell, the other newly formed cell getting neither one of those chromosomes. This error is called *nondis-junction*. When it occurs in one of the gametes, fertilization with the spouse's normal gamete in the zygote can result in three copies of that particular chromosome or only one copy of that chromosome. For example, there might be two sex chromosomes in one gamete. When it unites with a normal gamete, there will be a total of three sex chromosomes instead of the usual two. Should the gamete without any sex chromosomes unite with a normal gamete, the zygote will have only one sex chromosome. Mistakes of this sort can be fatal, depending on the particular chromosomes involved in the nondisjunction. When there are three instead of two chromosomes of a particular sort, the extra chromosome may produce an excess of certain biochemical products. Likewise, an absence of a particular chromosome may result in a deficiency in products necessary for normal development.

Other sorts of chromosomal rearrangements can take place. These all occur in, or just before, *synapsis*. In synapsis the corresponding chromosome pairs become intertwined and may then exchange genetic material. The types of chromosomal rearrangements are illustrated in Figure 3.2.

In a *deletion*, a twisted chromosome breaks off and the major portions then reunite, leaving the smaller segment to disappear. This can be serious because the chromosome will then be deficient in coding for some substance. If the healthy counterpart chromosome cannot compensate for the deficiency, the defect might be lethal. An *inversion* occurs when a broken chromosome segment becomes whole again after the broken fragment has rotated 180 degrees. This rearrangement changes the sequence of genes on a particular chromosome and impairs the chromosome's capacity during synapsis. A *duplication* occurs when only one chromosome receives genes from the other in crossing-over. This chromosome might then produce excesses in the particular substances whose coding has been duplicated. Finally, there is *translocation*, in which a fragment from one chromosome is displaced onto a nonhomologous chromosome so that the new chromosome has genetic material from a different chromosome in addition to its own. Translocation errors sometimes occur in Down's syndrome or mongolism and have the effect either of altering the timing for producing various biochemical substances or of making excesses of some products.

REGULATORY AND STRUCTURAL GENES

Thus far we have characterized genes as coding for some structures. It is now known that there are two classes of genes, those which code for protein structures, or *structural* genes, and those which control the

54

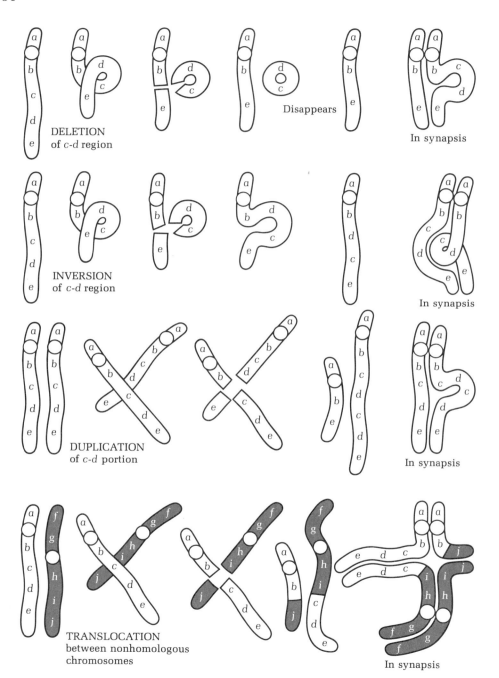

Figure 3.2

Types of chromosome rearrangements. (From Merrell 1962.)

onset and offset of other genes, producing no structures of their own, however. These latter gene types are called *regulatory* genes and are very difficult to identify. They may have played a very large role in evolution, however. Because there are relatively few differences in structural genes between species, it seems likely that regulatory genes produce species differences by affecting the timing of onset and offset of structural genes. Of course, differences within species may also be affected by structural genes.

GENES AND GENOTYPES

Corresponding genes at a particular location or locus on homologous chromosomes may differ in their structures or functions. These corresponding genes are called *alleles,* and those at a given locus A can be designated $A1$ and $A2$. Sometimes in a population of individuals there are more than two alleles for a particular genetic locus, although any one individual can have only two of the variants. When this occurs, the other variants can be labeled $A3, A4$, and so on. The genotype refers to genes in combination; hence, an individual with the genes $A1$ and $A2$ has the genotype $A1A2$.

GENOTYPE AND PHENOTYPE

While the genotype refers to the genes themselves, which are not usually directly observed, the phenotype refers to the visible consequences of the genes or genotype. Thus, traits or aspects of an individual such as eye color, weight, height, intelligence, and voice quality are phenotypes. Those interested in the genetics of behavior are concerned with the relationships between genotype and behavioral phenotype.

DOMINANT AND RECESSIVE GENES

An individual has two homologous genes for each autosomal locus. Sometimes these two genes are not identical but one is dominant over its recessive counterpart. Dominance and recessiveness refer strictly to the gene's effects on phenotypes. *Dominant* genes produce a constant phenotype, regardless of the gene with which they are paired. *Recessive* genes show their phenotype only if paired with another recessive gene.

Dominant genes are conventionally designated by capital letters and recessive genes by lowercase letters. For example, in a recessive form of deafness the presence of the D gene either as a homozygote DD or as a heterozygote Dd results in normal hearing, and D is said to be dominant to d. Only when the genotype is homozygous dd will the individual be deaf.

In the case of Dd heterozygotes, however, two different gametes will be formed. Half of the gametes will contain the D gene and half will contain the d gene. It is a matter of chance which one of these gametes will be involved in fertilization. Let us now consider some of the possibilities that can arise with the mating of two individuals of different or similar genotypes.

Figure 3.3 provides examples of the types of offspring that may result as a product of parental genotypes at one locus. In Case 1 both the mother and the father are homozygous for the dominant normal genes. They will produce zygotes that are all homozygous normal for the genes in question. In Case 2 one parent is homozygous normal and the other is heterozygous normal. In Case 2 matings, all the offspring will be normal phenotypically, but half of them, on the average, will be heterozygotes and, consequently, carriers of the deaf gene. Thus, the gene may be passed on to the next generation. In Case 3 both parents are

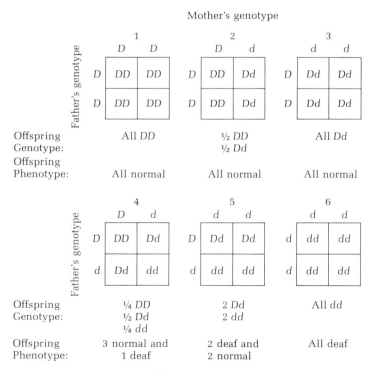

Figure 3.3
Genotypes of children from various mating combinations.

homozygous, but one is homozygous for the normal gene and the other is deaf and homozygous for the recessive gene. All children of such matings will be normal phenotypically but will be carriers of the recessive gene for deafness. In Case 4 both parents are heterozygote carriers of the recessive gene for deafness. One out of four of their children, on the average, will be homozygous for the deaf gene and thus will be deaf. In Case 5 one parent is a carrier of the deaf gene and the other parent is homozygous for the deaf gene. On the average, half of the children will be deaf in such matings and the other half, although phenotypically normal, will be carriers. In Case 6 both parents are homozygous for the deaf gene and all children will be deaf. Remember that the expected frequencies for Cases 2, 4, and 5 are only averages and will vary within particular families.

PEDIGREES

Analysis of pedigrees, or family trees, determines whether a gene for a trait is dominant or recessive. In analyzing a pedigree, one tries to determine the fate of each individual in a family with respect to the trait of interest. Investigators try to go back as many generations as possible in order to ensure precise judgments. Simplified pedigrees are shown in Figure 3.4.

Pedigrees are usually displayed so that squares represent males and circles represent females. Empty symbols indicate the absence of the phenotype or trait of interest and blackened symbols indicate the presence of the trait. The numerals at the side of the pedigrees refer to the generation of the family, and the arrow indicates the individual who was first identified (the proband, or index case). A horizontal line directly connecting two adjacent individuals in the pedigree indicates marriage or mating, and the vertical lines extending from the horizontal lines indicate the offspring of those matings. Sometimes the spouses are not included because they are presumed normal. Siblings are represented in the order in which they were born, from left to right.

In the example of dominant inheritance, the index male's older sister, father, and paternal grandmother all show the inherited trait. This is a pretty clear example of dominant inheritance. Barring mutations, with dominant autosomal inheritance, (1) no child is affected if both parents are unaffected; (2) only families with an affected parent can have an affected child; (3) both sexes are affected with the same frequency; and (4) the trait does not skip generations in the pedigree.

In the example of recessive inheritance, shown in the middle of the figure, the following conditions hold true: (1) all children are affected if both parents are affected; (2) parents who are unaffected can have affected children; and (3) the trait can skip generations (in this example

58

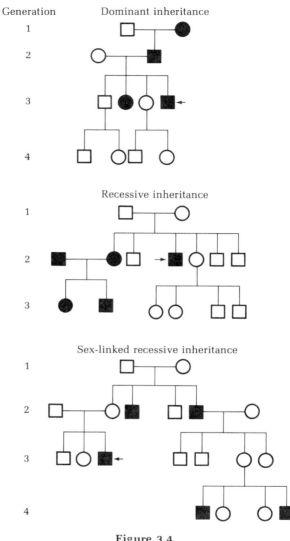

Figure 3.4
Some examples of dominant, recessive,
and sex-linked inheritance.

the trait is not present in Generation 1 but is present in Generation 2). In
interpreting this pedigree one can assume that both parents of Generation 1 were heterozygous carriers of the trait in question. As Case 4 in
Figure 3.3 shows, if four children are produced from such a mating, on
the average three will be unaffected and one will be affected. Two of the
unaffected will be carriers of the gene, however, and, should they in

turn mate with other carriers or affected individuals, some of their children could be affected.

Sex-linked inheritance is a bit more complicated. In this type of inheritance, certain traits appear to be related to the presence of the sex chromosome X. You will recall that the female sex chromosome constitution is XX and the male is XY. X and Y are not homologous chromosomes, although they are both sex chromosomes. Thus, if a male has a gene for a particular trait on his X chromosome, there is no opposing X chromosome to compensate for whatever that gene is coding for. If a trait is recessive and sex-linked, then a female might be a carrier of the particular gene on one of her sex chromosomes; however, since she does have a homologous sex chromosome, the recessive gene must be present on both to be evident.

In the example in Figure 3.4, note that (1) only males have the trait (this is the first clue that the trait could be sex-linked); (2) not all male siblings of affected individuals have the trait (this is because half the time the carrier mother will transmit her normal X chromosome to the child and half the time she will transmit the abnormal chromosome); and (3) in recessive sex-linked traits, fathers never pass the sex-linked deviant gene to their sons (this is because they pass their Y to their sons and not their X).

The examples given in Figure 3.4 were made easily understandable for didactic purposes. Often the patterns of inheritance are less clear-cut. Sometimes genes are incompletely penetrant, which means that the individual has the gene but the trait is not expressed. This can occur for a variety of reasons, the main one being that other genes the individual happens to inherit may compensate for the defect of the gene of interest. Incomplete penetrance can also occur when a critical environmental factor is not present to allow the expression of the trait.

MULTIPLE GENES

When the presence of genes at two or more loci is necessary for the expression of a particular phenotype, *polygenic* inheritance occurs. In the two-locus case it is easy to work out statistical expectations, but pedigrees based on a limited number of families may deviate considerably from expectations and more sophisticated techniques must then be employed.

Let's consider an example of polygenic inheritance in which the presence of homozygous recessive genes at two loci is believed to be necessary for the expression of the trait. We assume that each genetic locus is independent of the other, so that the transmission of one gene has no effect on the transmission of the gene at the other locus. If we grandiosely assume that 16 offspring are produced from such a mating, only 1 of the 16 children, on the average, will be homozygous for the two recessive gene pairs and thus identified as being affected (Table 3.1). Families that produce few children may be carriers of the genes of interest, but only a fraction of such families will express the trait. In general, pedigree analyses are of diminished use in such cases, and one must look for other indications that recessive inheritance might be operating. One way of doing this is to study families that have already produced at least one affected child. The prime indication of recessive inheritance under these circumstances is consanguinity. If the parents are themselves biologically related, the likelihood that both parents will be carriers of the recessive genes is increased.

Table 3.1

Genotypic combinations of offspring from parents who are each carriers of autosomal recessive genes for a trait determined by two genetic loci

		Mother's genotype = AaBb			
		AB	Ab	aB	ab
Father's genotype = AaBb	AB	AABB	AABb	AaBB	AaBb
	Ab	AABb	AAbb	AaBb	Aabb
	aB	AaBB	AaBb	aaBB	aaBb
	ab	AaBb	Aabb	aaBb	aabb

Genotypes produced	Frequency	
AABB	1	
AABb	2	
AAbb	1	
AaBB	2	
AaBb	4	
Aabb	2	
aaBB	1	
aaBb	2	
aabb	1	Affected
	16	

Notice that we have moved from individual pedigrees to populations of families. We now can compare the frequency of inbreeding among the parents of affected individuals with the frequency of inbreeding in control populations. This technique has been very useful, particularly in the area of mental retardation, where it has been found that retarded offspring are more frequently the products of consanguineous unions than are normal controls.

Population Genetics

As we move from the examination of pedigrees to the study of populations, a derivative set of principles needs to be applied.

HARDY-WEINBERG EQUILIBRIUM

A central concept in population genetics is the Hardy-Weinberg law, which describes the frequency of different genotypes among the individuals in a population. We can see how this works by returning to the example of two heterozygotes who mate in Figure 3.3. In this case we will assume that we know the genotypes of the parents.

Of every 4 individuals produced from this mating of two heterozygotes, on the average, 1 will be affected with the disorder. Let p stand for the proportion of D genes in the parents and q stand for the proportion of d genes in the parents. In this case, p and q are each equal to 0.5; thus, $p + q = 1$. The following is a presentation of the genotypes:

	Mother	
	D	d
Father D	$DD = p^2$	$Dd = pq$
d	$Dd = pq$	$dd = q^2$
	$p^2 + 2pq + q^2 = 1$	

Working backwards, we observe that the recessive phenotype, and hence the genotype dd, occurs in .25 of the cases. This value equals q^2. Thus, $q = .5$. Since $1 - q = p$, p also equals .5. We would then predict p^2 or .25 of the individuals would have the DD genotype, $2(pq)$ or .50 of the offspring would have the Dd genotype, and q^2 or .25 of the children would the dd genotype. This is exactly what we find.

In this example it might be argued that the Hardy-Weinberg equilibrium told us no more than we already knew about the frequency of expected genotypes. Let's consider an example in which we do not know the parental genotypes. Suppose that a particular. abnormality occurs in 1 percent of the population. Let us assume too that the abnormality is caused solely by a recessive gene and that parents randomly mate with each other. Then $q^2 = .01$ and $q = .10$; p must then equal .90. Applying the Hardy-Weinberg formula, we get the following: if p^2 equals all those who are genetically normal with respect to the abnormal gene, then $(.9)^2$ or .81 of the people in the population will be homozygous normals, $2(pq)$ or .18 of the people will be carriers of the gene, and .01 of the population will be homozygous for the recessive gene and therefore abnormal.

We see from this example that the number of carriers of the recessive abnormal gene in the population is 18 times the number of people actually affected with the disorder. The general rule is, the rarer the genetic disorder, the greater the *ratio* of carriers to those affected. Discouraging those with an infrequent recessive disorder from reproducing would not appreciably reduce the frequency of the disorder in the next generation, since most of the abnormals in the next generation will come from the mating of heterozygous carriers.

INCIDENCE AND PREVALENCE

One of the more difficult problems bedeviling workers in estimating gene frequency is the problem of ascertainment. How does one estimate the number of people actually affected in the population? It is not as easy as it might appear. Estimates based on those who come to the attention of physicians or other authorities ignore those who do not. This problem has plagued workers in psychopathology. Many middle-class individuals seek private treatment for their troubles and do not enter public institutions. In other social groups many cases may not come to medical attention at all. Consequently, if data only from public institutions are used, the frequency of these disorders will be underestimated.

It is important to distinguish between incidence and prevalence. *Incidence* refers to the proportion of individuals who ever exhibit a given trait. *Prevalence* refers to the frequency of individuals having the trait of interest at any one particular time. Thus, if we were to determine the number of individuals with schizophrenia on 1 May 1980, we would be specifying the prevalence of the disorder on that date. If we want to know how many of them have been schizophrenic in the past or will become schizophrenic in the future, we must determine the incidence of the disorder. One way to do this is to examine birth registers from long ago, following the fates of those individuals born in a specified year.

Sometimes differences between prevalence and incidence rates are great. For example, manic-depressive psychotic episodes are usually short-lived; consequently, individuals may remain in hospitals for only brief periods of time. Because only a fraction of cases will be in the hospital at any one time, it may appear that this form of psychosis is fairly rare. If incidence figures are examined, however, the disorder appears to be fairly frequent. On the other hand, schizophrenia is more likely to be chronic and patients stay in hospitals for longer periods of time. Consequently, the distinction between prevalence and incidence figures will not be so great.

It is always difficult to determine accurately the incidence of particular disorders, and this difficulty complicates the understanding of modes of genetic transmission. That is why it is important to understand how subjects were ascertained for inclusion in a particular study and why incidence figures based on the relatives of normal probands are desirable. In most instances, cases come to the attention of investigators because of the presence of an affected individual already in the family. As a result, the likelihood that any pedigree will have affected members is increased, and therefore the ratio of affected to unaffected members in the family will be increased. Families with no affected offspring are not ascertained by this method. Furthermore, the effect of this bias is especially apparent in one-child families, although it tends to decrease as family size increases. If parents come to the attention of investigators after they have one child, it is most likely that this child was affected by the disorder and the parents want to know about the risk that future children will be affected. Consequently, one-child families will have a disproportionate number of affected offspring.

One way of correcting for ascertainment bias is to exclude the index cases from an estimate of gene frequency and the mode of genetic transmission. Let's consider eight families of sibship size 2 that have

Table 3.2

How affected families are ascertained

Family	Children
1	AA
2	AN
3	AN
4	AN
5	NA
6	NA
7	NA
8	AA

Note: A = abnormal, N = normal.

been brought to the attention of investigators because each has an affected child (Table 3.2). Suppose that in two families both children are affected and that in the rest 1 child is affected. The total number of affected offspring is 10 of 16, giving a risk estimate of 62.5 percent. This uncorrected estimate leads to the conclusion that the disorder is closer to autosomal dominant inheritance than to recessive inheritance. If the index case in each family is excluded from the calculations, however, then 2 of 8 individuals are affected, or 25 percent of the offspring. This figure is in accord with recessive inheritance. Corrections of this sort are usually made for all sibship sizes separately, before the frequency and mode of genetic transmission are estimated.

MORBIDITY RISK

Still another problem confounds estimates of the frequency of genes or disorders in the population, namely, age of onset. Many genetic disorders begin at various ages, often tending to occur only in specific portions of the life span, such as late adulthood. An examination of the risk to other family members must take into account the ages of those family members, because some unaffected relatives may become affected later. Common examples of late-onset psychological disorders include Huntington's chorea, schizophrenia, and manic-depressive psychoses. The Weinberg short method is one technique for estimating *morbidity risk,* or the risk of being affected.

Let us take the example of schizophrenia, which seldom occurs in childhood or after forty-five years of age, and see how one might correct for this bias (Table 3.3). First one must determine the number of individuals already affected with the disorder in the sample under study

Table 3.3

Weinberg short method for calculating morbidity risk

Age	Number affected	Total sample size	Risk completed	Corrected sample size
0–14	0	200	0	0
15–45	25	400	0.5	200
46+	40	600	1.0	600
Total	65			800

Morbidity risk estimate, $m = \dfrac{\text{Number affected}}{\text{Corrected sample size}} = \dfrac{65}{800} = 8.1\%$

and order them by age. These individuals are presumably from families that have one other affected person already.

From this fictitious sample it is apparent that 8.1 percent of the first-degree relatives of schizophrenics are at risk for developing schizophrenia themselves. This estimate ignores those under fifteen and is based on the assumption that those people who are between fifteen and forty-five have, on the average, completed only half the period under which they are at risk. Consequently, the effective sample size for that age group is reduced by half. In this example sex distributions by age of onset have also been ignored and both sexes have been lumped together. When there is a sex difference in age of onset or in the frequency of the disorder, it is more appropriate to do these corrections for each age and sex separately.

DETECTION OF CARRIERS

Better than the statistical determination of risk is the actual knowledge of the carrier of the gene or genes, whether or not the person displays the disorder at the time of the investigation. One of the most promising areas of study in genetics is the detection of these carriers. In general, detection of carriers requires information about the gene itself or some "marker" that indicates the presence of the gene.

One of the greatest advances in the detection of carriers came with the development of a technique called *electrophoresis*. Genes code for amino acids, which then combine to make proteins. Some amino acids are negatively charged and others are positively charged. Thus, a protein can be placed in a supporting medium, such as a starch gel, and a current passed through the protein. Those proteins which are positively charged as a function of their average overall electrical charge will tend to migrate towards the negative pole, and those negatively charged on average will move towards the positive pole. After the migration is completed, the protein can be stained and a "fingerprint" of it can then be identified. This technique was very important in identifying the specific amino acid abnormality of sickle cell anemia.

Another way that carriers can be identified is to give those who might be carrying the abnormal gene a provocative test. This usually involves the administration of a substance that the gene presumably is unable to metabolize properly. One common provocative test is the glucose tolerance test for diabetes mellitus, a disease that causes defects in eliminating blood sugars at the usual rate because of insufficient insulin secretion. A basic tenet of genetics is that even recessive genes that are not phenotypically visible under the usual conditions may still be working abnormally.

Figure 3.5 gives glucose tolerance curves for three groups of individuals, none of whom had been diagnosed as having diabetes. The
controls were subjects who had no parents diagnosed as diabetic; the
second group were the offspring of one diabetic parent; and the last
group were offspring of two diabetic parents. As soon as thirty minutes
after the administration of the glucose load, the curves are shown to be
diverging. This suggests that those with one or more affected parents
rid themselves of the glucose in their blood at a slower rate than did the
fully normal controls. Those with two affected parents had slower rates
of elimination than those with only one affected parent (Neel et al.
1965).

It should be pointed out that, while the data were statistically able to
discriminate average glucose tolerance curves of these three different
groups, there was considerable overlapping of the curves of the individuals in different groups. As a matter of fact, interpretation of these
data suggested that diabetes mellitus was due to abnormalities at more
than one locus—a polygenic effect.

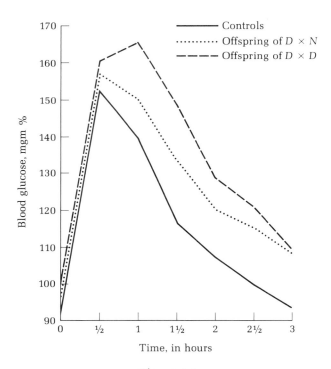

Figure 3.5

Glucose tolerance curves for offspring of diabetic (D)
and non-diabetic (N) matings. (From Neel et al. 1965.)

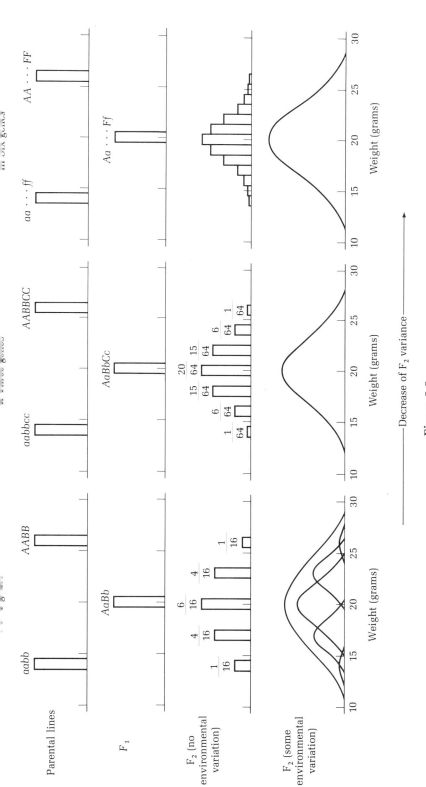

Figure 3.6

Crosses between two lines differing by two genes, three genes, or six genes. Distributions are shown for P, F$_1$, and F$_2$ generations in the absence of environmental variation. The bottom line shows the F$_2$ distributions as they would appear with some environmental variation. In each case, the homozygous "lightweight" parental line has a weight of 14 grams. In Case 1, alleles A and B each cause an increase of 3 grams in weight each time they occur in an individual. In Case 2, alleles A, B, and C each add 2 grams. In Case 3, alleles A, B, . . . , F each add 1 gram. (From W. F. Bodmer and L. L. Cavalli-Sforza, *Genetics, Evolution, and Man.* San Francisco: W. H. Freeman and Company. Copyright © 1976.)

POLYGENES

As indicated earlier, many traits of interest to psychologists are due to the action of genes at more than one locus on the chromosomes. Genes for intelligence seem to follow this pattern, as do genes for traits such as height and weight. In polygenic inheritance the genes at a particular locus are inherited in the usual fashion, but it is the genes in combination at multiple loci that determine the phenotypic effect. Each gene in polygenic inheritance contributes a smaller amount to the total phenotypic effect than it does to traits involving only single loci.

When traits are influenced by polygenes, the effects often approximate a normal distribution. This distribution often appears continuous and can be distinguished from discontinuous distributions, in which one either has the trait or doesn't have it.

One way to visualize a polygenic effect is to look at a trait involving two, three, or six loci. Figure 3.6 shows two separate inbred lines that differ from each other on every relevant locus. These two groups of animals are called the parental generation. If those two different homozygotes mate, they will produce the first filial generation, or the F_1 generation, which will be heterozygous for these genes at every locus. If, in turn, these F_1 hybrids mate, they will produce the second filial generation, or the F_2 generation. This generation will again yield homozygotes like those in the parental generation, as well as a range of intermediate types.

You can see that when the F_1 individuals are mated to each other the range of offspring begins to approximate a bell-shaped distribution—the more genes that enter into the trait, the closer the distribution is to a bell-shaped curve. The lowest portion of the figure shows what the distributions would look like if there were also some environmental variation. The environmental variation would make the weight differences caused by the genotypes less discrete, and, consequently, the distribution would be smoother.

Similarity Between Relatives

Obviously relatives share more similar traits than do nonrelatives. But how similar are relatives genetically? We know that both parents transmit exactly half their chromosome complement to each child and no more. Therefore the genetic similarity between each parent and each child is one-half. To see how similar siblings are to each other, consider Table 3.4.

Suppose that the trait under investigation came from one genetic locus and that the mother was of genotype $A1A2$ and the father was of genotype $A3A4$. These genes need not be functionally different from

Table 3.4
Gene overlap with relatives

	Mother	Father
Genotype	$A1A2$	$A3A4$

	Children	
	1	2
	$A1A3$	$A1A3$
	$A1A4$	$A1A4$
	$A2A3$	$A2A3$
	$A2A4$	$A2A4$

each other; the use of different labels for each of the genes merely identifies the parent from which the genes come. The first child can inherit either $A1$ or $A2$ from the mother, but not both. Likewise, the child can inherit either $A3$ or $A4$ from the father, but not both. Each gene in each pair has a fifty-fifty chance of being inherited. Thus, the child will have one of four equally possible genotypes; these possibilities are listed separately for child 1 and 2 in Table 3.4. Suppose the firstborn child has genotype $A1A3$, which is underscored. Child 2 can have the same genotype or one of three other genotypes. Counting the genes rather than the genotypes, however, one can see from the other underscored genes that there are four possibilities out of eight that the second child will resemble the first. Thus, on the average, two full siblings will share about 50 percent of the genes at each genetic locus. This principle applies to every genetic locus, so that siblings will average 50 percent genetic overlap overall.

While this example shows an average of 50 percent genetic overlap by descent, the percent of genetic overlap in terms of the functions of the genes can be higher. Imagine that both parents are homozygous for the same genes so that $A1, A2, A3$, and $A4$ are not functionally different from each other. In terms of similarity by descent there would still be 50 percent overlap, but in terms of gene function there would be 100 percent overlap.

The likelihood that parents will resemble each other in terms of their genes is related to their own degree of genetic relatedness, as well as to the degree of genetic variation in the population. An inbreeding coefficient, F, is a measure of the degree of genetic similarity; this will be taken up briefly later.

How similar would the grandchildren of these mothers and fathers in the chart be to their grandparents? Each grandchild will inherit only

$A1, A2, A3$, or $A4$ from a given grandparent via the parent so that, on the average, there will be one-fourth genetic overlap between each grandparent and each grandchild. And so it goes from generation to generation; parent-child overlap is one-half; grandparent-child overlap is one-fourth; and great-grandparent-child overlap is one-eighth. Each generation halves the degree of genetic relationship of the preceding generation.

One way to estimate the degree of genetic overlap between relatives is to count the number of steps between relatives by going back to the common ancestor and multiplying each step by 0.5. If there are two common ancestors, the degree of genetic overlap must be summed before the degree of genetic relatedness is computed. For example, first cousins are children of siblings; their degree of genetic relatedness is one-eighth.

Figure 3.7 shows how this is computed. Let X stand for one of the grandparents, A and B for the two children of that grandparent, and C and D for the grandchildren of X. To get the degree of genetic relatedness between C and D, we count the steps back from C through A to X to B to D, multiplying each step by one-half:

$$(0.5)(0.5)(0.5)(0.5) = \tfrac{1}{16}$$

We do the same for the other grandparent, since these two first cousins have two common ancestors, and again the answer is one-sixteenth. Summing the two values gives us one-eighth degree of genetic relatedness. You might try computing this for uncles and nephews or for half-siblings. The answers should equal one-fourth in both instances.

It is important to know the degree of genetic overlap between individuals in order to interpret many of the correlations between relatives for various psychological and physiological traits. For example, a correlation of .80 on a trait for pairs of siblings when there was nearly random mating of parents would not be consistent with a pure genetic

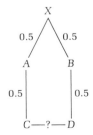

Figure 3.7
Computing the degree of genetic relatedness.

hypothesis, since the siblings' degree of genetic relatedness is only one-half. Consequently, one would conclude that an appreciable amount of nongenetic influence is making them more similar than they should be. Of course, such a high degree of similarity in a trait between relatives doesn't preclude the presence of a substantial genetic influence, but it does mean that there is at least some environmental influence that is making them more similar than they should be.

Herein lies a real strength of behavior genetic predictions for psychology. One can make specific estimates of how similar relatives should be based on their degree of genetic relatedness. In the simplest genetic model, genes are solely responsible for the trait in question and parents randomly mate. Thus, siblings should correlate .50 and grandparents and grandchildren should correlate .25, as should uncles with their nieces or nephews and half-siblings with each other. Departures too far from the predicted relationships can then be interpreted as indicating nongenetic influences or more complicated forms of inheritance. If the individuals are more similar than they should be, it is likely that environmental factors common to the relatives are making the individuals more similar. If the relatives are less alike than they should be on the basis of genetics, the presence of nongenetic influences is also suggested. In this case, however, there are more complicated genetic models that could be advanced to explain the findings.

Specific predictions are generally more desirable than *relative* predictions, which do not say how much more or less similar subjects should be to each other but simply predict that individual A will be similar to B. Genetically based models, which make specific predictions, tell exactly what the relationships should be, not just more or less.

For example, identical twins are not concordant for schizophrenia 100 percent of the time, but there is evidence that schizophrenia has a substantial heritable component. Since identical twins have 100 percent gene overlap, the fact that they are not perfectly concordant for schizophrenia is proof that genetic factors cannot completely account for the development of schizophrenia. Hence, some of the best, if not the best, evidence for a nongenetic component to schizophrenia comes from studies in which predictions are based on the degree of genetic relatedness.

Genetic Diversity

When one examines the extent of genetic diversity between individuals by electrophoretic methods, it turns out that at about 30 percent of loci two people will have genes that differ. Furthermore, about 16 percent of loci within an individual will be heterozygous. These observations, made simultaneously by Harris (1966) and by Lewontin and Hubby (1966), caused a great stir, because it was hard to understand why there was so much genetic heterogeneity. The answer to this question is still not resolved, but genetic heterogeneity does indicate that there is plenty of opportunity for different genes to undergo selective increases or decreases in frequency over generations. If one gene is advantageous such that those carrying the gene are at a selective advantage to leave more offspring, then the gene should become more frequent in the population over generations.

The selective forces that cause genes or genotypes to be at a relative advantage or disadvantage can be either biological or cultural. Most of the time these forces are hard to detect because they are not intense enough or they may have been operating only at one particular time in the past.

A classic instance of selective advantage is the case of sickle cell anemia. Normal hemoglobin in red blood cells makes these cells especially susceptible to the ravages of one form of malaria in Africa. It was noted that, where malaria was common, sickle cell anemia was also prevalent, even though the anemia almost invariably resulted in death. When the sickle cell gene happened to be paired with the normal gene for hemoglobin, however, it produced an individual with increased resistance to malaria.

This *heterozygote advantage* has the effect of maintaining the sickle cell gene at high frequencies in African populations. As malaria comes under control through better public health measures, however, the heterozygote advantage will disappear and the frequency of the sickle cell gene will decrease. Of course, if a cure for sickle cell anemia is discovered, the gene might remain at its current frequency in that population.

The heterozygous combination of the sickle cell and normal hemoglobin gene is one of the few documented cases of heterozygote advantage in human populations (there are many examples in animals), but it is a forceful one. This advantage occurs under extreme selection pressure to succumb to the effects of malaria. In Western civilization it is hard to find an equivalent genetic defect that could become so frequent because we cannot identify strong selection pressures working against survival of a normal homozygous genotype. There are nevertheless some diseases, such as asthma, cystic fibrosis, and schizophrenia, that appear to have some genetic basis and are relatively frequent in the population. If there is a genetic basis to these disorders, there might be some, as yet undetected, selective advantage for the carriers of these genes in a subdued or heterozygous form.

Of course, it is possible that each of these disorders was even more common in the past when there was a selective advantage. Now these genes may be in a transient state from even higher frequencies in the past to lower frequencies in the future, and we may be observing these genes along their downward path. We should be alert, however, to the possible positive effects of apparently deleterious disorders, particularly in some subdued form.

There are other instances in which cultural, and not biological, factors are determinative in decreasing or increasing the frequencies of certain genes in populations. A gene for one form of albinism is inherited as an autosomal recessive and is relatively common among some North American Indian tribes, including the Hopi of Arizona. Under most circumstances albinism is associated with reduced reproductive fitness, since many more diseases occur with greater frequency among persons possessing the gene than among those without it. Given the deleterious nature of the gene, it is surprising that albinism was so frequent among the Hopi (about 1 in 200 individuals was affected).

Pedigree analyses showed that among the Hopi albinism was viewed very favorably for cultural reasons and females preferred to mate, both inside and outside of marriage, with albinos. Consequently, the albinos tended to produce disproportionately more offspring than normally pigmented individuals. Since the Hopi are a relatively isolated breeding population, there was also an excess of inbreeding among them to further increase the likelihood that carriers of the albino gene would mate with each other and produce albinos (Woolf and Dukepoo 1969). Thus, cultural forces can also contribute to selective advantages or disadvantages for particular genes or genotypes.

We have limited our illustrations of selective advantage to genes at one locus, but it should be remembered that the unit undergoing selection is the individual and his or her aggregate genotype at all loci. With so much genetic variability within individuals, the chances are that some genetic combinations are advantageous and others are disadvantageous or neutral. When each locus is examined in isolation for signs of selection, this variability is sometimes ignored (Mayr 1970). Only when there are strong selection pressures can the selective effects of genes at particular loci be detected.

Reducing Heterogeneity by Genetic Analyses

One of the major obstacles to understanding genetic influences in both psychology and medicine is the frequent lumping together of seemingly identical disorders that really have different underlying genetic causes. We may talk of schizophrenia as if it were a single specifiable disorder, but it is possible that different genetic and environmental combinations can produce a similar phenotype. Thus, it may be more appropriate to think in terms of schizophrenias rather than schizophrenia. Each form of schizophrenia may be due to genes at different loci, and some may not be due to genetic differences at all. In manic-depressive psychoses, to be described in a later chapter, it was shown that at least two genetically independent forms of the disorder had been lumped together. These had superficially appeared to be similar, but it was shown that these two forms did not tend to occur with the same frequency in the same family.

One example of how clearer genetic differentiation has led to better understanding is the case of gargoylism, the disorder apparently depicted in the gargoyles of Gothic cathedrals (Herndon, Goodman, and David, cited by Neel 1955). The characteristics of gargoylism are those of moderate dwarfism—a large head, prominent forehead, and plump face, as well as a variety of other signs.

The interesting fact is that some other symptoms did not occur regularly in the disorder. Genetic analysis of pedigrees showed that some families seemed to follow a sex-linked pattern in which only males were affected and that other families seemed to follow a pattern of autosomal inheritance. When all of the diagnostic signs were separated by the presumed mode of genetic transmission, there was more clarity than when the two modes were lumped together. The differences between the diagnostic signs associated with the two types appear in Table 3.5.

The most noteworthy observation in this table is that clouding of the cornea occurred only among those pedigrees in the autosomal inheritance group and never among those pedigrees following a sex-linked pattern. Dwarfing was also much more common and deafness less common in the autosomal form. Thus, with genetic analyses it was possible to reduce the diagnostic variability by establishing different subtypes, within each of which the disorder was more homogeneous and regular in its form. The same will probably need to be done for many psychological traits as well.

We shall close this chapter with a summary of factors leading to genetic diversity. As indicated earlier, *mutations* are the original source of all diversity. Mutations occur because of errors in the transcription of the genetic code and may arise from a variety of causes. Without *selection*—that is, the relative advantage of the newly mutated gene in producing disproportionate numbers of offspring—the gene will have only a small chance for survival over many generations (Stern 1973). The context in which the genetic mutation occurs is also important. In very small breeding populations there is a greater chance that the gene will become established over generations than in larger breeding populations.

Random *genetic drift* can also play an important role in changes in gene frequency, particularly in very small populations. As an extreme example, suppose only one couple in a population was allowed to have offspring. The chance combination of the parents' own genes as well as

Table 3.5

Frequency of certain physical findings in gargoylism by probable mode of inheritance

Clinical signs	Group 1, auto-somal recessive, 96 cases		Group 2, mixed, 129 cases		Group 3, sex-linked, 21 cases	
	Number	%	Number	%	Number	%
Corneal clouding	78	81.3	64	49.6	0	0
Dwarfing	70	72.9	60	46.5	7	33.3
Deafness	5	5.2	22	17.1	9	42.9
Limited joint extension	86	89.6	115	89.2	14	66.7
Typical facies	83	86.5	104	80.6	18	85.7
Cranial deformity	81	84.4	122	94.6	20	95.2
Hepatosplenomegaly	70	72.9	93	72.1	17	80.9
Mental defect	68	70.8	97	75.2	11	52.4
Spinal deformity	66	68.8	99	76.7	6	28.6
Hernia	44	45.8	73	56.6	11	52.4
Short neck	44	45.8	56	43.4	10	47.6
Otitis media	32	33.3	51	39.5	8	38.1
Hypertrichosis	28	29.2	35	27.1	5	23.8
Enlarged sella turcica	21	21.9	45	34.9	4	19.1

Source: From J. V. Neel, "On Some Pitfalls in Developing an Adequate Genetic Hypothesis," *American Journal of Human Genetics.* Reprinted by permission of the University of Chicago Press. Copyright © 1955.

the genes they transmit to their offspring could have a profound effect on the nature of the gene frequencies for subsequent generations. The same thing occurs in small breeding populations, when even by chance some parents have more offspring than others in the small population. Chance factors could then play a role in the change in gene frequencies for subsequent generations.

The groundwork has now been laid for the sections on individual and group differences that follow. The next chapter will take up the history of and theories about intelligence. We shall see that concepts of intelligence are still evolving and that we are a long way from arriving at definite answers about its nature.

II

INDIVIDUAL DIFFERENCES

4

Individual Differences in Intelligence: History and Theory

Intelligence Tests

The invention of the intelligence test was probably one of the most important psychological developments of the twentieth century. Without knowledge of a subject's past biological and social history, or the organic condition of the brain, it is possible to make reliable and valid inferences about current intellectual functioning for a very large segment of society. It is rare to find a trait of practical psychological utility that is uncorrelated with intelligence. Furthermore, the intelligence test is able to predict future intellectual, academic, and socioeconomic status with a substantial amount of success.

Actually, formalized testing procedures to assess fitness have been around for a long time—perhaps four thousand years. DuBois (1970) recounts the history of testing in China, where aspirants to civil service were required to pass a series of written examinations. In the fourteenth century, the first examination took place in the local district. It lasted a day and a night, requiring knowledge of Confucian classics and the composition of poems and essays. Anywhere from 1 to 7 percent passed and were allowed to take the next examination. The second again required composition of prose and verse, and about 1 to 10 percent passed. The final examination took place in Peking, where perhaps 3 percent passed. Those who passed all three became mandarins, eligible for public office. Taking average percents passing for the three examinations, one may conclude that about 5 per 100,000 aspirants finally achieved the status of mandarin. During the early 1900s the examination was abolished in favor of progress through the university.

Modern scientific inquiry into intelligence and its correlates began with the publication of *Hereditary Genius* by Francis Galton in 1869. Himself a child prodigy and younger half-cousin of Charles Darwin, Galton noted that individuals and families differed from one another in intellectual abilities and that eminence tended to run in families. His ideas in this regard are worth noting.

> I began by thinking over the dispositions and achievements of my contemporaries at school, at college, and in after life, and was surprised to find how frequently ability seemed to go by descent. Then I made a cursory examination of the kindred of about four hundred illustrious men of all periods of history, and the results were such, in my own opinion, as to completely establish the theory that genius was hereditary [p. 23].

Using Quetelet's mathematical description of the bell-shaped curve, Galton argued that any naturally occurring trait would have a mean and a normal distribution about the mean. Thus, the more remote a particular measurement from the mean, the rarer its occurrence. By applying that law to mental faculties, he developed a scale of abilities and called an individual who ranked first among approximately four thousand individuals "eminent." For those of even rarer ability, he assigned more extreme ratings.

Galton regarded social and professional life as a continuous examination and believed that success was achieved in proportion to aggregate merit. He believed that the world allotted marks according to "originality of conception, for enterprise, for activity and energy, for administrative skill, for power of literary expression, for oratory" (pp. 49–50). He argued that, after learning to overcome our initial astonishment at our early and rapid progress in arithmetic and reading, we take a more sober view of our difficulties in calculus and rhetoric. We learn our place among our competitors both in and out of school. Finally, we learn to accept our status in life and take pride in the fact that we are doing about as well as we can, given our capabilities.

Using data on distinguished individuals, including judges, statesmen, scientists, poets, artists, commanders, literary figures, and religious leaders, derived from dictionaries of famous men and newspaper obituaries, Galton applied his scale of merit to their relatives. Table 4.1

Table 4.1

Percent eminent kinsmen of eminent relatives

	Judges	States-men	Com-man-ders	Lit-erary	Scien-tific	Poets	Artists	Di-vines
Father	26	33	47	48	26	20	32	28
Brother	35	39	50	42	47	40	50	36
Son	36	49	31	51	60	45	89	40
Grandfather	15	28	16	24	14	5	7	20
Uncle	18	18	8	24	16	5	14	40
Nephew	19	18	35	24	23	50	18	4
Grandson	19	10	12	9	14	5	18	16
Great-grandfather	2	8	8	3	0	0	0	4
Great-uncle	4	5	8	6	5	5	7	4
First cousin	11	21	20	18	16	0	1	8
Great nephew	17	5	8	6	16	10	0	0
Great-grandson	6	0	0	3	7	0	0	0
All more remote	14	37	44	15	23 ·	5	18	16
Number of families containing more than one eminent man	85	39	27	33	43	20	28	25
Total number of eminent men in all the families	262	130	89	119	148	57	97	75

Source: From Sir Francis Galton, Hereditary Genius (1869). Reprinted by World Publishing Company, 1962.

presents summary statistical pedigrees of the relatives of the eminent individuals in his study.

Noteworthy is the clear decline in eminence with increasing distance from the proband. Though Galton's understanding of genetics was inaccurate by current standards, he correctly recognized that heredity varied in proportion to the closeness of descent. His interpretation of these findings was that genetic factors were responsible for the attainment of eminence and that environmental influences were negligible.

Galton's conclusions have been criticized on a number of grounds. Pedigree studies alone cannot provide definitive evidence for genetic influence on behavior traits, and Galton's minimization of possible environmental influences is therefore unwarranted. The most glaring inadequacies of Galton's interpretation are his incomplete treatment of the rarity of eminent females (although he does provide data on a very small number elsewhere in his book) and his inability to disentangle genetic and environmental influences. It is now clear that accomplishment depends not only on innate endowments but also on opportunities for education and social mobility. This is not to say that Galton's emphasis on genetic factors has been proven incorrect, but rather that a more adequate treatment of environmental influences would be necessary to justify his interpretation.

Interesting also was Galton's discussion of the marks obtained by those who gained honors in mathematics at Cambridge University. The honors were earned in a grueling examination lasting five and a half hours a day for eight days. The examination was divided into classics and mathematics, but only the findings for the latter are presented here. Galton argued that mathematics training prior to entering Cambridge was of negligible importance since honors were repeatedly won by those who had little exposure to the necessary mathematics before entry. Table 4.2 combines the mathematics scores over a two-year period of students who won honors at Cambridge.

Table 4.2

Scale of merit in mathematics for those
earning honors at Cambridge University

Test scores	Number of candidates in the two years, taken together, who obtained those marks
7500 to 8000	1
7000 to 7500	0
6500 to 7000	0
6000 to 6500	0
5500 to 6000	1
5000 to 5500	3
4500 to 5000	1
4000 to 4500	2
3500 to 4000	5
3000 to 3500	11
2500 to 3000	8
2000 to 2500	11
1500 to 2000	21
1000 to 1500	38
500 to 1000	74
Under 500	24

Source: From Sir Francis Galton, Hereditary Genius (1869). Reprinted by World Publishing Company, 1962.

What is striking about these data is the enormous differences in performance among this select group of students. One year the lowest man on the list of honors scored 237, while the highest obtained a score of 7634. The second highest score in this year was 4123. The 32-fold arithmetic difference between the highest and the lowest "honor" student was regarded as an underestimate of the actual difference between them, since a large part of the examination was taken up in the mechanics of writing and gave no advantage to the more gifted. Besides the 200 men listed in the table, there were approximately 600 others who failed to make honors on the examination; one can only imagine the poor performance of these hapless souls.

The lesson to be learned from these data is that under most circumstances it is difficult to discern large differences on a scale of ability but that when environmental tasks are sufficiently challenging, as in the case of higher mathematics, remarkable differences among people begin to be distinguished.

Starting from the not unreasonable perspective that all information comes ultimately from the senses, Galton concluded that impairments in these areas would perforce lead to deficiencies in intellect. Reinforced in this view by the observation that mentally retarded individuals often display deficits in these areas, Galton suggested that the more intelligent would have superior sensory and motor functions.

Others followed in Galton's footsteps. In America, James McK. Cattell (1890), who first coined the term "mental test," developed a series of ten measures of intelligence. These included the following:

1. *Dynamometer pressure.* The power of a hand squeeze was regarded as a psychophysiological measure.

2. *Rate of movement.* The rate of hand movement has a large mental component also.

3. *Sensation areas.* This test measured the distance on the skin by which two points must be separated so that they can be distinguished.

4. *Pressure causing pain.* This measure was thought valuable in the diagnosis of nervous diseases and in studying abnormal states of consciousness.

5. *Least noticeable difference in weight.* This was regarded as a psychological constant.

6. *Reaction time for sound.* This test presented an auditory stimulus and required pressing a telegraph key.

7. *Time for naming colors.* Because reaction time was essentially reflexive, it seemed that a process more purely "mental" should be recorded.

8. *Bisection of a 50-centimeter line.* This was regarded as a measure of the accuracy with which space is judged.

9. *Judgment of 10-second time.* This provided a measure of the accuracy with which time is judged.

10. *Number of letters repeated upon once hearing.* This was a measure of attention and memory.

Studies to validate these tests against criteria such as school grades in normal populations proved singularly unprofitable (Wissler 1901), but more recently some of these tests have been modified and successfully incorporated into the investigation and measure of "biological intelligence" by Halstead (1947) and Reitan (1955). For example, since the motor cortex of the hemisphere contralateral to the hand controls motor movement, one can compare the relative strengths of hand squeeze (making allowances for normal differences between left and right hand) to determine whether there has been damage to the motor cortex.

BINET-SIMON SCALES

The greatest practical advance in intelligence testing came in the form of the Binet-Simon scales. Asked by the minister of public instruction in Paris to develop a test that could distinguish normals from subnormals, Binet and Simon devised a series of items that was easy to administer, of a heterogeneous nature, and bore principally on the faculty of judgment. Binet and Simon (1905) considered judgment the cardinal characteristic of intelligence, and, indeed, all other aspects of intelligent behavior paled before it. They said of this aspect of intelligence:

> To judge well, to comprehend well, to reason well, these are the essential activities of intelligence. A person may be a moron or imbecile if he is lacking in judgment; but with good judgment he can never be either.... Laura Bridgman, Helen Keller ... were blind as well as deaf, but these [handicaps] did not prevent them from being very intelligent. Certainly this is demonstrative proof that the total or partial integrity of the senses does not form a mental factor equal to judgment [in Shipley 1961, p. 886].

Difficulty of items increased with age, and a heterogeneous batch of questions and tasks was employed. Though the Binet scales have gone through a number of revisions since 1905, the concept of item heterogeneity and preference for complex problem-solving tasks have been preserved in these scales. In many ways this test has set the standard for measuring intelligence so that virtually all new measures purporting to be intelligence tests have paid obeisance to the Binet scales by presenting correlations between the new measure and the Binet. What follows is a brief description of the thirty items in the first Binet scale.

1. Visual coordination—do head or eyes follow a moving match?

2. Tactile prehension—is child able to pick up and bring object to mouth?

3. Prehension provoked by visual perception—does child grab object he sees?

4. Distinction between inedible and edible objects—does child try to eat chocolate and refuse to eat pieces of wood?

5. Unwrapping of candy

6. Following of simple commands

7. Naming of objects

8. Naming of objects from pictures

9. Naming of designated objects—can child name objects pointed to in pictures?

10. Comparison of two lines of unequal length

11. Repetition of three digits

12. Comparison of two weights

13. Suggestibility—does child refuse to follow command that is absurd?

14. Vocabulary

15. Repetition of sentences

16. Identification of differences between objects—how are fly and butterfly different?

17. Identification of pictures from memory

18. Drawing of a design from memory

19. Repetition of digits

20. Similarities—how are a poppy and blood alike?

21. Comparison of lengths

22. Placing of five weights in order

23. Identification of weight that has been removed

24. Rhyming

25. Completion of sentences

26. Construction of sentences—child is asked to construct sentence including three specified words

27. Social comprehension

28. Reversal of hands of clock

29. Paper cutting

30. Definition of abstract terms

Binet and Simon intended to measure "pure" intelligence by disregarding, so far as possible, items related directly to schooling. In 1908 they modified the scale to differentiate among normal children as well as discriminate between the mentally deficient and normals. The 1908 version also grouped items by age from three to thirteen years. An item was placed at an age level where approximately 75 percent of the children passed. Validation of the scale was accomplished by noting if retarded children were less likely to pass items at a particular age and scholastically advanced children were more likely to pass items beyond a particular age level.

Stanford-Binet Intelligence Scale.   In 1916 Lewis M. Terman published an American translation and revision of the Binet. Two major American revisions of the scale have been made since then. The 1937 version had two equivalent forms, L and M. The 1960 revision had only one form, L-M; it extended the test up to the superior adult level; and it replaced the IQ based on mental age alone with the concept of deviation IQ.

As indicated before, a test item was placed at an age where 75 percent of the standardization population answered correctly. Typically, there were 6 items at each year level; therefore each item was worth 2 months in mental age. Subjects were then administered the entire test and the number of items passed was multiplied by 2 months' mental age. Thus, an individual who passed 50 items would obtain a mental age of 100 months. This 100 months was then divided by the subject's chronological age (in months) and multiplied by 100 to obtain the IQ. For example, a child of 7 years and 6 months (90 months) with a mental age of 100 months would obtain an IQ of 111, derived from the following formula:

$$IQ = \frac{\text{Mental age}}{\text{Chronological age}} \times 100 = \frac{100}{90} \times 100 = 111 \text{ IQ}$$

The item content of the Binet test seems to counter the claim that good judgment was the essential feature of intelligence, for items involving perceptual-motor coordination and memory were also included. The contradiction is evident in Binet's 1909 comments about intelligence:

> The mental faculties of each subject are independent and unequal; with a little memory there may be associated much judgment.... Our mental tests, always special in their scope, are each appropriate to the analysis of a single faculty [quoted in Spearman 1927, p. 24].

The introduction of item heterogeneity at each age level meant that different faculties were measured at different ages, and this is in contradiction to Binet's thesis. If faculties are independent, then what is the utility of the mental age concept, which merely corresponds to that chronological age for which the particular number correct is the average? The overall performance, which is indexed by the mental age, is simply an average of heterogeneous performances. While the overall performance may be of some practical utility in prediction, it would be difficult to argue that an accurate picture of an individual's intelligence was being obtained.

Thurstone (1926) pointed out another contradiction of the mental age concept. For one definition of mental age, the test can be given to all people of a particular chronological age and the average number correct can be obtained; this would correspond to the mental age associated with that particular number correct. But if one starts the other way around and identifies all people with a particular number correct, and then finds the mean age of those people, that age very likely will not correspond to the same chronological age that was obtained in the first instance. This is because the regression of mental age on chronological age is not the same as the regression of chronological age on mental age.

There were other criticisms of the IQ concept based on mental age. The most important of these was the belief that there was a limit beyond which IQ based on mental age could not increase significantly with age. On memory for digits, the limit was fourteen years; for vocabulary, it was twenty-two years (Wechsler 1958). Since the denominator of the equation contained chronological age, adults who continued to answer the same number of items correctly would obtain decreasing IQs.

Wechsler's solution to the problem was the introduction of the deviation IQ and followed the lead of Thurstone (1926). Wechsler (1958) suggested that

> ... a person's intelligence at any given time is defined by his relative standing among his age peers. This assumes that though an individual's absolute capacity may change, his relative standing will not, under ordinary circumstances [p. 33].

According to Wechsler's solution, individuals at a particular age were administered the test, and the mean on the test was defined as a score of 100 and normally distributed with a standard deviation of 15. Thus, an individual who obtained a score 1 standard deviation above the mean earned an IQ of 115.

Wechsler (1958) remarked on the advantages of deviation IQs as follows:

> In the first place, they [deviation IQs] define levels of intelligence strictly in terms of standard deviation units and hence can be interpreted unequivocally. Second, they dispense with the necessity of making any

assumptions with regard to the precise relation between mental and
chronological rate of growth, and in particular to the linearity of the
relation. Third, they dispense with the need of committing oneself to any
fixed point beyond which scores are assumed unaffected by age, that is, to
a fixed average adult mental age. Finally, all IQ's so calculated, if numeri-
cally equal, may be assumed to be identically equivalent irrespective of
the age at which they have been determined [p. 37].

Wechsler (1958) recognized that the introduction of the deviation IQ
brought additional problems. Since individuals were now being compared with age peers, the aged needed to answer fewer items correctly
than young adults (at the peak of their intellectual powers) to obtain the
same IQ score. For example, an individual who obtained an IQ of 100 at
twenty years of age would earn an IQ of 113 for answering the same
number of items correctly at sixty-five years of age.

Wechsler was also critical of the Stanford-Binet because it contained
different tests at each age level. Thus, at one age an individual might be
exposed to mostly verbal items and at another to a higher proportion of
perceptual-motor items. Wechsler proposed to administer identical
subtests at all age levels, varying only the difficulty of the items within
a subtest. This solution, of course, does not ensure that the same ability
will be measured at different levels of difficulty, but on inspection the
problem-solving strategies within a subtest do appear to be similar.

Wechsler Tests. The 1939 version of the Wechsler test was called the
Wechsler-Bellevue Intelligence Scale; subsequent revision has resulted
in the Wechsler Adult Intelligence Scale (WAIS), published in 1955.
The revision essentially improved the norming procedures, provided a
greater range of item difficulty, and eliminated items judged ambiguous on the earlier version.

The WAIS yields three separate IQ scores; verbal, performance, and
full scale. The full-scale IQ essentially represents the average of the
verbal and performance IQs. These two subscales have been used extensively in the comparison of cerebral functioning of the left and right
hemispheres. By good fortune, it appears that for most individuals
verbal IQ skills are disproportionately represented in the left hemisphere, while performance IQ skills are more characteristic of right
hemisphere functioning. Thus, individuals suffering from lateralized
impairments of one or the other hemisphere would be expected to display selective deficiencies on one of the subscales (Reitan 1959). These
subscales have been particularly useful for the assessment of individuals who have suffered traumatic head injuries.

The subtests included in the WAIS are:

Verbal IQ	Performance IQ
1. Information	1. Digit symbol
2. Comprehension	2. Picture completion
3. Arithmetic	3. Block design
4. Similarities	4. Picture arrangement
5. Digit span	5. Object assembly
6. Vocabulary	

Group Intelligence Tests.   With the success of the individual testing movement in America came a parallel development in group intelligence testing. The selection of men in World War I was the major impetus here, since the mentally deficient were to be excused from participation in the war and it was desirable to select officer candidates of greater than average intelligence.

The army psychologists, under the direction of Robert M. Yerkes (1921), developed two group intelligence tests, the Alpha and the Beta. The Alpha was designed for literate, English speakers and the Beta was designed for illiterate or non-English speakers. The Alpha was composed of eight parts and covered such areas as following directions, arithmetic, practical judgment, synonyms-antonyms, disarranged sentences, number series completion, analogies, and information. The Beta consisted of a group of nonverbal performance tests, which included mazes, cube analyses, digit symbols, picture completion, and geometrical construction. The Alpha emphasized verbal and the Beta emphasized nonverbal intellectual functions; yet both were designated intelligence tests. This was consistent with the view that intelligence could be measured by a variety of roughly equivalent item types and that, since intelligence was essentially adaptational, there were multiple pathways to a particular correct solution. Thus, the emphasis was on achieving the correct solution and not on the method employed.

Spearman's (1927) unitary theory of mental abilities stemmed from his correlational analysis of a series of tests purporting to measure different functions. A not surprising result was that the tests tended to intercorrelate positively. He argued that the extent of the intercorrelation resulted from the fact that they were all tapping an underlying general factor, or g.

Spearman theorized that the difference between a positive, but imperfect, correlation and a perfect correlation of 1.00 occurred because each test had a specific component, or s, along with the general factor, or g. The Venn diagram in Figure 4.1 illustrates Spearman's theory. The tests were said to intercorrelate to the extent they were saturated with g. Test 2 correlates only to a small extent with Tests 1 and 3 because it does not have a high saturation of g. Spearman also argued that the correlation of

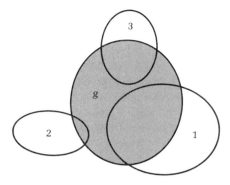

Figure 4.1
A model of Spearman's theory.

tests among themselves could be predicted rather precisely from their correlations with g. If Test 1 correlates .4 with g and Test 3 correlates .2 with g, then the product of those two correlations would give the correlation between Tests 1 and 3. Hence, the predicted correlation of Test 1 and Test 3 = .4 × .2 = .08.

Spearman's theory was indirectly a defense of Binet's choice of heterogeneous test items, since almost all mental tests tapped g to some extent and, consequently, it was not critical that items appear to have identical content. He also acknowledged, however, that many tests would intercorrelate over and beyond their correlation with g. For example, two tests of cancellation, one requiring the cancellation of X's from a line of letters and the other requiring the cancellation of E's, would intercorrelate over and above their correlations with the underlying g. He called these intercorrelations *group factors*. Such factors might reflect some special abilities or be due to excessive similarities in the test items themselves.

Spearman's own definition of cognition or intelligence contained two important qualitative components: (1) the eduction of relations and (2) the eduction of correlates. The eduction of relations is the capacity to extract a relation between two givens, such as "black—white," and the eduction of correlates is the capacity to apply this educed relation to a new situation such as "tall—?"). This, of course, is what we call reasoning by analogy, and, indeed, Spearman argued that analogy tests were among the best indexes of g. Sternberg (1977) has started investigating the component processes of analogical thinking for the very reason that it seems to be such a good index of g.

Spearman's quantitative methods came under fire from many different camps. A telling criticism came from Thurstone (1938), who applied techniques of multiple factor analysis to ability data. He concluded that there were a dozen primary mental abilities and that Spearman's g emerged only as a second-order factor. (Factor analysis starts with the actual variables, intercorrelates these variables, and identifies clusters among these intercorrelations. These clusters are called factors. When the original factor analysis utilizes the oblique method of factor rotation, it is also possible to intercorrelate the factors themselves with the resulting clusters of factor intercorrelations, called second-order factors.)

As Cattell (1941) pointed out, since g could be obtained as a second-order factor, both Spearman and Thurstone could be regarded as correct. There remained the question of the utility of the primary mental abilities concept, however, and its merits were hotly debated.

Kelley (1928) criticized Spearman on the grounds that the statistical procedures used to evaluate the presence or absence of g were faulty and that there had been some bias in the selection of tests used to demonstrate its presence. Kelley, like many others, argued that multiple factors were necessary to account for the intercorrelations between mental tests and that the ubiquity of g could not be demonstrated.

Others, such as Thomson (1948), suggested that a sampling theory of traits would satisfy many of the findings about the intercorrelations of mental tests without resort to g. Essentially the argument held that each behavior is composed of a number of elements and that those behaviors sharing common elements would intercorrelate with each other in proportion to their degree of sharing. This "sampling theory" left unspecified the nature of the common elements, but they could be genetic, neural, or environmental components.

The use of several factors rather than one general factor has not been shown to have a clear social or practical advantage, and one form of factor analysis, called principal components, will extract a first-order factor akin to g with data such as Thurstone had. McNemar (1964) suggests that, since these special abilities have not been found superior to general intelligence measures for predicting socially useful outcome variables typically employed by psychologists, such as grades in school and differential performance on the job, there seems little need to discard the concept of the primacy of g.

Exactly what g might be has eluded precise definition. One view is that all mental tests are in actuality complex, despite attempts to simplify. All tests will therefore contain common elements, and the commonality shared by all mental tests is what emerges as g (Thomson 1948). Another possibility is that, since the same or different problems can be solved by alternative mechanisms (there is more than one way to skin a cat), perhaps one ability is prepotent in an individual and this is what is being applied in various tasks of a seemingly heterogeneous nature. Since most tests merely record whether an answer is correct or not, the alternative and functionally equivalent processes leading to correct solution are rarely investigated.

Another view that is in keeping with the genetic material to be presented in the next chapter is that g is a quality of brain—for example, "good protoplasm." This inherited quality permits the acquisition, retention, and retrieval of appropriate knowledge towards the solution of problems.

One quality of the brain that appears to be related to problem solving success is the extent of dendritic arborization. Dendrites are processes that connect cells to each other. Each of the 11 billion brain neurons may average ten thousand synapses on those dendrites, which make connections to many other neurons. In fact, the number of possible interconnections is astronomical. Rats exposed to enriched environments have many more such arborizations than do environmentally deprived animals. These enriched animals are also more capable in problem solving (Greenough 1975).

Guilford (1967), however, contends that, if any two ability tests can be shown to be uncorrelated, it is sufficient to vitiate the fundamental nature of g. He has devised many ability tests that do not intercorrelate and therefore has actively pursued the multiple abilities concept in his "structure of intellect" model. This model is based on the orthogonal method of factor rotation and is illustrated in Figure 4.2.

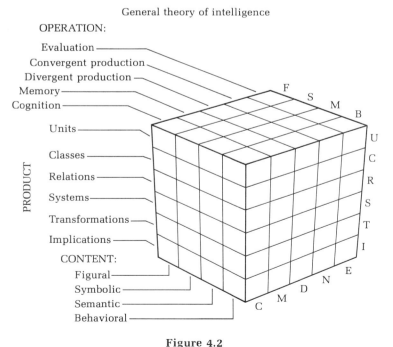

Figure 4.2
The structure of intellect model.
(From Guilford 1967.)

The solid cube contains the conjunctions of three sets of categories, which are given here:

Content	Operations	Products
1. Figural (nonverbal)	1. Evaluation (judgment)	1. Units (things, figures on grounds, chunks)
2. Symbolic (letters and numbers)	2. Convergent production (giving the correct answer)	2. Classes (common properties in diverse objects)
3. Semantic (verbal)	3. Divergent production (creative flexible fluency)	3. Relations (connections between two things)
4. Behavioral (social intelligence)	4. Memory	4. Systems (complexes, patterns of individual parts)
	5. Cognition	5. Transformations (shrinking, inverting)
		6. Implications (expectations)

Cattell (1971) has criticized Guilford's model on a number of points. The product classes could be replaced by other factors with equally good credentials, and the content categories are not mutually exhaustive or independent. Further, the specified operations omit several other possibilities. More importantly, Cattell holds that many of Guilford's tests, which appear to exist as statistical entities, bear little relation to the real world. Cattell suggests that a better procedure is to sample the behavior throughout the twenty-four hours of the day and find how such performances

> ... are spaced, i.e., whether one performance is very different from another or so close as to be considered a virtual duplicate.... For example, a psychologist could ... blow up a specific factor into a group factor (a primary) by multiplying the number of separate tests in quite a small specialized area. Only moderate ingenuity is required to invent ten different measures of efficiency in putting on and lacing one's shoes, and thus (since they are likely to mutually intercorrelate highly) produce a broad primary ability (covering ten variables) for putting on shoes [p. 28].

Horn and Knapp (1973) have uncovered an even more serious objection to Guilford's theory, namely, that his factor analytic techniques are not objective. Within his factor analytic technique even randomly generated hypotheses about which tests should or should not intercorrelate can be made to conform to the structure of intellect model Guilford proposes. This nearly devastating criticism requires that much of the data on which Guilford built his theory be reanalyzed using different factor analytic techniques.

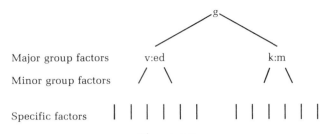

Figure 4.3
Vernon's schematic for ability factors.

HIERARCHICAL THEORIES OF MENTAL ABILITY

Burt (1949) and Vernon (1950) have proposed hierarchical models of intelligence. Vernon's model is shown in Figure 4.3. As in Spearman's model, g is at the top of the hierarchy and both verbal-educational (v : ed) and practical-mechanical (k : m) are immediately below. At the lowest level are specific factors, which Vernon acknowledges probably could be further subdivided. However, Vernon is of the opinion that these specific factors may be of little practical utility, since they appear to have little real-life variance. He suggests that it may be more useful (at least for the applied psychologists) to work with the broader factors that have consistent and reasonably substantial correlations with real-life criteria.

FLUID VERSUS CRYSTALLIZED LEVELS OF MENTAL ABILITY

Cattell (1971) has suggested that g could be subdivided into two major classes of abilities: fluid and crystallized. Fluid abilities are constitutionally or genetically based, while crystallized abilities are derived from cultural experiences. Excellent fluid abilities are a necessary, but not sufficient, condition for superior crystallized abilities; poor fluid abilities result in deficient crystallized abilities.

Evidence for this point of view comes from a number of sources, including findings, that, with age, performance on perceptual tests reaches a plateau earlier than performance on verbal tests, such as vocabulary or numerical ability tests; and that brain injury after maturity affects certain test performances more than others. Some test performances (mainly crystallized) depend on the location of the lesion, while others (mainly fluid) are affected regardless of lesion location. Also, after maturity, recovery is accomplished more readily in functions related to crystallized abilities than in those related to fluid abilities. Cattell (1971), like Hebb (1949), suggests that the abilities that are recovered after brain injury are abilities with substantial cultural components. Another important finding is that curves for the decline of mental ability with age differ for the two types of tests. The perceptual tests show a decline beginning at about twenty-five years of age, while the crystallized verbal tests could continue to rise throughout most of the life span.

Horn (1967) provides good descriptions of both sorts of abilities as well as samples of test items that are used to tap these abilities. Fluid abilities are believed to be relatively independent of specific cultural experiences and can be tested on those of non-Western cultural background. Tests of induction in which a general rule is to be discovered from a list of particulars, tests requiring detection of figural relationships, tests of memory span, and tests involving paired associates are all measures of fluid abilities. Of course the mode and content of presentation must be appropriate to the specific culture; it would not make sense to give an illiterate inductive reasoning problems such as, "What follows: A, 1, C, 2, F, 3?" It ought to be possible, however, to invent problems that could test for the equivalent inductive reasoning function in different cultures.

The crystallized abilities are closely tied to the store of gradually accumulated knowledge as represented in vocabulary, mathematics, and social reasoning. Tests calling for specific informational content are especially good measures of crystallized abilities.

The distinction between the two broad types of abilities cannot be sharply drawn, however, since it is often possible to solve a problem using either the fluid or crystallized modes. For example, a problem that could be solved using intuitive understanding might also be susceptible to solution with the help of algebra. The best evidence supporting the distinction between the two types of abilities does not even come from a detailed exegesis of the nature of the specific items, but rather from the fact that the growth and decline of these two types of abilities seem to follow different trajectories. The fluid abilities reach their peak in adolescence or early adulthood, whereas the crystallized abilities continue improving into late middle age, especially for those who have kept up with the esoteric aspects of their culture. More will be said about the fluid-crystallized distinction in Chapter 13.

Information Processing

Historical accident is probably responsible for the fact that those interested in intelligence and intelligence tests have remained isolated from experimental psychologists interested in the general processes of cognition. It is now being realized that this isolation makes no sense, for any theory of intelligence will ultimately be a theory of cognition. Figure 4.4 provides a general model of information processing, which emerges from cognitive psychology and is in the form of a flow diagram (Kausler 1974). Sensory information is first received and transduced, and then enters a short-term sensory store. This sensory store is on the periphery of the nervous system, as are the sensory receptors. Its action is evident in the afterimage you see when you turn off a bright light after staring at it for a moment. It seems that we identify features of stimuli by reading off of this short-term sensory store before it decays or is masked by new stimulation. The features that are detected from this store may then enter short-term memory or a rehearsal buffer that has very limited capacity. The rehearsal buffer actively goes over the information residing therein, as one does when rehearsing a new telephone number. The rehearsal buffer and short-term memory have limited capacity—too many things cannot be sequentially rehearsed at one time, and information decays rapidly if it is not continually activated or does not make contact with long-term memory. If the information has some larger meaning for the subject, it enters long-term memory, which presumably has nearly unlimited capacity.

It is important to make a distinction between structural and control processes in a general model of cognition. The structural features include the physical aspects of the system, and these "prewired" processes remain relatively fixed over situations. The control processes involve manipulation of information in the system and may be very

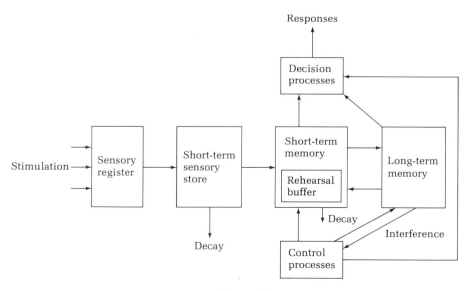

Figure 4.4
General model of memory (After Kausler 1974.)

dependent on previous experience, although they are probably not completely independent of the structural features of the system.

Figure 4.4 contains only the barest outlines of the model, and many researchers are investigating and further elaborating the component processes. Failures in intelligent performance can result if any of the component features are impaired either because of structural reasons or because of inadequate experiences. The system, however, is probably somewhat self-correcting in that impairments in one aspect of the system may be compensated by alternative control process strategies for processing the same information.

The information-processing approach focuses on what the subject brings to the situation in order to acquire knowledge about the world. The importance of this approach is that it acknowledges that differences in structural or control processes may account for the varying degrees to which people can extract or retain information about the environment.

PIAGETIAN THEORIES OF INTELLIGENCE

Piaget's approach to the study of intellectual functioning has for the most part employed the *methode clinique*. Having worked on the standardized method of administering intelligence test items, he was impressed by the types of errors children made in trying to solve intellectual problems. Finding consistency in the kinds of wrong answers children gave, he asked about the misapprehensions necessary to draw these incorrect conclusions. He noted that the answers given by older children differed qualitatively from those of younger children. By permitting the child's own answers to determine the next questions to be asked by the experimenter, Piaget was able to evaluate the processes and operations required for the answer given. Piaget concluded that the grasp of certain concepts showed an invariant sequence and that attainment of a more advanced stage always was associated with successful completion of an earlier stage. Some of the conservations associated with age are given in Figure 4.5. Note, for example, the weight problem, in which the child is asked, "Which is heavier, those objects lying horizontally or those same objects arranged vertically?" Most children below age eight focus on either the vertical or the horizontal dimension alone and answer either that the vertical blocks are heavier because they are taller or that the horizontal bocks are heavier because they are wider. The knowledge that weight is conserved regardless of shape is much more common among children older than eight. It appears that the various conservations form an ordinal scale. Children who are aware of conservation of weight also are aware of conservation of number, substance, length, and area, but they may not be able to solve the conservation of volume problem.

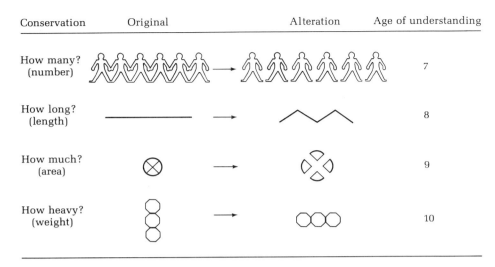

Conservation	Original	Alteration	Age of understanding
How many? (number)			7
How long? (length)			8
How much? (area)			9
How heavy? (weight)			10

Figure 4.5

A sampling of Piaget's conservations in which the child must recognize that number, length, area, and weight are conserved despite alterations in appearance.

Piaget himself was mainly concerned with normative child development and did not attempt to delineate individual differences in the attainments of the conservations. As is often the case, however, good data on normative development must be available before one can study departures from the norm. More recently, workers have attempted to psychometrize the conservation problems by presenting them in a standardized fashion (Tuddenham 1970). They have not found complete ordinality in the sequence of conservation attainments, but, in general, Piaget's theory has been confirmed. It has also been shown that the attainment of the conservations is not independent of general intelligence.

Table 4.3 presents data obtained by Tuddenham (1970) in his attempts to psychometrize the conservation items on a sample of 200 children in the first through third grades. The intercorrelations are given for some of the conservation tests. The volume item uses a fixed quantity of water, which is poured from a short, stubby glass to a thin, tall glass, and asks the child which glass contains more water. The tests of general intelligence employed in the study were Raven's Progressive Matrices, a nonverbal test in which the subject must complete a visual pattern, and the Peabody Picture Vocabulary Test (PPVT), which asks the subjects to identify from a series of pictures a particular item—for example, "Find the pitcher." It is noteworthy that the general intelli-

Table 4.3

Intercorrelations of some conservation items and intelligence test measures

	Volume (water pouring)	Length (chains)	Number (counters)
Length	.46		.40
Number	.60		
Age	.18	—	—
Father's occupation	.32	—	.19
Peabody Picture Vocabulary Test (PPVT)	—	.20	.35
Raven Progressive Matrices	.50	.27	.40

Note: Minimum of forty-three children entering into each correlation. Dashes mean no data available.
Source: From Tuddenham 1970.

gence measures correlate positively with the attainment of the conservations and that these correlations are only slightly lower than the interrelations of the conservation items among themselves. The Progressive Matrices test correlates positively with the entire scale of six to eight items .60, and the PPVT correlates with the entire scale .21. A number of investigators are taking a psychometric approach to Piagetian problems, and we can expect more data on this matter to appear in the not too distant future.

DISTRIBUTION OF INTELLIGENCE

More recent individual intelligence tests by convention set the mean for intelligence at 100 and the standard deviation at 15 (Wechsler). The Stanford-Binet, however, originally had a mean of 100 and a standard deviation of 16 because items were selected in such fashion that the average mental age of children at a particular age coincided with their chronological age (McNemar 1942). In contrast to the WAIS and the WISC, the standard deviation of 16 for the Stanford-Binet was originally an accidental function of the range and difficulty of the items chosen for inclusion on the test.

With representative sampling, the form of the distribution of correct responses is approximately bell shaped, but there is a "bump" at the low end and an excess of individuals at the high end. The bump at the low end is due to factors such as rare genetic occurrences and diseases or injuries to the brain that produce mental retardation. More will be said about these later.

CONSTRUCTING TESTS

Although we have discussed different views about intelligence, we have not described the logic behind intelligence test construction. Item writing is an art in itself, and usually many more items need to be written than are eventually accepted. The details of test construction differ, depending on whether the test is being used for children or adults. First we shall describe the construction of adult tests.

After the domain of the test has been identified, items are written and administered to groups of subjects. Item statistics are then developed, the most critical of which is the percentage of subjects that passed a particular item. Most of the items on the test should not be too easy or too hard. If too few pass or fail items, the test will not adequately distinguish between individuals. At the same time, if there are too many items of medium difficulty (e.g., 50 percent passing), the test will not be very discriminating at extremes of the score distribution.

Another item statistic of importance is the correlation between the passing or failing of a particular item and the total score on the test. Item passes should show positive correlations with total scores. Intercorrelations between items should also be positive, but not extremely high. If intercorrelations between items were extremely high, the incremental information derived from including more items would decrease.

For children, item statistics besides those mentioned in the preceding paragraphs become necessary, and the construction of the test becomes more complicated. Since intelligence is expected to increase with age, a greater proportion of the subjects should pass as age increases. Consequently, many items will be either too easy or too hard for children within a specified age group. In order not to frustrate the child, tests are usually terminated when a specified number of items, graduated in difficulty, are failed in succession. There are many other considerations of importance; detailed discussions of test construction can be found in Anastasi (1976) and Cronbach (1970).

The item statistics mentioned here are predicated on the view that intelligence is a general factor. A different theoretical model of intelligence, such as Thurstone's, which presumes a number of independent abilities, would add one further consideration in constructing tests— that items within a factor intercorrelate fairly highly among themselves but have fairly low intercorrelations with items on other factors.

Most tests are constructed to measure the percentage passing or failing particular items. It should be noted, however, that answering an item correctly or incorrectly is only one criterion for the assessment of intelligence. Thorndike et al. (1926) have pointed out that intelligence can be measured in terms other than "altitude." If individual A can answer more items of equal difficulty than individual B in an untimed format, A could be regarded as more intelligent and would be said to have greater "breadth." Also, if A can answer more easy items than B in a timed format, A could be regarded as more intelligent because of being speedier.

Speed, however, is especially complicated, since individuals may differ in the time spent on solving particular problems. Some may abandon items too difficult for them sooner than others, and others may abandon problems that they could eventually solve if they were more persistent (Furneaux 1961). Nevertheless, speed as an index of intelligence is beginning to receive much more attention than previously, the idea being that those who can process information faster than others are more likely to accumulate necessary information over time and, consequently, obtain higher intelligence test scores.

A major problem in all test construction is to develop items and tests that are unidimensional. Without unidimensionality, one cannot be sure what a particular score means. Imagine that there were two dimensions to test performance. Two subjects could get the same score in different ways. One subject might be high on one dimension and low on the other, while the second might have the opposite pattern of strength and weakness. Various scaling techniques for assessing unidimensionality are discussed in Guilford (1954).

SOCIAL CLASS, INTELLIGENCE, AND MOBILITY

A number of studies have shown that occupational class is associated with intelligence; those in higher occupational classes tend to have higher IQs. It has also been shown that the IQs of children are related to the social class of their fathers. Figure 4.6 provides an example of findings in this area. Waller (1971) recovered the IQ scores of fathers and their adult sons, all of whom had been routinely tested during their high school years in Minnesota. The figure gives mean IQs of the 130 fathers and 172 sons as a function of the father's social class. The data for fathers show that social class differences in IQ are substantial. The fathers in the highest social class average 114 IQ, while those in the lowest class average only 81 IQ. Their children's IQs demonstrate the usual regression towards the mean. The children of fathers from the highest social class obtain the highest average IQ scores, but the average IQ scores of those children fall below those of their fathers. Similarly, those children coming from the lowest social class obtain higher IQs than their fathers.

What about social mobility? Will children having much lower IQs than their fathers drop in social class while those children with higher IQs rise in social class? This question can be answered from Waller's data, since the sons now are an average of twenty-seven years old.

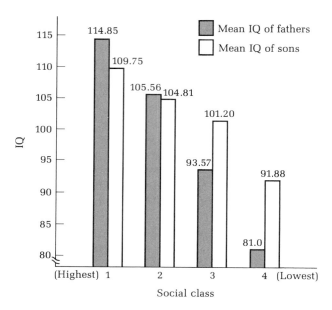

Figure 4.6

Relationship of IQ and social class in two generations. (After Waller 1971.)

Waller found that, indeed, differences in IQ between father and son were related to differences in the social class of the two. Children with lower IQs than their fathers went down in social class as adults, and those with higher IQs went up (r = .37 between difference in father-son social class and difference in father-son IQ).

If each generation of children distributes itself as the parents have been distributed, it will be necessary for individuals from lower classes to move upwards and those from higher classes to gravitate downwards in order for social class equilibrium to be maintained in successive generations. If a value near the mean for intelligence in a parental occupation is taken as the "appropriate" level for a particular occupational class, it is possible to calculate the proportion of fathers who are too high, too low, or correctly placed within an occupational class. Similarly, it is possible to group the children by parental occupational class and calculate the proportion whose IQs are above, equivalent to, or below their parental occupational class. For his data in Britain, Burt (1961) calculated that about 55 percent of parents were correctly placed, whereas only 33 percent of children were correctly placed. This means that a large proportion of the "incorrectly placed" children will have to move up or down in social class.

Burt's (1961) analyses are cited here primarily for illustrative purposes. They can be faulted seriously because many of the parents were *rated* on intelligence rather than actually tested, and any systematic biases of the raters could have affected the finding. One such indication of rater bias is found in the unusually wide differences in average intelligence between the parental occupational classes, suggesting that raters may have overrated the intelligence of the higher professionals and underrated the intelligence of the unskilled workers. For example, Gibson (1970) tested scientists at Cambridge University in England and found the mean WAIS IQ equal to 126.5. This is about 13 IQ points lower than the value obtained for a roughly corresponding group by Burt. However, while the exact percentage for mobility by intelligence is wrong, it is likely that the principles exemplified by Burt's analysis are correct.

Conclusions

From this review of some of the history and theories of intelligence, it is apparent that intelligence is not yet well understood. Disagreements among leaders in the field were apparent as early as 1921, when a symposium on the topic was held (Thorndike et al. 1921). There were almost as many different definitions as there were symposiasts. Thorndike defined intelligence as the "power of good response from the point of view of truth or fact." Terman held that "an individual is intelligent in proportion as he is able to carry on abstract thinking." Henmon argued that the definition of intelligence ought to be broad and include the "capacity for knowledge and knowledge possessed." And according to Haggerty,

> ... intelligence does not denote a single mental process capable of exact analytic definition. It is a practical concept of connoting a group of complex mental processes traditionally defined in systematic psychologies as sensation, perception, association, memory, imagination, discrimination, judgment and reasoning [Thorndike et al. 1921, p. 212].

Wechsler (1975) disagrees with previous definitions of intelligence because they have tended to mistakenly equate intelligence with the specific tasks employed to assess it. For him, dealing effectively with the test tasks, regardless of their specific natures, is a global capacity and is not to be equated with reasoning, spatial ability, memory, and so on. Intelligence includes good judgment, effective and worthwhile behavior, and nonintellective factors such as moral and esthetic appreciation.

Following Wechsler, one might ask whether a definition of intelligence is really possible and how it is to be identified independently of the tasks used to assess it. Experimental psychology endorses an information-processing view of intelligence, which is essentially value free, in contrast to Wechsler's definition, which is value loaded, specific to time and place. Information-processing approaches are "empty" because they focus on processes—sense receptor $\rightarrow$ encoding $\rightarrow$ decoding—and the intermediary and control processes necessary to produce a response. According to this view, failures in performance depend on insufficiencies in information storage or retrieval or the application of inappropriate control processes. Ultimately, however, the information-processing view ought to explicate how information is transduced in the mind. Perhaps then we will be in a better position to offer a definition of intelligence.

5

Individual Differences
in Intelligence:
Genetic Contributions

There has been much debate concerning the heritability of intelligence or, more accurately, the heritability of IQ scores. Some investigators have argued that intelligence is highly heritable, while others have argued the contrary (e.g., Kamin 1974). The best empirical evidence seems to fall somewhere between these two extreme views, as this chapter will show.

A perusal of the items on intelligence tests appears to indicate that these items do not measure any important differences in biological background but are more apt to measure differences in culturally specific experiences. The answers to questions such as "Why do deaf children have difficulty learning to speak?" or "What is the color of a ruby?" appear to be highly dependent on specific cultural experiences.

The view of intelligence test constructors, however, is that most of the items on intelligence tests could have been learned or overlearned by almost all individuals for whom the test is appropriate. This view argues that the more intelligent have extracted more information from their environments, either by doing it at a faster rate, remembering or synthesizing information better, or by exposing themselves to more information by virtue of their own actions, curiosity, and motivation. Ultimately, the logic of intelligence test construction places much of the responsibility for learning on the individual and not on the environment for providing and ensuring the acquisition of the information. The assumption is that, except for those who have been "extremely" deprived, there has been ample opportunity to acquire the necessary information and the reasoning powers to arrive at correct solutions to problems on the test.

This chapter first presents information about genetic factors in intelligence by explaining heritability quantitatively and then discusses evidence concerning the heritability of intelligence. The next chapter will take up the case of environmental influences on intelligence test scores more directly.

Heritability

Geneticists typically express the proportion of phenotypic variance accounted for by genetic factors in a population as the heritability of the trait, that is, the proportion of total variance that is genetic. The total phenotypic variance can be computed by the following formula (after Jensen 1969):

$$V_P = \frac{(V_A + V_{AM}) + V_D + V_i}{V_H} + \frac{V_E + 2\,\text{Covariance}_{HE} + V_I}{V_E} + \frac{V_E}{\text{Error}}$$

where

$$V_P = \text{phenotypic variance in the population}$$
$$V_G = \text{genic (or additive) variance}$$
$$V_{AM} = \text{variance due to assortative mating}$$
$$V_D = \text{variance due to dominance deviation}$$
$$V_i = \text{variance due to epistatic interactions}$$
$$V_E = \text{environmental variance}$$
$$\text{Covariance}_{HE} = \text{covariance of heredity and environment}$$
$$V_I = \text{variance due to statistical interaction of genetic and environmental factors}$$
$$V_e = \text{variance due to error of measurement (unreliability)}$$

Phenotypic variance. This refers to the variance of the trait as measured in the population.

Genic variance. This is the additive variance due to genes at one or more loci that have a constant effect, irrespective of the allele with which they happen to be paired. In many ways this is one of the most important sources of genetic influence for a trait such as intelligence. These additive genes are what makes for parent-child resemblance. The additive genetic effect of an individual on his offspring is the product of his genes alone; it is not dependent on the genetic complement of the mate, since additive genes are not at loci where they can be recessive.

Variance due to assortative mating. Assortative mating is the mating of pairs more similar for some phenotypic trait than would be expected from random mating alone. Normally, the variance due to assortative mating is part of the additive variance but can be estimated separately. Among other things, assortative mating affects the genetic structure of a population by producing siblings that are more alike than siblings produced in random mating.

Assortative mating correlations for intelligence vary, but the average estimate is about .50 in the general population. What this means is that the intelligence of spouses in the population correlates about .50. Vandenberg (1972) provides an extensive review of assortative mating for human behavior traits, and Spuhler (1968) does the same for human physical traits.

Assortative mating has a number of interesting genetic consequences, because it increases the variance for the trait in the offspring generation without affecting the overall average for the trait in the population. While the specific proportions of genes do not change at all in assortative mating, the proportions of different genotypes do (there is more homozygosity for the assorted trait). Of course for traits that are not perfectly heritable, regression toward the mean will reduce the expected variance increase in the next generation.

Consider a population of four individuals with IQs of 80, 90, 110, and 120, respectively. Suppose that the mean IQ of offspring of matings of any two of these people will equal the average of the parents' IQs (the midparent average). Suppose that each individual mates with every other, so that there are six matings altogether. The mean IQ of the six children will be 100, which is the average of the parents' IQs, and the SD will equal 9.1. Now let us restrict the matings so that only the two lowest in IQ mate with each other and the two highest in IQ mate with each other. The mean IQ of the two offspring will again equal 100, but in this case the SD will equal 15.0. Hence, the offspring resulting from perfect assortative mating will be more variable relative to each other than were the offspring resulting from random mating.

Of course assortative mating is never perfect, and this extreme difference would not be so clearly evident in populations where assortative mating is lower. Nevertheless, the general principle still holds, namely, that assortative mating increases the variability among children.

Assortative mating increases parent-child and sibling correlations because it increases the variance between families. In other words, the similarity between parents and children will increase in relation to their similarity to other families. Greater variance may have important consequences for civilizations because it increases the proportion of high or low scorers on a trait and the success of a civilization probably depends more on the proportion of high scorers than on the average level of a population. It seems likely that those with high intelligence scores are the ones to make the technological and creative advances that can then disseminate through the population and be used by those of lesser ability. An extensive discussion of assortative mating can be found in Jensen (1978).

Dominance deviation. The deviation of children's average value from the parents' average value on a metrical trait often indicates dominance deviation. Because alleles at some loci are recessive to others, the effect of a recessive allele can be unseen because it happens to be paired with a dominant allele. Thus, a parent with recessive alleles for a trait may not resemble a child even when that recessive gene is transmitted, because it is camouflaged by a dominant gene transmitted by the other parent. Dominance deviation is usually estimated from studies of inbreeding. Workers such as Jinks and Fulker (1970) have suggested that dominance deviation plays a large role in intellectual functioning.

Epistasis. Variance due to epistasis is the result of interactions within an individual's genotype. For example, an individual may have received two recessive genes at a particular locus reducing the efficiency of the manufacture of a particular gene product, but a gene at another locus may be able to restore that efficiency. This component is also responsible for some of the lack of resemblance between parent and child.

Environmental variance. This variance refers to all influences that are not genetic and include both prenatal and postnatal influences, biological as well as cultural. It does not include the error variance, however.

Covariance of heredity and environment. The covariance of heredity and environment is defined as twice the correlation between heredity and environment multiplied by the square root of the product of the heredity and environmental variances. It can be expressed in the following form:

$$\text{Cov} = 2r_{HE} \sqrt{V_H \times V_E}$$

The covariance of heredity and environment must be distinguished from the interaction of heredity and environment. The covariance of heredity and environment means that different genotypes are selectively *subjected* to different environmental treatments. In gene-environment interactions, on the other hand, different genotypes *respond* differently to the same environment.

Plomin, DeFries, and Loehlin (1977) have discussed three conceptually distinct types of gene-environment covariance. The *passive* type is one in which the parents give their children both good genes and good environment (or both bad genes and bad environment). The *reactive* type occurs when teachers and others respond differently to children of different genotypes by systematically furnishing different environments to children of different perceived potentials. The *active* type of covariance is one in which the child actively seeks out environments that are suitable to his or her genetic propensities. In practice, of course, it may be difficult to distinguish these three different sources of genetic-environment covariance, and many outcomes may be a mix of all of them.

To be sure there is some genetic-environment covariance for a trait like intelligence. More intelligent children are likely to be given increased opportunities for educational advancement and to be treated specially by their families and teachers. In a discussion of whether the covariance term belongs on the genetic or environment side of the equation, Jensen 1969 points out there is no right answer to the question:

> To the degree that the individual's genetic propensities cause him to fashion his own environment, given the opportunity, the covariance (or some part of it) can be justifiably regarded as part of the total heritability of the trait [P. 39].

Interaction of heredity and environment. This variance occurs because different genotypes respond differently to the same environment.

Error. Variance due to error is always present when there is some unreliability in the measures used. It is often possible to partially correct for unreliability with a trait like intelligence by obtaining an estimate of reliability and dividing the observed correlation by the reliability coefficient.

Confusion about the meaning of heritability is all too frequent. There are two senses in which heritability is used. Heritability in the narrow sense includes only the variance due to additivity and assortative mating. Animal and plant breeders refer to heritability in this narrow sense because selection of future generations of animals depends on narrow sense heritability only. Suppose one were to select cattle with the intention of increasing the average weight of the next generation. Assume that the narrow sense heritability of weight in this population is .5 and that the mean weight of cows in this total sample is 1500 pounds. If only those cattle weighing exactly 2000 pounds were selected to produce the next generation of stock, the expected weight of the next generation would equal $1500 + .5(2000 - 1500) = 1750$ pounds.

Heritability in the broad sense is more frequently employed in human behavior genetics. It includes all the terms listed in the heritability formula given on page 106, not only the proportion predictable from selective breeding.

HERITABILITY FORMULAS

There are many formulas for calculating heritability coefficients, not all of which yield identical values under all circumstances. Some heritability estimates are used for identical and fraternal twins or siblings reared together or apart and others are used for parent-child relationships. In actuality, it is possible to generate heritability formulas for any degree of genetic relationship, no matter how close or distant. Heritability estimates can range from 1.00 for perfect heritability to 0.00 for no heritability.

Most heritability estimates have been derived for identical and fraternal twins reared together. One of the simplest to calculate is Falconer's (1960) formula, $h^2 = 2(r_I - r_F)$, where h^2 equals the heritability, r_I equals the intraclass correlation for identical twins, and r_F equals the intraclass correlation for fraternal twins. The essential idea in all the twin formulas using identical and fraternal twins is that, since identical twins have about twice as many genes in common as do fraternal twins, the observed difference in the correlations for the two types of twins should be doubled. The Falconer formula assumes that there is random mating among the parents of the subjects and that only additive variance is responsible for the correlations. Another assumption is that the identical twins do not share more similar environments than the fraternal twins. Occasionally, the Falconer formula can yield values greater than 1.00 or less than 0.00. These values mean that some assumptions have not been met. A full discussion of heritability and the formulas applicable to various degrees of kinship is contained in Jensen (1973a).

Heritability estimates for parent-child relationships are simple to compute if the childen were adopted at birth. In this instance the heritability is equal to twice the correlation between parent and child. The correlation is doubled because a single parent transmits only one-half of her genetic complement to the child. It is always good, however, to obtain separate estimates for mother-child and father-child. Since the mother and child were together during the time the child was a fetus, there is a remote possibility that the heritability estimate might be inflated. Since father and child do not share the prenatal environment, agreement between the two estimates will increase confidence that the heritability estimates are reliable.

An important assumption in all heritability estimates is that shared environmental influences are not responsible for the heritabilities obtained. In the case of twins reared together, the assumption is that the identical twin correlations are not disproportionately inflated by environmental influences common to the twins.

Perhaps an even more important consideration is that heritability values are specific for the particular sample of subjects and measures used to obtain those estimates. One cannot make generalizations from one set of heritabilities because subject characteristics or test unreliabilities affect the heritabilities obtained. Furthermore, high heritability does not necessarily imply little potential environmental influence. Other environments, with more extreme effects, may be found or generated in another population and heritabilities may therefore be decreased.

There is considerable evidence that identical twins reared together are treated more alike than fraternal twins, but the evidence seems to suggest that this fact plays no detectable role in accounting for the greater similarity of identical over fraternal twins (e.g., Loehlin and Nichols 1976). A reading of the evidence suggests that many parents treat identical twins more alike not because of systematic attempts to do so but because identical twins behave more similarly than do fraternal twins. Of course many parents do make a consistent effort to treat identical twins more alike, but there is no indication that these children are any more or less alike than those whose parents have systematically attempted to treat the twins dissimilarly.

Just because a trait is highly heritable for a particular population, one should not conclude that it is difficult to modify nongenetically. Recessive genetic disorders that often produce mental retardation if untreated, such as phenylketonuria (PKU) or galactosemia, will not result in mental retardation if they are detected early enough that special diets can be introduced to prevent the accumulation of toxic substances in the brains of affected individuals. Our task at this point is merely to assess the evidence for genetic influences on intelligence. Later chapters will discuss how the genetic potential for intelligence can be modified.

KINSHIP CORRELATIONS

Erlenmeyer-Kimling and Jarvik (1963) have provided estimates of the various correlations among kinship members. They reviewed over fifty studies correlating the mental abilities for relatives on a variety of mental tests given over two generations. Figure 5.1 gives the median correlations for these studies. While the entire figure deserves careful scrutiny, we shall focus on those findings related to biological relatives reared together and apart.

Since the expected correlation for monozygous twins, whether together or apart, is 1.00, the fact that the observed correlations are less is evidence for nongenetic influences. These nongenetic influences include the unreliability of the tests used to measure intelligence, which will always lower the correlations obtained, as well as the differences due to dissimilarities in prenatal and postnatal environments.

The remainder of this chapter describes efforts to disentangle the relative influences of genetics and environment on intelligence, with

112

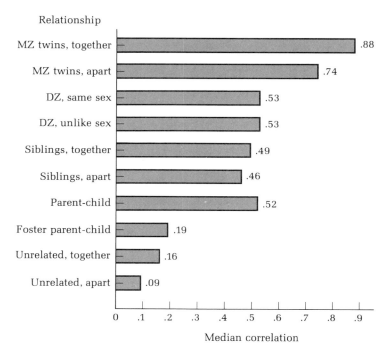

Relationship

MZ twins, together — .88
MZ twins, apart — .74
DZ, same sex — .53
DZ, unlike sex — .53
Siblings, together — .49
Siblings, apart — .46
Parent-child — .52
Foster parent-child — .19
Unrelated, together — .16
Unrelated, apart — .09

0 .1 .2 .3 .4 .5 .6 .7 .8 .9

Median correlation

Figure 5.1
Summary of IQ correlations for various degrees of kinship.
(Slightly modified from Erlenmeyer-Kimling and Jarvik 1963.)

the emphasis on genetic evidence. The next chapter will focus on influences on intelligence from an environmental perspective.

Genetic Influence on Intelligence

There are two extremely powerful and many less powerful approaches to estimating genetic components in intelligence. The most useful techniques involve either the study of children adopted early in life whose biological and adoptive parents have been tested with intelligence measures, or studies of monozygotic (MZ) twins who have been separated early in life. These two approaches will be considered in succession, and afterwards some of the less informative approaches will be described.

ADOPTION STUDIES

Essentially, the adoption design compares biological parent-child correlations for intelligence with adoptive parent-child correlations. A correlation between biological parent and child that is greater than zero suggests that genetic factors account for the relationship. A biological parent-child correlation that exceeds the adoptive parent-child correlation suggests that variations in genetic endowment are of greater influence than variations in environment, since at the time of testing the child has lived most of his postnatal life with his adoptive parents. It should be remembered that a single parent transmits only 50 percent of his genes to his child; therefore one cannot expect a perfect correlation of 1.00, even when genes are the sole determinant of the trait in question. Thus, in adoption studies the highest correlation expected between a single parent and child is only about .50 rather than 1.00, even with complete heritability. This is in contrast to an upper-limit correlation of 1.00 for monozygotic twins.

If the average of the two parents is used to predict the children's IQs rather than the single parent-child correlation, the maximum expected correlation is .707 under conditions of random mating, perfect test reliability, and perfect heritability. Of course when parents and children are tested on different measures, correlations will be reduced still more since it is doubtful that the two tests will measure precisely the same thing in the same manner. The .707 correlation comes from the averaging of the expected .50 between each parent and child. The formula for combining these correlations is $\sqrt{(0.5)}$, or .707.

To date there are no studies that have completely fulfilled the adoption design. In virtually all studies intelligence data on the biological father have been completely lacking, and therefore parental education or occupational level has been substituted. Problems arise because putative biological fathers, even in intact families, may actually be misidentified by the biological mother (Sing et al. 1971), and she may also report unreliably on his education and other matters. Nevertheless, correlations for intelligence between the biological father's reported education and child (whom he has usually never seen) are typically substantial in adoption studies.

In general the best adoption studies cover adoptions during the first year of life and have passable data on biological and adoptive families, few biases in the selection of biological mothers giving up their children for adoption, and sufficient information to pit biological and environmental determinants of children's IQ scores against one another. Following is a review of some of the best studies.

Burks (1928) compared 178 white adopted children, placed during the first year of life in adoptive homes, with a control group of 105 "own" children (children from intact families raised by their biological parents). Subjects were matched on sex, age, locality, and occupation of father. Many other measures of educational and social status were also obtained and will be reported in the next chapter. The major finding for our purposes now is that the adoptive midparent mental ages correlated only .20 with their adoptive children's IQs, whereas the biological midparent mental ages correlated .52 with those of their own natural children. The difference between these two correlations is statistically significant and supports the view that hereditary influences are more important than environmental influences in accounting for parent-child resemblance in intelligence.

Strikingly similar results to those of Burks were obtained by Leahy (1935). She matched 177 white children adopted before six months of age to 175 "own" control children for sex, age, father's occupation, education of parents, and residential size. Like Burks, she obtained a variety of educational, cultural, and intellectual measures for the parents, which will be reported in the next chapter. Using midparent mental age scores, Leahy found that the adoptive parent-child correlation was .18 but that the biological parent-child correlation was .60. As with the Burks study, Leahy's findings convincingly support a genetic basis to the resemblance between parents and children in intelligence. What both studies lacked, however, was information on the intelligence of biological parents of the adopted children.

An interesting feature of Leahy's findings relates the mean IQs of children to the occupational category of the parents. These data are reproduced in Figure 5.2. Among the adopted children the mean difference in IQ between the highest and lowest occupational categories is 4.8 IQ points, whereas there is a 16.5 IQ point difference from highest to lowest occupational category in the control group. Additionally, at the professional level the control children average about 6 points higher than the adopted children, while at the slightly skilled day laborer level the adopted children have the higher mean IQ by about 6 points.

These results can be explained in simple genetic terms. If one assumes that the group of children given up for adoption has near average genetic potential for intelligence (or at least a genetic potential higher than that of the children from the lowest socioeconomic classes), then the children adopted into professional homes should have an average genetic potential lower than that of the natural children of professionals. Likewise, the children adopted into homes of the lower occupational categories should have an average genetic potential higher than that of the natural children of this class of parents. All of this makes for larger regression effects in the adoptive families than in control families and can account for these findings.

Only a few studies have information on the biological parents of adopted children. In some ways these studies can be more valuable, since they offer the opportunity to pit biological parent-child correlations against adoptive parent-child correlations for the same set of children. The first study in this regard was that of Skodak and Skeels (1949), which obtained IQ data on 100 adopted children in a longitudinal study and IQ scores for 63 of the natural mothers of those children. The results of this study showed both hereditary and environmental

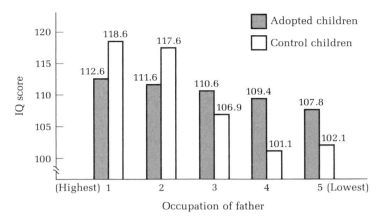

Figure 5.2
Intelligence of adoptive and control children classified
according to occupation of father. (After Leahy 1935.)

influences to be important. While the natural mothers of the adoptive
children had a mean IQ of only 86, their children averaged between 107
and 117 at various ages during repeated testings. This increase in mean
IQ from the biological mothers to the children is quite significant and
suggests a substantial environmental effect.

However, serious questions have been raised about the validity of the
appreciable increase in the IQ scores of the children over their biological mothers. The scores of the biological mothers appear too low, for
their educational attainments did not differ from those of other women
in Iowa, where the study was conducted (Tyler 1965). A strong hereditary influence was also found, since the IQs of the biological mothers
correlated .44 with the IQs of their adopted-away children at the final
testing in adolescence. Furthermore, biological mothers' education correlated .38 with the IQs of the children, whereas the adoptive parents'
education correlated only .04 with their adopted children's IQs.

Without considering the supposition that the IQs of the biological
mothers were underestimated, Jensen (1973b) asked whether the high
mean IQ of the children was inconsistent with that expected for high
narrow and broad heritability. We shall use here estimates of
heritability that are slightly less than those given by Jensen. Remember
that heritability estimates represent the portion of phenotypic variance
accounted for by genetic factors and, conversely, that $1 - h^2$ is the
proportion of phenotypic variance due to environmental influences and
measurement error. Let's assume for our purposes a narrow heritability
of .6 and a broad heritability of .7 for IQ scores and see if the results of
the Skodak and Skeels (1949) study are inconsistent with those
heritability values.

The biological mothers of the adopted children average 85.7 IQ. Although the IQs of all the biological fathers are unknown, let's assume that there was assortative mating for IQ in this group, as in most studies, with r = .39 (Jinks and Fulker 1970). The expected mean IQ of the biological father would then equal .39 (85.7 − 100) + 100 = 94.5. The midparent IQ mean would then equal 85.7 + 94.5/2 = 90.1.

The formula for estimating the regression of offspring on parents for a heritable trait is given by Crow and Kimura (1970) as the following (for IQ specifically):

$$\overline{IQ}_{off} = \overline{IQ}_{pop} + h_n^2 (\overline{IQ}_{par} - \overline{IQ}_{pop})$$

where

$$\overline{IQ}_{off} = \text{mean IQ of children}$$
$$\overline{IQ}_{pop} = \text{mean IQ of population}$$
$$h_n^2 = \text{narrow heritability}$$
$$\overline{IQ}_{par} = \text{midparent mean IQ}$$

Thus, 94.16 = 100 + .6 (90.1 − 100). Hence, the predicted mean IQ of the offspring was 94.2, but the observed mean for the most comparable test was 107, a discrepancy of 12.8 IQ points. These results suggest a substantial improvement of the children over their parents. But is this improvement incompatible with a narrow heritability of .6 and a broad heritability of .7, if the children were placed in very superior environments?

If .7 of the variance in IQ is due to broad heritability, then variance due to environment and measurement error is (1 − .7) = .3. If the total variance in IQ = 15^2 = 225, that proportion of the variance due to nongenetic influences is .3(225) = 75. The standard deviation of IQ for nongenetic effects will then be $\sqrt{75}$ = 8.66. Thus, 1 standard deviation of environmental advantage would be expected to elevate IQ scores about 8.7 points (ignoring measurement error).

Skodak and Skeels (1949) report that indeed the adoptive parents were very superior to individuals in the general population. If the homes averaged about 1.5 SDs above the mean for environmental factors, then the IQ discrepancy in this study would not be inconsistent with estimates of heritability that are moderately high. Although one cannot unequivocally demonstrate that degree of superiority of the adoptive families over the generality, this analysis does indicate the plausibility of the argument as an explanation for the Skodak and Skeels findings.

Scarr and Weinberg (1979) have recently reported a new study in which the IQs of adopted adolescents or young adults (N = 150) and the IQs of their adoptive parents were correlated. These correlations were compared with those of another group of equivalently aged children ($N = 237$) and their natural parents. All the adopted children were adopted before one year of age, the average age of adoption being 2.6 months. The average scores of both the adoptive family members and the control family members were decidedly above the norm. The parent-child and sibling correlations for WAIS IQ were as follows:

	Biological families			Adoptive families		
	Mother	Father	Children	Mother	Father	Children
Child IQ Score	.41	.40	.35	.09	.16	−.03

In the biological families the parent-child correlations are all statistically significant and are much higher than the corresponding parent-child correlations in the adoptive families. The correlations in the column labeled "Children" refer to the correlation of genetically related siblings in the case of the biological families and the correlation of genetically unrelated children reared in the same family in the case of the adoptive families. Again, in the biological families, where the siblings are genetically related, the correlation is higher than for the adoptive families, in which the children reared together are not genetically related. Thus, these correlations suggest a substantial heritable component to general intelligence as measured by the WAIS.

Various social and demographic factors, such as parental education, occupation, and income, were also used to predict the children's IQ scores. In the adoptive families, these measures were of only a little value in predicting the adopted children's IQs. This fact is important because it indicates that socioeconomic class has little independent effect on IQ scores in this population.

The results from the Texas Adoption Project (Horn, Loehlin, and Willerman, in preparation) yield estimates of heritability for general intelligence that are lower than those obtained in previous adoption studies. This study differs from all others in that IQ scores were available for the unwed mothers who gave up their children at birth, as well as for any natural children the adoptive parents had. Presented here are the correlations for full scale IQ; the numbers of pairs entering into the correlations are given in parentheses. Although over 400 unwed mothers received a nonverbal IQ test in the total sample, the table shows correlations for only the 53 who received one of the Wechsler intelligence scales. Correlations involving the nonverbal test will be presented elsewhere.

	Unwed mother	Adoptive mother	Adoptive father	Children
Adopted Child IQ	.32(53)	.19(455)	.17(457)	.25(364)
Natural Child IQ	.09(71)	.23(162)	.42(162)	.35(46)

The results indicate in every case that the correlation based on genetic relatedness is higher than the corresponding nongenetic correlation. Thus, unwed mothers correlate more highly with their adopted-away children than they do with the natural children of the adoptive parents. The adoptive mother and father correlate more highly with their natural children than with their adoptive children. The genetically related sibling sets correlate more highly with each other than do the unrelated children reared together.

The correlation that is most deviant involves the adoptive mother and her natural child (r = .23). It is unclear why this correlation is so low. One possible explanation is that the decision to adopt a child after the birth of a natural child was made more often in families where the mother-child correlation was lower than expected. This might have been because something went awry in the mother-child relationship or with the child himself. Evidence supporting this proposition comes from the correlation between the adoptive mother and her natural child when the natural child is born after the adoptive child. In this case, there would be no ascertainment bias because the birth of the natural child could not have affected the decision to adopt in the first place.

When the natural child is younger than the adopted child, the adoptive mother-natural child correlation equals .39 (n = 74). This value is higher than the adoptive mother-natural child correlation of .23 when all the natural children are included. This explanation is admittedly speculative and ad hoc, but it could be properly tested in future adoption studies.

MONOZYGOTIC TWINS REARED APART

Closely related to the adoption design are studies of identical twins reared apart. Since monozygotic twins are presumed to have 100 percent of their genes in common, nonconcordance for a particular trait can be attributed to nongenetic influences. Studying monozygotic twins who have been separated makes it theoretically possible to determine the relative influence of genetics and of environment on the trait in question. Three such reliable studies involving a total of 69 pairs have been reported (Newman, Freeman, and Holzinger 1937; Shields 1962; and Juel-Nielsen 1965). In contrast to the adoption design, in which it is essential to obtain multigeneration data on parents and children, the twin methodology requires data only on the twins themselves.

Jensen (1970b) has analyzed the data derived from those studies. The Newman, Freeman, and Holzinger (1937) study obtained data on 19 adult sets in the United States. Nine of these sets had been separated by six months of age, and the rest had been separated by twenty-five months. The Stanford-Binet (1916) form was administered to all the sets. Juel-Nielsen (1965) studied 12 Danish sets; 9 of these sets were separated by one year, and the oldest set was separated at less than six years. All of the sets were administered the Danish version of the Wechsler-Bellevue Intelligence Scale. Shields (1962) used a British sample and administered the Raven's Mill Hill Vocabulary Scales and the Dominoes test, which is a nonverbal measure of intelligence.

Table 5.1 gives Jensen's summary of the data from these studies. The average absolute difference between the twin sets was 7.09 IQ points, compared with the expected absolute difference between siblings reared together of 12 IQ points and the average absolute difference between all possible pairs of individuals in the population of 17 IQ points. In part, the difference of 7.09 points is due to the unreliability of the tests themselves. Terman and Merrill (1937), for example, found an average difference of 4.68 IQ points for the *same* individual tested on two occasions with the equivalent L and M forms of the 1937 Stanford-Binet.

Another study by the late Sir Cyril Burt (1966) of 53 sets of identical twins reared apart reported findings that were similar to those shown in Table 5.1. Those results were not included in Table 5.1, however, because there is some dispute over the legitimacy of the original data. Charges of faking have appeared (e.g., Kamin 1974), and a detailed appraisal of the data by Jensen (1974a) has demonstrated at least some

Table 5.1
Statistics on IQs of MZ twins reared apart

Study	N(pairs)	Mean IQ	SD	$\bar{d}$	$r_{intraclass}$
Shields	38	93.0	13.4	6.72	.78
Newman, Freeman, and Holzinger	19	95.7	13.0	8.21	.67
Juel-Nielsen	12	106.8	9.0	6.46	.68
Combined	69	96.1	12.7	7.09	.74

Source: Revised from A. R. Jensen, "The IQs of Identical Twins Reared Apart," *Behavior Genetics* 1 (1971): 133–147, p. 137. Plenum Publishing Corporation.

computational and careless errors. Since the verisimilitude of the data appears questionable, it is probably more judicious to disregard the study. This is especially unfortunate because Burt used the largest single series of cases, and one cannot be sure that the data are, in fact, worthless. But science must at the start depend on facts before the making of inferences. Fortunately, there are three other studies in the literature that are not subject to similar criticisms.

One must conclude that the evidence for a genetic component in intelligence seems indisputable and that the twin and adoption studies described here are in agreement. But Jensen (1970b) is careful to point out that the ideal design for monozygotic twins reared apart is rarely realized completely:

> There is never truly random assignment of separated twins to their foster homes. Some separated twins are reared, for example, in different branches of the same family. And twins put out for adoption rarely go into the poorest homes. Furthermore, separated twins have the same mothers prenatally and to whatever extent there are favorable or unfavorable maternal conditions that might affect the twins' intrauterine development, these conditions are presumably more alike for twins than for singletons born to different mothers. On the other hand, twin correlation due to common nongenetic factors is counteracted to some unknown extent by effects occurring immediately after fertilization which create inequalities in the development of the twins [p. 134].

TWINS REARED TOGETHER

The twin method, first proposed by Galton in 1875, compares concordance rates for traits by zygosity. Because monozygotic (MZ) twins have 100 percent of their genes in common and dizygotic (DZ) twins share only about 50 percent of their genes, the logic is that any difference between MZ twins is due to environmental, or nongenetic, influences and that differences between DZ twins are due to both genetic and environmental sources.

The comparison of MZ and DZ twins reared together for estimation of genetic and environmental influences is not without its difficulties. Typically, any correlated hereditary and environmental influences will make MZ twins more similar and DZ twins less similar. If, for example, parents of MZ twins could not easily distinguish one twin from the other, they might be treated more alike than DZ twins that can be distinguished. Also, a gene-environment interaction might make the DZ twins much less similar and lead to an overestimation of the genetic effects. For example, if slight genetic differences in a trait permitted one DZ twin to thrive while the other languished, the DZ twins would become more dissimilar and the genetic effects would be exaggerated

(Loehlin and Vandenberg 1968). Studies on this matter, however, suggest that, while MZ twins are treated more alike than DZ twins, such treatment has little effect on the observed differences in MZ and DZ correlations (Loehlin and Nichols 1976). Although she dealt with personality traits and not with intelligence test scores, Scarr (1968) found that young twin girls mistakenly identified by their mothers as being of a different zygosity from their true zygosity nevertheless behaved according to their true zygosity. That is, MZ twins mistaken by their mothers as being DZ behaved as correctly identified MZ with respect to the traits in question, and vice versa.

The fact that the intraclass correlations for the identical twins do not equal 1.00 indicates that nongenetic influences on intelligence are present. While these correlations are in part attributable to unreliability of the tests, other evidence suggests that this cannot be the whole story. Prenatal influences as well as a host of later influences may be implicated.

Besides the adoption and separated twin designs, there are others that can estimate genetic influences on traits. Cattell (1960) has taken the sorts of data described above as well as data on half-siblings reared together and apart to develop the Multiple Abstract Variance Analysis (MAVA). The MAVA combines single-generation data from these diverse sources to give estimates of hereditary and environmental influences on a trait. Very large sample sizes are required to yield reliable estimates, however.

The MAVA method estimates the influence of genetic and environmental factors on a trait by partitioning the source of its variation. In a simplified form, four components of variation, two environmental and two genetic, are distinguished. The four components include the following:

σ^2_{we} = variance *within* environment—the variance within a family as a result of being reared in that particular environment. This component would include, for example, how the firstborn child affects and is affected by the other siblings in the family, or how the parents differentially treat their children.

σ^2_{wg} = variance *within* genetic—the variability that exists within a family because members do not have identical genetic makeup.

σ^2_{be} = variance *between* environment—the variability between the average value for a family and the average value for all other families due to the common environmental experiences of all family members.

σ^2_{bg} = variance *between* genetic—the variability that exists between the average value for a family and the average value for all other families because the family members have a common genetic makeup and thus are more alike.

The observed total variance $= \sigma_{total}^2 = \sigma_{we}^2 + \sigma_{wg}^2 + \sigma_{be}^2 + \sigma_{bg}^2$. The preceding is a simplification of the model, since terms relating to interaction and covariation between the individual components are not included. Although these additional terms are included in the model, they are too cumbersome to be considered here.

Cattell (1960, 1971) described the MAVA method in some detail. In the few instances where it has been applied, he concludes that, for fluid intelligence at least, about four-fifths of the variation between individuals is due to genetic influences and about one-fifth is due to environmental influences. For crystallized intelligence, he suggests that the genetic component is somewhat less—between two-thirds and three-quarters.

All workers in the field have neglected some potential approaches that appear to be more easily fulfilled than the complete adoption design. Some of these are subsets of it and may be called incomplete family designs. Briefly, the adoption design requires (1) that biological parents do not rear their own child and (2) that nonbiological parents rear the child. Variations on this design can obtain meaningful correlations from the following sources of data:

1. *Stepmother-child correlation.* If the stepmother is introduced early enough, this correlation can provide an estimate of environmental influence. Educational or intellectual data on the biological mother would provide a direct estimate of genetic influence.

2. *Stepfather-child correlation.* If the stepfather is introduced into the home early, this correlation can also provide an estimate of environmental influence. Educational or intellectual data on the biological father would provide a direct estimate of genetic influence.

3. *Father absent—child correlation.* Data from this source are fairly common and do not require that the mother remarry. Besides providing a direct estimate of genetic influence, the biological father-child correlation can be contrasted to the mother-child correlation in the family. The difference between the mother-child correlation and the father-absent correlation, if in favor of the mother-child correlation, would yield an estimate of environmental influence.

4. *Mother absent—child correlation.* This correlation follows the logic of correlation 3.

5. *Biological parent—child not adopted (but reared in orphanage or foster home)* correlation. This correlation again provides a direct estimate of genetic influence, but it presents a number of complications related to the reasons why the child failed to be adopted. Munsinger (1975) reviews some studies of siblings reared in orphanages.

It seems probable that all the variations of the adoption design will become more widely used in the future. Already, in the study of psychopathology, such designs have caused a minor revolution in the thinking of social scientists who formerly depreciated genetic contributions to psychopathology (see Chapter 9).

INBREEDING AND INTELLIGENCE

Recall that dominant genes are detectable either as homozygotes or as heterozygotes, whereas recessive genes are recognized only when they are homozygous. In general, if a seriously deleterious genetic mutation occurs, it is likely to be eliminated from the population much more rapidly if it is dominant than if it is recessive. The reason for this is that the probability of obtaining two deleterious recessive alleles at a particular locus is the square of the probability of obtaining one deleterious gene. Thus, in a randomly mating population, if a deleterious gene occurs with a frequency of .01 in the general population, then the likelihood that the gene will be homozygous is $(.01)^2$, or .0001. If this deleterious gene is dominant, it will be expressed 1 time in 100 times. If the gene is recessive, it will need to be paired in order to be expressed, and this pairing will occur only 1 time in 10,000 times.

When relatives mate, however, the likelihood that the offspring will be homozygous for the gene increases tremendously if one relative is carrying the deleterious gene. The probability that two alleles at a particular locus are derived from a common ancestral allele is expressed as the coefficient of inbreeding, or F. The details of calculating F need not occupy us here, but the F values for the offspring of various matings between relatives are as follows: parent and child or siblings, $\frac{1}{4}$; uncle and niece or aunt and nephew, $\frac{1}{8}$; first cousins, $\frac{1}{16}$; second cousins, $\frac{1}{64}$; and third cousins, $\frac{1}{256}$. Concretely, for an F value of $\frac{1}{4}$, an offspring of a brother-sister mating will be homozygous for an allele common to both parents 25 percent of the time.

Inbreeding, which has been shown to have deleterious effects in lower animals, also appears to be deleterious for humans (Lindzey 1967b). It is widely believed that nearly everyone carries about one lethal recessive gene in the heterozygous form (Cavalli-Sforza and Bodmer 1971). One country in which inbreeding occurs with high frequency is Japan, where 6 percent of matings are between first cousins. Schull and Neel (1965) analyzed WISC scores of over 2000 Japanese children on one island, among whom 486 were the products of first-cousin marriages. These inbred children obtained WISC IQs about 3 to 5 percent lower than the other children. In addition, a variety of other physical defects occurred with greater frequency among the inbreds.

Reed and Reed (1965) report on a smaller number of consanguineous matings. They found that 10.7 percent of the 205 surviving children of first-cousin matings were retarded, as were 36.3 percent of the 11 surviving offspring of uncle-niece matings and 60 percent of the 5 surviving children or father-daughter and brother-sister matings. Death rates among the children of these matings were also exceedingly high; 13 percent of the children of first-cousin matings had died before age two, as had 31 percent of the children of uncle-niece matings and 17 percent of brother-sister and father-daughter matings.

Adams and Neel (1967) reported on 18 children who were products of incestuous mating (12 brother-sister and 6 father-daughter), ascertained by an adoption agency *prior* to the birth of the children. These parents were matched for socioeconomic status to control parents who also gave up their children for adoption. Among the 18 offspring of incestuous matings, 5 had died before the age of six months, 2 were severely retarded, and 3 gave evidence of borderline intelligence. Of the controls, none had died or were institutionalized, nor were any severely retarded (Lindzey 1967b).

These three studies are consistent in their findings of the deleterious effects of inbreeding, but it is difficult to prove that impaired intellectual functioning is a direct effect of inbreeding. It is possible that other physical impairments suffered by these inbred children could have affected intellectual functioning as a byproduct.

It should be pointed out that there is an important distinction between assortative mating and inbreeding. Assortative mating refers to the increased likelihood that individuals with similar values on some *phenotypic* measure will mate. If the trait on which they assort is partly heritable, it will have the effect of increasing homozygosity only for the particular genetic loci involved in producing that trait. In contrast, inbreeding refers to the mating of relatives, and this will have the effect of increasing homozygosity at all genetic loci. Thus, inbreeding refers to assortative mating on the basis of *genotypes* and not on the basis of phenotypes.

WHAT'S INHERITED

While the evidence for a substantial heritable component to intellectual performance appears rather persuasive, the degree of this influence is still a source of bitter dispute. Some argue that the heritability is high, and others argue that it is low. At the heart of the problem, however, is the fact that no one understands exactly what is inherited. The nature and heterogeneity of intelligence tests or the units used to grade intellectual performance do not lend themselves to ready classification or deeper analyses. Consider the following question: "How are an orange and banana alike?" Evidence suggests that the probability of correctly answering this question or a group of questions like this one has a heritable component. But because few would subscribe to the heritability of immanent ideas, it seems more likely that what is inherited are physiological processes that affect the likelihood of answering this question correctly.

If speed of neural conduction were heritable in humans (as it is in lower animals), then speed of neural conduction might be related to the speed of information processing. Those who process information at a faster rate might be those who are more likely to acquire and retain the information necessary for answering this question correctly. It is time for researchers to begin exploration in this area. We need to find physiological correlates, or better yet, mechanisms that permit the kind of detailed physiological and experimental investigations that will enable us to go beyond gross IQ measures.

SPECIAL ABILITIES

Thus far we have reviewed data on the inheritance of general intelligence. Some workers have suggested that more fine-grained analysis of intellectual functioning would reveal differential heritabilities for special cognitive traits. Twin studies using Thurstone's test of Primary Mental Abilities (PMA) have been performed, and agreement between the studies appears reasonably adequate. For verbal and space abilities, all show moderate to high heritabilities. For number, Blewett's (1954) study shows negligible heritability, while Vandenberg's (1962) two separate studies give moderate to high heritabilities. Reasoning appears to be more heritable in Blewett's study than in the others. It seems possible that some of these separate abilities are differentially heritable and that it might be fruitful to examine their inheritance in other ways, perhaps using an adoption design.

The difficulty with determining the heritabilities of special abilities, however, is that most studies have relied on factored tests such as Thurstone's PMA or the Differential Aptitude Tests (DAT). The specific factors on these subtests seem to measure more of a general factor common to all the tests than each of the specific factors that constitute their labels. Thus, it is impossible to tell whether the heritabilities obtained reflect much more than the differential loadings of each of the factored tests on the general factor. This problem can be corrected by looking at the heritabilities of each of the residual factors after the general factor has been removed. This has not yet been done with tests such as the PMA and DAT, although Nichols (1965) has reported significant heritabilities for subtests of the National Merit Scholarship Qualifying Test (NMSQT) after the general factor has been removed.

Loehlin and Vandenberg (1968) and Vandenberg (1965) have reported an ingenious technique for uncovering the structure of genetic and environmental influences. Although most studies have found both genetic and environmental influences to be important, it is possible that the *associations* between one trait and another result solely from common genes or common environment. The logic of Loehlin and Vandenberg's procedure is fairly straightforward, but it is best understood by means of a concrete example.

Suppose sets of twins were administered the verbal and space subtests of the PMA. The difference between a pair of twins on verbal may be related to their difference on space; a positive correlation indicates that common influences are operating. Since MZ twins are identical genetically, if the MZ twin higher on verbal was also higher than his cotwin on space, the relationship must be due to common environmental experiences affecting both traits. A similar positive correlation of twin differences among DZ sets could be due to both genetic and environmental forces. It is possible to subtract the correlation found for the MZ sets from the correlation found for the DZ sets. Because the MZ correlation represents only environmental influences and the DZ correlation represents both genetic and environmental influences, the difference between the MZ and DZ correlation would be an indication of genetic effects only or gene-environment covariance.

Loehlin and Vandenberg correlated the MZ twin set differences between all the subtests of the PMA and found that verbal, word fluency, and reasoning had a common environmental component. That is, if an MZ twin was higher than his cotwin on verbal, he also tended to be higher than his cotwin on word fluency and reasoning. The correlations for these differences were only moderate, ranging from .27 to .48, but they nevertheless suggest that common environmental influences are at work for these primary mental abilities. In general, the authors also found that subtracting MZ from DZ correlations still gave evidence of strong genetic effects.

They also had data from a second source and performed a similar analysis there. Again they found a pattern of correlations similar to the earlier data, but this time it appeared that number seemed to also go along with the other three. In evaluating their findings, Loehlin and Vandenberg conclude that there is less environmental than genetic intercorrelation overall.

Generally, two approaches to the study of genetic influences on behavior can be distinguished, one gene centered and the other trait centered. Thus far we have discussed only the trait-centered approach. We have taken a trait of interest—for example, general intelligence—and asked what the genetic influences on this variable are. We may also begin with a known genetic or chromosomal disorder and ask what its consequences are for intellectual functioning. The disorders best suited for study from a gene-centered perspective have a high survival rate, which permits testing in childhood or adulthood. In addition, intelligence should be high enough to permit testing of a wide range of behavior, and the population frequency should be high enough so that samples from diverse sources can be compared. If the biochemical pathways for the disease are already known, it should be possible to make specific physiological interpretations. If a means of treatment is available, treated cases should have higher IQs than untreated cases (Anderson and Siegal 1968).

TURNER'S SYNDROME

One chromosomal disorder that appears to be associated with consistent deviations in intellectual functioning is Turner's syndrome. Although genetic aberrations that seem consistently related to mental retardation are being discovered with increasing frequency, they appear to belong more properly in the chapter on mental retardation and will not be discussed here.

Turner's syndrome (Figure 5.3) is associated with nondisjunction of the X chromosome so that affected females (the disorder occurs only among females) have only one sex chromosome (XO) instead of the normal two (XX). Although Turner's females have a vagina, it is infantile; their ovaries are either rudimentary or absent, and they will not menstruate. Estrogen therapy in teenage will permit the development of secondary sex characteristics and the experience of normal sexual activity, but affected females will always be infertile.

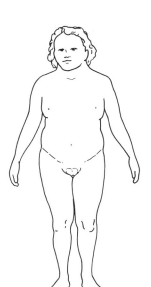

Figure 5.3
Turner's syndrome.

Individuals with Turner's syndrome are short, averaging about five feet tall, and there may be a variety of congenital anomalies present. Among these are a webbed neck, deficient lower jaw, shieldlike chest, and heart abnormalities (McKusick 1969).

Women with Turner's syndrome appear to have a specific pattern of intellectual abilities, which includes normal verbal intelligence and deficiencies in spatial organization that Money (1964) has called space-form blindness. Figure 5.4 plots the verbal comprehension and perceptual organization quotients for 37 Turner females. Only 5 of the 37 women have perceptual organization quotients that exceed their verbal comprehension quotients. Furthermore, the modest correlation between the two quotients suggests moderate independence of these factors among these people.

There does not appear to be any specific personality disorder associated with Turner's syndrome, but affected women have been regarded as being very "feminine" in the sense that they appear extremely passive and submissive. Recently Garron (1972) compared Turner cases to other dwarfed women and controls of normal stature. He found that passivity and submission was characteristic of very short women in general and did not appear to be specific for Turner's cases.

The space-form blindness is not characteristic of other sex chromosome anomalies. Klinefelter's syndrome, which has a sex chromosome complement of XXY, is not associated with specific space-form deficiency. It is, however, associated with an increased incidence of mental retardation and various personality aberrations, including homosexuality (Money and Ehrhardt 1972).

The specific space-form blindness of individuals with Turner's syndrome may be a consequence of a neurophysiological deficit associated

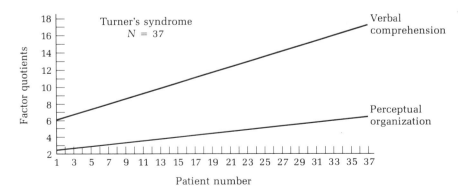

Figure 5.4

Distribution of two specific-factor quotients in thirty-seven cases of Turner's syndrome. (From Money 1964.)

with the abnormality. Some investigators (Alexander and Money 1966) have noted that women with Turner's syndrome display intellectual impairments similar to those of individuals with parietal lobe injury. The parietal lobe of the brain does control many of the skills involved in spatial organization, so a comparison of the two disorders seems warranted.

Conclusions

Taken as a whole, genetic influences on general intelligence appear quite substantial. This does not mean that environments do not hinder or enhance intellectual functioning. Nor does the fixity of genes mean that the modification of genetic potential is limited. On the contrary, it seems likely that an understanding of the nature of the genetic mechanism and the biochemical products of genes will permit phenomenal progress.

Perhaps the most important and difficult problem yet to be investigated in the genetics of intelligence is what exactly is inherited that permits intelligence test scores to follow genetic lines. It is obvious that the phenotypic qualities of intelligence tests bear little relationship to the physiological processes underlying intellectual performance. Until we adequately develop genetic markers or identify neurophysiological correlates of intellectual functioning, we will not make much more progress than we have already.

6

Intelligence and Environment

This chapter explores the effects of environmental variation on intellectual performance and the effects of intelligence on sociocultural achievements in Western civilization. Unfortunately, it has been notoriously difficult to specify environmental factors that have a substantial causal influence on general intellectual functioning. To be sure, there is a plentitude of studies reporting positive relationships between sociocultural advantage and intellectual performance, but the mass of these studies involves parents rearing their own children and thus confounds genetic transmission from parent to child with cultural transmission from parent to child. Indices of environment do exist, but crude indices generally show relationships to intellectual functioning of about the same magnitude as do more fine-grained measures.

Intercorrelations Among Environmental Indices

If one considers the sociocultural environment in the crudest terms—according to socioeconomic indices derived from prestige ratings of occupation, annual income, and years of education—one finds that the intercorrelations between these indices tend to be fairly high. For example, Cattell (1942) intercorrelated these measures and found average values in the low .80s and .90s. Kahl and Davis (1955) factor-analyzed nineteen measures of social class and found that most were substantially intercorrelated but that income correlated less well than the other measures. Likewise, there is considerable agreement that prestige ratings of occupations accord very nicely from country to country, even when communist and nonindustrialized nations are included. Hodge, Trieman, and Rossi (1966) found that correlations of prestige ratings of occupations in twenty-three foreign countries averaged about .91 with similar ratings made in the United States. The lowest correlations between foreign prestige ratings and those in America were found for the Belgian Congo and Poland, but these were still very high ($r = .79$ in both instances).

That parental socioeconomic status (SES) correlates with offspring intelligence is little disputed. Representative of these findings are those from the Collaborative Perinatal Study, in which over twenty-six thousand children from twelve institutions throughout the country were routinely administered Stanford-Binet IQ tests at age four. The socioeconomic status index used in this study was essentially the average of rankings on parental occupation, family income, and head-of-household education. The findings are shown in Figure 6.1.

The results of this study show increasing mean IQs with increasing SES for blacks and whites alike. The findings also indicate that the mean difference between blacks and whites increases as SES increases.

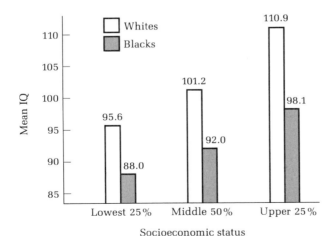

Figure 6.1

Mean IQ by race and socioeconomic status in four-year-old children. (After Broman, Nichols, and Kennedy 1975.)

Thus, in the lowest SES group the mean difference between blacks and whites is 7.6 IQ points, and in the highest group the mean difference is 12.8 IQ points. Correlations between the parental socioeconomic index and IQs of the children were .38 for whites and .24 for blacks. With sample sizes of such magnitude, the difference in the correlation coefficients is significant. The difference suggests that parental socioeconomic status is a better predictor of childhood IQs for whites than for blacks, but Loehlin, Lindzey, and Spuhler (1975) have reviewed many other studies of SES-IQ correlations in which racial differences in the magnitude of the correlations were not observed.

Family Characteristics

ADOPTION STUDIES

Although the focus in the previous chapter was on genetic effects on intellectual functioning, the powerful adoption and separated twin designs can also provide the most useful information about the role of environment in intellectual functioning. This is because familial influences under the usual circumstances are confounded by the fact that natural parents contribute both their genes and their environments to their children.

Table 6.1 gives some parent-child correlations from the Burks (1928) adoption study. As described in the previous chapter, Burks compared the adoptive families of children placed during the first year of life with a control group of biological parents rearing their own children. The two groups were matched on sex, age, locality, and paternal occupation. This adoption study is especially important for determining the independent influences of familial environmental factors, because there was no evidence of selective placement of the children in adoptive homes (correlations of occupational ratings of biological and foster fathers = .02). Two other relevant adoption studies (Leahy 1935; Skodak and Skeels 1949) give some evidence of selective placement. Selective placement has the effect of raising both the adoptive parent-child and the biological parent-child correlations because the adoptive parents have similar characteristics to the biological parents.

For every comparison in Table 6.1, the control parent-child correlation exceeds the adoptive parent-child correlation. The adoptive parent-child correlations average about .20, and this value can be taken as an estimate of the average influence of the typically measured environmental factors on the intellectual functioning of the children. Other studies show higher correlations between some family variables and intellectual functioning in children, but, since the natural parents reared the children in these studies, the influences of genetics and environment may have been confounded.

Table 6.1

IQs of adopted and control children as a function of environmental and hereditary factors

Variable	Adopted		Controls	
	Correlation	N	Correlation	N
Father's intelligence	.07	178	.45*	100
Mother's intelligence	.19*	204	.46*	105
Mid-parent intelligence	.20*	174	.52*	100
Father's vocabulary	.13*	181	.47*	101
Mother's vocabulary	.23*	202	.43*	104
Father's education	.01	173	.27*	102
Mother's education	.17*	194	.27*	103
Income	.23*	181	.24*	99
Parental supervision[1]	.12*	201	.48*	104
Number of books in library	.16*	194	.34*	100
Culture index[2]	.25*	186	.44*	101

[1] Six-point scale from little parental supervision to very exceptional care.
[2] Composite of parental vocabulary level, education, cultural interests, library size, and artistic tastes.
* Statistically significant.
Source: After Burks 1928.

The Leahy (1935) adoption study also gives information about environmental correlates of intelligence in the adopted and control children. In this study there was evidence of selective placement in that the educational levels of the biological and foster mothers correlated .25 for the 94 of 194 families for which such data are known. Nevertheless, the results of Leahy's study are remarkably similar to those of Burks (1928).

Table 6.2 gives the findings from the Leahy study, which matched adoptive families in which children were adopted before six months of age with control biological parents rearing their own children for sex, age, father's occupation, education of parents, race, and residential size. Again, the adoptive parent-child correlations are on the order of .20, while the control parent-child correlations average close to .50. Leahy points out that the IQ scores of the adopted children are actually less variable than the IQ scores of the control children. This fact decreases the adoptive parent-child correlations, but it can be corrected for statistically. When this is done, the average adoptive parent-child correlations increase by about .04. Thus, despite these corrections, the adoptive parent-child correlations are still substantially below those of the control parent-child correlations.

Another interesting feature of Leahy's work was the identification of those adoptive and control children who came from the most stimulating environments (arbitrarily defined as those environments in which all of the environmental traits measured were 1 SD above the mean

Table 6.2

IQs of adopted and control children as a function of environmental and hereditary factors

Variable	Adopted		Controls	
	Correlation	N	Correlation	N
Father's intelligence	.15	178	.51	175
Mother's intelligence	.20	186	.51	191
Mid-parent intelligence	.18	177	.60	173
Father's vocabulary	.22	177	.47	168
Mother's vocabulary	.20	185	.49	190
Father's education	.16	193	.48	193
Mother's education	.21	192	.50	194
Environmental status score	.19	194	.53	194
Cultural index of home	.21	194	.51	194
Child training index	.18	194	.52	194
Economic index	.12	194	.37	194
Sociality index	.11	194	.42	194

Note: All correlations are statistically significant.
Source: After Leahy 1935.

for the entire group). The seven adopted children coming from those homes averaged 113.3 IQ, while the eight controls coming from such an environment averaged 127.5, a statistically significant difference. These data indicate that the environmentally advantaged adoptive children only exceed the average for the total adoptive group by about 2.8 IQ points, since the mean IQ for all adopted children was 110.5. The very high mean IQ of 127.5 for the advantaged control children, in comparison with the total control group mean of 109.7, cannot be solely interpreted as a result of environmental advantage because these are homes in which the parents are also likely to be of very high intelligence. Leahy (1935) concludes that the "measurable environment does not shift the IQ by more than 3 to 5 points above or below the value it would have under normal environmental conditions" (p. 304).

SEPARATED IDENTICAL TWINS

The previous chapter discussed the IQ correlation data for twins reared apart. Although the twins were quite similar to one another in general, one might still ask whether differences in environmental advantage account for whatever differences in IQ exist. One study of separated identical twins provides data on the socioeconomic characteristics of the adoptive homes into which these children were placed. It is therefore possible to correlate the differences in environmental or social advantage within a twin pair with their difference in IQ.

Newman, Freeman, and Holzinger (1937) rated the social environments of their 19 sets of separated identical twins (18 of the 19 sets had been separated before twenty-five months of age). They found that within each twin set the difference in Binet IQ and the difference in social advantage correlated .51. This is a rather high value, and at first glance it seems to indicate that social advantage is a very important influence on IQ. But it should be recognized that this correlation accounts only for differences *within* twin sets and not for differences *between* one set and another. As noted in the previous chapter, these twin sets correlated .67 for intelligence.

Understanding the differential meanings of environmental influences *between* one set and another and environmental influences *within* a set is important. Suppose three sets of identical twins reared apart had the following IQs, respectively: 100 and 101, 110 and 112, and 120 and 123. Further, suppose that in each pair the member with the higher IQ were reared in a more socially advantaged home. If the IQs of the twin sets were correlated in the usual fashion, the correlation would be near 1.00 (because the IQs of each twin set do not overlap the IQs of the other twin sets). If, however, one asks whether the *differences* in IQ *within* twin sets correlated with *differences* in their social environments, one would also find a very high correlation. There is nothing contradictory in these data since the second correlation, taken in perspective, accounts for very little of the between-set differences (which average 10.5 IQ points) but substantially accounts for whatever within-set differences exist (which average 2 IQ points). The conclusion to be drawn from the Newman, Freeman, and Holzinger findings is that there is a moderate relationship between familial environmental advantage and IQ differences within sets of identical twins but that this relationship tells little about the effects of environmental advantage on differences between one twin set and another.

These data should give some idea of the extent to which the range of environmental influences accounts for differences in intellectual functioning. It should also instill caution in those who would undertake the task of increasing intellectual functioning in disadvantaged groups merely by using extensions of "common sense" to provide an intellectually stimulating environment. It is hard to imagine a structured part-time environmental enrichment program that would approach the environmental intensity found in the homes of these parents of adopted children. Yet genetic factors still seemed to have a prepotent influence in the adoption studies, as evidenced by the higher natural parent-child correlations.

Now let's explore some of the effects of environmental inputs on intellectual functioning according to their time of onset.

PRENATAL AND PERINATAL INFLUENCES

Among the classes of prenatal and perinatal environmental influences that may have effects on mental functioning are nutrition, diseases, and complications surrounding delivery. Without doubt, the incidence of fetal death, malnutrition, disease, and birth complications is strikingly related to social class factors; those in the lowest classes are much more likely to incur insults from these sources than those from the highest classes (Birch and Gussow 1970).

Illustrative of the social class relationships to perinatal factors are data fron New York City on perinatal mortality according to social class and race. Figure 6.2 shows, for each race, approximately 50 percent greater perinatal mortality in the lowest social class than in the highest. Since the distribution of social classes for the blacks is weighted toward the lower end, the black-white differences are particularly striking. It is noteworthy that the perinatal mortality rate for the highest social class of blacks is barely lower than the mortality rate for the lowest class of whites. One possible explanation for this finding is that a mother's ability to produce healthy live-born infants may be determined during the months in which she herself was a fetus and a youngster. This is the time when the prospective mother's own sex cells and physiological substrates for normal childbearing capacities are being formed. Early deprivation may then increase the risk in childbearing later, despite improved socioenvironmental conditions after puberty. Data of this sort

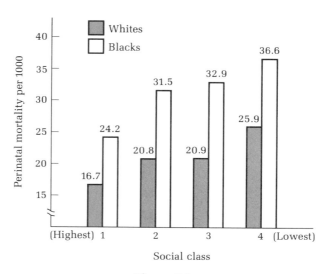

Figure 6.2

Perinatal mortality rates by social class and color in New York City, 1961–1963. (Adapted from Yerby 1966.)

suggest that an early start is necessary to markedly decrease perinatal mortality. Improved obstetrical treatment for already mature, but previously deprived, females seems little likely to rapidly alter perinatal mortality and morbidity.

It should also be noted that not all casualties die. Some infants suffer from milder insults that produce impairment rather than death. This proposition has been most forcefully stated by Lilienfeld and Parkhurst (1951) in their formulation of the "continuum of reproductive casualty," in which they point out that pathological factors in pregnancy and birth may produce a range of disorders from death at one extreme to cerebral palsy, mental retardation, and milder behavioral disorders at the other end.

NUTRITION

Questions about the role of nutrition in intellectual development can be framed from a number of different perspectives. One important question is whether undernutrition that occurs during prenatal development but is corrected later leads to intellectual deficits. All too often, poor prenatal nutrition continues postnatally, and it is therefore difficult to distinguish the prenatal from the postnatal effects. An opportunity to make this distinction presented itself in western Holland, where a famine occurred during World War II between mid-September 1944 and mid-May 1945 (Stein et al. 1972). This famine had a very clear beginning at the onset of Nazi reprisals against the Dutch resistance and ended with the liberation by the Allies. Because the famine was confined to western Holland, it was possible to compare those conceived and born in the midst of the famine to those Dutch conceived and born outside of the famine areas.

Since virtually all males reaching the age of nineteen years are examined for possible induction into the Dutch military, Stein et al. (1972) were able to obtain the Raven Progressive Matrices scores of those born during the famine as well as the date and location of their birth. The intelligence test scores of those inside and outside the famine areas and born or conceived before, during, or after the famine were then compared. The results failed to indicate any increase in either mild or severe mental retardation as a result of conception or birth during the famine, suggesting that maternal undernutrition had no long-term effects on intellectual functioning. The reader should be cautioned, however, that these results apply only to the survivors. There was other evidence, especially among the lower classes, that the birthweights of children affected by the famine were substantially lower than those outside the famine areas. Thus, it is possible that more severely malnourished fetuses aborted long before birth and that only the less undernourished survived.

A study of Korean girls adopted into American homes investigated the effects of early malnutrition on later growth, IQ, and scholastic achievement (Winick, Meyer, and Harris 1975). The girls had been admitted to an adoption agency in Korea before age two and adopted by age three. Three groups of children were identified—those who were malnourished, those who were moderately nourished, and those who were well nourished at the time of their admittance into the agency. When measured at school age in the United States, all groups were above the Korean norms for height and weight, although the malnourished group was still smaller, on the average, than the well-nourished group. The same findings held for IQ and scholastic achievement. All the groups were above U.S. norms for these tests, but the ordering of the groups related perfectly to their original nourishment status. Thus, this study shows that placement in an enriching environment can effect the expected *level* of performance but that the rank ordering of the groups will remain much the same. The findings also suggest a prolonged effect of early malnourishment, but, of course, this study differs from the Stein et al. (1972) study, in that malnourishment was largely confined to the prenatal period in the latter study. Readers should recognize the parallel between the Winick, Meyer, and Harris study and the IQ adoption study of Skodak and Skeels (1949), which showed that the children obtained much higher scores than expected from their biological mothers' IQs but that the rank orderings of the children in terms of their mothers' IQs was still partially preserved.

Many studies of malnutrition and intellectual development have taken place in countries where undernutrition is endemic. With increasing sophistication, studies using better controls (such as unaffected siblings) have been employed but these studies too have potentially serious biases. (Why did one child in the family become undernourished while another did not?) More recently, an even more sophisticated approach promises less ambiguous answers in this area. These newer studies will involve the addition of nutritional supplements to the diets of some of the deprived and not others.

TWIN STUDIES

Many studies have explored the relationship of birth weight to intelligence in identical twins. It is believed that birth-weight differences between identical twins result from competition for the scarce maternal nutritional resources. If lower birth weight relates to lower IQ within the twin sets prenatal nutritional factors might be implicated. Results from these studies have been mixed with the finding by some that the lower birth-weight twin of the pair has a lower mean IQ and the finding by others that no differences exist between the pairs (see Kamin 1974). It has already been unambiguously established that in general twins have lower IQs than singletons and that triplets have even lower IQs (Record, McKeown, and Edwards 1970). But there is some doubt that the lower IQs were due to prenatal factors alone, since these twins also shared a common postnatal environment that might have diminished their individual contact time with adults and thus suppressed their intellectual growth. Other data in the Record, McKeown, and Edwards (1970) study support this interpretation. They obtained the verbal reasoning scores of eleven-year-old children in Birmingham, England, and compared the scores of typical twin pairs, twins whose cotwin had died at or near birth, and singleton births. Like others, they found that the typical twin sets averaged between 4 and 5 IQ points lower than the singletons, but, for the twins reared as singletons, scores were only 1.3 IQ points below those of the singleton population. They concluded that "any increased difficulties associated with prenatal development or birth of surviving twins have little or no influence on their verbal reasoning at age 11" (p. 18).

One problem with the study was that children who were judged ineducable, were in private schools or in special schools for the handicapped, or were judged as subnormal did not take the examination. Further, the investigators point out that the proportion of individuals not taking the examination was somewhat higher for the multiple births, so that some selection bias may have been introduced. Nevertheless, it is not clear that this bias should have affected the comparison of the typical twins and the twins reared as singletons.

One other study on the topic (Myrianthopoulos et al. 1971) obtained four-year and seven-year IQs of twins whose cotwin had died at or near birth, typical twin sets, and singletons, using the data from the Collaborative Study. Their results conflict with those of Record, McKeown, and Edwards. Myrianthopoulos et al. found that the singleton-reared twins behaved as typical twins in that both types of twins had lower mean IQs than the singleton controls. This study gives perhaps the most convincing evidence that prenatal influences (those associated with twinning) are deleterious to later intellectual performance.

Early Childhood Influences

Early childhood environmental influences are both biological and social and it is sometimes difficult to assign definitive cause specifically to either the biological or the social component. One example of this difficulty comes from the work on intersibling spacing and birth order.

INTERSIBLING SPACING AND BIRTH ORDER

A number of findings suggest that firstborns show superiority to later-borns on tests of intelligence and achievement (Breland 1973). Other studies, however, have failed to confirm these findings (see Schooler 1972). It is true that when samples are selected for exceptional achievements there is clearly an excess of firstborns and only children (Breland 1973). In part, many of these findings are based on artifacts due to (1) failure to adequately control for social class (thus, in any population selected for high achievements, there will be an excess of individuals from higher social classes who are more likely to come from smaller families); and (2) failure to take into account secular changes in family size and birth rate. This failure is especially apparent in studies of individuals born during the baby boom following World War II. Because many new families were starting up then, any study using samples born during that era would contain an excess of firstborns. Furthermore, should there be a trend toward decreasing family size, there will be an overrepresentation of early birth ranks in the smaller sibships (Hare and Price 1969).

One explanation for findings that first or early births have higher IQs than later-borns comes from a model suggested by Zajonc and Markus (1975) and Zajonc (1976). This model depends exclusively on postnatal environmental influences and suggests that the intellectual environment in which a child is reared depends on the average mental age of the individuals already existing in the family. Since the mental age of adults is higher than the mental age of children, a firstborn child will enter a home with higher mental age than the home entered by later-borns. The sooner the second child follows the first, the lower the average mental age of the family into which the child is born and will be reared (since the mental age of the first child will still be low). The model takes into account the fact that spacing of children can have an effect. If there is long spacing between children, the earlier-born child will have gained considerably in mental age and the second child will not be at as great a disadvantage. The model also proposes a "last child" effect to explain the seemingly anomalous finding that last children or only children have lower IQs than would be predicted. The depression in IQ of such children occurs because they have not had the experience of being a teacher to a younger child, which, presumably, is intellectually beneficial to the older child.

The theory is very ingenious and has already been able to account for seemingly inconsistent data that were not available at the time the theory was proposed (Davis, Cahan, and Bashi 1977). Where the model may suffer is in its confusion of prenatal and postnatal environmental influences, since the second child in a family is not only reared second but comes from a mother who has had one previous birth. Should intrauterine exhaustion be operating, the second-born child might come from a less desirable intrauterine situation.

Unpublished data (Horn, Loehlin, and Willerman, in preparation), suggest that prenatal effects need to be considered as well. In this study many of the adoptive parents have two or more natural children. The Zajonc and Markus (1975) observations have been replicated in that the second-born natural children in these families have significantly lower IQs than the firstborn children (this is especially apparent if the second-born child is male). But in those families that have adopted first and then had a natural child, the natural child does not have a lower IQ (although the child has been reared second). This suggests that prenatal factors are important. While these new data do not conclusively demonstrate that the Zajonc and Markus model is incorrect, they do suggest that the birth order and IQ phenomenon may have prenatal as well as postnatal causes.

In one of the best-controlled studies of intersibling interval and intelligence (Holley, Rosenbaum, and Churchill 1969), children born within one year of the birth of a previous child were compared with those born two to five years after the birth of a previous child. These two groups were matched for hospital of birth, sex, race, and socioeconomic index. The results indicated that the birth weights of those born in rapid succession were lower, that their Bayley Motor scores at eight months were lower, and that their four-year Binet IQs were lower (about 5 IQ points) than those of children born after a longer interval. In addition, those born in rapid succession were twice as likely to show suspicious or abnormal neurological development on examination at one year of age. It appeared possible, however, that the results of the behavioral measures were simply products of the lower birthweights of those born in rapid succession. To test this notion, the authors selected only those matched pairs in which the birth weight of the child born in rapid succession was equal to or exceeded the birth weight of its matched control. Reanalysis showed that the differences between the rapid succession group and the controls were no longer statistically significant, although the rapid succession group still obtained IQs averaging about 3 IQ points lower than controls. They suggest that mothers may not have had time to restore the depleted supplies of critical nutrients for pregnancies coming in rapid succession and that rapid succession of pregnancies may be undesirable for this reason. An important point to note in this study is that some of the differences between the rapid succession group and the controls were observed at birth, thus challenging the hypothesis that socialization was sufficient to account for the lower IQs of the children.

CHILD-REARING PRACTICES

Many believe that child-rearing practices can account for the observed differences in intellectual performance between social classes and ethnic groups. One approach has been to look for differences in child-rearing practices of middle- and lower-class families; some studies have depended on parental reports or recall of child-rearing practices, while others have directly observed parental practices.

It is apparently not widely appreciated that parental recall of child-rearing practices or childhood behaviors is generally unreliable and that parents tend to recall the child in more favorable terms than deserved. This problem has probably compromised many reports based on recall of child-rearing practices and has helped to produce a maze of confusing and conflicting findings in the area of social class differences in socialization.

A careful study of recollections of childhood was conducted by Yarrow, Campbell, and Burton (1970). They had access to objective tests and contemporaneous ratings of children attending a particular nursery school between 1928 and 1958. Mothers of these children were contacted later and either interviewed or asked to complete questionnaires about events during the nursery school years. There were many findings from this study, and some are not easily summarized. Among the most pertinent was the finding that correspondences between the child's actual or rated contemporaneous performances and the mother's recollection of those performances were usually so low (median correlation about .33) as to make inferences drawn solely from parental recollections questionable. For example, after an interval of many years, mothers were asked to estimate their child's rank in intelligence in the nursery school. The correlation between the child's tested intelligence then and his mother's recent recollection was only .35. Equally important, however, was the fact that the mothers consistently tended to remember the child as being more intelligent in comparison with the other children than he actually was. In general, the authors found that for a variety of measures parents tended to rate their children more favorably on recall than contemporaneous observations indicated. The authors also review a number of other studies of parental recollections, and these too support the findings reported.

For this reason, studies that utilize direct observation of parent-child behavior take on increasing significance. These studies unfortunately are more difficult to conduct, since they typically require careful and reliable observations that take much more time than questionnaire or interview studies. But it appears that the payoff from such studies makes the effort worthwhile. Chapter 14 will review some of the observational studies on social class differences in parent-child interactions. The general finding from those studies is that middle-class mothers are more likely than lower-class mothers to supply the child with relevant information with which to solve problems and that middle-class mothers also seem to be more attuned to the child's own needs and qualities than are lower-class mothers.

FATHER ABSENCE

Individuals whose fathers were absent during childhood tend to show deficiencies in certain aspects of cognitive functioning, namely, in skills related to quantitative ability. These deficiencies can best be interpreted as being environmentally induced (see Biller 1971 for review). Carlsmith (1964) reports that Harvard freshmen whose fathers had served in World War II and were therefore absent during the early childhood of the students had lower math scores than verbal scores. This pattern is generally more characteristic of females in intact families and suggests that father-absent males develop more feminine styles of cognitive functioning than father-present males. Landy, Rosenberg, and Sutton-Smith (1969) report similar findings of relatively lower quantitative scores among a sample of female college students. Not only did complete father absence affect quantitative scores, but father absence due to night shift work also showed adverse effects on quantitative performance. Another study (Willerman 1973) showed that, while the child's age at the onset of father absence had no effect on verbal or quantitative test scores among college students, the duration of father absence correlated $-.30$ with quantitative scores and $-.22$ with verbal scores for 75 males; females were unaffected. It was also noteworthy that the effects of father absence were related to the reason for father absence. Those whose fathers were absent for military reasons showed no deficits, but those whose fathers were absent because of divorce were substantially affected ($r = -.53$ between length of father absence and quantitative scores for 35 males). Most of the military absences occurred in career military families. These data suggest that the disruptions preceding and following the separation were far less traumatic than those resulting from divorce.

It appears that father presence especially encourages the development of those problem-solving skills related to quantitative performance. This phenomenon may be due to the fact that the traditional role of the father stresses instrumentality or getting the job done, while the traditional role of the mother emphasizes the expressive or social aspects of child development.

Environmental Enrichment and Intelligence

One way of studying environmental influences on intelligence is to compare the effects of different training programs on intellectual performance. Many studies of this sort, especially with preschoolers, have been conducted, and findings and interpretations from these studies have resulted in some of the most bitter controversies in psychology. Knowledge of the criteria by which these studies are evaluated may help you understand why disputes abound.

Jones (1954) has proposed a series of precautions and criteria for the proper conduct of enrichment studies as they apply to the effects of schooling:

1. The experimental and control group should consist of matched pairs randomly assigned to one treatment or the other.

2. Homogeneous groups of subjects are needed, especially in pre-school studies, where small age differences can be very important. One must be especially cautious if selecting homogeneous groups that depart substantially from the normative means for the traits in question, since, upon retesting, statistical regression to the mean will most certainly be observed. Thus, if subjects selected because they originally scored below the mean on the trait in question are retested later (with or without an intervening treatment) and the trait is not measurable with 100 percent reliability, one can confidently anticipate that scores on retesting will be higher. Further, the more deviant the sample was originally, the greater the expected improvement in performance on retesting.

3. The criteria for matching the experimental and control pairs should include chronological age, initial IQ, and socioeconomic index. If children are matched solely on IQ, they may come from different socio-economic environments and the meaning of the IQ score may thus be different. For example, should a child from a lower socioeconomic class be matched to a child of equal IQ from a higher socioeconomic class, one couldn't be sure later that differential treatment effects were solely responsible for the results obtained.

4. The experimental situation should be described in detail. This is necessary so that others can be sure that positive effects of the enrichment experience didn't come from coaching on items similar to ones on the outcome tests.

5. The amount of practice with the tests themselves should be comparable for the two groups. If some groups have more retesting than others, their increased familiarity and comfort with the testing situation itself may contribute to improved performance.

6. The researchers should look not only for temporary increases in test performance but also for long-term increases. This requires more extensive follow-up evaluations. It is quite possible that early enrichment

might result in a rapid but temporary acceleration in performance (the "hothouse" effect) without continued maintenance of the advantages over time (the "fertilizer" effect) (Vandenberg 1968a).

Let us take one of the most interesting and controversial studies of environmental enrichment and examine it according to the criteria of Jones (1954) concerning the adequacy of proper design. Although the following may appear unduly critical, it is well to remember that this was a pioneering and courageous study in early enrichment and has had an enormous influence on the field.

Skeels and Dye (1939) transferred thirteen children from an Iowa orphanage for normal children to an institution for feebleminded women before the children were three years of age. These children were established in wards of brighter, inmate girls. These wards had few or no other "house guests," and the inmates as well as the attendants showered the children with a great deal of attention and took them on outings. Among other activities, the wards competed to see which would have its baby talking and walking first. The infants had all originally tested below 90 IQ (mean IQ = 64) at an average age of eighteen months and were transferred at an average of nineteen months of age. By the time of the first post-transfer test at an average age of twenty-nine months, the children had a mean IQ of 90, an average increase of 26 IQ points in just ten months. Another testing at about thirty-eight months showed that the thirteen children had continued to increase their IQs to a mean of 92. After six months of living with the feebleminded caretakers, one child of 35 IQ at seventeen months obtained an IQ of 87 on the first post-test, an increase of 52 IQ points. Another child who scored 46 IQ at thirteen months obtained an IQ of 77 after six months in the new institution.

Although Skeels and Dye did not have a control group, they did provide data on what they called a contrast group. After they had collected the data on the enriched group, they identified twelve children who had remained in the orphanage but who also had been tested prior to age two and were in residence in the orphanage at least until age four. On initial testing at about seventeen months, these children averaged almost 87 IQ, 23 points higher than had the experimental group on original testing. When they were retested at about four years of age, they obtained an average IQ of 60, a drop of almost 27 points from their first testing. Again, there were remarkable changes from the first to last testing; three of these children showed drops between 42 and 45 IQ points.

The results of this study were interpreted as indicating that an enriched environment (the home for the feebleminded) could make children with delayed or retarded development normal. A second and equally important conclusion was that continued residence in the orphanage could result in large depressions in intellectual performance. A follow-up study of the total sample of children twenty-six years later was completed by Skeels in 1966. The results showed remarkable differences in adulthood between the two groups of children. Eleven of the thirteen experimental children had subsequently been placed in adoptive homes, and the total group of experimental children on follow-up averaged 96 IQ. None of the contrast group was adopted, although one was later placed with his grandparents, who were described as providing only marginal support.

> All 13 children in the experimental group were self-supporting, and none was a ward of any institution, public or private. In the contrast group of 12 children, one had died in adolescence, ... four were still wards of institutions, one in a mental hospital, and the other three in institutions for the mentally retarded.... The contrast group completed a median of less than the third grade. The experimental group completed a median of the twelfth grade. Four of the subjects had one or more years of college work, one received a B.A. degree and took some graduate training [Skeels 1966, pp. 54–55].

Skeels describes the orphanage experience as follows:

> The orphanage experience can most graciously be described as deplorable. Overcrowding of living facilities was characteristic.... Thirty to thirty-five children of the same sex under six years of age lived in a "cottage" in the charge of one matron and three or four entirely untrained and often reluctant girls of 13 to 15 years of age.... The waking and sleeping hours of these children were spent in an average-sized room (approximately 15 feet square), a sunporch of similar size, a cloakroom, ... and a single dormitory. The latter was occupied only during the sleeping hours.... With so much responsibility centered on one adult the result was a necessary regimentation. The children sat down, stood up, and did many things in rows and unison. They spent considerable time sitting on chairs ... and ... there was the misfortune of inadequate equipment.... [Skeels 1965, p. 4]

Now let's examine the study according to Jones's (1954) criteria for an adequate design in enrichment studies. To begin with, subjects were not randomly assigned to one treatment or another (Criterion 1). In addition, groups differed initially by 23 IQ points, and sex differences in the assignment of subjects were large and unexplained (ten of thirteen in the experimental group were girls, while only four of twelve in the contrast group were girls). Subjects were not homogeneous with respect to age (Criterion 2)—the range of ages for the experimental group on initial testing was seven to thirty months; the range for the contrast groups was twelve to twenty-two months. Relevant to Criterion 3 was the fact that subjects were not matched for initial IQ and chronological age. Within the experimental group, the older half at initial testing averaged 12 IQ points lower than the younger half. Similarly, the older half of the contrast group averaged 5 IQ points lower than the younger half.

A description of the enrichment situation (Criterion 4) was provided. The authors described some of the daily and routine activities of the children. There was no suggestion that these children were coached on the test items. There were some unsystematic differences in the number of tests given to each child, but the authors attempted to correct for this by making comparisons among those who had taken the same number of tests (Criterion 5).

With respect to follow-up (Criterion 6), Skeels obtained IQs for many of the experimentals soon after adoption and, of course, admirably obtained information on their status and the status of the contrast group as adults.

According to the criteria of Jones (1954), the Skeels and Dye study only stacks up moderately well. Nevertheless, the improvement in intelligence for those reared by the feebleminded caretakers is truly astounding. What might account for the improvements? Since infant tests are poor predictors of later IQ, any infant group initially selected for lower intelligence will show some improvement on retesting. It appears, however, that the improvements are far too great to be accounted for solely by statistical regression to the population mean. It is noteworthy that Skeels and Dye reported that the children displayed little in the way of neurological abnormalities. One would expect that, in a group of children with such low IQs, some would have shown deviations in neurological development. The lack of neurological deviation suggests that the low IQs might have been due to the wretched conditions under which the children were reared in the orphanage. In the deprived environment of the orphanage, it is likely that the infants were listless and apathetic and thus performed far short of their potentials. Given the more stimulating environment provided by the feebleminded caretakers, they became active and interested. With this interpretation, it is not difficult to account for the substantial improvements in intelligence, even in the short space of ten months.

For some unexplained reason, the contrast group initially was not severely depressed in intelligence. Remaining in the orphanage eventually appears to have worn the group down, producing only later the listless, apathetic children with low IQs like those found originally in the experimental group.

What are the implications of the study for environmental enrichment of other deprived groups? Clearly, the wholesale application of these findings to minority groups in the United States is not warranted, because children from these minority groups as a whole do not give any indications of lower performance on infant tests (this fact will be discussed in Chapter 14). But other studies confirm that children in poor orphanages do show substantial depressions on infant tests. Dennis and Najarian (1957) compared infants reared under extremely poor conditions in an orphanage in Lebanon with a control group at a Lebanese well-baby clinic. The IQs of the orphanage infants averaged only 63, while the controls averaged 101. Likewise, a study showed that rural Guatemalan infants reared in windowless huts, rarely spoken to or played with, and having no toys averaged only 50 on the Cattell scales of infant development at one year of age (Kagan and Klein 1973). The interpretations of the findings from these orphanages and severely deprived populations is that conditions of this sort reduce the potential and expected IQs of children. Continued residence in such environments is likely to produce mentally impaired children later (Hunt 1961).

One must be cautious, however, in using these findings to indict all institutional environments. Tizard and Rees (1974) have shown that nurseries and orphanages with adequate facilities and competent personnel produce children averaging within the normal range of intelligence.

There are a number of case reports in which children have been reared in wretched early environments and then removed and reared in superior homes. These children often show very large gains in intelligence and social competence. Koluchová (1972), for example, reports on a set of identical twin boys reared in almost complete isolation by a cruel and disturbed stepmother. When located at age seven, the children could barely walk because of rickets, had not been out of doors, used gestures for communication, and had mental ages estimated to be about three years. Placed in a good institution and then in a good adoptive home, the children progressed rapidly. By the age of eight years and four months, the twins averaged 80 and 72 IQ, respectively; at eleven years they averaged 95 and 93 IQ, respectively. According to a follow-up report (Koluchová 1976), the children averaged 100 and 101 IQ at age 14. The implications of this work are clear: (1) children reared under deplorable conditions can benefit dramatically from an improved environment, and (2) it may not be too late, even at age seven, to change a negative prognosis to a good one. Such findings challenge the notion of critical periods and the lasting effects of very early deprivation. Many other challenges to such notions can be found in Clarke and Clarke (1976).

Rapid gains of this sort can pose problems for theories of intelligence. For example, if Koluchová's estimated mental ages of the twins when they were discovered are compared with the twins' mental ages after sixteen months in a normal environment, it appears that the twins gained about thirty-six months mentally, in a normal environment. How may this be explained? Since no test could properly be administered when the children were first seen, it is possible that their mental ages were grossly underestimated. It is also possible that biological maturation had been normal and that stages of cognitive development not originally observed were nearly normally developed. Hence, the twins may have been able to acquire information and problem-solving skills more quickly than younger children. This kind of phenomenon has been observed in cotwin control studies (see Plomin and Willerman 1975), where one twin is given enriched experiences prematurely while the other one is not. Generally, the findings are that the prematurely enriched child acquires the new skills much more slowly than the cotwin who is given the enriched experiences at a more age-appropriate time.

INTERACTIONS BETWEEN CONSTITUTION AND ENVIRONMENT

A question of some importance is what factors make some individuals better able than others to overcome the adverse aspects of their environment. It is well to remember that not all children undergoing deprivation succumb; some go on to perform at average or superior levels later. One such example comes from my own work in predicting IQ from scores on infant tests (Willerman, Broman, and Fiedler 1970). From over three thousand white infants tested at 8 months of age on the Bayley scales of infant development, two groups of children were identified. The first group included infants who were markedly retarded on both the mental and the motor components of the infant measures, scoring at 8 months no better than the average 6.5-month-old infant. The second group consisted of 8-month-old children who were extremely advanced on the infant scales, scoring at least at the 9.5-month level. These children were all routinely administered the Stanford-Binet IQ test when they were four years old, and the incidence of low IQ (IQ < 80) was obtained according to the social class of the parent. The results of this study are shown in Figure 6.3.

The findings from this study indicate that among infants retarded at eight months there was a marked social class effect in the incidence of mental retardation at age four; the retarded infants from the lowest social class were about seven times more likely to be retarded at age four than were retarded infants from the highest social class. The other relevant finding was that advanced infants showed no social class effects in the incidence of mental retardation later. It was as if the advanced infants in the lowest social class had the capacity to overcome the adverse effects of their environments. What could this "capacity" be? This is an unanswered question, and it is, in fact, difficult to formulate empirical propositions to test various hypotheses about this capacity. One hypothesis is that such children are superior in extracting

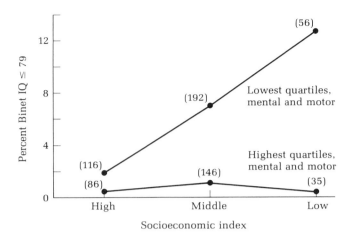

Figure 6.3

Percentage of children with IQ ≤ 79 at four years as a function of quartile category on mental and motor tests at eight months and social class (N in parentheses). (From Willerman 1970.)

information from their environments and that even the "depriving" environments of the lower classes may contain an abundance of relevant information for the taking if the child has the appropriate talents to do so.

It is also of some importance that only about 2 percent of the retarded infants from the highest social class were retarded later. This suggests that "compensatory" experiences of the sort that higher social class families can provide help to prevent mental retardation later.

These findings are not unlike those of a study (Holden and Willerman 1972) which found that neurologically abnormal one-year-old infants from the lower classes were far more likely to be retarded at age four than neurologically abnormal infants from higher social classes. Furthermore, the differences in the incidence of four-year mental retardation according to social class were far greater for these damaged infants than they were among normal controls matched to the damaged infants according to social class. Thus, 5 percent of the higher-class damaged infants were retarded, while 35 percent of the lower-class damaged infants were retarded (a 30 percent difference). Among the controls, none of the higher-class infants were retarded, and 14 percent of the lower-class controls were retarded (a 14 percent difference). The results of this study suggest that neurological abnormality has greater deleterious consequences for later intellectual functioning among the poorest classes than it does for those in the highest classes. Other studies by Drillien (1964) and Werner et al. (1967) are consistent with this interpretation.

These results lead to the conclusion that many retarded infants can respond favorably to an appropriately enriching environment, regardless of whether their retardation is constitutionally or environmentally based. But it is important to note that the enrichment can help to avoid intellectual retardation only; it has not been shown that retarded infants can be made into geniuses. Nor do all retarded infants respond positively to enrichment. Some infants are so impaired that they are insusceptible to attempts at remediation. These infants, however, may comprise only a subset of the retarded; thus, there may be hope for a large proportion of those identified early.

ENRICHMENT PROGRAMS FOR THE CULTURALLY DISADVANTAGED

It is quite another thing to demonstrate that children from culturally disadvantaged environments who give no indications of early retardation will respond favorably and with great magnitude to enrichment programs. Jensen (1969) suggests that the environment has a threshold of adequacy, below which retardation will almost inevitably result. Above that minimal level, however, there is little indication that environmental effects will appreciably add to intelligence test scores. According to Jensen (1969):

> ... especially large upward shifts in IQ which are explicitly associated with environmental factors have involved young children ... whose initial social environment was deplorable to a greater extreme than can be found among any children who are free to interact with other persons or to run out-of-doors. There can be no doubt that moving children from an extremely deprived environment to good average environmental circumstances can boost the IQ some 20 to 30 points and in certain extreme cases as much as 60 or 70 points. On the other hand, children reared in rather average circumstances do not show an appreciable IQ gain as a result of being placed in a more culturally enriched environment.... In brief, it is doubtful that psychologists have found consistent evidence for any social environmental influences short of extreme environmental isolation which have a marked systematic effect on intelligence [pp. 59–60].

My own view is that the environmental threshold for adequacy is not clear-cut and that some early enrichment programs for disadvantaged, but not deplorably deprived, groups do show substantial improvements in intelligence test scores in comparison with those of control groups. These increases, however, are often short-lived. Follow-up testing of these children during elementary school tends to show progressive declines from their higher levels of accomplishment in the preschool programs. Recent reports of findings in the area of compensatory education can be found in Stanley (1972, 1973); only some of the

IQ studies that approach the criteria proposed by Jones (1954) shall be discussed here.

One such study in Ypsilanti has been reported by Weikart (1972). He randomly assigned three- and four-year-old children to one of three enriching curricula for a period of two years or to an untreated control group. The children were described as functionally retarded and as coming from disadvantaged families. The three curricula, which varied in their philosophies, were as follows: (1) the *cognitively oriented curriculum* was a structured program based on principles of "verbal bombardment" and derived from Piaget's theory of intellectual development; (2) the *language training curriculum* was developed by Bereiter and Engelmann (1966) and involved the direct training of language, arithmetic, and reading; and (3) the *unit-based curriculum* emphasized social-emotional goals and the teaching methods found in traditional nursery schools. Children were in classes for half a day, and the teachers conducted a teaching program in the home for ninety minutes every other week. One of the findings from this study was that the different curricula were equally effective, at least initially. In comparison with the controls, all the programs were successful in producing large and significant increases in IQ scores by the spring of the first year. By spring of the second year of the program, some of the large gains were lost, but the gains over the initial testing were still of significant proportions. Repeated testing after the children had entered public elementary school showed continuous and progressive declines in mean IQ, and by the spring of second grade there were no differences between the experimental and the control groups.

A summary of Weikart's findings can be seen in Figure 6.4, where the three different curricula have been combined into one experimental group. Note the slow, but progressive, increase in the IQ scores of the untreated controls and the progressive decrease in the IQ scores of the experimental children after their earlier higher scores in the program.

In another study, Karnes (1973) compared the effectiveness of five different intervention programs on four-year-olds from low-income families; there was no control group. We shall discuss the findings from only three of the most pertinent programs. The first program was the Karnes structured cognitive program, which emphasized compensation for language inadequacies under very well controlled conditions. The second program, much like a traditional nursery school program, was designed to promote social, motor, and general language development in the children. The third program was the one devised by Bereiter and Engelmann, emphasizing intensive oral drill in verbal and logical patterns. According to Bereiter and Engelmann's (1966) general procedure, the child first learns a particular verbal formula by rote and then learns to apply that formula to analogous examples of increasing complexity.

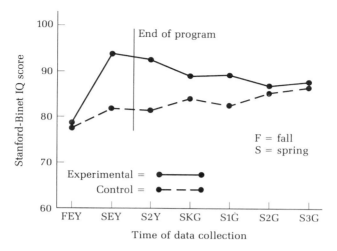

Figure 6.4

Mean Stanford-Binet IQs for enriched (experimental) and control children. (From D. P. Weikart, *Preschool Programs for the Disadvantaged*, ed. J. C. Stanley. Baltimore: The Johns Hopkins University Press. Copyright © 1972.)

After completing the first year of the program, two of the three treatment groups were scheduled to enter kindergarten. Those in the Karnes structured cognitive program (k_1) attended public kindergarten in the mornings and participated in a one-hour supportive program at the research center in the afternoon. Those in the traditional program (k_2) attended public kindergarten for a half-day, with no further intervention. Those in the Bereiter-Engelmann (B-E) program did not attend public kindergarten but continued to spend half-days at the research center. The findings of this study can be seen in Figure 6.5.

It is clear that the gains in IQ were substantial for each of the three programs during the first year—from 8 to 14 IQ points. During the second year of the program, only the Bereiter-Engelmann pupils, who did not attend public kindergarten, showed continued improvement; the other two groups showed slight drops in mean IQ. According to Karnes (1973):

> It seems clear that one year of preschool programming, no matter how immediately effective, did not equip disadvantaged children to maintain performance in the kindergarten setting. Regardless of the progress made, ... their relative performance deteriorated during the second year, which supports the current belief that typical public school kindergarten programming for disadvantaged children is inappropriate [pp. 123–124]

At the end of the first grade in public school, the Bereiter-Engelmann children showed a substantial drop in IQ. For these children, there were

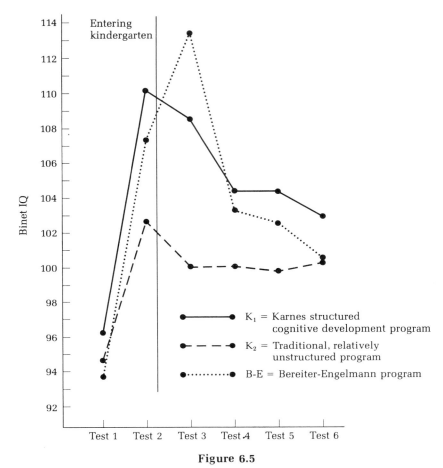

Figure 6.5

Mean IQs for three enrichment programs. (From M. Karnes, *Compensatory Education for Children Ages 2 to 8*, ed. J. C. Stanley. Baltimore: The Johns Hopkins University Press. Copyright © 1973.)

further declines during second and third grades, and by the third grade there was little differentiation between the three treatment programs. Overall improvements from initial testing to the last testing in third grade were between 6 and 7 IQ points. It is clear that the public school experiences were insufficient to maintain the large initial increases in IQ.

Using IQs and other measures, a very well designed study by Miller and Dyer (1975) compared four preschool enrichment programs, each having a different educational philosophy, to each other and to a control group of untreated children. The preschool programs lasted for the prekindergarten academic year, and a subset of children was then placed in follow-through classes that would presumably provide further enrichment during the school years. Although the preschool programs had a significant effect initially, by second grade the entire effect had vanished. Furthermore, the follow-through program appeared to have little, if any, effect on test scores in grade two.

Heber et al. (1972) have reported longitudinal findings on what is perhaps the most intensive intervention program. Children of low-IQ black mothers, all with initial IQs of less than 75, were assigned to either an experimental (n = 20) or a control condition (n = 20). After three months of age the experimental children spent each weekday at a community school with a paraprofessional caretaker from the same community on a one-to-one basis. The caretakers and the mothers were given training in child rearing throughout the program. The mothers were also provided with vocational training to build their self-confidence as well as to increase their employability. Heber et al. give a very thorough picture of the intervention program, which included perceptual-motor, cognitive-language, and social-emotional training before twenty-four months of age. After twenty-four months, the children also received training in academic subjects, such as reading and math problem solving. The children in the program also received nutritious meals at the school and medical care, if necessary.

Both the experimental and the control children were administered a variety of intelligence tests, starting from about six months of age and continuing, at regular intervals, until sixty-six months of age. From about eighteen months on, the experimental children began to exceed the controls, and, from about thirty months, the difference between the two groups remained approximately constant. At twelve months of age the children in both groups averaged over 110 IQ, but soon afterwards the IQs of the control children began to decline. The Wechsler Preschool Performance Scale of Intelligence (WPPSI) was administered to both groups of children at fifty-one, fifty-seven, and sixty-three months of age. The experimental children obtained mean IQ scores of 114, 111, and 110 at those ages, respectively, while the controls averaged 85, 81, and 88, respectively. Follow-up performance in the school years for these children has recently been reported (Heber 1976) and shows that the superiority of the experimental children was maintained until nine years of age.

This brief summary of the four preschool enrichment programs shows that they may be effective in raising IQ scores but that there may be sharp declines from the formerly higher IQ levels after attendance in public school. It appears that the more intensive and structured the program, the more emphasis on the acquisition of cognitive-academic skills as opposed to social-emotional skills, the more likely the program will be effective during the preschool years (Weikart 1972).

Why is it that the early gains are sometimes not sustained after the children enter the public schools? Can the public schools into which these children are placed be so pernicious and deficient? One possible explanation comes from the fact that test items tap different content areas or abilities at different ages. Drops in IQ might result later because the training programs have tended towards item-specific learnings that were keyed to the ages of the children while they were in the programs. Intelligence tests are constructed to elicit representative *samples* of what the child knows or can do and not to test *all* that the child knows or can do. If the training programs were closely tied to skills measured by the test items, then the test results are not small samples of what the child has learned but indications of nearly all that the child has learned. For middle-class children with above-average IQs, such test scores may represent only small samples of what they know, and, consequently, changes in item content will have little effect on their scores.

This analysis further suggests that children who have equivalent IQ scores but who come from widely differing backgrounds may differ in their relative degrees of impairment. It seems likely that a child from a higher social class environment is, with respect to biological integrity of the brain, more likely to be impaired than a child of equal IQ from a low social class environment. Confirmatory data for this proposition has been reviewed earlier in this chapter (Drillien 1964; Holden and Willerman 1972; Werner et al. 1967; and Willerman, Broman, and Fiedler 1970).

The preceding review of environmental influences on intellectual performance has generally indicated that, except for children in extremely deprived environments, it is difficult to demonstrate strong positive relationships between enriched environments and intelligence. This is not to say that environmental differences do not produce substantial effects on other aspects of behavior. For example, Bronfenbrenner (1974) has pointed out that cross-cultural studies of behavior show that children can behave so differently on some measures that their countries of origin can be identified with virtually no error.

It is quite possible that some structured intervention programs for underprivileged children have been neither intense enough nor early enough. The entire social and intellectual environment may have to be drastically altered before mean IQ differences can be substantially diminished or eradicated (e.g., Heber et al. 1972).

Preliminary evidence bearing on the issue of drastic environmental change and intellectual performance comes from Israel, where Smilansky (1974) is studying children of various ancestries living in kibbutzim. On the kibbutzim, children do not live with their parents but reside in a children's house with a cohort of age mates under the caretaking of a woman trained in child rearing (Devereux, Shouval, and Brofenbrenner 1974). Although the parents can spend a great deal of time with their children during the early evenings, it is clear that the role of the parents in the upbringing of their children is systematically and substantially reduced.

For many years Israel has had to face the problem of large differences in intellectual, educational, and occupational achievement between Jews of different cultural ancestry. Generally, there are large mean differences in IQ favoring Jews of European ancestry over Jews from the Arabic countries. These differences are comparable to, or even larger than, the black-white differences observed in the United States. Smilansky (1974) has shown, however, that among children reared on the kibbutzim mean IQs are above average and unrelated to country of origin. Thus, children whose parents came from the Arabic countries perform about as well as children whose parents came from Europe. This is an extremely important finding because it shows that mean differences can be eradicated by altering the entire life space of the children. There are few enrichment programs in the United States that are even remotely comparable in comprehensiveness to the kibbutz experience of Israel; nor is it clear that a large proportion of families would want to participate in such a program if one were available. Even in Israel only a small proportion of citizens (about 4 percent) are members of kibbutzim.

Individual differences in intelligence have not been eradicated by the kibbutz experience, however, even though mean differences have been. In general, the standard deviation for IQ test scores on the kibbutzim approach those for children in the standardization samples. Thus, individual differences in intelligence are still present, but they are no longer related to country of origin.

COTWIN CONTROL STUDIES

A neglected approach to the testing of environmental influences is the cotwin control method. This technique applies different treatments to each member of an MZ set to see if they will produce later differences in behavior. Because genetic differences within a set are eliminated, one can clearly observe the effects of the environmental treatment.

There are fewer than a dozen cotwin control studies in the literature (see Plomin and Willerman 1975 for a review), and they can be classified into three function categories. The earliest and largest category includes attempts to demonstrate that maturation interacts with training. Gesell and Thompson (1929), Strayer (1930), and Hilgard (1933) used the same pair of identical girls at different ages. They trained first one cotwin and then the other in the same skills; the major emphasis was on the age at which each cotwin was trained. The trained behaviors included stair climbing, vocabulary, memory for objects, speech, and reading ability. These studies all give tenuous support to the hypothesis that certain developmental processes can be accelerated but that maturation is also important, since the later-trained twin generally learned more rapidly than did the earlier-trained twin. As Mittler (1971) noted, timing is crucial to this "maturational" application of the cotwin method. If training occurs too early, no child will profit; if training occurs too late, both twins will have already changed by maturation and the effect of training will be minimal. The second category, which includes fewer studies, has tried to compare the effectiveness of different training programs. For example, Naesland in Stockholm (see Vandenberg 1968a) separated identical twins during their first years in elementary school to test two different instructional programs. The third category of cotwin studies simply asks to what extent the environment can produce differences in genetically identical individuals (see Mittler 1971 for examples).

One problem in the application of cotwin control methodology is the reluctance of parents to permit the drawing of blood from the youngsters for serological determinations of zygosity. More recently, however, it has been shown that parental ratings of the physical similarity of infant twins (Cohen et al. 1973) and self-ratings by adolescent twins (Nichols and Bilbro 1966) are from 93 to 98 percent accurate in determining zygosity. Thus, it is now possible to use parental ratings rather than serological tests for zygosity determinations. Another problem is an ethical one, since one twin might be deprived of the enriched experience or be delayed in receiving it. It seems possible to circumvent this problem, however, by simultaneously teaching both twins different desirable skills rather than depriving or delaying the training of one.

Theoretically, the advantage of the cotwin control method is that it permits the application of intensive environmental treatments to small samples of children, because within-set genetic variability is eliminated. Moreover, the intensity of treatment permitted by the cotwin method may yield larger mean differences, which may be better to work with than the slight, but significant, mean differences obtained by experimental studies using large numbers of subjects in less intensive situations.

Intelligence as a Predictor

The previous chapter pointed out that IQ scores obtained during the preadult years have a considerable degree of predictive validity. The relationship of IQ scores to future attainment will now be reviewed in more detail.

IQ AND ACADEMIC PERFORMANCE

Study after study has shown positive relationships between IQ scores and academic success as measured by either school grades or class rank. These correlations have averaged about .50 and are far from perfect. That they haven't been higher is due to a number of causes; grades themselves are not infallible, and students vary in motivation, personality, family attitudes, and other nonintellective factors that contribute to school performance.

One study that is representative of the findings in this area was conducted by Conry and Plant (1965). They administered the WAIS to two groups of students. In the first group WAIS scores were obtained when the students were high school juniors (N = 98) and then correlated with their class rank at graduation. In the second sample WAIS's given to college freshmen (N = 335) were correlated with their grades at the end of the first semester of college. The findings for both samples are shown in Table 6.3.

The results of this study indicate that the WAIS scores predict both high school rank and first-semester college grades but that the WAIS does a better job of predicting for the high school group. Perhaps the major reason for this is that the high school group was more heterogeneous in ability, averaging 107 IQ (SD = 12.4), while the college sam-

Table 6.3

Correlations of rank in class and grades with WAIS scores

WAIS subtests	Rank in high school	College grades
Information	0.54	0.48
Comprehension	0.55	0.33
Arithmetic	0.45	0.19
Similarities	0.50	0.39
Digit span	0.37	0.04
Vocabulary	0.65	0.46
Digit symbol	0.34	0.15
Picture completion	0.33	0.20
Block design	0.29	0.19
Picture arrangement	0.22	0.07
Object assembly	0.17	0.12
Verbal	0.63	0.47
Performance	0.43	0.24
Full scale	0.62	0.44

Source: Adapted from Conry and Plant 1965.

ple averaged 115 IQ (SD = 8.0). Thus, the high school sample included a larger proportion of students with fairly low intellectual ability than did the college sample. In addition, the verbal subtests and verbal IQ were better predictors of school performance than were the nonverbal tests. This fact is not surprising, since most of what is to be learned in school depends more on verbal skills than on nonverbal skills. It has frequently been pointed out that children who have the same total IQs but who have different patterns of verbal-performance abilities will also have different experiences in school. Those with deficiencies in verbal skills are much more likely to come to the attention of school authorities than those with deficiencies in nonverbal skills.

In general, correlations between intelligence test scores and scores on scholastic achievement tests are higher than the correlations between intelligence and school performance as measured by grades or class rank. This difference occurs because scholastic achievement test scores are more reliable than any other measured of scholastic performance, motivation is usually high during achievement test taking, and teachers' judgments do not enter into the scoring.

IQ AND EDUCATIONAL ATTAINMENT

The simple correlations between IQ and educational attainment in adults are positive, averaging about .70 (Matarazzo 1972). The correlation may be somewhat lower among females, however (McCall 1977). This high correlation is inflated partly by the fact that SES contributes independently to both intelligence and educational attainment. Information bearing on the interrelationships of SES, ability, and educational attainment are given by Jensen (1971), using data from Project TALENT collected by Flanagan and Cooley (1966).

Figure 6.6 gives the probability of entering college for whites as a function of ability as measured by high school tests of scholastic aptitude and parental SES. The results indicate that females are less likely to enter college than males of similar ability and SES. However, you can see from the figure that high-ability individuals from the lowest social class are more likely to enter college than individuals with low ability from the highest social class. Analysis of variance shows that ability is more important than SES in determining the probability of entering college, regardless of sex. Jencks (1973) has summarized findings from three studies that compared early test scores of youngsters between the ages of eleven and seventeen with their educational attainments as adults. He found correlations averaging about .5, suggesting that IQ had considerable predictive validity for later educational attainments. In a study by Bajema (1968), IQ scores of 437 males who

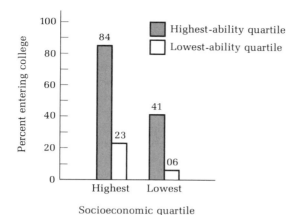

Figure 6.6
Probability of entering college as a function of
socioeconomic quartile and ability quartile. (After
Flanagan and Cooley 1966.)

were given a group intelligence test in the sixth grade were located at
age forty-five. The correlation between their early test scores and later
educational attainment was .58.

INTELLIGENCE AND OCCUPATION

Many studies have pointed to positive relationships between intelligence test scores and occupational attainment (see Duncan, Featherman, and Duncan 1972), and ratings of occupational prestige correspond closely to the mean IQs of those in the occupations.

An important study by Thorndike and Hagen (1959) obtained the test
scores of about ten thousand applicants, averaging twenty-one years of
age, to aviation cadet training during World War II. The examination
was primarily a scholastic aptitude test, with an emphasis on technical
and mechanical matters. The qualifying scores for acceptance in cadet
training were set at a level that could be reached by approximately half
of the high school graduates. Thus, these individuals as a group were
somewhat above average in their general educational and intellectual
achievement.

Twelve years later, these ten thousand men were located and asked to
complete a questionnaire on their current occupational status. Table 6.4
gives the mean wartime test scores obtained on selected groups of these
men according to their occupations about a dozen years later. The general intellectual test included tests of reading comprehension and gen-

eral information, with stress on vocabulary knowledge of technical and academic topics. The numerical fluency tests emphasized speed and accuracy in simple numerical operations as well as skill in reading dials and tables. The visual perception tests required speedy matching of visual forms and the reading of aerial photographs. The mechanical tests emphasized abilities related to spatial visualization and mechanical experience. Finally, the psychomotor tests involved complex coordination. The means for each of these tests have been set at a value of zero with a standard deviation of 100.

Examination of the data in Table 6.4 shows that some occupations

Table 6.4

Selected occupational group means on five score composites

	General intel- lectual	Numer- ical fluency	Visual percep- tion	Mechan- ical	Psycho- motor
	(G)	(N)	(Ps)	(M)	(Pm)
Accountants and auditors	28	54	−4	−46	−16
Advertising agents	26	−12	34	−15	−12
Airplane pilots	−16	−20	18	64	43
Architects	44	4	74	8	14
Artists and designers	−7	−12	51	−4	8
Bricklayers	−24	−5	−38	10	−32
Carpenters	−44	−17	−4	24	−1
Claim adjustors, insurance	−13	−5	−9	−44	−20
Clergymen	13	1	−17	−4	0
Clerical, machine operators	−30	−6	−1	4	−16
College professors	75	38	38	−33	1
Contractors	−7	−10	−10	34	5
Crane operators	−66	−84	−37	−19	−29
Dentists	28	29	15	−19	1
Dispatchers, control tower operators	4	37	31	31	41
Draftsmen	1	−14	31	14	15
Drivers, bus and truck	−53	−11	−23	−14	−20
Earth movers	−71	−70	−22	−3	−37
Electricians, instruments and equipment	−33	−43	−12	17	7
Engineers, chemical	106	42	30	19	20
Engineers, civil	75	31	56	36	14
Engineers, electrical	65	6	9	32	11
Engineers, industrial	44	41	34	−4	4
Engineers, mechanical	93	34	44	52	23
Engineers, sales	57	33	35	39	40
Engineers—trainmen, RR	−50	−37	−31	21	−1
Farmers, general	−6	−7	−29	38	−36

Table 6.4 (continued)

	General intel- lectual	Numer- ical fluency	Visual percep- tion	Mechan- ical	Psycho- motor
	(G)	(N)	(Ps)	(M)	(Pm)
Firemen	−29	−29	−6	−10	15
Handicraftsmen, jewelry, etc.	6	−4	15	26	5
Laborers	−33	−36	−13	−18	−24
Lawyers	39	22	−7	−42	−21
Mechanics, appliances & cameras	−19	9	17	32	54
Mechanics, engine	−28	−27	−29	28	−25
Mechanics, vehicular	−72	−65	−7	19	−6
Miners, drillers	−43	−4	73	75	80
Optometrists	14	34	−3	−14	15
Painters	−63	−12	−24	−25	−22
Personal service, other	−49	−42	−25	−33	−29
Pharmacists	29	39	−9	−7	15
Physicians	59	20	18	2	0
Plumbers	−42	−21	−31	−7	−5
Policemen, detectives	−50	−26	−20	−32	−4
Principals, high school	25	10	−13	−8	−24
Public relations men	9	0	−4	−32	−9
Radio and TV repairmen	−33	−37	21	2	5
Salesmen, insurance	−5	8	14	−17	2
Salesmen, real estate	6	17	6	−50	−32
Scientists, biological	33	12	25	−7	−21
Scientists, physical	80	22	23	5	−8
Scientists, social	64	33	21	−49	−26
Sheet-metal workers	−11	−55	−27	25	−24
Steel workers	−29	−37	−23	−8	−31
Surveyors	−25	−32	40	38	8
Teachers, elementary	−9	18	−27	−75	−32
Teachers, high school English, languages, social studies	−50	−37	−20	−102	−18
Teachers, high school mathematics and science	35	11	−4	−1	−2
Teachers, high school, other	−8	10	6	0	4
Telephone installers	−19	−20	5	5	−2
Treasurers and comptrollers	55	96	−35	−30	−12
Undertakers	−14	23	−35	−30	−12
Veterinarians	−8	−2	−20	−16	−5
Welders, lead burners	−61	−52	−32	−3	3
Writers	42	0	2	−50	−24

Note: Expressed as standard scores for which mean = 0, standard deviation = 100.
Source: From R. L. Thorndike and E. Hagen, *Ten Thousand Careers*. Copyright © John Wiley and Sons, 1959.

have distinctive ability profiles. For example, accountants have high scores on numerical fluency and low scores on the mechanical test. Airplane pilots showed superior abilities on the mechanical and psychomotor tests. College professors showed high scores on the general intellectual test and low scores on the mechanical tests. Chemical engineers were superior on all of the tests. In general, the ability profiles correspond to our images of the abilities and skills required for entry into each of the occupations. The fact that the ability tests were administered before most of the men had entered their occupations suggests that individuals tend to enter or to remain in occupations that call for specific abilities.

After reviewing studies on correlates of IQ, Matarazzo (1972) provided a table representing approximate average correlations of IQ with various occupational and educational outcomes. His findings are presented in Table 6.5.

Note that the lowest correlation in Matarazzo's table is for IQ and job success. This occurs partly because the range of ability is restricted within an occupation; those already in a particular occupation have been preselected for ability. In addition, the difficulty in reliably and validly defining job success within an occupation undoubtedly contributes to the low correlation.

McCelland (1973) has taken the finding that correlations between intelligence and job success tend to be low or nonsignificant as a cause célèbre for the dismantling of the intelligence test industry. He fails to note, however, that poor prediction of job success *within* an occupation

Table 6.5

Validity coefficients of IQ

Exemplars	r
IQ with Adaptive Behavior Measure	
IQ × mental retardation	0.90
IQ × educational attainment (in years)	0.70
IQ × academic success (grade point)	0.50
IQ × occupational attainment	0.50
IQ × socioeconomic status	0.40
IQ × success on the job	0.20
Related Variables	
IQ × independently judged prestige of one's occupation	0.95
IQ × parents' educational attainment	0.50

Source: From *Wechsler's Measurement and Appraisal of Adult Intelligence*, 5th and enlarged edition by Joseph D. Matarazzo. Copyright © 1939, 1941, 1944, 1958 by David Wechsler; © 1972 by The Williams and Wilkins Company. Reprinted by permission of Oxford University Press, Inc.

is a separate issue from the prediction of occupational attainments across occupations. By the time individuals have already entered a job, considerable selection has already taken place, often attenuating the distribution of IQs in the occupation as well as restricting the range of acceptable performances. Additionally, it would be too much to ask that intelligence be the sole source of adequacy in job performance. Motivation, carefulness, and many other nonintellective factors should and do contribute to job success.

At the same time, McClelland makes a valuable point. In our love affair with intelligence tests, we often neglect the more difficult problem of assessing competence. Presumably, competence includes intellective and nonintellective factors alike. Were we to develop scales for competence, it seems likely that the prediction of job success, even within an occupation, would be improved. It should be added, however, that competence is not likely to be unidimensional, and it does not appear that we will be able to develop a "competence quotient" that will have nearly the utility that the IQ score has now.

INTELLIGENCE AND LEARNING

Intelligence and Learning Ability. If intelligence tests are measures of what has been learned, it seems likely that intelligence test scores would relate substantially to tests of learning ability. Since IQ tests control for chronological age, it follows that those with higher IQs have learned more than those with lower IQs over a specific time span. There are, in fact, two separate but related ways of interpreting the IQ in this regard. IQ can be related to the *speed* of learning a task that all subjects ultimately can learn, or it can be related to the ultimate *level of complexity* that subjects can reach, given sufficient time.

Most studies that relate intelligence to learning ability have focused on tasks that are not exceedingly complex. Thus, one might predict near-perfect performance from virtually all subjects with tutelage, although some might take a long time to reach that level. Other studies have used tasks that appear to have a large motor component rather than a large intellectual component. On these measures, not all individuals may be able to attain near-perfect performance. Differences in individual reaction time would not be eradicated, even with years of practice, for example.

Evidence suggests that learning ability is not unitary. Intercorrelations between learning scores for different experimental tasks are almost always low or statistically nonsignificant. For example, Husband (1939) intercorrelated the scores obtained by 100 college students on fourteen different learning tasks as well as on an intelligence test. The tasks could be subdivided into motor tasks, such as mirror drawing;

rote learning tasks, such as memory for faces; and ideational tests, such as the recall of a prose passage. The intercorrelations between all the tasks tended to be low, averaging about .15. Those classified as motor tests intercorrelated among themselves about .19; the rote learning tasks intercorrelations averaged .20; and the ideational tests intercorrelated about .25. The highest single correlation was for the rote learning of Persian and English paired associates presented visually and Hindu and English paired associates presented via the auditory mode ($r = .53$). These, of course, can be regarded as virtually identical tests. The intercorrelations between IQ and the experimental tasks were usually quite low and ranged from .06 to .32. Another study by Husband (1941) lengthened such experimental tasks fourfold, with the idea of increasing the reliabilities of the measures. The intercorrelations were again very low, however, averaging only about .20.

Thompson and Witryol (1946) correlated Otis intelligence scores with learning of a finger maze and found correlations ranging from .03 to .28, depending on whether trials to reach the criterion, errors, or time to learn the maze was used as the outcome measure. All of these correlations were insignificant.

Gain Scores. Another approach has examined speed of learning or gains in learning from an initial pretest to a final test and kept the number of practice trials constant (see Woodrow 1946). The results have generally indicated that gain scores from initial to final testing on a variety of learning measures were not predictable from IQ. Furthermore, gain scores for one measure were not correlated with gain scores for other measures, so that there was little indication of a unitary general factor for speed of learning. For example, those who learned to memorize nonsense syllables rapidly could not be expected to learn a pursuit tracking test with equal speed.

In part, the results of such studies have been compromised by the fact that difference or gain scores can be extremely unreliable, even when scores for the initial and final tests are themselves highly reliable. Guilford (1967) gives the formula for the reliability of gain scores as

$$r_{gg} = \frac{r_{ff} + r_{ii} - 2r_{fi}}{2(1 + r_{fi})}$$

where r equals the correlation coefficient or the reliability, g refers to the gain or difference scores, f refers to the final score, and i refers to the initial score.

A concrete application of the formula might help you to understand its meaning. Suppose that the initial and final tests both had test-retest reliabilities of .9 and that the correlation between the initial and final score was .5. The formula would then be

$$r_{gg} = \frac{.9 + .9 - 2(.5)}{2(1 + .5)} = \frac{0.8}{3.0} = .27$$

The critical feature to note in this formula is the correlation between initial and final score. If that correlation is high, as in this example, then even with a reliable measure, the reliability of the difference score will be very low.

When we turn to intellectual tasks that more closely resemble academic subjects, the intercorrelation between any pretest measure and any final measure tends to be very high. Referring to the above formula, then, we see that if we want to measure the increment of learning from some initial measure to a final measure on academic type tests, we are not likely to be successful. Those who score high initially can improve relatively little, while those who score low initially can advance much further on retesting. It is therefore possible for IQ to correlate substantially both with some initial score on an achievement test and with the final score on that achievement test but be negligibly correlated with the gain score on that test.

It is possible to artificially remove the correlation between IQ and initial performance and the correlation of initial and final score on achievement tests, but the results of such a procedure can be difficult to interpret. For example, Tilton (1949) criticized previous work on two counts: (1) most tests had low ceilings so that those initially scoring high had little room for improvement, and (2) most studies of learning rate took place over too short a time span. Intelligence test scores of school-age children are the result of years of cumulative learnings, whereas the total time involved in the studies of learning rate tend to be much briefer.

To vitiate these criticisms, Tilton used two samples of students. The first group, seventh graders in social studies, was given a social studies achievement test. Only those items from the test on which less than 25 percent initially passed were used as the measure of initial performance and in the subsequent analyses. After eleven weeks of schooling, the test was readministered; the intercorrelation between the gain scores after the eleven weeks and Otis IQ scores of the children was .49.

The second group, twelfth graders taking a course in American history, was given a history achievement examination. For his analyses, Tilton used only those items on which less than 45 percent of the subjects passed initially. One year later the test was readministered, and again Tilton found the correlation of Terman IQ with gains on the history exam to be .49.

The problem with this procedure of eliminating initial items on which there is room for large differences between people is that it artificially reduces the correlation between initial and final score. Thus, the correlation between intelligence and gain score becomes almost equivalent to the simple correlation between IQ and final score. If one conceptualizes a continuum for answering an item—an incorrect answer might be a near miss for one individual and just a wild guess for another—one can see that some people might be closer to getting the item correct than others. The artificial removal of much of the variability in the pretest measure would obscure the correlation between the initial scores and the final scores.

After reviewing the literature on learning rate and gain scores, Cronbach and Snow (1969) conclude that the reliability of learning rate scores cannot be determined and that the entire concept of learning rate is false, educationally, psychologically, and psychometrically. Their analyses are exceedingly complex and are beyond the scope of this book, however, so they will not be discussed here. In sum, Cronbach and Snow believe that the problem of controlling for individual differences in initial scores is almost intractable.

Some evidence suggests that intelligence plays a more important role in solving unfamiliar and difficult intellectual problems than in solving relatively straightforward problems. For example, Osler and Weiss (1962) gave a concept attainment task to two groups of children, one of average intelligence and the other of superior intelligence. The children, were given examples of a specific concept and then asked to identify the concept itself. When the children were given hints about what to look for, there was little difference in the speed with which the two groups correctly identified the concept. When the children were not given such hints, however, those with high IQs were far more successful in identifying the concept than those with average IQs. The authors thus conclude that problem finding is more related to intelligence than is problem solving. Unfortunately, little is known about the skills involved in generating hypotheses for unfamiliar problems.

Verbal Mediation.   An area of research called verbal mediation has exposed some of the factors that influence learning. *Mediation* generally refers to all those processes that occur in the brain between the reception of sensory stimuli and the overt responses to those stimuli. Jensen (1971c) has provided an extensive review of verbal mediation research, showing, for example, that labeling or assigning names to things helps in learning. Instructions to label are especially helpful for preschool and primary school children, but not for older individuals. Pyles (1932) showed that younger children could learn to identify nonsense shapes if they were first instructed to assign nonsense names to those shapes. In any form of paired associate learning (of which the Pyles study is but one example), three components can be identified. The first is learning to discriminate between one stimulus and another; the second is the discrimination learning of the response items when they are different from each other (in this case the response of picking up the correct item was already known); and third is the linking of the stimulus and response terms. It is quite possible for an individual to learn each of these components at a different rate, but, theoretically, the intercorrelation between these rates ought to be positive. Jensen (1963) and Flavell, Beach, and Chinsky (1966) found that children who spontaneously applied labels to the items to be discriminated learned discriminations more quickly than children who didn't label. Further, when retarded children were instructed to assign labels to stimuli, their learning of paired associates improved. This work has suggested that richness of verbal associations and spontaneous use of such associations may generally enhance a person's learning ability (Jensen 1971c).

It should be noted, however, that *verbal* mediation is not solely responsible for differences in intelligence test performance. Many studies have shown that congenitally deaf children are not very deficient in nonverbal intellectual skills (see Chapter 10). Of course deaf children probably utilize nonverbal forms of labeling to assist them in learning.

Much research is being focused on training children to increase their spontaneous use of verbal mediation techniques. While it is often possible to get children to employ verbal mediation vigorously in the experimental situation, it is more difficult to get them to use these techniques outside of that setting.

The verbal mediation line of research is compatible with the findings of Osler and Weiss (1962) about the importance of hypothesis generation in tests of concept attainment. Little is known, however, about the causes of differences in the spontaneous generation of hypotheses or labels. One proposition, which is not readily testable, comes from an extension of Chomsky's (1972) theory regarding the acquisition of grammar. Since toddlers make such astonishingly rapid strides in the acquisition of language, Chomsky suggests that there is a brain mechanism that causes the child to consider only a limited subset, rather than all potential hypotheses, in inferring grammatical rules of the language.

At first blush the idea of preadaptation for intelligence seems excessively fanciful, but Bruner (1973) has pointed out that the accomplishments of infants involve

> ... problems of high complexity ... on the basis of encounters with the environment that are too few in number, too unrepresentative or too erratic in consequence to be accounted for either on the basis of concept attainment or the shaping effects of reinforcement. Initial "learning" has a large element of preadaptation that reflects species-typical genetic instructions [pp. 1–2].

It may be that the more intelligent have lower thresholds than the less intelligent for the generation of potentially adaptive and accurate hypotheses.

Conclusions

The data reviewed in this chapter do not support the conclusion that intelligence test scores are easily manipulable, except for those who have undergone extreme deprivation. Intervention programs in the United States have had some temporary success in raising IQs, but after one or two years of public schooling those gains disappear. The only programs that appear to have been successful in raising IQs are those experiments by Heber et al. (1972) and Smilansky (1974). Both programs involved a reorganization of the life space of the children for a major portion of the day, a reorganization that has not been approximated by most preschool programs.

To acknowledge that there is a substantial heritable component in IQ does not preclude the possibility that effective environmental enrichment programs may be found; the heritability of intelligence is far from perfect. Since heritability estimates of a trait are specific to the *frequency* and *range* of environments included in a study, it is possible that there are currently existing environments that occur too infrequently to have much influence on overall heritability estimates but that could be made more frequent if identified. On the other hand, it is quite possible that new types of environments will be necessary to improve IQ scores.

7

Educational Achievement Differences

Nowhere are individual differences more obvious than in the classroom. Especially in the early school years, pupils and teachers alike have the opportunity to observe others under fairly standard conditions—questions are asked and pupils reply; students are graded on written and oral performances and compare grades.

As children progress in school, their heterogeneity may become less apparent. As students begin to select their own courses, become more secretive, satisfy course requirements, and fulfill other conditions in order to enter advanced courses, variability among class members decreases. Yet the differences remain sufficiently large to see readily at all class levels.

Range of Academic Achievement

The monumental study by Learned and Wood (1938) gives an idea of the enormous range of individual differences even at the secondary school and college level. Identical tests of school-related factual knowledge were administered to thousands of high school seniors and college students in Pennsylvania between 1928 and 1934. Because the authors were more interested in the breadth of factual knowledge than in the problem-solving skills of the students, the tests more closely approximated achievement tests than intelligence tests.

One of the examinations, the general culture test, took about four hours to complete and included 1222 multiple-choice questions covering fine arts, history, and social studies; questions about foreign literature; and questions about natural science. The results of this test for three grade levels are given in Figure 7.1. The figure gives the 10th, 25th, 50th, 75th, and 90th percentiles for each grade. As expected, there is a regular increase in scores with each successive grade, so that the 75th percentile for one class is about equivalent to the 50th percentile of the group above. It is noteworthy, however, that about 10 percent of the high school seniors scored higher than about 75 percent of the college sophomores and higher than 50 percent of the college seniors on this test.

Learned and Wood asked what the composition of a graduating class would be if knowledge attained (as measured by the tests) rather than completion of four years of college was used as the criterion for graduation. Taking the 80th percentile score for college seniors as the criterion for graduation and ignoring the actual class year, they found that the "revised" graduation class would be composed of 28 percent of the seniors, 21 percent of the juniors, 19 percent of the sophomores, and 15 percent of the freshmen. (The numbers don't add up to 100 percent

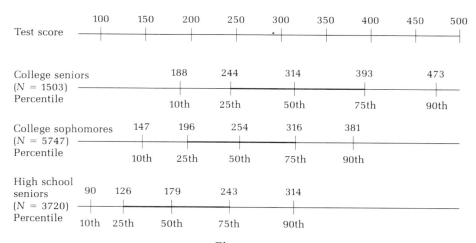

Figure 7.1

General culture test scores of students in high school and college taking the identical test. (After Learned and Wood 1938.)

because of differences in class sizes.) Since 15 percent of the freshmen were sufficiently knowledgeable to deserve graduation, one wonders about the purpose of requiring these students to continue in the usual academic curriculum.

Other analyses by Learned and Wood (1938) dealt with the average test scores of students with different majors and of students from different colleges. In general, the engineering majors scored higher than any other majors and, as expected, there were wide differences in the average scores of students from different colleges. Under special scrutiny were education majors intending to teach high school students. Learned and Wood point out that a large proportion of these prospective teachers knew less than many of the high school students that they would soon be teaching. They doubted that these teachers were of the intellectual caliber to be successful high school teachers.

The range of achievement for children in elementary school is little different. Figure 7.2 gives the 10th, 50th, and 90th percentiles and raw scores for one subtest, reading to note details, of the standardized Gates Basic Reading Tests for fifth and eighth graders. One can choose a specific raw score from the fifth grade and look at its percentile for that grade and for the eighth grade. For example, a raw score of 80 correct in grade five gives a percentile ranking of 90 percent, which means that about 10 percent of fifth graders obtained such a score or better. Even in grade eight, a raw score of 80 exceeds the scores of nearly 50 percent of the students. Thus, 10 percent of the children in grade five did better on

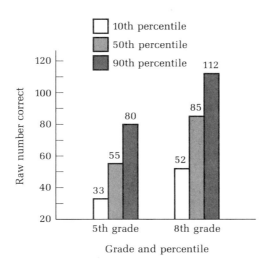

Figure 7.2

Percentiles and number correct raw scores for reading to note details from the Gates Basic Reading Tests (1958.)

this test than nearly 50 percent of the children in grade eight. As far as reading to note details is concerned, the fifth graders who scored in the upper 5 to 10 percent could easily be doing the work of most eighth graders.

These findings raise important questions about the relationship of teaching to learning. No doubt many pupils are learning much more or less than the instructor intends to teach. Failures of pupils to learn are often blamed on the teacher, and, indeed, in many circumstances the responsibility for inadequate learning can be attributed justifiably to the teacher. But these data also suggest that the teacher cannot be wholly responsible for the performance of the pupil. Many pupils may have advanced beyond the level at which the teacher is teaching the class, and perhaps the teacher should not be held any more responsible for the inadequate performances of some students than for the superior performances of other students.

Evidence from the Coleman report (Coleman et al. 1966) supports the proposition that teachers have less effect on children's school performance than previously believed. Coleman et al. tested over six hundred thousand children in some four thousand schools throughout the country, obtaining data on the teachers and the school facilities as well. One conclusion, among many others, drawn from the findings was that teacher variables played a negligible role in the scholastic achievements of children. The most important variables affecting school performance were those related to the home and those qualities of the child that were presumably present before the child entered school. Among the most important factors in this regard were the socioeconomic characteristics of the parents. More will be said about this report later.

Aptitude-Achievement Test Distinctions

Considerable controversy has centered around the merit or legitimacy of distinctions between aptitude or intelligence tests and scholastic achievement tests. While it is usually possible to distinguish between the two kinds of tests by examination of the item content or of the purposes which they serve, they generally intercorrelate with each other to about the same degree that one intelligence test does with another or that one achievement test does with another. Thus, on the basis of intercorrelations, it is usually difficult to distinguish between intelligence and achievement tests. The following discussion describes the clearer distinctions between the two types of test and then tackles the problem of more subtle distinctions. An excellent discussion of intelligence-achievement test distinctions can be found in Jensen (1973a).

BREADTH OF ITEM CONTENT

Perusal of achievement test items shows them to be tied closely to school learnings. Items typically selected for inclusion are representative of school subjects. Intelligence tests, on the other hand, generally cover a variety of learnings outside the classroom. Jensen (1973a) suggests that these tests call for a good deal of incidental learning, whereas achievement tests measure knowledge of what has been explicitly taught. Thus, being able to answer intelligence test items correctly does not depend on formal schooling, whereas a large component of achievement test items would rarely be learned outside the classroom. It is unlikely, for example, that the computation of square roots would be learned without formal teaching. Much of what intelligence test items call for is derivable from everyday experiences of living. For example, a child might be asked what is absurd about a boy's having feet so big that he had to put his pants on over his head. An absurdity of this sort is not explained in school. It is also reasonable to give nonverbal intelligence tests to illiterates or those from other cultures, but it doesn't make sense to give scholastic achievement tests to unschooled individuals.

RESPONSE TO DRILL AND PRACTICE

Because scholastic achievement tests sample from more circumscribed areas than intelligence tests, they appear to be much more susceptible to coaching. One could use achievement tests to identify a student's weaknesses in specific subjects and then work with the student on those specific academic skills. Intelligence test items, on the other hand, are so heterogeneous and interchangeable that it is difficult to imagine how one could explicitly train for an intelligence test; one intelligence test might include a completely different array of problems from those on another intelligence test.

This is not to say that coaching and other measures will not raise IQ scores, especially soon after coaching or drill. These improvements are generally short-lived, however, and do not result in long-term IQ improvements. Departures from the standard administration that tend to minimize the failures of preschool disadvantaged children can produce increases in IQs (Zigler and Butterfield 1968), but there is no good evidence that these departures will help older children or those who are not disadvantaged.

MATURATIONAL REQUIREMENTS

Some intelligence test items at early ages are closely tied to maturational factors. The Stanford-Binet, which can serve as the prototype intelligence test, required that difficulty of items increase with age. If the proportion of those who correctly answered a particular item did not increase with age, the item was eliminated from the test. This applied to items even at the preschool ages.

In many ways the passing of some intelligence test items depends on the maturation of the nervous system. It is very difficult to teach a five-year-old to copy a diamond, even though most five-year-olds can copy a square or circle. Without explicit instruction, however, a seven-year-old can copy a diamond (Jensen 1973a). Similarly, the meaningful incorporation of new experiences depends on the child's already existing level of cognitive development and maturity. The child is not a blank slate upon which explicit instruction can be certain to result in correct understanding. As Piaget has shown, the child's current conceptual world affects what aspects of information the child extracts from his world and how he interprets them and incorporates them into his already existing conceptual scheme. While it might be possible to drill young children so that they will correctly answer more items on a specific intelligence test, the result would be more of a parody of intelligence than a reflection of how it typically works. Children can give correct answers to questions because they have memorized the answers rather than understood their deeper meanings. A very young child could be taught, for example, to give an apparently sophisticated reply to a question such as "What is the meaning of justice?" But it is unlikely that a year later the child could still give a coherent and correct explanation of justice. There must be an accretion of relevant experiences (which requires the passage of time) before a deeper sense of the complexity of that question can emerge. Jensen (1973a) speaks of the incorporation of new information into some already existing "conceptual slot." If the network of associations is insufficiently rich, the new information will be retained for only a short time.

THE NATURE OF TEST ITEMS

Achievement tests generally have a larger proportion of items that call for factual information than do intelligence tests, although this distinction is not always clear-cut. Schlesinger and Guttman (1969) have developed a classification system for achievement and intelligence test items. According to this scheme, achievement items call for the application of an explicit rule to a specific case, whereas intelligence items require the generation or discovery of the rule itself. For example, the completion of the statement "A young bear is called a _____" requires that the subject know that he is to give the name of a young bear. The question is whether or not the child knows that name. On the other hand, the completion of the analogy "Bear is to cub as cat is to _____" requires first the discovery of the rule (select the "young of") and then the application of the rule to the specific situation. The important distinction, then, is between rule applying and rule inferring.

Intelligence tests and achievement tests generally have a mixture of the two types of items, although there is more emphasis on rule inferring in intelligence tests and on rule applying in achievement tests. One subtest on the Wechsler intelligence tests, for example, asks for information and requires mainly rule application (e.g., "From what animal do we get milk?"). Reasoning plays little role in answering such questions; you either know the answer or you don't. Similarly, achievement tests might require first the generation of an appropriate rule and then its application. A mathematics achievement test, for example, might include a story problem in which the appropriate rule to apply is not immediately obvious and the major problem for the subject is to discover the correct rule. Thus, the distinction between intelligence and aptitude tests on this matter is not entirely clear.

RECENCY OF LEARNING SAMPLED

One of the more subtle distinctions between intelligence and achievement tests is the recency of the learning sampled. Achievement tests measure recently acquired knowledge, while intelligence tests sample from earlier learning. On the college board exams, there is a mathematics section that calls for knowledge usually taught in eighth grade; yet the test is called a mathematics aptitude test. If the same questions were administered in eighth or ninth grade, they would be called achievement test items (Cleary et al. 1975).

The higher the grade, the more difficult it is to draw distinctions between intelligence and achievement tests. When achievement items require the subject to *discover* the correct approach to problem solution, there is a good deal of overlap with intelligence test items. In early grades, many achievement tests merely assess whether the subject has the basic skills, such as the ability to read or to count; little in the way of rule inferring is called for. Later, achievement tests assume that the subject has these basic skills and begin to draw more on rule inferring. As Jensen (1973a) points out, "It is always possible to make achievement tests correlate more highly with intelligence tests by requiring students to reason, to use the data provided, and to apply their factual knowledge to the solution of new problems" (p. 23).

HERITABILITY

Another possible difference between intelligence and aptitude tests concerns differences in heritability. One study of identical twins reared apart has suggested that twins are more similar on intelligence tests than on achievement tests. Newman, Freeman, and Holzinger (1937) found that on achievement tests identical twins reared together correlated .89, identical twins reared apart correlated .51, and fraternal twins reared together correlated .70. The correlation on scholastic achievement tests for identical twins reared apart was much lower than the correlations for identical twins or fraternal twins reared together. This finding suggests that environmental influences play a very important role in achievement test performance for two major reasons. First, the fraternal twins reared together correlate much more highly than do the identical twins reared apart. Second, there is a large drop in the correlation coefficients when identical twins reared together are compared with those reared apart.

Were these the only findings on the issue of differential heritability for the two kinds of tests, one might conclude that a very important distinction has been made. The problem is that other conclusions follow from the fact that the heritability of intelligence is higher than the heritability of scholastic achievement. For one thing, if environmental influences within the family play a larger role in achievement tests, then siblings reared together should correlate more highly on achievement tests than on intelligence tests. Since siblings share only about 50 percent of their genes, they should therefore correlate only about .50 for intelligence if intelligence is 100 percent heritable. However, if environmental influences within the family play an important role in achievement, then siblings reared in the same environment should correlate much more highly than .50 on achievement tests. Although there is little information on correlations of siblings reared together on achievement and intelligence tests, the data that are available do not indicate a substantial difference in heritability for the two types of tests.

Jensen (1973a) compared intelligence and achievement scores of siblings in Berkeley, California. Correlations for Lorge-Thorndike IQ ranged from .34 to .44 and from .22 to .45 for the achievement tests. On the average, the heritability estimates averaged about .80 for the intelligence tests and about .63 for the achievement tests. These heritability values are obtained simply by doubling the sibling correlations for the tests. Siblings reared together may not provide a good estimation of heritabilities when it is suspected that environmental influences are of importance, but these data do not strongly support a hard and fast distinction between these two types of tests.

Another study (Willerman, Horn, and Loehlin 1977) reported that genetically unrelated children reared together in adoptive homes are no more alike on achievement tests than they are on intelligence tests. This finding suggests that environmental variation has no greater influence on achievement tests than on IQ tests.

In summary, the evidence that achievement tests have a smaller heritable component than IQ tests is not clearly supported. In fact, it could be argued that many of the same information-processing mechanisms are operative in both types of tests and that these are the mechanisms which investigators should begin looking for.

Except for differences in content, then, there are few clear distinctions between intelligence tests and achievement tests. This is not to say that the difference in content is unimportant. If a child scores well on an IQ test but does poorly on an achievement test, one infers that the child may be suffering from disabilities, either physical or emotional, that are impairing the acquisition of concrete academic skills. Because achievement tests are subdivided into specific skills, it is possible to identify where the specific problem lies and perhaps attempt to alleviate the problem. If a child scores low on an intelligence test but high on an achievement test, one concludes that the child is expending much effort in acquiring the concrete skills tapped by the achievement test. When a child scores high on both intelligence and achievement tests, one assumes that the child is living up to his potential. However, a child who scores low on both types of tests tends not to get the necessary attention.

The correlations between intelligence and achievement tests are far from perfect. As a result, it is possible to change the scores on one test without necessarily changing the scores on the other. IQ scores have not yet been improved without considerable effort, but there is some reason to think that some of the specific skills tapped by achievement tests can be improved more easily. Thus, it seems desirable to develop instruction techniques that focus on the scholastic achievement acquisitions. While it may not be possible to make substantial improvements in skills that rely on abstract conceptualizations, the basic skills of reading and arithmetic should not be so difficult to improve.

Computer-Assisted Instruction

Some programs have been successful in teaching the skills required for reading and arithmetic. Some of the most successful use computer-assisted instruction (CAI). Computer-assisted instruction provides the sensitivity to individual differences among children that educational philosophy has been urging for years. It permits children to proceed at their own pace and can provide immediate reinforcement and correction of errors.

CAI can be of the most use when there are specific facts and skills to be learned. Not surprisingly, CAI has met with moderate success in the teaching of elementary reading and arithmetic, where the teaching principles are relatively well understood, the subject matter is concrete, and the goals are readily specified. In the higher grades and college it becomes more difficult to specify each of these elements and to identify the specific skills that are supposed to be acquired by the student. At the college level, the focus is often on a theoretical orientation or a way of approaching problems that may be independent of the content of the particular subject matter. It is hard to imagine just what one could teach using CAI in a college course in introductory philosophy, for example.

Fletcher and Atkinson (1972) report the scores on standardized reading tests for a group of first graders given a CAI reading program and for a control group exposed to a traditional reading program. The two groups were initially matched on a reading readiness test and then randomly assigned to one or the other reading group. The children given the CAI program spent eight to ten minutes a day at the computer during the second semester of their first year. At the end of this semester the children were administered standardized reading tests. The results indicated that the children exposed to the computer-assisted instruction were substantially more advanced than the control children. On the Stanford Achievement Test the CAI group had an average grade placement of 2.3 years; the controls averaged 1.9 years. On the California Cooperative Primary Reading Test the CAI group averaged 2.5 years, while the controls averaged 2.0 years. Thus, in about a five-month period the CAI group outgained the controls by almost five months.

Other research summarized by Atkinson (1974) suggests that after three years of early CAI reading experiences using the Stanford program with disadvantaged students, those exposed to the program averaged about 1.2 grades higher on standardized reading tests than children in traditional programs. This increase represents a substantial superiority of CAI over traditional methods. The program developed by Atkinson and others at Stanford is also relatively inexpensive, costing only about fifty-five cents per student per day, although the basic cost of a large computer is so great that it is difficult at this stage to make the initial capital outlay. The program does not rely solely on the computer to provide all reading instruction, however, and the teacher does play an important role. In the middle and late 1960s effective programs were developed that minimized the teacher's function, but they were too expensive for widespread application.

Suppes (1964) has made a strong argument for the application of CAI. He points out the huge range of individual differences within a classroom and the tremendous difficulty any teacher has in providing appropriate instruction for each of the students. In one study kindergarten children were taught fourteen letters of the alphabet and how to combine them into simple word phrases. The slowest learner in the class of thirty-eight children took 2506 trials to reach criterion, while the fastest learner took only 196 learning trials. These extreme scores did not seem to exaggerate the range of differences in the class, for the mean number of trials to reach criterion for the whole class was 967, with a standard deviation of about 400. There is little doubt that a teacher would have great difficulty accommodating this range of individual differences. Under such circumstances the teacher is often forced to teach at the level of one particular group in the class; inevitably, students at other stages must then suffer.

Suppes and Morningstar (1969) have provided an evaluation of the Stanford CAI program in mathematics for the first six grades in the states of California and Mississippi. Unlike the Fletcher and Atkinson (1972) study, this one did not match subjects on pretest scores and randomly assign them to CAI and control treatments. Instead, assignments to one or the other treatment were made either by school or by class. All children received the arithmetic portion of the Stanford Achievement Test batteries before and after exposure to the different treatments. In general, differences between experimental and control groups were negligible on the pretest measure. The average gain scores of the two groups from pretest to post-test were then compared separately for the two states. In California the children who had the CAI treatments outperformed those exposed to traditional methods in grades two, three, and five; in the other grades the differences were insignificant. In Mississippi the CAI group outperformed those given the traditional treatments at every grade. Thus, it appeared that CAI was generally beneficial but that its superiority was more evident in Mississippi than in California.

The superior performance of the CAI groups, however, must be judged in relation to the successes of the children who were exposed only to the traditional programs. On pretest measures the children in the two states did not differ in grades one through three, but in grades four through six the Mississippi children scored much lower on the SAT than did the children in California. Thus, the fact that the Mississippi CAI program seemed more successful than the California program is partly due to the relatively lower performance of the Mississippi control children and not only to the CAI program. On the basis of other considerations, the authors hypothesize that the educational and socio-economic environments in the Mississippi schools were less affluent than in California schools and go on to suggest that CAI may be especially beneficial to those coming from such disadvantaged circumstances.

Initially, there was an enormous amount of optimism concerning the application of CAI to the educational enterprise. More recently, the benefits of CAI are being seen from a more temperate perspective. The writing of effective computer programs is closely tied to an understanding of the nature of learning and memory as well as to the elements of the computer program itself. It is unlikely that computer programs will ever replace the teacher entirely, and such endeavors, whether potentially effective or not, appear to be so costly that widespread application seems improbable anyway. There is little doubt, however, that cost-effective programs can be written for important components of the educational process, and these can alleviate the teacher's burdens in accommodating the individual differences within the classroom.

There is also some suggestion that individual differences can be intentionally manipulated with CAI within the classroom itself. Atkinson (1974) has made the point that one ought to decide on the instructional objectives with respect to classroom individual differences in advance. For example, the goal might be to improve the class's overall performance, to minimize the variance of the class, or to raise the class's overall performance while keeping the variance of the members in the class below some particular level. CAI techniques can be used to achieve any of these instructional objectives.

Atkinson (1974) compared the performance of children in a CAI reading program, in which different children spent different amounts of time at the computer, with the performance of control children in CAI, all of whom spent equal time at the computer. The children were compared according to each of the objectives mentioned in the preceding paragraph. Atkinson found that when the most able students spend proportionately more time at the computer the overall class average increases substantially. At the same time, however, the variability in the class increases proportionately, and the even wider range of classroom differences may make for even greater teaching difficulties. On the other hand, when the less able students spend more time at the computer, variability within the class is reduced but at the cost of reducing the overall class performance. It is also possible to raise the overall class performance while keeping class variability below some desired limit by balancing the time that better and poorer students spend at the computer, but when this is done the overall class gain is less than it could be if the most able students spent the most time at the computer.

Whether one wants to increase overall class gain or reduce class variability is more of a practical question than a scientific one. On the one hand, it might be argued that efforts should be concentrated on the most able, since they are the ones who will make the greatest contributions to society. On the other hand, these children need the programmed instruction less than others, since the most able can utilize other instructional techniques, including self-instruction, to their own advantage. From the perspective of the parent, however, the teacher's problem with class variability is irrelevant. Parents want to see their child advance to the highest level possible and would probably balk at the suggestion that their child be held back in the interests of reducing class variability.

Cognitive Entry Behaviors

Recently, Bloom (1976) and his colleagues have tried a rather novel approach to disconnecting the typically strong relationship between achievement scores at Time 1 and Time 2. The essence of Bloom's notions center on the concept of *cognitive entry behaviors,* or behaviors that the student needs to know in order to learn something else. For example, in order to do well in algebra, one needs to know basic arithmetic operations, exponents, commutative and distributive laws, and so on. It is unlikely that one could do well in algebra without successfully grasping these skills, which may be regarded as "prealgebra" skills. Bloom gives students a diagnostic prealgebra math achievement test to determine what deficiencies they have in these prealgebra skills and then corrects the students' deficiencies before they enter the algebra course proper. When this is done, the correlation between the pretest math scores and the post-test math scores after completion of the algebra course diminishes, sometimes dramatically. Since much of mathematics is cumulative, it is not surprising that correction of deficiencies will lead to a reduced relationship between pre- and post-test performance. The important point of this work, which has been extended to other school subjects besides mathematics, is that it focuses on what one first needs to know in order to know something else. Sometimes, of course, the necessary prior learnings cover such broad areas that it may be difficult to correct all the deficiencies, except by putting the pupil through large portions of the entire curriculum again. For example, what are the cognitive entry behaviors for a course in philosophy? It is likely that they include a good vocabulary, sensitivity to nuances in meaning, logical thinking, and perhaps much more. If students don't have these cognitive entry skills, it may be very difficult to teach them in any reasonable period of time. Thus, the application of this technique may not be universal, but it does seem promising for many subjects where the preskills can be more easily remedied.

Aptitude-Treatment Interactions

In the educational process it has always seemed plausible that the method of presenting instructional material interacts with the student's own ability patterns. Thus, students with one pattern of strengths and weaknesses should profit better from one instructional technique, while another group with a different pattern of traits should profit more from another instructional technique.

The way to test hypotheses of this sort is to look for statistical interactions. The minimum requirement for such an analysis is that there be at least two groups of subjects that differ on the dimension of interest and at least two different instructional techniques. If subjects in group A do *significantly* better on treatment 1 than subjects in group B, while subjects in group B do *significantly* better than group A subjects on treatment 2, then one may conclude that a significant *aptitude-treatment interaction* (ATI) has been obtained. The situation just described is an example of a *disordinal* interaction, which is the one more pertinent to investigations of ATIs. In an example of *ordinal* interactions, subjects in group A outperform subjects in group B for both instructional treatments, but the difference between the two groups is much greater under one treatment than under the other. The distinction is presented graphically in Figure 7.3.

On the left-hand side of the figure, one can see that group A slightly outperforms group B with the first instructional approach but that the difference between the two groups becomes much larger under treatment 2. This is called an ordinal interaction. It does not follow from this interaction that treatment 1 should be provided for one group and treatment 2 should be provided for the other group. If the costs of each treatment are equivalent and there are no extenuating circumstances, all subjects should receive treatment 2, because the average perfor-

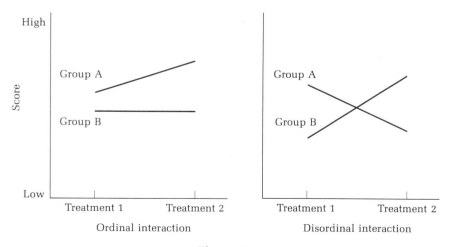

Figure 7.3
Examples of ordinal and disordinal interactions.

mance of both groups is higher here. The right-hand side of the figure tells a different story, however. If those in group A do significantly better on treatment 1 and significantly worse on treatment 2, then subjects in group A should be provided with treatment 1 and subjects in group B should be provided with treatment 2. Again, this decision assumes that the costs of the two treatments are roughly equivalent. Should one of the treatments require extraordinary costs, a practical decision might be to provide the same treatment for both groups.

Note that under the conditions described we are interested in classifying, as opposed to selecting, subjects (Cronbach and Gleser 1965). In the public educational process, where education is provided for virtually all students, one does not have the option of refusing to teach students—all children must be taught the three Rs. Selection occurs when subjects with certain patterns of performance are chosen for treatment while others are discarded or ignored. An example of selection is the requirement of a minimum grade point average or aptitude score for entrance into a university. If a person does not meet the criterion and is refused admission, that person has, in effect, been discarded by the university.

Sometimes the distinction between selection and classification is hard to draw. For example, one university might reject a candidate for admission. This appears to be an example of selection. However, that student may have applied to another school with less demanding standards and be accepted. From the broader view, the applicant has not been denied treatment (entrance to the university), but has been *classified* for one treatment rather than the other.

The main concern in elementary school and high school is to classify subjects appropriately rather than to select them. What is the evidence that assignment of different classes or groups of subjects to different treatments produces disordinal interactions? The answer—in brief—is not much. Bracht (1969) reviewed ninety different research studies in which there were 108 possibilities for disordinal interactions and found only 5 instances in which disordinal interactions occurred. While there were other studies showing ordinal interactions, these were of less interest because they did not lead to the assignment of different treatments to different groups. When only one treatment is to be used, the best idea is to give the treatment that provides the overall superior benefit at the least cost to all children. Cronbach and Snow (1969) also conducted an intensive and critical review of the research on ATIs and concluded that "there are no solidly established ATI relations even on a laboratory scale and no real sign of any hypothesis ready for application and development" (p. 193).

Cronbach and Snow do not conclude, however, that we should give up hope. They point out that

One reaction to this regrettable stage of affairs would be to abandon ATI research on the grounds that such effects are nonexistent. We urge against this defeatist course. It is inconceivable to us that humans, differing in as many ways as they do, do not differ with respect to the educational treatment that fits each one best. To abandon the ATI model is to assume that there is only one path toward educational development, and that individual differences have no implication save the fatalistic one, of telling the educator that some pupils will advance more rapidly than others no matter what he does [p. 193].

More recently, Cronbach (1975) has reviewed the ATI literature, again reaching the conclusion that the evidence for ATIs is still very sparse. He suggests, however, that personality-instructional technique interactions might yield more promising findings. He reports one study by Domino (1971) in which college students were given two scales of the California Personality Inventory (CPI)—Achievement via Independence (Ai) and Achievement via Conformity (Ac). Those scoring high on Ai reported that they do their best work when they can set the tasks for themselves. Those scoring high on Ac reported that they do best when others set the requirements for them. Domino had four different introductory psychology classes taught by the same instructor; in two classes the instructor pressed for conformity and in two the instructor encouraged independence. Domino found that, when the instructor's emphasis matched the achievement style of the students, the students did better than when the demands of the teacher and the style of the student differed. These effects were found for examination, course grades, and student satisfaction.

Findings of this sort are interesting in their own right, but they appear to contribute little insight into interactions between certain personal attributes and differential responsiveness to instruction. When motivation and not cognitive complexity is the primary factor affecting the acquisition of some skill or concept, one would anticipate that personality interactions would be important. But it should be noted that this anticipation is a far cry from the original conception of ATIs, in which motivation is presumed generally high for all subjects and the problem is to discover the appropriate channel or technique for imparting concepts or information most effectively.

Sources of Inequality

Earlier in this chapter the extraordinary range of individual differences in school-related subjects was documented. Many have blamed the schools themselves for these differences, citing such factors as inequalities in teacher quality, curricula, and pupil-teacher ratios. Many have ignored the well-established observation, however, that the variance of individual differences within schools is much greater than the variance of individual differences between schools. In concrete terms, children within a particular school generally differ among themselves much more than the average child in one school differs from the average child in another.

In 1966 the Report on Equality of Educational Opportunity (EEO) appeared, casting doubt on the premise that differences in schools produced differences in scholastic achievement. In general, differences in school or teacher quality were found to be of negligible importance in comparison with the role of family background. This monumental study had sampled over six hundred thousand children in four thousand schools throughout the country, and the results were interpreted as a severe blow to the theory that schools could reduce the gaps in scholastic achievement between children of different ethnic and socioeconomic groups. The following review presents only a few selected findings from that study. The interested reader is urged to consult the original report and the books edited by Mosteller and Moynihan (1972) and by Sewell, Hauser, and Featherman (1976), which discuss and reanalyze many aspects of the original findings.

A convenient way of presenting some of the statistical results of the EEO report is by use of standardized regression coefficients. These coefficients, like correlations, range from −1.00 to 1.00, with 0.00 indicating no relationship between the variables. The coefficient tells us how much change (in standard deviation units) we could expect in verbal achievement scores if we increased the score on a particular input variable (e.g., parents' education) by one standard deviation while all other input variables remained unchanged. Table 7.1 gives the standardized regression coefficients for a selected number of factors in verbal achievement scores (Smith 1972). The factors are divided into three groups: those relating to home background, those relating to facilities and curricula, and those relating to teachers' characteristics. It should be noted that these regression coefficients do not imply any causal relationships. Causality would need to be demonstrated via experimental procedures.

Table 7.1 shows figures for only a few of the many variables used, but the selected variables do give a fair idea of the results of the original study. The table presents findings for black and white sixth, ninth, and twelfth graders in the North, but the conclusions drawn from the findings would not differ much if the data for the entire country were presented.

Looking at the entire table, we see that family background measures relate more highly to verbal achievement scores than do any of the other measures in the table. The facilities and curricula measures have small and generally insignificant relationships with scholastic

Table 7.1

Standardized regression coefficients for selected independent variables on verbal achievement scores of northern black and white students

	Sixth grade		Ninth grade		Twelfth grade	
	Black	White	Black	White	Black	White
Family background						
Reading material in home	.11*	.12*	.08*	.11*	.04	.17*
Sibling number	−.08*	−.10*	−.13*	−.14*	−.09*	−.09*
Parents' education	.10*	.19*	.09*	.23*	.14*	.19*
Facilities and curriculum (after controlling for all other variables)						
Per-pupil expenditure	.01	.01	.01	.06	.00	.03
School size	−.01	.01	.08*	.02	−.15*	−.10
Tracking	—	—	.00	−.01	.03	.00
Teacher characteristics (after controlling for all other variables)						
Teachers' SES level	.00	.01	.04	.00	.09	.00
Teachers' experience	.02	.04	−.08	−.02	−.01	.04
Teachers' verbal score	.01	.02	.03	−.01	.04	.05
Teachers' race	.04	.03	−.10	.03	−.10	.00

* Statistically significant.
Source: After Smith 1972.

achievement scores. School size does show a significant relationship to verbal achievement among black ninth and twelfth graders, but the relationship is positive among the ninth graders and negative among the twelfth graders. Thus, the standardized regression for black ninth graders can be interpreted to mean that an increase of 1 SD in school size would result in an increase of .08 SD in verbal achievement, whereas the coefficient for black twelfth graders indicates that an increase of 1 SD in school size would produce a drop in scholastic achievement equivalent to .15 SD.

Clearly, the only variables that have consistently significant effects on verbal achievement are those related to the home. These home variables are presumably ones that the schools can do little about. It is also clear that the home variables show consistently stronger relationships among whites than among blacks. This may be because (1) the black children gave less reliable information about their home background, which had the effect of reducing the observed relationships, or (2) actual differences between homes of blacks had little influence in producing *differences* in the verbal achievement of the children. One or both of these explanations may be partly or wholly correct. Chapter 6 discussed the finding that black children from higher social class homes show disproportionately lower IQ scores than do white children from seemingly similar high socioeconomic backgrounds. It may be that many of the critical black experiences affecting various intellectual achievements are not as closely tied to specific differences in socioeconomic status as they are for whites.

SCHOOL DIFFERENCES

Another way of assessing the potential role of schools in reducing individual differences among children is to calculate ratios of between-school variance to within-school variance. Then the average amount of variation within each school can be compared with the average amount of variation between one school and another. Controlling for race, one finds that the percentage of total variance in verbal achievement scores of sixth to twelfth graders that lies between schools in the North is from 8 percent to 14 percent (Coleman et al. 1966). This means that most of the variation in verbal achievement scores is due to differences between children within the same school and not to average differences between one school and another. If race is ignored, however, the variance between schools may be as high as 36 percent (Mayeske et al. 1972), but even then there is substantially greater variation within the typical school than there is between one school and another. By ignoring race, one exaggerates the potential influence that school differences might realistically have in altering verbal achievement. For schools that are nearly all white or all black, mean differences between one school and another on verbal achievement may be very large. That is why the percentage of variation accounted for by differences between schools is so large when the racial composition of the schools is ignored.

SCHOOL BUSING

In 1954 the Supreme Court ruled in Brown v. Board of Education, Topeka that public schools must desegregate because separate but equal school facilities are impossible to achieve. As a result of this decision, interracial school busing became necessary and a furor arose.

The idea of school busing was not new; it had been around for over a hundred years. In the 1800's, when school attendance was made compulsory and efforts to improve the quality of education in rural areas resulted in consolidated school districts, busing (carriage style, of course) became widespread. In 1838 Massachusetts enacted a statute providing financial support for school transportation, and by 1913 all forty-eight states had such statutes (Mills 1973).

Current justification for school busing rests on three issues of substance: (1) legal, (2) moral, and (3) educational and social benefits. The legal justification follows from the Brown decision. Moral justification is more controversial. There are those who support the concept of neighborhood schools and oppose busing mainly because of the inconvenience, not because of racial or socioeconomic prejudice. Others oppose busing because of racial or ethnic prejudices and because they fear that their children will have inferior educational experiences or be threatened by intergroup social conflicts. The following discussion shall focus mainly on the last of these three issues, namely, the educational and social benefits that might accrue to children in integrated schools.

Many of the theorized social benefits expected from school integration were derived from Allport's book, *The Nature of Prejudice* (1954), which sets forth the argument that prejudice can be reduced by *equal status contact* between majority and minority group members, particularly if these contacts are sanctioned by institutional supports. There are two separate but related issues that should be addressed in this context. What are the effects of school desegregation on minority group members, and what are the effects on majority group members?

Armor (1973) provides a selective review of the evidence that school desegregation has positive effects on minority group students. Specifically, he was interested in evidence that school desegregation enhances race relations and black scholastic achievements, aspirations, self-esteem, and opportunities for higher education. His interpretation of the data is that school desegregation has no significant positive effects on any of these variables, except the likelihood of obtaining a college education. It seems clear that minority group children are much more likely to enroll and stay in college if they have attended a desegregated public high school.

Pettigrew et al. (1973) criticized both the data base and the negative interpretations that Armor drew from his own results and the findings of others. These authors point out that little distinction was made between desegregation and integration. If desegregated schools maintained some form of tracking, it is quite possible that racial segregation still occurred in the classroom and that the only points of contact between the races might have been passing each other in the school halls. According to Pettigrew et al., integration requires the active *interaction* of majority and minority pupils both inside and outside the classroom. This means that research studies of desegregation must provide descriptions of the actual policies and practices inside the school instead of simply stating the proportions of majority and minority pupils in the school. Even in schools that have an integrated teaching faculty and genuinely favorable attitudes toward pupil integration, there is strong evidence that children prefer to spend their time with children of their own race (Shaw 1973). Thus, one can find signs of voluntary segregation inside a school that is ostensibly desegregated. (One of the most obvious examples occurs when pupils segregate themselves by race in school lunchrooms.)

There is some evidence that desegregation may produce slight improvements in the academic achievement test scores of minority pupils. There is little or no evidence that aptitude scores are much affected by desegregation (Coleman et al. 1966). While the self-concepts of minority group children in desegregated schools appear to decrease (Gerard and Miller 1971), this effect may not be entirely undesirable. Pettigrew et al. (1973) point out that decreased self-concept may actually mean more realistic and effective self-appraisals and thus may lead to better academic performances.

It is not possible to summarize cogently the results of desegregation studies, for the data and the results have been constrained by governmental and school board decisions that often wreak havoc with the conduct of desegregation studies. Ideally, desegregation studies would include random assignment of minority and majority pupils to schools and would describe teacher and pupil attitudes, socioeconomic conditions in the accepting school, and so on. These ideals have not been realized in any published desegregation study and are not likely to be realized in any future study. With limitations of this sort, it may never be possible to determine with confidence the effects of desegregation on school performance, achievement, and attitudes. A thorough summary of the effects of desegregation can be found in St. John (1975).

Longitudinal Stability of School Achievements

We now turn to the question of the stability of academic performance through the school years. The available data suggest that there is a good deal of consistency in school grades and scholastic achievement in the precollege years (Bloom 1964). In general, the correlations over periods longer than a year are quite high, with a range of about .54 to .93 between test scores or marks at one time and another. The long-term correlations are a bit lower among younger children than among older children. Garrett (1949) summarized a large number of studies on the prediction of college grades from high school grades and found that high school grades correlated with college grades about .56, whereas aptitude or achievement tests correlated with college grade point averages about .47. A combination of predictors, such as aptitude test scores and high school grades, will outpredict either one alone, although the superiority of combining both is not usually substantial.

More recent work has confirmed the finding that high school grade point average or class rank is better than aptitude test scores at predicting college grade point averages (Cleary et al. 1975), although the differences between the predictions are not great. It is not so surprising that high school grades are superior to aptitude test scores at predicting college grades since school grades represent a lot more than aptitudes alone—motivation, diligence, and study habits all contribute to school grades but play a less important role in aptitude test performance.

Tests to Predict Differential Achievement

A number of investigators have been interested in developing tests that can predict achievement in different school subjects. It seems likely, for example, that those with good numerical skills would shine in mathematics courses and those with good verbal skills would do better in English courses. Results from studies that have correlated scores on aptitude tests with either scholastic achievement test scores or school grades in different subjects have not yielded entirely consistent findings. While specific aptitude scores might outpredict more broad-based measures of aptitude, the differences between the two types of test are not substantial (Tyler 1965). In part, this is due to the fact that different abilities are not entirely independent of each other; there are always positive intercorrelations between abilities, if the sample of subjects is very heterogeneous. Likewise, most school subjects call for components of each ability; subjects differ only in the relative proportions of each ability called for.

Clearly, the most important single ability is verbal. On the average, verbal ability correlates with grades more highly than any other ability. For example, Nunnally (1959) reported that the verbal scale of the Primary Mental Abilities test (PMA) outpredicted space, reasoning, and numerical ability for school grades in spelling ($r = .54$), social studies (.50), and shorthand (.44). For grades in typing, numerical (.32) and reasoning (.27) were superior to verbal ability (.19). Typing ability, of course, calls for motor skills as well as intellectual skills, so that the general level of all correlations is lower than for the more academic subjects.

The finding that the verbal component generally relates more strongly than others to school grades is also true of correlations between different ability measures and scholastic achievement tests. For example, Cattell and Butcher (1968) gave the PMA to 278 school children. The verbal component of the PMA correlated more highly with all the Stanford Achievement Test subtests (paragraph meaning, word meaning, spelling, language, arithmetic reasoning, arithmetic comprehension) than did any of the other PMA abilities except that the PMA numerical component had a higher correlation with arithmetic comprehension.

Inside and outside the academic classroom, abilities have positive relationships with achievements. Cattell and Butcher (1968) correlated PMA scores with teachers' ratings of personal adjustment, interest in school subjects, behavior records, leadership, achievement, and interest in sports. All PMA measures correlated positively with these ratings. The PMA verbal and reasoning subtests made the greatest contributions to the behavior ratings. For example, verbal correlated with personal adjustment .31, with interest in school subjects .54, with the behavior record .25, with leadership .46, with social adjustment .37, with achievement in sports .28, and with interest in sports .28. Reasoning correlated more highly with personal adjustment (.35), the behavior record (.29), and achievement in sports (.30). The differences in abilities measured by these tests point to the fact that there are different ways of looking at and experiencing the world and that lifestyles vary as a function of these ability differences.

Imagine what the antecedents of a high verbal score must have been. Behind it all must be a desire to know and understand the world. As an aid to understanding, we acquire labels for things and concepts. If we do not have that underlying need to understand, we do not bother to acquire these labels. While it is true that we can be motivated temporarily to direct our energies and talents to the accomplishment of specific and limited goals, good verbal abilities tap so much more and from such a wide experiential array that specific bits of knowledge or vocabulary will not suffice to produce good scores on verbal tests. Good verbal skills depend on a sustained interest in ideas and concepts, and this means that differences between those of higher and lower ability must extend to basic differences in what is noticed and extracted from the information in the environment.

Personality and Achievement in School

Personality variables also make a significant contribution to achievement in school. Some personality factors may be positively related to achievement in school, and others may be negatively related. Further, personality factors such as extroversion may be positively related to school achievement in the early years and negatively related later (Cattell 1971).

Figure 7.4 gives correlations of personality and ability factors with various measures of school achievement and school-related behavior using the High School Personality Questionnaire (HSPQ), the PMA, and Cattell's culture fair intelligence test (Cattell and Butcher 1968). Except for the total achievement score, all other measures are based on teachers's ratings of the children and thus are not entirely objective. The thirteen personality factors include all of Cattell's factors except factor B, which is actually a very brief intelligence test.

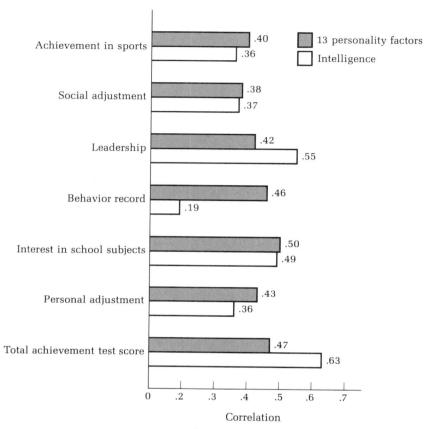

Figure 7.4

Predictions of school-related achievements from personality
and ability tests. (After Cattell and Butcher 1968.)

The figure indicates that personality factors make a very substantial
contribution to these school-related behaviors. The thirteen personality factors outperform the ability factors in predicting many of
the outcomes, falling behind only on leadership and total Stanford
Achievement Test scores. A statistical analysis of the improvement in
prediction afforded by the addition of this broad array of personality
factors to the ability measure indicates that about twice as much variance
is accounted for by both the personality and the intelligence measure
than is accounted for by the ability measure alone. Among the individual
personality factors making a positive contribution to school achievement
are extroversion in the early grades and introversion in college. Cattell
(1971) suggests that the positive correlation between school attainments
and extroversion in the early grades is due to the socially interactive

nature of the elementary school classroom. Later, many accomplishments depend on individual reading and self-motivation. In the early grades, docility contributes positively to school performance, whereas independence and a critical attitude positively affect performance later. Superego strength also contributes positively, perhaps because it is responsible for conscientiousness in doing homework. Self-sufficiency is also important, since self-sufficient students are not dependent on teachers but are willing to solve problems on their own.

There is no doubt that one's achievements after secondary school depend on many factors other than ability. High-level scholastic performance and later occupational successes depend heavily on motivational and other personality factors, since differences in intelligence among those already at higher levels are much less than differences in the general population. The old adage that outstanding achievements require more perspiration than inspiration beyond some minimal degree of intelligence may go too far, but it is clear that hard work, persistence, and zesty involvement in one's work contribute substantially to one's ultimate attainments.

Teacher Expectancies

INTELLIGENCE

Earlier we reviewed evidence from the Coleman report (Coleman et al. 1966) that teachers had little demonstrable influence on the aptitude test scores of school children. However, in this study the classroom was used as the unit for analysis. Thus, while there might not be good evidence that the teachers influence the aptitude scores of children within the classroom as a whole, there is the possibility that individual children within the classroom are differentially affected by differences in teachers' attitudes and expectancies. Furthermore, even if the aptitude scores of children within the class are not affected by differential teachers' expectancies, grades, achievement test scores, or behaviors other than those measured on standardized tests could be so affected.

A provocative but methodologically unsound study by Rosenthal and Jacobson (1966, 1968) induced a flurry of interest in the topic of teacher expectancies. These authors administered Flanagan's Tests of General Ability (TOGA) in May to children in grades one through six. A randomly chosen 20 percent of the pupils were designated as "spurters," and their teachers were told that this test would identify children who would bloom intellectually during the following year. The experimenters, however, knew that this test had no capacity to identify spurters. The next year these children were readministered the TOGA, and the scores of those children whose teachers had been told that they would "spurt" were compared with those of the remaining groups of children. The gain scores from pretest to post-test were also compared, and the authors reported that the spurters in grades one and two, but not in grades three through six, showed significant gains on the second test. Rosenthal and Jacobson concluded that the teachers' expectations prompted them to treat the spurters differently and thus caused unusual IQ gains.

Were it not for the ingenuity of the original conception, the study would not have received the widespread attention it did. The study was so seriously flawed that one reviewer remarked that it would have been found unacceptable for publication if submitted to a journal of the American Psychological Association (Snow 1969). Another said that the study was "so defective technically that one can only regret that it ever got beyond the eyes of the original investigators" (Thorndike 1968, p. 708).

Only some of the problems of the study can be touched upon here. First, the TOGA does not have adequate norms for very young children, and these were the only ones for which the putative expectancy effects were found. In addition, some of the children obtained pretest IQs at the imbecile and moron levels, and a year later some of these children scored in the range of 150 IQ. Thus considerable doubt is cast on the original measurements themselves. Second, many of the teachers could not even remember the names of the children they were told would be spurters. Third, the two grades for which the expectancy effect was presumably demonstrated contained only seven and twelve experimental children, respectively. Fourth, the statistical analyses of the data were incorrectly done. And finally, the tests were scored for the number correct only, so that teachers' urgings to the spurters to attempt more items might have explained the findings entirely.

The conclusion that many critics have reached—namely, that there was no expectancy effect—has been supported in subsequent attempts to replicate the original study. Fielder, Cohen, and Feeney (1971) administered the TOGA to children in grades one through six two weeks before the beginning of the second semester, telling the teachers that certain pupils (randomly selected) were about to enter a period of "unusual intellectual growth." When the TOGA was readministered four months later, there were no signs that the selected pupils had significantly improved over the control subjects. Two other attempted replications reached essentially the same conclusion (Claiborne 1969; Jose and Cody 1971), and Claiborne even failed to find any differences in the interactions between the teachers and those children who were designated as bloomers.

Other studies using intelligence tests did report some mildly positive interactions between expectancy and IQ gain. Conn et al. (1968) used a design similar to that of the original study and found correlations between gains in certain aspects of intellectual functioning and sensitivity to emotional expression as measured by another test. There was no check of whether the teachers actually remembered the names of the children who earlier had been designated as bloomers. Another study by Evans and Rosenthal (1969) did indicate that teachers had "remarkably inaccurate" memories of the names of children in the experimental condition.

Still other studies have used tests other than the TOGA and found some slight effects of differential teacher expectancies. One study by Mendels and Flanders (1973) used the Cognitive Abilities Test (CAT) among first grade disadvantaged children, finding some slight effect (accounting for only 2 percent of the variance) for teacher expectancy. However, the teachers remembered the names of less than half the children designated as bloomers and incorrectly remembered 33 percent of the control children as spurters.

In summary, it is yet to be established that differential teacher expectancies lead to differential gains in the intellectual performance of children. It should be noted, however, that such studies assume that actual changes in teachers' behavior toward specific children will produce noticeable gains in intellectual performance over a fairly short period of time. Implicit in this model of intelligence is the assumption that certain children have in some way been blocked from utilizing their intellectual skills and that higher teachers' expectancies will result in either an immediate unblocking of this previously suppressed intelligence or a very rapid improvement in information processing such that the children will gain in just a few months or a year all that they have lacked in the previous years. Although such a theory is incompatible with current theories of intelligence, it is not incompatible with a theory that long-term teacher expectancies will eventually produce changes in intelligence test performance after a few years.

While it may be true that many children do not function up to capacity because of emotional blocks, there is no model of intelligence that would lead one to conclude that changes in teachers' behaviors can improve a child's intelligence test performance in less than a few years. As a matter of fact, the observation of large genuine spurts in the intellectual performance of a randomly selected group of pupils over a short time span would require a complete reorganization in our current theories of intelligence and would necessitate a paradigm shift in our thinking about the nature of intelligence in general.

Styczynski (1975) has also pointed out that experimentation on the self-fulfilling prophecy (that teachers' expectations cause children to behave in ways consistent with those expectations) which uses longer-term follow-ups usually neglects to inform subsequent teachers that these children are destined to be bloomers. Thus, such experiments essentially test the effects of an earlier expectation on later performance and not a continuing expectation. Furthermore, she adds that several studies have been initiated in the middle of the school year, after the teachers have already had the opportunity to develop expectations about their pupils which may then be resistant to change.

SCHOLASTIC ACHIEVEMENT

Although there is little reason to believe that teacher expectations affect intelligence test scores, it seems likely that on school measures where motivation and interest play an important role, teacher expectations will affect achievement. However, studies in the area of academic achievement have been plagued by some of the same difficulties found in the work using intelligence tests. One investigator (Schrank 1968, 1970) deliberately misinformed teachers of airmen in a preparatory school that a particular class was either a high- or a low-ability group, when in truth the airmen were randomly assigned to the different classes. In the 1968 study the results indicated that the airmen in the so-called higher-ability class outperformed those in the lower groups on the examinations issued to the instructors. Another of Schrank's (1970) studies initially informed the instructors that the assignment had been random and failed to find any differences in the mathematics performance of the classes. Schrank compared the results of the two studies and concluded that teachers' expectations and interactions significantly affect the performance of students. The significance of these two studies cannot be denied, but it is important to note that the findings apply to the class as a whole and not to individual members within the class. Teachers vary in the intensity of their efforts, and it would not be surprising to find teachers taking a more active interest in classes in which they believe the students to be more talented.

The earliest study on the influence of teachers' expectations was by Pitt (1956), who used fifth grade boys, all with IQs above 94. A third of the teachers were provided with actual IQ scores of their students, another group of teachers received IQs 10 points below their students' actual scores, and another third were provided IQs 10 points higher. Six months later, standardized tests failed to reveal different scores on reading comprehension, vocabulary, or arithmetic achievement as a function of this misinformation, but spelling grades appeared to be higher for those labeled as having higher IQs. Since a positive effect of teachers' expectancies is evident in only one subject, it therefore cannot be regarded as strong indication that teachers' expectancies play a powerful role in academic performance generally.

Flowers (1966) matched seventh grade children on IQ and academic achievement scores and shifted one group to a higher section than their scores had warranted. At the year's end, standard achievement tests and an IQ test were readministered, and no significant differences were observed.

In sum, there is no strong indication that differential teachers' expectancies will alter the performance of students on standardized academic achievement tests, although there is some slight indication that grades (which are more subjective) might be altered on occasion.

Conclusions

The evidence reviewed in this chapter exemplifies the enormous range of individual differences in scholastic performance. Since socioeconomic success is so closely tied to education, it is important to understand the origin and maintenance of the factors that influence academic performance. It is clear that motivation plays an important role in those aspects of academic achievement that are influenced by diligence and hard work. Reading, writing, and arithmetic skills, especially in the early grades, can probably be acquired with effort by those for whom such skills do not come easily, and there is need to determine the conditions that will enable students to use their time profitably. There is little reason to think, however, that later academic performance, which strongly depends on adequate conceptual ability as well as on hard work, is as susceptible to educational innovations. This does not mean that efforts to find successful interventions should be curtailed, but it does warn that such interventions will not be found easily, especially ones that result in meaningful, not just statistically significant, effects.

8

Individual Differences
in Personality

Defining Personality

The term *personality* is not easily definable, and there is little agreement as to what constitutes its proper domain. Some say that all *enduring* qualities of an individual, including physical appearance, intelligence, aptitudes, interests, values, and psychopathology, belong under the rubric of personality (Guilford 1959). Others limit the term to noncognitive behavioral traits, thus excluding intelligence, interests, aptitudes, and various bodily features. Recent trends, however, suggest that only when cognitions are considered seriously will there be a comprehensive theory of personality (Mischel 1973). This view is based on the recognition that all behavior manifested in personality originates in the mind and that to pursue the study of personality the mind should not be neglected. Further, the objective situation surrounding a person's behavior may differ drastically from the subjective meaning the person gives it, since facts do not speak for themselves.

There is no single correct definition of personality. Rather, one's definition depends on the uses to which the definition is to be put. For example, those who limit personality definitions to observable behaviors often slight psychodynamic views, which emphasize unconscious processes, or biophysical views, which focus on biophysical systems. Those with a social-cultural orientation emphasize the role prescriptions and expectations of the actor, paying scant attention to the personal style that the actor brings to the situation.

Allport (1960) asks what units should be employed in the study of personality. Different investigators prefer different units, but there are few coordinating definitions to spell out how one unit is related to another. There are no units that can be converted directly into others, as centimeters can be converted into inches. Allport's units include intellectual capacities, syndromes of temperament, unconscious motives, ideational schemata, interests and values, expressive traits, pathological trends, and factorial clusters. Inquisitive investigators can spend a lifetime working on one of these units without ever coming to terms with coordinating definitions. Moreover, the units themselves are composites of more elemental units, and little is known about how the elemental units organize among themselves to yield the more complex units. This is not to say that some investigators haven't tried. Cattell (1965) offers perhaps a prime example of an effort to construct a theory of personality by starting with more elemental units and build to a more molar level. Nevertheless, there is so far no indication that his units are any more useful than others'.

For the purposes of this chapter, we will say that personality refers to consistent individual differences in either style or content of behavior. The components of the behaviors of interest will be influenced in varying degrees by biophysical factors, learning, psychodynamic processes, and cultural factors. It remains to be determined by empirical investigation how these different components operate separately and in interaction to produce the behaviors of interest.

Much of the current turmoil in personality theory and research stems from questions of (1) content versus style and (2) consistency versus inconsistency across situations. Distinctions between content and style often boil down to the difference between adaptive behaviors and expressive behaviors. Adaptive behaviors are often contingent upon reinforcement and modeling or imitation effects and have a predominantly voluntary quality. These behaviors are concerned with getting the job done—for example, writing a letter, throwing a ball, or taking a test. Expressive behaviors are the involuntary aspects of accomplishing those tasks—for example, handwriting speed and size, agility in throwing, or anxiety during test taking. Unfortunately, the distinction is not unambiguous, since one can voluntarily focus on some stylistic components of one's behavior and, occasionally, thereby alter them. Thus, one can write with smaller or larger letters, change one's throwing style, or talk oneself out of feeling anxious. In large part, content aspects of behavior have been the province of learning psychology, and stylistic aspects have been the subject for personality. Nowadays the distinction is blurred because learning psychologists have demonstrated that expressive movement can be brought under the control of reinforcement contingencies and modeling.

The issue of consistency or inconsistency in personality is no less controversial at this point. For centuries personality theorists have been trait theorists, assuming that individuals possess traits that are by definition (1) consistent across situations and (2) enduring. Recently, these two assumptions have been challenged strenuously (Mischel 1968, 1973), and the power of trait descriptions to account for, or predict, behavior in real-life situations is in question.

It is of the utmost importance to personality theory that consistency across situations be demonstrated, for it could be argued that without cross-situational consistency there can be no theory of personality. In that case, what we now call personality would not exist independently of contemporaneous environmental influences and learning.

Why are beliefs in substantial personality consistency so strong? Perhaps we construe consistency across situations because it helps to simplify our world. Appreciating individuals in all their complexity and inconsistency may be too demanding for our intellectual faculties.

Mischel (1968) suggests that personality consistency is construed for the following reasons:

1. We have limited information-processing capacities.

2. We explain away inconsistencies when they are observed.

3. We mistakenly generalize from the consistency in physical appearance and intellectual talents to the personality domain.

4. We usually observe others in the context of regular environments or social roles.

5. It is difficult to obtain convincing disconfirming data. For example, if an individual is construed as hostile, then any passive behavior is construed as an indication of an underlying conflict over the issue of aggression and not as lack of hostility.

6. We attempt to reduce inconsistent cognitions (cognitive dissonance) and impose consistency.

7. Once we form an impression, we are reluctant to alter it.

Another problem is that it is difficult to specify and agree on what behaviors connote or denote a particular personality trait. The result is that self-ratings of personality do not correlate well with peer ratings of personality. For example, Jackson (1967) carefully constructed a test called the Personality Research Form (PRF), which was based on Murray's (1938) list of twenty needs. He then had subjects who took the PRF and their friends complete one-item ratings representing each of those twenty needs. Thus, a subject was asked to rate himself on how aggressive he was, for example, and a friend rated that subject on the same item. Then the self-ratings and the friends' ratings were correlated with the subjects' scores on the PRF. Correlations between the self-ratings and the scores on the PRF ranged from .23 for need dependence to .76 for need order, with a median correlation in the .40s. The correlations between the friends' ratings and the subjects' PRF scores were even lower, ranging from a low of .16 for need understanding to a high of .64 for need order, with a median correlation in the low .30s. If one assumes that subsequent work using outside criteria will not yield substantially higher correlations, then it is clear that the limitations on predictive potential are considerable.

Closely allied to the concept of traits is the classification of individuals into *types*. While general traits are summary labels for limited components of behavior that all individuals can be said to possess in some degree or another, types are discrete combinations of traits, each characterizing a relatively small number of individuals. As Allport (1937) says, individuals can have a trait, but they can only fit a type. What this means is that types, even more than traits, exist in the eye of the observer and require the synthesis and inference from diverse sources in order to form a coherent and consistent conceptual framework. However, Mischel (1968) has shown that types, no less than traits, are often likely to be categories of the perceiver rather than properties of the subject.

The trouble with type descriptions is that they must ignore inconsistencies and counterexamples in the characterization. In part this flaw is due to our limited information-processing capacities, which cause us to simplify in order to store in memory something that can more easily be retrieved.

Modern Constitutional Psychology

Constitutional psychology is the psychological study of aspects of human behavior in relation to the morphology and physiology of the body (Sheldon 1940). In the early 1900s Ernst Kretschmer (1925) began to classify individuals according to a limited number of physical characteristics and to relate these physical characteristics to temperamental types and the two major forms of psychosis, manic-depressive and schizophrenic psychoses. He suggested three main body types, although mixtures occurred with great frequency. The three types were *asthenic*, or thin, frail, and linear; *athletic*, or muscular and vigorous; and *pyknic*, or rotund. A fourth category was called *dysplastic*; such individuals were unusually deviant in body build such as to appear strange.

Sheldon (1940) carried on in the tradition of Kretschmer, using photographs to develop ratings of body build (called somatotypes) that were somewhat more reliable than Kretschmer's. The somatotype is a standard series of full-length photographs from three views: front, profile, and rear. Sheldon argues for three components of physique: *endomorphy*, characterized by softness and predominance of fat; *mesomorphy*, characterized by a predominance of muscle and bony development; and *ectomorphy*, characterized by linearity and fragility of physique. Each component was rated on a scale of 1 to 7; 4 represented an average rating and 1 represented a low rating. Thus, a 4-4-4 would indicate an individual with average ratings on all three components, and a 1-1-7 would indicate a subject with a high rating on ectomorphy and low ratings on the other two components.

After developing a stable means of assessing body build, Sheldon identified fifty human personality traits from the literature and intensively studied thirty-three college men for a year. Each subject was rated on these fifty traits, and clusters of positively intercorrelated traits were identified. In order to be included in a cluster, a trait had to correlate .60 or more with the other traits in the cluster and correlate −.30 or less with traits in other clusters. The resultant scale had three components: (1) *viscerotonia*, which referred to individuals who were relaxed, loved physical comfort, eating, and approval, and were generally complacent; (2) *somatontonia*, which referred to individuals who were assertive, energetic, and loved physical adventure and risk; and (3) *cerebrotonia*, which referred to individuals who were generally introverted, secretive, restrained, and self-conscious. Items from Sheldon's temperament scale are given in Table 8.1.

Inspection of the item content on the temperament scale suggests that many of the viscerotonia items are the opposite of the cerebrotonia items; it is therefore unlikely that these are separate dimensions. For example, item 1 asks about relaxation of body movement for viscerotonia and about restraint in body movement for cerebrotonia. Item 3 describes slow reactions for viscerotonia and fast reactions for cerebrotonia. Similarly, items 8, 9, 15, 17, 18, and 19 indicate viscerotonic responses that are virtually opposites of cerebrotonic responses. It seems profligate to label these as independent temperament dimensions when it appears that one bipolar dimension of viscerotonia-cerebrotonia will do to describe the trait.

Humphreys (1957) has vigorously criticized the statistical and empirical bases of Sheldon's theory and findings. Types represent ideal descriptions of a hypothetical person, which a given individual's score can be said to remotely or closely approximate. Necessarily, an individual who represents the ideal of a type (i.e., a "7"), must perforce be low on the alternate types. Likewise, there can be no individuals who

Viscerotonia	Somatotonia	Cerebrotonia
( ) 1. Relaxation in posture and movement	( ) 1. Assertiveness of posture and movement	( ) 1. Restraint in posture and movement
( ) 2. Love of physical comfort	( ) 2. Love of physical adventure	( ) 2. Physiological overresponse
( ) 3. Slow reaction	( ) 3. The energetic characteristic	( ) 3. Overly fast reactions
( ) 4. Love of eating	( ) 4. Need and enjoyment of exercise	( ) 4. Love of privacy
( ) 5. Socialization of eating	( ) 5. Love of dominating, lust of power	( ) 5. Mental overintensity, hyperattentionality, apprehensiveness
( ) 6. Pleasure in digestion	( ) 6. Love of risk and chance	( ) 6. Secretiveness of feeling, emotional restraint
( ) 7. Love of polite ceremony	( ) 7. Bold directness of manner	( ) 7. Self-conscious mobility of the eyes and face
( ) 8. Sociophilia	( ) 8. Physical courage for combat	( ) 8. Sociophobia
( ) 9. Indiscriminate amiability	( ) 9. Competitive aggressiveness	( ) 9. Inhibited social address
( ) 10. Greed for affection and approval	( ) 10. Psychological callousness	( ) 10. Resistance to habit and poor routinizing
( ) 11. Orientation to people	( ) 11. Claustrophobia	( ) 11. Agoraphobia
( ) 12. Evenness of emotional flow	( ) 12. Ruthlessness, freedom from squeamishness	( ) 12. Unpredictability of attitude
( ) 13. Tolerance	( ) 13. The unrestrained voice	( ) 13. Vocal restraint and general restraint of noise
( ) 14. Complacency	( ) 14. Spartan indifference to pain	( ) 14. Hypersensitivity to pain
( ) 15. Deep sleep	( ) 15. General noisiness	( ) 15. Poor sleep habits, chronic fatigue
( ) 16. The untempered characteristic	( ) 16. Overmaturity of appearance	( ) 16. Youthful intentness of manner and appearance
( ) 17. Smooth, easy communication of feeling, extroversion of viscerotonia	( ) 17. Horizontal mental cleavage, extroversion of somatotonia	( ) 17. Vertical mental cleavage, introversion
18. Relaxation and sociophilia under alcohol	18. Assertiveness and aggression under alcohol	18. Resistance to alcohol and to other depressant drugs
19. Need of people when troubled	19. Need of action when troubled	19. Need of solitude when troubled
20. Orientation toward childhood and family relationships	20. Orientation toward goals and activities of youth	20. Orientation toward the later periods of life

Note: The thirty-two traits with parentheses constitute collectively the short form of the scale. *Source:* From Sheldon 1942.

are low on all types (i.e., 1-1-1). Humphreys (1957) pointed out that, after suitable statistical corrections had been made for measurements error and curvilinearity in the data, knowledge of any two of the dimensions predicted the third. Thus, there was no statistical evidence for three independent dimensions. Humphreys also noted (as others had) that in most of his work Sheldon himself made the ratings of both physique and personality. This fact could have spuriously increased the magnitude of the correlations obtained.

Despite the above-mentioned criticisms, studies by other investigators have nevertheless supported many of Sheldon's conclusions. Support, as indicated by the degree of correlation between physique and temperament, has generally been of considerably less magnitude, however (see Rees 1973 for an extensive discussion of much of the physique-temperament literature). For example, Walker (1962) rated somatotype photographs of 125 preschool children in a nursery school at Yale University. Nine behavior rating scales were devised, and teachers were asked to rate the children on the scales. In advance, Walker generated a series of 292 predictions about relations between physique and scores on the behavior scales. Of these predictions, 21 percent were confirmed statistically and 3 percent were disconfirmed statistically. The mesomorphic boys and girls both tended to be dominant and assertive, energetic and fearless, but the girls combined these traits with sociability and the boys combined them with hostility and impulsiveness. The ectomorphic children were described as aloof and emotionally restrained. The endomorphic children showed substantially less relationship to personality traits, and six of the ten significant findings were opposite from those predicted for endomorphy. Additionally, statistically significant relationships between body build and personality were generally much more common among boys than girls; more than a third of the predictions were confirmed for boys, and less than 10 percent were confirmed for girls. This is perhaps not so surprising when one considers that body type is more likely to influence the interactions of boys, because their style of interacting often involves body contact and physical competition.

The likelihood of becoming a delinquent is related to body build. Cortes and Gatti (1972) found delinquents to be significantly more mesomorphic than nondelinquents. Similarly, Glueck and Glueck (1956) found that delinquent boys matched to nondelinquents on age, SES, race, and intelligence were far more likely to be mesomorphic (60 percent versus 30 percent) and less likely to be ectomorphs (15 percent versus 40 percent) than nondelinquents.

For neurotic men in the British armed forces (Rees and Eysenck 1945; Eysenck 1947), individuals diagnosed with hysterical type-disorders (known to correlate with extroversion) were more likely to be endomorphic than ectomorphic, with the mesomorphs falling between the two. Those soldiers with disorders related to introversion (anxiety, depression, obsession) were more likely to be ectomorphs. Rees (1950) completed a similar study with women patients in the clinic and obtained results like those obtained from the servicemen.

Lindzey (1967a) has suggested four possible causes for the positive findings between physique and temperament.

1. *Common environmental events produce predictable outcomes.* Child-rearing events may produce changes in morphology as well as in behavior. For example, maternal overprotectiveness may be related to obesity and placidity.

2. *Body type affects reinforcement contingencies.* This theory argues that certain body types are more likely to be differentially reinforced for their behaviors. For example, mesomorphs who are also aggressive may be positively reinforced, but ectomorphs who are aggressive may get negative reinforcement.

3. *Stereotyped expectancies lead to stereotyped results.* This theory postulates that expectancies of correlations between morphology and behavior shape children to behave in accordance with those expectations. For example, because fat people are widely believed to be jolly, they may be characteristically exposed to situations inducing jolly behavior. Unfortunately, this theory does not explain how the stereotypes originally arose.

4. *There are joint biological influences on physique and behavior.* This theory holds that the link between physique and behavior is due to intimate genetic connections between the two. Some genetic disorders, such as Downs syndrome, produce consistent deficits in intellectual functioning as well as a characteristic body type, and many studies have demonstrated genetic influences on personality traits. Except for simple genetic disorders that affect intellectual functioning and body build, however, there has been no demonstration of a direct connection between the genes for body build and for behavior.

Until recently, American psychology has been reluctant to study physique-behavior relationships, perhaps because there is a certain sense of hopelessness about changing one's physique. American psychologists tend to be more proccupied with changing behavior than those in other countries. It seems, however, that resistance to the idea of biological influence on behavior is decreasing. With convincing demonstrations of genetic influences in psychopathology and mental retardation, many workers are now willing to countenance the possibility of genetic components in the normal ranges of behavior as well.

Table 8.2

Examples of different types of rating scales for sociability

Numerical ratings	Strongly agree				Strongly disagree
I like to be with others.	1	2	3	4	5
People are generally friendly.	1	2	3	4	5

Graphic ratings	Extroverted				Introverted
	├────┼────┼────┼────┤				
Check off your location on the scale.	1	2	3	4	5

Cumulated-point ratings

Check off those adjectives that apply to you.	___ outgoing	___ lighthearted
	___ gregarious	___ remote (−)
	___ sympathetic	___ friendly
	___ cooperative	___ lonely (−)
	___ isolated (−)	___ energetic
	___ generous	___ withdrawn (−)

Forced-choice ratings

Check off only one of each pair.	___ friendly	___ lighthearted
	___ isolated	___ lonely

Personality Measurement

QUESTIONNAIRES

Psychologists use various techniques in their studies of personality (Table 8.2). Ratings are perhaps the most popular form for the study of personality. Often they involve an *observer* who rates some aspect of another's behavior in a quantitative form either along a continuum or along ordered categories on the continuum. Sometimes subjects rate themselves. Guilford (1954) provides a detailed discussion and taxonomy of rating scales.

Numerical Scales. The subject is asked to circle a number associated with a particular adjective. For example, one might be asked to describe a sexual experience as 5—exquisitely pleasurable, 4—pleasurable, 3—so-so, 2—uninteresting, 1—tedious, or 0—dull and boring. Often the numerical ratings are not included on the rating scale; the subject merely checks the appropriate adjectives and the researcher later assigns the numerical values to the labels.

Graphic Scales.   The subject is asked to check off on a continuum the point that most characterizes the trait being rated. For example, a subject might mark a point midway on a continuum of favorable to unfavorable to indicate that the particular trait is neither favorable nor unfavorable.

Cumulated Point Scales.   This procedure is typically employed in a checklist format. A series of adjectives is presented for each domain in which the researcher is interested and the rater is asked to check those adjectives which apply to whatever is being rated. The summed value for the adjectives or the number of adjectives checked (with appropriate weightings for plus and minus adjectives) usually serves as the score for that individual.

Forced-Choice Ratings.   Instead of requiring the rater to indicate whether or not the subject has a particular trait or how much of the trait the subject possesses, this scale requires the rater to indicate which of a *pair* of traits the target has. The researcher equalizes the trait pairs in advance for social desirability or favorableness and also determines in advance which of the pair of traits is useful or predictive for his purposes. The rater, not having this information, cannot bias his ratings in order to make the target appear more or less favorable.

Guilford (1954) points out that the following errors and biases can compromise the validity of rating scales:

1. *Error of leniency.* Those whom the rater knows well or is ego-involved with tend to be rated higher (or lower) than they should.

2. *Error of central tendency.* Raters are reluctant to make extreme judgments and therefore there is excessive clustering of ratings in the middle of the scale.

3. *Halo effect.* According to Guilford, this error is made by *everyone* asked to make a series of ratings. The rater tends to rate the target according to the *general* impression he has of the target rather than on the basis of each individual trait.

4. *Logical error.* There is a tendency to give similar ratings on traits that seem related logically in the minds of the judges.

5. *Contrast error.* Judges may rate others in the direction opposite from the way they perceive themselves.

6. *Proximity error.* Judges rate traits that are adjacent to one another on the rating form as more alike, although their degree of actual similarity is presumably no greater than that of traits that are more remote from one another.

The most popular self-report inventory for psychiatric patients is the Minnesota Multiphasic Personality Inventory (MMPI), devised by Hathaway and McKinley (1943). This 550-item questionnaire was originally given to diagnosed psychiatric patients in Minnesota and to visitors to hospitals there. The items are keyed "True," "False," and "Cannot Say." Items were retained in the MMPI if they significantly discriminated between the patient and control populations. Thus, if 35 percent of diagnosed schizophrenics reported that "There is something wrong with my mind," whereas only 5 percent of visitors endorsed that item, it would be retained as a significant discriminator of schizophrenia on the MMPI. One item is not enough for diagnosis, however, so each scale actually has a number of items that each make some discrimination between the diagnosed group and the control population. Some individuals are not truthful, however, and many of the self-report inventories like the MMPI depend on honest replies to the questions. The MMPI does have validity scales to check for dishonesty or grossly deviant self-perceptions. For example, there is a scale on the MMPI that includes items that almost everybody endorses (e.g., "I do not always tell the truth") Virtually everyone who answers honestly would agree with that item, although there may be exceptionally rigid individuals who do always tell the truth. The scale has 15 items, and, should a subject answer more than 7 of the items in the direction opposite from that predicted, the results of the entire MMPI will be thrown into doubt. These validity checks have not proved to be very successful, however, and there is no good way of correcting for dishonest self-appraisal.

Sample items similar to those on some of the MMPI scales are given in Table 8.3. Interpretation has reached a level of sophistication that permits computer scoring and writing of the psychological report. In

Table 8.3

Items similar to those on the MMPI scales

Scale	Item
Lie	I sometimes get angry. (False)
Hypochondriasis	I wake up happy most mornings. (False)
Depression	I rarely feel energetic. (True)
Hysteria	I have never fainted. (False)
Psychopathic Deviancy	I hated school. (True)
Psychasthenia	I have self-confidence. (False)

Note: The "True" or "False" in parentheses is the answer that may indicate presence of the disorder.

general, computer reports do about as well as or better than skilled clinicians in providing a valid description of the person against some outside criterion, such as psychiatric diagnosis.

PROJECTIVE TESTS

Projective tests are relatively unstructured or ambiguous sets of stimuli to which the subject is asked to respond in some fashion. The idea is that unconscious determinants will affect the manner in which the subject perceives and interprets the ambiguous stimuli. Presumably there is a relationship between these unconscious determinants and the subject's personality. Perhaps the two most popular projective tests are the Rorschach inkblot test and the Thematic Apperception Test (TAT). Sample items similar to those on the Rorschach and TAT are given in Figure 8.1.

Unfortunately, there is no straightforward connection between the unconscious processes revealed by projective tests and other behaviors. For example, subjects giving aggressive interpretations are not necessarily highly aggressive otherwise. Perhaps the expression of aggression in fantasy reduces the need to act aggressively, but, more generally, this discrepancy means that pathways from test performances to criterion behaviors include influences not predictable from the test performances themselves.

This does not mean that projective tests cannot be useful, either as adjuncts to other tests or as vehicles to the explication of psychological processes of interest. But projective tests, like other tests, can be "edited" by subjects in ways that serve to disguise true feelings.

An interesting study in this regard was done by R. A. Clark (1952) on sexual arousal, fantasy, and guilt. In the first experiment, a group of college men were asked to rate slides of nudes according to sexual attractiveness while a control group rated neutral slides. Afterwards, both groups were administered the TAT and the experimenter made ratings of sexual fantasy and sexual guilt. Those exposed to the slides of nudes showed fewer signs of sexual fantasy and sexual guilt than the controls, a result contrary to common-sense predictions. But a second experiment was performed using males at a beer party with results that were just the opposite. This time those drinkers shown the nudes displayed much more TAT sexual fantasy and guilt than the drinkers who did not see the nudes. Under normal social constraints the expression of sexual fantasies can be inhibited, but under the uninhibiting conditions of a beer party these fantasies may be expressed. This study illustrates that projective tests (which are rarely administered under such extreme

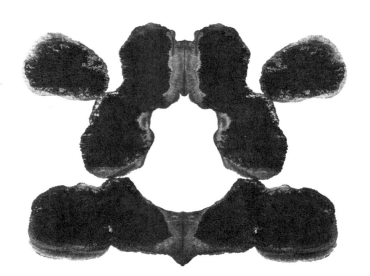

uninhibiting conditions) cannot be regarded as the royal road to the unconscious, but they may be used profitably as another source of information about the subject.

BEHAVIOR OBSERVATIONS

Observations of behavior may be made under naturalistic settings, controlled settings, or contrived settings (Wiggins 1973). Naturalistic settings may be immediate or retrospective. Examples of the former might include the settings in which anthropologists typically work or fieldwork in general; examples of the latter might include the elementary school experiences of adult criminals or the psychopathological childhoods of adult schizophrenics. Controlled settings involve situations that the experimenter has devised for the laboratory, whereas contrived settings, although likewise controlled, have the appearance of being natural to the subject.

Instruments typically used for the recording of behavior observations are ratings and/or electromechanical devices. Before any instrument is employed, however, decisions about the units of measurement to use must be made. In general, observational ratings tend to use more molar or global units than electromechanical devices, which usually record only amplitude, duration, and frequency of response. It is clear that the recording instruments may therefore influence the type of data collected as well as the results obtained.

TRAITS

After this brief overview of instrumentation and measurement of personality, we now turn to the research findings based on trait theories of personality. Following this we shall examine the criticisms of trait theories as well as review some of the literature on situational influences on personality. The traits studied vary from experimenter to experimenter. Except for Murray (1938), most recent trait theorists relied on factor analysis to identify or verify their traits.

Table 8.4 gives examples of the traits identified by different trait theorists, often using different experimental and statistical method-

---

Figure 8.1

Stimulus cards like those used in the two most popular projective tests, the Rorschach (top) and the Thematic Apperception Test (bottom). (TAT card reprinted by permission of the publishers from Thematic Apperception Test by Henry A. Murray, Cambridge, Mass.: Harvard University Press. Copyright © 1943 by the President and Fellows of Harvard College; © 1971 by Henry A. Murray.)

Table 8.4
Traits of different personality theorists

Eysenck (self-report)	Murray's needs (continued)
1. Neuroticism	13. Nurturance
2. Introversion-extroversion	14. Order
3. Psychoticism	15. Play
	16. Rejection
Norman (peer ratings)	17. Sentience
1. Extroversion	18. Sex
2. Agreeableness	19. Succorance
3. Conscientiousness	20. Understanding
4. Emotional stability	
5. Culture	Cattell (life history and questionnaire)
Murray's needs	1. Outgoing-reserved
1. Abasement	2. Intelligence
2. Achievement	3. Stable-emotional
3. Affiliation	4. Assertive-humble
4. Aggression	5. Happy-go-lucky–sober
5. Autonomy	6. Conscientious-expedient
6. Counteraction	7. Venturesome-shy
7. Defendance	8. Tender-minded–tough-minded
8. Deference	9. Suspicious-trusting
9. Dominance	10. Imaginative-practical
10. Exhibition	11. Shrewd-forthright
11. Harmavoidance	12. Apprehensive-placid
12. Infavoidance	

ologies. Eysenck's (1967) theory of personality is perhaps the easiest to describe and has received some experimental support. He has identified and studied intensively two factorially independent dimensions of personality, extroversion-introversion and neuroticism, or emotionality. (The third dimension, psychoticism, has received little support [Bishop 1977]). The extroversion-introversion distinction refers to putative differences in central nervous system arousal level and in reactions to stimuli; extroverts tend to dampen incoming stimulation and introverts tend to amplify stimulation. The neuroticism dimension refers to differential arousal in areas of the brain that control the autonomic nervous system; those high on the neuroticism dimension respond autonomically with greater intensity and emotional instability than those low on the neuroticism dimension. Eysenck's view is that extremes on each of these dimensions are associated with the development of different forms of psychopathology, while less extreme scores characterize normal personality types. For example, because highly introverted and neurotic or emotionally unstable individuals condition more rapidly and have more intense autonomic reactions than less introverted and neurotic individuals, they should be especially prone to acquire phobic responses.

This is not the place to discuss the monumental accretion of evidence both for and against the theory, and the reader is referred to Eysenck's 1967 book, *The Biological Basis of Personality*, for a sympathetic rendering of the data. One of the major problems in generalizing from the theory is that correlations between personality and proneness to conditioning generally tend to be small (Trasler 1973), even when positive results are obtained. Furthermore, Claridge (1973) has suggested that introversion-extroversion is not an independent dimension but follows from the weighting of the individual on the neuroticism and psychoticism dimensions.

Norman's (1963) five personality factors emerged from factor analytic investigations and appeared to be convincing, generalizable, and stable. The basic assumption, of course, was that these five dimensions represented real characteristics of the subjects being rated rather than fabrications or constructions by the rater. However, when Passini and Norman (1966) had college students rate *strangers* whom they could see but could not communicate with, the raters used the same five factors to describe the "imagined" personalities of the strangers. Not surprisingly, the self-ratings of the subjects had little relationship to the personality descriptions given by the observers. These data confirm the view that personality traits may exist as much in the eye of the beholder as they exist as properties of individuals themselves.

One of the most complex personality theories is that of Murray (1938), who generated a taxonomy of needs shown in Table 8.4. For him, needs were hypothetical concepts that served to organize perceptions and behaviors so as to satisfy those needs. Murray sought to distinguish between the objective and perceived demands of situations and emphasized the subject's role in making his environment. As a clinician trying to understand the individual patient, he noted where there were discrepancies between the subjective and the real demands of a situation; these discrepancies are often sources of real conflicts for the individual.

CONSISTENCY

The cross-situational consistency of traits was challenged in the classic studies of Hartshorne and May (1928) on honesty and deceit. They devised tests of moral knowledge (if you're hungry at a party and only light refreshments are served, what's the right thing to do?) and many *conduct*, or performance, tests in which children were given the opportunity to cheat. After intercorrelating the scores on the different tests, they concluded that there was little evidence for a general trait of honesty. When consistency was found, it appeared due to the similarities in the situations and not to a generalized trait of honesty.

Burton (1963) reexamined the Hartshorne and May data and found that many of the tests they employed were of very low or unknown reliability. With low reliability, one could not even expect to find that subjects would perform similarly on retesting with the same test, let alone that these tests would intercorrelate highly. Burton then selected only those tests with reliabilities of at least .70 and factor-analyzed the test intercorrelations. This time the factor analytic results indicated a general trait of honesty that accounted for 35 to 43 percent of the variance. Thus, he concluded that there was evidence for a generalized trait of honesty but that it was neither very general nor very consistent.

Family Studies of Personality Resemblance

SPOUSE CORRELATIONS

Studies of family resemblance in personality have relied almost exclusively on traits identified by questionnaires. A considerable body of evidence shows that people tend to marry assortatively; that is, people tend to marry those who are more similar to them than would be expected on the basis of chance alone. This similarity is not limited to obvious spouse correlations like age ($r = .76$) or religion ($r = .77$) (Hollingshead 1950) but also applies to many physical, intellectual, and personality parameters.

Assortative mating has both genetic and social consequences. To the extent that assortative mating is observed for traits with genetic components, the distribution of the trait in the population will differ from the distribution that would be expected as a result of random mating. In the case of intelligence, the fact that people tend to mate assortatively produces an excess of children in the next generation who are of especially high or low intelligence. This occurs because matings of exceptionally intelligent people will produce children that distribute themselves about a mean much higher than the mean of the general population. Likewise, low IQ matings will produce a distribution of children about a mean much lower than the IQ mean of the general populations.

Spuhler (1968) presents assortative mating coefficients for 105 different physical characteristics derived from a large number of studies. For weight, correlations range from .08 to .32, over seven studies, with an average of about .21. For height, the range of correlations over twenty-seven different populations is from .07 to .63, with an average of about .21.

Assortative mating has social consequences even if there are no heritable components to the traits for which there is positive assortment. Under positive assortment, spouse sets will, on the average, be more different from other spouse sets than they would be under conditions of random mating. Should there also be parent-child resemblance due to environmental factors, entire families will differ, on the average, from one another more than they would under conditions of random mating.

Assortative mating for personality characteristics has not been extensively studied. Both Vandenberg (1972) and Spuhler (1968) have given assortative mating coefficients for personality traits. Personality traits that have been studied include neurotic tendency, introversion, self-sufficiency, and dominance. Correlations are almost always low and positive, ranging from a low of −.07 for dominance to a high of .34 for neurotic tendency, with the average being about .18. By contrast, spouse correlations for intelligence average about .4. In part, the lower correlations for personality are due to the considerably lower reliability and validity of personality measures, but the lower correlations are probably also due to the fact that intelligence and education are more important dimensions for choosing a mate.

Comparisons between stable and unstable marriages show substantial differences in assortative mating. Cattell and Nesselroade (1967) compared 102 stable marriages and 37 unstable marriages, using the Sixteen Personality Factor questionnaire, and found much more negative assortative mating for the unstable marriages. The results of this study are shown in Table 8.5. Whether the dissimilarity between the partners in the unstable marriages preceded the marital unhappiness or was a consequence of it is unknown.

Looking at assortative mating coefficients alone without the addition of psychological theorizing appears to be less fruitful than it could be. One can imagine that opposites on a particular personality dimension may be happy under some circumstance and unhappy under other circumstances. The combination of two highly emotional people might not make for a very happy marriage, since such a combination might lead to excessive conflict. On the other hand, two unemotional spouses or one emotional and one unemotional spouse might be a felicitious combination. The assortative mating coefficients would be high for both the two emotional spouses and the two unemotional spouses; yet the consequences could be different for each combination. The overall correlation coefficient ignores these opposite consequences and simply averages the results. More work on the detailed patterns of relationships needs to be done in this very interesting area of investigation.

Table 8.5

Spouse correlations for stable and
unstable marriages for the 16 PF

Variable	102 stable marriages	37 unstable marriages
Outgoing-reserved	.16	−.50*
Intelligence	.31	.21
Emotional stability	.32	.05
Assertiveness	.13	.31
Enthusiasm	.23	−.40*
Conscientiousness	.33	.19
Venturesomeness	.23	.12
Tender-mindedness	−.15	−.13
Suspiciousness	.18	−.33*
Imaginativeness	.22	−.01
Shrewdness	.18	.27
Guilt proneness	.11	.36
Radicalism	.27	.34
Self-sufficiency	.15	−.32*
Self-concept control	.27	−.02
Tenseness	.16	−.11

* Significant difference between the stable and unstable marriages.
Source: From R. B. Cattell and J. R. Nesselrode, "Likeness and Completeness Theories Examined by the 16 PF Measures on Stably and Unstably Married Couples," *Journal of Personality and Social Psychology* 7 (1967): 351–361. Copyright © 1967 by the American Psychological Association. Reprinted by permission.

TWIN AND SIBLING RESEMBLANCE

There are many studies of twin resemblance (see Vandenberg 1967 for a review) on personality measures but few sibling studies. You will recall that twin studies are especially valuable for the estimation of heritability. However, the evidence that identical twins are treated more similarly than fraternal twins has compromised the results of personality studies of twins, since the greater similarity of identical twins in personality may be explained by greater similarity in treatment. There are two ways of dealing with the problem—by studying twins either reared apart or separated for long periods of time, or by determining whether twins who are treated more similarly by their parents resemble each other more closely than those treated less similarly.

Twins Reared Apart or Separated.   Table 8.6 gives the personality correlations for identical twins reared together or apart on self-report inventories, as well as correlations for those separated five years or more.
The studies yield somewhat inconsistent results, but there is no evidence that those identical twins separated for long periods are less alike
than those who have been together. In fact, the trends over the studies

Table 8.6

Personality correlations for MZ twins reared together and apart on self-report inventories

Study	Reared	N	Trait measured	Cor-rela-tion
Newman et al. (1937)	Apart	19	Woodworth-Matthews (Neurot.)	.58*
Newman et al. (1937)	Together	50	Woodworth-Matthews (Neurot.)	.56*
Shields (1962)	Apart	42	Maudsley Extraversion	.61*
Shields (1962)	Together	43	Maudsley Extraversion	.42*
Shields (1962)	Apart	42	Maudsley Neuroticism	.53*
Shields (1962)	Together	43	Maudsley Neuroticism	.38*
Wilde (1964)	Apart (5 yrs.)	38	Amsterdam Neuroticism	.52*
Wilde (1964)	Together	50	Amsterdam Neuroticism	.55*
Wilde (1964)	Apart (5 yrs.)	50	Amsterdam (Hypochondriasis)	.75*
Wilde (1964)	Together	38	Amsterdam (Hypochondriasis)	.46*
Wilde (1964)	Apart (5 yrs.)	50	Amsterdam Extraversion	.19
Wilde (1964)	Together	38	Amsterdam Extraversion	.58*
Canter (1969)	Apart (5 yrs.)	15	EPI Neuroticism	.18
Canter (1969)	Together	25	EPI Neuroticism	.53*
Canter (1969)	Apart (5 yrs.)	15	EPI Extraversion	.67*
Canter (1969)	Together	25	EPI Extraversion	.10
Canter (1969)	Apart (5 yrs.)	15	EPI Sociability	.91*
Canter (1969)	Together	25	EPI Sociability	.51*
Canter (1969)	Apart (5 yrs.)	15	EPI Impulsivity	.20
Canter (1969)	Together	25	EPI Impulsivity	−.03
Price (1969)	Apart (5 yrs.)	57	EPI Neuroticism	.69*
Price (1969)	Together	45	EPI Neuroticism	.45*
Price (1969)	Apart (5 yrs.)	57	EPI Extraversion	.57*
Price (1969)	Together	45	EPI Extraversion	.29

* Statistically significant.

suggest that twins reared apart or separated for long periods resemble each other more closely than those reared together.

The observation that identical twins reared together may be less alike than those reared apart has been called a contrast effect and has suggested that identical twins living together may seek to forge separate and sometimes complementary identities, with varying degrees of success.

Even if these twin data support the view that some personality traits have a heritable component, there is no evidence that there are genes that directly code for the traits in question. It is quite possible that positive correlations are essentially epiphenomena of heritable similarities in other characteristics (such as body build) that, in interaction with the environment, account for the personality similarities. Only if the genes for these traits or their biochemical products are themselves identified could we conclude that one inherits genes for these traits directly.

The question of whether increased similarity in treatment for identical twins is responsible for their great resemblance on tests of personality has been examined in detail by Loehlin and Nichols (1976). They used data obtained on twin applicants for National Merit Scholarships who were administered the California Psychological Inventory (CPI) and whose parents completed a child-rearing questionnaire. Loehlin and Nichols found that parents did treat identical twins more alike than fraternals but that there was no relationship between the degree of similarity in parental treatment and the degree of similarity in personality for either the identical or the fraternal sets. This means that twins who were dressed alike, slept in the same room, and so on were no more alike in personality than those who were dressed differently or slept in different rooms.

Twins Reared Together. The twin correlations in the Loehlin and Nichols (1976) study are shown in Table 8.7. The identical twins are generally more similar to each other than the fraternals, the median correlation for the identicals being about .50 and the median for the fraternals being about .30. While the overall results indicate that identicals are more similar than fraternals, there is no consistent evidence that some CPI scales are more heritable than others. This is challenging to any genetic theory of personality, since some traits ought to be more heritable than other. Another analysis by these authors made the story even more complicated. They could not identify environmental influences common to members of a twin set that made them more alike in personality. They conclude that "the relevant environments of a pair of twins are no more alike than those of two members of the population paired at random" (Loehlin and Nichols 1976, p. 91).

It may be that the psychological traits measured by the CPI are too far

Table 8.7

Intraclass correlations on California Psychological Inventory scales for identical and fraternal twins taking the National Merit Scholarship Qualifying Test

CPI scale	Identical		Fraternal	
	Males (199 pairs)	Females (288 pairs)	Males (124 pairs)	Females (193 pairs)
Dominance	.57	.49	.12	.36
Capacity for status	.55	.61	.35	.54
Sociability	.52	.54	.23	.33
Social presence	.53	.54	.14	.31
Self-acceptance	.42	.55	.12	.37
Well-being	.54	.45	.32	.26
Responsibility	.58	.43	.30	.40
Socialization	.52	.55	.16	.48
Self-control	.56	.57	.27	.36
Tolerance	.60	.47	.30	.38
Good impression	.48	.46	.30	.28
Communality	.31	.43	.28	.11
Achieve. via conformance	.47	.44	.06	.27
Achieve. via independence	.58	.50	.39	.41
Intellectual efficiency	.57	.48	.29	.38
Psychological-mindedness	.48	.37	.28	.18
Flexibility	.45	.51	.24	.18
Femininity	.41	.31	.26	.14

Source: Loehlin and Nichols 1976.

removed from those genetic and environmental factors known to affect personality. But Horn, Plomin, and Rosenman (1976) suggested that, since many of the same CPI items appear on multiple scales, the elimination of item overlap might yield differential heritabilities. Using 198 sets of adult male twins, they did demonstrate differential heritabilities when item overlap was removed. Those traits having to do with sociability and compulsivity seemed to be the most heritable, while philosophical attitudes and intellectual interests seemed to be among the least. It is clear that much more work will need to be done to elucidate genetic and environmental factors that affect personality dimensions.

CRITICISMS OF THE PERSONALITY QUESTIONNAIRE METHOD

While these findings raise doubts about the value of twin studies in estimating the inheritance of personality traits, the questionnaire method itself is susceptible to much criticism. Questionnaires come off a poor second to paper and pencil measures of intellectual abilities.

Fiske and Butler (1963) provide a detailed analysis of the two classes of paper and pencil tests and a comparison is shown in Table 8.8.

Because subjects are often unaware of what is expected of them on personality tests, interpretations of the test situation may vary considerably from subject to subject. The ambiguities described in the table for personality questionnaires may be detrimental to any trait measures of personality. Perhaps a solution might lie in the development of ability tests of personality in which the subject is aware of what is expected and knows what a good or poor performance represents (Wallace 1966).

The value of requiring maximal performance on intelligence and achievement tests is not strongly disputed; yet it is unlikely that a subject's daily activities demand the intellectual prowess required on ability tests. Efforts are underway to devise personality tests modeled on an ability format. A recent study (Willerman, Turner, and Peterson 1976) compared two paper and pencil measures of angry expression to see which better predicted laboratory measures of anger. One paper and pencil measure of angry expression asked how subjects typically behaved when angry, and the other asked subjects to say what they would do if they were to get as angry as possible. The first measure is similar to those used in traditional studies of personality in which typical performance is called for. The second is more akin to ability measures, in that maximal performance is requested. The results indicated that the maximal measure could outdo the typical measure in predicting laboratory anger.

The neglect of motivational factors in the administration of personality tests may contribute significantly to the difficulties that personality measurement finds itself in. For example, Fiske (1971) reports a study designed to measure impulsiveness. (Impulsiveness has been defined variously as having difficulties in inhibitory control, persistence, sensa-

Table 8.8
Differences between ability and personality tests

	Ability	Personality
Instructions	Subject told to do his best	Subject told to be "honest"
Questions	Usually clear	Vary from ambiguous to clear
Answers	Right and wrong answers	No correct answer
Set	Subject knows what's expected	Subject often unaware of examiner's expectations
Motivation	Subjects highly motivated	Motivation may vary considerably
Goals	Examiner wants *maximal* performance of subject	Examiner usually interested in modal or *typical* performance

tion seeking, and short decision time.) Fiske had four different tasks for impulsiveness: (1) a cancellation test—drawing a line through each occurrence of any of four letters in a long string of letters; (2) making an X that crossed within each of many small circles; (3) counting randomly placed dots within a square; and (4) successively subtracting 7s from 300. The tests were given under one of two conditions, both without time limits. The first condition included standard instructions, and no effort was made to induce additional motivation. The second condition offered a fee of two dollars and a bonus for good performance. The results indicated two things. First, there were no substantial differences in the average error scores of the subjects under the two conditions. The second and more important finding was that the intercorrelations among the various impulsiveness measures were insignificant and often negatively intercorrelated under the standard condition but positively intercorrelated under the incentive condition. Had the study used only the standard nonmotivating instruction, the interpretation of the findings would differ drastically from those following from the incentive instructions. High motivation may elicit a trait that might not be seen under conditions where motivation is lower.

Recent tests of the cross-situational consistency of personality traits have generally yielded negative or weak positive findings. An example of the poor cross-situational consistency of traits is provided in the innovative work of Endler and Hunt (1966) on anxiety as a trait. Essentially, they asked subjects to indicate how anxious they would be under a particular set of circumstances in different situations—for example, how anxious the subject would be after spilling coffee on himself at home, in a ritzy restaurant with a date, or while at work with colleagues. Trait theorists believe that subjects would feel least anxious about spilling coffee at home but expect an anxious person to be anxious in many situations.

Analysis of variance can be applied to data of this sort to determine what proportion of the variability in anxiety is due to situations in which the subject finds himself and what proportion is due to the level of anxiety generally characteristic of the individual. Bowers (1973) has summarized the findings from eleven studies evaluating the relative magnitude of the personal and situational variables on behavior. He found that traits accounted for only 12.7 percent of the variance, situations accounted for only 10.2 percent of the variance, and interactions between persons and situations accounted for 20.8 percent of the variance. The remaining variability in self-report was essentially unpredictable with the measures used. What these results mean is that only about 43 percent of the variability in behavior is "explained" by either a person's traits, the situation he finds himself in, or interactions between the two. These data suggest that traits do not do a very good job of predicting how a person will react over a variety of settings. And, finally, the most important single influence is the interaction between traits and situations. Bowers (1973) interprets this to mean that both the person and the situation need to be specified simultaneously for predictive accuracy.

The problem with this statistical approach is that it misses the mark with respect to the question of whether or not rank orderings of individuals among themselves over different situations remain much the same, irrespective of the relative influence of situations. This is the main question in the issue of cross-situational consistency in personality. Suppose one obtained measures of anxiety on two individuals in two different situations, the first situation nonthreatening and the second anxiety provoking. In the first situation both individuals would obtain relatively low anxiety scores, but in the second situation both scores would increase dramatically. Now suppose further that the first individual obtains a slightly higher anxiety score on both occasions. The approach that Bowers has taken would lead to the conclusion that situations are more important than persons. From another perspective, however, one could conclude that individual differences in personality are very important, because the rank ordering of the two individuals remained the same over both situations. A discussion of this problem and one statistical solution can be found in Golding (1975).

Mischel (1968, 1973) has chosen to emphasize that traits are poor predictors of behavior, while Bowers has emphasized the power of interactional influences on behavior. Wachtel (1973) has defended traits from a different perspective. He is critical of the representativeness of the situations used in experimental studies to test the efficacy of trait theory. He points out, for example, that experimental situations in the laboratory are relatively simple and clear in contrast to the everyday situations in which we have to interpret effects and behaviors of others that are much more ambiguous and susceptible to distortion. Furthermore, the typical research study involves an experimenter who is instructed to behave in a specified fashion towards the subject, independently of the subject's own behavior. This situation is a far cry from the usual dynamic interpersonal situations in which we mutually create the environment and situations to which we are exposed. Thus, when an individual reports that he is always being exploited the situationist is likely to identify the exploitation itself as the stimulus, while the psychodynamically oriented would ask why the individual repeatedly gets himself into such situations.

In addition, it is difficult to specify in advance what is meant by "different situations." Just imagine designing an experiment on stress and behavior where a stressful condition and a control condition are planned. Suppose that the stress is to be an angry remark by a frail female confederate and no differences between the two conditions are observed. It is likely that the experimenter will not stop there, but try to increase the stress, perhaps by using a mesomorphic Neanderthal to deliver the angry remark. If the manipulation is now successful, the experimenter concludes that the treatments are now different.

The lesson to be learned from this example is that it is almost always possible to construct or find situations where differences between treatments can be obtained and thus damage a trait theory. But we do not know whether the treatments presented are ecologically representative or artificially manipulated, occurring only rarely under natural circumstances. To draw meaningful conclusions that situations are more or less important than traits, it will be necessary to develop an ecology of situations and learn how different situations are distributed in the natural world.

Recently a novel defense of trait theory has emerged (Fishbein and Ajzen 1974; Jaccard 1974). Instead of indicting personality traits, the defenders have focused on the response side of the relationship. They point out that behavioral responses are subject to some of the same sort of measurement difficulties and biases that characterize personality traits in paper and pencil tests. Just as a single test item may be a poor indicant of a trait, so might a single outcome or behavioral measure be ambiguous or of little validity. These theorists have devised multiple-act rather than single-act criteria that are meant to indicate the presence of a particular trait. For example, Jaccard (1974) asked undergraduate females to think of another female whom they regarded as dominant and to indicate five behaviors they thought she had performed that related to her being dominant. Then the students were asked to do the same for behaviors that a nondominant female may have performed. Jaccard identified forty behaviors suggestive of dominance or non-dominance and incorporated them into a multiple-act criterion scale. Subjects then completed standard personality questionnaires as well as this behavior scale, which asked whether or not the subjects had performed any of the forty behaviors. The results indicated that correlations between dominance scores on the standard questionnaires and each of the single-act criteria averaged only about .20, but that the correlations between the standard questionnaires and the multiple-act criterion scale averaged about .60.

Thus, trait theory is not dead. Situationists have forced a reexamination of the trait position, however, and have destroyed the myth of extreme cross-situational consistency. Reason persuades us that excessive cross-situational consistency is, in fact, a sign of irrationality. For example, to experience a compulsion to wash one's hands regardless of whether or not they are dirty is not only a sign of cross-situational consistency but also a sign of a neurotic disturbance. Mentally healthy individuals are expected to be influenced by situational circumstances.

Rational behavior essentially means responding appropriately to the peculiar circumstances of a particular situation. Nevertheless, we do expect that the inferred dispositions called traits should perhaps imperfectly shine through across many situations.

WHERE IS CONSISTENCY?

When extreme groups are selected on a personality scale there is often much better prediction. For example, Hathaway and Monachesi (1963) gave the MMPI to a large sample of ninth graders in Minnesota. About four years later the subjects with official records of delinquency were identified, and their earlier MMPI profiles were reexamined to determine if certain personality profiles were associated with delinquency. The base rate for delinquency among all the boys was 34 percent, but among the 4.1 percent of boys with the highest scores on the psychopathic deviate and hypomania scales (in that order), 54 percent were later identified as delinquent. For the 1.7 percent of boys with very elevated scores on these two scales, 60 percent subsequently became delinquent.

Occupational interests is another area of personality in which consistency or stability over time is observed. D. P. Campbell (1969) has summarized the findings of the Strong Vocational Interest Blank (SVIB):

> Test-retest correlations over 30 days average slightly over .90, dropping to about .75 for over 20 years for adults and to .55 over 35 years for men first tested at age 16. Correlations over the four years of college usually are in the .60's.... When the SVIB is used for those below the age of 21, the possibility of future change must be recognized [p. 21].

One of the earliest of the interest inventories, the SVIB was developed in the 1920s and enjoys great popularity even now. Strong (1943) argued that, if individuals enjoy the same activities as do those already in a particular occupation, then those individuals too would be suitable for that occupation. Thus, if working engineers would enjoy scientific activities such as authoring a technical book but would not enjoy authoring a novel, or would like being an architect but not an auctioneer, then an individual with similar preferences might choose engineering as a suitable occupation.

These seemingly simple-minded empirically derived keys for particular occupations have been surprisingly successful. For example, Strong (1955) has shown that the SVIB administered in college predicts what occupation the student will be engaged in eighteen years later. Strong uses a rating system in which individuals score A for a particular occupation if they have interests very much like the interests of a high proportion of those already working in that occupation. Those who have interests represented by only about 2 percent of those already in that occupation score C on that scale. Strong found that in comparison to the original college sample, five times as many men in a particular occupation eighteen years later had A interest patterns for that occupation while in college.

Actually, theorists such as Mischel (1968) who favor situational influences over traits as predictors would not find the stability in occupational interests incompatible with their own views. Virtually all situationalists accept the fact that cognitive traits (those which involve intellectual abilities) do display considerable stability over time (see Mischel 1968 for a review).

TEMPERAMENTS

Because the evidence does not support strong personality consistency as measured by conventional personality tests, increasing attention has been focused on the conceptually more basic level of *temperaments*. Temperaments are meant to reflect the biological foundation, which in interaction with learning and other environmental factors produces the conventional personality traits. Buss and Plomin (1975) have made the following assumptions about temperaments: (1) individuals begin life with a small number of broad, *inherited* dispositions to act in certain ways; (2) the environment reacts to and modifies these dispositions (within limits); and (3) temperaments are more concerned with stylistic than content aspects of personality.

The classic work of Allport and Vernon (1933) on expressive movement illustrates what is meant by stylistic aspects of behavior. The authors asked twenty-five adult males to write, walk, draw, count, read, tap, stroll, estimate distances, and perform many other simple tasks. They then constructed a composite factor of expansiveness based on the sum of nine behaviors and correlated each of these with the sum of the other eight, yielding the following correlations:

Area of total writing	.69
Total extent of figures	.67
Area of blackboard figures	.64
Slowness of drawing	.52
Area of foot squares	.48
Overestimation of angles	.45
Movements during idleness	.39
Length of self-rating checks	.38
Length of walking strides	.37

These correlations for expansiveness of movement indicate moderate consistency. They describe *the way in which* individuals go about various tasks and not the actual content of the tasks or the accuracy with which the various tasks are performed. These are the aspects of personality with which Buss and Plomin are mainly concerned.

Allport's (1961) definition of temperament is still generally accepted and is as follows:

> Temperament refers to the characteristic phenomena of an individual's nature, including his susceptibility to emotional stimulation, his customary strength and speed of response, the quality of his prevailing mood, and all the peculiarities of fluctuation and intensity of mood, these being phenomena regarded as dependent on constitutional make-up, and therefore largely hereditary in origin [p. 34].

Cattell and Warburton (1967) defined *temperaments* as those personality traits which do not change much with changes in incentive or complexity. *Abilities* are those traits whose scores change as a function of complexity, and *dynamic personality traits* are those which change as a function of incentive or motivation.

The question of what aspects of personality should be called temperaments can also be answered from the perspective of evolution. Diamond (1957) identified behavioral dispositions found in both animals and man, and Buss and Plomin slightly modified his list, proposing three empirical and two rational criteria for a temperament. The *empirical* criteria are that the trait be (1) inherited, (2) stable during development, and (3) present in adulthood. The *rational* criteria are that the trait be (1) adaptive and (2) present in animals close to man. Three temperaments seem to fulfill these criteria:

Activity—sheer energy output
Sociability—the tendency to approach others
Emotionality—the tendency to be aroused

Activity. Activity has been studied according to a variety of methodologies, mechanical devices, observational ratings, and self-reports. Animals can be bred for activity level, and activity is clearly adaptive, since it permits the organism to seek out rather than passively await the arrival of necessary supplies. Human studies on the inheritance of activity level have relied mainly on twin studies and family correlations. In general, activity has been shown to have an inherited component, although parental ratings of activity level tend to yield higher heritabilities (e.g., Willerman 1973) than do experimental measures of the activity of the twins (e.g., Scarr 1966).

Buss and Plomin (1975) summarized the results of nine longitudinal studies of activity level, five of them using children less than a year old. These five studies are consistent in showing that activity level in infancy is unstable. This instability is compounded when attempts are made to relate infant measures of activity to later measures, when activity is assessed differently. For example, Thomas, Chess, and Birch (1970) labeled high-active infants as those who moved during sleep or wriggled when the diaper was changed. At ten years of age high-active children were those who played ball and engaged in other sports or could not sit still enough to do homework. It seems clear that comparison of activity level across ages starting from infancy is not reasonable. On the other hand, one should expect some longitudinal stability of activity level at later ages, when the behaviors assessed are more comparable. This is exactly what Buss and Plomin found. Activity level measured after the first year of life does show moderate stability, although the longitudinal correlations bounce around from study to study. There is less information on stability of activity level during adulthood, although Gottschaldt (in Vandenberg 1967) does say that he found stability over fifteen years from adolescence to adulthood. In short, there does seem to be some support for qualifying activity level as a temperament.

Sociability.   This is the only temperament with a directional component—the tendency to approach others and be responsive to them. Sociability is clearly adaptive, in that it serves to promote cooperation and must have aided survival through evolution. One expects that those who are sociable will get positive reinforcement for approaching others and, within limits, that sociability will be reinforcing to companions so that a positive feedback loop will be established. Differences in sociability are present early in life, and lower animals show large differences in sociability. Schaffer and Emerson's (1964) work with cuddling and noncuddling infants demonstrates this difference. They showed that some infants seemed to find cuddling rewarding, while others appeared restless and resistive during cuddling. It is not clear, however, that these differences are due solely to sociability; it might be that the more active infants resist restraint more than less active infants.

Twin studies of sociability suggest that sociability is moderately heritable, and the two twin studies of infant sociability imply that it is present early in life (Freedman 1965; Wilson, Brown, and Matheny 1971). Longitudinal studies of sociability show moderate correlations over time. For example, Kagan and Moss (1962) found that interview ratings on withdrawal from social interaction between twelve years and adulthood correlated .65 for males and .56 for females.

Emotionality.   Emotionality is a particularly difficult concept to define. Under normal circumstances it has three components (Izard 1972): (1) an innately determined neural substrate, (2) a characteristic neuromuscular expressive pattern, and (3) a distinctive subjective quality. Too often psychologists have focused on the neural substrate alone, as if sympathetic nervous system arousal were identical with emotion. It is now known from work both with animals (Solomon and Wynne 1954) and with humans that individuals deprived of sympathetic nervous system innervation still display behavior or report experiences that can be described as emotional (Cannon 1939).

Schachter and Singer (1962) beautifully demonstrated the role of cognitions in emotions when they gave epinephrine (a sympathetic nervous system stimulant that produces palpitations, tremor, and sweating) under the pretense that it was a vitamin supplement for vision. Some subjects were correctly informed about the stimulating effects of the drug, others were told that there would be no side effects, and still others were not told anything about side effects. After the drug was administered, each subject was placed in a room to wait for the drug to take effect. A confederate of the experimenter, also supposed to be waiting for the drug to take effect, joined the subject in the room. Depending on the experimental condition, the confederate displayed either of two types of behavior: euphoria or anger. After the confederate had completed his routine, the subject was asked to rate two items: how angry and how happy he felt at present. The results indicated that those subjects who were exposed to the euphoric accomplice and who were accurately informed about the drug effects were less likely to rate their arousal as happiness than were those misinformed or uninformed about the biological effects of the drug. Likewise, subjects who were exposed to the angry accomplice and who were ignorant about the side effects reported more anger than those who were correctly informed. Schachter and Singer (1962) interpreted the results as indicating that it was not the autonomic arousal per se that determined the emotional state but rather the cognitive appraisal and labeling of the emotional arousal. When accurately informed about the side effects of the drug, subjects did not need to label the arousal they were feeling as either euphoria or anger and therefore were not especially susceptible to the emotional behavior they observed. When misinformed or uninformed about the drug effect, subjects used what was going on around them as cues to label their arousal as a particular emotion.

Unfortunately, emotions are particularly difficult to study from the perspective of individual differences because they are usually fleeting and appear closely tied to environmental stimuli. Further, a distinction must be made between tonic and phasic arousal. *Tonic* arousal refers to resting levels of arousal and is somehow related to chronic levels of physiologic activity, while *phasic* arousal refers to temporary reactions in response to stimuli.

Buss and Plomin (1975) equate emotionality with phasic autonomic reactivity rather than with tonic levels of arousal. They point out that there seems to be a developmental sequence for emotionality; newborns display only what can be described as distress, and it is not until about three months of age that they display signs of pleasurable emotions— cooing, smiling, and so forth. Of course anger and affection appear even later, and these emotions must be related to the maturation of the cognitive apparatus. Emotionality is clearly adaptive in that it permits reactions like fight or flight, and animals can be bred for emotionality. Twin studies of emotionality have generally found a significant inherited component, but most of these studies have been interested in general emotionality and have not experimentally induced emotionality. There is little longitudinal data available on emotionality from adolescence on (Tuddenham 1959).

The importance of learning in emotionality is clearly seen in the large gender differences in the expression of affect. Buss and Plomin (1975) point out that in infancy and the preschool years there are essentially no gender differences in emotionality but that in the school years and later females show many more signs of fearfulness. Nevertheless, their argument that emotionality should shine through the overlay of learning is warranted, because both boys and girls show some longitudinal consistency in emotionality when the data are separated by sex. The gender difference suggests that the cognitive meaning for various stimulating events is mediated through learning, and it thus seems clear that we can learn to overcome many of our fears.

TEMPERAMENTS AND CHILD REARING

The inherited dispositions called temperaments are likely to modify and become modified by the environment. In the process of socialization, children at the extremes of the temperament dimensions are probably subjected to parental attempts at modification. Parents try, for example, to make low-active children more active and high-active children less active, etc. That these temperaments show significant heritabilities suggests that attempts at modification have not been entirely successful.

The merit of the Buss-Plomin theory of temperaments is that it is grounded in empirical findings and that the temperaments are few enough to serve as organizing principles or source traits for a theory of personality. From even a cursory review of the many traits described in this chapter, it seems that we are in need of organizing principles that simplify and yield testable propositions with explanatory power.

Cognitive Styles

Our sensory apparatus and brain are like filters through which we apprehend our world. Variations or defects in the filters affect what we notice or how we interpret events. If different individuals apprehend the world differently, it follows that they will also behave differently. Research on these filter mechanisms and consequent behavioral differences has been of considerable interest to a number of investigatory groups. The field is broadly called *cognitive styles* and can be considered to exist on the borderline of intellectual function and personality.

We do not apprehend our world directly, but information is transmitted and modified by passage through the nervous system and brain. Limitations on the resolving power of the nervous system would of course affect how and what we experience. For example, we see moving pictures as being continuous when they pass our eyes at the rate of 24 frames per second. At this rate the resolving power of our visual system cannot distinguish the rapid changes in successive still pictures from continuous movement.

Variations and defects in these filter mechanisms can be due to genetic factors or environmental factors or both. It has been shown that different cultures often have slightly different color-naming systems. Some fail to distinguish certain primary colors from one another, and these confusions often correspond to genetic differences in their visual receptor systems (Bornstein 1973).

It is also possible that various experiential events would lead us to be more or less sensitive about certain aspects of the environment. If one is in a haunted house, one is more prepared than under normal circumstances to interpret any sudden.changes as being dangerous and frightening.

Much of the work described on the following pages had its origin in traditional work on perception. This work has since expanded to areas of personality in which correspondences between certain aspects of perception and personality have been obtained.

GLOBAL VERSUS ANALYTIC COGNITIVE STYLES

Early work by Herman Witkin and Solomon Asch was stimulated by the observation that some airplane pilots would enter clouds right side up and emerge from them upside down without awareness that their position had become inverted while in the cloud. This observation led to investigations on the perception of the upright and to a vast body of research showing how perception of the upright related to other intellectual and personality factors.

Over the years a number of different tests were used to conduct these researches. The Body Adjustment Test (BAT) required a subject seated in a tilted chair in a tilted room to adjust the chair to the true upright. The Rod and Frame Test (RAT) required a subject to sit in a darkened room in which only a rod and surrounding frame were illuminated. The subject was first exposed to a rod and a frame that both deviated from the true vertical and asked to adjust the rod to the true vertical. It turned out that individuals who could not adjust the tilting chair to the true upright when the room was tilted were the same ones who could not adjust the rod to the true vertical when its surrounding frame was tilted. These individuals were labeled as field dependent, because they seemed unable to separate the "figure" from the "ground" in which it was embedded. Those who did a good job of adjusting the chair or the rod to the upright were called field independent, since they were not overly influenced by the field in which the figure was placed (Witkin et al. 1954).

Another test, called the Embedded Figures Test (EFT), yielded roughly the same kind of results. In this paper and pencil task the subject was required to identify or locate a particular figure that was hidden in a complex background. Those who performed poorly on this task also did poorly on the other tasks.

The concepts of field dependence and field independence underwent further changes over time (Witkin et al. 1962), especially when EFT performance was found to correspond to performance on adjustment to the upright. It appeared then that poor scorers on all these tests were individuals who were less psychologically differentiated than those who scored well—that is, the poor scorers had a global rather than an analytic cognitive style. As Witkin and his associates put it:

> In a field-dependent mode of perceiving, perception is dominated by the overall organization of the field; there is relative inability to perceive parts of a field as discrete. This global quality is indicative of limited differentiation. Conversely, a field-independent style of perceiving, in which parts of a field are experienced as discrete from organized background, rather than fused with it, is a relatively differentiated way of functioning. Persons whose field-dependent perception suggests limited differentiation in their experience of the world about them also show limited differentiation in their experience of their bodies. Further, they tend to use the social context in which they find themselves for definition of attributes of the self.... Finally, persons who are perceptive in a field-dependent fashion are also likely to use such global defenses as repression and denial, suggestive of limited differentiation, whereas field-independent perceivers tend to use specialized defenses, as intellectualization and isolation, suggestive of developed differentiation [Witkin, Goodenough, and Karp 1967, pp. 291–292].

In interpersonal relations field-dependents are more sociable, prefer to be physically close to others, and have well-developed sets of social skills. Field-independents tend to be more impersonal, do not appear to be very interested in others, and prefer nonsocial situations (Witkin and Goodenough 1977).

Longitudinal studies of subjects on these different measures of field dependence and independence showed moderate stability over time. In one group of boys tested at eight and again at thirteen years, the correlation for scores on the RFT was .76; for the girls tested at the same ages, the correlation was .48. For a group of males tested at ten and again at twenty-four years of age, the correlation was .66 for scores on the RFT (Witkin, Goodenough, and Karp 1967). The other perceptual measures yielded roughly corresponding findings. This is not to say that there were no changes in the absolute scores of subjects as they grew older. In fact, subjects tended to become more field independent until age seventeen, after which scores seemed to level off or move slightly in the direction of more field dependence until age twenty-four. These authors also report that geriatric subjects are extremely field dependent.

There has been considerable discussion about the construct of field dependence and independence. Questions about how it differs from general intelligence have been raised, and there is the possibility that changes in equipment or procedures can affect the results obtained (Vernon 1972).

Factor analyses and intercorrelations of intelligence subtest scores with the various measures of field independence by Witkin et al. (1962) showed that verbal intelligence measures did not correlate highly with scores on the measures of field independence. However, among adults two performance IQ subtests, picture completion and block design, did correlate positively and substantially with scores on the EFT, .72 and .80, respectively. Both picture completion and block design call for a type of disembedding. In picture completion the subject is to identify a part that is missing from a picture, and in block design the subject is to construct a block design from randomly arrayed blocks while looking at a picture of the design to be constructed. The results of the block design subtest were so promising that this measure is often used as a substitute measure of global or analytic style. It is a bit strange, however, that the block design subtest appears to be relatively independent from the verbal subtests in Witkin's analyses, because block design correlates about .50 with verbal IQ scores in children and about .61 with verbal IQ scores in adults in the manuals for those tests. The greater selectivity of the subjects used in Witkin's investigations might account for this finding.

Many of Witkin's provocative findings have been applied to cross-cultural settings. It has been found that hunting-and-gathering societies are more field independent than sedentary agricultural societies. Similarly, societies in which there are loose child-rearing structures and where self-reliance is encouraged as opposed to an emphasis on obedience, have many more field-independent members than do societies that have authoritarian child-rearing structures and an emphasis on obedience. Furthermore, societies in which there might have been some genetic selection for field independence appear to be more field independent than other societies (Witkin and Berry, in press).

This latter finding is of extreme interest, because the Eskimo obtain fairly high scores on measures of field independence (Berry 1966; MacArthur 1967). Furthermore, there is no sex difference in scores. Other studies usually find sex differences in teenage and thereafter showing that boys are more field independent than girls. The fact that there were no sex differences among the Eskimo and that their scores compare favorably with those obtained from industrialized societies has suggested that the environment of the Eskimo may either foster or select for those who are more field independent. Witkin and Berry (in press) point out that indeed girls are given considerable independence in Eskimo society and that the environment calls upon individuals to make sharp visual differentiations on the basis of skimpy information, differentiations that may affect survival. One must be able to distinguish the polar bear or the igloo from the snow, and such distinctions may have life or death consequences.

LEVELING VERSUS SHARPENING

Investigators at the Menninger Foundation in Topeka, Kansas, have been studying a cognitive style called leveling versus sharpening (Gardner et al. 1959).

One approach to the leveling-sharpening distinction is to have subjects rate the size of a series of squares that differ in area. After five squares have been rated, a new, larger square is surreptitiously substituted for the smallest. Some subjects fail to assign to the new square a rating that indicates it is larger than the old square. Others recognize that the square is larger and appropriately assign it a new and higher rating. After this new series is rated, another new and larger square is substituted for the smallest, and so on. Those who fail to recognize the new, larger squares, and who are called levelers, also appear to have less distinct memories than those of subjects who do recognize the new squares. Levelers tend to blend experiences rather than distinguish changes in stimuli. The sharpeners often are hypersensitive to changes and notice minutiae, while the levelers seem to be simplifiers. The sharpeners also do better on such tasks as the EFT.

Other dimensions of cognitive style have been investigated. Cognitive complexity is one (Bieri 1955), and reflection-impulsiveness is another (Kagan 1966). Reviews of work in cognitive styles can be found in Kagan and Kogan 1970; Messer 1976; and Zelniker and Jeffrey 1976.

The importance of this work in cognitive styles is to show that many of the insular categories used to distinguish academic areas may limit the richness of the hypotheses and findings. Perceiving and remembering are not necessarily separate processes, because the same organism is usually doing both simultaneously. The fact that those who do poorly on tests of field independence also appear to be somewhat dependent in their social relationships would not have been discovered if investigators had remained insulated from other areas of investigation. Scientists often need to go wherever the problem takes them and thus may have to acquire new areas of expertise or collaborate with investigators who belong to different disciplines.

PERSONALITY AND ABILITY

There are other intimate relationships between some personality dimensions and ability, although it is not possible now to say whether there is a causal connection between the two. Cattell (1971) has identified several personality dimensions, called *ability factor simulators*, that correlate with performance on ability tests. While there are more than two, the focus here shall be on cortertia and temperamental independence. Cortertia and temperamental independence can be fac-

Table 8.9

Correlations of second-stratum personality factors with WAIS measures

WAIS measure	Personality factor			
	Extroversion	Anxiety	Cortertia	Temperamental independence
Information	.16	−.22	.15	.43
Comprehension	.23	−.17	.18	.44
Arithmetic	.14	−.18	.24	.33
Similarities	.11	−.13	.15	.34
Digit span	.03	−.04	.05	.18
Vocabulary	.19	−.12	.12	.47
Digit symbol	.13	−.16	.13	.19
Picture completion	.06	−.15	.19	.30
Block design	.09	−.17	.23	.32
Picture arrangement	.04	−.05	.20	.24
Object assembly	.00	−.03	.23	.22
Verbal IQ	.18	−.19	.20	.48
Performance IQ	.10	−.15	.26	.38
Full-scale IQ	.16	−.20	.25	.47

Note: Correlations greater than .12 are statistically significant at $p < .05$.
Source: From Turner, Willerman, and Horn 1976.

torially derived from the intercorrelations produced by other traits on the 16 Personality Factor Test (16 PF). *Cortertia* refers to cortical alertness and is characterized by cheerfulness, alertness, and a readiness to handle problems at a cognitive rather than at an affective level. *Temperamental independence*, of which field independence is a subsidiary perceptual manifestation, is characterized by criticalness, flexibility, self-assurance, and self-control.

Turner, Willerman, and Horn (1976) administered the 16 PF and the WAIS to 249 adoptive parents and correlated these two personality factors and another two (extroversion and anxiety) with WAIS subtest scores. The results are shown in Table 8.9. Extroversion bears only low, but generally positive, relationships to intelligence test scores. Anxiety shows consistently negative, but low, relationships to the intelligence measures. One of Cattell's ability simulators, cortertia, also shows generally low, but positive, correlations with ability. Temperamental independence, however, yields fairly high correlations with virtually all subtest measures of intelligence. Although it is not known how personality and ability interact, these results clearly indicate that some personality factors can be regarded as closely allied to abilities and that intelligence does not exist in a vacuum.

Longitudinal Studies of Personality Development

ADVANTAGES AND DISADVANTAGES

Conducting longitudinal studies of personality development is an ambitious and precarious undertaking. It often means that data must lay dormant for many years until follow-up information can be collected. It often requires commitment to variables and hypotheses that may have seemed interesting and worthwhile at the initiation of the study but that years later may be outmoded or have already been supported or discredited by researchers using other methods. Also, new hypotheses emerge in later years that are often untestable because the appropriate data had not been collected earlier. Preventing sample attrition over the years is another problem, since families may no longer be interested in cooperating or may have moved away.

Despite these difficulties, those studies which have covered a large portion of a life span provide a unique body of data that can answer questions of personality continuity and change over the life cycle. A major stumbling block, however, is that comparisons of results between different longitudinal studies is close to impossible, since the studies usually test different hypotheses and obtain different kinds of data. When comparisons between studies are made for those variables that appear comparable, findings agree only about half the time (Block 1971).

For the most part, researchers have been interested in continuity of personality over time. Continuity implies positive and at least moderate correlations between traits measured early and later, and these correlations are valuable for making predictions. If early signs of deviance are predictive, then one might explore means of altering the expected outcome.

RETURN TO TYPES

Block (1971) has suggested that researchers ought to be interested not only in personality *continuity* over time, but also in correlates of personality *change* over time. He has pointed out that in any one study some subjects may show continuity over time and others may not. Combining results for all subjects may obscure important relationships within subsets of the sample. Using a method called the Q-sort, he studied a group of subjects who had participated in either of two longitudinal studies from the Institute of Human Development in Berkeley, California.

The Q-sort is a technique that permits the correlation of persons rather than tests over time. Judges review case histories of each subject and then sort standard statements into nine different piles according to how closely each statement characterizes the person. The number of statements that can be assigned to each pile is specified in advance and is meant to fit a normal bell-shaped distribution. Thus, piles one and nine have the least number of statements and pile five has the largest number of statements. Some of the statements are:

> Is critical, skeptical, not easily impressed.
>
> Is a genuinely dependable and responsible person.
>
> Has a wide range of interests.
>
> Is a talkative individual.

Suppose that the first statement in the preceding list was very characteristic of subjects one and two and thus was assigned to pile nine for each of them. If the other statements likewise were assigned to similar piles, these two subjects could then be regarded as similar in personality and would be classified as the same type.

Block identified 180 Q-sort statements of personality that subjects in high school and during adulthood (mid-thirties) had been rated on in the Berkeley longitudinal studies. He then factor-analyzed these statements on each of the 171 subjects. The factors obtained in this instance represented similar people. Block identified five male and six female types by this method and then examined all the data that had been collected on the subjects from infancy on, looking for differences between the types. Only 63 of the 84 males and 70 of the 87 females were classifiable into types; the remainder he called residuals. Examples of the male types follow.

Ego Resilients. These subjects had relatively high IQs and parents who seemed to enjoy a good relationship with each other. The mothers of these subjects were judged intellectually superior and cooperative. During junior high the subjects were regarded as bright, dependable, productive, and having a wide range of interests. In senior high school and adulthood similar traits were described as characteristic of them. During adulthood they attained more education and improved in socioeconomic status more than the others, were satisfied in their occupations, and were judged markedly well adjusted.

Belated Adjusters. These were children from lower socioeconomic homes with little parental intellectual stimulation. During junior and senior high they were generally belligerent and negativistic. By contrast, as adults they were dependable and sympathetic and had lost their rebelliousness. Although their IQs in high school were lower than the mean for the other types, these subjects did improve substantially in socioeconomic status as adults. However, they did not have high achievement orientation as adults, and they still lacked long-term goals. Block suggests that they adjusted relatively well because they preferred an easily predictable, if circumscribed, life. There was little correspondence between the personality descriptions of these subjects obtained in high school and those obtained in adulthood.

Illustrations of the female types follow.

Cognitive Copers. These girls showed a gradual improvement in personal adjustment over the years—from being thin-skinned, uncomfortable with uncertainty, and ruminative in junior high to being less distrustful and overcontrolled in senior high. By adulthood they were introspective, valued independence, and were aesthetically sensitive. They were also more warm, talkative, and straightforward. Their educational achievements and socioeconomic progress exceeded all others, and they appear to have blossomed over the years. The label of cognitive copers is applied because they seem to have approached life in an essentially intellectual fashion.

Dominating Narcissists. These girls were self-indulgent throughout the years, but as adults their self-indulgence became more socialized and appeared as assertiveness. Thus, described as less well adjusted than the other types during adolescence, they improved considerably as adults. As adults they were pragmatic, knowing what they wanted and not beset by the nagging doubts that might befall others in making decisions. Their parents had an unhappy relationship with each other, the father being dominant and self-indulgent and the mother retiring and somewhat dysphoric. The label of dominating narcissist is meant to refer to their continuing self-absorption and aggressiveness in advancing their own desires.

Block found that some personality types in adolescence appeared to be related to a positive adult adjustment while others did not. What seemed to distinguish those with more favorable outcomes from the rest was the capacity for routine self-examination and introspection. Those who seemed well adapted during the school years but who did not subject themselves and others to scrutiny became less well adjusted later. Additionally, Block points out that the early home environment was a potent influence on the developmental outcome. It was not socioeconomic factors so much as the relationship between the parents themselves and their orientation toward the child that seemed to count in the end.

Some of the personality types displayed a good deal of consistency, while others did not. Remember, however, that comparisons of results from different longitudinal studies do not always show good agreement; hence, it is quite possible that these types may not be replicable in other studies.

Conclusions

The utility of traits determined by questionnaires as predictors of stability or change in behavior is rightly being challenged. Given the findings of the situationists, it is clear that predictability from traits alone will always be less than 100 percent, even under the best of circumstances. It appears, however, that behavioral predictions can be improved appreciably if some of the criteria applied to items on psychometric tests are also applied to behavioral outcome measures. It must also be acknowledged that the predictability of traits for behavioral outcomes may only be high for a subset of individuals measured on those traits and not for everyone (Bem and Allen 1974).

9

Psychopathology

Psychopathology is not to be equated with deviance, although all individuals with psychopathology can be regarded as deviant. Those forms of deviance which often involve superior personal or social adaptation, such as high intelligence, are not regarded as psychopathological; only those whose behavior is deviant *and* maladaptive are viewed as having psychopathology. There are varying philosophies about the origins of different forms of psychopathology, some emphasize organic factors and thus imply a disorder in the biological substrate, and others focus on the learning of maladaptive responses. These two orientations shall be pitted against each other wherever appropriate in the discussion that follows.

The abnormal behaviors to be treated in this chapter fall into four broad traditional classifications—psychoses, neuroses, character disorders, and childhood disorders. Each of these classes of behavior is further subdivided—psychoses into schizophrenia and affective disorders, neuroses and character disorders into subdivisions that will be described later, and childhood disorders into hyperactivity and specific learning disabilities.

Schizophrenias

These disorders are marked by disturbances in thinking, mood, and behavior. The thinking disturbances involve unusual forms of logic (e.g., Napoleon was a man, I am a man, therefore I am Napoleon), delusions, and hallucinations. The mood changes include extreme ambivalence and constricted or inappropriate emotional responses. The behavior may be withdrawn, childish, or bizarre. To some extent, nonschizophrenics experienced one or all of these disturbances on occasion. For example, many have hallucinations, say, while driving at night, or have marked mood changes for which there is no ready explanation. What distinguishes those who are diagnosed as schizophrenic is the frequency and duration of these unusual experiences, in the absence of obvious external causes, such as fatigue or drugs.

Schizophrenia may be classified in a variety of ways. The most popular classification was devised by Bleuler in 1911, based on clinical signs, and includes four major subtypes:

1. *Paranoid schizophrenia*—characterized by hallucinations or delusions

2. *Catatonia*—characterized by marked disturbances of motor ability, either violent activity and excitement or generalized inhibition, stupor, mutism, negativism, or unusual posturing

3. *Hebephrenia*—characterized by disorganized thinking, shallow or inappropriate affect, unpredictable giggling, and regressive behavior and mannerisms

4. *Simple schizophrenia*—characterized by a slow and insidious reduction of external attachments and interests. Apathy and indifference predominate, and there are few of the dramatic features found in the other major subtypes.

The distinctions between these subtypes are not always clear, since in the course of the disorder individuals may display signs of each subtype and may ultimately end up in a subtype different from that noted upon initial examination. A further complication, to be amplified upon later, is that many individuals display traits that can be described as schizophrenic-like or schizoid but do not comprise schizophrenia in its full-blown form. These schizoids display a "rigidity of thinking, blunting of affect, anhedonia, exquisite sensitivity, suspiciousness, and a relative poverty of ideas" (Heston 1970, p. 251). It has been suggested that these individuals have a milder form of schizophrenia and may fall into what is known as the schizophrenic spectrum.

FREQUENCY AND DISTRIBUTION

The incidence of schizophrenia has been calculated in many studies and shows considerable variability from country to country (although there is no society free of schizophrenia), from investigator to investigator, and from one method of calculating incidence figures to another. In the United States a generally accepted estimate is .85 percent, or slightly less than one per hundred. If the entire life span is used, the frequency of the disorder does not differ much according to sex, but before the age of twenty-five there is a predominance of males diagnosed with the disorder; after age thirty-five many more females are so diagnosed. There is some question about the diagnosis of schizophrenia in childhood; many investigators argue that childhood schizophrenia is due to organic brain disease and associated with mental retardation (Pollack 1967). Reviewing the genetic evidence for childhood schizophrenia, Hanson and Gottesman (1976) conclude that there is little evidence for genetic factors in schizophrenia that begins before age five, but childhood onset after age five may simply be an early expression of the adult form of the disorder. Furthermore, Hauser, DeLong, and Rosman (1975) have recently used radiographic techniques to find visible brain atrophy in the left hemispheres of children who have an early-onset form of schizophrenia called infantile autism. This finding tends to solidify the view that brain lesions are critical in very early onset expressions of the disorder.

These findings are in contrast to adult schizophrenia, which is not frequently associated with diagnosable brain disorders, although there is some evidence that this view may be altered in the light of new findings (Haug 1962). Schizophrenics are also found in excess in the lowest social classes (Hollingshead and Redlich 1958), but it should not be concluded that the stresses associated with the lowest social classes necessarily precipitate schizophrenia. Two other studies (Goldberg and Morrison 1963; Dunham, Phillips, and Srinivasan 1966) have shown that the social class origins of schizophrenics do not differ from the social class origins of the general population, but that the schizophrenics, during the course of their adult lives, tend to drift downward in social class.

FAMILY MORBIDITY RISK

The likelihood of having schizophrenia varies with the severity of schizophrenia in the proband and the degree of family relationship to the index case. First-degree relatives of schizophrenics are anywhere from five to fifteen times more likely to develop schizophrenia than the general population, and second-degree relatives are about three times more likely. Data of this sort can be explained from either a genetic or an environmental perspective, and it takes the more effective behavioral genetic methodologies involving twin and adoption studies to determine if familial concentrations for the disorders are due to heredity. But it is worth noting that the risk of having schizophrenia does not differ according to whether the schizophrenic parent was the mother or the father (Kallmann 1938). This suggests that deleterious maternal child-rearing practices do not increase the child's risk for schizophrenia.

TWIN STUDIES

Comparisons of concordance rates for monozygotic and dizygotic twins have shown that MZ twins are more concordant for schizophrenia (Rosenthal 1970). The results indicate a concordance rate for schizophrenia anywhere from three to six times higher among MZ than DZ sets. The fact that MZ concordance rates are below 100 percent, however, suggests that the genetic disposition alone is not sufficient to produce schizophrenia. It has also been demonstrated convincingly that twin concordance for schizophrenia is strongly related to the severity of the schizophrenia in the index twin. Rosenthal (1961) reorganized the twin data of Slater according to severity of schizophrenia and found 100 percent concordance for schizophrenia for the extremely and moderately severe cases and only 26 percent concordance for the mild

Table 9.1

Concordance rates for schizophrenia in MZ twins reared apart

Date	Investigators	Age at separation	Number of pairs	
			Concordant	Discordant
1938	Kallmann	soon after birth	1	
1941	Essen-Moller	7 yrs.	1	
1945	Craike & Slater	9 mos.	1	
1956	Kallmann & Roth	not given	1	
1962	Shields	birth	1	
1963	Tienari	3 yrs.		1
	Tienari	8 yrs.		1
1965	Mitsuda	infancy	5	3
1967	Kringlen	22 mos.		1
	Kringlen	3 mos.	1	
	Total		11	6

Source: From E. Slater and V. Cowie, The Genetics of Mental Disorders. London: Oxford University Press, 1971.

cases. Gottesman and Shields (1966) found 67 percent concordance in the cotwins of index MZ twins hospitalized for more than one year and only 20 percent concordance for those hospitalized less than one year.

Since 1938 seventeen sets of MZ twins have been collected who were either reared apart or separated before eight years of age (Slater and Cowie 1971), in which at least one twin was diagnosed as schizophrenic (Table 9.1). Of these seventeen sets, eleven cotwins were also diagnosed as schizophrenic, which is about the same rate of concordance as determined from MZ sets not reared apart. These data offer perhaps the strongest evidence that schizophrenia has a genetic component.

ADOPTION STUDIES

Adoption studies likewise have clearly supported the theory that schizophrenia has a genetic basis. The first study to be reported using adoption methodology is that of Heston (1966). He located forty-seven children who had been born between 1945 and 1951 while their schizophrenic mothers were patients in psychiatric hospitals in Oregon. These children were reared either in foster homes or by paternal relatives not known to be schizophrenic. The children of schizophrenic mothers were matched to other children from the same foundling homes according to age and eventual type of placement. The results are shown in Figure 9.1.

As can be seen, five of the forty-seven children of schizophrenic mothers were diagnosed as schizophrenic (these five had been hospitalized), while none of the fifty children of nonschizophrenic mothers was so diagnosed. Of great interest was the additional finding that the children of the schizophrenic mothers had a variety of disorders, including mental retardation and antisocial personality previously thought to be unassociated with schizophrenia.

It should be pointed out, however, that the psychiatric status of the fathers in this study was unknown, except that they had not been hospitalized for a psychiatric disturbance. This type of information is crude, and other data presented later will show that many nonhospitalized individuals are themselves disturbed. Furthermore, the evidence suggests that psychiatrically disturbed persons are more likely to mate with others who are disturbed. Consequently, there is a good possibility that the strange varieties of abnormalities in the offspring in this study were related to genetically transmitted abnormalities on the paternal side, although this is not known for sure.

Heston also reports anecdotally that many of the twenty-one children of the index cases with no psychiatric impairments tended to lead more spontaneous and colorful lives and had more creative jobs and imagi-

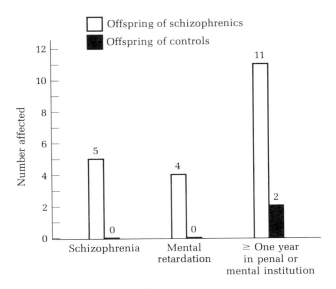

Figure 9.1

Outcomes for individuals born to schizophrenic mothers (N = 47) and reared in adoptive or foster homes and control adopted children born to normal biological parents (N = 50). (After Heston 1970.)

native hobbies than the children of nonschizophrenic mothers. This finding jibes with other reports that the relatives of schizophrenics are in fact more creative than others. Perhaps this represents the positive side of manifestations of "schizophrenia genotypes," when they are expressed in a subdued form.

Another study of adopted children was performed by Rosenthal et al. (1968) in Denmark, where very thorough psychiatric and adoption records are kept. These workers located thirty-nine individuals who had given up their children for adoption and who also had diagnoses of schizophrenia (N = 38) or manic-depressive psychosis (N = 1). These parents were matched to a control group who had likewise given up their children for adoption but who had no psychiatric history. The controls were matched to the subjects according to sex, age, age at transfer to the adopting family, and socioeconomic status of the adopting family.

The two groups of children were given intensive personal examinations lasting two days by interviewers who knew nothing about the psychiatric status of the biological parents. Rosenthal points out also that the adopted children rarely knew the psychiatric status of their biological parents. Table 9.2 provides the major findings collected by 1967 in this ongoing study.

Table 9.2

Schizophrenic-spectrum disorders in adoptees who had
a biological schizophrenic or manic-depressive parent,
or both biological parents without psychiatric history

Diagnosis of adoptee	One parent psychotic ($n = 39$)	Parents without psychiatric history ($n = 47$)
Schizophrenia:		
Hospitalized	1	0
Never hospitalized	2	0
Borderline schizophrenia	7	1
Near or probably borderline	0	2
Schizoid or paranoid	3	4
Not in schizophrenic spectrum	26	40

Source: From Rosenthal 1970.

Among the thirty-nine children with a psychotic parent, three adoptees were diagnosed as schizophrenic (although only one of these had been hospitalized) and seven were diagnosed as borderline. Thirteen of the thirty-nine children of psychotic parents were diagnosed in the schizophrenic spectrum, whereas only seven of the forty-seven children of parents without a psychiatric history were so diagnosed. A follow-up of an expanded group ($N = 76$) of this population found that 31.6 percent of the adopted-away offspring of psychotic parents had disorders in the schizophrenic spectrum, whereas only 17.8 percent of the controls were similarly diagnosed (Rosenthal et al. 1971).

These data for schizophrenia confirm those of Heston and clearly require an explanation that takes into account genetic factors. It should be noted, however, that had Rosenthal et al. relied on psychiatric records alone, they would have missed two of the three schizophrenic offspring and all of the borderline cases. This again casts doubt upon the reliability of using hospital records of psychiatric involvement alone for the control groups. If an individual can be diagnosed as psychotic from interviews and testing without having been hospitalized, it follows that some of the biological parents without psychiatric histories in the control group (who were not themselves examined) might have been diagnosed as psychotic had they undergone testing. Although one can be fairly confident that those with psychiatric records were psychotic, one cannot be sure that those without such records were not. The Horn et al. (1975) findings are relevant here. They collected MMPIs on 363 mothers who had given up their children for adoption and found significantly elevated scores on the schizophrenic and psychopathic deviate scales of the MMPI, suggesting that those who give up their children for adoption may have more psychopathology than those in the general population.

ADOPTEES' FAMILY METHOD

A study by Kety et al. (1968, 1976) in Denmark started with the adopted children themselves, locating those diagnosed as schizophrenic who had been given up for nonfamilial adoptions between 1924 and 1947. A control group of nonfamilial adoptees without psychiatric history was matched to the schizophrenic adoptees according to sex, age, age at transfer to the adoptive parents, pretransfer history, and socioeconomic status of the adopting family. All the adoptive and biological relatives who were judged schizophrenic after the records search had been themselves hospitalized with a psychotic disorder. The major results are shown in Table 9.3.

Note that the table is composed of four groups of individuals, the biological relatives of the index and control cases and the adoptive relatives of the index and control cases. The table shows that 21.4 percent ($\frac{37}{173}$) of the biological relatives of the index cases are in the

Table 9.3

Distribution of schizophrenia-spectrum disorders among the biological and adoptive relatives of schizophrenia index cases

	Biological relatives	Adoptive relatives
Index cases	37/173	4/74
Controls	19/174	7/91
p	.006	N.S.

Subsample of 19 index cases and 20 controls separated from biological family within 1 month of birth (1968)

	Biological relatives	Adoptive relatives
Index cases	10%(N = 93)	4%(N = 45)
Controls	0%(N = 92)	2%(N = 51)
p	.002	N.S.

Numerators = number with schizophrenia, uncertain schizophrenia, or inadequate personality.
Denominators = number of identified relatives.
Source: From S. S. Kety, D. Rosenthal, P. H. Wender, and F. Schulsinger, "Studies Based on a Total Sample of Adopted Individuals and Their Relatives: Why They Were Necessary, What They Demonstrated and Failed to Demonstrate," *Schizophrenia Bulletin* 2 (1976): 413–428.

schizophrenic spectrum, while only 10.9 percent ($\frac{19}{174}$) of the biological relatives of the control cases are so diagnosed. In contrast, there is no difference in the frequency of schizophrenia spectrum disorders among the adoptive relatives of the index cases and the frequency among the adoptive relatives of the control cases. These results suggest that there is an appreciable portion of schizophrenia spectrum disorders only among the biological relatives of the schizophrenics.

Actually, an examination of the data separately for the parents, siblings, and half-siblings of the adoptees shows that the excess in psychopathology in the biological relatives of the schizophrenic adoptees is entirely due to the increased frequency of psychopathology in their half-siblings. The probable reason for this is that most of the half-siblings were directly interviewed, while the psychiatric status of the parents often had to be obtained through records. At the time of this study, many of the biological parents had already died and five of the biological parents of the schizophrenic adoptees had committed suicide, whereas none of the biological parents of the controls had done so. Although these five biological parents were not formally diagnosed as psychotic, other evidence suggests that at least some of them were. While these suicides are not included in the table, they do seem to increase the probability that there is a hereditary connection in the transmission of psychopathology.

Karlsson (1966) examined the biological and adoptive siblings of schizophrenics in Iceland who had been adopted before one year of age and obtained results similar to those of Kety et al. He found that six of twenty-nine biological siblings of the schizophrenics were also diagnosed as schizophrenics.

The adoption data reviewed here strongly support a genetic etiology to some forms of schizophrenia, although there is a possibility that psychopathology in the adoptive parents plays some role in the precipitation of schizophrenia in adopted children. Wender, Rosenthal, and Kety (1968) examined the biological and adoptive parents of schizophrenic and normal control adoptees in Denmark. Using psychiatric interviews and psychological tests, they found that the biological parents of the schizophrenic adoptees had the greatest amount of psychopathology, as expected, but also that the adoptive parents of the schizophrenics manifested more psychopathology than did the adoptive parents of normal controls. It was impossible to determine whether the increased psychopathology in the adoptive parents of the schizophrenics preceded or was a consequence of the schizophrenia in their adoptive children.

A similar but better controlled study in the United States compared biological parents of schizophrenics, adoptive parents of other schizophrenics, and biological parents of children with nongenetic forms of mental retardation and found elevated rates of psychopathology only in the biological parents of the schizophrenics (Wender et al. 1977). One advantage of this later study was that the inclusion of the comparison group of parents of nongenetic retardates afforded some control for the possibility that having a deviant child itself could have accounted for the earlier findings. Differences in the outcomes of the earlier and later studies by Wender and his colleagues were explained in terms of methodological differences that may have made the first study less valid.

It would not have been surprising to find that the stress of having a schizophrenic adoptive child could induce some psychopathology in the adoptive parents (Liem 1974). Nevertheless, Rosenthal (1970) concludes that

> ... the evidence has turned up so consistently and so strongly in favor of a genetic hypothesis that the issue must now be considered closed.... We need to concern ourselves with the mode of genetic transmission and the biological-psychological mechanisms involved. We know too from the twin studies [because there is less than 100 percent concordance for MZ twins] that nongenetic factors play an important role, and we must identify these and determine how they relate to the expression of the genetic factors" [pp. 131–132].

GENETIC MODELS

.Many workers have tried to identify the mode or modes of genetic transmission in schizophrenia, and no one theory has found widespread favor (see Slater and Cowie 1971 for review). The two major competing theories are that the disorder is polygenic, involving a threshold phenomenon in which a sufficient loading of the "schizophrenic" genes is necessary to produce the schizophrenic disorder, or that the disorder is due to a single autosomal gene that in double dose invariably produces schizophrenia but that in heterozygotes is associated with schizophrenia in only about 25 percent of individuals. Slater and Cowie suggest that it is difficult to prefer strongly one model to the other, as there are no data available that can specifically exclude either possibility.

A major stumbling block in discovering the mode of genetic transmission through adoption studies is that one usually does not know the psychiatric status of the coparent (spouse or mate) of the index parent. It is quite likely that many of them are also disturbed, although never hospitalized. This ignorance is equivalent to trying to predict the eye color of a child from the eye color of the mother, without knowledge of the father's eye color.

Rosenthal (1974) tried to remedy this situation by interviewing those coparents he could locate who were originally in the Kety et al. (1976) study. It turned out that 35 percent of the coparents located were diagnosed as having a psychiatric disorder within the schizophrenic spectrum. Another 19 percent were diagnosed as having psychopathy. Thus, over 50 percent of the coparents were psychiatrically disturbed. When the data in the original Kety et al. study were reanalyzed according to whether or not a coparent was in the schizophrenic spectrum, large differences emerged. If the coparents were in the schizophrenic spectrum, 60 percent of the children were also in the spectrum; if the coparents were not in the spectrum, only 9 percent of the children were in the spectrum.

It is clear that much more will have to be known about the partners in studies of this sort before it will be possible to establish precise modes of genetic transmission.

DIAGNOSIS

Not the least of the difficulties in identifying the mode of genetic transmission is the fact that different investigators have not agreed on the diagnosis of schizophrenia. Even when psychiatrists try to classify the same patients into broad categories, such as psychotic, neurotic, or organic, agreement between the doctors rarely exceeded 80 percent (Zubin 1967). In those studies with high agreement rates, there is the strong possibility that raters did not made their diagnoses independently. When raters tried to make differential diagnoses within each of the broad categories, Zubin found that agreement dropped to about 50 percent. Thus, without some standardized nomenclature for diagnosis, we may not be able to make much progress.

In recent years relatively structured interviewing procedures have minimized examiner idiosyncracy and increased diagnostic reliability. It has also become clear that European workers generally require more signs of psychopathology in order to diagnose an individual as a schizophrenic than do Americans. A successful effort to identify a set of symptoms that diverse diagnosticians can agree upon was made by Carpenter, Strauss, and Bartko (1973). Investigators in nine different countries interviewed a total of 1202 patients using a standardized and structured interview schedule called the Present State Examination. The patients were randomly divided into two equal-sized cohorts, A and B. Twelve of the most telling signs and symptoms of schizophrenia across all the countries as determined from cohort A alone were then applied in cross-validation to cohort B, where they were equally as successful in discriminating between the schizophrenics and the nonschizophrenics. An important feature of this work was that the authors were able to compare their hit-or-miss rates with the number of symptoms displayed by the patients. For example, if the criterion for schizophrenia were considered to be four or more of the symptoms, 91 percent of the schizophrenics (as initially diagnosed by various means in each of the countries) were correctly classified as schizophrenic again, but about 33 percent of the nonschizophrenic patients were also misclassified as schizophrenic. If the criterion were placed at eight or more of the symptoms, however, about 21 percent of those previously diagnosed as schizophrenic were again diagnosed as schizophrenic, while none of the nonschizophrenics was misdiagnosed as schizophrenic.

Shields and Gottesman (1972) asked seven diagnosticians from four countries to independently review the psychiatric histories of 114 twin individuals. In each twin set, at least one twin had at some time in the past received a diagnosis of schizophrenia. Using as their criterion of diagnostic success the difference in the concordance rates for the MZ and DZ pairs, they found that a diagnostic approach which was neither extremely stringent nor extremely liberal produced the most discriminating differences between the concordance rates for the MZ and DZ pairs.

These results indicate that there is a core concept of schizophrenia that experts from diverse backgrounds can agree upon. If future investigators in every country used these same diagnostic criteria, at least for research purposes, it would be easier to make comparisons among different studies. Since the number of schizophrenics that are classified according to the most stringent criteria is less than the total number of schizophrenics, there will be a loss in sample size. Nevertheless, the trade-off of smaller sample sizes for increased agreement may be just what is needed for research. If one were to conduct a biochemical study of patients having eight or more of the signs, one could be reasonably sure that those individuals were schizophrenic and the possibility of replication with a different sample would be increased. The twelve discriminating signs or symptoms are shown in Table 9.4.

It should be remembered that support for a genetic hypothesis in schizophrenia is only the first step in understanding how schizophrenia comes about. It remains to be specified how the gene or genes are acting—that is, what biochemical products they produce, how these products differ in either degree or type from the biochemical products of the normal gene at that locus, and how the abnormal product produces the symptoms of schizophrenia. If the disorder is polygenic, it is going to be especially difficult to isolate the culprit biochemical gene products; each of the genes may be producing only small deviations from the norm. If the disorder is due to only one gene, there may be more hope for identifying the biochemical abnormality.

This is not the place to review the research on the biochemistry of schizophrenia. While there have been many reports suggesting that schizophrenics can be distinguished from nonschizophrenics biochem-

Table 9.4

Items from the Present State Examination (PSE) corresponding to the twelve signs or symptoms favoring a diagnosis of schizophrenia

Sign or symptom	PSE observation or question
Restricted affect	Blank, expressionless face. Very little or no emotion shown when delusion or normal material is discussed which would usually bring out emotion.
Poor insight	Overall rating of insight.
Thoughts aloud	Do you feel your thoughts are being broadcast, transmitted, so that everyone knows what you are thinking? Do you ever seem to hear your thoughts spoken aloud? (Almost as if someone standing nearby could hear them?)
Waking early (—)	Have you been waking earlier in the morning and remaining awake? (Rate positive if 1 to 3 hours earlier than usual.)
Poor rapport	Did the interviewer find it possible to establish good rapport with patient during interview? Other difficulties in rapport.
Depressed facies (—)	Facial expression sad, depressed.
Elation (—)	Elated, joyous mood.
Widespread delusions	How widespread are patient's delusions? How many areas in patient's life are interpreted delusionally?
Incoherent speech	Free and spontaneous flow of incoherent speech.
Unreliable information	Was the information obtained in this interview credible or not?
Bizarre delusions	Are the delusions comprehensible?
Nihilistic delusions	Do you feel that your body is decaying, rotting? Do you feel that some part of your body is missing—for example, head, brain, or arms? Do you ever have the feeling that you do not exist at all, that you are dead, dissolved?

Source: From W. T. Carpenter, J. S. Strauss, and J. J. Bartko, "Flexible System for the Diagnosis of Schizophrenia: Report from the WHO International Pilot Study of Schizophrenia," *Science* 182 (21 December 1973): 1275–1278. Copyright © 1973 by the American Association for the Advancement of Science.

ically, virtually every one of the "breakthroughs" reported have been disconfirmed upon attempted replication (see Levitt 1972).

A number of workers have been trying to find drugs that can induce schizophrenic-like symptoms in normals, hoping that these "model psychoses" will provide a clue to the mechanisms behind schizophrenic behavior. Many have thought that psychedelic drugs, such as LSD and mescaline, produce a symptom picture sufficiently close to schizophrenia that elucidation of how those drugs act on the brain would be helpful in understanding schizophrenia. By now it seems clear that these psychedelics do not mimic schizophrenia that closely. They seem to cause little disturbance in thinking per se but appear to have their major influence on perceptual processes. Further, Hollister (1962) has shown that judges can reliably distinguish between tape-recorded interviews of schizophrenics and of those on psychedelics.

The closest we have come to a model psychosis is with the repeated and heavy administration of amphetamine. For example, Griffith et al. (1972) administered amphetamine orally in ten-milligram doses hourly to seven previously heavy users of amphetamines who had been carefully screened so as not to have even the mildest signs of schizophrenia. Within two to five days every subject sustained a paranoid psychosis that was indistinguishable from the real thing.

Snyder (1974) sums up the similarities between amphetamine psychoses and schizophrenia:

1. Those with amphetamine psychoses are regularly misdiagnosed as having paranoid schizophrenia.

2. The schizophrenic-like symptoms of amphetamine psychoses are not the result of sleep loss or activation of latent schizophrenia.

3. Phenothiazine tranquilizers are useful in treating both amphetamine psychoses and schizophrenia.

4. Amphetamine in small doses will activate the symptoms in incipient or mildly symptomatic schizophrenics but will not have this effect on schizophrenics in remission, manic-depressed patients, or normals.

Where the parallelism of amphetamine psychoses and schizophrenia breaks down is in the fact that amphetamine invariably produces paranoid states and never produces hebephrenia or catatonic states. Snyder (1974) suggests that this may be due to the central stimulant action of the drug, which produces a hyperalert individual who is energetically searching for some "explanation" for the strange feelings he is experiencing. The result is his "paranoid insight." If the stimulating effects of amphetamines can be cleaved biochemically from other effects, perhaps other types of schizophrenia can be produced. Snyder goes on to draw parallels between the action of amphetamine on the neurotransmitter substance, dopamine, and the way that phenothiazine tranquilizers affect the same neurotransmitter system. Although there are many links missing in the explanatory chain, much biochemical work is proceeding along these lines.

BEHAVIORAL ASPECTS OF SCHIZOPHRENIA

Hundreds, if not thousands, of studies have shown schizophrenics of one kind or another to be deficient on a monumental array of experimental tasks (see Eysenck 1973). In many circumstances, however, the subjects' cooperation or motivation was minimal, their contact with reality was impaired, or long-term hospitalization had contributed to their social disarticulation. Furthermore, few distinctions had been made in terms of the severity or chronicity of the illness and in terms of whether the patients were paranoid or nonparanoid schizophrenics; the prognosis for the less chronic and paranoid patients usually appears to be more optimistic (Chapman and Chapman 1973). Likewise, little distinction was made between those aspects of schizophrenia which were learned or were a consequence of the disorder and those aspects which were causal in the disorder. Experiments requiring that the presumptive psychological deficits be converted into superior performance in the experimental situation would probably have avoided much of this fuzziness and resulted in fewer experimental dead ends.

Perhaps the greatest difficulty in theorizing about schizophrenia is to account for the many patches of intact performance in the field of bizarre behavior. For example, although the intelligence of severely schizophrenic individuals may be somewhat below average (Payne 1973), one is struck by the preservation of average or even remarkable intellectual superiority in many schizophrenics, especially those diagnosed as paranoid. It is certain that clinical schizophrenia in all its concrete manifestations is not inherited. After all, one cannot have a delusion about being Napoleon unless one has learned about Napoleon.

One theory of schizophrenia that appears to be heuristically promising is that of Meehl (1962), who has tried to account for the genetic evidence and the heterogeneity of behavioral symptoms that schizophrenics display. He postulates that four behavioral characteristics are central to the concept of schizophrenia, although schizophrenics differ in the degree to which they display any of the symptoms.

1. *Cognitive slippage.* This refers to disturbances in thinking, such as believing that one's nose is growing inward. Cognitive slippage is probably the hallmark of schizophrenia, since the other features can be found in a variety of other psychotic and nonpsychotic disorders.

2. *Interpersonal aversiveness.* This refers to social fear, distrust, expectation of rejection, and conviction of one's worthlessness.

3. *Anhedonia.* This is a marked and widespread defect in the capacity to experience pleasure.

4. *Ambivalence.* With this characteristic, one has contradictory thoughts or feelings simultaneously.

To be sure, we can all recall occasions under which we have experienced each of these characteristics, but it is the pervasiveness and duration of these experiences that characterize schizophrenics. Meehl suggests that only some form of an "integrative neural defect" in some parameter of single-cell functioning, admittedly amorphously described, can account for this collection of features. He goes on to say that only the neural defect is inherited and calls this inheritance schizotaxia. When the neural defect is exposed to existing child-rearing regimes, however, it invariably results in the learning of these core behavior traits, which Meehl calls schizotypy. If the rearing environment is favorable and the individual has the good fortune to inherit an otherwise vigorous and healthy constitution, he may never manifest the symptoms with sufficient intensity to be diagnosed as schizophrenic.

There has been little progress in identifying the nature of the integrative neural defect, although some of the work described above (Snyder 1974) tends to implicate the neural transmitter substances.

ATTENTIONAL DYSFUNCTIONS

For some time investigators have suggested that attentional disturbances are central to the development of schizophrenia. Correlations between attentional deficits and schizophrenia have been repeatedly observed in severely affected samples but less frequently in mildly affected samples. The kinds of tasks used in these studies include concept formation, span of apprehension, vigilance, and tasks that test one's ability to be unaffected by distractions.

Asarnow et al. (1977) tried to distinguish between attentional deficit as a primary consequence and as a secondary consequence of schizophrenia by looking at individuals who had a high risk of developing schizophrenia. They compared ten foster children whose biological mothers had been diagnosed as schizophrenic, ten foster children whose biological mothers had no known psychiatric disturbance, and a control group of normal children reared by their natural parents. The two foster groups had been removed from their natural homes at the age of eight, and all children were about sixteen years of age when tested on the attentional tasks. The results indicated clear differences between the two foster groups, especially on attentional tasks of greater complexity. The normal control group often performed better than either one of the two foster groups.

This study does not rule out early environmental factors in the genesis of schizophrenia, since the foster children lived with their parents until eight years of age. However, because the family environments of these children since age eight were judged by the authors to be quite adequate, one cannot make the argument that contemporaneous disruptions were responsible for the deficits observed.

Only a subset of the ten children of schizophrenic parentage would have been expected to display these attentional disturbances, and it is remarkable that statistically significant differences were achieved with such a small sample size in this study. The causal mechanism in attentional disturbance still remains elusive. If attentional deficit is found to be a core feature of schizophrenia, investigators will still need to examine its biological correlates.

Justice cannot be done to other ideas about the nature of schizophrenic deficits in the space available. Eysenck's (1973) *Handbook of Abnormal Psychology* and Salzinger's (1973) book on behavioral studies of schizophrenia provide up-to-date and comprehensive discussions of research on the psychological aspects of schizophrenia.

LONGITUDINAL AND FAMILY STUDIES OF SCHIZOPHRENIA

It has been noted repeatedly that schizophrenics come from families that display more psychopathology than average, but it has been especially difficult to determine whether parental psychopathology contributes to schizophrenia through the genetic or the environmental side of the parent-child relationship (or both). The adoption studies previously described suggest that the known and established contributions tend to come from the genetic side of the relationship, but it seems implausible that environmental influences should not also contribute to schizophrenia, at least in some patients. Indeed, the families of schizophrenics often seem riddled with psychopathology. For example, in an intensive study of families of schizophrenics under twenty years of age, Lidz, Fleck, and Cornelison (1965) suggested that 60 percent of the parents had schizophrenic tendencies and transmitted to their children irrational distortions about the nature of reality, both within and outside the home.

A longitudinal approach that seems very promising is to study children who are at high risk for schizophrenia (Mednick and Schulsinger 1974). Those considered to be at high risk are the children of schizophrenic mothers, about 12 percent of whom are expected eventually to become schizophrenic; some others are expected to become behaviorally deviant, although not schizophrenic. This design might be able to illuminate how the genetic defect is associated with the learning of the core behavioral features of schizophrenia.

One problem is that only a small proportion of high-risk subjects become clinically schizophrenic. Thus, a large initial sample is required to capture a sufficient number of eventual schizophrenics to make comparisons possible. This type of research has an important advantage over family studies in which the children have already become schizophrenic. In the former type, it is possible to say something about early differences between those who do and those who do not become schizophrenic, uncontaminated by the fact that the subject is currently schizophrenic (Garmezy 1974).

Some of the high-risk children in this study have already developed psychotic disorders, and one finding of considerable interest has emerged. Those who now have a psychosis had unusually rapid onset autonomic nervous system responses in an aversive conditioning situation. These rapid responses were accompanied by rapid autonomic recoveries as well. Mednick and Schulsinger (1974) suggest that these findings may be a key to the development of schizophrenia. They argue that the rapid autonomic responsiveness would facilitate the development of avoidance behaviors, which would help to alleviate distress. The quick autonomic recovery of schizophrenics would be a potent reinforcer for learning avoidant responses, since their discomfort would be rapidly diminished. Thus, thinking disturbances in schizophrenics, that is, not dealing with reality, might be a way of avoiding distressing autonomic consequences by misinterpreting the true nature of the stimuli.

Affective Psychoses

There is significantly less research on affective disorders than there is on the schizophrenic psychoses. One reason for this is that many individuals with affective psychoses improve with or without treatment, at least temporarily, and therefore do not remain in residential psychiatric facilities long enough to be studied easily. The major diagnostic categories for the affective psychoses are:

1. *Depressive psychosis*—characterized by depressed mood, anergia, poverty of ideas and interests, motor retardation, and often delusional beliefs of worthlessness and guilt.

2. *Manic psychosis*—characterized by elation of mood, motoric hyperactivity, flight of ideas, talkativeness, rapid speech, and irritation when obstructed from carrying on activities, often accompanied by delusions of grandeur. This disorder occurs rarely.

3. *Manic-depressive psychosis*—characterized by the presence of signs of both manic and depressive psychosis.

Psychotic depression differs from neurotic or reactive depression in that reactive depression is often associated with an identifiable and real loss of an important affectional object, while psychotic depression is less frequently associated with such a loss. Recently, however, it has been demonstrated that the distinction between psychotic and reactive depression in terms of a demonstrable loss of an important object may be due to the psychotically depressed individual's failure to report the loss because of his profound disturbances. Careful questioning of psychotic depressives after recovery, however, shows little difference between the incidence of such losses reported by the psychotic depressives and by the neurotic depressives (Leff, Roatch, and Bunney 1970; Paykal et al. 1969). Among neurotic depressives, however, the depth of reactive depression is never so deep as it is among psychotic depressives, is not associated with delusions, and less frequently requires hospitalization.

There is some question as to where *involutional* depression belongs. It occurs, by definition, among those in middle age and predominantly in women, but except for age and clinical history the symptom picture is not easily distinguishable from psychotic depression. The disorder seems to be precipitated by the patient's increasing awareness of growing old, realization of unfulfilled expectations, diminished physical attractiveness, and by being needed less in the rearing of children. Since some of these losses are real, it is difficult to assign these patients to one or the other category.

Hopkinson and Ley (1969) reported on genetic evidence for depressive psychosis that might also shed some light on involutional depression. They examined the incidence of affective disorders among the first-degree relatives of patients with affective disorders according to the age of onset of the disorder. Twenty-nine percent of the first-degree relatives of those who sustained their affective psychosis before forty years of age were likewise afflicted with affective disorders, whereas only 12.5 percent of the first-degree relatives of those with later-onset affective disorders could be so diagnosed. These data suggest that involutional depressions, which tend to occur after age forty, can be distinguished from other psychotic depressions, but it should be noted that the incidence of affected first-degree relatives of the late-onset cases is still substantially higher than the incidence in the general population.

FREQUENCY AND DISTRIBUTION

It is difficult to obtain consistent estimates of the frequency of affective psychosis. There has been no attempt to obtain separate estimates for each type of affective psychosis; all types have usually been lumped into the broader category of manic-depressive psychosis. The median estimate of frequency is about 0.7 percent, or slightly less than the 0.85 percent frequency for schizophrenia (Rosenthal 1970). Affective psychosis occurs anywhere from 1.5 times to twice as frequently among females than males, although it is possible that early suicide in males before the disease is diagnosed may account for some of the sex difference.

FAMILIAL MORBIDITY RISK

The risk of manic-depressive psychoses in the first-degree relatives shows wide variation from study to study. The median rates of affective psychoses as determined by Rosenthal (1970) are 7.6 percent for the parents, 8.8 percent for the siblings, and 11.2 percent for the children. If borderline cases are also included in the estimates, the risks are increased by about 2 or 3 percent for each of the preceding values. Second-degree relatives likewise show rates of manic-depressive psychosis that are far above the rates in the general population.

Affective psychoses might be genetically heterogeneous, since probands with unipolar depression (no indication of mania) are much more likely to have first-degree relatives who display unipolar depression than relatives who display bipolar (manic-depressive) psychosis. Similarly, the first-degree relatives of bipolar cases are much more likely to display the bipolar form of the disorder than the unipolar form.

Estimating family morbidity risk for affective psychoses is further complicated by the fact that the risk of suicide is elevated, not only among the manic-depressive probands themselves, but also among the first-degree relatives of the cases. Perris (1966) estimates that perhaps 3 to 5 percent of the first-degree relatives of depressive patients commit suicide. Many of these individuals may never have been formally diagnosed as having an affective psychosis, but the implication clearly is that they might have been so diagnosed at a later date if they had not committed suicide.

TWIN STUDIES

Relatively few twin studies on affective or manic-depressive psychosis have been made. The existing studies all show, however, that MZ twins are substantially more concordant than the DZ twins for the diagnosis. The data are summarized in Figure 9.2. The median estimate for concordance of MZ twins is about 66 percent, whereas the median concordance for DZ sets is about 18 percent. The high MZ concordance rates may be somewhat inflated by the fact that the more severely affected individuals were more likely to be in psychiatric hospitals than less severely affected individuals and thus were more likely to be included in the twin studies. Had those with the milder forms of the disorder been included, the proportion of discordant MZ twins might have been larger.

The most complete twin study of manic-depressive illness was recently reported by Bertelsen, Harvald, and Hauge (1977) in Denmark. Through various twin registries they identified all twins born between 1870 and 1920 who had received a diagnosis of manic-depressive illness. Using a strict diagnosis of manic-depressive psychosis, they found

STUDY

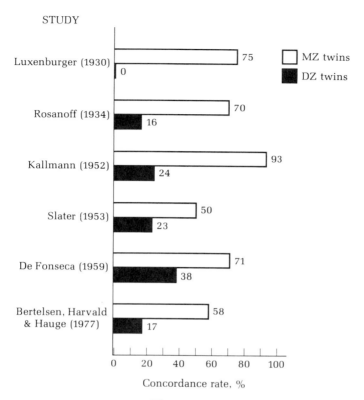

Figure 9.2

Twin concordance rates for affective psychoses.

that 58 percent of the MZ twins (n = 55 pairs) and 19 percent of the DZ twins (n = 52 pairs) were concordant for the disorder. Using a less stringent criterion for manic-depressive illness, they found that 85 percent of the MZ twins and 37 percent of the DZ twins were concordant. These workers also confirmed the specificity of the bipolar and unipolar distinction in affective psychoses. When the MZ proband had the unipolar form of the disorder, eleven of the twelve concordant cotwins also had the unipolar form. When the MZ proband was bipolar, fourteen out of twenty of the concordant cotwins also had the bipolar form of the disorder.

ADOPTION STUDIES

Cadoret (1976) culled from a larger study of adoptions eight biological mothers having a diagnosis of affective disorder. Of their children, three were subsequently diagnosed with a depressive disorder (37 percent), while only 5 percent of the seventy-five biological mothers who had other psychiatric diagnoses had a child who eventually was diagnosed as depressed. Thus, these data point also to a hereditary component in the development of depression.

A recent adoption study of bipolar affective psychosis in Belgium strongly supports the view that manic-depressive illness is under substantial genetic control (Mendlewicz and Rainer 1977). The biological and adoptive parents of twenty-nine manic-depressive adoptees were interviewed blindly, as were the biological and adoptive relatives of normal adoptees. Two additional control groups were employed. One control group consisted of bipolar cases reared by their natural parents, and the other control group was composed of individuals who had polio and who also were reared by their natural parents. The last control group was included to test the hypothesis that rearing a disabled child increases the risk for psychopathology in the parents. The results indicated that 31 percent of the biological relatives of the manic-depressive adoptees had affective disorders whereas only 12 percent of the adoptive relatives of these individuals had affective disorders ($p < .05$). Twenty-six percent of the parents of the nonadopted bipolar cases also had affective disorders. Thus, the biological relatives of adopted-away bipolar cases were at about the same risk for affective disorders as were biological relatives who reared affected children. Among the other control groups, 10 percent of the adoptive relatives and 2 percent of the biological relatives of the normal adoptees were diagnosed with affective disorders. Among the biological parents of the polio cases, 10 percent were judged to have psychopathology in the affective spectrum.

ETIOLOGY

It has been possible to develop both behavioral and biochemical models in infrahuman primates and in humans that closely mimic many aspects of depressive behavior (Akiskal and McKinney 1973). For example, Kaufman and Rosenblum (1967) separated infant pigtail monkeys from their mothers when the infants were between four and five months old for a period of four weeks. For the first day or two after separation, the infants appeared to be acutely distressed (screaming, searching, acting restless). Five or six days later this stage was followed by depression, in which the infants were hunched over, almost rolled into a ball, and generally withdrawn, not unlike manifestations of human depression. It is also possible to produce depression in humans and primates by the administration of reserpine and other drugs. These drugs have in common the depletion of a class of neurotransmitters called biogenic amines. These biogenic amines are secreted by presynaptic neurones in the central nervous system and affect the firing of the postsynaptic neurones. Drugs that are effective in the treatment of depression are known to increase the availability of these amines.

Akiskal and McKinney (1975) propose an integrative model for the development of depression, acknowledging that genetic, pharmacological, and experiential factors can all lead to the final path of depression. In essence, stress factors, such as hopelessness or learned helplessness (Seligman 1975), promote the development of a hyperaroused state, which has neurophysiological consequences in an area of the brain called the diencephalon. This area includes the thalamus, hypothalamus, and the pituitary, among other organs. The hyperaroused state produces alterations in biogenic amines or intraneural sodium that help to cause depressions. These alterations in biogenic amines can also come from genetic influences and likewise can lead to depression. Thus, Akiskal and McKinney's argument is that depression can be caused by a number of factors, which can operate in interaction or separately, but all of which have their field of action in the diencephalon.

In 1973, Akiskal and McKinney had proposed that the distinction between reactive and psychotic depression might be only a matter of degree and might not be due to any fundamental differences in cause. Additionally, they suggested that severe depression, which seems to be so common during middle age and later, is possibly due to the increased stresses associated with aging and a genuine decrease in the availability of biogenic amines with age.

They also suggested that mania and depression are on a continuum, sharing the same basic dysfunction, but that mania is associated with abnormal increases in the biogenic amines while depression is associated with decreases in the biogenic amines.

Psychoneuroses

Perhaps more than for the psychoses, the understanding of the psychoneuroses has been compromised by the lack of interrater agreement for specific diagnostic categories. Such agreement rarely exceeds 60 percent, and usually it is much lower. There is even lower consistency of diagnosis across time (Zubin 1967). Sarason (1972) says that neurosis nowadays suggests

> ... disturbance with a moderate level of psychological pain and anxiety.
> ... the term implies a disorder that restricts, to some extent, the individual's overall judgment, his ability to achieve good contact with reality, and his capacity to relate effectively with others in the environment. The psychiatric diagnosis would be applied to a person who is fundamentally distrustful of his own general level of competence and basic merit, and of

the basic friendliness and accepting nature of the environment.... In general, neurotic behavior is inappropriate, inadequate, and unsatisfying. It may even be rather infantile. It results in subjective and objective discrepancies between a person's potential and his social behavior and achievements.... Neurotics tend to behave in what Dollard and Miller (1950) called a "stupid" manner, that is they tend to respond repetitively and rigidly in interpersonal relationships and seemingly, do not profit from experience [p. 256].

The diagnostic categories to be discussed are:

1. *Obsessive-compulsive neurosis*—characterized by "a recurrent or persistent thought, image, impulse, or action that is accompanied by a sense of subjective compulsion and a desire to resist it" (Carr 1974).

2. *Anxiety neurosis*—characterized by diffuse apprehension and fear, often free floating, the cause of which the individual is unable to specify.

3. *Phobic neurosis*—characterized by specific fears that the individual recognizes as unwarranted.

4. *Hysterical neurosis*—characterized usually by multiple somatic complaints that have no evident organic etiology, often distinguished from "conversion symptoms," which are unexplained somatic complaints involving only the nervous system (e.g., paralysis, amnesia, or unconsciousness).

FREQUENCY AND DISTRIBUTION

The determination of accurate frequency figures for the psychoneuroses is an especially difficult task because most individuals with such disorders are never institutionalized. If they are treated for the disorder, they often see private practitioners. Usually the neurotic sees no one for treatment. In the case of phobias, Agras, Sylvester, and Oliveau (1969) found a prevalence in the general population of about 71 per 1000. The highest rates were at age fifty, but different phobias had different peaks. Fear of snakes was highest at age twenty, fear of crowds at age sixty, and fear of injections between the ages of ten and twenty. A history of conversion symptoms was found in 27 percent of normal postpartum women (Farley, Woodruff, and Guze 1968). The disorder is much more common in women than in men.

FAMILY MORBIDITY RISK

There are two ways of estimating family morbidity risk for the psychoneuroses. The first is to obtain clinical information on relatives of the patients and to make diagnoses from that information. The second way is to administer objective personality tests to the relatives to see if they differ from the relatives of controls. Two studies have administered the Maudsley Personality Inventory (MPI) to the relatives of psychoneurotics. In both cases the relatives did not obtain elevated scores on the neuroticism dimension of this scale, as would be predicted from a genetic hypothesis (Coppen, Cowie, and Slater 1965; Rosenberg 1967).

A likely reason for the lack of elevated neuroticism scores among the relatives is that measures of neuroticism are very sensitive to the current state of the subject. Ingham (1966) readministered the neuroticism scale to 119 former neurotic inpatients, of which some were clinically judged to be much better. The neuroticism scores of these improved patients dropped significantly, although they were still somewhat higher than the scores for the general population. If the relatives of the neurotics in the Coppen, Cowie, and Slater and the Rosenberg studies were even less affected than the improved former inpatients of Ingham, it would not be surprising that elevated neuroticism scores were not observed.

Clinical family studies of morbidity risk for the psychoneuroses, in contradiction to those using objective test measures of neuroticism, have consistently revealed elevated rates of psychoneurosis among the first-degree relatives of psychoneurotics. Brown (1942) found 16.4 percent of the parents and siblings of psychoneurotics to be likewise psychoneurotic and another 16.8 percent to have what he described as an anxious personality (which included traits of timidity, excessive worry, and phobia). In a control group, he found only 1.1 percent to be neurotic and another 10.1 percent to be anxious personalities. Thus, Brown's data suggest that the rates of psychoneurosis are elevated among relatives of psychoneurotics. However, this study is compromised by the fact that Brown did not personally interview all relatives but often relied on reports by other relatives. Other clinical studies by Oki (1967) and Sakai (1967) in Japan have likewise revealed elevated rates of psychoneurosis among the families of psychoneurotics.

TWIN STUDIES

Slater and Shields (1969) reviewed six twin studies of psychoneurosis, finding average concordances of about 55 percent for MZ twins and 31 percent for DZ twins. Shields (1973) points out, however, that the MZ-DZ differences might be inflated because investigators often knew of the diagnosis of the index twin as well as the zygosity of the twins. Slater and Shield's (1969) own twin study cannot be criticized on these grounds, since they made diagnoses on the basis of summaries that did not mention diagnosis of zygosity. They found significantly higher concordance rates for anxiety neurosis than for the other categories of neurosis. Forty-one percent of the MZ cotwins of anxiety neurotics were also diagnosed as anxiety neurotic, while only 4 percent of the DZ cotwins of anxiety neurotics were so diagnosed. Among the other forms of neurosis there was zero concordance for both the MZ and the DZ twins.

Thus, the results seem to indicate greater heritability for anxiety neurosis than for the other neuroses. The evidence for the heritability of neuroses generally is not strong, however, nor is there a good indication that genetics plays a predominant role in their cause. Consequently, many investigators have suggested that the contribution of genetics to the neuroses is very limited and that learning plays a much more important role in the neuroses than in the psychoses. For example, Jones (1924) successfully treated a boy's fear of rabbits by systematically feeding the boy in the presence of the animal, gradually moving the boy closer to the rabbit on successive feedings.

It comes as no surprise that anxiety neurosis has a heritable component, because it seems likely that intense autonomic reactivity should play a role in its development. Assuming that autonomic reactivity has a heritable component, one can imagine that a high reactor would be affected severely by just a moderately aversive stimulus while an autonomically phlegmatic individual would hardly respond to the same aversive stimulus.

Carr (1974) points out that high levels of autonomic arousal are also present in obsessive-compulsives, which appear to be reduced only when the patient is permitted to perform his compulsive act. Carr argues that compulsives expect undesirable outcomes. One treatment for compulsive neurosis is to help patients reduce their subjective probabilities regarding aversive outcomes.

ENVIRONMENTAL INFLUENCES

It seems likely that there are a number of paths toward becoming autonomically imbalanced. They can be genetic or environmental in origin, but the central feature appears to be anxiety, which mobilizes the affected individuals to find behaviors that are anxiety reducing. Some will happen upon obsessive-compulsive rituals, others will phobically avoid the stimuli that either realistically or symbolically represent the threat, and still others will be so overwhelmed by the autonomic response that there is no way for them to avoid the reactions; consequently, they develop anxiety neurosis.

It appears that stress may be a critical factor in the development of many illnesses, including neurosis as well as illnesses that have been regarded as exclusively nonpsychological. Selye (1956) showed that animals placed in conditions of extreme stress underwent predictable changes in endocrine function and that these changes increased the likelihood of death. Less traumatic life changes also appear to increase the incidence of disease, particularly if many of these changes bunch together in a short time period. Relatively ordinary events, such as loss of job, divorce, and loss of loved ones, have been found to be associated with increased illness, although the relationships between such events and illness have not been strong (Rahe et al. 1974).

Extreme psychic trauma may be related to later illnesses. Eitinger and Strøm's (1973) carefully done study of Norwegian ex-prisoners of Nazi concentration camps found higher mortality and morbidity during the twenty-one years following their release from the camps. Considering only those who survived the twenty-one years after liberation, the authors selected 498 ex-prisoners to compare with a matched group of nonprisoner controls on the frequency of fourteen medical and psychiatric disorders for these twenty-one years. Unfortunately, standard medical and social service agency records had to be used, so that the reliability of each diagnosis is uncertain. Nevertheless, the results of this study indicated elevated risk for the ex-prisoners for each of the fourteen conditions investigated. The results for those four conditions with previously established psychological components are shown in Figure 9.3. The diagnosis of "neurosis and nervousness" is of course vague, but this diagnosis and the diagnosis of ulcers show especially striking differences between the two groups. The fact that medical disorders such as "diseases of bones, joints, and muscles" also showed

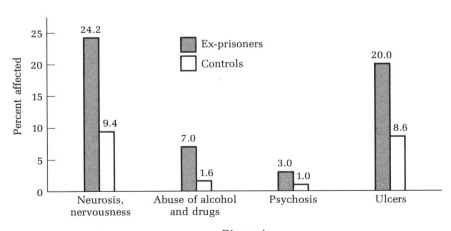

Figure 9.3

Psychologically related disorders in Norwegian ex-prisoners of Nazi concentration camps and controls, 1945–1966. (After Eitinger and Strøm 1973.)

similar relationships to imprisonment indicates that the distinction between psychological and nonpsychological medical disorders may be
strained. These results confirm the view that specific traumatic environmental stress does increase the likelihood of developing an illness
such as neurosis later.

Character Disorders

PSYCHOPATHY AND CRIMINALITY

Psychopathy is a label applied to individuals who seem to be chronically in trouble with the law. They seem to have few affectional ties, are
often callous and impulsively hedonistic, and appear to profit little
from punishment. What is particularly perplexing about the
psychopath's behavior is its self-defeating quality; the gains to be
realized from the behavior often do not appear to be worth the risk.

A useful distinction is drawn between the primary and the secondary
psychopath. The primary psychopath displays little anxiety or guilt
about his behavior, and the secondary psychopath often gives indications of neurotic maladjustment, anxiety, and guilt. In the secondary
psychopath, the antisocial behavior seems to be a consequence of needs
for punishment or recognition rather than a cause.

It appears that a disproportionate number of identified psychopaths
come from environments in which the rearing conditions are far from
satisfactory. Broken homes, poverty, alcoholism, and other signs of familial maladjustment are common in the histories of psychopaths (Robins 1966). These conditions are deplorable, and folk wisdom tells us
that psychopathy is simply a natural outgrowth of being reared in such
an environment. What folk wisdom cannot easily explain is why the
majority of individuals reared in such environments do not become
psychopaths and why some children within a family become
psychopaths while others are spared.

Frequency and Distribution. It is particularly difficult to obtain estimates of psychopathy or criminality in the general population because
"successful" psychopathy may go undetected, and criminality is often
unreported. Rates of psychopathy in various census studies reviewed
by Rosenthal (1970) give frequency estimates ranging from .05 percent
to 15 percent, a 300-fold difference. These discrepancies are partly due
to different diagnostic preferences and different methods of ascertain-
ing the sample. Without agreed-upon methods for diagnosis, reliable
frequency estimates of psychopathy cannot be established. The only
point that seems to be undisputed is that psychopathy or criminality
occurs much more frequently among males than among females, although how much more frequently is uncertain.

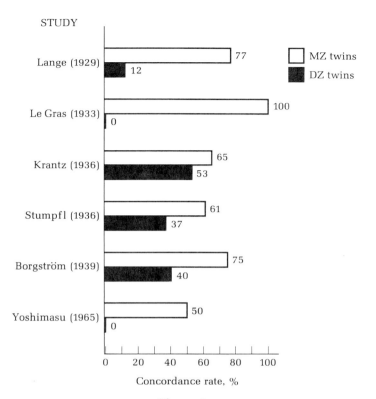

Figure 9.4

Twin concordance rates for criminality. (After
Slater and Cowie 1971.)

Twin Studies. Unfortunately, twin studies of psychopaths per se have
not been conducted. The usual procedure has been to equate
psychopathy with criminality and study concordance rates for criminality. It is not clear what proportion of criminals would actually be
diagnosed as psychopaths, although it is probably a majority among
incarcerated criminals.

Slater and Cowie (1971) have summarized the results of various twin
studies of criminality. These results are shown in Figure 9.4. All six
studies represented in the figure found greater concordance among the
MZ sets than among the DZ sets. Lange (1931) was so persuaded by his
findings suggesting high heritability for criminality that he published a
book called *Crime as Destiny* to emphasize the genetic determination of
criminality.

Adoption Studies. Crowe (1972) has recently reported an adoption
study involving female criminal offenders whose children were given

up for adoption in the state of Iowa. These children were matched to control adopted children for age, sex, race, and age at adoption. For estimates of criminality in these children, Crowe used arrest records obtained from the state; he did not personally interview the children. The results of this study are shown in Table 9.5. The findings indicate that about 13 percent of the children of the criminal probands had arrest and conviction records, whereas only about 2 percent of the children of the controls had been arrested and convicted. The other indications of criminality are likewise elevated among the children of probands, supporting the interpretation that criminality has a heritable component. The 13 percent figures for arrest and conviction for children of the probands may be an underestimate, however, since Crowe examined only records in the state of birth. Interstate mobility is probably substantial, and those who might have been convicted elsewhere were not ascertained. Since the children were adopted at an average age of eighteen months, one cannot be certain that even this short stay with the criminal probands was not an environmental influence on their future behavior (see Crowe 1974 for a discussion).

An adoption study from Denmark also supports the notion of an hereditary component to psychopathy. Schulsinger (1972) defined psychopathy in terms of impulsiveness, acting out, and manipulativeness occurring in adulthood; those with neuroses and psychoses were not considered psychopaths. Fifty-seven psychopaths who had also been adopted were identified and matched to a control group of adoptees on the basis of age, age at first transfer to adoptive home, and adoptive parent social class. The psychiatric hospital records in Denmark were then searched for both the adoptive and biological relatives

Table 9.5

Arrest records of adopted-away offspring of female criminal offenders compared to those of adopted-away controls

Arrest records	Probands	Controls	p
Number of subjects checked for records	52	52	
Subjects with records	8	2	0.046
Total number of arrests	18	2	
Subjects arrested as adults	7	2	0.084
Subjects with convictions	7	1	0.030
Subjects with two or more arrests	4	0	0.059
Subjects incarcerated for an offense	5	0	0.028
Total time incarcerated	3.5 yrs	0	

Source: From R. R. Crowe, "The Adopted Offspring of Women Criminal Offenders," *Archives of General Psychiatry* 27 (1972): 600–603. Copyright © 1972 by the American Medical Association. Reprinted by permission.

of the index and control cases. If there was evidence of a psychiatric history, the data were transcribed and reviewed blindly in order to arrive at an unbiased diagnosis. The major results of this study are shown in Figure 9.5.

Cases were divided into those who gave probable, but incomplete, evidence of psychopathy and those who were clearly psychopathic according to the diagnostic criteria. The results indicated a significant excess of core psychopathy as well as elevated rates of disorders in the psychopathic spectrum (criminality, drug abuse, and alcoholism, among others) in the biological relatives of the index cases in comparison with the biological relatives of the controls. The adoptive relatives of the index and control cases did not differ in the frequency of psychopathy or psychopathic spectrum disorders. Thus, the evidence appears consistently to support the view that psychopathy has an inherited component.

A recent adoption study of registered criminality in Denmark also points to a genetic component. Hutchings and Mednick (1974) compared two groups of adopted children, one with criminal records and the other without. Of the 143 criminal adoptees, 49 percent had a

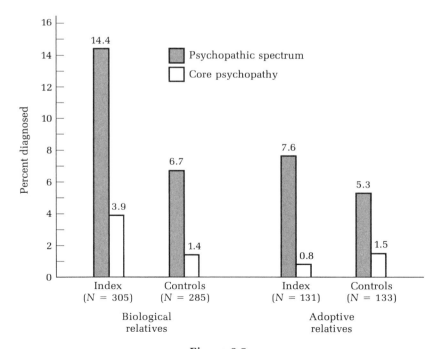

Figure 9.5

Psychopathic disorders in the biological and adoptive relatives of psychopaths and controls. (After Schulsinger 1972.)

biological father who was also a registered criminal. Only 28 percent of the biological fathers of the noncriminal adoptees had a criminal record. However, the authors also point out that 23 percent of the adoptive fathers of the criminals had criminal records, while only 10 percent of the adoptive fathers of the noncriminals had criminal records. Further analyses indicated that registered criminality in the adoptees was promoted by both genetic and environmental influences, although the hereditary ones seemed slightly more potent than the environmental ones.

It should be noted that these data were obtained from arrest records and are not equivalent to a diagnosis of psychopathy. While it is likely that some of the criminals were in fact psychopaths, one cannot determine an exact proportion in these data.

Behavioral Studies of Psychopathic Criminals. It was first demonstrated by Lykken (1957) and then corroborated by Schachter and Latané (1964) that primary psychopaths differ from others in their relative indifference to punishment. For example, Schachter and Latané (1964) had psychopathic prisoners, nonpsychopathic prisoners, and normal controls learn a maze in which each choice point was associated with four alternatives. Only one of the alternatives was correct at each choice point, but of the three incorrect choice points one was associated with a moderately painful shock. The investigators found no difference between the three groups in the rate of learning the maze, but the primary psychopathic prisoners, in contrast to the others, seemed not to learn to especially avoid the one incorrect alternative at each choice point associated with shock. It was as if the primary psychopath did not take special notice of the shock associated with the specific incorrect alternative because it was not particularly distressful to him.

Another study supported the notion that psychopaths are less affected than others by the threat of punishment. Hare (1965) placed psychopathic prisoners with an experimenter who said that he was going to count from one to twelve and that when the number eight was reached there was going to be a painful electric shock. The subjects' skin conductance levels were recorded as an index of autonomic arousal during the counting sequence. Hare found that the psychopathic prisoners seemed to show less autonomic anticipation of the electric shock than did nonpsychopaths and that the anticipatory signs of autonomic reactivity seemed to appear only just before shock onset at number eight. The nonpsychopathic prisoners showed elevated skin conductance levels at numbers much earlier in the sequence. If autonomic reactivity helps to make salient fear and anxiety, as well as serving as an autonomic reminder that trouble is in store, then those who do not have this autonomic assist are likely to be less affected by a future threatening event than those who do have this assist.

Hare's (in press) review of new research in this area has confirmed the finding that psychopaths display reduced skin conductance levels under the threat of pain. Slightly before this reduction, however, it appears that they also show heart rate acceleration. One interpretation of this finding is that the increased heart rate assists the psychopath in tuning out the environment and thus in being less severely affected by the aversive stimulus. An important point to note here is that the nervous system operates as an integrated whole and that studies limited to only one mode of response at a time could not detect this interesting interaction. Whatever the causes of this peculiar response to threat, it does demonstrate an unusual characteristic of psychopaths that can be found at a physiological level, and that is good news. This mechanism of avoiding aversive stimulation may be learned, but psychopaths may be more adept at learning this than nonpsychopaths for a variety of genetic and environmental reasons.

What Is Inherited in Criminality? Although there is evidence of a genetic component in criminality, one cannot conclude that criminality is inherited. Criminality is in part dependent on the social codes of a particular society, and what is defined as criminal changes from time to time. A genetic theory has to account for four facts: (1) the disproportionate number of psychopaths that come from the lower classes, (2) their lack of fearfulness, (3) the often impulsive and unplanned aspects of psychopathic behavior, and (4) the lack of empathy for the discomfort and pain they cause others.

If one supposes that the psychopath inherits an autonomic nervous system that is typically less aroused, but more labile, than normal, then one can explain some of the psychopaths' behavior. Lower arousal could be responsible for lack of fearfulness and planning; greater lability could account for the seemingly impulsive nature of many psychopathic acts. The callousness and deficient empathy of psychopaths could be explained by an autonomic nervous system that does not assist them in representing psychologically the pain they are causing others, perhaps because they have acquired techniques for reducing environmental impact upon themselves. That psychopathy occurs more frequently in the lower classes than in other classes may be a consequence of a realization that many of life's most desirable objects are inaccessible to the lower classes and to get them easily requires illegality. With less of an autonomic deterrent, psychopaths are more willing to transgress.

While this theory seems to account for some of the facts of psychopathy, it should be noted that no clear autonomic defect has yet been demonstrated in psychopaths and that there are some indications from electroencephalograms that a disproportionate number of them may have brain abnormalities. Thus, there is reason to think that psychopaths are actually a heterogeneous group and that the theory will account only for a portion of those labeled as psychopaths.

ALCOHOLISM

Alcoholism is not only a personal problem, it is also a social problem of gigantic proportions. A study of 588 homicides in Philadelphia showed that in 64 percent of the cases alcohol was present in either the victim or the offender (Wolfgang 1958). Blood alcohol levels for drivers killed in single-car crashes indicate that a majority have detectable blood alcohol levels at autopsy.

Definitions of alcoholism vary, but virtually everyone agrees that it involves a pathological dependence on ethanol. Since there is no uniformity in the course of the disorder, it is difficult to specify exactly when an individual is to be diagnosed as alcoholic. If there is physiological dependence such that withdrawal produces tremors, seizures, delirium tremens, or hallucinations, the diagnosis of alcoholism is straightforward. Likewise, when individuals drink despite strong medical contraindications or the possibility of job loss or marriage disruption, alcoholism can be diagnosed. There are a number of early warning signs of alcoholism, such as surreptitious or morning drinking, but these can represent temporary responses to environmental stresses and the diagnosis must be provisional.

Frequency and Distribution.   It is estimated that there are between 4.5 and 10 million alcoholics in the United States. There are wide differences between frequencies of alcoholism in different ethnic groups—Chinese and Jewish groups have low reported frequencies; the Irish have a high frequency. The frequency of alcoholism differs considerably from country to country as well, and it is much more frequent among males than females.

Family Morbidity Risk.   Åmark (1951) obtained risk figures for alcoholism using alcoholic probands and controls in Sweden. He found 26 percent of the fathers, 2 percent of the mothers, 21 percent of the brothers, and 1 percent of the sisters of alcoholics to be alcoholics themselves. Among the controls, the frequency of alcoholism was 3.4 percent for males and 0.1 percent for females. These data show that the frequency of alcoholism is far higher in the relatives of alcoholics than in controls and that males are substantially more likely to become alcoholics than females. Many other studies have likewise confirmed higher rates of alcoholism in the relatives of alcoholics than in the relatives of controls.

Twin Studies. One problem in the twin studies of alcoholism is that investigators have studied twin concordance rates for drinking habits rather than for alcoholism per se. In any representative sample of twins, alcoholism will be fairly rare and thus there is little evidence on twin concordance for alcoholism alone in large twin studies.

Kaij (1960) studied 174 pairs of male twins in Sweden listed on a twin register. He personally interviewed most of them and developed a five-point scale for drinking habits, ranging from total abstention to chronic alcoholism. Chronic alcoholism was defined as an overwhelming desire for alcohol after ingestion of a small dose, regular blackouts, and physical dependence as manifested in withdrawal symptoms. He then rated each set of twins according to their degree of drinking similarity on this scale, calling those with identical ratings concordant. He found that 53 percent of the MZ twins and 28 percent of the DZ twins were concordant for degree of drinking. Partanen, Brunn, and Markkanen (1966) found that MZ twins were slightly, but significantly, more concordant than DZ twins for heavy drinking in Finland.

Adoption Studies. Four adoption studies on alcoholism have been reported, and, unfortunately, their results do not agree. In New York State Roe (1945) studied thirty-six adopted children who had a biological parent described as a "heavy drinker" and twenty-five control adopted children whose biological parents were judged as normal. The average age of the adopted children at the time of the study was 30 years. The children with heavy-drinking parents were placed at an average of 5.6 years, and the control adoptees were placed at an average age of 2.6 years; this difference in age of placement was significant. Also, significantly more of the control children than experimental children were placed in urban environments. None of the index children was judged an excessive drinker, and only 7 percent were regular, although not necessarily excessive, drinkers. Of the control adoptees, 9 percent were judged regular, although not necessarily excessive, drinkers. Thus, there was no indication from these data that the children of the heavy drinkers were at increased risk for alcoholism later.

Goodwin et al. (1973) studied fifty-five men in Denmark who had separated from their biological parents within the first six weeks of life and who had a natural parent that had been hospitalized for alcoholism. These adoptees were matched to two groups of control adoptees. The first group of control adoptees had biological parents with no alcoholic or psychiatric history; the second control group of adoptees had a natural parent who had been hospitalized for a psychiatric condition not involving schizophrenia or alcoholism. The idea was to control for the possibility that psychiatric hospitalization might have a significant influence on the outcome measures, regardless of whether or not alcoholism was involved. The index cases and controls averaged thirty years at the time of the study. A preliminary analysis of the two control groups failed to reveal any differences between them, so they were combined in the subsequent analyses.

The findings indicated that 18 percent of the children of alcoholics were themselves judged to be alcoholics, while only 5 percent of the control adoptees were similarly judged. There was no indication that moderate to heavy drinking short of alcoholism was elevated significantly in the index children.

The authors attempt to reconcile their findings with those of Roe by pointing out that Roe had only twenty-one male children of heavy-drinking parentage and only eleven males of normal parentage. They suggest that the sample size might have been too small to obtain reliable estimates of the frequency of alcoholism among the adoptees. More importantly, in Roe's study the index biological parents were diagnosed not as alcoholic but as "heavy drinkers," and it is not clear what proportion of them would actually have been diagnosed as alcoholic. All of the Goodwin et al. cases had received a hospital diagnosis of alcoholism, and their results seemed to indicate that only alcoholism and not heavy drinking has a heritable component. Goodwin et al. also note that a much greater proportion of Roe's children were placed in rural environments, where alcoholism rates are known to be considerably lower than in urban areas. With these criticisms in mind, it could be argued that the Roe study was not an adequate test of the heritability of alcoholism.

Goodwin et al. (1977) conducted a comparable study with adopted-away daughters of alcoholics. The results of this study failed to demonstrate a heritable component to alcoholism. Sample size for the index cases was small ($n = 49$) for such a rare trait, and perhaps a larger sample size would have made for a better test of the genetic hypothesis. At any rate, failure to find elevated rates of alcoholism in the adopted-away daughters shows that the basis for alcoholic behavior is very complex.

A recent adoption study by Cadoret and Gath (1976a) had only six biological parents with a primary or secondary diagnosis of alcoholism and seventy-eight control biological parents who had either another psychiatric diagnosis or no psychiatric diagnosis. Three of six of the adopted-away offspring with alcoholic biological parentage had a diagnosis of alcoholism, whereas only one of the adopted-away offspring of the seventy-eight control biological parents had a diagnosis of alcoholism. Thus, this study supports the Goodwin et al. findings of a hereditary basis to alcoholism.*

A Half-Sibling Study. Schukit, Goodwin, and Winokur (1972) identified primary alcoholic patients admitted to the alcohol units of two hospitals. The diagnosis of primary alcoholism meant that they were free of other psychiatric disorders not related to alcoholism. Sixty-nine of the patients who also had half-siblings were identified as the probands. Forty-four of the sixty-nine probands were black, and the average age was forty years. These probands and their relatives were interviewed about alcoholism in the family, and the statistical findings were derived from those interviews.

Many of the probands had a biological parent who was also alcoholic. Since the probands were half-siblings, they shared either this alcoholic biological parent or the nonalcoholic biological parent with their half-siblings. The investigators found that 48 percent of the half-siblings who shared the alcoholic biological parent were themselves alcoholic, whereas only about 9 percent of those half-siblings who shared the nonalcoholic biological parent with the proband were diagnosed as alcoholic. Furthermore, the frequency of alcoholism in the half-siblings was independent of whether or not the half-sibling lived with the alcoholic parent during childhood. These results strongly suggest a biological component in alcoholism, but, unfortunately, diagnoses of alcoholism were made not from direct interviews with all relatives but from reports made by other relatives. The data would have been more persuasive if diagnoses had been based on face-to-face contacts with all relatives. Nevertheless, the data generally support the notion of a genetic component to alcoholism, though it is not yet clear what is inherited.

Other Genetic Studies on Alcoholism. Mice can be bred for alcohol preference and tolerance. Some mice strains seem to prefer alcohol to other substances and are less susceptible to intoxication when they ingest it (McClearn 1972).

* Bohman (1978) recently conducted an adoption study in Sweden which strongly supports the view that alcoholism has a heritable component but that criminality does not. He noted that alcoholism and criminality tended to occur conjointly in about one-third of males. If a biological parent of an adoptee was only a criminal and not an alcoholic, however, there was no increased risk for either criminality or alcoholism in the adoptee. If the biological parent was either an alcoholic only or an alcoholic and a criminal, the risk in adopted-away children for alcoholism alone or in conjunction with criminality was higher than the risk in control adoptee samples. Since previous adoption studies of criminality have not distinguished clearly alcoholic criminals from nonalcoholic criminals, it is possible that the genetic component to criminality has been overestimated as a result of its frequent coexistence with alcoholism.

The ability to tolerate alcohol also differs widely between ethnic groups. For example, Wolff (1972) showed that native Japanese, Taiwanese, and Koreans respond with a rapid facial flush and many symptoms of discomfort after ingesting amounts of alcohol that have a negligible effect on Caucasians. He also showed that infants from the Oriental ethnic groups likewise displayed much more facial flushing than Caucasian infants when given small amounts of alcohol, thus ruling out differential postnatal experience with alcohol as being a cause for the difference. In a later study, Wolff (1973) gave alcohol to American Indians and Americans of Oriental ancestry. He found that the American Indians and the Orientals responded with facial flushing to about the same degree and that both groups responded with more flushing than Caucasians.

It has been suggested that flushing and the attendant discomforts account for the low rates of alcoholism among Orientals. The problem is that a simple hypothesis of this sort cannot account for the very high rates of alcoholism among the American Indians, who respond with similar symptoms to alcohol ingestion. Wolff (1973) admits that he has no cogent explanations for the relationship between his findings and the frequency of alcoholism according to ethnicity. He does suggest, however, that in the socially cohesive cultures of the Orientals the visible flushing might elicit sanctions against further intoxication, whereas among the American Indians, whose cultures have been for the most part destroyed, flushing might be socially reinforced and consequently lead to more drinking.

Environmental Factors.   Although the evidence from lower animals and from adoption and half-sibling studies suggests that alcohol preferences have a genetic component, it seems unlikely that the frequency of alcoholism can be explained by genetic factors alone. According to Sarason (1972), alcoholism is on the decline among groups that formerly had high rates of alcoholism (Irish and Swedish-Americans) and is on the increase among groups that formerly had low rates (second- and third-generation Italians). In all probability, these generational changes reflect changing child-rearing and cultural attitudes towards drinking and drunkenness.

Summarizing the findings from a booklet published by the National Institutes of Health (1967), Sarason points out that excessive alcohol intake is minimized when:

1. children are exposed early in life to alcohol, but in diluted amounts and usually within the context of some family or religious ritual;

2. the beverages usually ingested have a low percentage of alcohol;

3. the beverage is considered mainly as food and is usually taken with meals;

4. parents drink only moderately;

5. no moral importance is attached to drinking;

6. drinking is not considered proof of virility or adulthood;

7. abstinence is socially acceptable;

8. excessive drinking is socially acceptable; and

9. the culture group agrees on the point when drinking has gone too far and should be stopped.

The evidence seems to suggest that learning factors cannot be neglected in understanding alcoholic addiction. For many years it was thought that opiate addiction could not be established in lower animals and that the capacity to become an addict was a uniquely human attribute. Nichols (1972) pointed out, however, that an important distinction between human and animal addiction was that animals were administered the drug while humans could give themselves the drug. In 1955 he developed a device by which animals could give themselves opiates and was able to establish that animals could become addicts. He suggests that alcoholic drinking is maintained in the same way as any other reinforced behavior. It is an operant response performed because it is rewarding to the subject.

Childhood Disorders

HYPERACTIVITY AND LEARNING DISABILITIES

These disorders have received a good deal of attention in recent years. It is difficult to discuss them separately, as they often appear simultaneously in the same individual. As soon as children enter school, behavior deviations that impair their learning or obedience come under scrutiny. If these children do not show general intellectual retardation, they are often diagnosed as having minimal brain dysfunction (MBD). It is important to note that the diagnosis of MBD is an inference about a putative infirmity of the brain that is meant to explain these behavior disorders. In many instances, neurological examinations show no "hard" evidence for brain impairment and the diagnosis is made either on "soft" neurological signs, such as motor incoordination, or on a perinatal history that suggests some possibility of trauma.

The determination of the extent of brain injury is clearly a signal-detection problem. As diagnostic techniques improve, or as environmental challenges become more demanding, hitherto undisclosed behavioral impairments will be detected. Whether or not a child is diagnosed as having MBD is partly dependent on historical accidents of technological and educational advances. For example, it has been reported that dyslexia (specific disability in reading) is comparatively rare in Japan, and it has been suggested that the reason for this is the logographic character of the Japanese writing system (Makita 1968). Logography is easier to learn than the alphabetic system because it maintains a one-to-one relationship between symbol and word. The finding that American black children seriously deficient in reading could be taught to read Chinese logographs fairly rapidly suggests that their reading retardation may be associated partly with the alphabetic nature of our written language (Rozin, Poritsky, and Sotsky 1971).

Even when brain injury can be demonstrated in children with MBD, there is not always a one-to-one relationship between the location and character of the brain injury and the behavioral consequences. As Birch (1964) points out:

> We never see an individual whose disturbed behavior is directly a consequence of his brain damage. Instead we see individuals with damage to the nervous system, which may have resulted in some primary disorganization, who have developed patterns of behavior in the course of atypical relations with the developmental environment [p. 8].

Hyperactive children have short attention spans and are easily distracted. They are unable to persist in a single activity for a long period of time, are impulsive and unable to delay gratification, and appear to be chronically unhappy and tense.

Incidence and Frequency.   Minimal brain dysfunction and hyperactivity have been used interchangeably in diagnosis, and it is therefore difficult to give precise estimates for either one of the disorders. Estimates of hyperkinetic disorders range from perhaps 3 percent to 15 percent in children, and they are substantially more frequent among boys than girls (Wender 1971).

Twin Studies.   There has been no large twin study of hyperactive children, although one (Willerman 1973) has reported on activity level concordance among mostly preschool-age twins using a hyperactivity questionnaire completed by the parents. In that study it was shown that activity level had a heritable component (MZ twins correlated .92 and DZ twins correlated .57). The children in the highest 20 percent of the activity scale were culled and labeled hyperactive, and then the MZ-DZ correlations were recomputed; the MZ twins correlated .71 and the DZ sets correlated .00, suggesting a heritable component to activity level even at the higher levels.

Adoption and Family Studies.   Cantwell (1972) and Morrison and Stewart (1971) have reported family studies of hyperactive children. In both studies the family members of these children reported higher frequencies of hyperactivity when they themselves were children as well as more alcoholism, hysteria, and sociopathy in comparison with controls.

Morrison and Stewart (1973) interviewed the natural parents of hyperactive children, the adoptive parents of another group of hyperactive children, and a control group of parents whose children gave no signs of hyperactivity. From the psychiatric interviews they made diagnoses of the hyperactivity of the relatives when they were themselves children.

There was clearly an excess of childhood hyperactivity among the male biological relatives of the hyperactive children and some suggestion of an excess among the female biological relatives of the hyperactive children. Almost 13 percent of the biological fathers, grandfathers, and uncles of the hyperactive children were judged to have been formerly hyperactive, whereas only 3.4 percent of the adoptive male relatives of the hyperactives were so judged. Among the control male relatives of nonhyperactive children, only 0.8 percent were diagnosed as formerly being hyperactive. Elsewhere the investigators report that the biological relatives of the hyperactive children were almost twice as likely as the relatives of controls to have psychiatric diagnoses in areas other than hyperactivity, especially alcoholism. These data strongly suggest a heritable component to hyperactivity, but the authors point out that the diagnoses were made from interviews and, although they took precautions against bias, it is possible that biases still could have entered into the diagnoses.

Safer (1973) reviewed the social service and medical charts of siblings and half-siblings of seventeen foster children diagnosed as having minimal brain dysfunction in Baltimore. These seventeen index foster children all had aberrations in learning, attention, and behavior, IQs of over 70, and no evidence of organic cerebral insult. Hyperactivity and short attention span dominated the clinical picture. In nearly every case the parents had mismanaged the care of these children and had lost legal custody. These index children had been placed in foster homes at an average age of 2.2 years; their full siblings had been placed at 3.0 years; and their half-siblings had been placed at 4.8 years. All half-siblings had the same mother but not the same father. The results indicated that nine of nineteen (47 percent) of the full siblings and only two of twenty-two (9 percent) of the half-siblings were likewise diagnosed as having minimal brain dysfunction. This finding strongly suggested a genetic component to MBD, because the half-siblings shared only 25 percent of their genome with the index cases whereas the full siblings shared about 50 percent of their genome with the index cases.

A recent adoption study in the state of Iowa by Cunningham et al. (1975) also points to hereditary influences in the development of childhood psychiatric disorders. These researchers identified a group of biological parents who had given up their children for adoption early and divided them into two groups, based on whether either biological parent had a psychiatric diagnosis (N = 59) or not (N = 55). Because diagnoses of the parents had to be made from the adoption records, one cannot be confident of the validity of the diagnoses. The adopted children were about seventeen years old at the time of interview, although some were as young as twelve and as old as twenty-four. Psychiatric diagnoses of the children were made by a psychiatrist who was unaware of the psychiatric status of the biological parents.

Results indicated that 50 percent of the male offspring from disturbed parentage were themselves moderately to severely disturbed, whereas only 9 percent of the adopted male offspring of the control parents were similarly diagnosed. Among the female offspring, the authors originally reported that there were no differences according to parentage. In a more recent reanalysis of their data, however, Cadoret et al. (1976) pointed out that the female offspring of the affected parents were more likely to have had somatic complaints as children than the female offspring of the controls.

Interpretation of the data in this study is made more difficult by the facts that the biological parents had a variety of disorders and that there are simply insufficient numbers of cases in any one diagnostic category to make assertions about the exact resemblance of parents and their children for a particular diagnostic category. It is worth noting, however, that 14 percent of the adopted-away offspring of the affected parents were diagnosed as having been hyperactive, while only 2 percent of the adopted controls had been so diagnosed.

Further analyses of the data (Cadoret and Gath, 1976b) showed that, if a biological parent had a diagnosis of antisocial personality or alcoholism, 15 percent of their adopted-away offspring were diagnosed as hyperactive. If the biological parents had either no psychiatric diagnosis or a psychiatric diagnosis other than alcoholism or antisocial personality, only about 5 percent of the offspring were diagnosed as hyperactive. Thus, these findings are consistent in showing a heritable basis for hyperactivity. But they also support the view that hyperactivity may be a childhood manifestation of other forms of disorder in adults.

Treatment. The most popular treatment for hyperactivity in children has been to administer stimulants, mainly amphetamines such as Dexedrine and Ritalin. These drugs have been successful in about 75 percent of cases, and only about 13 percent of the children have shown toxic side effects (Millichap 1973). It might appear paradoxical that stimulants are given to already hyperactive children, but these drugs in appropriate doses help concentration and attention even in normal individuals. Many of us know of college-age friends who have found these drugs successful as assists in studying. For a comprehensive discussion of hyperactivity and minimal brain dysfunction, see Wender (1971).

Family Studies of Learning Disability.   Several genetic studies have been conducted in the search for etiological factors in learning disabilities. Hallgren (1950) studied 116 affected children and 160 other family members who were also affected. His results showed substantial familial clustering of the specific disabilities and provided strong evidence for a genetic etiology.

Owen et al. (1971) reviewed the literature on twin studies of learning disabilities. They found that all twelve MZ twins in the literature were concordant for the disorder and that only seven of seventeen sets of fraternal twins were concordant. The results strongly suggest a genetic basis to learning disabilities, but precisely what is inherited has not been shown.

One suggestion is that the brains of these children mature at slower rates than those of normal children (maturational lag theory), leading to poorer academic performance (Kinsbourne 1973). Rossi (1972) has described a genetically transmitted neurochemical deficit in a small group of learning disabled children who improved rapidly with chemotherapy.

It may be of utility in understanding the etiology of learning disabilities to divide cases into two groups, those with severe disabilities and those with moderate disabilities. This was done with some success in a study by Byrne, Willerman, and Ashmore (1974), which identified children of normal nonverbal intelligence who came to a speech disability center. It was found that those children with *severe* speech disabilities had many signs of having had perinatal and early childhood traumas that might have been related to their speech disorders. Those with *moderate* disabilities, on the other hand, showed only about one-third as many perinatal or early childhood events that might have been deleterious. Most striking was the finding that only 17 percent of the families of the severely affected reported a history of speech disability in another family member, while 55 percent of the moderately affected families reported some family history of speech disability. This suggested that there were at least two distinctive etiologies to speech disabilities; the severe form seemed due to substantial physiological trauma or rare genetic mutations, while the moderate type could be due to either genetic or environmental causes (since other family members displayed similar speech disorders). These findings parallel those of Roberts (1952), who pointed out that the siblings of severely retarded individuals were on the average of normal intelligence but that the siblings of moderately retarded individuals averaged only about 80 IQ.

He suggested then that the severe defects were due to genetic mutations, rare recessive genes, or brain injuries during the course of development and that this is why the same events are unlikely to be duplicated among relatives. The moderate cases were called cultural-familial retardates, who may either represent the lower end of the normal polygenic continuum or have retardation related to cultural factors (or both). This study design is not capable of distinguishing between the cultural and genetic influences among the moderately affected individuals.

It has been suggested by Wender (1971) that some children with learning disabilities, like those with hyperactivity, might benefit from treatment with stimulants. He points out that therapeutic trials with these stimulants take only about three weeks and are relatively inexpensive. He claims that these drugs will sometimes work for learning disabled children and that they ought to be tried before the children are subjected to psychotherapy or to remediation by the other training techniques.

Conclusions

This chapter has examined the evidence for genetic and environmental influences on various forms of psychopathology. On balance, the weight of the studies strongly implicates genetic factors in the severe psychoses and in some of the developmental disabilities of childhood. Other disorders, such as alcoholism and psychopathy, may have some genetic components, but it is not clear how the genetic factors might interact with the environment to produce the syndromes. While there is some evidence for genetic factors in anxiety neurosis, the other forms of psychoneurosis appear to have strong environmental causation. But no adoption studies of psychoneurosis have been conducted, and perhaps it is more judicious to delay final evaluation of the role of genetic factors until such studies have been accomplished.

10

Mental Retardation
and Other Handicapping
Conditions

This chapter will focus on three major handicapping conditions: mental retardation, blindness, and deafness. Mental retardation will occupy the bulk of the chapter, for it is largely a behavioral concept, although it often has its roots in biological determinants. The other two conditions, which are basically medical disorders, are of interest to the psychologist mainly because of their behavioral consequences. Since the blind and the deaf have drastic restrictions in their sensory channels for processing information, one can learn something about the effects of deficits in these channels on behavior in general.

Mental Retardation

ADAPTIVE BEHAVIOR

Mental retardation, as currently defined by the American Association of Mental Deficiency, "refers to significantly subaverage intellectual functioning existing concurrently with deficits in adaptive behavior and

manifested during the developmental period" (Grossman 1973, p. 11).
The most important point to note in this definition is that the diagnosis
of mental retardation requires deficits in *both* intellectual functioning
and adaptive behavior. Adaptive behavior refers to the capacity to perform various duties and social roles appropriate to age and sex. Among
the adaptive behavior indices for the young child might be self-help
skills such as bowel control or dressing oneself; for the adult one index
might be the extent to which the individual can work independently on
a job.

One can find individuals who are deficient in only one of the two
components required for the diagnosis of mental retardation. For example, some are intellectually retarded but not adaptively retarded. These
individuals have been called quasi-retarded and are disproportionately
found among minority group members. Others are adaptively retarded
but not intellectually retarded. These individuals have been called behaviorally maladjusted (Mercer 1973).

Table 10.1 gives some samples of adaptive behaviors associated with
each level of retardation (profound, severe, moderate, and mild) for
individuals of different ages. The level of adaptive deficit is determined
by locating the pattern of behaviors that most closely resembles the
highest level of routine functioning for a given individual and then
checking the ages at the left to determine the approximate level of
deficit. Interpolations based on clinical experience would be required
for individuals at ages between those given. In this table the adaptive
behaviors are only examples, and one would need to consult more
complete tables or other standard adaptive behavior measures, such as
Doll's Vineland Social Maturity Scale (1965), or Cain, Levine, and
Elzey (1963) for more refined descriptions. Keep in mind, however, that
the adaptive behaviors of particular individuals not only reflect their
physiological capacities but also develop in the context of differential
opportunities and motivations to use those adaptive potentials. It is also
important to recognize that physical disabilities independent of intellectual retardation can be responsible for failure to perform many of the
adaptive behavior items.

INTELLIGENCE

Traditional criteria for mental retardation have employed intelligence
tests primarily for diagnosis. Earlier classifications of mental retardation have included terms like *idiot, imbecile,* and *feebleminded,* but
these terms connote a variety of surplus meanings and nowadays more
descriptive and less emotionally loaded terms are used. Table 10.2
provides the old and new labels and the corresponding IQ levels asso-

ciated with the labels. The IQ levels are determined by individually administered intelligence tests and not by group tests, since one can never be sure in group administration whether failures to understand directions or motivational deficits are responsible for poor performances. Since the Stanford-Binet has a standard deviation of 16 and the Wechsler tests have a standard deviation of only 15, it is necessary to give separate corresponding IQ levels for each grade of mental retardation.

FREQUENCY OF MENTAL RETARDATION

In virtually all studies of the prevalence of mental retardation, IQ, and not adaptive behavior, has been employed as the index. Prevalence is usually defined as the number of cases per thousand of the population at risk. It is not always easy, however, to determine the number at risk or the number of mentally retarded individuals within any single population. Sometimes the rates of institutionalization for retardation vary with socioeconomic status, but whether the higher classes institutionalize their defective children more or less frequently than the lower classes may vary unpredictably from country to country. If only institutionalized populations are used, one does not know how many defective children have been kept at home.

Abramowicz and Richardson (1975) reviewed twenty-seven community studies of severe mental retardation (IQ < 50), starting with a report by Lewis (1929), and found that the prevalence rate for severe retardation was about 4 per 1000. No social class correlates of severe retardation were observed; thus, children from the lower classes were no more likely to be severely retarded than children from the higher classes. This lack of social class effect is not the case for the prevalence of moderate retardation, which may be a magnitude higher in the lowest social class than in the highest.

Moderately retarded children have often been termed cultural-familial retardates, largely because one cannot be sure whether socioeconomic or genetic factors are responsible for the elevated frequency of such children among the lowest social classes. More will be said about the moderately retarded later.

Another interesting finding of the Abramowicz and Richardson review was that there were no substantial changes in the prevalence of severe retardation over the past forty-five years. Improved health services and obstetrical techniques may have diminished the likelihood of having a severely retarded child, but those improvements may also have permitted many severely retarded children to survive who would have died earlier.

TWO BROAD CLASSES OF MENTAL RETARDATION

Researchers in mental retardation have established the existence of two generally distinct forms of intellectual deficiency. These two forms have been labeled variously as high-grade versus low-grade defectives, cultural-familial retardates versus those with major gene defects, and normal versus pathological defectives.

Although the essential ingredients of the hypothesis concerning the

Table 10.1

Adaptive behaviors by age

Age and level	Behaviors
≥3 yrs: profound	*Independent functioning*—drinks from cup with help; opens mouth in anticipation of feeding
	Physical—sits unsupported; reaches for objects
	Communication—initiates sounds; smiles back
	Social—recognizes familiar persons and interacts nonverbally
3 yrs: severe	*Independent functioning*—attempts finger feeding; "cooperates" in bathing or dressing
6 yrs: profound	*Physical*—stands alone; coordinates hand-eye movements
	Communication—knows one or two words (e.g., *Mama, ball*)
	Social—responds to others in a predictable fashion; plays patty-cake
3 yrs: moderate	*Independent functioning*—tries to feed self with spoon; indicates wet pants
6 yrs: severe	*Physical*—walks alone steadily
9 yrs: profound	*Communication*—may use four or six words; uses gestures (points)
	Social—plays with others for short periods; recognizes others
3 yrs: mild	*Independent functioning*—feeds self with spoon with considerable spilling; puts on socks and underclothes
6 yrs: moderate	*Physical*—climbs up and down stairs, but not alternating feet; transfers toys to others
9 yrs: severe	*Communication*—uses simple two or three word sentences; names simple common objects
12 yrs: profound	*Social*—interacts with others in simple play activities; shows preferences for some persons over others
6 yrs: mild	*Independent functioning*—feeds self; puts on clothes, although may need help with buttons
9 yrs: moderate	*Physical*—hops and skips; takes steps with alternating feet
12 yrs: severe	*Communication*—has speaking vocabulary over 300 words and uses grammatically correct sentences
≥15 yrs: profound	*Social*—participates in simple group games
9 yrs: mild	*Independent functioning*—feeds self adequately with spoon and fork; can butter bread and tie shoes

different forms of deficiency were evident early in the twentieth century (Pearson and Jaederholm 1913–1914), the complete proposal was most clearly advanced by Roberts (1952) in his lecture to the British Eugenics Society. Summarizing the results of investigations in the area, Roberts concluded

> that the higher-grade defectives, roughly the feebleminded, are the lowest part of the ordinary distribution of intelligence in the population, no more abnormal than the geniuses and near-geniuses at the other end of the

Table 10.1 (continued)

Age and level	Behaviors
12 yrs: moderate ≥15 yrs: severe	*Physical*—runs, skips, hops; can throw ball to hit target *Communication*—has complex sentences; generally speaks clearly and distinctly *Social*—participates in group activities spontaneously *Economic activity*—may be sent on simple errands and make simple purchase with note *Occupation*—prepares simple foods (sandwiches); can set and clear table *Self-direction*—may ask if there's work to do; may pay attention for 10 minutes or more
12 yrs: mild ≥15 yrs: moderate	*Independent functioning*—feeds, bathes, dresses self *Physical*—good body control *Communication*—carries on simple conversation; uses complex sentences *Social*—interacts cooperatively and/or competitively *Economic activity*—can be sent on errands without notes; adds coins and dollars with fair accuracy *Self-direction*—initiates most of own activities; may be conscientious in assuming responsibility
≥15 yrs: mild	*Independent functioning*—cares for personal grooming *Physical*—goes about hometown or local neighborhood in city with ease *Communication*—uses telephone and may write simple letters *Social*—initiates some group activities primarily for social or recreational purposes *Economic activity*—can be sent to several shops to make purchases *Occupation*—can cook simple foods; can engage in semiskilled or simple-skilled job *Self-direction*—initiates most of own activities; but needs guidance for tasks with responsibility (e.g., health care, care of others)

Note: By selecting the pattern most closely resembling the highest level of *routine* functioning for a given individual, one can determine the approximate level of deficit.
Source: From H. Grossman, *Manual on Terminology and Classification in Mental Retardation*, 1973. Reproduced by permission of the American Association on Mental Deficiency.

Table 10.2
IQ classifications for different levels of mental retardation

Retardation		IQ	
Old label	New label	Binet	Wechsler
Idiot	Profound	≤ 19	≤ 24
Imbecile	Severe	35–20	39–25
Moron	Moderate	51–36	54–40
Feebleminded	Mild	68–52	69–55

scale. Below that come the pathological variants, roughly the idiots and imbeciles, owing their mental state to some major accident of heredity or environment [p. 72].

The classic studies in this area that permitted the formulation of the preceding conclusions were essentially of two types. The first type used the normal curve to predict the number of cases in the general population that should fall into any given IQ score interval. An analysis of data gathered on the school children of Stockholm (Pearson and Jaederholm 1913–1914; Pearson 1930–1931) showed that the fit of the normal curve to actual population intelligence figures was three times closer if children from "help classes" (for those with mild and moderate retardation) were included. Inclusion of the severely retarded, however, created a surplus at the very lower end of the distribution. In Roberts's (1952) study of 3361 Bath, England, school children, expected frequencies predicted by the normal curve were compared with the number of cases that actually occurred within designated IQ intervals. The expected frequencies and the actual incidence figures did not differ for IQ above 45. For IQs of 45 and below, however, the actual number of cases was found to be eighteen times greater than the expected number.

The second type of study that suggested a distinction between these two broad classes of mental retardation used expected correlations between relatives sharing varying proportions of their genes (e.g., 50 percent for first-degree relatives and 25 percent for second-degree relatives) to predict resemblances between retardates and their relatives. The assumption that the proportion of gene overlap will be proportional to the correlation between relatives in intelligence allows prediction of the average resemblance that should exist between relatives on a polygenically determined trait. Roberts (1952) found that the correlation between moderately affected retardates and their siblings was .53, while the correlation for the severely retarded and their siblings was not significantly different from zero. A similar study by Penrose (1939) produced parallel findings, although the correlation for moderate retardates and their siblings was slightly lower (.42). In plainer terms, both studies confirmed that the average resemblance between moderate retardates and their siblings was of the order predicted by the polygenic model but that this was not the case for the severely retarded and their siblings. It should be pointed out, however, that these studies have generally neglected the possibility that the average resemblance between moderate retardates and their siblings can be interpreted from either a genetic or an environmental perspective.

Figure 10.1 provides a graphic description of Robert's (1952) findings. This figure gives the IQs of the siblings of the moderately and severely affected cases separately. Clearly, the siblings of the severely deficient cases are close to the normal mean and distribution of intelligence, but the siblings of the moderately retarded score about 20 points lower than the average. The fact that the siblings of the severely affected cases also show an excess of severe retardation has been interpreted as indicating that some of the siblings were likewise afflicted by whatever rare genetic or environmental events had afflicted the first severely retarded sibling.

CAUSES OF MENTAL DEFICIENCY

One partitioning of the causes of mental retardation is given by Penrose (1971) and is shown in Table 10.3. The most outstanding feature of the table is the fact that there is no explanation available for almost 50 percent of mental retardation in the population.

There is little doubt that extreme environmental deprivation increases the risk for mental retardation, both in intellectual and in adaptive behaviors. For example, children reared in substandard orphanages

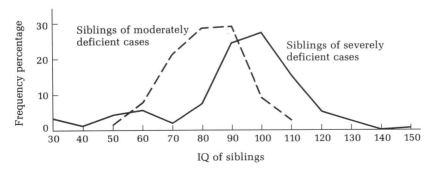

Figure 10.1

Frequency distributions of the IQs of 562 siblings of 149 moderately retarded and 122 severely retarded individuals. (From Roberts 1952.)

Table 10.3

Partitioning the causes of mental retardation

Genetic	Percent
Recessive	5
Dominant	1
Polygenic	15
Sex-linked	1
Total genetic	22
Chromosomal	
Down's syndrome	10
Other autosomal	2
Sex chromosomal	3
Total chromosomal	15
Environmental	
Specified diseases, infections, brain damage	5
Various environmental influences	15
Total known environmental causes	20
Total unknown causes	43

Source: After Penrose 1971.

for prolonged periods are at a much greater risk than other children (Skeels and Dye 1939). How extreme the deprivation must be is not clearly established.

It is difficult to achieve a consensus on the meaning of deprivation. Everyone agrees that extreme social isolation and prolonged nutritional deficiencies are detrimental to the development of intellect. But what about cruel or abusive parents? How could one demonstrate that such parents are unequivocally deleterious to the development of a healthy intellect? The specification of environmental influences and their functional relationships to behavioral outcomes is still one of the most challenging tasks facing investigators.

Of the known genetic causes, polygenes are believed to be the largest single contributor to mental retardation. This is not surprising, given the consistent findings for a substantial polygenic basis to general intelligence. Unfortunately, the number of polygenes entering into intellectual functioning is almost impossible to determine, and, since each polygene is presumed to make only a small contribution to overall intellectual functioning, the potential for eliminating the polygenic causes for mental retardation is limited. Because the effect of a polygene is so small, correcting any negative consequence, even if identified, would probably have only a negligible effect on the overall distribution of mental retardation. Consequently, many have argued that only selective eugenic programs will be successful in eliminating mental retardation in the polygenic range. Rather than trying to understand the specific contribution of each of the polygenes, the argument goes, one should simply discourage those with an unusual accumulation of negative polygenes from reproducing. This way the negative polygenes simply become less frequent and therefore less likely to lead to mental retardation in successive generations.

The actual number of polygenes that enter into intellectual functioning is difficult to determine because the brain is susceptible to adverse influences from distant parts of the body as well as from direct effects; consequently, there can be both distal and proximal polygene effects. In the case of phenylketonuria, a known recessive disorder leading to retardation to be described later, the primary defect is due to an inactive enzyme (phenylalanine hydroxylase) in the liver. Thus, focusing on the biochemical processes of the brain alone will not be sufficient to eliminate all the causes of mental retardation.

DOWN'S SYNDROME—A CHROMOSOMAL EXAMPLE

Down's syndrome probably accounts for 10 percent of all cases of mental retardation and is almost always of the severe type. In all instances the disorder is due to an extra quantity of the genetic material from chromosome 21. You will recall from Chapter 3 that the 22 pairs of autosomes and the pair of sex chromosomes have been assigned numbers according to size from largest to smallest. In about 90 percent of the cases, the disorder is due to an entire extra chromosome 21 (an event known as *trisomy 21*) produced as a result of nondisjunction. As described in Chapter 3, both the egg and the sperm undergo a reduction division (meiosis) before fertilization; it is here that the disorder due to nondisjunction has its origin. Instead of each going into separate eggs or sperm, the two chromosome 21s enter the same sex cell. The process of fertilization and duplication then continues in the usual fashion for the cell with the double chromosome, but every one of the cells of that zygote now contains an extra twenty-first chromosome (two from the abnormal cell division and one from the normal gamete of the other parent).

The incidence of the nondisjunction form of Down's syndrome is strongly related to maternal age, although the disorder can also occur as a result of nondisjunction on the paternal side. It has been estimated that the nondisjunctive form of the disorder has an incidence of only 1 in 1500 for mothers under thirty years of age. For women between thirty and forty, the incidence is about 1 in 477. For women of forty to forty-four years, however, the frequency is about 1 in 130. For women over forty-four, the frequency of the disorder may be as high as 1 in 16 (Lindjsö 1974). It has been recommended that women over thirty-five undergo amniocentesis in the twelfth to fifteenth week of pregnancy to determine whether the fetus is afflicted with Down's syndrome, since the disorder can be reliably identified then. If the mother is found to be carrying an affected fetus, she can have the option of abortion. Indications are that the maternal nondisjunction in Down's syndrome may be related to an excessive quantity of maternal antibodies against the mother's own tissue (Fialkow 1967).

The second type of chromosomal abnormality producing Down's syndrome is called the *mosaic* form, which results in nondisjunction after fertilization and after at least one duplication of the zygote. If nondisjunction occurs at the second duplication, two of the four cells will have the normal complement of 46 chromosomes and one of the two remaining cells will have only 45 chromosomes (monosomy) and will die out. The remaining cell will have 47 chromosomes and will duplicate normally from then on. Thus, approximately one-third of the cells of the entire individual will finally be trisomic, and two-thirds will be normal. In this form of Down's syndrome it is necessary to test for the trisomy in a number of different cells, for some will be normal and only some will be abnormal.

The third type of Down's syndrome is the *translocation* type, which results when all or a part of the twenty-first chromosome becomes attached to one of the chromosomes in the 13–15 group or in the 21–22 group. In about one-third of such cases one of the parents is a genetically balanced carrier of the disorder. This parent appears normal but has only 45 separate chromosomes; the translocated chromosome functions as a normal chromosome 21, and there is only one other unattached normal chromosome 21. Thus, while there are 45 separated chromosomes, the parent really has 46 independently functioning chromosomes. During meiosis of the egg or sperm, the translocation may enter the same cell as the other chromosome number 21 so that after fertilization there will be a total of three such chromosomes (two from the translocation parent and one from the normal parent). The affected child will, however, have only 46 separated chromosomes. However, if the fertilized cell by chance has the other normal chromosome from the 13–15 group or the 21–22 group and the normal chromosome number 21, the offspring will be normal. If the mother is the translocation carrier, there is about a 15 percent chance that the offspring will have Down's syndrome. If the father is the translocation carrier, the risk is only about 5 percent. The difference is probably due to the relatively reduced viability of the translocated sperm. The translocation form is unrelated to maternal or paternal age.

IQs of children with Down's syndrome tend to be higher if the children remain at home than if they enter institutions. For children at home, the average IQ is 40 to 50. For those in institutions, IQs tend to be below 35 (Lodge and Kleinfeld 1973). Johnson and Olley (1971) have reviewed studies of behavioral comparisons of those having Down's syndrome and a variety of retarded control groups, finding no consistent differences between them and other groups matched for IQ. They point out, however, that there have been too few studies to draw firm conclusions on this matter. It is clear that more studies in this area need to be done. If we cannot identify information-processing deficits specific to well-identified syndromes like Down's, we are probably not going to make much progress in understanding the nature of the intellectual and sensory deficits among other groups of retardates. Presumably, intellectual deficits leading to low IQ can be the result of many different causes, and the low IQ score is only the final common path for these varied etiologies.

Other trisomies leading to mental retardation have also been identified (trisomies 13 and 18), and there are others involving partial deletions of a particular chromosome. One, called the *cri du chat* ("cry of the cat") syndrome is due to a deletion on the short arm of chromosome 5. It can be identified readily in infancy, when the child makes a high-pitched kitten-like cry and has a number of other stigmata that make the child easily diagnosed. This peculiar cry tends to disappear later, and the disorder is associated with severe mental retardation. No monosomies have been identified (except those involving the sex chromosomes) that produce mental retardation. Apparently all autosomal monosomies are lethal.

DOMINANT GENES

Most dominant genes that might be associated with mental deficiency are the result of fresh mutations, usually because the disorders themselves are so incapacitating that they do not permit reproduction and therefore passage to the next generation. Other dominant gene disorders are incompletely penetrant on occasion, so that a carrier may be only mildly affected and consequently may reproduce. In these cases the child is often more severely affected than the parent.

RECESSIVE GENES

Many disorders leading to mental retardation are associated with recessive genes. Dewey et al. (1965) tried to estimate the number of different recessive genes that contribute to mental retardation by examining families in which the parents were of normal intelligence but had produced at least two children with IQs of less than 50. Excluded were families in which the children had disorders known to be caused by other than recessive genes (e.g., Down's syndrome, trauma, infection). Using data from Wisconsin institutions and from Penrose's (1939) survey in Colchester, England, the authors estimated that about 12 percent of the mentally retarded in this group of children with IQs of less than 50 had disorders due to recessive genes; the remainder of the retardates were regarded as sporadic cases of unknown origin (traumas, other environmental causes, incompletely penetrant dominant genes, chromosomal aberrations). The authors estimated that the number of different recessive genes leading to mental retardation in the 12 percent was somewhere between 114 and 330. The attempt to understand the specific metabolic defects among each of these recessive disorders is a massive undertaking, and Cavalli-Sforza and Bodmer (1971) have suggested that even the estimate of 330 different recessive genes may still be too low. As would be predicted, Dewey et al. (1965) also noted an excessive amount of consanguinity among the mentally retarded families with recessive gene disorders.

PHENYLKETONURIA (PKU)—A RECESSIVE EXAMPLE

It was Garrod's (1909) discovery of inborn errors of metabolism that suggested that a single gene deficiency leads to a single enzymatic deficiency and then to a clinical abnormality. When Følling (1934) described ten mental retardates, some of whom were siblings, who secreted phenylpyruvic acid in their urine, the suggestion was clearly confirmed. Later, Jervis (1939) showed that the disorder was due to an autosomal recessive gene and found that phenylalanine hydroxylase in the liver was inactive in these patients (1953). A fairly effective preventive therapy was then developed that involved diets low in phenylalanine so that the culprit amino acid would not accumulate (Armstrong and Tyler 1955; Bickel, Gerrard, and Hickmans 1954). A newborn screening test for PKU was developed in 1963 (Guthrie and Susi). Since the test yields some false positives, careful follow-up must be done to confirm that the infant genuinely has PKU.

Although PKU accounts for only about 1 percent of the mentally defective population, it has received a great deal of attention because an understanding of the exact pathway from the enzymatic defect to its effects on the central nervous system may provide a model for understanding the mechanisms behind other recessive disorders. As yet it is not clear how excessive phenylalanine levels impair the central nervous system.

One way in which a positive newborn screening test can be confirmed is by examining the parents for elevated levels of phenylalanine.

It is possible to detect heterozygous carriers of the disorder by determining the amount of phenylalanine in the blood either after fasting or
after a dose of the amino acid. Schematic results for the identification of
heterozygosity are shown in Figure 10.2.

These data on detecting heterozygosity show quite clearly that the
average heterozygote carrier has substantially more phenylalanine in
the blood plasma than do normal controls. While there is some overlap
between the controls and the carriers, the likelihood that *both* parents of
an infant with high phenylalanine levels also have high levels themselves would be small if chance alone were operating.

Knox (1972) has provided a comprehensive review of the symptom-
atology and biochemistry of PKU. In the first few weeks after birth,
blood phenylalanine levels are thirty times higher than normal; a
bit later mental retardation is evident; and reduced pigmentation,
eczema, or seizures may occur. The majority of untreated patients are in
the profoundly retarded range; a few may be severely retarded; and
some may be only moderately retarded.

Early detection and treatment of the disorder with a diet low in
phenylalanine reverses all the circulating biochemical abnormalities,
although previously existing structural defects cannot be eliminated.
IQs of children treated early tend to be in the low 90s, and, for some

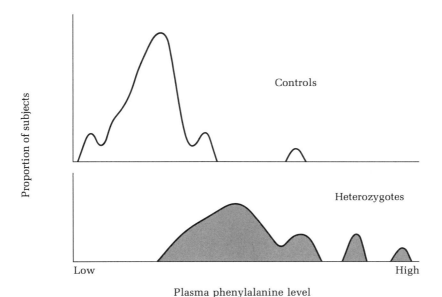

Figure 10.2

Plasma phenylalanine levels in heterozygote carriers
of the PKU gene and in normal controls.

reason, the IQs still fall slightly below those of unaffected siblings (Berman and Ford 1970; *Collaborative Study of Children Treated for Phenylketonuria,* 1975). It is quite important to begin treatment early in infancy, since late treatment is likely to be ineffective in correcting any intellectual deficits.

SEX-LINKED GENES

A chapter in Robinson and Robinson (with the collaboration of Omenn and Campione, 1976) gives details of many other genetic and chromosomal disorders leading to mental retardation. One disorder of special behavioral interest is the *Lesch-Nyhan syndrome* (Lesch and Nyhan 1964), which is caused by a sex-linked gene. Boys who suffer from this disorder have hyperuricemia (high uric acid levels in the blood) and usually test below 50 IQ. The striking and puzzling feature about them, however, is their self-mutilation. Omenn describes affected children who bite off their lips while crying out in pain so that the teeth must be removed. These children appear happy only when bindings restrain them from biting their lips. Nyhan (1973) points out that their tested mental development is probably an underestimate, for they appear to have a good sense of humor and may be quite engaging. There is no effective therapy for the disorder.

Unfortunately, recessive disorders are not easily eliminated from the population. The vast majority of individuals carrying recessive genes is heterozygotic; consequently, the genes are not readily detected. The rarer the disorder, the greater the ratio of carriers to affected cases. To give but one example, if a fully penetrant recessive disorder occurs once in 1000 times, there will be about 61 heterozygous carriers of the gene in that population of 1000. If the disorder is even rarer, such that it occurs only once in 10,000 times, there will be 198 heterozygous carriers among those 10,000. Devising detection programs, even if the heterozygote state can be determined, is a major undertaking.

CONCENTRATION IN FAMILIES

Mental retardation is very much a family affair. Regardless of one's theories of mental retardation, it does tend to concentrate in families. The monumental study by Reed and Reed (1965) of more than 82,000 relatives of 289 mentally retarded white probands in Minnesota institutions between 1911 and 1918 showed this clearly. The criterion for mental retardation used in the study was an IQ below 70 if an IQ score was available, or strong indications of scholastic retardation in lieu of an IQ score.

The probands were divided into four categories according to the probable cause of mental retardation. The *primarily genetic* group had well-defined chromosomal or genetic abnormalities, or there was evidence of parental consanguinity. The *probably genetic* group contained probands whose family consisted of three or more consecutive generations that had at least one mentally retarded individual. The *environmental* group was composed of individuals who were retarded because of infections, traumata, or other events. The fourth group had *unknown* causes for their mental retardation. Results from this study are shown in Table 10.4.

The first thing to note is that the incidence of mental retardation in the parents and siblings of the retarded probands was substantially higher than the incidence of retardation in the children of the probands (only 57 percent of the probands reproduced). This fact probably indicates a bias in the institutionalized proband population. Parents who were themselves retarded or who had another retarded child would be more likely to institutionalize their offspring because they would have fewer resources for caring for the child in the home than would other parents. Thus, the least biased retardation risk figures are probably those for the children of the institutionalized probands.

The incidence of retardation in the children of probands in the primarily genetic category is about half of that in the children of the

Table 10.4

Percentages of mental retardation in the relatives of retardates according to the category of retardation

Relationship to retarded and generation level	Category of retardation of the patient				
	Primarily genetic	Probably genetic	Environ-mental	Un-known	Total
First-degree relatives					
Parents	35.1	69.1	26.0	18.2	33.4
Siblings	33.8	44.1	20.0	14.9	26.3
Children	12.5	27.6	—	9.7	16.3
Second-degree relatives					
Grandparents	6.0	20.9	0.9	0.2	5.9
Uncles and aunts	10.4	21.5	3.9	4.0	9.0
Half-siblings	17.2	22.5	—	12.5	16.8
Nephews and nieces	6.7	10.3	0.4	1.6	4.8
Grandchildren	5.3	9.4	—	1.6	4.4

Note: Dashes in the body of the table indicate that there were fewer than twenty persons in that category.
Source: From E. W. Reed and S. H. Reed, *Mental Retardation: A Family Study*. W. B. Saunders Company. Copyright © 1965.

probably genetic category. This relationship is to be expected, since the primarily genetic group contains many recessive disorders and products of consanguineous unions who would not be likely to duplicate the circumstances of their parents' genetic situation with their own partner (e.g., mate incestuously or with another carrier of the same recessive gene).

The actual percentages in each of the categories are broad estimates for the incidence of mental retardation among the families of mentally retarded probands and can be seen to fluctuate considerably, depending on other classifications too detailed to discuss here. For example, in the probably genetic category, the incidence of retardation in the offspring of the probands is three times higher for an illegitimate child than for a legitimate child. This difference might be due to a variety of differences in the spouses in the two types of matings (such as consanguinity), but it serves to indicate the difficulties involved in making very confident interpretations of this aspect of the data.

Reed and Reed provide only a limited discussion of social deprivation and its role in the development of mental retardation. One might anticipate that particularly for the probably genetic category, whose members come from three successive generations of retardation, environmental factors might be of considerable importance. Reed and Reed do provide, however, an extremely interesting table about the intelligence of children of at least one retarded parent. The results of the Reeds' analysis are shown in Figure 10.3.

This figure gives mean IQs according to which parent is retarded. If only the father is retarded, then 7 percent of the children are retarded. If

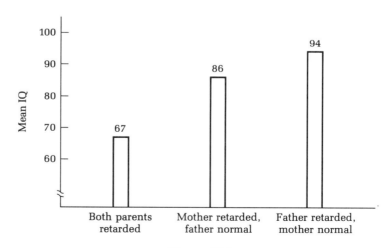

Figure 10.3

Mean IQs of offspring according to parental
retardation. (After Reed and Reed 1965.)

the mother is retarded and the father is not retarded, then 18 percent of the children are retarded. About 61 percent of children of unions of two retardates are themselves mentally retarded.

The greater frequency of retardation when only the mother is retarded than when only the father is retarded must be the result of a maternal effect. Since the mother is the primary agent of socialization, she probably has a greater influence on the intellectual development of the child than does the father. Thus, a mentally retarded mother would have a greater effect than would a mentally retarded father. This finding, however, is subject to another competing interpretation, known as the threshold hypothesis (e.g., Freire-Maia, Freire-Maia, and Morton 1974). Since there is evidence that males are more susceptible than females to mental retardation, it could be argued that affected females must have a greater "dose" of deleterious genes in order to be mentally retarded. If so, then, on the average, mentally retarded males would be less likely to produce mentally retarded children since they would pass a lower dose of deleterious genes than would mentally retarded females. As a corollary, the male offspring of such matings would be more likely to be retarded than would the female offspring. Freire-Maia, Freire-Maia, and Morton compared the maternal effect hypothesis to the threshold hypothesis, using the data of Reed and Reed (1965), and found that the threshold hypothesis seemed to be upheld while the maternal effect hypothesis was not.

The Reeds performed another interesting analysis on the frequency of mental retardation in the "unselected" relatives of the original probands, concluding that "1 to 2 percent of our population composed of fertile retardates produced 36.1 percent of the retardates of the next generation, while the other 98 or 99% of the population produced only 63.9 percent of the retarded persons of the next generation" (Reed and Reed 1965, p. 48).

CATTELL'S PARADOX

For some time it has been known that there is a negative relationship of about $-.20$ between IQ and family size (Cattell 1951). This relationship has been interpreted as suggesting that the intelligence of the population should be declining with successive generations, for the least intelligent are producing more children. Data on this proposition, however, have not supported the prediction of secular decreases in IQ; this has been called Cattell's paradox. The solution to the paradox was given by Higgins, Reed, and Reed (1962), using the Minnesota data. They too confirmed that there was a negative relationship between IQ and family size, but they demonstrated that this relationship takes into account only fertile individuals—those who have produced at least one child. If one takes into account the many nonreproducing individuals, one sees a slight positive relationship between IQ and family size. What turns the relationship around is the fact that there is a great proportion of retarded individuals that never reproduce. There is no need to worry that the intelligence of the population is declining, although one might justifiably be concerned about the fact that retarded individuals contribute a disproportionate number of retardates to the next generation. A study by Bajema (1963) using IQ scores obtained from school records in Michigan yielded conclusions that were very similar to those of Higgins, Reed, and Reed.

PSYCHOLOGICAL THEORIES OF MENTAL RETARDATION

MA-IQ Distinctions. Before beginning a discussion of psychological theories of mental retardation, we must make an excursion into the differential meanings attributed to mental age (MA), chronological age (CA), and IQ. The concept of MA comes from the developers of the Stanford-Binet test and refers to the level of cognitive functioning achieved by a child. The expected MA for children of a given age is closely tied to CA in that the average child of five is expected to have a MA of five and the average child of eleven is expected to have a MA of eleven. Note that MA is defined in terms of *average* performance at a given CA and does not mean either that individuals above or below that CA cannot obtain the same MA or that children of a given CA cannot obtain MAs above or below that level.

Furthermore, although two people may have identical MAs, there is considerable latitude for how that MA is reached. For example, it is possible for a seven-year-old to obtain a MA of eight by passing all items at the seven- and eight-year levels and none thereafter. Another child of equal CA can obtain the same MA by passing all items at age seven and two of six items at ages eight, nine, and ten, passing none thereafter. While one would say that the second child displayed more scatter in intellectual performance than the first, in terms of MA level, the two children would be indistinguishable in terms of the IQ score.

Although it is not difficult to understand the procedure by which MAs are obtained, there are a number of problems attending its interpretation. First, the age variability for passing an item is related to the age level at which it is placed. An item of moderate difficulty for three-year-olds may be extremely difficult for two-year-olds and quite easy for four-year-olds, but an item placed at the twelve-year-old level may be passed by children as young as seven or eight and not passed by some adults.

Second, the fairly linear relation of MA to CA tends to deteriorate after age fourteen or so. For example, while it is usually easy to find items that many more six-year-olds than five-year-olds will pass, it is harder to find items that many more fifteen-year-olds than fourteen-year-olds will pass.

Third, it is of some dispute whether two individuals of equal MA but differing CA are equal in terms of *level* of mental development. For example, a child of ten with an MA of six is retarded, while a six-year-old with the same MA is average in intelligence. These children are likely to differ on many physical and personality dimensions as well.

In comparisons of retarded individuals and controls, the problems of choosing the controls have been vexatious. If the normal controls and the retarded are of equal MA, the controls will be of younger age and higher IQ. If the normal controls and the retarded are of equal CA, the controls will be of higher MA and IQ. Although IQ is theoretically independent of CA, in a group of equal MAs, IQ is negatively correlated with CA. It is impossible to control CA and MA simultaneously and to allow IQ to vary. Only if CA itself were found to be unimportant to learning or to any other relevant outcome measures could the problem be reduced to the influence of two separate psychological variables, MA and IQ. Zeaman and House (1967) reviewed the literature on CA as an independent variable in studies of learning and found that the influence of CA shows "unreliable, zero, and negative correlations, unless accompanied by large MA differences.... The evidence on this matter is not overwhelming, and may be variously interpreted, but we do wish to suggest that our basic assumption of the irrelevance of CA is not without empirical support" (p. 194).

Other indications that CA itself may be of little value in understanding mental development comes from evidence reviewed elsewhere in this book (Chapter 11) showing that children of a given CA can have funds of information far beyond that expected for their age and certainly far beyond what has been explicitly taught in school. What CA presumably represents is both physiological maturation and opportunity; those with higher CAs are physiologically more mature than those with lower CAs and have been exposed to the sources of information that serve as the fundamental data ingredients for information processing. Physiological maturity may be very important in young children, since brain maturation itself may be necessary for the accomplishment of certain cognitive tasks (e.g., five-year-olds can copy a square but not a diamond, while seven-year-olds can usually copy both).

Whether MA or IQ is the more important index for understanding the cognitive process in retardation is an empirical question. To be sure, it is IQ and not MA that defines mental retardation; aside from that distinction, however, can it be shown that one index is more useful than the other? Harter (1965, 1967) demonstrated in a discrimination learning experiment that MA and IQ could make independent contributions to the prediction of learning. She argued that MA represented the amount of prior learning, and, if that fund of information were useful in solving a new problem, MA would predict the speed of learning. In this model IQ is regarded as an index of the relative speed with which the subject characteristically acquires new strategies, skills, or concepts and therefore would also predict speed of learning in experimental situations. The distinction, admittedly, is not an easy one to draw, but imagine a thought experiment in which subjects were asked to solve a problem for which no prior information is of use. The theory hypothesizes that IQ, but not MA, will determine the rate at which this new problem is learned. If the imaginary experiment required only the application of old information and not the acquisition of new strategies, however, it would be anticipated that MA and not IQ would determine the speed of learning.

This example is fanciful, and the actual situation is undoubtedly more complicated. Furby (1974) elaborated on Harter's interpretation, arguing that IQ represents an index of the speed of *habituation* of the orienting reflex (OR), which is a built-in attention response to a salient novel stimulus. The idea here is that if one habituates slowly to the most salient cues in a problem-solving situation, one has less time or opportunity to consider the subtle cues. If the most salient cue also happens to be the necessary one for solving the problem, then IQ will play little part in the rate at which the problem is solved. If the subtle cues are more important, however, IQ will be critical. In Furby's words,

> ... one of the major differences between "retarded" and "normal" children in regard to problem-solving performance is that lower-IQ children respond more to the salient cues or schemata than do the higher-IQ children because ... their OR habituation (both simple and serial) is slower than that of higher-IQ children.... One major determinant of rate of cognitive development, and thus IQ scores, would appear to be the speed of OR habituation, and thus the ability to use less salient schemata and to form new ones within a given period of time. Consistent with this interpretation of IQ, it is suggested that one major determinant of level of cognitive development, and thus of MA score, is the number of schemata already acquired [1974, p. 121].

· Note that an essential feature of this interpretation hinges on the speed of information processing and is fully compatible with the findings on relationships between speed of habituation in infancy and later intelligence (Lewis 1975) and the research of Hunt, Lunneborg, and Lewis (1975).

Learning.   The influential work of Zeaman and House (1967; Zeaman 1973) bears critically on the preceding interpretation. In comparisons of mentally retarded and normals during problem solving, they found that retardates and normals differed mainly in the length of time it took them to "catch on" to the correct cues for solving the problem. Once the retardates caught on, it appeared that the rate at which they solved the problem was little different from that of the normal controls. In examining backward learning curves (Hayes 1953) for discrimination learning, these authors showed that retardates performed at essentially guessing levels for longer periods of time than did normals. Once the retardates started moving toward the correct solution, however, they did not differ from normals in the number of trials it took to reach criterion.

The way backward learning curves work is as follows. Suppose one subject took twenty-five trials to reach criterion and another took fifty trials. One simply ignores the actual number of trials to reach criterion but plots backward the learning curve from the trial on which the criterion was reached, irrespective of the number of that particular trial. Thus, the backward curves can be constructed using notations such as "criterion minus one trial," "criterion minus two trials," and so on. While there may be little doubt that the two hypothetical subjects differed in the number of trials they took to reach criterion, the important point that this technique exposes is whether or not the *rate* of learning in the immediate vicinity of the criterion differed for the two subjects. This approach also permits the investigator to equate subjects by using the notations of criterion minus one, criterion minus two, and so on, and to construct group learning curves. Figure 10.4 shows a group learning curve based on the data of Zeaman and House (1963). It is quite clear that the learning slopes are very similar for the quick learners and the slow learners (the dip at the end for the learners reflects the fact that one trial beyond criterion is usually plotted also).

Zeaman and House (1963, 1967; Zeaman 1973) have highlighted an alternative approach to the understanding of mental processes in retardation. Instead of simply contrasting retardates to controls on a variety of measures, they have tried to estimate the parameters of information processing in mathematical terms for the mentally retarded alone. These mathematical statements represent a meaningful advance, for they can lead to independent and unexpected predictions and insights when the mathematics is manipulated independently from the data on which it was originally based.

Zeaman and House have labeled the following parameters as deserving more investigation: (1) *Alpha*, which represents the bias for preferring old to new information when there is limited space in short-term memory; (2) *Beta*, which refers to the maximum buffer size and is equal to the number of chunks of information that can be rehearsed actively in short-term memory (Simon 1974); (3) *Delta*, which refers to the rate at which information is lost from short-term memory; and (4) *maximum breadth of attention*, which is essentially a measure of the speed of

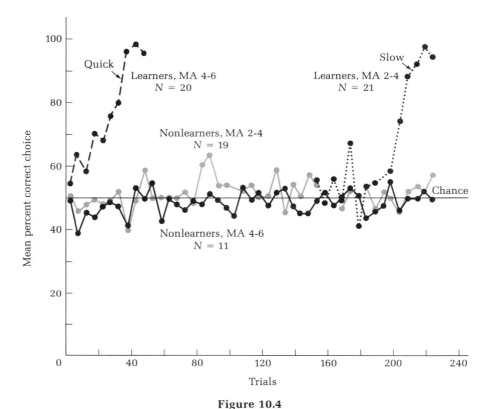

Figure 10.4

Intelligence and discrimination learning. (From Zeaman and House 1963.)

scanning information in the stimulus or in the short-term memory store. Zeaman and House believe that the difficulty that retardates have in solving visual discrimination problems lies in the attention and retention processes rather than in learning per se.

Learning Versus Memory.   Traditional psychology has maintained a distinction between learning and memory, but this distinction is now becoming blurred. If learning is defined as a change in response probabilities as relevant experiences accumulate, then the subject obviously must have access to some memory store of the preceding events in order to increase the probabilities of correctly responding on the next trial.

Learning and memory, however, are critically dependent on attention to the relevant cues in the environment and on encoding them in a fashion that ensures retrieval when necessary. It is possible to attend to the relevant stimuli and yet not encode them in a manner permitting access. For example, a string of nine digits is usually difficult to recall without grouping them into chunks of three or so. A subject can attend to all digits, yet fail to group, and consequently not recall all the digits.

Clustering. There is considerable evidence that retardates fail to chunk stimuli so as to facilitate their later retrieval. Spitz (1973) reviewed the studies on this matter, pointing out that, when stimuli are presented in random order, mature individuals of normal intelligence will cluster them so as to facilitate recall; retardates don't do this as often. However, when the stimuli are already grouped for the retardates (e.g., all animals, all foods, etc.), there is a dramatic improvement in recall. The problem is that retardates do not spontaneously cluster, when caught unawares, even after training in clustering. A review of clustering phenomena can be found in Jensen (1971c).

Retardates not only fail to cluster spontaneously but also seem unable to process information at the rate that normals do. For example, one study (see Spitz 1973) varied the numbers of randomly arrayed dots displayed for one second and asked subjects to estimate the numbers of dots shown. The retardates could make correct discriminations when four or five dots were shown but not when six dots were presented. If exposure time was increased to four seconds, these subjects were able to discriminate up to six dots. Other studies of memory processes in both visual and auditory modes confirm the proposition that the short-term memory capacities of retardates are clearly less than those of controls.

It would be foolishly optimistic to believe that the varieties of mental retardation can be attributed to some single and sovereign information-processing deficiency. While many investigators acknowledge the distinction between the cultural-familial form of mental retardation and the more severe forms representing major environmental deviations or single-gene disorders, it is likely that this differentiation will be insufficient for the task of identifying information-processing deficiencies. Just as geneticists have discovered separate biological causes for many forms of mental retardation, psychologists will probably have to further differentiate mental retardation into very specific classes of information-processing deficiencies. Thus, some retardates may have difficulties in the peripheral processing of information; others may have deficiencies in short-term memory capacities (perhaps of a very specific nature); and others may lack processing characteristics not yet specified. What seems needed is a set of tests sampling each of the relevant aspects of information processing so that further subdivisions may be made within the domain.

The majority of studies in mental retardation have focused on comparisons between retardates and controls, and have been satisfied simply to determine whether or not the groups differ on some specific information-processing variable of interest to the experimenter. Within retarded groups, however, it might be that only some of the subjects have the deficiency of interest to the experimenter; consequently, group comparisons may not produce statistically significant results. If the specific deficiency is rarely found among the group of retardates, the wheat may be discarded with the chaff. While there may yet be discovered a "big theory" that accounts for much mental retardation, it is more likely that many little theories will need to be adduced instead.

Developmental Versus Defective Retardation.   Zigler (1967) has identified two orientations toward mental retardation. The first view, called the developmental view, regards the familial retardate as essentially a normal individual of low intelligence whose cognitive growth is essentially like that of the normal child, except that its rate is slower and its ultimate level is lower. In this model, equating retardates and normals for MA (by using younger normal controls) should not produce differences on many cognitive processing measures. The second view regards all retardates as defective and as suffering from some specific physiological deficits. When MA is controlled, one should still observe behavioral differences between retardates and controls.

It is difficult to summarize the results of the many studies that assess the relative merits of one or the other position. It should be noted, however, that if the familial retardates simply represent the lower portion of the normal distribution of intelligence, and if intelligence has a genetic component, then these individuals will need no more "explaining" than those who are in the normal or above-normal range. That is, in order to understand familial retardates, one will need to understand those biological processes that relate to intellectual functioning in general and not just to familial retardates.

Primary Versus Secondary Retardation.   Jensen (1970a) has distinguished two types of familial mental retardation: Level I retardation is the primary form and results from deficits in simple associative or rote learning abilities; Level II retardation is the secondary form and is due to deficits in abstraction or conceptual abilities. Severe deficits in Level I always lead to retardation as measured on IQ tests, because some minimal memory is necessary for the advanced conceptual abilities generally called for on these tests. Level II retardation is not usually associated with deficits in Level I abilities, although it can be because Level I retardation would affect Level II processes.

Among the pieces of evidence prompting Jensen to propose this distinction is the finding that differences between retardates and normals or superior subjects are often minimal on rote learning measures but large on tests calling for abstraction abilities. In one study of associative learning ability (Jensen 1963), for example, special classes of retardates averaging 66 IQ were compared with one group of children averaging 103 IQ and with another group of gifted children averaging 143 IQ. Although the rote learning scores of the three groups differed as expected, the retarded were much more variable than the other groups. In fact, some of the retarded subjects learned some tasks faster than the average gifted subject. The results were interpreted as suggesting that some of the retardates had deficits not in Level I abilities but only in Level II abilities.

A theory of this sort has some heuristic value, for it helps to explain why many retarded have adaptive abilities that are inconsistent with their low scores on IQ tests (e.g., Cooper et al. 1967). Likewise, Mercer's (1973) observations that minority group children testing in the retarded range on standard IQ measures do not show deficits in adaptive behavior can be accounted for in this model. In Jensen's view, this lack of deficits in adaptive behavior is due to the fact that a major proportion of minority group retardates are deficient only in Level II abilities, which are less important than Level I abilities in adaptive behavior. Anglo retardates, on the other hand, are more likely to be deficient in Level I abilities than in Level II abilities.

Motivational and Emotional Factors.   A distinction must be made between the primary and secondary *effects* of mental retardation, regardless of the severity of retardation. Zigler, in a series of influential papers (e.g., 1967, 1973), has pointed out that retardates must be viewed as whole persons. Many of the behavioral deficiencies attributed to them are the consequence of experiences of being unable to cope as successfully as normals. Institutionalization, rejection by peers and parents, excessive failure—all operate synergistically to impair further intellectual performance. Zigler's argument is not that mental retardation has no causal factors independent of motivation and emotion, but that these extraintellective factors all contribute to the further impairment of the retardate's functioning.

Zigler has pointed out repeatedly that the intentions of retarded subjects may foil those of the experimenter—the retardate may be concerned about the meaning of the social interaction between him and the experimenter, while the experimenter just wants to know whether the subject can solve the cognitive problem presented. Many subjects, especially retardates, do not always appreciate the significance of a particular experiment and see it more as an opportunity for social interaction than anything else.

In this regard, Zigler has observed that retardates are especially outer directed. On some occasions they perform in a fashion that serves to maintain the social interaction, even if that means failing to learn the problem. On other occasions, some retarded children may be wary and distrusting of adults and consequently have a negative set about the situation. Zigler has noted that these two competing motivational factors can play a role in the cognitive performances of subjects and thus must be controlled or manipulated within the experiment. To the extent that retardates are outer directed, they will not concentrate on the task at hand. Thus, they are in double jeopardy—they will concentrate less on the task and be more susceptible to the nature of the social interaction than will individuals of normal intelligence.

SOCIAL DISADVANTAGE

There is yet one thorny issue that we have not faced squarely in dealing with mental retardation, particularly with the milder forms. The question concerns the manner in which we are to understand observations that social class and social deprivation interact powerfully with constitutional determinants in producing a mentally retarded child or adult. It has been shown elsewhere in this book (Chapter 6) that developmentally retarded or organically damaged infants are more likely to become mentally retarded if they come from lower-class homes than if they have come from upper-class homes, while developmentally advanced infants tend not to become retarded regardless of the homes in which they have been reared. Such observations, if confirmed, suggest that even the milder forms of mental retardation have an organic or genetic basis but that many individuals who are not mentally retarded have the same or similar degree of organic impairment as some who are. These nonretarded individuals have, by good fortune, matured in an enriching environment that provided them with the information that they would not have been able to acquire on their own. In this model, the organism is not seen as a passive recipient of information from the environment under normal circumstances. The normal infant finds an abundance of information available for him to actively process and transform; the abnormal infant must obtain the same information more passively from the environment.

This model might also help to explain Mercer's (1973) finding that intellectually retarded minority group members are less likely to be adaptively retarded than are retarded majority group members. The minority group retardates have low IQs for the same reasons that the majority retardates do, but the necessity for earlier independent functioning that so often is required of minority children functions as the equivalent of a stimulating environment, or at least as an environment that forces the acquisition of skills necessary for adaptively successful behaviors.

ADULT STATUS OF RETARDATES

Many studies have indicated that the adult outcomes for mild and moderate retardates are not so bleak as might be predicted. Follow-up studies have shown that these individuals are usually off welfare rolls and bear responsibility for a family. For example, Baller, Charles, and Miller (1967) found that 65 percent of retardates who were originally in special classes in Nebraska and who averaged 60 IQ were self-supporting thirty years later. Another 24 percent were potentially self-supporting, and only 6.5 percent were in institutions. In another group of subjects of borderline intelligence (having IQs of about 81), 94 percent were self-supporting and 3 percent were partially self-supporting. Only 1 percent of these cases were institutionalized.

Personality factors and work habits are of critical importance to the adult adjustment of mild and moderate retardates. Robinson and Robinson (1976) point out that specific work skills count less than perseverence, cheerfulness, cooperation, self-confidence, good social behavior on the job, and respect for supervisors. When these behaviors are lacking, outcomes are much poorer.

It seems clear that the demands of job and family are less exacting than those of school life, where there is a premium placed on problem-solving efficiency and mistakes seldom go unrecognized. Adult life outside of school usually has much more robustness, permitting compensation for mistakes and fresh chances after failures. It seems that educators ought to concentrate on cultivating good work and social habits, since they probably have less to do with heredity but make for successful adult outcomes. In this way, much can be done to improve the chances of those who are intellectually retarded.

Deafness and Blindness

During the course of evolution, the senses of vision and hearing have become increasingly important, as has the central integration of the two. Both systems are delicately tuned and consequently are very susceptible to insults from a variety of causes, both environmental and genetic. One estimate of the distribution of childhood causes of these diseases comes from Fraser (1965) and is shown in Figure 10.5. On the whole this figure suggests that environmental factors, such as infections and trauma, and genetic causes are about equally responsible for these disorders. Fraser has estimated that about twenty-five different genetic loci are involved in deafness and somewhere between forty-seven and fifty-nine different genes are involved in blindness. The vast majority of the genetic causes are probably recessively transmitted.

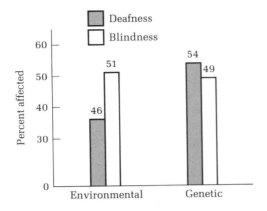

Figure 10.5

Etiology of childhood deafness and blindness according to presumed cause. (After Fraser 1965.)

DEAFNESS

It is estimated that around 1 in 1000 individuals in Western countries is profoundly deaf (Fraser 1971). Were hearing impairments of a less severe nature included, the proportion would increase substantially. In view of the high frequency of hearing disorders, it is surprising that most of us have little direct acquaintance with the deaf. This is because fairly self-contained deaf communities exist in virtually all cities of substantial size, and most of the social lives of the deaf are centered in such communities. We shall have more to say about deaf communities momentarily.

Deafness can be subdivided into a number of different etiologies according to the locus of the impairment and the degree of severity. Hearing disorders can be roughly classified as occurring because of (1) *Conductive* deficits in the mechanical conduction of the sound waves caused by impairments in the external auditory canal, (2) deficits in the *sensory-neural* apparatus that carries the mechanically transduced sensory information to the brain, and (3) deficits in the *central* processing mechanism of the brain itself. Similarly, it is possible to identify different hearing disorders that are limited to certain sound frequencies or to specific genetically related degenerative changes in the sensory apparatus.

It is especially important that a thorough diagnostic evaluation be made for hearing disorders so that the genetic forms can be identified. Because assortative mating among the deaf is extremely high, those with identical recessive gene disorders will produce only deaf children. On the other hand, if the deaf parents have different recessive disorders, the risk of having deaf children is considerably reduced. About two-thirds of matings between genetically deaf parents result only in hearing offspring; thus, there is cause for optimism for many genetically deaf parents. In the remaining families, there are about equal numbers of those producing only deaf children and of those producing both hearing and deaf children (see Nance and McConnell 1973 for a review).

Infections have been responsible for a large proportion of congenital or early childhood deafness, with rubella (German measles) being the largest single contributor. This infection is relatively innocuous in children or adults but can be devastating to a fetus during the first half of fetal development. The pregnant mother may appear only mildly ill during the infection, yet about 10 percent of such infected mothers produce children with congenital rubella syndrome. In addition to a variety of vascular and eye lesions, these children often have microcephaly and mental retardation. During the rubella epidemic of 1964, almost two million individuals contracted the disease and a significant number of them were pregnant women. Other common infections associated with childhood deafness are meningitis and syphilis. Prematurity and Rh incompatibilities also are significant contributors to the frequency of deafness.

Intellectual Functioning.   Intellectual testing of the deaf presents a special problem, since virtually all congenitally deaf individuals have language deficiencies that exceed those found for any other group, handicapped or otherwise. The deaf do not have a language as we know it, and only a small proportion have a reading level sufficient to comprehend any paragraph in this book. Thus, intelligence testing of the deaf has relied on nonverbal intelligence measures, usually with some provision for more detailed directions to make sure the subject gets the point of the test. Results of studies of congenitally deaf or early childhood deaf individuals generally indicate no dramatic difference from hearing controls on nonverbal tests (Meyerson 1963), and in a minority of studies the scores of the deaf subjects may even exceed the normative averages.

It is difficult for hearing individuals to imagine the magnitude of the task of learning language for a deaf individual. Furth (1973) suggests an exercise that might help the hearing individual comprehend the difficulty of this task. Imagine trying to learn a language by watching television with the sound turned off in a foreign country with an unfamiliar tongue. It is demanding to learn to read lips facilely, and Furth claims that very few congenitally deaf individuals ever become proficient at this.

Academic Achievement.   It is probably fair to say that almost the entire preoccupation in the teaching of the deaf in the early school grades is with language learning and reading. That schools for the deaf have been unsuccessful in this endeavor is absolutely clear. Figure 10.6 gives

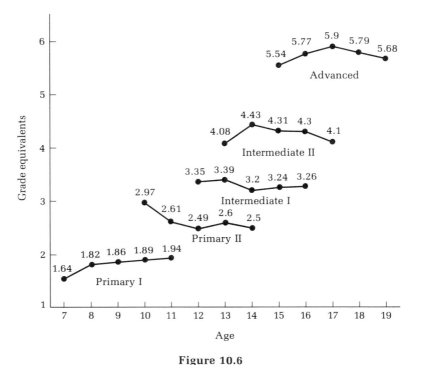

Figure 10.6

Grade-equivalent test performance according to age and test battery for deaf children. (After Gentile and DiFrancesca 1969.)

the grade-equivalent scores of severely deaf children on the paragraph meaning subtest of the Stanford Achievement Test (Gentile and DiFrancesca 1969). Five different batteries of varying difficulty were given according to age and performance in school; there was considerable overlap in the ages of children given different batteries, however. The two most important things to note about Figure 10.6 are, first, that the absolute scores of the paragraph meaning subtest were low in relation to the ages of the children, and second, that there was no increase in the paragraph meaning scores as a function of age within each battery. In fact, as Furth (1973) points out, the scores of the subjects are close to meaningless. Each battery is designed for children of a specific grade level range (e.g., the advanced battery is recommended for grades seven through nine), and it is difficult to assign grade equivalents accurately for extremely low scores within a particular test. Although the children taking the advanced battery scored slightly above grade five, it is important to recognize that chance alone would produce a score of 4.8. This restriction of range at the lower end applies to all the other batteries shown as well, so that the mean scores are all inflated. Furth

(1966) provides data similar to this for the Metropolitan Elementary Reading Test, with which the same conclusions were reached.

A follow-up study by Hammermeister (1971) also yielded similar conclusions. The study included sixty subjects who had graduated from a residential school for the deaf and were retested on the paragraph meaning and word meaning subtests of the SAT seven to thirteen years after they had first been tested. The results indicated no significant change in paragraph meaning scores over the years—the subjects were still scoring at the fifth-grade level on the average (there were, however, a few who were reading above the tenth-grade level). On the word meaning subtest, which is essentially a test of vocabulary, there was a slight, but significant, increase in scores over time. At the first administration in school the subjects averaged 5.08, and at follow-up they averaged 5.72. Thus, there are indications of vocabulary growth during adulthood, just as occurs with normal subjects. In those areas which require the extraction of meaning from semantic and syntactic relationships between words, however, there is no indication of improvement over time.

Thinking. Many believe that language is an essential ingredient of thought and that, consequently, those without a conventional language must have deficiencies in their thinking processes. There is considerable evidence, however, both theoretical and empirical, which indicates that thinking can go on without language and that most of what is called thinking takes place out of awareness anyway, at such a rapid rate as to prohibit verbal labeling.

There has been a great deal of research on thinking deficiencies in the deaf (see Furth 1964, 1971), with the general conclusion being that the thinking processes of the deaf and the hearing do not produce vastly different types of performances. Some concepts are especially difficult for the deaf to acquire, such as the idea of opposites, but by and large there is considerable overlap between deaf and control groups. The types of tasks used in these studies are heterogeneous and include, among others, learning of rules (choosing only extreme values), understanding transitive relations, (seeing if the child can conclude $A > C$ from the information that $A > B$ and $B > C$), and remembering what was seen.

The current view of the relationship of thinking to language is that language can facilitate the acquisition of concepts and that some concepts may not be expressible in nonlanguage terms, but that our preoccupation with language qua thought derives largely from a nonrelativistic perspective and deserves remediation itself. The deaf child does have a symbol system, perhaps largely represented in concrete gestures and kinesthetic cues. These symbols are facilitators of thinking, as are linguistic symbols for the hearing. It is the task of educators of the deaf to help the child form conventional symbols, in addition to those that will be generated spontaneously, so that communication will be enhanced.

The last point to be made is that deaf individuals and their families can find wisdom and support in the communities for the deaf formed in almost all cities of substantial size. It is especially important for hearing parents of deaf children to become acquainted with these communities, for such parents usually have special difficulty adjusting to the deafness of their child.

BLINDNESS

Definitions of blindness vary according to the purposes of the investigator or the purposes of the classification system. If the investigator is concerned with visual acuity, a Snellen chart, which presents letters in various spatial orientations, is often used. The legal definition of blindness under these circumstances is usually taken as 20/200. This means that the individual can identify the letters with his better corrected eye at 20 feet that the normal individual can identify at 200 feet. The field of vision may also be affected—for example, the subject may have a blind spot, or *scotoma,* in some portion of the visual field but have comparatively normal vision in other parts of the field.

Blindness is usually not an all-or-nothing affair. Most individuals in schools for the blind are able to identify shadows or light from dark. Nevertheless, this minimal vision is usually insufficient for the student to enter a typical public school. Others with very poor vision as measured by the Snellen chart can still read large print close up, or they can make more effective use of the minimal visual cues available to them than can others with the same scores on the Snellen. For the most part, findings in this section concern those who have the most severe degrees of visual impairment, at least since early childhood.

Many forms of blindness have their origins in genetic factors (Francois 1961), but these factors are too complicated to discuss here. On the environmental side, there are also many causes of blindness. One form, called retrolental fibroplasia, is particularly tragic because it was caused by a medical advance during the period from 1942 to 1954. Premature infants were given high concentrations of oxygen for prolonged periods in order to enhance their chances for survival. While this measure did improve survival rates, the oxygen concentration was permanently devastating to the retinal cells and caused an explosion in the incidence of blindness. Now oxygen concentrations are carefully monitored for premature babies, and the disorder has been almost completely eliminated.

Touch and hearing are the major modes of experiencing the world for the blind. It is impossible for the congenitally blind to understand many objects and events in the same fashion as the sighted. Touch is limited by the size and nearness of objects, and, while some smaller objects can be manipulated in one grasp, others are too large for the span of the hand and the fingers must travel over them in a sequential fashion. Still other objects are too large or too distant (e.g., the sky) to permit even this attempt at understanding. Since sight is almost instantaneous in the construction of a percept, the sighted experience sensation of a quality totally unavailable to the blind. Although many blind appear to use terms for sensations derived from sight in an appropriate manner, their meaning has usually been inferred from context and is different from our own.

Sensory Compensation.   Some have believed that blindness makes the other senses more acute. There is little evidence for this belief, however, although there are indications that the blind can sometimes make more efficient use of the intact senses that they have (Hayes 1941; Lowenfeld 1971).

One active area of research for many years was the apparent obstacle sense of the blind. It turned out that the blind were responding to changes in sound frequencies reflecting from obstacles. When the ears were plugged, the blind could maneuver no better than sighted individuals under comparable circumstances (Cotzin and Dallenbach 1950). Thus, the tapping of a cane not only provides cues for what is ahead by an extension of touch but also permits the sound of the tap to rebound off obstacles.

Intelligence.   Tests for the blind have usually consisted of many of the verbal items used on the various IQ tests, such as the Stanford-Binet and the Wechsler tests. Even now these tests are probably the ones used most frequently in the assessment of blind children. Hayes (1941) provides an extensive review of the results of such tests. He found that the blind tended to score in the lower portion of the average range, although there were many who performed in the superior category. More recently Tillman (1967) compared blind and sighted individuals on the Wechsler tests, finding superior performance by the blind on some subtests (digit span, especially) and inferior performance on others (comprehension and similarities). It appears, however, that the blind were deficient only on certain items of the comprehension and similarities subtests.

In recent years there has been interest in intelligence tests that utilize touch and that can be used as an adjunct to the verbal scales. Various analogues of Wechsler subtests have been constructed in which embossed or textured surfaces are used in place of the colored or line surfaces of the original. Subjects may be required to touch a completed figure and then reproduce it, or to construct a design from randomly arrayed elements (Shurrager and Shurrager 1964). Since these verbal and non-verbal tests intercorrelate as highly among the blind as do similar tests among the sighted, there may be a factor analogous to Spearman's g entering into intellectual functioning among the blind.

Witkin et al. (1968) compared blind adolescents and sighted adolescents who were blindfolded on a battery of tactual analogues to non-verbal intelligence subtests. On the tactile embedded figures test subjects felt a particular design with their fingers and then tried to locate it again in a complex design in which it was embedded. An auditory embedded figures test worked in a similar fashion. Subjects first heard a short three-to-five-note tune and then tried to identify it embedded in a more complex melody. On the tactile block design test, which was a direct analogue of the Wechsler subtest, the subject felt the reference design and then constructed the same design from the set of blocks. Another task was the tactile matchsticks test, in which matchsticks were arranged in the form of a lattice and the subject was required to reduce the total number of squares by removing a specified number of matchsticks. Finally, to test body concept, the subject was given a ball-shaped piece of clay and instructed to form a man or woman. Except for the auditory embedded figures test, intercorrelations between the tests were moderate to high (ranging from .54 to .76). The test of music memory correlated insignificantly with the other tests, although it did correlate with scores on the attention-concentration factor (arithmetic and digit span) of the Wechsler tests. These results suggest that auditory embedded figures are best conceived of as measuring the capacity for sustained auditory attention.

In comparison with the sighted controls, the blind were significantly better on the auditory embedded figures and worse on the tactile embedded figures and the clay models. There were some congenitally blind, however, who produced clay figures that earned the highest score possible.

The scores on the Wechsler digit span subtest were vastly superior among the blind subjects. Hayes (1941) had also observed this phenomenon, although not so clearly, in his earlier review of digit span. The importance of this finding extends beyond the work with the blind, because it indicates that an extreme deprivation can result in a dramatic improvement in at least one aspect of intellectual functioning. Unfortunately, the consequences of blindness are so great that it might be impossible to produce a deprivation of this magnitude under more nearly normal circumstances.

Achievement Tests. In general, achievement test results with the blind have suggested some retardation in the early school years followed by catching up later. Usually achievement tests are presented either orally or in braille (see Lowenfeld 1971), and items that are particularly inappropriate for the blind are usually eliminated. Intercorrelations between intelligence test and achievement test results are about the same for blind as for the sighted.

Vision and Development.   Some of the most interesting work with the blind has been used to test hypotheses about the relative influence of hereditary and environmental factors on development. Congenitally blind individuals provide a ready-made experiment in natural deprivation, so that it is possible to determine whether certain behaviors emerge among those deprived of sight in the same way that they do among normal individuals. For example, research into the origin and development of smiling has been undertaken by a number of investigators (see Freedman 1974), with the idea of pitting the maturational argument against the environmental argument stressing the role of imitation and learning. Studies indicate that smiling is present in blind or deaf-blind infants at near-appropriate ages of onset, although the smile may be more fleeting for the blind than for the sighted (Freedman 1974).

Other investigators have examined the lasting effects of early blindness or strabismus (crossed eyes) on visual perception after surgical correction. Senden (1960) reported that individuals congenitally blinded by cataracts showed marked visual disturbances in pattern recognition immediately after surgery, but that there was some evidence of pattern recognition for objects that the patients were familiar with through touch. Evidence now suggests, however, that, while there is some improvement in pattern recognition over time, critical neurons or their interconnections may have been destroyed permanently during the period of blindness (Hebb 1972).

Lasting effects of strabismus have also been observed. Individuals whose strabismus was not surgically corrected before three years of age showed deficits on a task akin to binocular fusion (Banks, Aslin, and Letson 1975). This finding suggests that there is a critical period for the proper development of binocularity and that later surgical correction will not be totally successful in enhancing binocular development.

Conclusions

Although blindness and deafness represent extreme departures from normal sensory experiences, the blind and the deaf are often surprisingly successful in adapting to their environments. Environmental deprivation usually refers to sociocultural forms of deprivation that appear to be far less extreme than deprivation of these major senses. Yet tests appropriate for the deaf and blind show surprisingly fewer deficits than one might naively expect for such deviations. On the other hand,

while some of the cultural-familial deficits we have discussed elsewhere appear trivial by comparison, the magnitude of their consequences are often as profound as or more profound than the consequences of being blind or deaf. Obviously, we shall need to rethink the
nature of environmental deprivation and construct models that predict
that clear and unambiguous deficiencies can result in less ultimate
impairment than dysfunctions that are not total but that permit the
individual to continue to limp along with his deficiencies.

The findings concerning mental retardation show both genetic and
environmental factors to be present. The task of eliminating mental
retardation is overwhelming. The only action that can dramatically reduce retardation in the next generation is to prevent the retarded from
reproducing. This form of prevention challenges basic beliefs about
individual freedom and thus meets with resistance. Even with such a
policy, the majority of retardates cannot be identified before birth, and,
as a consequence, the problem of mental retardation will be with us for
a long time to come.

11

Intellectual Superiority, Genius, and Special Talents

Perhaps there are no more fascinating subjects in the study of human individual differences than those who represent the highest extremes on measures of achievement. Their extraordinary accomplishments earn for them a place in the pages of history, to be admired and revered. For want of a better term, we shall call such individuals geniuses. This chapter shall consider not only those who, by virtue of their accomplishments, have been recognized and esteemed by their contemporaries and history, but also those with extraordinary intelligence or specific talents who may not have achieved widespread social recognition.

We shall begin by focusing on the antecedents and the consequences of superior intelligence or giftedness. Presumably this is a personal quality that may or may not lead to socially esteemed accomplishments, although it appears that individuals of superior intelligence are more likely to make high achievements and eventually to acquire the label of genius.

Early Development of Intellectually Precocious Children

The very early mental and personality traits of intellectually precocious children have been the subject of considerable speculation, but thus far little objective data are available on their performance. This state of affairs is easily understandable, since such children are typically identified only in the school years or later and one must necessarily rely on inaccurate or unverifiable retrospective information derived from historical biographies or parental recollections. Without the aid of systematic observations during the preschool years, judgments of the early development of intellectually precocious children in relation to that of the total population are subjective and comparisons among the precocious are unreliable.

Regardless of whether genetic arguments or environmental arguments apply to the development of intellectual precocity, such precocity must be developed over time; these children do not disclose their complete array of competencies as neonates, although they may begin to display their extraordinary abilities rather early. At least two theories about the development of brilliance can be advanced. The first view can be seen as an extension of Chomsky's (1972) position that the "grammar" of intelligence exists preadapted to the brain. In this model the environment is seen as acting as a releasing stimulus (in the ethological sense) of the grammar, with genetic variability affecting either the threshold neural firing patterns or the availability of the intelligent behavior for release. This model suggests that the toddler confronted with a problem is tuned to consider only a limited subset of, rather than all, potential hypotheses as solutions. Notions of "critical periods" of optimal learning likewise imply preadaptation or tuning for selection of appropriate stimuli from the environment.

Overreactions to the doctrine of innate ideas persuaded many to throw the baby out with the bath water, because it was not generally recognized that such preadaptation could be genetically encoded into the brain through evolution, not as already fully formed ideas, but as specified and adaptive ways of taking external stimulation and transforming it at a number of levels along the path from sense receptor to the brain.

Furthermore, the acknowledgment that general intelligence has a substantial heritable component raises an important question that has not been widely recognized—namely, how is genetic information transformed so as to lead to *predictable* individual differences in intelligence? Because the translation of genetic differences to IQ test differences is not yet understood, many superficially criticize intelligence tests and charge that the questions reflect no more than culture-specific learnings. Were IQ items tapping no more than culture-specific learnings, however, it would seem impossible to account cogently for the findings of adoption and twin studies, which indicate a substantial heritable component to intelligence.

Observations of precocious development are difficult to explain in terms that ignore concepts of pretuning or preadaptation. In the area of musical talent, especially, there are documented cases of preschool children whose accomplishments surpass those of intelligent adults with years of formal training (Scheinfeld 1965).

An alternative hypothesis about the origins of intellectual precocity is that gifted children have learned unusually efficient problem-solving strategies and academic motivations. This position may seem more appealing, since it emphasizes learning and is potentially susceptible to experimental verfication. Cox (1926) has provided evidence consistent with, but not sufficient for, this view. She perused biographies of historical geniuses and found that a large proportion were distinguished from the general population by having parents of high social class who assiduously encouraged their children in their accomplishments.

The trouble with data of this sort is that they do not exclude either genetic or environmental causes and they tell us little about the direction of effects (Bell 1968), that is, whether parental encouragement precedes or follows the child's achievements. Many gifted children display accomplishments so early in life that it is difficult to attribute them to parental treatment. As Dennis (1947) has suggested, traits that appear very early in life are more likely to be related to biological than to psychological factors, and, if it can be shown that gifted children display unusually advanced behaviors in the toddler stage or earlier, the persuasiveness of explanations emphasizing environmental influences is diminished.

Moreover, there has been little progress in the assessment of the relevant environmental factors influencing intellectual performance. Evidence from tools and other artifacts associated with early man one million years ago (Oakley 1972) and cave paintings in France and Spain more than ten thousand years old (Wendt 1972) indicate the existence of substantial intelligence before man ever left the caves. It may be that we have lost sight of the really critical factors in the development of high intelligence in our emphasis on cultural artifacts, such as early reading and writing, and the presence of amenities around the home. The fact that outstanding accomplishments can be documented prior to the invention of writing suggests that environmental assessments that typically employ variables such as quality of housing, number of books and magazines around the home, and the like may be missing the mark and that other environmental factors are critical in influencing the development of high intelligence.

Information Processing and Intelligence

Experimental cognitive psychologists have regarded man as an information processor for some time now (see Neisser 1967). These psychologists have been concerned with the ways in which stimuli are detected, integrated, coordinated with internal representations in memory, and altered and abstracted for adaptive behavior, as well as with the general nature of the transformation processes. Although individual differences in intelligence have been largely ignored by cognitive psychologists, the processes they study must surely be essential to performance on intelligence tests. Recently, some investigators have begun applying the techniques and methods of experimental cognitive psychology to the explanation of individual differences in performance on intelligence tests (Estes 1974; Hunt and Lansman 1975; Hunt, Lunneborg, and Lewis 1975).

In contrast to the psychometric approach, which emphasizes the presentation of seemingly "novel" problems to the subject, the experimental cognitive psychologists often use stimuli that are highly overlearned by the subjects. These psychologists use techniques that rely primarily on speed or reaction time as outcome measures. The units they employ are milliseconds (thousandths of a second). Since milliseconds (msecs) are the units used to measure the speed of neural transmission, it might be possible to say something about the relative lengths of neural paths that must be traversed for particular problems to be solved.

The following discussion shall only briefly describe the results of some pioneering experiments that used the methods of experimental cognitive psychology for the analysis of differences in intellectual processes. The studies to be described are only a sample of the recent research, but they provide insights into what might be done in a field calling for more exploration.

Hunt, Lunneborg, and Lewis (1975) were interested in two general aspects of intellectual functions: (1) the speed with which overlearned codes could be aroused or retrieved from long-term memory and (2) the speed with which internal representations in short-term memory (a memory stage that only holds specific bits of information for a few seconds) could be created, altered, and integrated. Their general procedure was to compare college students who were either in the upper or lower quartiles on a verbal aptitude test. Examples of experiments applied to each of these two problem areas shall be provided here, but the reader is encouraged to pursue this topic in more detail by referring to the original article.

SPEED OF RETRIEVAL FROM LONG-TERM MEMORY

In one experiment the subjects were asked to judge whether two stimuli were identical in name (*AA* or *Aa*) or different (*Ab*). Posner et al. (1969) had previously established that it takes about 70 msec longer to make a name identification (*Aa*) than a physical identification (*AA*). The materials were presented on a computer-driven display and the subject's preferred hand rested atop two keys, one marked "same" and the other marked "different." The incidence of error was less than 5 percent, and the percentage correct was the same for those who scored high and for those who scored low on the verbal test. The results indicated that high verbals responded more quickly than the low verbals on both the name identical trials and the physically identical trials, as was predicted, but the important point was that the *difference* between the speed of response to the name identical and the physically identical letters was less for the high verbals than for the low verbals. This finding suggested to the authors that "high overlearned codes are somehow more accessible to the high verbal subjects" (Hunt et al. 1975, p. 204).

SPEED OF INFORMATION PROCESSING

This study employed the Sunday and Tuesday task. Subjects were required to do simple addition problems or more complicated addition problems rapidly, using bases other than 10. For example, if Monday = 1, Tuesday = 2, and so on up to Sunday = 7, then what is the sum of Monday and Tuesday? (The correct answer is Wednesday.) More complicated problems of this type can also be asked, such as, what is the sum of Sunday and Wednesday? (The correct answer is Wednesday.) Subjects also performed additions using months of the year (base 12) or letters of the alphabet (base 26). Reaction times were again recorded, with the result that high verbals were significantly faster than low verbals in doing problems for days, months, and letters. There was no difference for simple addition problems in base 10. Since the order of days, months, and letters are overlearned by all college students, the results suggested that the differences between the two groups of students must be due to the speed at which the information is processed.

   Hunt et al. conclude that, although verbal aptitude is an indication of what people know and can do, the information-processing approach may be more helpful in describing and analyzing the nature of the advantage for the high verbals. In this case it appears that such individuals are more proficient in coding and manipulating verbal stimuli when knowledge per se is not an important factor.

The utility of the information-processing analysis of intellectual functioning is that it permits inquiries about what underlies psychometric intelligence. New classes of questions can now be asked: What are the built-in differences in information-processing styles that relate to intelligence test performance? Can individual components of information processing be altered or improved? What happens when people with different information-processing styles are exposed to similar environments over a long time? These questions undoubtedly have implications for the findings that intelligence has an inherited component and that it is difficult to account for observed differences in intelligence on the basis of differences in environmental factors alone. For psychologists interested in intelligence, the analysis of information processing is probably one of the most important new areas of research and theory. It also represents the first significant fusion of experimental cognitive psychology and differential psychology in the area of intellectual functioning.

Social Origins of the Intellectually Superior

Virtually all investigators have noted the high frequency with which the intellectually superior and geniuses originate in the highest social classes. Galton's (1869) analysis in Hereditary Genius concluded that 31 percent of the fathers of eminent men had themselves achieved eminence, and Cox's (1926) analysis of historical geniuses estimated that over 52 percent came from professional families or nobility. Terman's (1925) study of California children with Stanford-Binet IQs of 135 or more estimated that 29 percent came from professional families, while only 2.9 percent of the general population came from professional families. Visher's (1947) analysis of the most eminent men listed in the Directory of American Men of Science estimated that 45 percent of them had fathers in the professions.

More recent data on the social origins of intellectually superior children come from the Collaborative Perinatal Project, which identified 114 four-year-olds with S-B IQs of 140 or more (Willerman and Fiedler 1974; 1977). The mothers of these children had completed 2.5 years more education than had the mothers of the nongifted children in the sample. When the fathers' occupations were examined, the results were even more striking; within the gifted group, there was a substantial relationship between parental occupation and IQ ($r = .56$). When the 114 gifted children were classified into three groups on the basis of IQ category (140–149, 150–159, and 160–182), all ten fathers of the children in the highest IQ group obtained the maximum occupational rating.

There is also considerable evidence that the intellectually superior come from smaller families and tend to be firstborns as well. For example, Breland (1973) compared the order of birth in high school students scoring in the upper 5 percent on the National Merit Scholarship Qualification Test with the birth order of the remainder of the group taking the test (total $N = 687,043$) and found a higher proportion of firstborns among those scoring at the very highest levels than at the lower levels. Terman (1925) found an excess of firstborns among eminent American men of science and among children scoring in the gifted range. Hollingworth (1942) also found that ten of the twelve children she studied with IQs of 180 or more were either only children or firstborns. Helmreich (1968) summarized some recent findings on birth order, pointing out that all seven of the original Mercury astronauts were firstborns and that twelve of the fifteen candidates for the Gemini space program were the oldest or the only male offspring.

Genetic Studies of the Gifted

The classic studies of intellectual superiority were conducted by Lewis Terman and his colleagues, and no discussion of the topic can be complete without a review of their findings. Beginning in the early 1920s, a large group of intellectually superior school children was identified and followed longitudinally so as to characterize comprehensively their social and academic attainments throughout their lives. The findings of these researchers have already spanned more than forty years, and at least one more follow-up is planned. The five volumes on this project that have appeared over those years shall be taken up sequentially.

THE FIRST STUDY (1925)

Terman (1925) sought to identify those children who would score in the top 1 percent on IQ tests in the state of California. Teachers nominated the brightest children in each class, who were then tested on either a group or an individual intelligence test (Stanford-Binet) to confirm their superiority. Terman set the cutoff score at 140 IQ to identify the top 1 percent. A few children with IQs between 135 and 139 were also included if the testing conditions suggested that their "true" IQs were somewhat higher than the obtained scores or if they were siblings of those who had already qualified.

Over a thousand children were identified by these procedures (the specific Ns varied with the characteristics of each of the subsamples). As previously indicated, the social origins of these subjects were on the whole far superior to those of the general population. A breakdown by ethnicity showed disproportionately high numbers of individuals of English and Jewish ancestry. The relatives of the gifted children showed a considerable frequency of eminence, in line with the findings of Galton (1869). Contrary to popular beliefs that gifted children are more likely to be asthenic and of substandard health, these gifted children were larger and healthier than comparison groups of nongifted children. A more recent comparison of gifted children and their siblings suggests that it is not high IQ per se that is associated with larger size and better health but rather the general home environment of higher social class homes, which may provide better nutrition and care for the children (Laycock and Caylor 1964).

The Terman children were administered standardized achievement tests and tests of character, and their parents and teachers rated tham on many personality traits. The general findings indicated that the gifted children were indeed far superior to control children on virtually all measures. One of the largest differences between the gifted and control children was observed on the information test. This test was designed to tap knowledge of both a scholastic and nonscholastic nature, much as Learned and Wood (1937) had done. A total of 335 items asked about geography, hygiene, elementary science, language and literature, and history and the arts.

Table 11.1 sets forth the means and standard deviations of the total scores on the test by age of the child. It is noteworthy that the average gifted child at age eight obtained an information score about equivalent to that of the average twelve-year-old control. It appears that the average gifted child had mastered subject matter about 40 percent above his chronological age, although such children were accelerated in school grade by only 14 percent above the norm. Sex differences on the tests of

Table 11.1

Means and standard deviations on the information test for gifted and control children

Age (yrs)	Gifted (N = 632)		Controls (N = 463)	
	Mean	SD	Mean	SD
6 & 7	65	31	—	—
8	111	34	22	16
9	151	41	42	30
10	188	34	54	37
11	230	34	81	55
12	255	25	118	66
13	278	18	134	69

Source: From Terman 1925.

information were also very large. The gifted boys were far superior to the gifted girls in the science and history subtests and somewhat superior in the language and literature subtest.

Correlations of Stanford Achievement Test scores for different school subjects and the number of years in school for gifted children of homogeneous age were negligible. Terman correlated achievement test scores in spelling, information, reading, and arithmetic for all children having a chronological age of ten to eleven years with the amount of time they had been in school (range of schooling was from 2. to 6.5 years). In all instances the correlations were miniscule; the highest was for arithmetic, which correlated .13 with years of schooling. Thus, it was clear that these children learned much outside of the classroom and that formal school curricula bore little relationship to their performance.

Another interesting analysis involved teachers' rating of the character and personality of the gifted children and of the control children. The gifted exceeded the controls on virtually every trait rating, although the extent of the group differences varied with the trait being measured. The advantage for the gifted was especially apparent on traits of self-confidence, perseverance, achievement drives, originality, common sense, and, of course, intelligence.

FIRST FOLLOW-UP

In 1930 a volume appeared by Burks, Jensen, and Terman reporting on the subsequent development of the sample about eight years after the collection of the original data. A representative subset of the subjects was readministered IQ tests, which indicated a drop in IQ over the original high scores. The drop was especially apparent among the girls (about 13 IQ points); for the boys the drop averaged only 3 IQ points. Children of fourteen and over were also administered the Thorndike College Entrance Examination, which showed that these children exceeded the scores of entering Stanford freshmen by about one standard deviation. About 80 percent of the children had been accelerated in school. One hundred twenty-three siblings of the gifted were also tested on the Stanford-Binet, obtaining a mean IQ of 123. This score is close to the expected value, since IQ correlations for siblings are around .45 to .50. Thus, one would expect that siblings of the gifted, who averaged 151 IQ, should regress 50 to 55 percent in the direction of the mean IQ of the generality (IQ = 100).

A large portion of this volume deals with case studies of gifted subjects with special talents. One of the most interesting analyses concerns blind comparisons of the childhood writings of some of the children with the literary juvenilia of historically eminent authors. The results indicate that seven of the gifted children produced juvenile literary works that rivaled the childhood productions of historically eminent authors. One conclusion to be drawn from this is that the wealth of talent existing in the population is greater than anticipated. But whether or not promising children become eminent writers as adults depends on motivational and other factors. Basic talent may be present, but that alone is clearly insufficient for outstanding adult accomplishment.

SECOND FOLLOW-UP

Twenty-five years after the original data were collected, a volume by Terman and Oden (1947) appeared, reporting on the development of the subjects into the mature years. Further examination of the intelligence of the subjects was undertaken. To test the intelligence of this very able group, the Concept Mastery Test was designed. This test was constructed to have sufficient ceiling to discriminate among these gifted subjects. It was a verbal intelligence test composed of items requiring the production of synonyms and antonyms and of analogies. Scores of the gifted were compared with those of college students. It was found, for example, that Stanford seniors averaged 63 on this test (SD = 27), while the gifted averaged 96 (SD = 30). Thus, the gifted group averaged about one standard deviation above the scores of a highly selected sample of college students.

Another analysis evaluated vocational success. The primary criterion for success was the extent to which the subjects had made use of their superior ability. The subjects were divided into two extreme groups, A and C, representing the most and least successful of the subjects (150 in each group), respectively. As might be expected, the A's were all in professional and semiprofessional or managerial occupations, whereas only 11 percent of the C group had achieved as well. The A's were also much more likely to have been accelerated in school, and those who had been under fourteen in 1921–1922 had obtained Stanford-Binet IQs about 5 points higher than those of the C's at that time. There were no differences in intelligence for the A's and C's who had originally been tested in high school, however. By 1928 parent and teacher ratings of intellectual traits in these children had shown a substantial difference in favor of the group eventually to be designated as A. On the Concept Mastery Test in 1940, the A's averaged more than one-half standard deviation higher than the C's. The ratings also indicated that the A group had begun walking at an earlier age.

The social origins of the two groups differed markedly. The fathers of the A's were much more likely to have graduated from college and the children to have come from intact homes. Personality ratings of the two groups in 1940 showed that goal direction, perseverance, and self-confidence were reliably higher among the A's. Thus, there was a host of intellectual and social factors that differentiated the A's and C's. It is difficult to estimate the relative importance of the various differences in the failure of the C's to live up to their promise, but there is little doubt that social, as opposed to intellectual factors, were the major differences leading to the less adequate performances in the C group.

THIRD FOLLOW-UP

Thirty-five years after the original data were collected, another follow-up was made (Terman and Oden 1959). Appraising the achievement of the men, the authors conclude

> that the superior child, with few exceptions, becomes the able adult, superior in nearly every respect to the generality.... More than 85% of the group entered college and almost 70% graduated. The latter figure is about ten times as high as for a random group of comparable age. Graduation honors and elections to Phi Beta Kappa were at least three times as numerous as in the typical senior college class....
>
> Additional evidence of the productivity and versatility of the men is found in their publications and patents. Nearly 2000 scientific and technical papers and articles and some 60 books and monographs in the sciences, literature, arts, and humanities have been published. Patents granted amount to at least 230. Other writings include 33 novels, about 375 short stories, novelettes, and plays; 60 or more essays, critiques, and sketches; 265 miscellaneous articles on a variety of subjects. These figures on publications do not include the hundreds of publications by journalists that classify as news stories, editorials, or newspaper columns, nor do they include the hundreds, if not thousands, of radio, television, or motion picture scripts [pp. 143–147].

The achievements of the gifted women were not so striking, although their intellectual levels had been roughly comparable to those of the men in childhood.

> The careers of women are often determined by extraneous circumstances rather than by training, talent, or vocational interest.... But in spite of the fact that American women on the average occupy positions of lesser responsibility, opportunity, and remuneration than do the men, the gifted women have a number of notable achievements to their credit.... That 7 women should be listed in *American Men of Science,* 2 in the *Directory of American Scholars,* and 2 in *Who's Who in America,* all before reaching the age of 43, is certainly many times the expectation from a random

sample of around 700 women. Publications of the gifted women include 5 novels; 5 volumes of poetry and some 70 poems that have appeared in both literary and popular journals; 32 technical, professional, or scholarly books; around 50 short stories; 4 plays; more than 150 essays, critiques, and articles; and more than 200 scientific papers. At least 5 patents have been taken out by gifted women [pp. 144–145].

FOURTH FOLLOW-UP

In 1968, more than forty years after the original investigation, Oden published another follow-up of the gifted. The results were quite consistent with those obtained earlier. The men and women had achieved even greater eminence and recognition. Over fifteen hundred children of the gifted had also been tested, obtaining a mean Stanford-Binet IQ of 133. Over one-third of these children scored 140 or more.

The results of this series of studies clearly confirm the view that outstanding accomplishments can be predicted from IQ tests obtained in childhood. Without doubt, high IQs are not a sufficient condition for outstanding later attainments, as seen in the group of relatively unsuccessful C's. But if one were looking for a single childhood augury of outstanding later accomplishment, one could not do better than to obtain an intelligence test measure on the subject.

IQS ABOVE 180

Hollingworth (1942) conducted a special study of twelve children with IQs of 180 or above. While it is doubtful that a true ratio scale of merit could be developed that accurately assesses the relative value of different IQ levels, it is clear that these extraordinary children are far above that which is conventionally designated as giftedness. Hollingworth provides case histories of her subjects, an example of which follows.

One child obtained an IQ of 184 when tested at seven years. From about age four to seven he wrote about an imaginary land called Borningtown, peopling Borningtown with imaginary characters, laying roads, drawing maps, composing and recording the language (Bornish), and writing its history and literature. He was gifted in both music and art, invented many games, displayed mathematical ingenuity, and classified and diagrammed many things, including classifying parts of speech in various stories and poems. His classifications of words, numbers, colors, musical notes, and objects would fill a large volume. In 1926 he graduated Phi Beta Kappa from college at the age of sixteen. He did graduate work in chemistry and died in 1938 at the age of twenty-eight.

EXTENT OF SUPERIORITY

The psychometrics of quantitatively estimating the extent of superiority of such extraordinary children is no easy matter (Stanley, Keating, and Fox 1974). Standardized tests given to children within a particular grade usually have too low a ceiling to make fine distinctions among all those scoring at the 99th percentile. Absolute numbers correct of subjects all scoring at the 99th percentile on published norms can differ from each other as much as those of subjects scoring at widely different percentile levels, say the 99th and 65th percentiles. The only solution seems to be to give the subjects tests designed for individuals much older than they. The more difficult test permits finer distinctions to be made among the gifted subjects.

This is not to say that scores on such advanced tests are directly comparable for older and younger subjects. Older subjects may have acquired the basic techniques for solution of the problems through formal training, whereas the younger subjects may have to invent the solution on the spot.

Two skills that emerge especially early among the gifted are speaking and reading. Albert and Ayres (1969) have reanalyzed the published literature on the accomplishments of gifted children in these areas. They subdivided gifted children by IQ, rating those above 155 as *exceptionally gifted*. Published reports of onset and definitions of speech and reading varied with the investigators, but Albert and Ayres found that the *exceptionally gifted* children began speaking in "sentences" by about 14 months, that the *gifted* children began at about 17.5 months, and that the average child began between 2.5 and 3 years. Likewise, the exceptionally gifted learned to read at an earlier age than the gifted, and both learned to reach much earlier than the average child. One important conclusion to be drawn from the authors' analyses is that "gifted" children probably have quite heterogeneous behavior characteristics and that it is incorrect to treat them as a homogeneous group.

Another study (Willerman and Fiedler 1974, 1977) focused on whether there were behavioral differences that could be detected prior to the onset of speech or reading. The 114 children with Stanford-Binet IQs of 140 or more at four years of age were compared with the total group of children born at the same hospital ($N = 4649$) as part of the Collaborative Perinatal Study. On the Bayley Scales of Mental and Motor Development, routinely administered to all the children when they had been eight months of age, only slight, but statistically significant, differences in favor of the gifted children were observed. On both the mental and the motor scales the gifted children averaged about .30 of a standard deviation higher than the total group. We concluded that there was little on standardized infant scales that would efficiently augur the later intellectual accomplishments of these very superior children.

These 140 IQ children were also followed to seven years of age, when they were given the WISC and the Wide Range Achievement Test (WRAT). The results showed that these children were still superior in intelligence (IQ = 123) and that their scholastic achievements were far superior to those of the generality. While the actual grade placement of the superior children was about 2.0, their average spelling score was at 3.0, their reading score was at about 3.75, and their arithmetic score was at 2.4. Thus, these children were much further advanced in reading and spelling than in arithmetic. This may be because skills in arithmetic are more closely tied to formal school teachings than are spelling and reading skills, which can often be acquired outside of the school.

Many investigators are persuaded that these gifted children are indeed biologically superior to the generality. There are few data focusing specifically on gifted children that can be used to evaluate that belief. A study by Duncan (1969) employed a novel approach that may have some implications for the biological basis of high intelligence, however. She compared gifted and control children in the fourth through sixth grades on *rate* measures of performance. Among other tasks, she had the subjects rap on a table 100 times and walk in place 100 times, and she counted the number of words spoken in one minute by the children in response to a question. There is no more than a cursory description of each of these tasks, so one cannot be sure of the precise way in which the tasks were presented. Nevertheless, it was found that the gifted children, who averaged 138 IQ, performed at a faster rate on all measures than the control children, who averaged 110 IQ.

CONCLUSIONS

There is ample evidence that highly intelligent children tend to come from the highest social classes more frequently than expected. While it is not easy to specify the causal antecedents of intellectual superiority, it is clear that both social and genetic factors play roles in its development. From the data presented elsewhere on the inheritance of general intelligence, there is little doubt that genetic factors must be operating. Information on the performance *rates* of intelligent children suggests that they may process information more rapidly than the less intelligent, and it is possible that these rate differences also have a genetic basis. In infancy there is little indication on standardized tests that the intellectually precocious can be identified efficiently, although by the toddler stage such children are more advanced than children in general.

That infant tests have not been good predictors of later intellectual functioning has been something of a problem for those with a genetic perspective. It is always possible to argue that the skills tapped by infant tests are different from those tapped by intelligence tests, but this argument has something of a post hoc flavor and is not convincing to many. Recently Lewis (1975) has presented data that suggest that one dimension of performance in infancy might be predictive of later intelligence. The dimension is habituation, which is measured by having an infant attend repeatedly to a stimulus. During repeated exposures to a stimulus, the response of various physiological and behavioral parameters tends to decrease (habituation). It is as if after the infant has gotten a cognitive representation of the stimulus he is no longer interested in it. It is assumed that the faster the infant obtains a cognitive representation of the stimulus, the faster he will habituate. Lewis reports that habituation during the first year of life was related to Stanford-Binet IQs at age four ($r = .48$). Replication of these results would help to establish a biological basis for differences in intelligence.

Whether intellectually superior children achieve as adults commensurably with their early promise seems more a matter of social factors, such as family stability and parental social class, than of genetic factors. It is quite possible that, if we could identify the *social* factors that encourage the successful development of high achievement in adulthood among the intellectually able, we could increase dramatically the number of those individuals who eventually make positive contributions to society.

Gifted children are far superior to the average child, not only in terms of what they know, but also in terms of their cognitive operations. This cognitive advancement is not closely related to the number of years spent in the classroom. A study by Keating (1975) illustrates this phenomenon nicely. He had fifth and seventh graders of gifted and of average IQ perform a series of Piagetian conservation tasks and found that the bright fifth graders were more likely to have attained more mature mental operations than were the average IQ seventh graders. Since the bright fifth graders had spent fully two years less in school than the average IQ seventh graders, formal schooling does not seem to be the critical factor in the acquisition of more mature mental operations.

A further explication of the nature of intellectual superiority must take into account the quality and speed of information processing. Undoubtedly there are personality traits associated with intellectual superiority, but there are no indications that these traits are causal in its development. There is somewhat more evidence (to be presented in the following section) that personality traits play a larger role in high achievement—that which we label *genius* or award with eminence. We turn now to the nature and meaning of genius.

Genius

TWO PROBLEMS

While many have regarded genius as emerging either from divine inspiration or from madness, there is little or no evidence to support either proposition. In any case, the determination of genius is usually based on the consensus of acknowledged experts in the appropriate field. These experts often spend much of their lives working out the implications of the original work of genius.

There are two perennial problems in the discussion of genius and its occurrence. The first can be conceptualized as the "great man versus the inevitability of genius" argument. The great man argument is that if so-and-so had not made the discovery it might not have occurred at all. The inevitability argument is that if so-and-so had not created the work of genius someone else would have. Closely allied to these arguments is the second problem, namely, the distinction between works of genius in the arts and in the sciences. Many believe that if Shakespeare had not written *King Lear* it would not have been written; yet few would assert that if Watson and Crick had not discovered the double helical nature of DNA it would not have been discovered at all.

On the matter of the great man, there is considerable evidence in the sciences and technologies of multiple and independent discoveries that are essentially similar to one another (see Ogburn and Thomas 1922; Merton 1961). This evidence suggests that there is a Zeitgeist, or spirit of the time, that directs investigators and inventors to work on similar problems. Merton (1961) reports that he and Barber have undertaken the study of over 260 multiple discoveries, of which 179 are doublets (having two independent discoverers), 51 are triplets, 17 are quadruplets, 6 are quintuplets, 8 are septuplets, and 2 are nonaries. Merton describes in some detail the case of Lord Kelvin, who participated in 32 multiples, according to his own testimony. These 32 multiples involved an aggregate of 30 other codiscoverers, some of whom were themselves of unquestionable genius—Poincaré, Cavendish, and Helmholtz. Merton concludes that, although others would have made these discoveries had Kelvin not done so, Kelvin nevertheless qualifies as a great man—it took a considerable number of others to duplicate the 32 discoveries that Kelvin himself made (not to mention those of his which were singletons). Many singletons, however, are not genuinely so. An investigator may abandon a problem upon learning that a competitor has solved it. Thus, Merton's resolution to the great man-inevitability issue is that great men do exist but that they are those who produce in their lifetime many discoveries that can be duplicated only by an aggregate of other scientists.

This is not to say that the issue is now resolved. There is considerable dispute over what constitutes a multiple, since scientific discoveries are rarely couched in identical terminologies or structures. Furthermore, one needs a representative distribution of all discoveries to identify the proportion that consists of multiples (Jewkes, Sawers, and Stillerman 1969). It does appear, however, that great men participate in many discoveries and that an essential feature of the genius is his productivity. Another feature is the elegance and comprehensiveness with which discoveries of genius proportions are made. These discoveries may need little in the way of later modification to be of use—although they certainly may be improved upon in later years.

The second problem concerns the distinction between discovery in the arts and in the sciences. Stent (1973) suggests an important difference—that scientific discovery is susceptible to paraphrase, while artistic creations are not. To summarize the findings of great work in the sciences does no injustice to them, but summaries of important artistic compositions always detract from their value. The nature of the double helix can be expressed successfully in many forms, but a paraphrase of *Hamlet* makes the story seem trite. This difference exists largely because works of art often represent externalizations of the relationships between images, ideas, and affects, while works of science usually describe relations between external events only.

While few would deny the cumulative nature of scientific progress, evidence for accumulation in the arts is more elusive. It should be recognized, however, that certain established artistic styles and inventions are analogous to paradigms in the sciences. For example, it would have been useless to reinvent the tragic form already perfected by the Greeks, and a potential recreator of the tragic form would, of course, have been forestalled from doing so, since it had been invented already.

PERIODS OF EXCEPTIONAL GENIUS IN HISTORY

The advantage of being first in discovery comes into play here. Consider that a period of about three hundred years—from the seventeenth through the nineteenth centuries—produced composers that have yet to be equaled or surpassed. Bach, Beethoven, Brahms, and Mozart composed works that have never been rivaled, although today there are perhaps multitudes more composers than there were then. It must be that these individuals, talented as they were, were awarded such fame in part because they were first. There are limits on the number of good and different creations possible within a particular artistic form, and it may be that these composers nearly exhausted the musical forms in which they operated. Similarly, the tragic form brought to an apotheosis by the theory of Aristotle and the creations of Sophocles has never really been surpassed, despite the many playwrights and philosophers alive today. Can it be that genius was more frequent in the past, or is it that the times were ripe for the development of those ideas then and there is no necessity to reinvent them now? It is a fact that tragedians of the modern day are constrained to work within the framework of tragedy created two millenia ago.

Another important point concerns the climate for creativity and works of genius. Perhaps there was no more fertile period in thought than the golden age of Greece (530–430 B.C.). During this period Athenian Greece produced a number of geniuses that have been unrivaled since; among them are Thucydides, Socrates, Plato, Aeschylus, Sophocles, Euripides, Aristophanes, and Phidias.

Surprisingly, the population of Athens during the golden age was less than a quarter-million persons; the adult male citizenry numbered about 35,000 to 50,000 during any specific time during that period (McNeill 1963). Yet this small society produced a flowering of genius unparalleled by any society since. Galton (1869) estimated that if Victorian England had been so productive of genius there would have been 200 times more genius existing in England at that time than there actually was.

The explanation for this enormous productivity has baffled many historians and philosophers. During much of this period Athens was the financial and naval center for all of Greece, as well as being at war much of the time. A picture has been painted by McNeill (1963) of the Greeks embarking every summer on their new fleets of triremes to do battle with the Persians. Even low-born free citizens served on these vessels, which attacked and ruthlessly plundered some country or city formerly under the enemy's hegemony. McNeill has this to say about the accomplishments of Athens during that intellectually fertile time:

> The key to Athens' extraordinary career lay in her fleet.... Two hundred triremes allowed Athens to play the decisive role in the war.... The fleet had two further consequences.... It made Athens securely democratic and incurably aggressive. In the fleet, the poorest citizens played the main role, since the rowers who drove the ships into battle needed no equipment but trained muscles. Consequently, the democratic forms of Athenian government were enormously strengthened when Athenians too poor to equip themselves as hoplites acquired a vital military role as rowers. Moreover, the aggressiveness of the Athenian polis was enhanced when rowers' pay and plunder became, for a surprisingly large proportion of the Athenian citizenry, a necessary or at least highly desirable addition to family resources.
>
> Second, as Athenian citizens encountered foreign places and strange customs ... traditional beliefs and attitudes underwent rapid erosion.... The dedication of each citizen to the task of forwarding the greatness and

glory of Athens seemed a satisfactory and sufficient ideal for human striving.... With emotions tied securely to a familiar social frame, and with
minds freed from commitment to any particular view, the Athenians were
thus ideally situated for cultural creativity [pp. 280–282].

The Athenians were not gentle masters; despite their lofty accomplishments in philosophy and art, they were among the cruelest
and most exacting of rulers. No doubt the enormous sense of confidence
among all the citizens of the society, derived from their battlefield vic-
tories and the cultural novelties they encountered during their travels
abroad, contributed to their outstanding successes. Moreover, in an
attempt to identify the cultural correlates of creativity in general, Cattell (1971) points out that "frequent involvement in war," as assessed
for many cultures, is associated with a high degree of cultural creativity. He suggests that perhaps the intensity of life during those times is
transmitted to other fields as well, or that the breakdown of the conventional ways of thinking promotes the development of new questions
and lines of inquiry.

DEFINITION OF GENIUS

Albert (1975) has recently provided a detailed review of the concept of
genius, pointing out (1) that genius is derived from consensus of peers;
(2) that there is no single criterion of genius, but it is always built on
public acts that of necessity require peers to come to terms with the
ideas proposed; and (3) that productivity is a necessary ingredient of
genius and that the impact of the collective work of genius requires a
major shift in thinking rather than being simply an extension of what
went before. Although there is an emphasis here on social and intellectual impact, one should not be deceived into thinking that social impact is the goal of the creator. Geniuses strive or are driven to work on
problems that they recognize or create, but the problems they choose to
work on and solve are "deep" problems and the eminence accorded to
such individuals by peers is simply a byproduct of their works of
genius.
    According to this behavioral definition of genius as deriving from
public esteem, there are no hidden geniuses, snuffed out before they
had a chance to produce. This definition implies that genius is a product of *success* and is to be differentiated from high IQ scores or high
scores on creativity tests, which represent *capability* (Miles 1954). High
capacities must be galvanized into successful public achievements for
genius to be manifested. But high test scores can be studied in their
own right, because they represent capacities that are prerequisite, although not sufficient, for works of genius.

METHODS FOR THE STUDY OF GENIUS

Anastasi (1958) reviews six methods for the study of genius: biographical, case study, statistical survey, historiometry, intelligence test survey, and longitudinal study. Her book can be consulted for a detailed review of each of these methods. While we shall have occasion to employ data from the methods she describes, they will be considered only in passing and not enumerated directly.

A number of studies of historical geniuses have been conducted over the years. The study by Cox (1926) is perhaps the most renowned. She studied 301 historical geniuses born between 1450 and 1850, determining who was a genius and the degree of genius by the amount of space allotted to the individual in biographical dictionaries. The advantage of her study is that she and her colleagues had been trained in the methods of IQ administration and were able to estimate the childhood and adult IQs of the subjects. Previously there had been no attempt to assess the degree of intelligence "necessary" for the accomplishments recorded. Before that time there was little in the way of normative data on the accomplishments of children, so that individual judgments about the relative degree of precocity represented by these accomplishments was highly subjective and not easily or reliably assessed.

The necessity for training in child development, and particularly for normative knowledge of age-related milestones in childhood development in the generality, is particularly evident in Pearson's (1914) four-volume biography of Francis Galton. Here is a letter of Galton to his older sister written on the day before his fifth birthday, so you may judge for yourself about Galton's precocity:

> My Dear Adele,
>   I am 4 years old and I can read any English book. I can say all the Latin Substantive and Adjective and active verbs besides 52 lines of Latin poetry. I can cast up any sum in addition and can multiply by 2, 3, 4, 5, 6, 7, 8, (9), 10, (11).
>   I can also say the pence table. I read French a little and I know the clock.
>
> Francis Galton
Febuary [sic] 15, 1827

Terman (1917) comments that the only misspelling is in the month. The numbers 9 and 11 in parentheses are the result of Galton's belief that he had claimed too much. Thus, he scratched out one of the numbers and pasted paper over the other. Galton's statement that he is four years old on the day before his fifth birthday is probably indicative of an unusual striving for achievement, since it makes it appear that his accomplishments are even more precocious than they actually were.

On the basis of this and other evidence, Terman later concluded that Galton's childhood IQ could not have been far from 200.

Cox obtained two estimates for IQ for the historical geniuses, one for the years up to age sixteen and one for the years thereafter. By having multiple raters estimate the IQs of the subjects, she also was able to calculate interrater agreement reliabilities for the data. She found for the 282 subjects in her highest achievement category that the reliability ratings for the childhood IQ was .46 (mean IQ = 135) and for the adult IQ the reliability estimate was .53 (mean IQ = 145). It was also clear that the lower the original estimate of IQ, the lower was the reliability of that estimate. It is likely that this fact is related to the extent and quality of the data obtained for each of the geniuses and that these IQs cannot be regarded as being very close to the scores that the subjects would have earned had they actually been tested.

Simonton (1976) applied modern statistical methods to the data in Cox's book, pointing out that birth year (more recent) and data reliability (higher) are by far the most powerful determinants of ranked eminence among these subjects. He also found that when the geniuses were divided into "creators" versus social, military, and political leaders there was an inverted U-shaped function between achieved eminence and education, such that increased education was associated with more creative accomplishments only up to a point; after that, increased education was associated with lower ranked eminence. He also concluded that fathers' status had no direct impact on ranked eminence. It should be recognized, however, that his analysis applied only to the geniuses represented in the book and that different results might obtain were comparisons with the generality to be made.

CHARACTERISTICS OF LIVING GENIUSES OR EMINENT INDIVIDUALS

Since the 1940s there have been a series of studies that give test performances of living individuals identified as eminent. For example, Roe (1953) studied 64 eminent scientists selected by panels of experts in each field of science. Among those who agreed to participate were 20 biologists, 22 physicists, and 22 social scientists. She describes the modal scientist as a child of a middle-class family and the son of a professional man. He was likely to have been a sickly child or to have lost a parent at an early age. He had a very high IQ and in boyhood began reading extensively. He tended to feel lonely and was shy and aloof from his classmates. It was not until rather late in college that he decided upon his vocation as a scientist.

There were substantial differences among the groups on various personality and intelligence measures. On the Rorschach, the social scientists appeared deeply concerned with interpersonal relationships; the biologists were especially concerned with form; and the physicists seemed especially high in anxiety and concerned with space and inanimate motion. On ability tests administered to this group, the theoretical physicists were superior to all other groups on verbal and spatial tests. On the mathematics test it was impossible to measure the physicists, for the test was too easy for them. Mean verbal IQ was estimated at 163 for the entire group; spatial IQ was 140; and mathematics IQ was believed to be about 160.

The most comprehensive and detailed studies of eminent individuals were undertaken at the Institute of Personality Assessment and Research (IPAR) beginning in 1949 (see MacKinnon 1975 for a review). The essential purpose of the institute was to learn about the characteristics of persons who have highly successful private and professional careers.

Since 1950, IPAR has studied the intellectual and personality characteristics of eminently creative members of different professions. While many of these individuals might be called geniuses, we shall use the term *creative* as the original authors have. The usual approach has been to select outstanding members in a particular field by using peer nominations and then to compare these individuals, whenever possible, to contrast groups of persons in the same field who have not been outstandingly creative. Creatives and controls in each of these fields were often invited to Berkeley to participate in living-in assessments, where they could interact with the institute staff and each other as well as undergo behavioral assessments on objective and projective tests.

Table 11.2 presents the scores obtained by the creative groups studied at Berkeley and by various comparison groups on the Concept Mastery Test. As indicated earlier in this chapter, this test is a measure of verbal intelligence and is designed to be more challenging and to have a higher ceiling than conventional verbal intelligence measures given to the general population.

The data in this table permit only rough comparisons to standard IQ measures, but we note that Terman's gifted sample, who averaged about 150 IQ on the Stanford-Binet when tested as children, scored below both the creative writers and the creative women mathematicians on the Concept Mastery Test. The lowest mean score for the creatives is found among the creative architects, who score slightly better than the average college graduate at Berkeley. It is not surprising that the creative architects do not perform outstandingly well on this verbal test, for the talents necessary for creative accomplishments in architecture probably depend little on verbal intelligence. We may conclude that high verbal intelligence, while not a sufficient condition for outstanding creative accomplishment, is clearly associated with such accomplishment. Barron's (1969) conclusion is that a minimum IQ is

Table 11.2

Concept Mastery Test scores

Sample	N	Mean	SD
1. Creative writers (IPAR)	20	156.4	21.9
2. Creative women mathematicians (IPAR)	16	144.0	
3. Stanford Gifted Study	1004	136.7	33.8
4. Representative women mathematicians (IPAR)	28	124.5	
5. Graduate students, University of California	125	119.2	33.0
6. Research scientists (IPAR)	45	118.2	29.4
7. Medical students, University of California	161	118.2	33.1
8. Ford Foundation fellowship applicants	83	117.9	35.1
9. Creative architects (IPAR)	40	113.2	37.7
10. College graduates, University of California	75	112.0	32.0
11. Public Health Education applicants, University of California	54	97.1	29.0
12. Spouses of Stanford Gifted	690	95.3	42.7
13. Electronic engineers	95	94.5	37.0
14. Undergraduates, lower division, Stanford University	97	77.6	25.7
15. Military officers	343	60.3	31.6

Source: From *New Directions in Psychology 2* by Frank Barron. Copyright © 1965 by Holt, Rinehart and Winston. Reprinted by permission of Holt, Rinehart and Winston.

necessary to acquire the information for engaging in the profession. Beyond that minimum, there is little relationship between creativity and intelligence test scores.

Table 11.3 presents the mean scores of groups of creative professionals and controls on the California Psychological Inventory (CPI) as summarized by Barron (1969). This self-report scale was designed to have a mean of 50 and a standard deviation of 10 in the general population. The CPI profiles of the creatives suggest a high degree of personal effectiveness, with the creatives in each of the professions being especially flexible in their thinking and low in achievement through conformance.

Also interesting were the scores of the creative writers and their controls on the MMPI (Figure 11.1). Again, the test is standardized to a mean of 50 and a standard deviation of 10. We see here that the creatives given much more indication of psychopathology than do the controls; the scores of the creatives are elevated on every one of the psychopathology scales. We should note, however, that the ego-strength scores are also elevated among the creatives. This suggests that the creatives are elevated not only on psychopathology scores but also in their capacity to cope with their psychopathology.

Table 11.3

CPI scores of creative professionals and controls

CPI scale	Creative architects	Representative architects	Creative writers	Representative writers	Creative women mathematicians	Representative women mathematicians
Dominance	59	56	55	54	46	50
Capacity for status	60	57	60	57	52	54
Sociability	48	51	52	49	42	47
Social participation	58	53	60	57	52	52
Self-acceptance	61	56	63	54	44	51
Sense of well-being	48	54	41	48	50	50
Responsibility	51	54	52	50	55	55
Socialization	47	52	42	46	45	48
Self-control	45	53	45	52	51	53
Tolerance	50	54	53	47	56	56
Good impression	43	52	44	51	46	47
Communality	48	53	49	51	41	47
Achievement through conformance	50	56	50	54	46	54
Achievement through independence	59	58	63	60	65	64
Intellectual efficiency	51	54	54	52	54	55
Psychology-mindedness	61	57	60	59	68	65
Flexibility	59	51	60	55	69	56
Femininity	57	52	62	55	53	49

Source: From Barron 1969.

The average creative writer is in the upper 15 percent of the general population on *all* measures of psychopathology in this figure. If one combines these MMPI findings with CPI indications that the creatives tend to have a reduced sense of well-being in comparison with other writers or with the general population, one is led to a description of the creatives as being individuals who are struggling to reconcile their inner drives with the outer world. They are often psychologically uncomfortable but have a capacity to cope with that discomfort. It is here that one sees the evidence for the view that creativity is akin to madness. At the same time, however, one must recognize that the coping skills are generally elevated so that madness does not gain the upper hand.

Barron (1969) also reports on the results from the Myers-Briggs Type Indicator, which is a questionnaire developed on the basis of Jung's

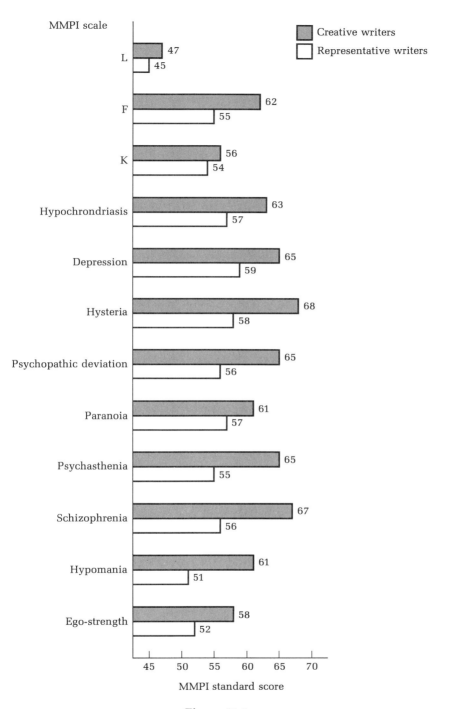

Figure 11.1

Average MMPI scores of creative and representative writers. (After Barron 1969.)

theory of psychological types. Jung proposed four fundamental psychological functions: thinking (ideational and intellectual), feeling (evaluation of things, whether positive or negative, and an emphasis on the subjective experiences of the emotions), sensing (the perceptual or reality function), and intuition (going beyond the facts in search of the underlying and nonobvious reality). The test found that only 25 percent of the general population emphasized the intuitive mode; yet 100 percent of the creative architects were classified as intuitive as against 59 percent of the representative architects. These data suggest that creatives are not inflexibly tied to the objective perceptual world of everyday experiences. They tend to direct their attention inward for the creative ideas, and only later, when they must come to terms with the objective world, do they need to provide justifications for their creative productions.

Cattell (1971), in reviewing his own work over the years on creative artists, literary figures, and scientists, finds further evidence of high ego-strength among the creatives. Like the IPAR studies, he also found (for scientists) that high scores on one psychopathology scale (schizothymia) were associated with high ego-strength scores.

PREDICTING CREATIVITY FROM CREATIVITY TESTS

Guilford (1967) and Torrance (1962) have been leaders in the development of creativity tests. Most of these tests involve the generation of *divergent* ideas, in which the emphasis is on quality and quantity of output and in which there is no single "correct" answer but many appropriate answers. An example of a test focusing on divergent productions is the Unusual Uses Test, in which the subject is asked to list as many uses as possible for a commonplace object, such as a brick. The responses of the subject are then categorized according to their number and uniqueness to obtain a "creativity" score. While there has been a profusion of such tests, there has been little effort to validate these measures using outside criteria of creativity, such as judgments of creative productions in the professional world.

In defense of those working on divergent thinking tests, it should be pointed out that identifying criteria for creativity is much more difficult than identifying criteria for intelligence tests. Creative productions are by definition so rare and variegated that they do not lend themselves to easy classification on a uniform scale. Nevertheless, results of studies using measures of divergent thinking have afforded variable, but modest, contributions to the prediction of creativity.

Wallach and Wing (1969) performed one of the most extensive validation studies of creativity tests. The sample was composed of college students who had taken the SAT during high school. The authors gave the college students four creativity tests, two verbal and two visual. One of the two verbal tasks was the unusual uses task, and the other was a similarities task in which subjects were given the names of two objects and were asked to write down as many ways as possible that they were alike. The first visual task was to write down as many different things as an abstract visual stimulus suggested to the subject; the second test presented differently shaped continuous lines to the subject, who was asked to write down what the lines might suggest. Two scores were derived from each of the creativity tests, one based on the sheer number of responses and the other on the uniqueness of the responses (the rarity of the particular response in the entire series of 502 tests). Correlations between the creativity measures and the SAT scores were near zero, and correlations between the number of ideas and their uniqueness ranged from .36 to .66.

Wallach and Wing (1969) divided their groups into high and low thirds on the SAT, the productivity measure, and the uniqueness measure, and compared the high and low thirds on each of the measures for various outcome criteria.

These creativity tests correlate significantly with self-reports of creative accomplishments in art, writing, and science (r = .20), and these predictions are independent of and superior to predictions derived from the SAT. The lowness of these correlations, however, suggests that these creativity tests will not do a good job of identifying the potentially creative and productive individual. Nevertheless, for research purposes, these results clearly indicate that the creativity tests make an independent contribution to the prediction of creative accomplishments.

Another creativity test that has gained more impressive validation statistics is the Remote Associates Test (RAT) devised by Mednick and Mednick (1967). The test requires that the subject identify the common feature in three different stimuli by calling forth remote associations to each of the stimuli until a common associate is found. For example, the subject might be asked to identify the common associate in the following three words: big, gun, put (answer = shot). Among undergraduate and graduate college students and among mature research workers the RAT generally correlates with measures of verbal intelligence about .4. Were the samples less restricted in intelligence, the correlations would undoubtedly be much higher. The test also predicts creative accomplishments quite well. Mednick and Mednick (1967) report that the RAT has a correlation of .70 with faculty ratings of twenty architecture students and a correlation of .55 with research advisors' ratings of forty-three graduate students in psychology. In addition, research workers with higher scores on the RAT submitted more research proposals and got a higher proportion of them approved than did those with lower RAT scores. In the few studies where measures of verbal ability were also administered, there was little or no correlation between ability scores and creativity ratings. This finding suggests that the RAT can make an independent contribution to the prediction of creativity and that it clearly deserves more investigation.

Harrington (1975) made an important methodological contribution to the laboratory study of creativity by demonstrating that instructions for administrating creativity tests and the scoring criteria for creative productions are often ambiguous or irrelevant to real-life evaluations of creativity. Many creativity tests (excluding the RAT and a few others) score creative responses according to novelty and number without regard to the quality of the solutions proposed. Furthermore, they rarely inform the subject in advance about the qualitative criteria to be applied in scoring the responses. For example, subjects may not be told that the test will be scored for cleverness, or they may be told to pursue several goals simultaneously (e.g., produce many solutions, produce interesting solutions), when one goal might be reached at an expense of another. In addition, subjects often are not given clear instructions, so that subjective interpretations and motivational levels are left to vary outside the experimenter's control.

Harrington had male college students first complete a series of personality tests and then take (among other creativity tests) the Alternative Uses Test. The creativity tests were given with one of two types of instructions: (1) creative instructions (to produce novel and worthwhile responses with examples provided) or (2) standard instructions (with no directions to produce creative responses). Raters independently evaluated the quality of the creative responses under the two conditions, finding that the proportion of creative responses was clearly greater under the creativity instructions than under the standard instructions. More important, however, was the finding of many substantial correlations between personality traits and the number of creative responses under the creativity instructions. A sampling of the personality trait correlations with the number of creative responses under the two instructional conditions is given in Table 11.4. The Harrington (1975) study should be consulted for a more detailed listing of the personality correlations as well as many other interesting findings.

The results of these comparisons are clear. There are only a few significant correlations between personality traits and the number of creative responses under standard instructions, but there are many substantial correlations when the instructions are to be creative. The picture that emerges is that the creatives have high ego-strength, self-confidence, and high achievement needs, as well as low need for support from others. Harrington also reports correlations between the number of creative uses and SAT scores under the two instructional conditions (under both conditions the average correlation was about .42). Thus, the frequently reported finding of little correspondence be-

Table 11.4

A sampling of correlations between the number of creative uses
and some personality traits under two instructional conditions

Personality scale	Number of creative uses	
	Standard instructions (N = 55)	Creativity instructions (N = 50)
Adjective checklist (ACL)		
Self-confidence	.17	.53*
Adjustment	−.30*	.18
Achievement	−.08	.54*
Dominance	.07	.62*
Endurance	−.17	.44*
Order	−.10	.43*
Nurturance	.29*	.02
Exhibition	.21	.41*
Autonomy	.16	.48*
Aggression	.16	.14
Succorance	−.09	−.68*
Abasement	−.18	−.62*
Deference	−.24	−.54*
Special ACL scales		
Creative personality	.20	.69*
Creative abilities	.16	.64*

* Statistically significant.
Source: From D. M. Harrington, "The Effects of Explicit Instructions to "Be Creative" on the Psychological Meaning of Divergent Thinking Test Scores," *Journal of Personality* 43 (1975): 434–454. Copyright © 1975 by Duke University Press.

tween intelligence and creativity measures (e.g., Getzels and Jackson 1962) may be due partly to the failure of other studies in determining creativity, to evaluate the *quality* of the responses. Datta (1963) also found that, with explicit instructions for creative responses, ratings of the creativeness of the responses correlated substantially with supervisors' ratings of creativeness among research scientists (r = .71).

HERITABILITY OF CREATIVITY

There have been only a few studies of the heritability of creativity, if scores on divergent thinking tests are used as the criterion. Given the findings of Harrington (1975), which question the legitimacy of the usual administration of these tests, even those few studies are suspect. Reznikoff et al. (1973) administered ten divergent thinking tests and one brief verbal intelligence test to 117 pairs of teenage twins, about half of whom were identical. Only two of the ten creativity tests yielded significant heritabilities, and these were the RAT and the Similies Test (on which the subject is asked to think of three different endings for each of three incomplete sentences). The verbal intelligence test also yielded a significant heritability and it is not known whether parceling out the influence of intelligence from the two heritable creativity tests would eliminate even their significant heritabilities. The evidence from this study does not suggest clearly that scores on such tests are heritable and may indicate that environmental factors and error play a large role. In any case, we are left in the dark about the contribution of heritable factors to tests of creativity, since instructional sets may have altered the findings in unpredictable ways.

Musical Ability

In contrast to accomplishments in the sciences and in other intellectual endeavors, it is possible for a rare youngster, barely old enough to read, to perform on a musical instrument at a level exceeded only by a few adults with years of musical training. Thus, whatever the skills necessary for musical accomplishment, advanced absolute mental age does not seem to be required. Many infants are responsive to melodies, and there is a report that a nine-month-old infant was able to sing correctly notes played on the piano (see Shuter 1968 for a review). There are also reports of individuals with very low psychometric intelligence who display exceptional musicality (e.g., Anastasi and Levee 1959; Scheerer, Rothmann, and Goldstein 1945). Nevertheless, correlations between IQ and scores on musical aptitude tests are always positive in the general population.

GENETIC EVIDENCE

There is considerable evidence that musical talent tends to run in families. Pedigree studies have consistently confirmed this observation, but, as pointed out repeatedly, such studies can never provide conclusive evidence regarding the heritability of musical talent. One study can serve as an exemplar of the pedigrees associated with extraordinary musical accomplishments (Scheinfeld 1939). Scheinfeld queried three groups of talented musicians—world-class instrumental virtuosos (e.g., Jascha Heifetz, José Iturbi, Yehudi Menuhin, Arturo Toscanini), Metropolitan Opera singers (e.g., Kirsten Flagstad, Lauritz Melchior, Ezio Pinza, Lawrence Tibbett), and students at the Juilliard School of Music—about musical talent in members of their families. In virtually all instances, talent judgments were made by the musicians themselves (in a few cases the virtuoso was too young to make the judgment alone). The results of that study are shown in Figure 11.2.

Among the clearest findings of this study were the early age at which this talent was expressed (for the instrumentalists, it was under six) and the apparently high frequency of talent among the relatives of the talented probands. Other evidence found in this study was that the frequency of musical talent in siblings of the proband was a function of whether or not the parents were judged talented. In essence, the likelihood that siblings would be talented was strongly related to whether or not one, both, or neither parent was judged talented. Models for the inheritance of musicality from pedigree studies have been advanced (Scheinfeld 1965), but none is very simple and more precise data about musicality in the relatives are required for sophisticated genetic models to be developed.

Twin studies of musical ability have not been as helpful in sorting out genetic and environmental influences as might be anticipated. If musical talent depends on the expression of rare genes, then any twin sample unselected for musical talent would have too few of these genes to detect. From this perspective, twin studies would require at least one musically talented twin in every set as a proband, and no such study has yet been performed. If the genetic model for musical talent is a polygenic one, however, then it is possible to use twins unselected for talent, since the musicality genes would be distributed among them in sufficient frequency. Vandenberg (1962), Shuter (1968), and Stafford

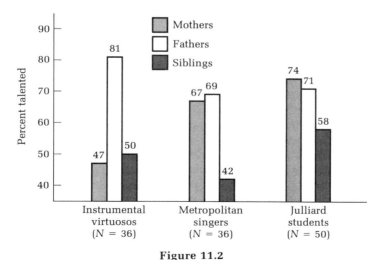

Figure 11.2

Musical talent in the relatives of outstanding musicians. (After Scheinfeld 1939.)

(1970) studied musically unselected pairs of twins on musical aptitude tests and found low heritabilities for overall musical aptitudes, except for musical memory, which showed moderate heritabilities (Musical memory is the ability to listen to a melody twice and judge whether it has been played the same or differently on the second rendition.)

PREDICTION OF MUSICAL ACHIEVEMENT

Evidence indicates that it is possible to predict fairly well the degree to which an unselected group of students will profit from instrumental music lessons. The most comprehensive study on this matter was conducted by Gordon (1967) in an effort to validate his Musical Aptitude Profile (MAP), a rather lengthy test that consists of three major parts— tonal imagery, rhythm imagery, and musical sensitivity—and a number of subparts. The first two parts have answers that are unequivocally correct; the last part is a test of musical taste. No previous knowledge of musical techniques is required, and there are no questions dealing with historical facts. On the first two parts, subjects need only indicate whether the stimuli presented are alike or different. The last part asks which of two renditions of a musical piece (presented on audiotape) represents a more tasteful musical performance.

Prior to instruction on a musical instrument, every child in eight classrooms in five different cities ($N = 241$) took the MAP. Throughout the study, teachers, judges, and students were kept uninformed about the students' aptitude test scores. Every student was then provided a musical instrument and given instruction as part of the regular school curriculum at least once a week over a three-year period. At the end of each year tape recordings were made of the students' performances, and judges rated their quality. At the end of the first year the correlation between the MAP and the judges' ratings of the musical performances of the children was .59; at the end of the third year the correlation was .74. Correlations of the teachers' ratings of the progress of the children and their MAP scores were always lower (.31 to .43). The results defin-itely indicate that musical aptitude tests can predict with considerable success the degree to which children will profit from musical instruction.

In an earlier study, Stanton (1935) validated the Seashore Measures of Musical Talent with applicants to the Eastman School of Music. The applicants were all administered the Seashore tests prior to entry, and their scores were kept secret by Stanton. On the basis of their scores on this test, the students were classified into five categories of musical aptitude. Among the outcomes examined was whether the student graduated from the music school four years later. Only 17 percent of those in the lowest rank on the musical aptitude test graduated, whereas 60 percent of those in the highest group graduated. Since students might not have graduated from the school for a variety of reasons besides musical aptitude, it is clear that these results support the validity of the Seashore battery, even in a group of generally talented music students. A discussion of this and other early research on the psychology of music can be found in Seashore (1938). A comprehensive review of music aptitude tests and their predictive validities, as well as a discussion of many other musical phenomena of interest, can be found in Shuter (1968).

Visual Artistic Ability

PROBLEMS

Despite continued and intense interest in the artist and his creations, there is still a dearth of information on the hereditary and environmental factors influencing artistic accomplishments. The reason for this is unclear, although many artists and art educators themselves have been reluctant to tackle the nature of artistic talent, preferring that it retain an aura of arcanum about it.

There are many difficulties in assessing the quality of artistic performances, and these difficulties differ from those in assessing musical compositions. In musical performance it is possible to have subjects perform the same musical piece and then compare their performances to some standard. Artistic productions, particularly abstract pieces, are so open-ended that it is difficult to apply a standard. The fact that a chimpanzee can compete in abstract artistic expression and that a programmed computer-generated drawing (Noll 1966) may be preferred to a Mondrian painting testifies to the ambiguity in artistic judgments. It is possible to obtain more agreement among raters of artistic products when subjects are asked to draw a specified object from a specified perspective (Skager, Schultz, and Klein 1966), but when constraints on the creative product are relaxed, the intercorrelations between raters may be only in the .30s (Getzels and Csikszentmihalyi 1966).

Outstanding artistic talents are often found to run in families (e.g., the Bruegels, Holbeins, and Wyeths), but evidence of this sort is insufficient for untangling genetic and environmental elements. While it appears that the talents necessary for artistic accomplishment should differ from one area to the next (e.g., sculpture and painting), there are rare individuals who have excelled in more than one artistic medium (e.g., Leonardo da Vinci and Michelangelo). This fact leads one to believe that there might be some factors central to artistic accomplishment in general.

ARTISTIC VALUES

Using the Allport-Vernon-Lindzey Study of Values, Getzels and Csikszentmihalyi (1968) showed that the values of college students enrolled in the Chicago Art Institute differed dramatically from those of other students. These art students demonstrated a single-minded interest in aesthetics to the virtual neglect of every other value of the test (such as economic, social, political, and religious) except theoretical. The average score on the aesthetic scale for all types of art students was about two standard deviations above college student controls with whom they were compared. Among the various subdisciplines of art students, those majoring in the fine arts obtained the highest score on the aesthetic scale and those majoring in art education obtained the lowest.

ART TESTS

Published art tests either measure aesthetic appreciation or call for samples of artistic work. Tests of the appreciation, or preference, type provide a standard drawing preferred by the vast majority of art experts and alternatives differing slightly from the original on some dimension, such as unity or symmetry, in a way that reduces the drawing's aesthetic value. The most widely used test of the preference variety is the Meier Art Judgment Test (1942). Not surprisingly, Meier (1939) found that, with increasing age and increasing education in the arts, judgments of the aesthetic values of the drawings increasingly resemble the judgments of experts. Another test of artistic appreciation, now out of date, is the McAdory Art Test (Siceloff and McAdory 1933), which correlates only .23 with scores on the Meier (Anderson 1951). Thus, judgments of artistic sensitivity depend on the art appreciation test used.

Anastasi (1961) reviews reports of correlations ranging from .40 to .69 between scores on the Meier and art grades or ratings of artistic creativity. Among older age groups, correlations between intelligence test scores and scores on art preference tests generally tend to be negligible. Among younger children, correlations tend to be significant but low (Burkhardt 1958). Positive correlations between artistic appreciation and intelligence among youngsters is probably due to the earlier acquisition of adult normative standards by those who are more intelligent. Eventually most individuals are exposed to artistic conventions, and the correlations then tend to diminish or disappear.

The Horn Art Aptitude Inventory (1945) is an example of a test calling for artistic productions under restricted conditions. The test is composed of two parts: (1) scribble exercises and doodle exercises, in which the subject makes quick sketches of common objects and geometric figures, and (2) an imagery test, in which the subject is provided with rectangles containing a few meaningless lines and is asked to compose designs that incorporate these lines. An item similar to one in the imagery test is shown in Figure 11.3.

The validity of the Horn test has not been firmly established, although Horn and Smith (1945) supply information indicating that the Horn correlated .53 with faculty ratings of performance over a three-year course in an art school and .66 with ratings of instructors in a one-year course for exceptionally able high school students. As can be seen from the sample drawing, the test calls for rather highly developed artistic skills and cannot be employed efficiently with younger children.

Data on the relationship of various perceptual and cognitive abilities to artistic preferences and productions are limited. Using 132 college students, Child (1965) has provided an extensive series of correlations between aesthetic preferences on a test of his own devising and a series of personality and cognitive measures. The strongest correlations with aesthetic judgment were two background variables, education in art and experience in art galleries (both .49). Art-related hobbies and family attitude toward art correlated only about .19. Only two perceptual tests, hidden figures and spatial relations, correlated significantly ($-.20$) with aesthetic preferences, and for these tests only the number of

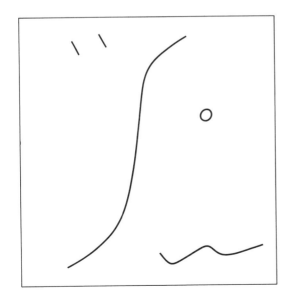

Figure 11.3

Sample test item
for artistic imagery.

incorrect responses correlated significantly. Among questionnaire measures of cognitive style, the strongest correlations were found for the introversion and intuition scales of the Myers-Briggs Type Indicator, with the more introverted and the more intuitive obtaining higher scores on the preference test. Again, the absolute levels of the correlations were low, only .29 and .21, respectively. The Scholastic Aptitude Test verbal scale also correlated significantly with the preference test scores (.24). The Child (1965) article should be consulted for a detailed discussion of these findings as well as many others.

The correlates of outstanding artistic productions are of greater interest. Getzels and Csikszentmihalyi (1966) found insignificant correlations between cognitive abilities and the quality of artistic products among art students, although these correlations were substantially attenuated by the low interrater reliabilities for the creative products.

A most important contribution to the understanding of the variables affecting creative productions was also made by Csikszentmihalyi and Getzels (1971) in a study that somewhat restricted the artistic productions of thirty-one fine arts students. About thirty objects were placed on a table and the artist was asked to select from those objects a composition that was eventually to be drawn. Three measures of *predrawing* performance were assessed by observers—the number of objects manipulated, the unusualness of the different objects selected, and the extent to which the subject explored each of the objects manipulated. The overall aesthetic value and the originality of the final artistic products correlated with the three predrawing measures from .35 to .58. This finding suggests that the predrawing measures that involve *problem finding* bear a substantial correspondence to the quality of the final artistic production. Furthermore, Getzels and Csikszentmihalyi (1975) report that, five years after the subjects' graduation from art school and seven years after the predrawing measures were obtained, expert ratings of the quality of artistic productions now in galleries and museums correlated in the .40s with the predrawing measures. Thus, it seems that variables in the problem-finding stage contribute to artistic success even after formal schooling is completed.

Meier (1939) proposed six interlocking factors that lead to artistic talent:

> Artistic aptitude is viewed as resting upon the possession of six factors: manual skill or craftsman ability, energy output and perseveration in its discharge, general and aesthetic intelligence, perceptual facility, creative imagination, and aesthetic judgment.... Of the six general factors the first three (skill, energy-perseveration, and intelligence) refer *primarily* to heredity. The latter three (perceptual facility, creative imagination, and aesthetic judgment) refer principally to acquired nature, but ... are con-

ditioned in their specific development by factors having a definite reference to heredity. This is particularly applicable to perceptual facility and
aesthetic judgment, less to creative imagination [p. 141].

The common feature in all creative achievements, whether scientific
or artistic, is a passion for doing work in a particular area. It is unclear
whether the passion is an antecedent or a consequent of outstanding
performance, but, whatever the endeavor, it must be present.

Mathematical Ability

Mathematical excellence is held in awe by almost everyone who has
been exposed to advanced mathematics. Many reading this book have
probably enjoyed great success with the elementary operations of
arithmetic but, upon confronting algebra and even more advanced
forms of mathematics, have faltered and fallen. Because mathematics is
unquestionably logical and because our society places a premium on
the exercise of logical reasoning, it is not obvious why so few can do
advanced mathematics. The logical nature of mathematical reasoning is
elucidated by Poincaré (1913), himself a mathematician of the first rank.

> A mathematical demonstration is not a simple juxtaposition of syllogisms,
> it is syllogisms placed *in a certain order*, and the order in which these
> elements are placed is much more important than the elements them-
> selves. If I have the feeling, the intuition, so to speak, of this order, so as to
> perceive at a glance the reasoning as a whole, I need no longer fear lest I
> forget one of the elements, for each of them will take its allotted place in
> the array, and that without any effort of memory on my part [in Ghiselin
> 1952, p. 35].

Similar conclusions can be drawn from studies of reasoning and
memory in the literature of cognitive psychology, namely, that once an
overall logical structure has been discovered the individual elements
originally necessary for the discovery no longer need to be focused
upon directly. They are recoded into chunks of larger conceptual
units, and these chunks may be recoded into even larger chunks (Miller
1956; Simon 1974). Once information is coded into chunks, it is possible to retrieve the individual elements by an unfolding process.

There is no information available on the capacity of mathematically
talented people to chunk information. For the range of subjects studied
in experiments unrelated to the investigation of talent, the number of
chunks, regardless of size, that an individual can retain in memory is
about seven, plus or minus two (Miller 1956). An ingenious study of
chess masters who play chess blindfolded suggests that it is the ca-

pacity to chunk into larger units that distinguishes them from less able players, and not the absolute number of chunks. Most chess masters and grand masters can play a number of chess games simultaneously while blindfolded. It was thought that this ability represented a remarkable capacity for visualizing the chess boards game after game, but, when chess masters were asked to reproduce chess boards on which the pieces had been arrayed randomly, they displayed no unusual talent. They had coded board positions in *genuine* games into meaningful larger chunks, because meaningful positions are what occur in genuine games. When pieces are arrayed randomly on a chessboard, the opportunity to chunk into large meaningful units is almost always lost; consequently, no special talents are noted (Chase and Simon 1973).

Mathematically talented people appear to *read* mathematics as others read words on the printed page. In reading, the individual letters and words are but a part of the understanding entailed in the concepts implied by those symbols. For concepts that we understand, the exact phrasing is no longer of substantive import and we need not resort to rote memory to recover the essential ideas represented by those symbols on the printed page.

Another feature of mathematics that many marvel at is that it can appear precociously. Mathematics, like musical talent, is a relatively closed system that is unrelated to broad everyday experiences; consequently, accomplishment does not depend on advanced age.

A major study of mathematically precocious youths is currently underway at Johns Hopkins University. In this study seventh and eighth graders under fourteen years of age in the Baltimore area can enter a mathematics competition in which they take a variety of mathematics tests as well as other personality and intellectual tests (Stanley, Keating, and Fox 1974).

The mathematically most able 35 boys in the first year of competition have been singled out for special study (there were too few mathematically able girls to study). In general these boys score in the 90th percentiles or higher for high school seniors on the SAT mathematics section and even score above the mean on the SAT verbal portion as well. Their scores on the nonverbal Raven's Progressive Matrices intelligence test are around the 99th percentile for British college students. On Terman's Concept Mastery Test 32 of 34 obtained higher absolute scores on the verbal reasoning subtest than on the vocabulary subtest. This finding confirms the view that experience and age may play an important role in the acquisition of vocabulary, while verbal reasoning processes may be advanced at a relatively early age. Furthermore, this finding illustrates the validity of distinguishing between vocabulary and verbal reasoning.

The personality profiles of these students suggest social maturity and psychological health. Thus, they are not psychologically odd by conventional standards. A selected number of the students have been placed in college math and science courses after consultation with the staff, and the results have been universally favorable thus far. Many of the teachers have been unaware that these students were youngsters, and course grades have almost always been above average. The descriptions of the students and their families conform quite closely to descriptions derived from Terman's (1925) study fifty years earlier.

Conclusions

The studies reviewed in this chapter display a remarkable consistency. They suggest that talented individuals may be intelligent, but that high intelligence is not sufficient for high accomplishment. Some studies suggest that there is a climate for creativity, and that this climate may involve self-confidence, whether merited or not, and perhaps a good deal of cultural conflict. Studies focusing on early passion for work in a particular area are required, since this passion seems necessary, although not sufficient, for high accomplishment.

III

GROUP
DIFFERENCES

12

Sex Differences

Innate Factors Versus Socialization

This chapter has two themes. The first is the contribution of innate factors to sex differences across a wide spectrum of interesting behaviors. The second theme is the role of socialization and situational factors in the genesis of many observed sex differences. To anticipate findings from our review, some important psychological sex differences may have their antecedents in innate factors, and many of the differences observed between male and female, both in their own behaviors and in the way they are socialized by the family and society, are the result of these innate differences. Boys and girls are groomed to assume and internalize their predicted adult roles (housewife-mother or breadwinner-protector). Although these adult divisions of labor do not have equivalents in childhood, it is the job of society and the family to develop the character of the child so that the child will eventually incorporate and value positively these predicted adult roles and responsibilities. This process takes a long time, and, as the child successfully internalizes the desirability of this division of labor, behaviors not in accord with these internalized demands produce a sense that something is wrong, that the person who manifests these deviant behaviors is inferior or deficient in some respect.

Many of the sex-typed socialization differences have their roots in the obvious sexual dimorphisms, such as childbearing and physical strength. In nonliterate societies, differential socialization reflected a division of labor that was necessary in adulthood. With the advent of birth control and other technological advances, however, sexual intercourse was no longer inextricably linked to childbearing, nursing did not necessarily mean breast-feeding, and factors such as strength had less influence on the ability to be the breadwinner.

Breast-feeding was one of the important factors keeping women around the home to care for very young children. Because it tends to inhibit ovulation, breast-feeding is also a moderately effective birth control technique and thus has served to keep children fairly well spaced. As a result, each child's chances of survival were increased and less of a burden was placed on the family to support its issue. Nowadays bottle feeding provides an acceptable substitute for mothers' milk, and artificial devices are even more effective methods of birth control than is breast-feeding. Thus, the moral justification for maintaining the social consequences of an innate sex difference such as the ability to breast-feed has begun to undergo an agonizing reappraisal.

It has also become difficult to predict adult sex roles with certainty. Women can enter previously all-male occupations, and many women find it no longer acceptable to remain in the home. Modern technological advances have wreaked havoc on the innate social order. New norms and modes of relating are necessary when physical labor is no longer exceptionally rewarded and anatomy is no longer destiny. Every labor-saving invention threatens prior justifications for maintaining the social consequences of innate differences.

From an evolutionary perspective of genetic selection, it would not be surprising to find that many of the personality differences observed between men and women have genetic antecedents in these previously inevitable divisions of labor. For example, highly active women might have found it unusually difficult to stay tied to the home and they may either have had fewer offspring or have been less successful in rearing children in subsistence societies with scarce resources. To the extent that the behavioral differences were associated with the sex chromosomes, there might have been selection for lower activity levels in women.

From the evolutionary perspective of "nature, red in tooth and claw," the concept of *parental investment* may explain some persistent sex differences. The concept refers to behavior that increases the chances of offspring survival at the cost of the parent's ability to invest in future offspring (Trivers 1972). It should be clear from this definition that the female must make a larger investment than the male in each offspring to ensure that her genes will be represented in succeeding generations. As a consequence, her best strategy in choosing a mate is to select one who will be better able to help in the rearing of the offspring (by giving signs of love to indicate that he will maintain an enduring attachment or by being of higher social status and therefore in a better position to provide for the child). A male should adopt a different strategy with the same goal in mind; he should inseminate as many females as possible and let each fend for herself. He need not be as discriminating in his choice of mates, for the biological cost of insemination is trivial.

That many species below humans behave in ways consistent with this view has been documented (Wilson 1975); whether such views are applicable to humans is still in dispute. But the concept of parental investment does help to account for some otherwise mysterious phenomena. Consider the finding that the sex ratio at birth varies with social class such that the lower social classes are more likely to produce females than males, while the reverse is true in the higher social classes (see Figure 14.3). Since the individual male is less important in maintaining population numbers, he should be more expendable in times of scarce resources. In times of abundance a preponderance of males may be desirable, since the ensuing competition among them for the rarer females increases the likelihood that those with the "best" genes will father the children. That males are generally less trustworthy in monogamous relationships is also in accord with their strategy for increasing the representation of genes in the next generation.

The evolution of culture and conscience may obscure built-in differential dispositions, and that is why the analysis of sex differences is so much more complicated in humans than in lower animals. If such dispositions are evolutionarily grounded, however, there may always be a necessity for societies to adopt cultural prohibitions in order to accomplish other important tasks. But as the goals of society change, previous prohibitions may be relaxed and new ones instituted.

Societies have been fairly consistent in sex-typing their members and similar differences have been fostered in many cultures, both literate and nonliterate. Barry, Bacon, and Child (1957) analyzed many cultures for differences in socialization pressures after infancy according to sex. The results of their analyses are shown in Figure 12.1.

The figure shows that child-rearing practices across cultures train girls to be nurturant and boys to be self-reliant. Boys are clearly subjected to greater pressures to achieve and girls are under greater pressure to be responsible and obedient. While the origins of these differential pressures are the subject of debate, the exceptions to the usual practices that can be seen in the table show that the socialization pressures are not inflexibly connected to biological differences.

It might be argued that tampering with the social consequences of

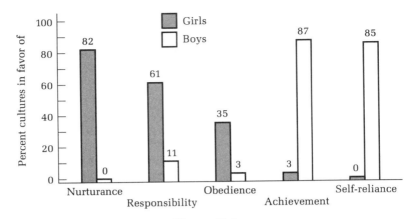

Figure 12.1

Cross-cultural ratings of socialization pressures on the different sexes. Some cultures could not be rated. (After Barry, Bacon, and Child 1957.)

innate differences by actively discouraging traditional sex-typing is risky. Human society does what it does because those actions have been adaptive in the past, and who can confidently prophesy the unintended consequences of any revolutionary change in the relations between the sexes and the structure of society? In reply, it could be said that the social changes already wrought by technological advances are at least as powerful as the intended consequences of diminutions of sex-typing. We produce technological revolutions at a pace far faster than any genetic changes can be expected, but humans are remarkable in their genetically bred plasticity and in their extraordinary capacity to adapt to change. Given our heritage of successfully adapting to past changes, it seems likely that we will eventually learn to adapt to the new challenges and that new norms for sex-typing will evolve to meet the uncertainties of the desexualization of adult social roles.

There will undoubtedly be limits on the desexualization of socialization because some important innate sex differences will still remain. The vulnerability of the female to sexual attack by the male and other consequences of physical differences between the sexes will justifiably influence parents to be more protective of their daughters than of their sons. Positive evaluation of childbearing will still be necessary, for humanity could not survive long if childbearing were completely eradicated or test-tube babies did not become the norm.

The fundamental problem guiding research in sex differences is what proportion of observed behavioral differences is "built-in" through the genetic program and what proportion is acquired postnatally through learning. One should not expect too much of the genetic differences between males and females. The two sexes have $\frac{45}{46}$ of their chromosomes in common, and the one that differs (the Y) contains the smallest proportion of genetic material. The X chromosome is more likely to be influential, however, because it is the third largest and contains much more genetic information than does the Y. Recessive genes on this chromosome are more likely to be expressed in males than in females because males are hemizygous (because they have no homologous X to compensate). The path from genes to morphology and behavior is treacherous, however, and many vicissitudes of hormonal turbulence can alter or even reverse the genetic program. There are a number of reports of individuals whose genetic sex is not entirely congruent with their assigned sex, and it is here that we begin our inquiry into the nature of sex differences.

Sexual Differentiation in Mammals

In the absence of the Y chromosome from the father, a fetus will differentiate to become a female. The presence of the Y chromosome, or, more precisely, a gene on the Y chromosome, causes the undifferentiated gonads to develop into testes. From then on the testes control further differentiation into maleness through the secretion of *androgen*, a male hormone. Silvers and Wachtel (1977) have recently reviewed evidence identifying the sex-determining gene on the Y chromosome as the same one that affects tissue graft incompatibility between opposite-sexed members of the same strain of rats or mice.

The idea that the Y chromosome serves only as a trigger for sexual differentiation into maleness is probably oversimplified. There is evidence that those with two Y chromosomes (XYY syndrome) are at increased risk for mental retardation, criminality, and disorders such as acne, and they are likely to be taller than average. Witkin et al. (1976) have recently suggested that the extra Y chromosome might be related to increased criminality because it is associated with lower intelligence. There is no good evidence that individuals with two Y chromosomes are at especially increased risk for violent crimes, however, as has been suggested by many researchers.

The testes perform two important functions during embryological differentiation: (1) they secrete a chemical called *Mullerian inhibiting substance*, and (2) they secrete *testosterone* (a male hormone). The Mullerian inhibiting substance prevents the differentiation of the Mullerian ducts, which would otherwise serve as the anlage out of which the female internal sexual apparatus would develop. Early in development the secretion of testosterone causes the internal differentiation of the male sexual apparatus, and later it causes the development of the external male apparatus (Money and Ehrhardt 1972). The secretion of these substances presumably has effects on the brain as well as on other parts of the body. We shall now explore some of the behavioral consequences of anomalies in the secretion of or response to testosterone.

ADRENOGENITAL SYNDROME (AGS)

AGS is a disorder caused by an autosomal recessive gene that produces an excess in the secretion of an androgen from the adrenal gland. In genetic females this hormone causes the external genitalia to differentiate in the masculine direction, although, because of timing, it has little effect on the internal sexual apparatus. Thus, affected individuals are female in the internal sexual apparatus but male externally. The external male genitalia, however, may vary from a fully developed penis and empty scrotal sack to a grossly enlarged clitoris or very small penis, depending on the extent of the adrenal hyperfunction. Since the external genitalia are incompletely differentiated, the alert physician can often identify the disorder and institute corrective surgery early. Thus, such children are now usually reared as girls. AGS occurs with equal frequency among boys, but the disorder is not easily recognized at birth. Because the hypersecretion of androgen does not cease at birth, however, both boys and girls with the disorder will have an extremely early puberty unless cortisone is administered postnatally to prevent the continued hypersecretion of androgen.

A very similar disorder to AGS is progestin-induced hermaphroditism, which was caused by the administration of progestin to pregnant women who seemed likely to abort (it is now rarely used). This hormone can also have a masculinizing effect on the external sexual apparatus, until its administration ceases with the birth of the child. Should the fetus be a genetic female, depending on the extent of genital masculinization, the child could either be labeled as a boy with undescended testes and reared as a boy, or recognized as a female and undergo corrective surgery and rearing as a female.

Recent interest in the AGS was prompted by findings that rhesus monkeys given androgens during pregnancy had female offspring who were "tomboyish" in their behavior (Young, Goy, and Phoenix 1965). Since both AGS and progestin-induced hermaphroditism involve excesses in prenatal androgens, it was thought that human females with these disorders might also display more masculine intellectual and personality characteristics. Ehrhardt and Money (1967) and Ehrhardt, Epstein, and Money (1968) reported on ten girls with progestin-induced hermaphroditism and fifteen girls with AGS, all treated successfully postnatally and reared as females. These twenty-five girls were matched to a group of normal girls on age, SES, IQ, and race. The girls and their mothers were interviewed, and the girls were given a variety of personality tests. In comparison with the controls, these girls were more tomboyish, enjoying rough-and-tumble activities with high energy expenditure. However, neither their parents nor they saw themselves as especially aggressive. Money and Ehrhardt (1972) suggest that the preference for more masculine activities may be due to the effects of androgen on the fetal brain.

Another study by McGuire, Ryan, and Omenn (1975) studied children and adults with corrected AGS, using both female and male patients as well as normal controls. The controls were matched for age, height, sex, urban or rural residence, and IQ. Tests of masculinity and femininity and questions designed to elicit tomboyism were given to the subjects. There was no indication that the AGS subjects differed from their same-sexed controls. Differences were observed between male and female AGS patients on the tests, but these differences paralleled the differences observed between the male and female controls. These authors point out that their data are difficult to reconcile with the earlier findings and add that a recent study by Ehrhardt and Baker (1974) had confirmed the earlier findings of greater energy expenditure and tomboyism among AGS females, thus making the results even more difficult to reconcile.

As is often the case in a new area of research, one is faced with a maze of confusing and inconsistent findings. The earlier Ehrhardt and Money (1967) study reporting tomboyism among the prenatal androgen patients fit nicely with preconceptions that the hormones should be doing something more than simply affecting morphology. Together with the findings on lower animals, these results made a good story. At this stage we cannot be sure whether the hypothesis deserves support or should be discarded. McGuire, Ryan, and Omenn (1975), however, have had the opportunity to conduct a better-controlled study. Hopefully, more research in this important area will be done.

ANDROGEN INSENSITIVITY SYNDROME (AIS)

The closest counterpart of the AGS is the AIS. In this syndrome testosterone is secreted normally, but genetic males are incapable of responding to it because of another genetic defect. These genetic males have external genitals nearly normal for females, although some aspects of the internal sex organs are incompletely developed in the feminine direction because the Y chromosome induced the development of testes, which then secreted the Mullerian inhibiting factor. In most instances these infants are reared as girls. This is particularly fortunate, for there is no known treatment for the disorder. It exists at the cellular level, and no amount of androgen supplementation will cause the body to masculinize. Money and Ehrhardt (1972) report that these women, as teenagers and adults, conform to our conventional concepts of femininity.

The overall findings from these studies suggest that it is not the genetic sex per se but rather the sex of rearing that is most important in the development of one's gender identity. In the case of AIS, the fact that the prenatal brain was probably not masculinized may have made the good adjustment to the female role possible, so that one must be cautious in drawing any definitive conclusions. The mixed results of the studies of AGS suggest the possibility that prenatal hormonal circumstances can affect temperament, but the results of the carefully done McGuire, Ryan, and Omenn (1975) study strongly indicate that the prenatal hormonal influences on gender identity and sex role identification are not very strong, if present at all.

Despite the conclusion in the previous paragraph that the sex of rearing seems to be the dominant influence on gender identity, there is a recent report of an extraordinary genetic defect in the Dominican Republic that serves to complicate the picture (Imperato-McGinley, et al. 1974). Twenty-four genetic males born with ambiguous external genitalia but with undescended testes and other indications of masculine internal genitalia have been identified. The genetic origins of this disorder can be traced back seven generations to a common ancestor. These individuals are usually reared as females, but at puberty the voice deepens, muscle mass increases, the testes descend, and the penis enlarges to become sexually functional. With those changes their sexual orientation appears to reverse and the gender identity in some becomes masculine, with sexual energies directed towards females. The genetic defect is not in testosterone but in the conversion of testosterone to dihydrotestosterone in certain tissues. Among some of these cases sex of rearing appears not to prohibit a drastic reversal of sexual orientation, although no detailed psychological studies have been reported to certify that the reversal is without complication. Since testosterone is present prenatally and there is masculine differentiation internally, brain development may have also been affected in such a manner as to make the transition at puberty less difficult than otherwise.

POSTNATAL ACCIDENT

Thus far we have discussed individuals with some abnormality in prenatal sexual differentiation such that there is a contrast between genetic sex and morphological sex. For scientific purposes, it would be ideal to have cases of individuals whose genetic sex and prenatal development were entirely congruent and normal, but who suffered some accident postnatally that required a reversal in the sex of rearing.

A rare case meeting these requirements occurred when one of two normal male twins had his penis accidentally ablated during circumcision at age seven months (Money 1975). The parents learned that surgery was possible to remodel the infant's sexual apparatus in the female direction, and at seventeen months the surgery was undertaken. From then on the parents made every effort to treat the infant in accordance with the newly assigned sex. By four years of age it was quite clear that the two twins were developing gender identities consistent with their assigned sex. The girl chose to help mother in the kitchen and preferred dolls and other feminine activities, while the boy preferred cars and trucks. The only possible indication that the prenatal androgens had some effects on the girl was that she tended to become dominant when playing with other girls. At age nine, Money reports, gender differentiation appeared successful. Around puberty the girl will have the final necessary surgery to construct a functional vagina so that she can experience and enjoy sex. Around that time she will also be told of the events leading to the sex reassignment.

From the results of the above-mentioned studies, it appears that gender differentiation is insufficiently advanced at birth to ensure gender identity in the appropriate direction. Much of gender differentiation goes on postnatally, and little of it appears irreversible at birth. The question of whether the prenatal hormones have an irreversible effect on brain development or temperament (activity level) is still open, although with lower animals it seems clear that prenatal hormones have a more influential role vis-à-vis sex-typed behavior.

Until now we have only discussed the effects of male hormones or their absence on personality development, neglecting the effects of female hormones on development. Only one study has presented evidence of behavioral correlates of female hormones administered prenatally. Yalom, Green, and Fisk (1973) identified a group of diabetic mothers who had been given progesterone and estrogen during pregnancy to reduce their propensity to miscarry because of deficiencies in these hormones. Two different age groups of boys were studied, six-year-olds and sixteen-year-olds. The sixteen-year-olds (N = 20) were compared to eight children of diabetic mothers not given these hormones and fourteen children of normal mothers resembling the subjects in age, sex, and social class. The twenty six-year-olds were compared only with a control group of seventeen children of normal mothers.

The general findings suggested that the children given these hormones were less masculine (less athletic, assertive, and aggressive) than the controls. One peculiar finding was that the untreated diabetic controls tended to be more masculine on these dimensions than the normal controls. This might be seen as somewhat confirmatory of the other findings, since mothers of these children were presumably deficient in the female hormones during the pregnancy. A problem in interpreting the findings for the sixteen-year-olds, however, was that differences between the treated children and the normal controls were often insignificant, whereas differences between the treated and untreated children of diabetic mothers often were significant.

For the six-year-olds, teachers' ratings showed the children of the treated diabetics to be significantly less assertive and athletic than the normal controls. But, again, the findings are peculiar in that sixteen of the seventeen normal controls were rated above the mean for their classes on these dimensions, while the treated children more closely approximated the expected fifty-fifty split. Thus, it might be argued that it is more necessary to account for the peculiarities of the controls than of the treated children. An additional finding was that the children of the treated diabetic mothers were marginally shorter than the controls, a fact that might have contributed to their more feminine behavior.

The findings of this study are surely unclear, but they reinforce the possibility that prenatal hormones do play a significant role in personality. We can only reiterate that these are important and groundbreaking investigations and that they should prompt more sophisticated research designs in the future.

PHYSICAL DIFFERENCES

At birth girls have a larger pelvic outlet, a higher proportion of body fat, and more advanced skeletal maturation than boys (Tanner 1970). Infant boys are heavier and more muscular than girls, and soon after birth their basal metabolism and calorie intake are higher. Since muscle has a higher metabolic rate than fat, the greater muscularity of boys may relate to their higher caloric intake (Eichorn 1970).

Work with lower animals also suggests that the hypothalamus may differ between the sexes, since it is especially susceptible to the effects of testosterone. There is an intimate and reciprocal orchestration between the pituitary and the hypothalamus in the release of various hormones, and Tanner (1970) points out that

> in all mammals investigated endocrinological and to a large extent behavioral maleness is dependent on the structure of the hypothalamus. If a male pituitary is grafted into an adult male whose own pituitary has been removed, then, when vascular connections with the hypothalamus have been established, the pituitary will secrete gonadotrophic hormones in a male, not a female cycle. The converse is also true [p. 115].

One cannot be sure that this phenomenon would also occur in humans, but at least on a priori grounds the possibility does not seem remote.

Throughout all of prenatal development it appears that males are more susceptible to a variety of insults. It has been estimated that 130 to 150 males are conceived for every 100 females, but that during pregnancy the males are more likely to be aborted, producing a sex ratio at birth of about 105 males to 100 females. The boys are much more likely to be born with major congenital malformations, and it has been suggested that the greater susceptibility to malformations among boys is due to the fact that they have only one X chromosome (i.e., they are hemizygous). Any defects or recessive genes with deleterious effects on this chromosome get expressed because boys do not have a "backup" X chromosome. Since girls have two X chromosomes, a deficiency in one may not be expressed because there is some likelihood that the second X will not have the same defect.

Figure 12.2 gives the rates of malformations by sex from the Collaborative Perinatal Study based on about 56,000 births. Except for congenital dislocation of the hip among the major malformations and strawberry/port-wine hemangioma among the minor malformations, the rates are clearly higher among the males. This should assure readers that the differences between males and females are not confined to the obvious anatomical ones. As newer and more sensitive diagnostic procedures become available, it seems likely that other anatomical and physiological differences between the sexes will be discovered.

From the first year of life males are more susceptible to a variety of diseases, including major cardiovascular diseases, malignant neoplasms, nutritional deficiencies, peptic ulcers, asthma, and parasitic and other infective diseases. The conclusion must be drawn that females are better buffered against the onslaught of disease. This buffering is probably due to the greater genetic heterozygosity of females, which permits deficiencies in one X chromosome to be compensated by adequacies in the other X chromosome. Males, on the other hand, have only one X chromosome and thus fewer biochemical resources to call upon in the event of life-threatening stresses (Thompson and Grusec 1970).

Male vulnerability is not limited to the perinatal years. Throughout the lifespan males are more likely to succumb. Some of this increased vulnerability is due to cultural factors, but it appears that biological factors also play a significant role. In an effort to minimize some of the sociocultural sex differentials, Madigan (1957) calculated death rates for Catholic priests and nuns teaching in educational institutions. Madigan found that the life expectancy among the priests was five to six years lower than among the nuns and that this difference was comparable to that found in the generality. Thus, the root of the difference seemed to lie in biological factors.

STRENGTH

One important difference between the sexes from age five on is in strength. Few studies of strength have been done with preschool children (Metheny 1941b) because it is so difficult to motivate them to exert

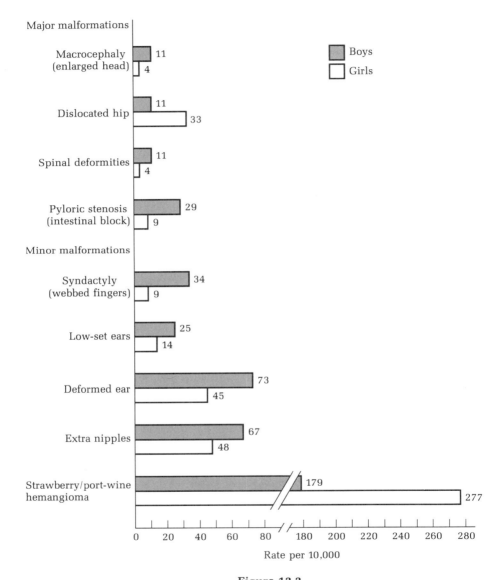

Figure 12.2

Congenital malformations per 10,000 births showing significant differences between males and females. (Myrianthopoulos and Chung 1974.)

themselves to the limit. However, grip strength as measured by a hand dynamometer shows that by age five boys are slightly stronger than girls, even after correcting for body size (Metheny 1941a). There are indications that the number of muscle cell nuclei and muscle fibers is greater in boys than in girls at this time, so that boys not only have more muscle mass then but also have a head start at puberty when testosterone increases and muscle mass and strength differences become enormous (Cheek 1968). It is not clear how the preferences for more vigorous motor activities among boys at this age contribute to the strength differences. Sociocultural pressures for large-muscle activity in boys undoubtedly play a role in the differences in muscle mass, but it may be that greater strength also leads to greater preference for vigorous activity. The strength differences are almost entirely limited to the upper extremities and the trunk, and there are only minor differences, if any, in the strength of the lower extremities. Women possess, on the average, 35 percent of men's strength. If this difference is corrected for the greater size of the male, women still possess only about 80 percent the strength of men (Asmussen 1973).

Regardless of the cause of the strength differences, they are likely to have implications for other behavioral differences between the sexes. Self-reliance ought to be enhanced when strength aids adaptive functioning. Strength should also play a role in increasing self-confidence on many important dimensions relating to the interpersonal and the object world. Especially among boys during the school years, strength and athletic prowess play an important role in social development. For example, Jones (1949) has shown that among boys aged eleven to seventeen popularity is correlated in the .30s with both dynamic strength (measured by jump tests, distance throw, and running) and grip strength. Social status, school achievement, and height had negligible relationships to popularity in this sample of boys. It is also generally true that school-age boys and men have more confidence than females in their task performance and rate themselves higher on measures of strength and potency (Maccoby and Jacklin 1974).

GENDER IDENTITY AND GENDER ROLE IN YOUNG CHILDREN

What do we mean by masculinity and femininity? In order to develop an understanding of these concepts, one must distinguish between the private experience and the public expression of one's masculinity and femininity. The private experience in the self-awareness of being male, female, or ambivalent is referred to as *gender identity*, while the public expression of behaviors associated with the private experiences is referred to as *gender role*. In most individuals these two coincide, but among some they may not (Person and Ovesey 1974). The following discussion shall first review the limited evidence concerning private experiences of sexual identity and then go on to public observations of these differences in young children. Findings among older children and adults shall be discussed later.

Private.   It would seem that one's private sense of masculinity or femininity must develop over time. To be sure, most children of speaking age can correctly name their sex, but there is little indication that such young children can unequivocally indicate knowledge that the anatomical difference is the essential ingredient of sex determination. For example, Levin, Balistrieri, and Schukit (1972) had lower-class children aged five to eleven try to identify sex from drawings depicting only the head (long or short hair) or only the clothed or nude body (genitalia visible) of a boy or girl. When hair or dress was the only cue, almost all children were able to correctly identify the sex. From the genital cue alone, however, the vast majority of five-year-olds were unable to make the correct identification. Only 23 percent of the five-year-olds made the correct discrimination; 52 percent of the seven-year-olds, 79 percent of the nine-year-olds, and 92 percent of the eleven-year-olds made the correct discriminations.

The authors then presented drawings in which there was a conflict between the visible genitalia and either hair or dress to see whether the children saw anatomy as being determinative. Only 16 percent of the seven-year-olds, 24 percent of the nine-year-olds, and 61 percent of the eleven-year-olds responded correctly in terms of genital dominance (data on the five-year-olds were not reported).

These results have a number of implications. First, the cognitive ability to make definitive sex discriminations is not common among five- or seven-year-olds and seems to develop over time. This finding throws into question Freudian theories, which are based on the assumption that three-to-five-year-old children have a deep understanding of anatomical differences as part of the Oedipal complex and penis envy. Second, it is hard to imagine that gender identity can be well developed in young children when they have such little cognitive appreciation for the basis of sex differences. Third, the results were derived from lower-class black and white samples, and higher social class samples might be able to make these discriminations earlier.

Another way to get a look at the "inside" or private aspect of sex differences is to ask children about their interests. In the It Test, children are given the opportunity to choose among a variety of sex-typed activities for a cutout doll of presumably ambiguous sex. This projective test reveals that boys from three on have clearly masculine interests; they prefer playing with masculine-type toys and are likely to see the ambiguous figure as being a boy. Girls prefer feminine toys and see the ambiguous figure as being a girl (Fling and Manosevitz 1972). Other studies clearly confirm the view that sex-typing with respect to toys begins occurring in the second year of life and is generally clearly established after age two (Maccoby and Jacklin 1974).

Public. When do behavioral sex differences emerge on the "outside" so that they are discernible to others? In the first year of life there are no experimentally established sex differences in large-muscle activities, but after that the results indicate either no differences or that boys are more active. Typical studies observe children in large play areas that have been marked off in a gridlike fashion. The results generally indicate that boys are likely to use much more of the space available than are girls, and that girls are likely to spend their time seated at craft or art projects (Maccoby and Jacklin 1974). Whether the greater amount of free-ranging activities among young boys is acquired or innate is still a subject of much dispute. The fact that most primates show similar sex differences in the pattern of gross motor activities, however, suggests the presence of an innate component.

Findings indicate that in the three-to-six-year range boys are more curious and exploratory than girls. In some respects this characteristic is confounded with activity level and such factors as fear and timidity. Although it is difficult to separate activity from exploratory behavior in any individual, there are striking consequences of these differences. Table 12.1 gives mortality figures from accidents among children aged one to four. It is clear that boys are much more likely than girls to die from accidents in that age range and that many of these sex differences are clearly present around age one. The reasons for pedestrian deaths among one-year-olds are different from the reasons for such deaths among three- and four-year-olds. One-year-olds tend to be run over by cars in their own driveways or in garages, while three- and four-year-olds tend to be run over while they are riding their tricycles or chasing after a ball in traffic. Drowning also shows a much greater frequency among boys, being three times more common at four years of age among boys than among girls.

There is little indication that the sex differences in accidental mortality by age one are due to differential child-rearing practices for boys and girls, although this possibility remains open. There are only weak indications that parents may be less watchful of boys than of girls at this age (Pedersen and Robson 1969), although during the school years parents are likely to be much more concerned about the safety and welfare of girls than of boys.

The most plausible explanation for the findings is that boys are more likely to be hyperactive than girls. It has been shown that hyperactive children (at ages later than one) are much more likely than nonhyperactive children to be involved in accidental poisonings (Stewart 1970),

Table 12.1

Mortality from leading types of accidents among children
aged 1–4, United States, 1972–1973

Type of accident	Average annual death rate per 100,000									
	Boys at ages:					Girls at ages:				
	1–4	1	2	3	4	1–4	1	2	3	4
Accidents—all types ..	38.0	44.5	40.7	36.5	30.1	25.4	32.9	27.9	21.9	18.9
Motor vehicle	13.6	12.7	13.3	14.7	13.9	10.2	10.8	11.2	9.3	9.4
Pedestrian (in traffic accidents)	6.5	3.6	6.3	7.9	8.3	3.3	2.3	3.5	3.6	4.0
Drowning*	8.3	8.8	10.2	8.4	5.6	3.6	5.1	4.6	2.8	1.8
Fire and flames	5.6	5.8	7.1	5.5	4.1	4.6	4.9	5.1	4.2	3.9
Inhalation and in- gestion of food or other objects	1.8	4.1	1.8	0.9	0.5	1.4	3.2	1.2	0.7	0.6
Poisoning	1.6	3.8	1.4	0.9	0.5	1.1	2.4	1.2	0.6	0.3
Falls	1.5	2.8	1.4	1.2	0.8	1.2	2.1	1.0	1.1	0.5
Firearm missile	0.7	0.4	0.8	0.7	1.1	0.4	0.2	0.4	0.7	0.4
Accidental deaths as a percent of all deaths	42%	34%	44%	49%	49%	36%	30%	38%	40%	41%

* Exclusive of deaths in water transportation.
Source: Reports of the Division of Vital Statistics, National Center for Health Statistics. Taken from *Statistical Bulletin*, Metropolitan Life May, 1975.

and it may be that the other accidents reported in the table are also related to a greater frequency of hyperactivity among the boys. This is not to deny that closer parental supervision could have prevented many of the accidents. But often hyperactive children dart away at the slightest failure of vigilance.

Physical aggression is one trait that is more common among boys than among girls as early as two or three years of age. Maccoby and Jacklin (1974) consider two social learning hypotheses concerning this sex difference: (1) girls are permitted only subtle and indirect expressions of aggression, such as cattiness, but not direct physical forms of aggression; and (2) because aggression is generally less acceptable for girls than for boys, girls develop greater inhibitions against displaying aggression. Both views support the notion that the innate propensity toward aggression does not differ between the sexes but that reinforcement and modeling serve to discourage the expression of aggression in girls.

Maccoby and Jacklin (1974) have reviewed the mixed evidence for each of these hypotheses, finding no strong evidence to support one or the other notion. They do suggest, however, that biological factors may be very important in the expression of aggression and in the reaction to the aggressive responses of others. They offer as evidence for a biological component the following:

(1) Males are more aggressive than females in all human societies for which evidence is available. (2) the sex differences are found early in life, at a time when there is no evidence that differential socialization pressure have been brought to bear by adults to "shape" aggression differently in the two sexes. (3) Similar sex differences are found in man and subhuman primates. (4) Aggression is related to levels of sex hormones, and can be changed by experimental administration of these hormones [in animals] [Maccoby and Jacklin 1974, pp. 242–243].

It is not clear that aggression differences are inherited directly. Aggressive responses among boys might be the result of high activity levels and experience in rough-and-tumble play. If the aggressive response is viewed as a "skill" or ability, the boys, by virtue of their greater gross motor activity, may have had more opportunity than girls to learn to express aggressive behavior because of more frequent encounters with frustrating events in the environment. The fact that mesomorphic preschool boys (Walker 1962) and mesomorphic adolescent boys (Cortes and Gatti 1972) are more likely to be aggressive and delinquent, respectively, than nonmesomorphs suggests that reinforcing factors are important in the acquisition of aggressive behaviors. For example, after the proverbial ninety-seven-pound weakling takes his body-building course, he too can become a bully. The boy already had the propensity to aggress; he simply did not have the skills.

It seems likely that strength factors are central to the expression of aggression. These factors are associated with propensities toward high-level motor activities and the exercise and expression of the competencies represented by greater muscle mass. The fact that males interact physically with others more than do girls suggests that provocations for aggression are more frequent among boys than girls. The combination of increased opportunity for provocation and greater skills in aggressive expression probably accounts for the greater propensity to aggress among boys than among girls.

The two competing views of the causes and maintenance of sex differences still revolve around the issues of biological predispositions and differential socialization of the sexes. Research with primates shows remarkable parallels to the sex differences observed in humans. This similarity leads one to believe that biological predispositions are not irrelevant in the genesis of sex differences. But these biological predispositions may be either amplified or countered in the course of development by differential socialization practices. Most parents would not want their children to engage extensively in sex-inappropriate behaviors, although there is evidence that prohibition of sex-inappropriate behaviors is greater in boys than in girls (Maccoby and Jacklin 1974). A major goal of socialization is to prepare children for the sex role behaviors they will engage in later, and parents obviously believe that they can influence the development of sex-inappropriate behaviors.

An overview of sex differences suggests that group differences in adulthood tend to have developed over time and not to have appeared full-blown at this later stage. While some of these sex differences are present at birth (e.g., birth weight and birth length are greater in boys) and others do not emerge until later, they generally become larger rather than smaller over time. There are not many sex differences appearing early that tend to disappear later.

Differential Socialization of the Sexes in Early Childhood

It is important to make a distinction between the acquisition and the performance of sex-appropriate behaviors. There is little evidence that girls cannot do what boys can do or vice versa. The fact that behavioral differences are not as great in early childhood as they are later suggests that young children are "bisexual" in their performance of sex-appropriate behaviors. Thus, a little boy can play with an available doll if he so chooses, and a little girl can wear a fireman's hat if she is motivated to do so. Boys are not encouraged, however, to play with dolls, and girls are not encouraged to play with a fireman's hat. Parents do not usually buy sex-inappropriate toys for their children, nor do they encourage sex-inappropriate behaviors when they are performed by their children. Indeed, throughout the life span there are few behaviors that members of both sexes cannot perform should they want to. The sex differences that do exist in the ability to perform various sex-appropriate behaviors often hinge on biological differences, such as strength and sexual anatomy, or on a history of earlier experiences that permitted the learning of certain skills by one sex and not the other.

How do boys and girls acquire the behaviors appropriate to their sex? Aside from the possibility that some aspects of the acquisition of sex-typed behaviors are innate, the general view is that children acquire their sex-appropriate behaviors through observational learning and reinforcement. Observational learning has been given importance because the direct reinforcements administered to a child after the performance of various acts (both sex-typed and others) are too few or too infrequent to account for the rapid acquisition of a large number of social skills in early childhood. Moreover, reinforcement theories alone cannot account for the first occurrence of a novel response, before the administration of a reinforcer. Observational learning, however, can account for the acquisition of novel responses (via direct observation of the behavior of others) and for the reinforcement that follows them (Bandura 1969).

While we may need to focus on parents, siblings, and peers as early sources of sex-typing models, we should not neglect the general cognitive ability of the child to decipher the relevant environmental events surrounding him or her. In this respect the acquisition of sex-typed behaviors does not differ from the acquisition of many other behaviors. It has been shown, for example, that mentally retarded children are less likely than normal children to acquire sex-appropriate behaviors at an early age (Clark 1963), and that children of above-average intelligence tend to acquire sex-appropriate behaviors at an earlier age than children of average intelligence (Kohlberg and Zigler 1967). Intelligence plays a less prominent role in sex-typed behaviors later, when the required mental age for their proper acquisition has already been reached by the vast majority of children.

No special resemblance between sex-typed interests of parents and the sex-typed behaviors of their name-sexed children has generally been found (Hetherington 1965; Mussen and Rutherford 1963). But one should not conclude that parental factors play no role in the acquisition of sex-typed interests and activities. Mussen and Distler (1959) compared five-year-old boys defined as either high or low masculine on the basis of the It Test. Each boy was then given a series of stories and asked to supply endings for each of the stories. For example, one story was about a boy who refused to go to bed and threw a toy to the ground. The child was asked what would happen next, and then the responses were scored for mother and father nurturance (warmth) and punishment. Although the boys did not differ in their views of their mothers, results indicated that the high-masculine boys regarded their fathers as both more nurturant and rewarding and more punishing than did the low-masculine boys.

To account for these results, Mussen (1967) proposed that the high-masculine boy identified with his father; that is, he tried to be more like his father "in order to recapture the feeling that he experienced in the presence of that model. Thus, by identifying with the parent, the child could administer to himself the rewards that originally were administered by the loved parent" (p. 94).

One should always keep in mind that the child (especially the boy who has identified or learned to imitate* a same-sexed parent) is not

---

* The terms *identify* and *imitate* are used interchangeably here, although many would like to see them distinguished. Bandura (1969) points out that virtually all distinctions are gratuitous and unnecessary. There is little need to posit different learning mechanisms for each; they seem susceptible to the same kinds of reinforcement contingencies; both

(*continued*)

performing as a miniature of that parent. There are many aspects of the same-sexed parent's behavior that are beyond the child's ken or cognitive equipment to understand. This is particularly so for boys, since their fathers are often away much of the day at jobs that are beyond the boy's cognitive maturity to appreciate. For girls, the identification can be simpler, since the mother is often around the home more and performs tasks that the daughter can more readily follow.

Furthermore, the child must have some image of the same-sexed parent in order to make the appropriate sex-typed identifications. Biller (1971) has reviewed the evidence on sex-typing in father-absent boys, showing that these boys generally had more feminine interests and behavior than did other boys (see also Lynn 1974). The studies of father-absent girls are fewer and more complicated, although there are indications of greater maladjustment and later marital disharmony among them than among other girls (Jacobson and Ryder 1969). Hetherington (1972) found that teenage girls whose parents had divorced or whose fathers had died differed from each other and from a control group of girls from intact homes in the way they responded to a male stranger conducting an interview with them. Girls with divorced parents sat closer to the interviewer and behaved somewhat seductively. Those girls whose fathers had died sat farther away and generally appeared more inhibited with the interviewer. Both father-absent girls and father-absent boys are at a disadvantage, since they do not get to see both parents play out their respective sex roles in interaction with each other. Sometimes the presence of a parent surrogate, such as an uncle or older sibling, can vitiate some of the adverse effects, however.

Toman (1970) has shown, for example, that the sex of siblings affects both the likelihood of divorce and the duration of marriage before a divorce. His theory was very simple. Individuals with siblings of the opposite sex have had the earlier opportunity to interact in situations similar to those in marriage and thus are at a greater advantage than if they had siblings of the same sex. A marriage between a male who had a younger sister and a female who had an older brother would tend to duplicate the experiences of their childhood. Toman devised a nine-point scale that quantified the degree of duplication of the family constellation in the marital situation. Thus, an older brother who had a younger sister and was married to a younger sister of an older brother would have the highest score, since both partners had childhood experiences that paralleled those in the marriage. Those who had only siblings of the same sex or who had siblings who were undesirable in

---

require symbolic mediation and can produce behaviors performed either in the presence or absence of the model; and both are affected by the same antecedent conditions. Personality theories have used the concept of identification, whereas experimental psychologists have used the term *imitation* to mean the acquisition of similar responses.

terms of birth order (e.g., a younger brother of an older sister) were given various intermediate scores. Only children were given the lowest scores. Toman then looked at divorces among twenty-three hundred families in Germany, which confirmed his expectation that those marriages which duplicated the best childhood constellations were least likely to end in divorce.

The point of this digression is to acknowledge the role of others besides parents in the socialization of children. Studies of children with either same- or opposite-sexed siblings also illustrate the importance of siblings in socialization. Cross-sex behaviors are more likely to be present if there is a sibling of the opposite sex than if there isn't (Brim 1958), and masculine behavior is likely to be greater among boys with older brothers than among those with older sisters (Koch 1956).

Late Childhood and Adulthood

Late childhood and adulthood are characterized by an overwhelming array of sex differences in activities, interests, and cognitive performance. Comprehensive summaries and integrative reviews of these differences are available (Garai and Scheinfeld 1968; Maccoby and Jacklin 1974), and it is unnecessary to attempt to duplicate those scholarly achievements. This is an area in which the facts are not changing so much as are the interpretations of those facts. Therefore, our focus will be on methodological and theoretical issues in the area. Along the way relevant facts shall be provided, however.

MASCULINITY-FEMININITY

The most popular means of assessing psychological sex differences has been through the administration of self-report questionnaires and tests of cognitive abilities. The general approach for the development of masculinity-femininity (M-F) scales is to write a number of items covering a wide array of behaviors and values. These items are then administered to males and females, and those items showing differences in endorsement frequencies between the sexes are incorporated into a scale. This is the method of contrasting groups and is a popular way to identify items for final inclusion in a scale. It is important to note that the criterion for inclusion of an item is the sex difference only. From this sex difference emerge concepts of masculinity and femininity that refer to differences in gender identity or sex role orientation, which can be different from one's biological sex.

The first important M-F scale was the 433-item scale of Terman and Miles (1936). The test was composed of the following "exercises":

1. *Word association test.* Stimulus words were presented along with four alternatives from which subjects were to select a response. The idea was that men and women would have different associations for these words. For example, men would associate "flesh" with "meat" and women would associate "flesh" with "pink."

2. *Inkblot association.* Ambiguous inkblots were constructed that could be taken as either a masculine or a feminine symbol—for example, a snake or a tulip.

3. *Information test.* Various items of information were canvassed, and those showing reliable sex differences were eventually incorporated into the scale. Four alternative answers to each item were provided, and even *incorrect* answers that showed sex differences were weighted in the scoring.

4. *Test of emotional and ethical attitudes.* The theory guiding the construction of this subscale was that women are more emotional than men, and that the relative contribution of the various emotions differs between the sexes (e.g., men are more angry; women are more sympathetic). Thus, the stimuli calling forth the emotions would differ (men and women do not fear the same things).

5. *Test of interests.* This test was composed of items covering occupations, people, movies, reading material, games, and amusements, as well as other items covering special interests.

6. *Tests of opinions.* This test was based on the belief that women and men differ in their opinions. It contained items such as "Blonds are less trustworthy than brunettes." As it turned out, this test was a very poor discriminator of the sexes relative to the other tests. Nevertheless, it was retained in the interest of making the scale as comprehensive as possible.

7. *Test of introvertive response.* Inspection of the items on this test suggests that it came closer to being a test of anxiety and emotionality than a test of introversion. This test also showed limited success in differentiating between the sexes but was nevertheless retained in the final scale.

The intercorrelations between the seven exercises were almost all negligible and insignificant, having a median correlation of about .12. Surprisingly, the authors combined the subtests into one scale anyway and gave a single M-F score. This move made little sense, for the truth to be learned from the findings of Terman and Miles (1936) is that there is no such thing as a unitary M-F personality dimension. The search for such a dimension is fruitless and represents a premature and unwarranted attempt to simplify the complexities of masculinity and femininity. Another problem with the scale was the rather low reliability of its subscales, ranging from only .32 to .90 for both sexes. This low reliability meant that many of the subtests could not be used for profile analyses in which a person's score on one subtest could be said to differ reliably from his or her score on another subtest.

This is not to say that the total score on the scale did not correlate with criteria in the expected directions. For example, the average masculinity score of passive male homosexuals (homosexuals who predominantly took the feminine role in their sexual behaviors) was about one standard deviation lower than that of a control group of males. Interestingly, the scores of active male homosexuals (those taking the masculine role) exceeded those of the normal male controls by a substantial margin. In general, however, correlations between M-F scores and various personality and physical dimensions were low or insignificant.

M-F scales were also developed by Strong (1943), Gough (1952), and Hathaway and McKinley (1943), among others. The underlying assumption of these scales was that there was a unitary bipolar dimension, with masculinity at one extreme and femininity at the other. We know now that the dimensionality of the existing M-F scales is not unitary, and it is doubtful that such a dimension actually exists. Factor analyses of the scales yield multiple factors, and the factors emerging are strongly related to the specifics of the item content. Lunneborg (1972) recently administered many of the popular scales to a group of over nine hundred subjects and found only four factors common to the two sexes on which the sexes differed: neuroticism, power, scientific interest, and (less significantly) religiosity. This finding suggests that these are factors that males and females tend to differ on. But Lunneborg points out that these factors (plus another ten factors specific to one sex or the other) accounted for only about 24 percent of the variance on the test items. Thus, the difference between the sexes on these factors is not very large. Lunneborg also points out that the Terman and Miles scale is the least discriminating of all the scales. This is not so surprising, for it is a very old scale and sex-typing has not been as clear-cut since then. A critical review of these scales can be found in Constantinople (1973).

Bem (1974) developed a scale of psychological androgyny (the coexistence of masculine and feminine characteristics in one) with the idea that possession of both characteristics was desirable for psychological health. The scale had two separate subscales, one for femininity and one for masculinity, that were reported to be statistically independent of each other. Thus, it was possible to obtain high scores on both masculinity and femininity or low scores on both. An androgyny score was also developed that was essentially a statistical test for the significance of the difference in endorsement frequencies of the masculine and feminine items. Bem (1975) later presented evidence that presumably supported the value of androgyny in psychological health (e.g., androgynous subjects were less conforming to sexual stereotypes in a situation where conforming to those stereotypes meant yielding to a clearly erroneous judgment). There was a serious, but now corrected (Bem 1977), flaw in the study, because she failed to distinguish those

who endorsed high numbers of both masculine and feminine items
from those who endorsed low numbers of each—both received equal
androgyny scores in her system. Spence, Helmreich, and Stapp (1975)
pointed out that there were important differences between those having
high amounts of both masculinity and femininity as measured by
another scale and those having low amounts of both. Those with low
amounts of both obtained very low scores on a measure of self- esteem,
while those with high scores on both obtained very high scores on the
self-esteem measure. Furthermore, the authors found that the masculinity and femininity subscales were uncorrelated with each other. This
means that the score on one subscale is unrelated to the score on the
other, and thus it is equally likely that individuals high on one will be
high or low on the other.

A promising approach to the psychology of sex differences is emerging from the phenomenological or experiential framework. Investigators in this area can objectify their findings, but their ideas spring
from the psychological experience of being male or female rather than
from a cataloguing of sex differences of the sort included on many
scales of masculinity and femininity. Phenomenological investigators
are also relatively unconcerned with the concrete details of differences
and work at a high level of abstraction.

Agency and Communion

One of the most interesting approaches to the experience of being male
or female comes from Bakan's (1966) concepts of agency and communion. Agency encompasses such characteristics as self-assertiveness,
separateness, instrumentality, mastery, and libidinal sexuality; communion is represented by interpersonal concerns and interests, connec-
tedness and union, and cooperation. The psychological world of men is
characterized by themes of agency, while the world of women is associated with themes of communion. Bakan emphasizes the dualistic nature of these two modes, regarding them as fundamental modes of
existence for all living creatures, and stresses that males and females
have both. It is only in the relative emphasis on one or the other mode
that males and females differ.

The ecology of being male or female, of course, encourages the
development of the different themes. The important milieus of most
men and women differ drastically. As Gutmann (1965) puts it:

> Male and female ego functions develop in and are coordinated to
> significantly different "habitats".... Consider the normative situation of
> men. Whether it be the large office, battlefield, or hunting ground, the
> milieux that men inhabit with other men, with prey, with ally and enemy
> share some central, recurrent qualities. These milieux are *impersonal*—

they do not take their order from the individual—and they are unpredictable, subject to the whims of nature, the "laws of the Market," or the inscrutable plans of remote leaders. Hence ... they daily depart from a milieu that bears the stamp of their own personalities, arrangements, and schedule ... and in some sense their task is to impose on constantly fluctuating circumstances a more personal and predictable order.... [W]omen are invested in domestic and maternal roles—in a life centered around familiar, strongly cathected people and routines, within the confines of home and neighborhood.... However restricted, the home is to some degree an extension of the homemakers' persona, and the home environment bears the imprint of the wishes, values, and techniques of the person central to its maintenance [pp. 229–234].

Empirical tests of some of the implications of these views have been provided by Carlson (1971), Cohen (1973), and Block (1973). Carlson tested many predictions derived from the theories of Bakan (1966) and Gutmann (1965). In one test, Carlson had men and women complete an adjective checklist and found that men described themselves in individualistic terms (e.g., ambitious) while women described themselves in interpersonal terms (e.g., friendly). As another test, Carlson asked, "What sort of a person do you expect to be in fifteen years?" Over two-thirds of the women responded with mention of the family, whereas only one-third of the men included family in their representation of the future. In still another part of the study, men and women were asked to write about important emotional experiences in their lives; over 70 percent of the men described these emotional experiences in agentic terms, whereas only 25 percent of the women used such terms. Many other derivations of the theories were also tested and confirmed.

Cohen (1973) showed the importance of the distinction between male-female and masculinity-femininity in a study of dream life. He obtained groups of college-age men and women who were either high or low on Gough's (1957) scale of masculinity-femininity and classified their dreams according to the dimensions of agency and communion. He found a slight tendency for males to have more dreams containing themes of agency, but he also found that scores on the Gough M-F scale were much more likely to predict agency themes than the biological sex of the subject.

Results from these studies suggest that biological sex represents only one of the coordinates of the psychological experience of masculinity or femininity. The psychological battle of the sexes may be more the product of the different normative psychological milieus that impose different ways of attending to and selecting the significant events of live than the product of any inflexible biological characteristic.

Consonant with the views of Bakan (1966), Block (1973) has provided cross-cultural and child-rearing antecedents of agency and communion as well as shown how a balance of agency and communion leads to the development of mentally healthy individuals. Following Bakan, she points out that for men the integration of agency and communion requires that self-assertion, self-interest, and self-extension be tempered with mutuality, interdependence, and joint welfare. For women realization of potential requires the inclusion of self-assertion and self-expression in the context of the communal orientation. "Unmitigated" agency or communion is undesirable for either sex. Using ideal self-descriptions of male and female university students in six different countries, she found that there were ten agentic adjectives consistent across cultures for the masculine ideal and no communal adjectives. For females, seven of the ideal self-descriptions included communal values and only one emphasized agentic values (vital).

Block also shows that child-rearing practices in four different samples of American children tend to foster these orientations according to sex. In addition, she presents evidence that an androgynous orientation—one containing both masculine and feminine qualities—among both sexes is associated with positive mental health and other desirable characteristics.

General Intelligence

Many investigators have been preoccupied with the question of sex differences on tests of general intelligence, failing to note that the best-known tests have been standardized so as to eliminate sex differences in IQ. These standardizations were accomplished either by deleting items showing large sex differences or balancing those items with others advantageous to the opposite sex. Differences in IQ or subtest performance found in specific studies are most likely due to characteristics of the local sample, actual inadequacies in the original standardization, or genuine historical changes over time. This is not to say that sex differences on subtests, even in reanalyses of the original standardization data, cannot be found, but rather that the question of sex differences in general intelligence can be investigated more profitably using tests that have not been designed so as to reduce or eliminate sex differences (McNemar 1942).

It should be remembered that test items are written by men and women who have either implicit or explicit theories about what items need to be represented on a general intelligence scale. The domain of potentially relevant items for such scales may not be adequately represented by item writers, and, as will be seen later, it is even possible to intentionally construct an intelligence test that maximizes sex differences. There are still other widely used intelligence tests, such as the Thurstone Primary Mental Abilities Test (PMA), in which sex differences were ignored in the construction.

In infancy there do not appear to be sex differences on scales of mental and motor development (Bayley 1965). Bayley standardized her Bayley Tests of Mental and Motor Development on a sample of over fourteen hundred infants from one to fifteen months of age in twelve different metropolitan areas, and this standardization should be regarded as the most representative test of the notion of sex differences in mental and motor development at these ages. Other studies using the same test have occasionally found sex differences, but these studies are based on less representative samples and in any case the differences are usually small (Goeffney, Henderson, and Butler 1971; Willerman, Broman, and Fiedler 1970). There is also some doubt that tests at these ages are strongly predictive of intelligence test performance later, or that they represent problem-solving abilities in the way that tests given at older ages do.

Most studies of preschoolers fail to show sex differences in general intelligence (Maccoby and Jacklin 1974), but when differences are observed they tend to favor girls. In virtually all instances, however, these differences are very small.

The 1937 revision of the Stanford-Binet was the target of an item analysis by McNemar (1942) to disclose sex differences. McNemar points out that the developers of the Stanford-Binet made an effort to eliminate those items showing large sex differences, although this was not always possible because of a paucity of items to replace the eliminated ones in the item pool. In the original item pool there were twelve items favoring girls and twenty-four items favoring boys. Six items favoring girls and six items favoring boys were eventually culled from the test, so that there were six items favoring girls and eighteen items favoring boys in the final version. The advantage to boys was more apparent than real, for many of the male items were duplicates or more difficult variants of ones appearing earlier that also had a male advantage.

Regardless of whether items are culled from the original item pool, there still remains the question of whether there are in theory differences in intellectual functioning between males and females. The question cannot be answered easily unless a comprehensive theory is provided about the domain of knowledge and problem-solving skills that are to be tapped by test items. If the items from this domain are unrepresentative, or if the domain itself is incorrectly specified, then sex differences might or might not emerge, depending on the mix of items.

Analyses of the subtests of the WAIS based on the national standardization sample with seventeen hundred subjects do indeed show sex differences on eight of the eleven subtests (Matarazzo 1972). The clearest differences are on arithmetic, where the advantage is in favor of males, and digit symbol, where females are superior. But even here the correlation between sex and subtest score is very low, only .17 for arithmetic and .18 for digit symbol. This means that, if one were trying to guess the sex of the subject from scores on these two tests, the success rate would be better than chance, but hardly encouraging.

While subtest or overall IQ differences have been slight, there are indications on specific items within subtests that sex differences are large. A recent study of sex differences in intelligence (Turner and Willerman 1977) analyzed the items on the WAIS for 264 pairs of spouses who are adoptive parents. These parents all live in Texas, are above average in intelligence (husbands' IQ = 114, wives' IQ = 111), and have a mean age of about thirty-nine years. It was found that twenty-one items on the WAIS significantly differentiated the sexes, with seventeen of them showing an advantage for the husband. In the majority of instances the sex differences, although reliable, were not large. The items showing the largest differences were all in favor of the males. The biggest difference obtained was on an information item, "At what temperature does water boil?" Only 30 percent of the women answered correctly, while 70 percent of the men answered correctly. This item, as well as most of the other items showing large sex differences, was found by Klingler and Saunders (1975) to load on a factor they labeled scientific information in a study that ignored sex differences. It is hard to understand why the sex difference on the temperature item is so large; it may represent an instance of local peculiarity in the sample that will not generalize, or it may be that the psychological milieus of men and women in this culture are even more disparate than we thought.

Wechsler (1958) believed that additional mileage could be gotten from the WAIS by developing a masculinity-femininity index based on the rather slight sex differences in subtest performances. He summed three scales on which men tended to score better (information, arithmetic, and picture completion) and subtracted from that the sum scores on three other subtests on which women excelled (vocabulary, similarities, and digit symbol) for his M-F index. The higher the index, the greater the masculinity score. Since the WAIS is designed to eliminate sex differences, it is not the best test from which to construct an M-F index for intellectual functioning.

McCarthy, Anthony, and Domino (1970) correlated scores on the WAIS M-F with other indices of masculinity and femininity and found that the WAIS M-F did not correlate with any of the others. These authors conclude that the WAIS M-F is without any practical utility. It should be added that none of the other M-F indices correlated highly with each other either. The search for a cognitive ability M-F index should not be ended, however, because there is evidence that these indices are helpful when based on tests not originally designed to eliminate sex differences.

SPECIFIC ABILITIES

There is a suggestion of sex differences in specific abilities of young children, but in all cases the differences are small. The data suggest that girls excel on measures of *verbal fluency,* but the findings are rarely consistent from study to study. On measures of quantitative ability, in preschool children and young school children, the differences are again negligible. By the age of twelve or thirteen, however, the advantage of boys in quantitative ability is consistently observed. This may be due to a variety of factors, including sex-typing, which encourages boys to be more involved in quantitative pursuits, or it may represent changes that are to some degree under the control of hormonal factors.

Measures of spatial ability generally do not show differences between boys and girls in the preschool years, but by age eight the superiority of males on these tasks begins to emerge (Maccoby and Jacklin 1974), and by adolescence the advantage for males becomes quite consistent. The larger sex differences in spatial performance occur with the onset of puberty. It is tempting to ascribe these differences to the accompanying hormonal changes, and, in fact, those changes may be responsible. On the other hand, puberty is the time when the fruits of socialization begin to be harvested, and it is difficult to separate the results of socialization from biological influences.

For the question of sex differences in special abilities, standardized tests containing a large variety of items that disregard sex differences have an advantage, namely, that they provide a wide range of items from which to draw a profile of sex differences in cognitive performance. For example, the Differential Aptitude Tests (DAT), which were not standardized to eliminate sex differences, show that high school girls perform much better than boys on tests of clerical speed and accuracy and language usage, while boys perform much better than girls on tests of mechanical reasoning and space relations (Bennett, Seashore, and Wesman 1968). The results of these tests for pupils in grade twelve are shown in Table 12.2.

The DAT is the sort of test that is promising for the development of an M-F index because sex was disregarded in its construction. There have been efforts to construct M-F indices for tests such as the DAT. For example, Horn and Turner (1974) administered the American College Test (ACT) and the Guilford-Zimmerman Temperament Survey to 108 male and 78 female Mexican-American college students. An M-F index was constructed, based on the mathematics and English portions of the test. The idea was that those with a higher score in English than in mathematics should be feminine and those with superiority in mathematics should be masculine. The results of this study confirmed the prediction, but just for the females. That is, females with a higher mathematics score than English score were more masculine than the other

Table 12.2

Mean Differential Aptitude Test (DAT) scores for twelfth graders by sex ($N > 4000$)

Sex	Verbal reason-ing	Numer-ical ability	Abstract reason-ing	Clerical speed and accuracy	Mech. reason-ing	Space relat.	Lang. usage: spell-ing	Lang. usage: gram-mar
Males	27.9	25.3	35.4	53.9	48.3	35.7	72.5	33.4
SD	10.3	9.1	9.6	12.6	9.5	12.4	16.1	10.9
Females	26.2	23.0	33.7	60.1	37.4	31.8	81.0	37.9
SD	10.3	8.4	10.1	12.8	8.5	11.5	14.1	10.9

Source: Reproduced from the Fourth Edition Manual of the Differential Aptitude Tests by permission. Copyright © 1968 by The Psychological Corporation, New York, N.Y. All rights reserved.

females, as measured by the Guilford-Zimmerman test. Studies by Milton (1957), Kagan and Moss (1962), and Ferguson and Maccoby (1966) also show correlations between M-F cognitive indices and masculinity-femininity.

Field independence is another ability that shows superiority among males (Witkin et al. 1962). Field independence refers to the ability to separate a target element, such as a hidden figure, from its complex background. On tests of this sort boys have been found superior from about age eight on, with the sex difference becoming marked in adolescence. There is evidence, however, that different tasks purported to measure the same ability do not intercorrelate as highly as expected (Vernon 1972); thus, the unitary nature of this ability is currently in question. Nevertheless, field independence has been found to correlate with other measures of cognitive ability (e.g., general intelligence) and personality (see Vernon 1972 for a review).

It has been suggested by Broverman et al. (1968) that the advantage of males on measures of field independence indicates a general male superiority on tasks that involve "an inhibition or delay of initial response tendencies to obvious stimulus attributes in favor of responses to less obvious stimulus attributes" (p. 28). They contrast this male superiority to the advantage of females on tasks that are overlearned repetitive behaviors that call for minimal central mediation. Broverman et al. point out that females are superior in speed of naming colors, canceling numbers, reading, coding, tapping, writing, typing, simple calculations, and other tasks of this nature. Men are found superior on mirror tracing, maze performance, counting backwards, choice reaction time, and others. The authors theorize that these sex differences have much to do with the balance of estrogens and androgens on sympathetic and parasympathetic nervous system pathways, but their interpretation has been challenged (Parlee 1972).

ACHIEVEMENT

A review of sex differences in cognitive ability does not indicate over-whelmingly large differences between males and females. Tests of general intelligence, even those which have not been designed to eliminate sex differences, show strengths and weaknesses for both sexes. Yet sex differences in important culturally recognized accomplishments are far larger than would be predicted by any ability or personality differences. Tyler (1965) asks:

> Why have women made so few major contributions to civilization? ... History has recorded the names and achievements of a large number of men but only very small number of women. Ellis (1904) in his study of British genius found only 55 women in his total group of 1,030 persons.... In the 1927 edition of *American Men of Science*, only 725 women were listed out of 9,785 entries, and out of the 250 names starred because of special eminence, only three were women....
>
> Even in fields traditionally assigned to women, the most eminently successful persons are likely to be men. Interest in the arts is accepted as a feminine trait, yet there are very few women who have distinguished themselves as creative artists. Even in dress-designing and interior decorating the leaders in the field are men. Most of the world's cooking may be done by women, but the great chefs of all time have been men. Though acting is a field that has been open to women for a long time, the great playwrights and producers are men [pp. 240–241].

The most parsimonious explanation for these sex differences in achievement is that sex-typed socialization practices work against the production of highly regarded cultural accomplishments by females. By the elementary and high school years, differential preoccupations in agentic or communal interests have already clearly emerged. For example, boys are three times more interested in adventure stories and mysteries than girls, and girls are ten to thirteen times more likely to read stories of home or school life than boys (Terman and Tyler 1954). Girls are also more anxious about failure and more cautious in risky situations, qualities that are probably detrimental to outstanding success. Females of equal intellectual ability and socioeconomic status to males are also less likely to enter college, which is often a prerequisite for any culturally appreciated attainments (Flanagan and Cooley 1966).

While these differences may have their ultimate origins in innate factors, it is clear that if women are to be men's equals with respect to cultural attainments the differentials in agentic and communal interests will need to be eradicated. A drastic restructuring of the social order will be required if the vast majority of women become agentic in their orientations. Western culture has enough slack in the system, however, to permit large numbers of females to develop agentic orientations without hastening the demise of psychological sex role differences in general.

Hormones and Behavior

Many investigators have become interested in the psychological changes accompanying the menstrual cycle. Studies suggest that the phase just preceding menstruation and the menstrual period itself are associated with dysphoric mood and irritability, a propensity for criminal activity, death from suicide and accident, admission to mental hospitals, and taking children to consult a physician (see Parlee 1973 for review). The midcycle period, during which ovulation occurs, seems to be associated with positive mood and self-esteem and with a relative absence of the negative signs just mentioned.

The two hormones that have received the most attention in those studies are estrogen and progesterone, since their relative proportions are highly correlated with the phases of the menstrual cycle. Estrogen rises abruptly just before ovulation in midcycle and then drops fairly precipitously. Progesterone shows a parallel precipitous rise a few days before ovulation, dips abruptly for a few days, and then rises to a high level, dipping again just before the onset of menstruation. Bardwick (1971) has reviewed the studies showing correlations between behavior and phases of the cycle, tentatively concluding "that high levels of estrogen are correlated with high levels of positive moods, and low levels of estrogen and progesterone are correlated with significant negative emotions" (p. 39).

An interesting study in this regard was that of Paige (1969), who compared cyclic mood changes of sexually active women not using chemical means of birth control with mood changes of women using one of two types of oral contraceptives. One group of women had never used oral contraceptives; another group used the "combination" pill (twenty days of pills containing estrogen and progestin, followed by seven days off the pill); and a third group used the "sequential" pill (fifteen days of pills containing only estrogen, followed by five days of pills containing both estrogen and progestin and then seven days without pills). All women were tested four times during the cycle—on the fourth, tenth, and sixteenth days of the menstrual cycle and two days before the next menstrual cycle. Paige theorized that, for women on the combination pill, the hormones are relatively constant for twenty days of the period and that mood should be relatively constant during that time. The sequential pill more closely approximates the natural menstrual cycle, so that both these women and those not on the pill should show high positive mood during midcycle and high negative mood just before and during menstruation. The results of her study tended to confirm her predictions. There were no cyclic changes in mood for those on the combination pill—they demonstrated a high level of hostility throughout the cycle, equal to menstruating women controls. On the other hand, the lowest levels of hostility were found on day sixteen for both the sequential-pill users and those not on the pill. Bardwick (1971) summarizes the findings by saying that "when the hormone levels are fairly constant during the cycle, as in women on combination pills, anxiety and hostility levels are correspondingly constant. When the hormone levels fluctuate during the cycle, emotions correspondingly fluctuate" (p. 37). Thiessen (in press) points out, however, that other hormones, such as aldosterone, are correlated with the mood changes and should be ruled out before the focus is placed exclusively on estrogen and progesterone.

During menopause there is also an increase in signs of negative mood. Interestingly, this is also a time of declining estrogen production. There have been a few attempts to provide estrogen supplements to women during menopause, and studies of such attempts seem to indicate that there are fairly consistent improvements in mood (see Bardwick 1971 for a review).

Conclusions

Throughout the primate order there are clear and consistent sex differences in behavior, and humans are no exception. The parallels are so great that we cannot regard them as mere coincidence. Our brains are just as much a product of nature as are the brains of any other primates. To be sure, evolutionary trends show that we are remarkably plastic and susceptible to cultural learnings. But it may be that the cultural sex-typed socialization practices of humans serve the same functions as do the innate differences in lower primates—namely, they inculcate through the cultural mode that which is innate among the lower animals.

Attention to human psychological sex differences is increasing because cultural inventions of a labor-saving nature have resulted in the desexualization of adult sex roles. If there are sex differences in the brain, it seems unlikely that the largest differences would be connected with the higher cortical functions, which are the most recent, evolutionarily. It seems more likely that large sex differences emerged earlier, in more primitive species, and thus are connected with those brain structures which we share with these lower species.

13

Age Differences

The purpose of this chapter is to review the evidence for continuity and change in intellectual and personality functioning throughout the life span. Age has been the traditional variable by which the course of development is marked, and it is necessary to acknowledge its prepotency in any treatment of human behavioral differences. The growth and decline of physiological, psychological, and social parameters are associated with age, which enters into virtually every functional relationship relevant to behavior. At the same time we ought not to mistake shadow for substance, for age itself tells little about the causes of continuity and change. We ought to be interested in the causes of the changes that take place over time, although it must be admitted that this has not preoccupied the majority of investigators in developmental psychology.

There are two broad issues at the pivot of much research on aging. The first concerns the degree of decline or preservation of different functions with age. The second concerns the degree to which declines, when observed, are due to central as opposed to peripheral mechanisms. Both of these questions are being actively investigated now, but both are far from closure.

A related and equally important question concerns the ecology of aging and the extent to which that ecology contributes to the declines observed. Aging individuals typically have few demands placed on them; responsibilities for self-management are often usurped; and motivation for maintaining their earlier independent status may not be preserved.

Studies on aging are particularly susceptible to sampling bias. Only a small proportion of individuals enter homes for the aged, and, although these people are an easy resource for investigations on aging, they usually show more decrement than do those not in homes. Consequently, the putative effects of aging may be overestimated. The *Handbook of the Psychology of Aging*, edited by Birren and Schaie (1977), which contains chapters by forty-two contributors, is an essential sourcebook for those seriously interested in questions of aging.

Methodological Issues

CROSS-SECTIONAL VERSUS LONGITUDINAL STUDIES

It is possible to distinguish two major approaches in the study of continuity and change over the life cycle. The *cross-sectional* approach collects representative samples of individuals of different ages and compares their performances on a number of presumably equivalent measures. Such cross-sectional studies have been particularly popular in the examination of changes in intellectual and personality functioning associated with the aging process.

In the case of intelligence, the use of deviation IQ scores in these studies is unreliable, for the IQ scores have already been corrected for age, and, consequently, any truly representative sample of subjects in different age groups should have mean IQs around 100. Instead, the proper analysis uses the *efficiency quotient,* or the EQ.

The EQ is usually determined by taking the raw or scaled score performances (not corrected for age) of the most optimally functioning age group and then comparing this level with the levels obtained by other age groups. A representative curve for changes in EQ as a function of age, taken from the WAIS standardization sample, is given in Figure 13.1. The optimally functioning group is between twenty and thirty-four years of age, and the older groups show a general decline in EQ with advancing age. That the curve shows some bumps, however, suggests that the decline may not be strongly predictable. Many other cross-sectional studies have yielded curves comparable to this one (see Matarazzo 1972 for a review), but this curve is somewhat deceptive in

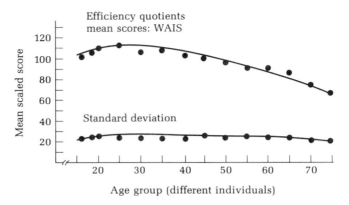

Figure 13.1

Full-scale scores of the Wechsler Adult Intelligence Scale for ages sixteen to seventy-five and over. These are scaled scores that, when used with Table 18 of the 1955 manual for the different age groups, yield an efficiency quotient for that age group relative to the twenty-to-thirty-four-year-old reference group sample. (From *Wechsler's Measurement and Appraisal of Adult Intelligence*, 5th and enlarged edition, by Joseph D. Matarazzo. Copyright © 1939, 1941, 1944, 1958 by David Wechsler; © 1972 The Williams & Wilkins Company. Reprinted by permission of Oxford University Press, Inc.)

that the EQs are confounded with differences in educational attainments for the different age cohorts and other generational differences that may have affected the extent of the decline. In general, a problem with cross-sectional studies is that they can confound genuine age-related differences with generational or cohort differences. Some examples of the effects of this confounding will be shown later.

Another important point is that the decline in overall performance observed here conceals the fact that some WAIS subtests show little or no decline and others show rather steep declines. Vocabulary level may increase rather than decrease with age, while those subtests having timed components may show precipitous declines, particularly for individuals over age sixty-five.

In *longitudinal* studies the same individuals are followed and retested over a number of years. In these studies generational or cohort differences are not confounded with age differences as they are in cross-sectional studies. More importantly, however, longitudinal studies permit the analysis of *intraindividual* variation over time, thus giving some perspective on stability and change within subjects rather than between subjects.

A disadvantage of longitudinal studies is that the results may be specific to the age cohort or to the unique characteristics of the cohort chosen for study; had subjects from a group born in a different epoch

been chosen, findings might have been different. Also, repeated measurements of the same subject over time may itself affect the results
obtained. Finally, the attrition of subjects over time may not be random.

SEQUENTIAL STRATEGIES

A model for combining the advantages of both the cross-sectional and
the longitudinal approaches has been proposed by a number of investigators, but has been explicitly stated by Schaie (1965) and in a series
of volumes edited by Goulet and Baltes (1970), Baltes and Schaie
(1973), and Nesselroade and Reese (1973). The design proposed is a
sequential one, in which individuals of different ages are simultaneously and repeatedly tested over a number of occasions. Imagine that
three age groups of individuals are simultaneously tested on three different occasions, say every ten years, and that these age groups are
fifteen, twenty-five, and thirty-five years old, respectively, at the first
testing. The age differences observed on any one of the three occasions
can be regarded as equivalent to cross-sectional data, and the changes
or patterns of scores for a particular age group over the three occasions
of testing can be regarded as longitudinal data. Finally, the middle
cohort on the second testing will be of the same age as the oldest cohort
was on the occasion of the first testing, so that it is possible to estimate
whether the experience of having been born during a particular historical epoch has differential effects (e.g., having been a child during World
War II as opposed to having been a child during the Korean War or the
Vietnam War). This model is shown in Table 13.1.

Table 13.1

Life span designs starting with three different age cohorts in 1975

Birth year	Year of testing		
	1975	1985	1995
1940	35 yrs	45 yrs	55 yrs
1950	25 yrs	35 yrs	45 yrs
1960	15 yrs	25 yrs	35 yrs —Longitudinal
	Cross-sectional		Cross-sectional sequential

The table lists three groups of subjects ranging in age from fifteen to thirty-five years on the occasion of the first testing in 1975. Any differences between the groups according to age in any one year of testing can then be regarded as cross-sectional differences. Because the testing is repeated every ten years, there will eventually be three cohorts for age thirty-five, each with a different year of birth. If all individuals of the same age at any time of testing are combined, regardless of their birth years, then it is possible to obtain some information about the effects of age independent of year of birth. Finally, if the same individuals are followed over the years, it is possible to obtain information about longitudinal changes within the subjects over time. It is important to remember that cross-sectional data always run the risk of confounding cohort differences with genuine age-related changes. Unless cross-sectional data are checked against sequentially collected information, one can never be sure that the changes observed are actually related to age per se. We shall now present the findings on intellectual functioning using each of these approaches.

Longitudinal Studies of Intellectual Functioning

A thoughtful review of cross-sectional and longitudinal studies on aging and intelligence can be found in Botwinick (1977). Only some of those studies shall be examined here.

Owens (1966) studied 127 male subjects who originally took the army Alpha examination when they were freshmen at Iowa State University in 1919. Subsequently 127 of these subjects were retested in 1950, and 96 of these were again tested in 1961. The correlations for the 96 subjects over the three testing occasions are given in Table 13.2 and demonstrate a considerable amount of stability over the forty-two-year period, especially for the total score on the Alpha. This group test requires only about twenty-five minutes when given under normal conditions. Despite its brevity, the test affords relatively reliable indices of the intellectual functioning of adults.

Owens also plotted changes in the performance level over the years for each of the major components of the Alpha. The results are shown in Figure 13.2. The vertical scale of this figure gives the mean scaled scores of the subjects in relation to the scores of the original normative population of the Alpha test after conversion to a mean of 5 and an SD of 1. Thus, on the occasion of the first testing in 1919 these subjects were about .7 of an SD above the standardization mean on the total score, improving to about 1.3 SD above the mean on the second testing and dropping negligibly and insignificantly on the third testing in 1961. Note that the only score that underwent serious decline between 1950 and 1961 was the numerical score of the Alpha. Still another

Table 13.2

Subtest and component test-retest reliabilities of the Army Alpha

	Retest reliability			Component predicted
	1919 versus 1950	1950 versus 1961	1919 versus 1961	
Following directions	.30	.46	.41	Reasoning (R)
Arithmetical problems	.69	.83	.68	Numerical (N)
Practical judgment	.56	.68	.60	Verbal (V)
Synonym-antonym	.64	.71	.56	Verbal (V)
Disarranged sentences	.48	.69	.52	Verbal (V)
Number series completion	.62	.61	.54	Numerical (N)
Analogies	.58	.83	.54	Reasoning (R)
Information	.63	.75	.59	Verbal (V)
Verbal component	.75	.87	.73	—
Numerical component	.71	.86	.73	—
Reasoning component	.57	.85	.58	—
Total	.79	.92	.78	—

Source: From W. A. Owens, "Age and Mental Abilities: A Second Follow-up," *Journal of Educational Psychology* 57 (1966): 311–325. Copyright © 1966 by the American Psychological Association. Reprinted by permission.

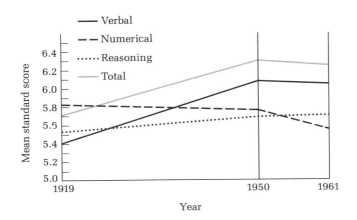

Figure 13.2

Test performance trends for components and total. (From Owens, "Age and Mental Abilities: A Second Follow-up," *Journal of Educational Psychology* 57 [1966]: 311–325. Copyright © 1966 by the American Psychological Association. Reprinted by permission.)

testing would be welcomed to see if this decline would continue. Owens points out that the decrement does not appear to be due to the timed nature of this subtest, since allowing subjects double time to complete the subtest did not significantly affect the relationships obtained.

The findings from this study support the contention that intelligence scores for adult subjects remain stable over time, but this consistency is far from perfect and permits considerable room for *individuals* to move about within the distribution. Owens did correlate changes in scores over time with various life history factors as reported by subjects in 1961. He found that socioeconomic success was related to improvement in scores on the verbal and reasoning components of the Alpha between 1919 and 1950, and that a factor labeled sensitive intelligence (e.g., likes reading, is tense) related positively to gains on the reasoning component and on the total score during the same period.

Kangas and Bradway (1971) present a thirty-eight-year follow-up of individuals originally tested in 1931 as part of the California sample for the standardization of the 1937 Stanford-Binet. These subjects were all preschoolers at that time, averaging about four years of age. Many of these subjects were subsequently retested in 1941, 1956, and 1969. During the last two testings the subjects were also administered the WAIS. Results for the Stanford-Binet retests are shown in Table 13.3 and show that preschool IQs do predict later intellectual functioning, but that the power of the prediction decreases as the interval between one testing and another increases. Thus, preschool IQs predicted moderately well IQs obtained in adolescence, but by 1969 the correlation had dropped substantially. As with the Owens (1966) study, the correlations obtained in adolescence correlated strongly with those obtained later, thus supporting the notion that IQs measured late in

Table 13.3

Correlations between Stanford-Binet test scores over four administrations

Test	Average age (yrs)	1941	1956	1969
1931	4.8	.65	.59	.41
1941	13.6		.85	.68
1956	29.5			.77
1969	41.6			

Note: N's vary from 109 to 111 subjects for the tests through 1956 and N = 48 for those retested in 1969.
Source: From J. Kangas and K. Bradway, "Intelligence at Middle Age: A 38-Year Follow-up," *Developmental Psychology* 5 (1971): 333–337. Copyright © by the American Psychological Association. Reprinted by permission.

childhood or adulthood show consistency over time. The early Stanford-Binet was almost equally predictive of the last Stanford-Binet score and the WAIS score, although correlations for the same test over time tended to be somewhat higher than correlations between different tests. WAIS performance IQs were clearly less predictable from earlier performance IQs than were the verbal IQs from earlier verbal IQs.

Kangas and Bradway (1971) also charted the changes in mean IQ scores over time, showing that there was a highly significant increase in mean scores over this thirty-eight-year period. The subjects averaged about 111 IQ on the first Stanford-Binet IQ in 1931 and about 130 on the retesting in 1969. On the WAIS full-scale IQ the subjects averaged 109 in 1956 and 118 in 1969. Thus, there was no indication of a decline in intellectual functioning on these measures over the years. It is, of course, hard to specify the cause of the increase in IQ, and previous practice with the tests may have played a role. Subtest scores of the WAIS were not reported. This is unfortunate, because inclusion of sub-test scores would have provided a more detailed picture of the lon-gitudinal pattern of changes in intellectual performance.

Tuddenham, Blumenkrantz, and Wilkin (1968) retested 164 men re-tiring from the army after twenty years of service who had first been tested about thirteen years earlier on the Army General Classification Test (AGCT). The correlation between the first testing, which occurred when the subjects were about thirty years of age, and the retesting thir-teen years later was .79. There was very little consistent evidence for a decline in performance over this period, except on the perceptual reasoning subtest (which required the subjects to match the edges of an irregular polyhedron with corresponding parts of a flat pattern). Even here the drop over the years was less than .25 of a SD.

A longitudinal study conducted in Berkeley was reported by Honzik, Macfarlane, and Allen (1948). The subjects in this study had been tested on a yearly basis between two and ten years of age and at wider intervals until age eighteen. The subjects represented a select group, as their Stanford-Binet scores in the early school years averaged about 118. Some of the results of this study are shown in Table 13.4.

Like many of the other longitudinal studies, the test intercorrelations tend to illustrate what is called a *simplex* pattern. Closely spaced tests show high intercorrelations, while more distant intervals between test-ings show lower intercorrelations. Note also that the intercorrelations between tests tend to be higher when the children are older at both testings than when they are younger.

One very interesting analysis in this study involved the distribution of the range of IQ changes between the ages of six and eighteen years. There were eight different testings during that period, and only 15 percent of the subjects obtained any two IQ scores that differed by 9 IQ points or less. Thirty-seven percent of the subjects showed changes of

Table 13.4

A sampling of correlations between test scores obtained at different ages

Test	Age	N	California preschool schedule			Stanford-Binet (1916)	Stanford-Binet (1937)		Wechsler-Bellevue
			3	4	5	7	10	14	18
California preschool schedule	1¾	234	.52	.38	.39	.29	.22	.07	.07
	3	229		.58	.57	.55	.36	.35	.35
	4	211			.72	.59	.66	.54	.42
	5	212				.73	.75	.61	.56
Stanford-Binet (1916)	7	208					.77	.73	.71
Stanford-Binet (1937)	10	107						.85	.70
	14	51							.73

Source: From M. Honzik, J. Macfarlane, and L. Allen, "The Stability of Mental Test Performance Between Two and Eighteen Years," *Journal of Experimental Education* 17 (1948): 309–334. Heldref Publications.

20 or more IQ points between one testing and another during that period. Thus, even fairly high intercorrelations between testings (at least of the magnitude shown here) permit considerable IQ change within individuals. There is little indication that the IQ score is "fixed" over the school years.

In normal samples, scores on infant tests tend to predict later IQ scores at only low levels, although the relationships between the two tend to be positive. A useful summary of the predictions of later childhood test scores from infant measures is given by McCall, Hogarty, and Hurlburt (1972). The median correlations between these tests are shown in Figure 13.3. It is clear that predictions of later IQ from infant scores obtained in the first six months are generally negligible, but there is a tendency for the infant tests to become more predictive when they are administered at a later age. For subnormal samples, however, early infant tests do a better job of predicting later IQ than do later infant tests (see McCall, Hogarty, and Hurlburt 1972 for a review).

The inadequacies of infant tests in predicting later IQs in normal samples is not due to low reliability, since test-retest reliabilities between adjacent tests given at one-month intervals tend to be very high. Anderson (1939) suggests that the reason that early tests poorly predict later IQ is that there is little *overlap* in content or function of the items between the early and later tests. At later ages item content or function

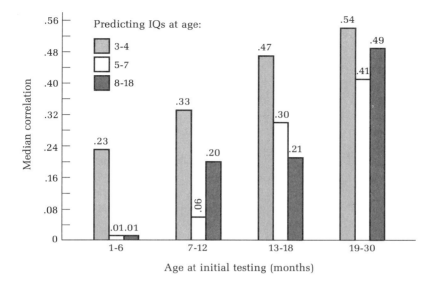

Figure 13.3
Median correlations between infant tests and childhood IQs
for normal children. (McCall, Hogarty, and Hurlburt 1972.)

changes far less over time and therefore widely spaced intervals between testings may still yield high intercorrelations.

There are other considerations that might help to account for the
generally lower predictiveness of early tests. Tests given in the early
years usually sample a smaller number of items than do later tests
because of limitations in the intellectual repertoires of children. More
importantly, however, the different maturation rates of many biological
processes mean that there might be greater variability both within and
between subjects for many biological and psychological processes. In
adulthood these maturational differences will no longer have an important contemporaneous role to play. For example, while some normal
three-year-olds do not speak, all normal adults do. Since maturation of
a particular function takes time, adjacent tests will find the same individual roughly near the same point on a particular maturational dimension. Consequently, there will be higher intercorrelations between the
adjacent tests than between the more distantly spaced tests. After maturation is completed, future development will be more predictable.

Since most of these maturational processes involving intellectual
functioning take place internally, they are not easily observable and
thus it is difficult to be more specific about them. On the other hand, for
an easily observable characteristic like height, rapid maturation and
differential onset of the maturational processes in adolescence make it

hard to predict adult height. Tuddenham and Snyder (1954) intercorrelated height measurements obtained in successive years between ages
two and eighteen for the children in a longitudinal study in Berkeley.
The results indicated (in contradistinction to Anderson's [1939] prediction) that adult height (at age eighteen) could be better predicted by
height at age six than it could be by height during the early adolescent
years (eleven or twelve for girls and thirteen or fourteen for boys).

Cross-Sectional and Sequential Strategies

Unfortunately, there are few studies employing the cross-sectional sequential strategies for intellectual functioning, and we will have to rely
on one major study reported by Schaie and Strother (1968), Schaie,
Labouvie, and Buech (1973), and Schaie and Labouvie-Vief (1974). In
these studies a longitudinal sample of members of a West Coast prepaid
medical plan were tested on three occasions, in 1956, 1963, and 1970.
There was considerable attrition over the two retests, so that only 32
percent of the original subjects were available for retesting in 1970.
There were 161 subjects, ranging in age from twenty-one to eighty-four
years, who were tested on all three occasions. Another group consisted
of individuals in the same original cohort but tested on only one of each
of the three occasions. The group test used was the PMA, which has
five subtests—verbal meaning, space, reasoning, number, and word
fluency—and tests of behavioral rigidity and psychomotor speed.

Composite PMA scores (this is a standard score with a mean of 50
and an SD of 10) for the longitudinal and independently sampled
groups are shown in Figure 13.4. This figure comes from a reanalysis of
the original data of Schaie and his colleagues that is somewhat easier to
follow than the analyses in the original reports. The solid lines represent longitudinal findings for those repeatedly tested, and the dashed
lines represent groups that were originally in the 1956 cohort but were
tested on only one of the three occasions. For example, the point at age
thirty-two in 1963 on the dashed line in cohort I represents people who
were not tested either in 1956 (when they were twenty-five) or in 1970
(when they were thirty-nine). The purpose of including those tested
only on a single occasion is that they help to evaluate effects due to
repeated testing experiences in the longitudinal cohorts.

Each of the seven panels contains different age cohorts, numbered I
through VII. For cohorts I through IV there are no consistent age declines in the longitudinal data, but beginning with cohort V (ages
53–67) there appear to be regular declines with age. The independently
sampled groups parallel fairly well the trajectories of the longitudinally
collected data, but their mean scores at each test tend to be lower. Any

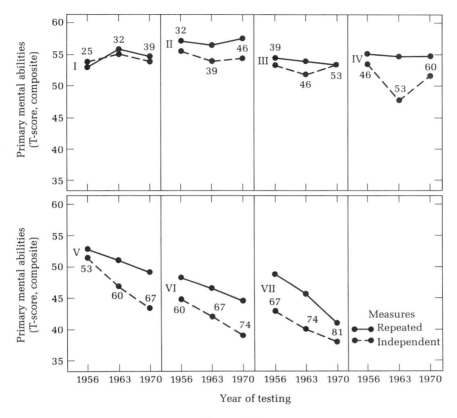

Figure 13.4

Botwinick's age change analysis of longitudinal (repeated) measures and independent sample measures drawn from data provided by Schaie. (Reported in different form in Schaie and Labouvie-Vief 1974; Schaie, Labouvie, and Buech 1973. From *Handbook of the Psychology of Aging*, ed. James E. Birren and K. W. Schaie. Copyright © 1977 by Litton Educational Publishing, Inc. Reprinted by permission of Van Nostrand Reinhold Company.)

differences between the levels of the longitudinal and independently sampled groups may be in part artificial because many of the longitudinal subjects dropped out over time and the more able ones might have been those more likely to return for reexamination. We shall have more to say about those who drop out of longitudinal studies later. The general picture that emerges from these data is that the longitudinal and independently sampled groups show similar patterns of decline but that these declines begin only after age fifty. There are no large discrepancies between the two methods of sampling; the differences are of degree rather than of quality.

TIME OF TESTING

The effects of the time of testing are neither very consistent nor very large. The question is whether individuals of a specific age differ as a function of the year in which the testing took place. For example, do those who were tested at age fifty-three in 1956 differ from those who were tested at age fifty-three in 1963 or 1970? By looking at people of the same age in successions of three panels, one can get an idea of the effects of the year in which the testing was done. For the longitudinal data, there is no evidence for a change associated with the year of testing through age forty-six. At ages fifty-three and sixty, however, those tested in 1970 did somewhat better than those tested at ages fifty-three and sixty in earlier years. The cross-sectional data lead to much the same conclusions, namely, that those tested at ages fifty-three and sixty in 1970 did somewhat better than those tested at fifty-three and sixty in earlier years. This difference may be due to greater education, general increases in test wiseness, better health, and so on.

CROSS-SECTIONAL FINDINGS

By summing test scores of people of a specific age, regardless of year of testing, it is possible to examine the effects of age, averaged over the three different years of testing. The largest difference between the cross-sectional and longitudinal data is for the ages of fifty-three and sixty-seven. The longitudinal data show a decline of about 3 standard score points, while the cross-sectional data show a decline of about 9 points. Botwinick (1977) suggests that this discrepancy might have been due to chance. Other than for that interval, the cross-sectional and longitudinal data seem to agree fairly well.

What about differences among subtests of the PMA? Do some tests show greater changes than others? The longitudinal data for verbal meaning, space, and reasoning are distinguished by the absence of any consistent evidence for decline, at least before age fifty-three or sixty. Number shows no change at any time. Word fluency is complicated because the 1956 cohort generally does better than those tested in later years and also because the cross-sectional findings do not appear to indicate large aging effects while the longitudinal data do. In interpreting their findings, Schaie and Labouvie-Vief (1974) note

> that most of the adult life-span is characterized by an absence of decisive intellectual decrements. In times of rapid cultural and technological change it is primarily in relation to younger populations that the aged can be described as deficient, and it is erroneous to interpret such cross-sectional age differences as indicating ontogenetic [age changes in the individual] change patterns [p. 317].

One inference to be drawn from this quotation is that changes in IQ over generations should occur if there is rapid sociocultural change but that in socioculturally stable groups change over generations should not occur. Successive cross-sectional representative samples of younger ages over a number of years fail to indicate consistent changes in IQ over time, especially when individually administered IQ tests are used. Other studies (reviewed by Loehlin, Lindzey, and Spuhler 1975) do suggest some improvements in IQ over the years, but these occur mainly when deprived populations have been exposed to large positive cultural influences. Whether or not improvement in IQ is to be expected in future generations is difficult to determine. While cultural changes may generally have a positive effect on IQ, some specific cultural changes may have a negative effect. There is certainly no good indication that for modern countries large increases in the IQs of future generations are to be anticipated in representative samples across a wide range of ages.

Fluid Versus Crystallized Abilities

The appearance of declines or improvements with age seems to be dependent on the particular subtest being used. Those subtests which call for fluid intelligence are the ones most likely to show decline, whereas those which call for crystallized abilities may show stability or improvements with advancing age (Cattell 1971). Horn and Donaldson (1976) have also reanalyzed the original data used to construct Figure 13.4, showing that declines are much steeper with age for the "fluid" than for the "crystallized" tests. The details of the theory of fluid and crystallized abilities are considered in Chapter 4. Briefly, most intelligence tests contain items that tap both fluid and crystallized abilities. Fluid abilities are those which in many ways are "perceptual" and which relate to basic operating characteristics of the organism. Items that test fluid abilities usually are either highly overlearned or novel to all those tested. We shall not try to define what exactly is meant by overlearning, for the meaning depends on the criteria employed. Individuals can be said to have overlearned the multiplication table to 9×9 in the sense that they make no mistakes. If the criterion is *speed* of saying the table, however, the same individuals might no longer be considered to have overlearned the table equally.

Crystallized abilities also involve an important dimension of intellect and may even appear superficially similar to fluid abilities, except that the former are strongly dependent on exposure to the general and esoteric elements of the culture. Thus, defining unusual words would depend on previous experience with the esoteric culture and could not be generated by drawing on one's fluid abilities ("natural capacities").

In general, fluid and crystallized abilities tend to be substantially correlated with one another and thus might appear to be two sides of the same coin. It has been shown, however, that the trace lines for the development of these functions appear to diverge with time. Although the evidence is neither overwhelming nor very consistent, it does appear that sometime in the late teens or early twenties fluid abilities reach their peak and begin to decline thereafter, whereas crystallized abilities continue to increase at least to late middle age and possibly later.

A report by Horn and Cattell (1966) is one of the major sources of evidence in support of this fluid-crystallized distinction. They administered a battery of tests to a sample of 297 persons from state prisons, state schools, and a state employment agency (72 percent male) in order to tap these different abilities. Schematic findings of that study are presented graphically in Figure 13.5.

The figure shows that fluid abilities tend to decline steadily from teenage on, whereas the crystallized abilities tend to increase at a roughly similar rate. The omnibus curve is essentially the average of the two separate abilities and is probably much closer to the usual mix of fluid and crystallized abilities of most traditional intelligence tests. The authors are aware that these findings come from cross-sectional samples and that longitudinal samples might yield somewhat different results. In addition, the fluid tests have a substantial response speed component, which may make for a steeper decline with age than if

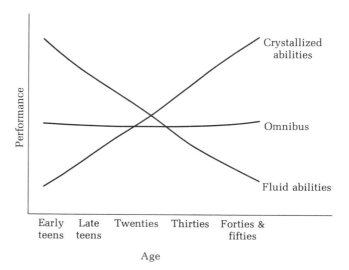

Figure 13.5

Performance as a function of age on tests of fluid and crystallized abilities. (From Horn 1970.)

these tests solely measured mental processes. Horn (1970), however, reviews other literature on the topic that suggests that these findings are consistent with other findings about age changes in fluid and crystallized abilities. It should be added, however, that the sample of subjects used in this study is unrepresentative of the general population and that information of this type coming from more representative samples would be welcome.

Sensation and Perception

The decline of fluid abilities with age closely parallels the decline of many sensory and perceptual processes with age. While the slope of the sensory-perceptual decline varies in regularity and extent for the particular modality and process under investigation, it is clear from the consistency of the regressions of these functions on age that few can escape decline on some sensory modality. A review of these age changes can be found in McFarland (1968) and in the handbook edited by Birren and Schaie (1977).

VISION

With age, the eye undergoes a series of metabolic and structural changes that lead to deterioration in vision and eyeball motility (Fozard et al. 1977). It is well known that farsightedness tends to increase with age, and it is possible to observe this change as early as age twenty. Adaptation to the dark shows a striking decrease with age, and in one study McFarland and Fisher (1955) observed a correlation of $-.89$ between age and dark adaptation. In such studies subjects are placed in completely dark environments for forty minutes or so and then a light is flashed at gradually increasing intensities until the subject is able to detect it reliably. The longer the subject has been in the darkened environment, the more light sensitive the subject will be.

Results of another study, by McFarland et al. (1960), are shown in Figure 13.6. In this figure the horizontal axis charts the amount of time subjects spent in the dark before exposure to the light stimulus, and the vertical axis gives the threshold of the light intensity needed for detection—the lower the curve, the less light is needed for detection. The results show very clearly, with virtually no overlap in the curves, that age is strongly related to dark adaptation. The blips on the left side of the curves refer to adaptation of the cones (which primarily function at daylight levels of illumination), and the remaining portion of the curves gives the adaptation curves for the rods (which operate mainly at nighttime levels of illumination).

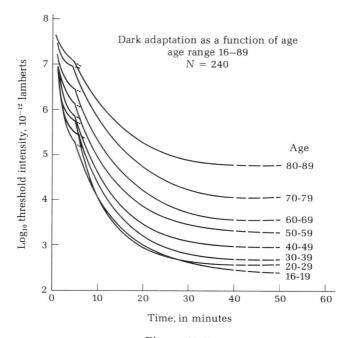

Figure 13.6

Dark adaptation as a function of age. (McFarland et al.
1960. Reproduced with the permission of the *Journal of
Gerontology*.)

Some of the visual loss with age is undoubtedly due to changes in the
eye itself—decreased visual accommodation; reduction of pupil size,
which in turn means less light falling on the retina; and yellowing and
opacity of the lens (McFarland 1968). Other indications are that central
neural mechanisms are also impaired with age; thus, it is difficult to be
specific about the exact sources for the visual impairments (Welford
1965; Walsh 1976).

AUDITION

Auditory sensitivity also declines with age. In order to measure this
decline, a sound stimulus (tone) is decomposed into its two components, frequency and amplitude, which can be varied independently.
Frequency refers to the number of cycles per second (cps) the tone
makes; *amplitude* is the extent or intensity of the excursion of the wave
form from its zero point. A common reference value for energy or
amplitude in these studies is 10^{-16} watts per square centimeter. Each

three-decibel increase is equal to a doubling of energy relative to this reference level, which is called *zero decibels.*

Figure 13.7 shows the decline of hearing with age for different sound frequencies. There is little decline in sensitivity (amplitude) for the lower frequencies on the left side of the curves, but there are rather severe losses for frequencies of 2000 cps or more. There is some indication that hearing loss in these higher tones is somewhat more severe in men than in women. This difference might relate to differential exposure to noise.

A recent review of the question of peripheral versus central deficits in audition can be found in Corso (1977). His tentative conclusion is that aging is associated with deficits at both locations but that the manner in which these deficits interact may vary at different age levels.

OTHER SENSES

McFarland (1968) also discusses the other major senses, finding that there is some evidence for increasing thresholds for the four basic tastes (bitter, sweet, sour, and salt), especially after fifty years. These increased thresholds are probably related to an absolute decrease in the number of taste buds. The ability to detect vibrations applied to the big

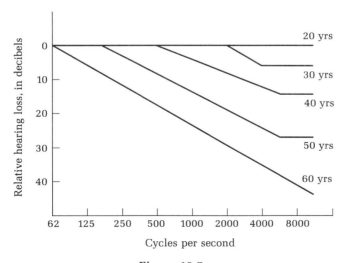

Figure 13.7
The progressive loss of hearing in relation to age, especially for the frequency ranges above 2000 cycles per second. (From Rosenblith and Stevens 1953.)

toe is also strongly associated with age, although this association is not found to the same degree for the index finger.

Engen (1977) points out that studies of taste and smell often yield contradictory findings. Diseases in other organs can affect taste sensitivities and thresholds. And the question of central versus peripheral deficits looms large here as well.

It would indeed be surprising if only the peripheral organs in sensory detection were affected adversely by age and that the central processing mechanisms were spared. There is evidence, in fact, that the central processing of information is also affected adversely, independently from the peripheral organs, and we shall review some of that evidence now.

Functional cells appear to decrease in the central nervous system as age advances. Other data suggest that the level of random neural activity increases with age, as does slowness of recovery from the effects of previous stimulation (Welford 1965). All of these changes would, of course, be likely to reduce the efficiency of the neural apparatus in distinguishing signal from noise in the system.

Central Processes

Much of the research on the psychological effects of aging has concentrated on discovering central mechanisms that may be differentially impaired by advancing age. It would not be surprising, of course, if all biological systems underwent aging effects, and data consistent with that hypothesis shall be presented later. Nevertheless, one might expect that some systems are more delicately balanced than others and thus have less tolerance for breakdowns in any of their biological components.

SHORT-TERM MEMORY

One technique that has recently been applied to the study of short-term memory processes in aging was originally developed by Sternberg (1966) to untangle motoric from central processes in reaction time measurements. Essentially this procedure asks the subject to remember a specific set of items (say numbers or letters), usually ranging from one to seven items. Then a single number or letter is shown on a screen and the subject is to indicate as quickly as possible whether the specific item presented is or is not part of the set of items held in short-term memory. The reaction times to the specific stimuli are recorded over a number of trials as a function of the number of items that the subject was asked to hold in memory.

This technique is used not to demonstrate that reaction times differ between different groups (which they do), but to plot the latency of the reaction time as a function of the number of items the subject was originally asked to remember. Sternberg (1966) found that the speed of search through short-term memory was linear, serial, and exhaustive. This means that each item in memory was accessed one at a time and that all items in the memory list were searched before a decision was made as to whether or not the specific item on the screen was part of the memory set. This latter procedure is counterintuitive, since one would have anticipated that, if the subject were required to remember the numbers 1, 3, and 5 and a 1 was presented on the screen, the reaction time decision would be faster than if a 5 were presented. That this is not the case may be due to the fact that making the decision per se takes time and that making a yes-no decision after each item might be more time-consuming than scanning the entire memory store and making only one decision.

Anders, Fozard, and Lillyquist (1972) used digits and applied the Sternberg procedure to three groups of subjects averaging twenty, thirty-eight, and sixty-eight years of age, respectively. The results of that study are shown in Figure 13.8. The vertical axis gives the reaction times to the stimuli and the horizontal axis gives the number of items the subjects were asked to remember before the specific stimulus was presented. There are two things to note about this figure. First, the point where the lines intercept the vertical axis is the fastest reaction time. One can see that the youngest subjects tend to be negligibly faster than the middle group and substantially faster than the oldest group. Second, and more important, the slope of the line is steeper for the older groups than for the youngest group. This means that the older subjects took more time to scan their immediate memories before the decision was made than did the younger subjects. The old-age group took about 71 msec to scan each item in memory, while the youngest took only 39

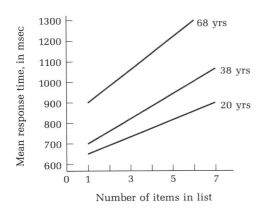

Figure 13.8

Response times for young, middle-age, and old-age subjects. (From Anders, Fozard, and Lillyquist 1972.)

msec. The two older groups did not differ significantly in their speed of scanning.

It is important to recognize that the intercepts and slopes are independently obtained in the Sternberg procedure. The fact that the elderly have slower motoric responses is not surprising but merely confirms everyday observation. The fact that it takes the elderly longer to process each bit of information *centrally* is of more interest.

Another study that investigated changes in short-term memory with age was reported by Inglis, Ankus, and Sykes (1968). They tested 240 subjects between the ages of five and seventy years on a dichotic listening task. This test, originally developed by Broadbent (1958), simultaneously and independently presented to both ears separate series of digits by means of earphones. It was found that subjects typically reported all the digits presented to one ear first before reporting those presented to the other ear. Thus, it was argued that there were two cognitive systems involved in this task. The first held and read out the material that was being processed actively; the second was a short-term memory store where the digits presented to the other ear were temporarily stored until the first system had completed its readout. Of relevance here was the finding that the older subjects made more errors in repeating the digits from the short-term memory system than in repeating the digits from the active processing system.

Inglis, Ankus, and Sykes theorize that, if the short-term memory component is impaired in aging, then the deficits in the aged will be found for the digits held in the short-term memory store. This is exactly what they observed. Recall of the first half-span of digits to one of the ears was almost constant for the different age groups, but there was a decline with age in the number of digits recalled in the second half-span. The highest-scoring group was composed of those aged twenty-one to thirty, and a fairly steady decline followed with increasing age. The important methodological point of this study was that a simple motivational explanation (less interest in the task by the aged) would not explain the specific findings readily. Thus, one may conclude that there are declines in the efficiency of the short-term memory store with increasing age.

LONG-TERM MEMORY

It has often been remarked that as adults age they tend to be more preoccupied with past than with present and future events. This change may be a way of coping with impairments in short-term memory, which put the aged at a disadvantage for dealing with current events and induce them to focus on the past.

Most models of memory posit at least two memory stages, the short-term and the long-term (Klatzky 1975). In contrast to short-term memories, information in the long-term store is believed to have no or very slow decay time, which may vary with the richness of the associational network into which the long-term memory was placed. Although it can be said that one's current telephone number is in long-term memory and easily retrievable, one is hard put to recall a previous telephone number because it is not richly interconnected with other associations. Other memories of more meaningful experiences can be shown to have little or no decay with time.

Nonexperimental studies of long-term memory in the aged are hard to interpret because the original conditions under which the information was first registered and stored are usually unknown (Botwinick and Storandt 1974). One is usually ignorant of the amount of practice and rehearsal of that information that took place during the intervening period, or of how well the information was learned in the first place.

Smith (1963) had some control of the level of initial performance in a study of long-term memory. She retested subjects who had originally learned all the correct answers to 107 questions in the Westminster Shorter Catechism sixty years earlier when they were under thirteen years of age. These individuals were retested in 1934, 1950, and 1960 on those same questions. There was only slight evidence of loss between 1934 and 1950, but there was a sharp drop in recall in 1960. In 1934 the subjects remembered or needed only one prompting to correctly recall 98 of 107 answers. In 1950 these subjects recalled 92 of those items under similar conditions. In 1960, however, they remembered only 73 of the answers. Thus, between the ages of sixty-three and seventy-three these people forgot much more than they had forgotten between the ages of forty-seven and sixty-three.

The fact that crystallized abilities seem to show less decline with age than do fluid abilities is also related to the question of long-term retention and age. Foulds and Raven (1948) showed that vocabulary scores (which measure crystallized ability) have negligible declines with age but that Raven Progressive Matrices scores (which measure fluid abilities) show rather steep declines. Presumably knowledge of word meaning is accumulated over the years and is more likely a measure of long-term retention than are the progressive matrices, which appear to tap mainly current information-processing abilities.

Shakow, Dolkart, and Goldman (1941) also showed that "old" memories tend to reveal less deterioration than "new" memories. This study is less satisfactory than the others, however, for there is no knowledge of the extent of rehearsal over the intervening years. Other studies on this matter are reviewed by Welford (1958), but we can conclude that there is less evidence for decline in long-term memory with age than there is for decline in short-term memory.

RECOGNITION MEMORY

Another area of investigation in memory processes is recognition memory. In recognition memory tasks, the subject is shown a series of stimuli and then asked to indicate whether or not each of the stimuli is part of a larger set of stimuli shown later. This kind of task is much easier to perform than recalling stimuli without any cues, a finding that suggests that people have more in their memory stores than they can retrieve unaided.

The distinction between recall and recognition is that recall requires an active search to locate the appropriate memory while recognition merely requires finding a match between what is presented and what is in memory. In recognition, the subject may need only to recognize a component of the full stimulus to generate a correct response. In recall, the subject must generate at least this component on his own. Undoubtedly this distinction is oversimplified, for even in recognition there has to be some active process of locating the appropriate match in memory.

Schonfield and Robertson (1966) exposed subjects ranging in age from twenty to seventy-five to two lists of twenty-four nouns or adjectives. After exposure to each of the lists, the subjects were to try to recall freely as many of the words they had seen or else to recognize whether or not each of these twenty-four words was part of a larger list of words presented to them. Results indicated a clear decline with age in free recall of the lists but no decline in recognition memory with age. Although those over age sixty could only recall about 54 percent of the words that those between the ages of twenty and twenty-nine could, the older subjects actually recognized slightly more of the words than did the youngest subjects.

Other studies show some decline in recognition memory with age, and the issue is still in dispute (Botwinick and Storandt 1974; Schonfield, Trueman, and Kline 1972). Nevertheless, it is clear that under some conditions it is possible to demonstrate steep declines in recall memory with age when there are none in recognition memory.

PSYCHOMOTOR SPEED

The distinction between psychomotor speed and some of the tasks we have been discussing that involve motor components is not great. In essence, *psychomotor tasks* are those which appear simple and seem to require little central problem solving in relation to the amount of time spent on the motoric activity itself. It turns out that the distinction between psychomotor tasks and other tasks is not easy to draw, since all psychological tasks require some central processing mechanisms. The apparent simplicity or complexity of the task may have little to do with the actual underlying complexities of the central or peripheral mechanisms involved. Nevertheless, a number of interesting findings that relate psychomotor speed to age have emerged and shall be reviewed here.

While it is a common observation that individuals tend to grow motorically slow with age, the cause is not obvious. Furthermore, not only do older people work more slowly than younger people in speeded tasks, but, when the directions are to work slowly, they can not work as slowly as can younger people. For example, Botwinick and Storandt (1974) had subjects ranging in age from twenty-one to eighty write "United States" as slowly as possible without lifting their pencils from the paper or dotting the *i*'s or crossing the *t*'s. Subjects in their twenties took 112 seconds to do this, whereas those in their sixties and seventies took about 21 seconds. Thus, there was a dramatic difference in the degrees to which older and younger subjects could work slowly when asked to do so.

A classic work on aging and psychomotor performance was reported by Miles (1931). He obtained the psychomotor performances of 331 males ranging in age from six to ninety-five on six different psychomotor tasks. The *manual motility* measure required the subject to grab a pencil from a hole, place it in another hole, and then return his hand to the starting point. The *extension-flexion* measure required the subject to lift his finger from an electric key and bring it down again as quickly as possible. The *rotary motility* measure required the subject to rotate the crank handle of a hand drill as many times as possible in ten seconds.

Another class of psychomotor tasks studied by Miles involved reaction times. The test of *pursuit reaction* required the subject to stop an electrically moving clock hand at the zero point when the hand was sweeping at a rate of two revolutions per second. In the *digital reaction* or *foot reaction* test, the subject was required to lift either his finger or the forepart of his foot and return it to its starting point on signal. The results of these measures are graphed in Figures 13.9 and 13.10. The arrows on the sides of Figure 13.10 point to the appropriate vertical axis from which to read the results.

Both figures show a decline in speed with advancing age. For manual motility, those in their eighties were 50 percent to 60 percent slower than the twenty-year-olds. The curves present average scores and fail to indicate that the elderly were much more variable than the younger subjects and that many of the older subjects were able to outperform the average fifty- or sixty-year-old. For the extension-flexion measure, those in their eighties took about three times longer than those in their middle twenties, but, again, one-third of the oldest subjects were able to outperform the average fifty-year-old. Rotary motility showed a similar effect with age. Reaction time measures appear to be better preserved

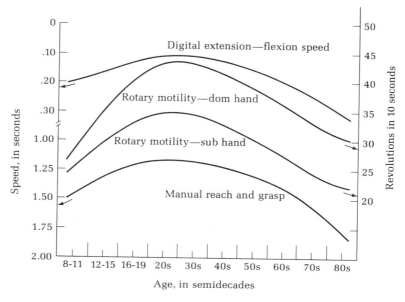

Figure 13.9

Changes in manual motility with age. (From Miles 1931.)

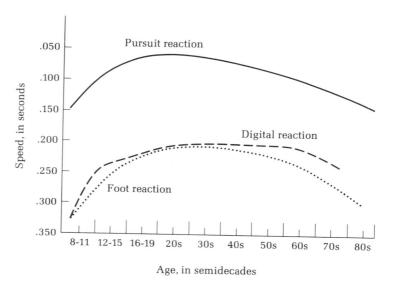

Figure 13.10

Changes in reaction time with age. (From Miles 1931.)

over the years than do motility measures. Digital reaction time shows no decline with age until age seventy. Both foot reaction and pursuit reaction begin to show declines earlier.

The causes for the declines with age are not yet understood. Speed of neural conduction is not believed to be sufficient cause, for Norris, Shock, and Wagman (1953) found only small changes in nerve conduction velocity as a function of age in nonbrain areas. Other physiological functions, such as cardiac output and maximum breathing capacity, show much steeper declines with age.

Welford (1958) points out that the motoric component of the psychomotor response does not appear to be the critical factor in the slowing down with age and that the deficits must lie at either the sensory or the central level. One experiment cited by Welford points to declines in central processes as being the critical factor. The study was by Crossman and Szafran (1956), who required subjects to sort an ordinary deck of playing cards according to different rules. Subjects sorted the pack into alternate piles as quickly as possible, into black and red piles, into the four suits, and into the four suits separating court cards from the rest. The alternative-piles sort was used as a measure of the basic speed of the sorting movements themselves; the other three sorts required decisions by the subjects involving two, four, and eight choices, respectively. The results of the time spent per card as a function of the number of choices are shown in Figure 13.11 for three different age groups.

Note that the sorting times when no decision had to be made did not differ by age. When a choice had to be made, however, the oldest group took substantially more time than did the younger two groups. It is perplexing, though, that there was no increase in the *difference* between the age groups with increasing number of choices. Welford (1958) adds that in many studies of coordinated psychomotor performances older subjects appear to be more accurate than younger subjects, as if there were some trade-off of speed and accuracy.

Declines in intellectual performance are closely related to speed; older people work more slowly than younger people, and timed tests show larger intellectual declines than do unspeeded tests. Christian and Paterson (1936) administered a 120-item vocabulary test with a fifteen-minute time limit to Minnesota college freshmen and older relatives of the students and found that older subjects obtained lower scores. The authors also observed, however, that older subjects attempted fewer items and that when only the first sixty items were analyzed (which all subjects had attempted) the age trends were actually reversed—the older subjects had a higher proportion of those items correct than did the younger subjects. Lorge (1936) also showed that on untimed intelligence tests there was less of a decline with age

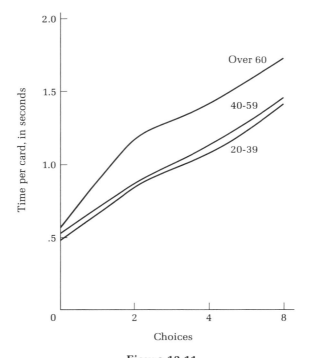

Figure 13.11

Times taken to sort cards into various numbers of categories.
(From Crossman and Szafran 1956.)

than on timed tests. Almost all intelligence tests confound speed and power, and we ought to be clear about the distinctions in discussing intellectual decline with age. Power tests are those which give ample time for solution; the question is whether or not the subject can correctly answer the items.

This is not to gainsay the importance of speed itself. Higher speed means that subjects can process information more rapidly. Thus, if exposure time is held constant, those with greater speed should acquire more information and be more fluent in their thought processes. Birren (1974) has criticized those who minimize the importance of speed in intellectual functioning. If processing time is slow, then information in short-term memory (which tends to decay rapidly normally) may be lost before it can be used. There is a vicious cycle in which reduced speed means that less information has the opportunity to be rehearsed and enter long-term memory. Birren also points out that we ought to appreciate the implications of slower speed among the elderly. They will not do well in environments that call for a speedy pace, but, if speedy response is not absolutely necessary, they may perform quite adequately.

GENETICS

Most theories of aging include some sort of genetic explanation to account for the general decline in functioning with age. At the molecular level, there is evidence that the ability of cells to repair themselves deteriorates with age. The number of cell divisions a particular cell can undergo *in vitro* is strongly related to the age of the organism from which it comes. For example, a cell from a human fetus can double in a test tube about fifty times before it dies, but cells drawn from older humans show proportionate drops in the number of duplications before death (Hayflick 1974). Only cells having qualities akin to malignancies appear to duplicate indefinitely. Furthermore, each species has its own finite number of duplications that are possible in tissue culture before demise. It is as if the number of duplications was preprogrammed and coded into the genome.

There are many different genetic theories of aging, and a valuable compendium of such theories can be found in Rockstein (1974). Virtually all hypothesize some accumulation of either wear and tear or probabilistic errors in the repeated cell duplications concomitant with a gradual decline in the capacity of cells to repair themselves after damage.

There is evidence that longevity is under some genetic control—children of long-lived parents tend to live longer than children of short-lived parents, and MZ twins show greater similarity in age of death than do DZ twins (Kallmann and Jarvik 1959). Table 13.5 sum-

Table 13.5

Differential life span data related to parental age

Author	Life span of offspring (in years)		Comment
	Short-lived parents	Long-lived parents	
Actuarial Society of America (1903)	39.44	41.77	Life expectancy of sons at age 27
Bell (1918)	32.8	52.7	Mean life span of sons and daughters
Pearl (1931)	40.9	45.8	Life expectancy of sons at age 20, related to father's age only
Yuan (1932)	31.5	39.8	Life expectancy of sons at age 20
Jalavisto (1951)	36.2	48.1	Life expectancy of sons at birth
Kallmann et al. (1956) ...	45.8	55.2	Mean life span of sons
Kallmann et al. (1956) ...	49.5	57.9	Mean life span of sons and daughters

Source: From F. J. Kallmann and L. F. Jarvik, "Individual Differences in Constitution and Genetic Background." In James E. Birren, ed., *Handbook of Aging and the Individual*. Reprinted by permission of The University of Chicago Press. Copyright © 1959.

marizes findings from studies of the relationship between parental longevity and life spans of children. Although these data used different methods of ascertainment and are derived from different countries and socioeconomic mixtures, the results are quite consistent. In all instances they show that children of long-lived parents are likely to live longer than children of short-lived parents. Alexander Graham Bell's study (1918) found that if both parents had died before age sixty the life span of the children was about twenty years shorter than if both parents had died after age eighty. It would have been interesting to analyze such data in terms of cause of death. Genetically determined longevity probably does not account for the major proportion of variance in life span, since noninherited diseases and accidents play a large role as well. But genetic longevity will begin to be more important as these other causes for death are diminished (Birren and Renner 1977).

Medical Factors

Of special importance in the decline in intellectual functioning with age is, of course, change in the brain. Cross-sectional samples show that brain weight may diminish by 10 percent or more between early adulthood and late old age (Horn 1970). Cerebral blood flow also declines with age (Wang 1973). Other signs of cellular degenerative brain changes also occur, so that one should not be surprised that intellectual declines may accompany aging. It is clear, however, that some individuals are spared the full ravages of aging in the intellectual realm, and, since there is not usually a close correspondence between the neuronal brain changes and intellectual functioning, one must look at the medical disorders that accelerate the decline.

BLOOD PRESSURE AND CEREBRAL BLOOD FLOW

High blood pressure and reduced cerebral blood flow appear to be associated with intellectual decline, both pointing to deficiencies in the circulatory system and perhaps reduced oxygen (anoxia) in the brain cells. Wilkie and Eisdorfer (1973) have shown negative relationships between Wechsler IQ subtest scores and blood pressure in individuals aged sixty to seventy-nine. The magnitude of the correlations is not great (in the −.20s on the average), but the findings are in the predicted direction for every single subtest of the WAIS. Furthermore, these authors showed that for those between seventy and seventy-nine survival was strongly related to blood pressure. Only 40 percent of those in the high blood pressure category returned for a repeated examination, whereas 80 percent of those with lower blood pressure returned.

Cerebral blood flow also showed some relationship to intelligence, especially among individuals with low education and low SES. Cerebral blood flow can now be estimated safely by having subjects breath radioactively labeled xenon and then recording the radioactivity with a scintillation counter from the head—the faster the radioactivity is picked up, the better the circulation (Wang 1973).

TERMINAL DROP

A series of studies have shown that deterioration in intellectual performance is predictive of death as early as five years before its occurrence (see Riegel and Riegel 1972 for references). This is really not surprising, since intellectual measures do tap underlying biological processes and any newly acquired impairments in brain structure or function should cause drops on these measures.

Riegel and Riegel point out that most longitudinal and cross-sectional studies may actually underestimate the extent of the decline with age, for they usually do not include a detailed analysis of those who either resist retesting or who die between retestings. These authors have shown that both retest resisters and individuals who failed to survive until the next examination had lower scores on earlier tests. Furthermore, there is usually little discussion of the subjects' reasons for resisting a repeated testing. Subjects may not feel well enough to participate in the testing, or they may prefer to avoid the stresses associated with a repeated examination because of a recognition that they are not as able as they used to be.

Similarly, personality measures of rigidity show that those who resist retesting or who fail to survive for retesting manifested more rigidity at the first examination than did those who are retested. This rigidity difference is especially salient among those under sixty-five years of age. For older subjects there is a general increase in rigidity scores with age, independent of survival or resistance to retesting.

Aging and Personality

PERSONALITY STUDIES OF CHILDREN

Not many researchers have been interested in the relationship of personality to age, although many have investigated the behavioral consequences of specific life stress events that occur along with age—marriage of children, retirement, job loss, menopause, and so on. This approach is somewhat at variance with the approach used with younger children, in which only variables such as age and sex are usually included in studies of the structure and stability of personality.

Consider some childhood equivalents to adult life stress events—entering school, the birth of a younger sibling, the departure of an older sibling, the loss of a parent. Except for the last event, it is not possible to locate studies that examine cohorts of children who were simultaneously being subjected to such life stress events, and virtually nothing exists on the direct effects of these events on the shaping of personality. Perhaps this lack reflects the bias that most such childhood events have only temporary consequences and therefore are of little interest. On the other hand, the consequences of adult life stresses might be more enduring because the aged are less resilient.

Studies of personality in young children follow a different pattern for other reasons as well. First, the behavioral repertoires of young children are more limited than those of adults. Second, it is not easy to find specific items constant across infancy and youth of which one can obtain frequency estimates as a function of age. For example, it would be meaningless to ask whether an infant has many friends. Third, the meaning of a particular behavior may change with age—an infant may cry because of physical discomfort, but a toddler may cry because of psychological distress. Fourth, self-report measures, which are the most common source of information about older children and adults, cannot be used with young children.

The consequence of these limitations is that one must look for genotypic continuity, despite phenotypic discontinuity, when studying younger children. Bronson (1966) has called this the notion of *central orientations*, which refers to the complex of traits, attitudes, and abilities that characterizes one's actions. She has identified two dimensions, akin to extroversion and impulsiveness, that do show continuity from about age five to age sixteen.

Another study demonstrated personality continuity between the toddler age and late adolescence. Shirley (1933) had published personality sketches of twenty-five toddlers she had studied during the first two years of life. Fifteen years later Neilon (1948) was able to locate many of those children and independently wrote new personality sketches of them derived from interviews and ratings. The children were separated by sex, and judges were asked to match the original toddler portraits with the new ones. For both boys and girls this matching was clearly successful, suggesting personality continuity between the ages of two and seventeen. However, some children were matched perfectly over the fifteen-year-period (by ten different judges), while others were never correctly matched. Thus, some children showed continuity and others did not.

Because of the difficulty of comparing behavior across time for children, no more shall be said on that topic here, except that there are two important volumes containing the findings for major longitudinal studies of personality, at least to early middle age (Jones et al. 1971; Kagan and Moss 1962).

PERSONALITY STUDIES OF ADULTS

A cross-sectional study of aging and personality using eighty-seven males between the ages of fifty-five and eighty-four was conducted by Reichard, Livson, and Peterson (1962). The study is of interest because of the extensive personality characterizations of the subjects and the form of factor analysis used which permitted the classification of individuals into types. The authors found five major types—mature, rocking chair, armored, angry, and self-hating. The first three were regarded as successful agers, while the last two were not. Different patterns of adjustment operated even among the successful agers. The mature types, even in retirement, were actively involved in their social worlds; the rocking-chair men, also successful agers, were more passive and had little ambition. One important point of the study was that there is a variety of patterns for successful aging and that it would be inappropriate to fit all individuals into the same prescriptive mold.

A major cross-sectional study on age changes in personality was recently reported by Swenson, Pearson, and Osborne (1972). They administered an automated version of the MMPI to fifty thousand adult outpatients at Mayo Clinic. None were acutely ill, and psychiatric patients were excluded. A sample of the findings is shown in Figure 13.12. High scores on the hypochondriasis scale mean self-reports of numerous physical complaints. It is noteworthy that the peak on this scale is for people only in their forties and fifties. The fact that actual declines in physical health are probably much greater after this age supports the psychological nature of this scale. The finding suggests that the acknowledgment of hypochondriacal complaints is an adaptive process in which declining expectations of good health follow along with actual declines. Similarly, there is not much evidence for increases on the depression scale with age, at least beyond forty. From the perspective of youth, aging may seem like a dreadful prospect, but for those who are aging it does not seem so terrible.

Hypomania and psychasthenia both show rather steep declines with age. Hypomanics are described as being impulsive, expansive, and distractable; psychasthenics are regarded as fearful, ruminative, and agitated. Declines on these scales bring bad news and good news. On the one hand, there is clearly a loss of vigor and energy, as suggested by the decline on the hypomania scale; yet there is considerably less ruminative doubting with age, as suggested by the decline on the psychasthenia scale.

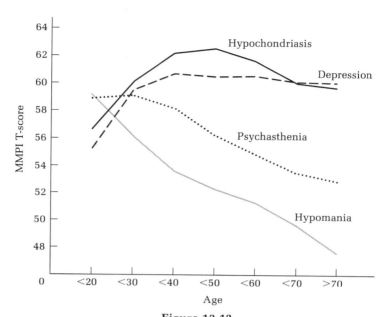

Figure 13.12

MMPI scores as a function of age. (After
Swenson, Pearson, and Osborne 1973.)

As with all cross-sectional findings, one cannot be sure that these
differences reflect genuine changes with aging or generational differences conditioned by sociological phenomena. Only in combination
with longitudinal findings could firm conclusions be established. Furthermore, findings of age or generational differences may be confounded with the personality scales employed. Had only measures on
depression and hypochondriasis been used in the Swensen, Pearson,
and Osborne study, the conclusion would be that there was little cross-
sectional evidence for aging effects. On the other hand, if only measures
of hypomania or psychasthenia were available, one would conclude
that there were fairly large age or generational differences. In light of
the evidence, it would be unwarranted to expect all personality measures to yield equivalent findings with respect to age changes or stability in personality.

The danger of drawing strong conclusions from data derived solely
from cross-sectional cohorts is exemplified by a study of Woodruff and
Birren (1972). They readministered the California Test of Personality
(CTP) in 1969 to middle-age subjects who had originally taken this test
while students at the University of Southern California in 1944. The
authors do not report test-retest correlations or scores for the individual

subscales of the test, but only the total score, which is presumed to be an index of overall adjustment. They found little evidence for longitudinal changes in overall adjustment for this twenty-five-year period. However, they also tested teenagers in 1969 who were about the same age as the original cohort had been in 1944. In comparison with the older subjects, the younger ones were considerably less well adjusted. What would have happened had only the data been available for the middle-age and teenage groups tested in 1969? If cross-sectional comparisons had been made on those data alone, one might have (unjustifiably) concluded that increased age is associated with better adjustment. It is only with knowledge of the 1944 test that one can demonstrate that the cross-sectional data alone lead to erroneous inferences. As it turns out, at least on the CTP, those tested both in 1944 and in 1969 were better adjusted than those tested in 1969 alone, independent of age. This difference is best regarded as generational rather than age related. Woodruff and Birren (1972) cite a number of other cross-sectional studies that also may have overestimated the role of age in personality.

Kelly (1955) retested subjects on a battery of tests twenty years after they had originally been given these tests when they were in their mid-twenties. He found test-retest correlations of about .32 for the Allport-Vernon scale. For the Bernreuter Personality Inventory, test-retest correlations were about .61 for ratings of self-confidence and .47 for sociability. On the Strong Vocational Interest Blank (SVIB), correlations over the twenty-year period averaged about .62 for the men and about .57 for the women. These correlations are somewhat lower than similar correlations reported by Strong (1951) over a twenty-two-year retest interval. Strong found that the average test-retest correlation for the SVIB was about .75. As might be expected, Strong found that the occupational interests of those originally tested when a bit older (about thirty years old) showed more stability than the occupational interests of those tested when relatively young (in the eleventh grade).

These results suggest moderate stability of attitudes and interests over two decades. It should be remembered that these tests are not perfectly reliable even after short test-retest intervals, so that correlations close to 1.00 cannot be expected.

A study by Pressey and Jones (1955) of moral codes and anxieties associated with age is of special interest. They tested individuals ranging from twenty to sixty years old over a thirty-year period, cross-sectionally finding increased conservatism with age. The important point, however, was that older subjects tested in 1953 obtained about the same scores as younger subjects had obtained in 1923. A cross-sectional analysis of only the 1953 data would suggest increasing conservatism with age, but the long-term data indicate that even youngsters in 1923 were more conservative than youngsters in 1953. Pressey and Jones conclude that there was no good evidence for increasing conservatism with age but that generational differences were responsible for the apparent age differences in conservatism.

In general, the issues occupying researchers who study the personalities of children and young adults are the same issues that are of concern to those studying older populations. Questions of cross-situational consistency, validity of personality test scores for predicting real-life or laboratory criteria, and the units most appropriate for measuring personality—all need to be resolved.

There has not been much psychological theorizing extending beyond the young adult years (see Neugarten 1977 for a review). Freud was largely interested in early childhood and adolescence, regarding adult personality as a predictable transformation of early experiences and biological dispositions. Erikson (1963) does have stages that extend through the adult and old age years, including, among others, intimacy versus isolation for early adulthood, generativity versus stagnation for middle adulthood, and ego integrity versus despair for late adulthood. These concepts have been useful for simplifying the complexities of adult behavior, but as yet there is no more empirical support for these stages than for other sets of stages or for other models of stability and continuity of personality in the adult years (Schaie and Parnham 1976).

SOCIAL ECOLOGY

One interesting question about the social psychology of aging concerns the extent to which a changing social ecology contributes to decline. There is a sequence of life events that occurs among almost all aging individuals, irrespective of their biological health, that might be expected to produce changes in lifestyle, goals, and opportunities. These events include loss of parents and friends, marriage of children, declining sexuality, retirement, and the approach of death. The frequent decline in and isolation from social interactions that tend to accompany aging are in part due to this reduction in the number of significant others. Cumming and Henry (1961) have termed the simultaneous withdrawal of the individual from society and the withdrawal of society from the aging individual *disengagement*. They regard the process of disengagement as an adaptive process in which there is a reduction in social roles, social relationships, and meaningfulness, which serves as preparation for the inevitable.

Much research has been generated on disengagement theory. The evidence is that for some individuals disengagement is an adaptive process associated with good psychological health, while for others it is not (Neugarten 1973). For some, continuation of an active life is associated with successful aging. Neugarten has argued that there are many ways to successfully or unsuccessfully age, and that these ways will depend on the previous lifestyle of the individual.

At its worst extreme, the social environment of the aged can be a depriving one of few challenges and few expectations. It is not clear how much an impoverished environment contributes to intellectual and personality declines. The fact that crystallized abilities tend not to decline with age suggests that social impoverishment may not be as widespread or devastating as it might appear. On the other hand, an impoverished environment may have deleterious effects in one area of functioning and not in another.

Conclusions

The evidence reviewed in this chapter suggests that there are clear declines in sensory and motor abilities and general information processing with age. While these declines are generally predictable, many individuals can escape their full ravages. Why some are spared the declines is an important area for future research and will necessarily include investigations from genetic, physiological, psychological, and sociological perspectives. It is also clear that traditional cross-sectional studies are not sufficient in themselves to chart the course of aging; one must be alert to biases in sample ascertainment especially.

There are few solid findings in the realm of personality and aging, except that declines in activity and energy are associated with older ages. There has also been little to report on the relationship of physical health to personality, and this is obviously an open area for future investigation. And finally, we know little about the relationship of intellectual functioning to personality in the older years. Most researchers have been interested in one or the other area and have not sought to connect the two. We can expect that there will be an increase of interest on aging, since medical advances will increase the proportion of aged and we will need to focus our attention on them more and more.

14

Racial and Ethnic Comparisons

Black-white differences in the United States have received an enormous amount of attention relative to comparisons among other racial or ethnic groups. This special interest does not result simply from the fact that blacks are the largest nonwhite minority (about 92 percent of all nonwhites) in the country. Rather, it can be traced to deviations of blacks from the majority population on a number of important and highly visible social parameters.

To define a race is no easy matter. In the past the emphasis has been on conspicuous morphological characters, such as skin color, hair texture, skull shape, and facial features. Among the major racial groups—Caucasoids, Negroids, and Mongoloids—reliance on these characters for nonprecise classification is scientifically respectable, since they tend to correspond to more objective measures of genetic differences as determined by blood-group genes. When racial hybrids are encountered, however, it often becomes difficult to classify individuals on the basis of the visible morphological characters alone, and the blood-group measures take on increasing importance.

While hybrids confound clear assignment of an individual to a specific race, interfertility between members of different races is required for the definition of race. The absence of interbreeding and gene flow between groups would constitute a species difference and not a race difference. Since there is no precise definition that can be used to identify races, arbitrary decisions must be made. As Baker (1974) puts it:

> One may argue that a population "A" is distinguishable from a population "B" if x% of the individuals constituting population "A" can be recognized as not belonging to population "B." It will be understood that the correct value to be assigned to x cannot be discovered by objective means; nevertheless, if a high figure (perhaps 75) is agreed upon by taxonomists, one can scarcely doubt that there is a distinction worthy of recognition as a subspecific or "racial" x [p. 99].

Genetic-racial variations are usually accompanied by a variety of cultural and behavioral differences. Undoubtedly the genetic and environmental dissimilarities mutually interact in a fashion that tends to maintain or even exaggerate these differences. This occurs because of positive assortative mating—we tend to mate with those who resemble us physically (Spuhler 1968) and culturally (Vandenberg 1972). Mating with those who resemble us is not limited to racial groups, of course, since there is substantial assortative mating within races as well.

Recent definitions of race for scientific purposes have taken on a dynamic flavor by emphasizing differences in gene frequencies between populations. Thus, races are defined as populations that differ in the incidence of some genes. Using gene frequencies helps us to think in nontypological terms; we can then see gradation between races and understand that assignment to one or another race is statistical rather than absolute.

Table 14.1 provides approximate frequencies for various genes obtained through blood samples in Caucasian and African Negro populations (Cavalli-Sforza and Bodmer 1971). There are some genes, such as Lu^a, that are not very useful in differentiating the races, and others, such as Fy^a, that are more efficient. While these blood type frequencies provide conclusive evidence for substantial genetic differences between Caucasians and African Negroes, their application to behavioral studies of blacks and whites in the United States is not immediately apparent.

By calculating the proportion of "Caucasian" genes in the American Negro, however, it is possible to estimate statistically the extent to which the American black has mated with the white American. The degree of Caucasian admixture in the American black for any particular genetic system can be estimated from the following formula:

$$M = \frac{(q_n - q_a)}{(q_c - q_a)}$$

where

M = degree of Caucasian admixture in the American Negro

q_n = gene frequency in the American Negro

q_a = gene frequency in the African Negro

q_c = gene frequency in Caucasians

Suppose that 15 percent of a particular sample of American blacks was found to have the Fy^a gene. Using Table 14.1, one could calculate the proportion of Caucasian admixture in the following manner:

$$M = \frac{(.15 - .06)}{(.42 - .06)}$$

= .25 Caucasian admixture of the Negroes in this population

To be sure, one could calculate the proportion of Negro genes in American Caucasians, but products of black-white matings have been categorized as Negro and reared largely in the Negro community when Negroid features have been recognizable. Only those with a very small proportion of Negro admixture would therefore be classified as Caucasian. Also, since blacks comprise only about 11 percent of the population, even with a fairly high proportion of Negro intermating it would be difficult to detect reliably such a small frequency difference among whites.

Table 14.1

Selected gene frequencies in Caucasians and African blacks

Gene	Caucasian	Black
0	.66	.71
M_s	.31	.49
P_2	.48	.11
r	.38	.12
Lu^a	.04	.03
K	.05	.003
Se	.52	.57
Le	.82	.32
Fy^a	.42	.06

Source: adapted from L. L. Cavalli-Sforza and W. F. Bodmer, *The Genetics of Human Populations.* San Francisco: W. H. Freeman and Company. Copyright © 1971.

Reed (1969) has summarized data on the proportion of Caucasian admixture in American blacks. Some of his findings are shown in Figure 14.1. He points out that there appears to be substantial regional difference in the degree of admixture and that estimates based on southern populations suggest much less admixture than in the North. It is uncertain whether the higher proportion of the Caucasian admixture in northern blacks occurred before or after migration to the North, but some evidence suggests that it was the more admixed who migrated. These were often house slaves and offspring of matings involving the slave master or other members of his family. These offspring would be appreciably more admixed and would generally have greater educational and other advantages. Reed concludes that the average amount of Caucasian admixture in the American black is about 21 percent.

But what does a Caucasian admixture of 21 percent in American blacks mean? We share, on the average, 25 percent of our genes with a single grandparent; thus a 21 percent admixture in blacks represents a value a bit less than having one white grandparent. Of course it is unlikely that all the white genes came from a single ancestor. This same percentage of admixture could be reached, for example, by having two grandparents who were each first-generation black-white hybrids.

Medical Disorders

The foregoing discussion shows that to identify the American black as a race completely apart from the Caucasian is an oversimplification that does injustice to the complexity of race. Nevertheless, even this crude classification shows correlations with a number of important outcome variables. When Chung and Myrianthopoulos (1968) reviewed comparisons of American blacks and whites with respect to congenital malformations, they found that the rates of congenital malformations differed substantially for some disorders. For example, harelip plus

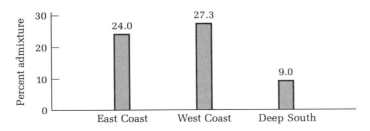

Figure 14.1

Estimates of Caucasian admixture in American blacks by geographical area. (Adapted from Reed 1969.)

cleft palate, webbed fingers or toes, and anencephaly (absence of brain tissue) are about three times more frequent among white infants than among black infants. Polydactyly (extra fingers or toes) is about nine times more frequent among blacks than whites.

Figure 14.2 gives death rates for selected causes in American whites and nonwhites for 1966. (Remember that 92 percent of nonwhites are Negroes). The figure shows some remarkable differences between whites and nonwhites. Suicide, leukemia, and arteriosclerosis are far more common among whites, and homicide, hypertensive heart disease, and tuberculosis are far more common among blacks.

One of the most striking and important differences between blacks and whites is in the rate of hypertensive heart disease. Black males are about three times more likely than white males, and black females are about twice as likely as white females, to suffer from the disease. The cause of this difference in rates is not known, but Boyle et al. (1967) have noted a significant positive relationship between skin pigmentation and hypertension among blacks in Charleston, South Carolina. Since skin pigmentation would seem to vary with degree of Caucasian admixture, some genetic mechanisms may be operative. Harburg et al. (1970) have suggested, however, that stress may contribute to the increased proportion of hypertension among blacks. They found that Detroit census tracts identified as high stress (e.g., having a high crime rate) were associated with more hypertension in blacks than were low-stress tracts. It is not clear whether skin color differences are associated with being in high- or low-stress black areas of cities, so that the causes of these relationships are not yet understood.

Perinatal Differences

The ratio of male to female births differs appreciably between blacks and whites, with blacks having a lower proportion of male births. One way of designating this proportion is by the *secondary sex ratio,* which is the number of male births divided by the number of female births multiplied by 100. Thus, a ratio greater than 100 indicates a greater number of male births than female births, and a ratio of less than 100 indicates fewer male births than female births. This secondary sex ratio is to be distinguished from the *primary sex ratio,* which refers to the sex ratio of conceptions. The primary sex ratio is much more difficult to estimate, although some argue that as many as 150 males are conceived to every 100 females.

Reviewing the natality statistics for the United States between 1963 and 1967, Malina (1973) reports that for whites the sex ratio was about 105.5 and for blacks it was 102.5. This difference has been observed consistently over the years and appears to have both genetic and en-

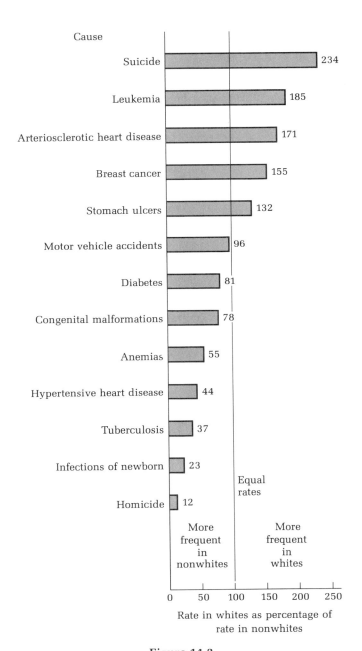

Figure 14.2

Relative death rates for selected causes in U.S. whites and nonwhites, 1966.
(From U.S. Department of Health, Education, and Welfare.)

vironmental correlates. Figure 14.3 gives secondary sex ratios in the Collaborative Perinatal Study by parental socioeconomic status and race (Willerman 1972). Note that at every point on the socioeconomic index the sex ratio for whites exceeds that for blacks. Among both blacks and whites, however, those from the lowest socioeconomic strata have a deficiency in the proportion of male births. One interpretation of these data is that males are more vulnerable than females and that the poorer prenatal conditions in the lowest social classes increase the likelihood that males will be aborted. This interpretation cannot account for the overall differences between blacks and whites, however, since high social class blacks also have a low sex ratio. Presumably prenatal conditions in this group were not poor, and therefore it should not have produced fewer males. It may be, however, that many of these mothers were born in low social class environments and that there might be some lasting legacy of poverty from early childhood.

There are many other differences between blacks and whites around the time of birth (see Malina 1973 for review). Blacks are almost twice as likely to have dizygotic twins than whites, although the likelihood of monozygotic twins is similar for both groups. Lower birth weight, birth complications, and infant mortality under one year of age are also much more frequent among blacks than among whites. Blacks also have higher bone density and earlier eruption of teeth than whites.

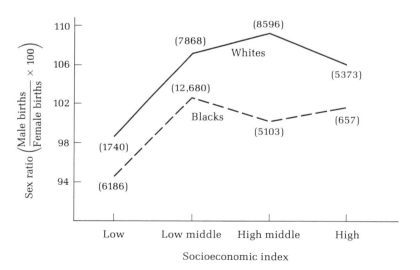

Figure 14.3

Sex ratio by race and socioeconomic index.
(From Willerman 1972.)

Intellectual Differences

While the foregoing review indicates substantial differences between blacks and whites, none of these has captured the attention of so many social science researchers as has the difference in intellectual performance between the groups. Our intention is to describe, with little interpretation, the results of comparisons of blacks and whites on intelligence tests so that the reader will have a clear idea of the consistency and the magnitude of the differences obtained. Afterwards the factors that may account for the differences observed will be discussed.

Shuey's (1966) comprehensive review of the evidence relating to black-white comparisons is probably the most detailed and complete. She reported on comparisons of preschool children, school children, adults, selected populations such as military recruits and veterans, delinquents and racial hybrids. It is worth quoting extensively from her summary, because it states with little interpretation the results of a half-century of research on black-white comparisons.

We have attempted to assemble and evaluate critically the research in the field of Negro intelligence as determined by psychometric tests. The survey covers a span of more than 50 years. Approximately 382 studies have been examined in which 81 tests were administered, and hundreds of thousands of Negro children and adults from various sections of the United States, as well as some 1600 from Ontario, Canada and the West Indian Islands of Jamaica and Grand Cayman, served as subjects [p. 491].

Young Children. Approximately 1700 colored and 13,900 white children between the ages of two and six served as subjects in 17 studies reported between 1922 and 1965.... The average IQ's of the various groups of colored children ranged between 83 and 101; the average IQ's of the white groups with whom they were compared ranged between 102 and 113. The combined average IQ of the colored subjects was 94, or approximately 12 points below that of the white Ss [pp. 491–494].

School Children Individual Tests. This review includes 43 investigations in which fourteen individual tests were administered to 9225 colored school children. In 23 of these researches white subjects were also tested; in two of them the colored average equaled that of the compared white groups.... The average IQ's of colored and white children who were examined between 1921 and 1944 were 85 and 99, respectively, a difference of 11 points; in the 1945 to 1965 period the respective colored and white IQ's were 83 and 102, a difference of 19 points [pp. 494–495].

Shuey reports similar racial differences for college students and members of the armed forces during World Wars I and II.

SOCIOECONOMIC STATUS AND RACIAL DIFFERENCES

Because SES differences in favor of whites are so visible, many investigators have attempted to control for it statistically in comparisons of black and white intellectual performance. One such effort was by Heber, Dever, and Conry (1968), who presented the data in Figure 14.4. These data indicate that the rate of low IQ (below 75) is much higher for blacks than for whites, even when parental SES is controlled. When mean IQ rather than prevalence is used, Shuey (1966) reports that

> where Negro pupils have been compared with whites of the same occupational or socioeconomic class and where children from two or more classes have served as subjects, a greater difference has been found between the racial samples at the upper than at the lower level.... The consistent and surprisingly large difference of 20.3 IQ points separating the high-status whites and the high-status colored is accentuated by the finding that the mean of the latter group is *2.6 points below* that of the low-status whites [pp. 519–520].

HERITABILITY OF INTELLIGENCE IN BLACKS

Few data exist on the heritability of intelligence in black populations. Perhaps the largest single study that individually administered intelligence tests to blacks and whites comes again from the Collaborative Perinatal Study. Nichols (1970) reported data on all twins, full sibs, and

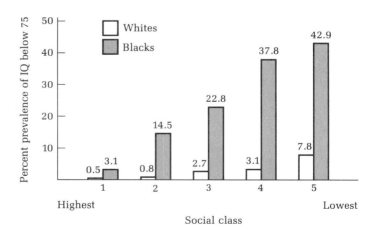

Figure 14.4

Prevalence of children below 75 IQ as a function of social class. (After Heber, Dever, and Conry 1968.)

half-sibs administered an abbreviated version of the Stanford-Binet Intelligence Scale (1960) at age four. The correlations are shown in Table 14.2.

All MZ twins in the collaborative study were in the process of being identified by blood type at the time the research project was being conducted, and fewer white MZ twins than black MZs had been blood-typed. The white full-sib correlation of .52 accords nicely with the theoretical correlation for full sibs of .50, but the intraclass correlation for black sibs of .37 is significantly lower than the value obtained for the whites. While the half-sib correlation for the whites of .44 is higher than the theoretical correlation of .25, the number of subjects is small and the difference between these two values is not statistically significant.

Using the MZ and the same-sex DZ twins for the calculations of Falconer's (1960) heritability estimate ($h^2 = 2[r_{MZ} - r_{DZ}]$) gives a .48 heritability for whites and a .22 heritability for blacks. Both are lower than most twin heritabilities reported in the literature for whites or blacks. It should be reiterated here, however, that the standard errors of heritabilities are very great when the N is small, so that it would be inappropriate to draw far-reaching conclusions from these findings.

Scarr-Salapatek (1971) collected twin data on black school children in Philadelphia. She determined zygosity by statistical procedures based on the Weinberg twin formula. This formula assumes that the number of opposite-sex twin sets (which are, of course, DZ) in any

Table 14.2

Intraclass correlations by race and degree of relationship on the four-year Stanford-Binet IQ

	Whites		Blacks	
	r_I	(pairs)	r_I	(pairs)
Same-sex pairs				
MZ twins	.62	(36)	.77	(60)
Same-sex DZ twins	.38	(25)	.66	(29)
Same-sex full-sib pairs	.56	(530)	.39	(450)
Opposite-sex pairs				
Opp.-sex DZ twins	.57	(40)	.44	(55)
Opp.-sex full-sib pairs	.48	(570)	.35	(520)
Same + opposite-sex pairs				
All DZ twins	.51	(65)	.52	(84)
All full-sib pairs	.52	(1100)	.37	(970)
All half-sib pairs	.44	(50)	.26	(150)

Source: From Nichols 1970.

completely ascertained population is known and that there is the same proportion of same-sex DZ sets as opposite-sex sets. Given those assumptions, doubling the proportion of opposite-sex sets leaves as the remainder the proportion of MZ sets. Assuming also that the correlation for opposite-sex sets equals that for same-sex DZ sets, one can calculate the theoretical MZ correlation by parceling out the opposite-sex correlation from the same-sex correlation.

Scarr-Salapatek (1971) suggests that there are two competing predictions about heritabilities for IQ in whites and blacks. If the lower mean IQ of blacks is due to social disadvantage, then it is expected that the lowest-class blacks would have the lowest heritabilities, since their genetic potential would be suppressed by the poor environment. The genetic differences hypothesis says that the mean IQ difference between races is genetic in origin and therefore heritabilities for IQ between social classes should be similar. Scarr-Salapatek interprets her findings as supporting the environmental disadvantage hypothesis, since the heritabilities for aptitude test scores were highest for the higher-class blacks.

The results of this study are compromised for a variety of reasons, the major one being that the heritabilities for some aspects of the aptitude tests are far lower than any ever reported, even for the advantaged white group. For example, the heritability for nonverbal aptitude among those white children was only .04. Many heritabilities for other social class groups could not even be computed because the opposite-sex sets correlated more highly than the same-sex sets and thus the theoretical MZ correlation was lower than the DZ correlation. Such findings are virtually unheard of and suggest that something during data collection had gone awry. It is likely that the faults are not the author's, since she simply culled the data from the standardized batteries of tests routinely given to the children in the Philadelphia school system. Sometimes under routine testing circumstances children are poorly motivated or misunderstand directions, and thus the validity of the test results is reduced. Another criticism is that the study did not fulfill a fundamental assumption of the Weinberg method of estimating zygosity, namely, that the proportion of male and female twin sets are about equal. Actually, females made up 59 percent of the 333 sets of black twins, a significant departure from the expectation (Erlenmeyer-Kimling and Stern 1973). Findings of this sort make the zygosity estimates of doubtful validity, and comparisons of putative MZ and DZ groups are therefore rendered questionable.

A small-scale study of black twins was conducted by Vandenberg (1969), using thirty-one sets of blood-typed MZ and fourteen sets of DZ twins. Twenty paper and pencil tests were administered, tapping a variety of verbal and perceptual abilities. Four of the tests (two involving reasoning and one each for numerical ability and perceptual speed) yielded significant heritabilities. Because statistical significance depends partly on sample size, the fact that only four of the tests yielded significant heritabilities is not particularly detrimental to genetic hypotheses. Also, the DZ twins were aberrant, since they obtained mean scores on the tests considerably below those of the MZ group. There is no apparent reason why this should occur; thus, the results should be interpreted very cautiously (Loehlin, Lindzey, and Spuhler 1975).

The largest twin study with black blood-typed twins has recently been completed by Scarr and Barker (in preparation) with a sample of school children aged ten to fifteen years in the Philadelphia area. One hundred and sixty sets of same-sex black twins and 212 sets of same-sex white twins were employed in the analyses. Among the five cognitive measures administered to the children were four that could be regarded as verbal or nonverbal measures of intelligence: the Raven Progressive Matrices Test and the Revised Visual Retention Test (both nonverbal), and the Peabody Picture Vocabulary Test and the Columbia Mental Maturity Scale (both verbal). In the discussion that follows, I have averaged all the correlations from those scales together to simplify the presentation.

The results indicated that MZ twins resembled each other more than did the DZ twins and thus suggested some heritability for those measures. The correlations for the black MZs averaged about .60, and the correlations for the black DZs averaged about .39. For the white MZs and DZs, the corresponding correlations were .56 and .23, respectively. Since the heritability for the measures can be estimated by doubling the MZ-DZ difference for each race separately, you can see that the heritability in the black sample is lower than in the white sample.

The major factor accounting for the reduced heritability among the blacks is that the black DZs resemble each other substantially more than do the white DZs. The explanation for this finding is not clear, but the authors suggest that environmental influences within the black family make for the greater similarity. That black same-sex DZ twins resemble each other more than do white same-sex DZ twins is consistent with Nichols's findings, previously shown in Table 14.2, in which the black same-sex DZ sets correlated .66 and the corresponding white DZs correlated only .38.

Suppose the hypothesis were that black families ignored or reduced differences between their same-sex DZ twins to a greater extent than white families (or, conversely, that white families tended to amplify differences between their same-sex DZ sets). What other predictions might follow? We might expect the same pattern to hold for opposite-sex DZs as well as for siblings. While Scarr and Barker do not have data bearing on these predictions, Nichols does, and none of these expectations is confirmed. In all other instances, the white pairs resemble each other more closely than the black pairs (Table 14.2).

We can no longer maintain a broad general hypothesis that, in comparison with white families, black families tend to reduce differences between their children. Probably the most parsimonious conclusion we can draw from these two twin studies is that there is evidence for low to moderate heritability for cognitive traits among blacks as among whites. Since heritability is not high, we can be confident in assuming that environmental factors have a substantial influence on cognitive ability. The nature of these influences, however, is not yet clear.

In summary, the four twin studies obtaining heritabilities for intelligence in blacks have yielded inconclusive results. The Nichols (1970) study did not have a very large sample of twins, and they were tested at only four years of age. Since the study from which these data were taken is a longitudinal one, it should be possible to repeat the twin analysis at age seven when the children are retested and more reliable data can be obtained. Vandenberg's (1969) study had only fourteen sets of DZ twins, which is too few to permit meaningful conclusions. The Scarr-Salapatek (1971) study had a much larger number of twins but used somewhat questionable estimates of zygosity for the calculation of heritabilities. The fact that the heritability estimates for the whites were strikingly deviant from those of previous studies of whites and the necessity for statistical procedures to correct for nonnormality in the distribution of scores make the heritabilities she derived difficult to interpret. The most satisfactory study is that of Scarr and Barker (in preparation). Results of this study demonstrated significant heritability for some cognitive traits among blacks, and the trends suggest that heritability for such traits may be lower among blacks than among whites.

RELATIONSHIP OF WITHIN-GROUP
TO BETWEEN-GROUP HERITABILITY

Our review (especially the data presented in Chapter 5) strongly suggests that the heritability of IQ for whites is significant. For blacks the data are much more limited, but indications are that the heritability for IQ is also greater than zero. If there are significant heritabilities within each of the races, need there be any heritability of the mean IQ differences between the races? A formal connection of within-group to between-group heritability has been postulated by DeFries (1972). In order to properly apply the formula, one must assume that the same genetic and environmental factors that cause differences among individuals within each race also cause the mean IQ difference between the races as well.

The utility of the formula, however, depends either on knowing which genes affect intelligence in the first place, or on the veracity of the assumption that the average gene differences within and between races that are already known behave as "intelligence" genes would if they were identified. But if the intelligence genes were already known, there would be little need to apply the formula, for we could focus directly on the genes themselves. If we don't know which specific genes affect intelligence, then we cannot evaluate the assumption that the genes we do know about behave as intelligence genes would. Consequently, the practicality of the formula is compromised, and we still do not know whether or not the mean difference in IQ between races is also heritable. Jensen (1973a) argues that if the heritability of IQ within each race is established it will be *plausible* that the mean difference between races is also heritable. His discussion of this matter is worth reading for those who are interested in this question.

HYBRID POPULATIONS

The study of racial hybrids has generally been predicated on the argument that, if black-white hybrids perform better than unmixed blacks or worse than unmixed whites on intelligence tests, then the higher IQ can be related to the higher proportion of white admixture.

Although it is possible to estimate the degree of admixture in black populations, it turns out that such estimates do not agree when different genetic loci are independently used to derive these estimates. A detailed discussion of the problem is given by Adams and Ward (1973). They point out that the extreme heterogeneity found in estimates of admixture in a single population is biologically unreasonable and, furthermore, that rank correlations of admixture estimates from one black population to the next are not consistent and depend strongly on the estimates of gene frequencies in the parent populations. Slaves were imported from eight different geographical areas of Africa, and no one area contributes more than a quarter to the total black population. With such heterogeneity, it is not surprising that unbiased estimates of gene frequency in the parent populations are hard to obtain.

As indicated earlier, most studies of hybrid populations have utilized estimates of black-white admixture based not on gene frequencies but on estimates of admixture from pedigrees or physical parameters, such as skin color. Judgments of skin color have often been made by the Milton-Bradley color top method, which uses adjustable amounts of colored papers (red, black, white, and yellow) on a top. The top is spun and each of the component colors is adjusted to yield a blend that matches the color of the subject's skin.

Summarizing studies on admixture and intelligence test performance through 1964, Shuey (1966) says,

... we find that in 12 of the 18 comparisons, the lighter in color or those identified as mixed, scored higher than the darker, the most Negroid in features, or the unmixed; in four other studies, the lighter or hybrid groups scored the higher in the majority of test situations, i.e., three out of four or three out of five, and in two comparisons, there was no evidence of a relationship existing between the amount of white ancestry or absence of Negroid characteristics and test score.... The test differences are typically not large, however, and in the opinion of this writer these studies make no important contribution to the problem of race differences in intelligence [p. 466].

A more recent study by Green (1972), using a sample of over a thousand adults, was conducted in Puerto Rico, where there appears to be less prejudice than in the United States. Skin color was judged on a five-point scale from apparently "pure" white to "pure" black and WAIS IQs were obtained. On each of the eleven WAIS subtests the darkest-skinned scored lowest. The differences on six of the eleven subtests reached statistical significance, but, again, there was a tendency for the lowest SES groups to be overrepresented by very dark-skinned individuals. Of interest was the finding that the three lightest-skin-color categories did not differ from each other in mean IQ on any of the subtests. If the ratings of skin color were reliable and the WAIS was a sufficiently sensitive instrument, there should have been some drop in IQ with increasing proportions of Negro genes.

Green says that members of the three lightest categories are not regarded as blacks but as Puerto Ricans, while members of group four may or may not be regarded as black, depending on the presence of other Negroid features, such as kinky hair; group five individuals would definitely be considered Negro. Green suggested that, since there was no consistent decline in IQ with darkening of skin color, it appears that the results follow more closely lines of prejudice rather than genetic lines. But it is possible to interpret the study differently. Because of initial social class differences long ago, there was probably more intermating between whites and the brightest blacks than between whites and other blacks. Thus, the brightest blacks would have become increasingly light over generations. This development would have left the less intellectually able blacks the least admixed and in the lowest social class groupings. In this case, there would be no direct genetic connection implied between the degree of admixture and intelligence. There would simply be a correlation between the two as a result of assortative mating for intelligence. This correlation might make it appear that there is a genetic connection, even when there is none. For example, blue eyes and blond hair go together with greater than chance frequency; yet each trait is controlled by different genes. It is because of assortative mating that the traits appear to be genetically linked.

The most sophisticated study in this area was recently reported by Loehlin, Vandenberg, and Osborne (1973). They obtained direct estimates of admixture as determined by blood grouping in school children. Blood samples from children in Georgia and Kentucky, broadly defined as black and white, were assayed, and genes that differed in frequency between the two racial categories were identified. There were no genes present in one group and absent in the other, but there were some genetic loci showing large differences in frequency. A battery of factored tests of mental ability was administered, and total scores on the tests were correlated with the presence or absence of the individual genes in the black and white groups separately. That is, within the white group some individuals would have a gene more characteristic of the blacks. If these genes were associated with lower IQs, then whites with this gene should have performed more poorly than whites without this gene. Similarly, blacks with genes more characteristic of the white group should have performed better than those blacks without that gene.

Table 14.3 gives correlations between the presence or absence of the

Table 14.3

Correlation of blood group genes with ability in whites and blacks in Georgia

Blood group	Percent of individuals with gene		Point-biserial correlations with ability	
	White (N = 50)	Black (N = 40)	White	Black
Fy^a	80	22	−0.21	−0.35
S	70	17	0.14	−0.03
C	58	10	0.11	0.31
Le^a	32	13	0.21	−0.32
E	32	20	−0.25	−0.12
M	72	63	−0.02	0.00
A_2	12	5	0.05	0.07
A_1	34	30	0.02	−0.25
K	4	5	0.36	0.01
B	6	17	−0.22	0.28
D	84	100	−0.03	0.00
c	82	100	−0.00	0.00
s	76	95	−0.18	0.27
Jk^a	68	90	−0.27	0.16
N	62	88	−0.00	0.08
P_1	54	97	0.11	−0.08

Note: Positive values indicate that the presence of the gene found more frequently in whites is associated with higher ability scores.
Source: From J. C. Loehlin, S. G. Vandenberg, and R. T. Osborne, "Blood Group Genes and Negro-White Ability Difference," *Behavior Genetics* 3 (1973): 263–270. Plenum Publishing Corporation.

particular genes and the average score on the factored tests for the Georgia sample. None of the correlations in either of the two samples are statistically significant, and often the sign of the correlation changes from one sample to the other. These results suggest that when direct measures of genetic admixture are employed there is no relationship between admixture and mental ability.

A study by Eyferth (1961) compared the illegitimate offspring of black and white servicemen stationed in Germany after World War II. All the children had German mothers, and the mothers were of approximately equal socioeconomic status. The results indicate no consistent overall difference in the IQ scores of the children as a function of the father's race (all mothers were white). While these results do not support a genetic interpretation of black-white differences in IQ, it must be noted that there were complicated interactions between race, age of child at testing, and sex. Sons of white fathers obtained slightly higher scores than sons of black fathers, but daughters of black fathers scored better than daughters of white fathers. Also, the results were inconsistent for the younger and older children; the race of the father made the largest difference for younger girls and older boys.

The results of this study cannot be readily interpreted because there was no information on the characteristics of the fathers, and selection of servicemen might have made them unrepresentative of blacks and whites in general. It should also be remembered that the children averaged only about 40 percent admixture of genes from blacks (i.e., the black servicemen probably had about a 20 percent admixture of genes from whites, only half of which would be transmitted to the offspring). Perhaps the IQ tests were not sensitive enough to detect such a small percentage of admixture, and thus a genetic interpretation cannot be firmly excluded. But this study offers no support for a genetic hypothesis accounting for black-white differences in IQ.

Another study (Willerman, Naylor, and Myrianthopoulos 1970, 1974) started from the assumption that, if racial differences in intelligence were due to genetic differences between races, then the children of interracial matings should have the same mean IQs, irrespective of the parents' racial combination. That is, children of white mothers and black fathers should average the same IQ as children of black mothers and white fathers. If, however, racial differences in intelligence were due to socialization, then the children of black mothers and white fathers should score lower than the offspring of white mothers and black fathers, since the mother is the primary agent of socialization during the early years.

There were 129 women in the Collaborative Perinatal Study who reported that the father of their baby was of a different race. The children of these mothers had been administered the research form of the Bayley Scales of Infant Development at eight months of age and an abbreviated version of the Stanford-Binet (1960) at four years of age. A variety of SES indices on the parents, as well as gestational ages and birth weights of the children, were also obtained. None of the SES or perinatal data yielded significant differences between the mating types; accordingly, it was not necessary to control for these factors in the analysis that followed. The data were analyzed by marital status of mother, sex of child, and maternal race.

No differences in infant test performance were observed at eight months of age, except that the interracial children of black mothers slightly outperformed the interracial children of white mothers on the Bayley Mental Tests. This difference was probably due to the fact that interracial children of white mothers gained less weight during the first few months after birth, and this lower weight might have impaired their performance on the Bayley scale. The importance of this finding is that there was no evidence of behavioral impairment in the interracial children of black mothers during infancy.

The results of the IQ analysis are set forth in Table 14.4. The data are displayed by race of mother, sex of child, and marital status. The major finding presented in this table is that the interracial children of white mothers obtained higher IQs than the interracial children of black mothers. Additionally, interracial children of unmarried mothers and boys performed more poorly than the children of married mothers and girls. Statistical techniques applied to these data in order to derive independent and "pure" estimates of the influence of each of these variables (mother's race, marital status, and sex) give somewhat differ-

Table 14.4

The IQ scores of four-year-old children categorized
by race of mother, sex of child, and marital status

Race of mother	Sex of child	Marital status	IQ score	SD	N
White	Male	Unmarried	96.2	15.0	20
White	Male	Married	102.8	16.3	23
White	Female	Unmarried	100.7	17.4	31
White	Female	Married	106.3	15.8	27
Black	Male	Unmarried	70.3	17.2	3
Black	Male	Married	85.9	8.0	8
Black	Female	Unmarried	94.8	13.5	8
Black	Female	Married	105.7	15.6	9
All whites			101.8	16.4	101
All blacks			93.1	16.9	28
All subjects			99.9	16.8	129

Source: From Willerman, Naylor, and Myrianthopoulos 1974.

ent values for the effects of these variables than are given in the table. The results of the statistical analysis showed that the "pure" effect of race of mother was 9.7 IQ points rather than the mean difference of 8.7 points given in the table. "Pure" effects of marital status were 7.0 IQ points (children of married mothers scored higher) and 7.5 IQ points for sex (girls scored higher), with all reported differences achieving statistical significance.

These results cannot be interpreted easily within a genetic framework and suggest that environmental influences account for a substantial amount of the mean difference in IQ between the blacks and the whites. Taken with the findings of Loehlin, Vandenberg, and Osborne (1973), these results suggest that genetic factors do not account for the mean differences in IQ between blacks and whites as judged from studies of racial hybrids. There is some question, however, about the representativeness of individuals entering into interracial matings. A discussion of the problem can be found in Willerman, Naylor, and Myrianthopoulos (1974).

Scarr and Weinberg (1976) studied black ($n = 29$) and interracial ($n = 68$) children adopted in white homes of very high SES in Minnesota. One of the easiest findings to follow in this rather complicated study is that of the correlations between parental education and children's IQs. The correlations of adopting mothers and fathers with their adopted children were .22 and .34, respectively. The corresponding correlations for the biological mothers and fathers and their adopted-away children were .31 and .45, respectively. Thus, the biological parent-child correlations were at least as high as or higher than the corresponding adoptive parent-child correlations. This finding suggests that there is a heritable component to intelligence among blacks.

The major complication in this study is that many of the children were adopted late, and one cannot be sure that early experiences did not contribute to the lower correlations between the adoptive parents and the adopted children. The children adopted during the first year of life did score higher on the intelligence tests than did those adopted later.

Another comparison of interest was between the IQs of the adopted children and the IQs of the natural children of the adopting parents. The natural children of the adopting parents averaged about 118 IQ, while the adopted children averaged about 106 IQ. The adopting parents averaged 119 IQ. Thus, the natural children of the adoptive parents were much closer in IQ to the adopting parents than were the adopted children. It is worth noting, however, that the mean IQs of the adopted children were still above average, and this was confirmed on scholastic achievement tests when such scores were available. It is hard to say, however, how much their performances on these measures were above that expected for black and interracial children in Minnesota, where the scores of minority group children tend to be higher than those of minority group children in many other parts of the country.

Scarr and Weinberg (1976) also compared the performances of interracial children and children of black-black matings. They found that the interracial children scored higher than the black children on the IQ tests. These results were also confounded, however, because the prior foster placement histories of the interracial children were more favorable than the prior placement histories of the black children. The proper interpretation of this study is ambiguous, and to determine the effect of placement history on IQ is virtually impossible.

SELECTIVE MIGRATION AND GEOGRAPHICAL DIFFERENCES

Not only are there consistent mean differences in IQ between blacks and whites, but blacks and whites vary in their intellectual performance as a function of geography as well. In general, those from rural areas and from the South perform less well than urbanites and northerners. Two hypotheses have been advanced for these findings; the first relates to better educational and other environmental opportunities in the North and in urban areas, and the second suggests selective migration of the more able to the cities and to the North. These notions are not mutually exclusive and may occur simultaneously.

Spuhler and Lindzey (1967) had the mean scores for black and white recruits on the army Alpha examination from twenty-three states and the per capita expenditures for education in each of those states during the early years of this century. The data showed that the scores for both whites and blacks from the South tended to be lower than the scores of their counterparts from the North. For every black and white comparison within a state, the mean Alpha score of the whites exceeded that of the blacks. When Spuhler and Lindzey correlated the Alpha test scores in each state with the per capita school expenditures for that state, they found that the correlation between Alpha scores for whites and school expenditures equaled .74 and that the correlation between Alpha scores for blacks and school expenditures equaled .70. The correlation between the mean scores of the whites and the blacks within the state equaled .73. All these correlations were significant and consistent with a hypothesis of environmental advantage. Unfortunately, these data do not imply a *causal* link between school expenditures and test performance.

Geographical differences on intelligence tests are present even prior to the school years. The collaborative study obtained four-year IQs for children from all twelve of its collaborating hospitals throughout the country, and the mean IQs as well as the average SES ratings show that both the blacks and the whites in the South have lower IQs and lower

SES ratings than do blacks and whites in the North. Thus, it would seem that educational expenditures cannot be implicated as a direct explanation for the lower performance of the black children, since these differences are present even before school age. One must consider the family and perhaps other mediating variables as well.

The *selective migration* hypothesis holds that the most able individuals leave the South for the greater opportunities in the North. Although this hypothesis can be applied with equal utility to migrating whites and blacks, studies to be reported here focus on migrating blacks alone. In general, the plan of these investigations has followed two courses: (1) the school performances of eventually migrating children and of sedentary children in the South have been compared via school records; and (2) migrants to the North have been compared to northern-born children, typically as a function of the number of years the migrants have been in the North.

It should be clear that these two approaches answer different questions. Comparisons of migrant and sedentary blacks in the South are more important for the selective migration hypothesis, while comparisons in the North say much more about environmental influences on performance as a function of being in the North. The value of a comparison of northern- and southern-born blacks for tests of selective migration is especially shaky, since virtually all northern blacks had predecessors who were themselves migrants. It is thus more accurate to say that the comparison is between earlier and later migrants. It is also worth noting that when studies are of school children and not of their parents (who are the ones making decisions about migration), even when the migrant parents are superior to the sedentary parents, differences between the children might not be detected because of regression of the children toward the population mean.

Using U.S. census data for the South Atlantic area, Hamilton (1964) showed that migration to the North of twenty- to twenty-four-year-old blacks was consistently related to amount of education. The college educated were about five times more likely to migrate than those with little education. Klineberg (1935) compared the school marks of sedentary and migrant blacks from Nashville, Birmingham, and Charleston, South Carolina, and found superiority of the migrants from Nashville and Charleston and inferiority of the migrants from Birmingham. All five other studies reviewed by Shuey (1966) have shown superiority of the migrants to the sedents. To account for the difference between Birmingham and the other cities in Klineberg's study, Shuey (1966) suggests that migration may have been caused by different factors in different communities.

One study involving comparisons of northern- with southern-born black children on intelligence tests is that of Lee (1951) in Philadelphia. Elementary school children there had been periodically administered the Philadelphia Tests of Mental and Verbal Ability. The results of these tests are shown in Table 14.5. Note the tendency for a decline in test scores moving from left to right and from top to bottom of the table and the relationship between length of time in the North and IQ score. The magnitude of the relationship is not great, and there are some instances of reversals of the trend. For example, on the test given in the sixth grade the new arrivals exceeded those who had arrived about two years earlier. It is unfortunate that neither the correlation nor the regression coefficient for duration and IQ was given so that the strength of the relationship could be determined. Nevertheless, it appears from these data that environmental factors do contribute to improved performance by the black migrants. Shuey (1966) summarizes the findings for comparisons of northern- and southern-born:

> ... selective migration does not account for *all* the difference between northern and southern Negroes. Our single best estimate was that approximately seven points separate the average IQ of southern colored children from northern children of their race. If this is correct, then about half or possibly a little bit more than half of this difference may be accounted for by environmental factors and the remainder by selective migration [p. 490].

Similar arguments for selective migration in the North-South IQ differential have been advanced for the overall black-white IQ difference. In the latter case, the argument is that the selective migration of blacks to North America involved those of inferior intellectual genetic stock. It appears that a definitive answer to this hypothesis will never be avail-

Table 14.5

IQs of black children born in Philadelphia or migrating from the South, after various periods in the Philadelphia school system

Sample	IQ in grade:					Number of children
	1A	2B	4B	6B	9A	
Philadelphia born, KG	97	96	97	98	97	212
Philadelphia born, no KG	92	93	95	94	94	424
Southern born, entered 1A	86	89	92	93	93	182
Southern born, entered 1B–2B		87	89	91	90	109
Southern born, entered 3A–4B			86	87	89	199
Southern born, entered 5A–6B				88	90	221
Southern born, entered 7A–9A					87	219

Note: IQ is measured by the Philadelphia Tests of Mental and Verbal Ability (norm group—all Philadelphia children).
Source: From Lee 1951.

able, since little is known about the original conditions of selection for slavery. It can be said, however, that, without opportunities for both upward and downward social mobility in Africa, even those from the lowest social class there might not have been genetically inferior in intellectual functioning. Demonstrating that black slaves were likely to be lowest in the African social hierarchy might not indicate much about their genetic potential for intelligence.

Summarizing the results of the studies of intellectual differences is no easy matter. At this point it appears that evidence from hybridization research does not firmly support the notion of a genetic basis to the intellectual differences between blacks and whites. At the same time, however, these studies do not conclusively refute the notion of genetically determined differences. Since more black children are being adopted into white homes now than before, it would seem to be only a matter of time before more studies such as Scarr and Weinberg's (1976) are completed. White children are very rarely adopted into black homes; thus, it is difficult to say much about the putative negative intellectual effects of being reared in a black environment.

Ultimately, if genetic factors are ever convincingly implicated in black-white differences on IQ tests, then the biochemical pathways by which these differences become expressed will need to be specified. We will have made a real advance when we can say that the presence or absence of gene product X will increase (or reduce) IQ by so many points regardless of the race. Should we reach that level of sophistication, we might then be in a position to ameliorate deleterious conditions of the individual's environment by increasing or decreasing that gene product.

Environmental Explanations for Racial Differences in IQ

Environmental explanations for the lower IQs of blacks have generally rested on notions of cultural differences or deprivations. These accounts have maintained that tests standardized on white populations have put black children at an unfair disadvantage. Arguments of this sort have a certain a priori appeal, since these cultural differences are easily visible to even the casual observer. Yet critical examination of the research literature does not support many of these contentions. This is not to say that these environmentally based explanations will not ultimately be found correct, but rather that current evidence does not support them convincingly.

There are leads, particularly in the area of early mother-child interactions, that appear promising in accounting for the IQ differences between blacks and whites. These hypotheses have not been sufficiently studied to merit complete confidence that they are right, but they appear meritorious enough to deserve intense investigation. Early parent-child interactions seem to be the most worthwhile and strategic area to study, since it is clear that the black-white differences on IQ tests are present before the school years. Poor schools, deleterious peer group interactions, the "street culture," and prejudice and discrimination against the black individual mostly occur after age five; to attribute the black-white IQ differential to these influences is to fly in the face of the evidence that IQ differences are present by age three or four. Certainly many of the these influences can be deleterious. They may do little to ameliorate already existing conditions, and they may maintain already existing differences. They undoubtedly have an effect on the character of parenting, since they are part of the socialization process of the parents, who are then in a position to transmit these influences to their children during the preschool years. But to focus on these environmental influences as causes of the black-white IQ differential seems unnecessarily indirect. This is not to say that these influences are not interesting to study in their own right, however, and we will review some salient theories based on them now.

CUMULATIVE DEFICIT

Originally advanced to account for the decline in IQ that accompanied increase in age of English canal boat children (Gordon 1923) and children in the Blue Ridge Mountains of Virginia (Sherman and Key 1932), the hypothesis of *cumulative deficit* goes as follows: as a result of inferior environmental conditions, disadvantaged children fall increasingly behind on tests as they get older. *Cumulative deficit* does not refer to the increasing *absolute* difference on tests between advantaged and disadvantaged children, but to *proportional* increases in the differences between these groups. As far as the hypothesis is concerned, it is not of great interest that a one-year difference in reading placement at age eight increases to a one-and-one-half-year difference at age sixteen, if the difference in standard deviation units increases proportionately. Of importance to the hypothesis is the fact that the *relative* performance of deprived children decreases with age, so that, for example, a difference of 1 standard deviation in IQ at age eight increases to a difference of 2 standard deviations at age sixteen. The distinction between relative and absolute differences in test scores is of crucial importance, and Jensen (1971a) has discussed this problem in great detail.

Many standardized achievement tests express scores in grade norms rather than according to some fixed value, such as a mean of 100 and a standard deviation of 15. Therefore there is a tendency to compare absolute rather than relative test performance. The way to correct this is to convert all grade-equivalent scores to standard deviations and express the differences in terms of these units. For example, the Coleman report (1966) notes that "... the lag of Negro scores [in verbal ability] in terms of years behind grade level is progressively greater. At grade 6, the average Negro is approximately $1\frac{1}{2}$ years behind the average white ... At grade 12, he is approximately $3\frac{1}{4}$ years behind the average white" (p. 273). When Coleman et al. expressed these differences in standard deviation units, however, they obtained a different picture. They report (1966) that "the Negroes are almost exactly one standard deviation below the whites in this region [the northeastern region of the United States] at each grade level [using the standard deviation of the white's scores as the measure]" (p. 273). Coleman et al. go on to ask:

> How can these two measures give such different results? The answer lies in the different meaning of a standard deviation at these grades. At the earlier grades, a standard deviation in white scores represents a smaller number of grade levels or years than it does at higher grades. Or in other words, the whites themselves are more widely dispersed in terms of grade levels at the higher grades than at the lower ones [p. 273].

Although it is the absolute difference that is so apparent to educators, it is the relative difference that bears directly on the cumulative deficit hypothesis.

Some studies central to the origins of the cumulative deficit hypothesis seem to have little relevance to black-white differentials, since they involve white children deprived to an uncommon extreme. For example, in Sherman and Key's (1932) study of mountain hollows in Virginia, it was true that children tested between the ages of six and eight obtained a mean IQ of 84 and that those tested between ten and twelve years averaged only 53 IQ. A description of the children's environment, however, indicates extraordinary intellectual deprivation by twentieth-century Western standards. Sherman and Key (1932) describe one of the communities as follows:

> This hollow is small, consisting of a small number of families living in scattered, mud-plastered log huts. There is no road, except for a trail, to the outside world.... With three exceptions, the adults are illiterate. They are descendants of the original settlers who *married relatives* and mixed very little with people outside of the hollows.... Most of the children do not know their last names. They identify themselves, for example, as Sadie's Bennie or Dicy's Willie [p. 279].

Besides the probable deleterious effects of inbreeding on intellectual functioning, these children had only a total of sixteen months of public school over a twelve-year period. One of the test items required that the subject find a ball presumably lost in a field; Sherman and Key report that most of the children had never seen a ball. These types of deprivations are only rarely seen in black-white comparisons and therefore do not easily generalize to a hypothesis of cumulative deficit among blacks.

There are some methodologically more sophisticated studies bearing on cumulative deficit among blacks. Kennedy, Van De Riet, and White (1963), for example standardized the Stanford-Binet (1960) on black children in five southern states. These children were in grades one through six and ranged in age from five to sixteen years. The authors found a progressive decline in mean IQ with age from a high of 86 at age five to a low of 51 at age sixteen. Schaefer (1965) points out that it is difficult to interpret this decline since the data were cross-sectional and because the children still in a low grade at age sixteen were likely to be retarded. Following Schaefer's suggestion, Kennedy (1969) reexamined a subset of children followed longitudinally over a five-year period and found no decline in mean IQ for them.

The Coleman report (1966), with one exception, also failed to find evidence for a cumulative deficit through twelfth grade in blacks. However, the report did not deal with biases resulting from the fact that children with lower IQs tended to quit school before reaching the twelfth grade. This fact would tend to increase the IQs of the remaining twelfth grade population. It is not clear that such a bias would vitiate the report's findings, but it would have been useful to have such information. In the nonmetropolitan South there was some evidence for cumulative deficit, since the black-white difference in favor of whites increases in grades six, nine, and twelve from a low of 1.5 standard deviations in the sixth grade to a high of 1.9 standard deviations in the twelfth grade. Other studies have been reviewed by Jensen (1974b), who concludes that there is no clear evidence for increasing IQ differences between blacks and whites with age.

Jensen's (1974b) own study of six thousand children in Berkeley, California, about 40 percent of whom were black, is perhaps the most sophisticated methodologically. He compared younger to older siblings in the school system, using the Lorge-Thorndike Intelligence Test. The test has three levels. The first two levels are for kindergarten through grade 3. They are nonverbal and use pictorial items exclusively. The third level is for grades four through six and has both verbal and nonverbal components.

Jensen (1974b) compared IQ scores of younger siblings and older siblings to permit some control for genetic and socioeconomic characteristics. The hypothesis was that if there were a cumulative deficit the older child would obtain a lower score than his younger sib. Jensen found that for verbal IQ there was a significant drop of almost 4 points among black older siblings, while white older siblings showed no decrements. This decline was limited to comparisons involving the verbal component, and there was no evidence for a significant progressive decline in the nonverbal area.

Jensen argues that only a small part of the black-white verbal IQ difference and none of the nonverbal IQ difference can be accounted for by the cumulative deficit theory, but noted that findings for Berkeley may not be generalizable to the entire United States. Many environmental advantages exist for children in that university community that are unavailable elsewhere.

Jensen (1977) tested blacks and whites in rural Georgia to see whether the absence of a substantial cumulative deficit in the relative prosperity of Berkeley, California, could be confirmed in an environment that was generally much more impoverished. The results clearly support the view that such depriving conditions are cumulatively deleterious for IQ scores. As in Berkeley, Jensen compared the performances of siblings between the ages of six and sixteen that were still in school. He found that there was indeed a substantial decrease in IQ for the older siblings and that this decrease was fairly linear. For every year difference between the older and younger black sibling, the older scored about 1.4 IQ points lower. Thus, a sixteen-year-old black who had a six-year-old sibling would be expected to score about 14 IQ points lower than his younger sibling. No such evidence for cumulative deficit was found in the white sample in this study. Jensen concludes that these findings are strong support for an environmentalist explanation for cumulative deficit in blacks in very depriving conditions. It should be pointed out, however, that the blacks in this study averaged only 71 IQ on the California Test of Mental Maturity. This average was almost two standard deviations below the score of whites living in the community, and the conditions in that community might have been far worse than the conditions of blacks in other parts of the country.

To summarize the findings for the hypothesis of cumulative deficit, it appears that there is no consistent evidence for such a notion in the North. When evidence is found, its magnitude tends to be small. The evidence in Jensen's Berkeley study, for example, amounted in a decline of only 4 verbal IQ points. No support for the hypothesis was found in the case of nonverbal IQ. In rural Georgia, however, the evidence for cumulative deficit was very strong. Shuey's (1966) review of all relevant earlier studies of IQs of black children as a function of age found that children between the ages of six and nine averaged 84 and that those between ten and twelve years averaged 83. This slight difference is meager support for a generalized cumulative deficit theory.

CULTURAL BIASES

It has been asserted that a variety of cultural differences between blacks and whites put blacks at a disadvantage on intelligence tests. One such bias is *linguistic;* blacks do not speak the same language as whites but speak black English. This language has a grammar of its own and superficially is so similar to standard English that both blacks and whites have mistakenly believed that black English was a substandard dialect. The argument of linguistic bias holds that unfamiliarity with standard English results in lower IQ scores for blacks. Presumably, then, the blacks would be at the greatest disadvantage on verbal IQ items.

Examination of the data on the relative performance of blacks on verbal and nonverbal intelligence tests does not support the contention that they are especially deficient in verbal skills. Jensen (1974c) points out that tests that are exclusively nonverbal, such as the Raven's Progressive Matrices, have demonstrated white-black differences as large as those on tests involving verbal components. Also, when the Stanford-Binet (1960) was rewritten and administered by a black in black English, black children did not perform better than when it was administered in the standard format (Quay 1971). Similarly, mean IQs of black children are not generally different as a function of the examiner's race. A detailed review of bias in mental tests can be found in Jensen (1974c).

While linguistic biases do not seem responsible for the IQ deficit, it is likely that what black children learn in their cultural milieu is different from what white children learn. Each subculture has its own goals, and it is likely that the goals of the black subculture(s) do not place demands on the same areas of achievement as do the goals of the whites.

PREDICTIVE VALIDITY OF IQ SCORES

The issue of racial or ethnic bias in intelligence tests is important. Proof of the absence or insignificance of bias would have large implications for the differential achievements of minority and majority group members. Rarely uttered in public, but frequently expressed in private, is the question of why American blacks have not risen in socioeconomic status at the same rate over the generations as have other immigrants to America. The answer to this complex question is not known precisely, but if intelligence tests are shown to be relatively unbiased, a proximal answer can be given. The answer is that the mean IQ of blacks has never reached the level eventually achieved by other immigrant groups. Indeed, if bias is small in the tests themselves, or if the predictive validities of intelligence tests are shown to be approximately equal in both majority and minority groups, then the hypothesis must be entertained that genuine increases in IQ scores would eventuate in higher socioeconomic status, provided the individuals value that goal. To be sure, higher intelligence is no guarantee of higher status, but it can be a big help. The evidence presented throughout this chapter suggests that much of the difference in IQ is due to environmental factors. The implication is that those factors need be altered in order to raise IQs. Chances are that rough equality in later socioeconomic accomplishments would then take care of itself, if social mobility is not vitiated by prejudice. A good test of this hypothesis may be possible when the experimentally enriched black children in the Heber (1976) study described in Chapter 6 reach adulthood. As you will recall, at age nine these children averaged more than 20 IQ points higher than control children.

It has been argued that IQ tests are culturally biased in that the test items are "unfair" to members of minority groups. Psychometrically, biases are measured in two ways. The first measures differences in predictiveness of the IQ test according to some external criterion, typically by the use of regression slopes. The second uses internal analyses of the test items to see if there are some on which one group is especially disadvantaged. Humphreys (1973) has compiled the data relevant to the question of biased predictiveness of intelligence tests in blacks and whites. He says that

> when the literature reporting regression comparisons is summarized, the following conclusion seems warranted: there is relatively little difference in the slopes or intercepts of regression lines as a function of the demographic groups that have been studied. Use of a single regression equation for these groups leads to no substantial degree of unfairness in drawing inferences concerning the criteria measures [p. 59].

Stanley (1971) has reviewed the evidence for college students and finds that college entrance examinations predict grades in school with about equal success for blacks and whites, regardless of whether the blacks are in segregated or integrated schools.

To investigate the possibility of cultural bias in test items, Jensen (1974c) has undertaken a detailed analysis of the PPVT and the Raven's Progressive Matrices in black, Mexican-American, and white elementary school children. Essentially, this analysis involves looking at the proportion of children from each ethnic group that passes each item of each of the tests. While one group could have a lower percentage passing each item, cultural bias would be indicated only if the rank order of item difficulty differed between the ethnic groups. That is, evidence of cultural bias would exist if there were items that one group had special difficulty in answering correctly, while the other groups did not. These two tests (PPVT and Raven's Progressive Matrices) are especially helpful in making such comparisons. The PPVT is generally re-garded as having the greater cultural loading because it requires the subject to find, from a set of four pictures, something that the tester has named, such as a table or a chair. Without knowledge of the English language, it would be almost impossible to answer these items beyond the chance level of success. The progressive matrices test, on the other hand, does not call for language skills and has been used in illiterate populations. The test calls for completion of a matrix from which a part has been deleted. Cultural loading should be distinguished from cultural bias. Cultural loading exists if a test score depends on exposure to aspects of a particular culture. Cultural bias exists if the test is differentially predictive of various external criteria, such as grades, or internal criteria, such as the rank order of item difficulties in different ethnic groups.

Using black, white, and Mexican-American children from California, Jensen (1974c) found that the rank order of item difficulty for these tests was virtually identical for the three ethnic groups. Thus, there was no evidence of cultural bias in these tests.

For those blacks testing in the mentally retarded range, however, IQ tests do a very poor job of predicting *adaptive behavior*. This refers not to scholastic performance but to whether retarded individuals are able to manage their affairs responsibly. For those testing in the retarded range, the prediction of scholastic performance, although successful, is of little utility. For the retarded, the important questions revolve around self-management and independence. This is an area of research that has been much neglected. Perhaps because the business of educators and psychologists involves schools to a great extent, they have shortchanged the behavioral measures that are much more difficult to assess. Mercer (1971) has recently devised an adaptive behavior scale, having a mean of 100 and standard deviation of 15, that is analogous to an IQ test. The scale includes questions about how successfully the subject is managing day-to-day responsibilities, such as holding a job or riding a bus alone. After identifying as "retarded" by IQ score adults from three ethnic groups—white, Mexican-American, and black— Mercer compared their performance on the adaptive behavior scale. When retardation was defined on either the IQ or adaptive behavior scale as a value of less than 70, every white (100 percent) who was retarded on IQ was also adaptively retarded. Of the Mexican-Americans who were retarded on the IQ test, only 38 percent were behaviorally retarded. Of the blacks who were retarded on the IQ scale, only 8 percent were behaviorally retarded. These findings indicate that, at least for low scorers, the IQ test is an excellent predictor of adaptive behavior impairments among whites but a poor predictor of adaptive behavior among Mexican-Americans and blacks. Furthermore, the findings suggest that the *meaning* of an IQ score differs for blacks and whites, at least within the low IQ range. The meaning of a test or any construct is given by its place in the *nomological* net, that is, by what it does and does not correlate with. If test A correlates with B and C in one group and only with B in another group, the suggestion is that the meaning of the test varies with the group. Research using adaptive behavior scales in racially heterogeneous populations of normal intelligence would help clarify the behavioral implications of IQ scores for the different racial and ethnic groups.

Parent-Child Relationships

It is plain that traditional SES measures employing parental education, occupation, and income tell us little about the psychological interior of the family. That the children of high SES black parents do very poorly in comparison with their white SES counterparts has already been discussed, and the basis for these black-white differences has yet to be established. Hess and Shipman (1965) have provided some of the most provocative forays into early mother-child interactions among black families. Discussing "cultural deprivation," they argue that the behavior leading to social, educational, and economic poverty is learned early in childhood and that the central feature is a lack of cognitive meaning in the mother-child interaction. They hypothesize that the lower-class home constricts the number and variety of alternative notions and thoughts that promote cognitive development. Following Bernstein (1960), they suggest that parental language crucially shapes the development of cognitive processes and that the language of the lower-class home is inadequate in this respect by middle-class standards.

The research plan of Hess and Shipman (1965) involved 163 black mothers and their four-year-old children. They were divided into four SES groups, from high (college educated; intact family) to very low (less than high school education; father absent; on welfare). The mothers were interviewed twice in their homes and then brought to the university for testing. The testing involved two object-sorting tasks and another task that required the mother and child to work cooperatively in copying some designs. Hess and Shipman recorded the mother-child interactions and found, first, that the total verbal output during the testing situation of mothers from the highest SES group was about 60 percent greater than the output of any of the other groups and that they tended to use a much higher proportion of abstract words in interacting with their children. Second, in comparison with the other groups, the highest SES mothers were much more likely to be person, rather than status, oriented. For example, mothers were asked what they would do if their child had some difficulty in school, both academic and social.

Person-oriented statements recognized the child's anxiety and pointed out the personal relationship of the teacher to the child. Status-oriented responses emphasized the authority of the teacher and the child's responsibility to be passive and compliant. Third, the investigators found that on the sorting tasks high SES mothers were much more likely than low SES mothers to offer approaches that were orderly and complex. This finding suggests that the high SES mothers had more differentiated strategies for information processing.

In summarizing their conclusions, Hess and Shipman (1965) say:

> The picture that is beginning to emerge is that the meaning of deprivation is a deprivation of meaning—a cognitive environment in which behavior is controlled by status rather than by attention to the individual characteristics of a specific situation and one in which behavior is not mediated by verbal cues or by teaching that relates events to one another and the present to the future. This environment produces a child who relates to authority rather than rationale, who, although often compliant, is not reflective in his behavior, and for whom the consequences of an act are largely considered in terms of immediate punishment or reward rather than their future effects and long-range goals [p. 885].

Using 137 of the 163 mother-child pairs of Hess and Shipman (1965), Brophy (1970) studied how the mothers taught the sorting tasks to their children. The children were taught to sort blocks on two of the following dimensions: color, height, type of marking, and shape. The verbal interactions of the mothers and children were recorded. Brophy was most interested in the specificity of the verbal labels the mothers used to describe the relevant aspects of the blocks and how they got their children to *focus* on the task. The data were analyzed according to the specificity of the labeling. Nonspecific labeling involved statements such as "Take the block and put it over there." Specific labeling included statements such as "Put the tall block with the X on it over there." In focusing the mother emphasized the salient features of the block so that the child would not attend to irrelevant dimensions. The results indicated substantial variability within the four SES groups on how the mothers taught their children, but there were still a large number of statistically significant differences among the SES groups. For example, when asked to sort by markings and height, the high SES mothers were two to three times more likely than mothers in the other SES groups to verbalize the dimensions on which to sort. According to Brophy, it is not the sheer amount of stimulation that is the crucial factor in the development of cognitive ability, but the way in which the organization of the stimuli distinguishes among cues.

Since the Hess and Shipman (1965) and Brophy (1970) studies used only blacks, there was no opportunity to make direct comparisons with white groups. Bee et al. (1969) studied SES correlates of maternal teaching strategies of four- and five-year-olds in a biracial sample. The higher-class group was all white, but the lower-class group included both black and white mother-child pairs. Thus, some comparisons between lower-class blacks and whites were possible. As in the other studies, mother-child pairs were observed in a series of problem-solving interactions. What Bee et al. found was that, in contrast to the lower-class mothers, the higher-class mothers, "regardless of the situation, used more instructions, less physical intrusion, less negative feedback, and were generally more in tune with the child's individual needs and qualities" (p. 732). They also compared the lower-class blacks with the lower- and higher-class whites on twelve variables and found on four of them that the lower- and higher-class whites were similar to each other and that both differed from the blacks. In contrast to the two white groups, the black mothers were less likely to give positive feedback, offer helpful suggestions to the child, and interact with the child. Another difference was that the black child was less likely than the others to ask for information while in the waiting room. These results suggest that there are both social class and racial differences in mother-child interactions and that it is necessary to have biracial samples representing all SES groups in order to disentangle the influences.

These three studies show striking differences between racial and social class groups in mother-child interactions, but it should be pointed out that generalizations to the entire black and white populations are unwarranted on a number of counts. The first, and probably most important, is that the SES groups are not representative of their racial groups. The Hess and Shipman (1965) and Brophy (1970) studies used an exclusively urban black sample, approximately 25 percent of whom had some college education. This proportion is undoubtedly higher than the proportion in the general black population. Second, when blacks are matched to whites for SES, as in the Bee et al. (1969) study, either the whites tend to be below the average SES for whites in general or the blacks tend to be above the black SES average. Especially in the case of genetic arguments about the causes of racial differences in IQ, it should be remembered that not even those on the side of genetics say that there are no blacks who are genetically more able than most whites. It is always possible to find some blacks who exceed some whites, so that selecting unrepresentative samples for study requires caution in interpretation and tells little about the distribution of the trait in the population from which the samples were drawn. Furthermore, it is likely that matching blacks and whites on gross SES variables often hides important stylistic differences within the families, and it is these differences that may play an important role in intellectual performance differences between the races (Trotman 1977).

Another issue is whether these studies of mother-child interaction showing large racial and SES differences exclude genetic interpretations. The answer clearly is that they do not. For example, in the Hess and Shipman (1965) and Brophy (1970) studies, the WAIS IQs of the mothers in the highest and lowest SES groups differed by about 26 IQ points. When parents rear their own children, however, it is almost impossible to disentangle the genetic and environmental influences on a behavior trait. As has been reiterated on a number of occasions, studies that confound genetic and environmental factors because of failure to cross-foster can never provide definitive answers to the kinds of questions we ask here. Thus, the high-IQ parents could have obtained their scores because of either genetic or environmental reasons. Nevertheless, the findings of striking behavioral differences in the total amount of verbal output, in whether a mother was person or status oriented, and in whether or not a mother was physically intrusive have not yet been shown to be under substantial genetic control.

Until genetic components are established, one can proceed on the assumption that these variables may have strong environmental components. To the extent that nonheritable socialization practices (e.g., maternal warmth, authoritarianism) promote styles of interaction that encourage or discourage intellectual development, is seems possible that some of the SES and racial socialization differences reported affect intellectual development from the environmental side.

PATTERNS OF ABILITY AMONG ETHNIC GROUPS

Ethnic is an ambiguous word, for it usually refers to groups distinguished by cultural features or national boundaries (Baker 1974) and these differences may or may not overlap with race differences. Thus, Swedes and Danes might be regarded as different ethnic groups but not necessarily viewed as different races. There is no clear demarcation between race and ethnic group, since they may overlap; when the criterion for group assignment is primarily social, however, the use of ethnic group is often preferred. The two terms shall be used interchangeably throughout this discussion.

In the past decade patterns of mental abilities among ethnic groups have become a prominent area of investigation. Perhaps one of the most intriguing studies in this area is one by Lesser, Fifer, and Clark (1965). They administered tests to 320 six-to-eight-year-old children from four ethnic groups in New York City (Chinese, Jewish, black, and Puerto Rican). These groups were each divided into middle- and lower-class samples and had equal representations of girls and boys. The tests were divided into four parts: verbal, reasoning, number, and space. The authors were interested in learning if patterns of specific strengths and weaknesses for each ethnic group could be identified. The results are shown in Figure 14.5.

These data suggest that distinctive patterns of ability characterize each ethnic group and that these patterns are independent of social class. It appears that social class affects only the *level* of performance and not the patterns of performance.

The four abilities were not statistically independent because there were positive intercorrelations between them within every ethnic group. Nevertheless, some of the differences among levels of perfor- mance on the different abilities are striking. Among the Jews, the verbal scores are clearly superior to the spatial scores. The blacks' perfor- mance shows an essentially flat profile, but their verbal scores are higher than all the other scores. This fact is important in light of argu- ments suggesting that blacks are especially disadvantaged in verbal abilities. The important conclusion to be drawn from these findings is that social class and ethnicity appear to operate independently, with social class affecting only the level of performance.

The differences between the social classes in levels of performance seem to vary with the ethnic group. Thus, among the Chinese the mid- dle- and lower-class groups do not differ substantially, whereas among the blacks the social class differences are great. This finding might be interpreted as suggesting that lower-class experience among the Chinese is not as deleterious to intellectual functioning as is the lower- class experience among blacks. However, it may be that the selective factors involved in locating middle-class blacks are such that they rep- resent a very small proportion of the total black population and thus constitute an exceptionally able group.

Stodolsky and Lesser (1967) asked whether individuals within each of the ethnic groups followed the profile pattern for their ethnic group as a whole. Among the Jewish group, 76 percent of the children ob- tained the pattern of highest on verbal, next highest on number, next highest on reasoning, and lowest on space. Among the Chinese chil- dren, 54 percent showed their group pattern; among blacks, 49 percent showed the group pattern; and among Puerto Ricans, 48 percent showed the group pattern. Except for the Jewish group, only about 50 percent of the individuals behaved in the same fashion as their ethnic group profiles. This fact is important, because we must be wary of trying to put each individual within a particular ethnic group into a mold that doesn't really fit.

It is difficult to assess whether the cognitive differences between the Chinese-Americans and the others have a genetic basis, but Freedman and Freedman (1969) have shown that some behavioral differences be- tween Chinese-Americans and white Americans are present almost from birth. They studied twenty-four Chinese-Americans and twenty-

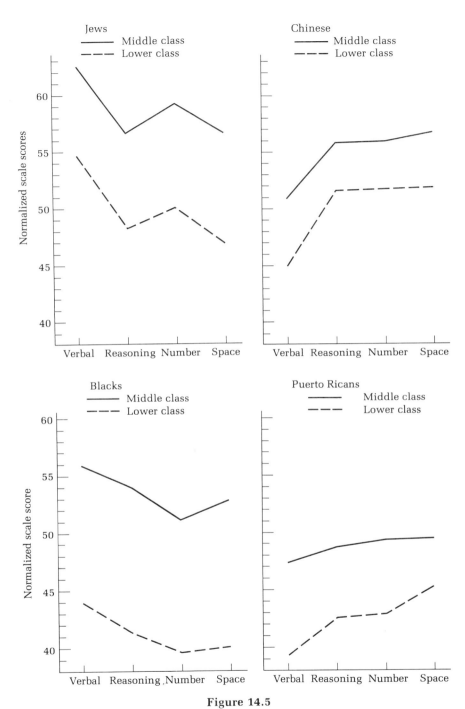

Figure 14.5

Comparison of test performances of middle- and lower-class children from four different cultural groups. (From G. S. Lesser, G. Fifer, and D. H. Clark, "Mental Abilities of Children from Different Social-Class and Cultural Groups," *Monographs of the Society for Research in Child Development*, Inc. Copyright © 1965.)

four white infants averaging about thirty-three hours old and compared them on a number of behavioral tasks. While there was substantial overlap between the two groups, the Chinese-American infants were generally less excitable and less labile. On one measure the tester placed a loosely woven cloth over the supine baby's face. The white infants typically struggled to remove the cloth by swiping at it and turning the face, while the Chinese-American infants tended to lie impassively. The authors' summary was that "the Chinese-American newborns tended to be less changeable, less perturbable, tended to habituate more readily, and tended to calm themselves or be consoled more readily when upset" (p. 1227). The early age at which these differences appeared is consistent with the presence of a genetic component.

Stodolsky and Lesser (1967) conducted a partial replication of the Lesser, Fifer, and Clark (1965) study in Boston with Chinese, black, and Irish children. For the Chinese and black children, the results virtually duplicated the findings in New York. The Irish children showed no consistent pattern of abilities, since the findings were different for middle- and lower-class Irish.

A study underway in Hawaii has examined patterns of *intercorrelations* for different mental tests in two ethnic groups, Americans of European ancestry (AEA) and American of Japanese ancestry (AJA). This approach differs the Lesser, Fifer, and Clark (1965) approach, in which *levels* of performance on different mental tests are compared in different ethnic groups. In the Hawaii study a battery of fifteen mental tests have been given to large samples of both ethnic groups, including parents and their children (DeFries, Vandenberg, and McClearn 1976). The domains covered by the tests include spatial, verbal, visual memory, and speed and accuracy. While mean scores on the different tests have not yet been reported, factorial loading patterns resulting from the intercorrelations of the tests are remarkably similar for the two groups (Figure 14.6). This similarity in factorial structure suggests that the manner in which the tests are construed by the subjects is similar regardless of ethnicity and that the tests are measuring the same mental abilities in the two groups.

The similarity in factor patterns here should not be seen as a contradiction to the findings of Lesser, Fifer, and Clark, for they were concerned with patterns of mean differences and not with intercorrelations between tests. To take a simple example, in one ethnic group verbal scores could be much lower than spatial scores, but the intercorrelation between the tests could be the same as when mean verbal and spatial scores are equal.

A study by Sitkei and Meyers (1969) also looked at patterns of intellectual performance among four-year-olds. The 100 children were stratified by race and social class into approximately equal-sized groups. The authors administered a large battery of tests derived mostly

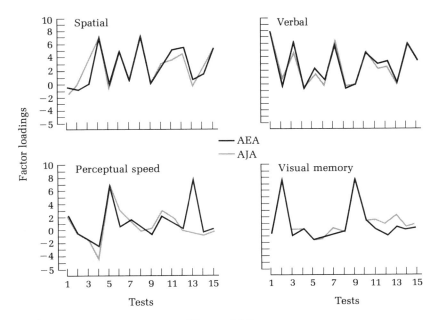

Figure 14.6

Loadings of fifteen cognitive tests in Americans of Japanese ancestry (AJA) and Americans of European ancestry (AEA). (From J. C. DeFries et al, "Near Identity of Cognitive Structure in Two Ethnic Groups," *Science* 183 [25 January 1974]:338–339. Copyright © 1974 by the American Association for the Advancement of Science.)

from Guilford's structure of intellect model and included measures of verbal comprehension, ideational fluency, perceptual speed, and figural and auditory memory. The results were somewhat surprising, since race and social class differences appeared only in skills that required the use of standard English. There were no distinctive profiles characterizing the social classes or ethnic groups. Comparing their findings to those of Lesser, Fifer, and Clark (1965), the authors suggest that Lesser's six-to-eight-year-old children may have had greater exposure to their subcultures than the four-year-old children, and, to the extent that learning of the subculture "style" is important, this difference in exposure may be responsible for the lack of agreement between the two studies.

The lack of pronounced differences by race or social class for many of the test measures in the Sitkei and Meyers study is not consistent with the findings from other studies of four-year-olds. One wonders if the tests were sufficiently sensitive to detect differences that might have been present.

Marjoribanks (1972) not only obtained test score profiles of children from different ethnic groups but also related performance on these tests to various environmental influences in their families. Marjoribanks sampled thirty-seven families from each of five ethnic groups in Canada: Canadian Indians, French Canadians, Jews, southern Italians, and white Anglo-Saxon Protestants. Eleven-year-old boys were tested on the SRA Primary Mental Abilities Test, and the author interviewed both mothers and fathers of these children in their homes. Figure 14.7 gives the mental ability profiles of the children in this study. The results are standardized to a mean of 50 and a standard deviation of 10. The verbal and numerical ability scores of the Jewish children exceeded significantly the scores of the children from all other ethnic groups, with the Protestant boys scoring second highest on both. The profile obtained for the Jewish children in this study bears a striking resemblance to the Jewish profile obtained by Lesser, Fifer, and Clark (1965).

On the basis of the home interviews, Marjoribanks (1972) rated the families of these children on eight parental environmental forces: achievement, activeness, intellectuality, independence, English, eth-

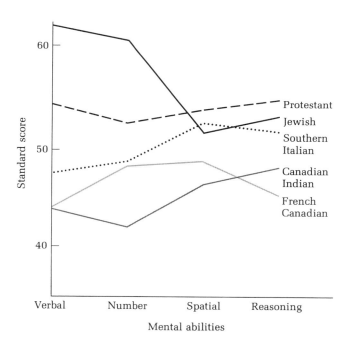

Figure 14.7

Profiles of mental ability test scores for each ethnic group. (From K. Marjoribanks, "Ethics and Environmental Influences on Mental Abilities," *American Journal of Sociology* 78:323–337. Reprinted by permission of the University of Chicago Press. Copyright © 1972.)

language (pressure to use the language peculiar to each ethnic group), father dominance, and mother dominance. He found significant differences in the profiles of environmental forces for the ethnic groups and tried to relate these influences to performance on the tests. All of the environmental forces correlated with the scores on the verbal component of the test, and most correlated with the numerical and reasoning components. For spatial ability there were fewer correlations with environmental forces, and those present tended to be smaller than the correlations with the other components. Since the ethnic groups differed on both test profiles and patterns of environmental forces, Marjoribanks tried to determine their independent and joint contributions to test performance differences between the ethnic groups. In general, he found that environmental forces related more to test profiles than did ethnicity, but that each made independent contributions to the test patterns. Marjoribanks did not report on the influence of each of these environmental forces *within* an ethnic group; presumably environmental influences would be considerably diminished in such an analysis. While it might be instructive to construct "ethnic" groups on the basis of profiles of environmental forces, such constructions would tell little about the relative contributions of genetics and environment to these test profiles.

Nevertheless, there are differences within ethnic groups that are often obscured by our comparisons between ethnic groups. An illustration of this is seen in the study of Gross (1967), who studied two groups of American Jewish children living in adjacent neighborhoods in Brooklyn: Sephardim, or Oriental Jews, and Ashkenazim, or eastern European Jews. The ancestry and traditions of these two groups are quite different. The Sephardim have lived for many centuries in Moslem countries, and, from about the sixteenth century on, there has been a parallel decline in the cultural creativity of the Arab and Sephardic cultures. In fact, these two cultures were inextricably bound during those years, so much so that one nineteenth-century observer reported that the Sephardic Jews were "Arab in all but religion" (Gross 1967, p. 11). The eastern European Jews have a long tradition in commerce and trade and have capitalized on and contributed disproportionately to technological and scientific achievements in the past and present.

Gross compared the performances of children from these two groups on a battery of intelligence and perceptual-motor tests. The children, averaging about seven years old, were enrolled in separate religious day schools, each serving one of the traditions. Assessed by family income, all children were at least middle class. The Ashkenazic mothers and fathers, however, had, on the average, about 1 and 1.4 years more education, respectively, than the Sephardic parents. The forty-two eastern European Jewish children significantly exceeded the forty-eight Sephardic children on the Stanford-Binet (116 to 110), the

Peabody Picture Vocabulary Test (113 to 96), and the Bender Visual Motor Gestalt Test (9.7 errors to 10.8 errors).

Both groups are clearly middle class and above average on the Stanford-Binet IQ, so that one cannot speak about "cultural deprivation," in the usual sense, when referring to the Sephardic children. Gross relates the difference between the two groups to

> longstanding cultural ideas.... Both groups may share middle-class status and a high level of achievement motivation.... The Sephardi's achievement drive may be directed to the accumulation of wealth while the Ashkenazi may retain his ... commitment to book-centeredness [p. 34].

Gross attacks the concept of cultural deprivation that blames the schools and that emphasizes deficiencies in financial resources and goods. He points out that anthropologists who have studied the Shtetl (Ashkenazi European Jewish community) have observed that the curriculum in those schools

> was uninteresting, the hours long, the teaching pedagogically unsound, and the teachers without compassion. Yet the system produced scholars, philosophers, scientists, and people whose lives were devoted to learning [p. 14].

The critical differences between the two types of Jews seem to be in the pervasive respect for learning, and it is Gross's suggestion that much of what is called cultural deprivation is related more to child-rearing practices than to school quality.

Lumping the Ashkenazic and Sephardic Jews together obscures important differences between them. Whenever global distinctions are made, there is the danger of homogenizing within-ethnic group differences and imputing intraethnic commonalities that may exist only in the minds of the observers.

The largest comparison of ethnic group mental test performance is given in the Coleman report (1966) of verbal and nonverbal tests. This was a survey of nearly twenty thousand school teachers and their pupils throughout the United States. In first grade, except for the Oriental children, all nonwhite groups scored lower than the whites on the verbal tests; on nonverbal tests, Indians, Mexican-Americans, and Orientals scored above the mean of 50. Results of this sort force us to refine our concepts of cultural deprivation; if such "deprivation" exists, it obviously does not affect all areas of intellectual functioning equally, nor does it affect all ethnic groups proportionately. By the twelfth grade, all nonwhite ethnic groups except the Orientals had lower average test scores than the whites.

Again, ethnically and genetically diverse groups have been incautiously lumped together, and substantial amounts of information may have been lost in the process. Subdividing ethnic groups can reveal striking differences. For example, Weyl (1969) gives the occupational attainments of various American ethnic minorities based on data from the 1960 census. In contrast to the Coleman data, the Orientals have been subdivided into Japanese and Chinese. Weyl devised an index figure in which 100 refers to the ethnic group being represented in the particular profession in proportion to the population expectations; a value of 50 means that only half as many as expected are represented in the profession; and a value of 200 means that twice the expected number are represented in the profession. Table 14.6 gives the indices for selected ethnic groups and shows that, while both the Chinese- and the Japanese-Americans are overrepresented in the professions, the Chinese-Americans are much more likely than the Japanese-Americans to be architects, engineers, college professors, and natural scientists. Both groups do not have proportionate numbers of lawyers or clergymen. Perhaps these deficiencies indicate some disadvantage with respect to the English language and differential involvement in religious practices. The Indians exceed expectations in some areas of occupational performance; in the professions of artist and writer, clergyman, and nurse, Indians are overrepresented. Were we to subdivide the Indians into various tribes, we would expect differences among them to emerge as well.

Table 14.6

Index figures of the contribution of five ethnic groups to American professions in 1960

Profession	Number in thousands	White	Negro	Indian	Japanese	Chinese
All	7325	107	38	76	139	189
Accountants	473	112	7	38	166	174
Architects	30	110	5	0	232	506
Artists and writers	133	110	16	133	209	136
College Professors	177	107	32	0	143	537
School teachers	1682	103	76	86	120	318
Engineers	870	111	5	57	124	303
Natural scientists	150	109	20	0	205	438
Lawyers and judges	210	111	11	19	54	53
Clergymen	312	104	66	124	89	23
Physicians	230	108	21	10	182	302
Nurses	591	106	54	124	116	76
Technicians	493	107	36	86	201	197

Source: From Weyl 1969.

There is more than ample evidence that ethnic differences on psychometric tests are reasonably consistent over studies. While these data may have important implications for educational and child-rearing practices, we still do not understand how these differences arise. Again, we must suggest interethnic adoption studies as the method appropriate for disentangling the biological and social factors involved.

BLACK-WHITE DIFFERENCES IN INFANT PRECOCITY

Many secondhand reports have suggested that early infant precocity is negatively related to later intelligence test performance. But the original data come from only two sources: (1) Bayley's (1933) findings in her longitudinal study of white, largely middle-class children in Berkeley, California, and (2) reports of precocity in African infants. These latter findings are then related to the findings of lower IQs among blacks in Africa and the United States.

Bayley repeatedly tested infants on the Bayley scales of infant development and on intelligence tests from the first months of life through adulthood, and has presented intercorrelation matrices of the findings. Of the many intercorrelations reported, one for infant performance between four to six months and IQ at sixteen to eighteen years of age was negative $(r = -.30)$ for boys only. This correlation was not statistically significant (Wilson 1973) and has not been confirmed in other studies.

The reports of precocity in black African infants has been the subject of considerable dispute. Warren (1972) has provided the most critical appraisal of the research findings. The early reports of Geber and Dean (1957) prompted most of the interest in this area, since the black infants in these studies were said to display remarkable motor accomplishments—for example, 100 percent of the infants had developmental quotients greater than the white standardization mean of 100. These data were presented without white controls, and the question of tester bias in these studies is not adequately dealt with. Despite the criticism of Geber and Dean's studies, there does seem to be considerable evidence that African black children are precocious relative to white standards. Warren's (1972) critique tallies ten studies favoring that hypothesis and two against. A recent study by Leiderman et al. (1973) also strongly supports the finding of black African infant precocity, especially on the motor scale of the Bayley test.

The evidence of remarkable precocity in American black infants is entirely lacking, however, and it is not clear in what way the African data relate to performance of blacks on IQ tests in America. In America, Bayley's (1965) revision of her scales shows the black infants to be superior in motor development to the white infants at every month from one to fourteen, although there were no significant differences between the groups on the mental scale. The differences in favor of the black infants on the motor scale are less than $\frac{1}{2}$ standard deviation in every instance but one. These consistent motor differences are generally very slight and may relate to the other indications of more rapid physical development in blacks (Malina 1973) mentioned earlier in this chapter.

The theory that advanced infant development is related to later intellectual inferiority stems from a notion derived from cross-species comparisons. Species with early infant precocity and maturity are those who tend to be lower in the phylogenetic order, and those species with prolonged infancies, such as the apes, are historically closer to man. Infancy is regarded as the period of greatest neuronal plasticity and thus the time for greatest learning, but the generalization to normal development *within* a species is not supported. The most extensive data on infant development and later intelligence come from a study by Broman, Nichols, and Kennedy (1975), which is based on the test performance of over twenty thousand children. The study shows, for both whites and blacks, that infant motor performance at eight months relates positively to IQ at four years—$r = .23$ for whites and $r = .25$ for blacks. Likewise, intellectually very superior white children (IQ of 140 or more) have slightly but significantly advanced mental and motor development at eight months compared with the development of the total population at that age (Willerman and Fiedler 1974).

The possible deleterious consequences of "artificial" induction of infant precocity are seen in the studies of biochemical supplementation with thyroxine, which produces more rapid physical maturity and advanced infant performance in rats (Schapiro 1968). These supplemented animals perform more poorly during their later development, however, and Schapiro has suggested that the early maturity results in a loss of neuronal plasticity and consequently impairs learning ability later. Studies of this kind can be extremely useful in understanding the relationship of learning to its physiological substrata, but they correspond only indirectly to the within-species discussions of precocious development. The most reasonable conclusion, therefore, seems to be that advanced infant precocity in humans is positively related to later intellectual development, although the relationship is not a strong one.

Conclusions

Black-white comparisons consistently show that American blacks score lower than whites on tests of intelligence. Unambiguous reasons for this deficiency have not been established. Those with environmental biases can point to a number of early differences in child-rearing and teaching practices (e.g., Hess and Shipman 1965) that could account for the difference. Those with a genetic bias, on the other hand, can point to studies of heritability of intelligence in blacks (e.g., Nichols 1970), which can be interpreted to mean that IQ scores in blacks do have a heritable component. But definitive answers will come from the applications of more informative study designs involving adoption methodology (e.g., black children adopted into white homes).

What if future research indicates that the lower IQ scores in blacks have a genetic basis? Some will feel that this spells disaster for our society unless we alter our system of rewarding intellectual achievements with socioeconomic benefits. Others will not find it so disconcerting, because demonstrating heritability for a trait means that there are biochemical gene products giving rise to the differences and that ultimately these products can be identified and a "therapy" found. It is perhaps less difficult to disconnect intellectual ability from socioeconomic success by means of policies that equalize income (Jencks et al. 1972) than it is to find biochemical correctives for polygenically determined traits. We should not forget, however, that the pedestals upon which intelligence and socioeconomic success have been placed cause the neglect of other traits that are of substantial import to human happiness, such as altruism, sympathy, warmth, and understanding. To encourage the development of these traits and the ending of prejudice seems fully as important as the search for the causes of racial differences in intelligence test performance.

Bibliography

Abramowicz, H. K., and Richardson, S. A. 1975. Epidemiology of severe mental retardation in children. *American Journal of Mental Deficiency* 80: 18–39.

Adams, J., and Ward, R. H. 1973. Admixture studies and the detection of selection. *Science* 180: 1137–1143.

Adams, M. S., and Neel, J. V. 1967. Children of incest. *Pediatrics* 40: 55–62.

Agras, W. S., Sylvester, D., and Oliveau, D. 1969. The epidemiology of common fears and phobias. *Comprehensive Psychiatry* 10: 151–156.

Akiskal, H. S., and McKinney, W. T., Jr. 1973. Depressive disorders: toward a unified hypothesis. *Science* 182: 20–29.

_____. 1975. Overview of recent research in depression. *Archives of General Psychiatry* 32: 285–305.

Albert, R. S. 1975. Toward a behavioral definition of genius. *American Psychologist* 70: 140–151.

Albert, R. S., and Ayres, D. B. 1969. Studies in early cognitive development among the gifted, and the exceptionally gifted: similarities, differences and possibilities. Paper presented at the annual meeting of the Western Psychological Association, Vancouver, B.C.

Alexander, D., and Money, J. 1966. Turner's syndrome and Gerstmann's syndrome: neuropsychologic comparisons. *Neuropsychologia* 4: 265–273.

Allport, G. W. 1937. *Personality*. New York: Holt.

_____. 1954. *The nature of prejudice*. Reading, Mass.: Addison-Wesley.

_____. 1960. What units shall we employ? In *Personality and Social encounter*, ed. G. W. Allport, pp. 111–129. Boston: Beacon Press.

_____. 1961. *Pattern and growth in personality*. New York: Holt, Rinehart & Winston.

Allport, G. W., and Vernon, P. E. 1933. *Studies in expressive movement*. New York: Macmillan.

Åmark, C. 1951. A study in alcoholism: clinical, social-psychiatric and genetic investigations. *Acta Psychiatrica et Neurologica Scandinavica Supplement*, no. 70.

Anastasi, A. 1958. *Differential psychology*. 3d ed. New York: Macmillan.
————. 1961. *Psychological testing*. 2d ed. New York: Macmillan.
————. 1976. *Psychological testing*. 4th ed. New York: Macmillan.
Anastasi, A., and Levee, R. F. 1959. Intellectual defect and musical talent. *American Journal of Mental Deficiency* 64: 695–703.
Anders, T. R.; Fozard, J. L.; and Lillyquist, T. D. 1972. Effects of age upon retrieval from short-term memory. *Developmental Psychology* 6: 214–217.
Anderson, J. E. 1939. The limitations of infant and preschool tests in the measurement of intelligence. *Journal of Psychology* 8: 351–379.
Anderson, R. G. 1951. A note on the McAdory and Meier art tests in counseling. *Educational and Psychological Measurement* 11: 81–86.
Anderson, V. E., and Siegel, F. 1968. Studies of behavior in genetically defined syndromes in man. In *Progress in human behavior genetics*, ed. S. G. Vandenberg, pp. 7–17. Baltimore: Johns Hopkins Press.
Armor, D. J. 1973. The double standard: a reply. *The Public Interest* 29: 119–131.
Armstrong, M. D., and Tyler, F. M. 1955. Studies on phenylketonuria, I: restricted phenylalanine intake in phenylketonuria. *Journal of Clinical Investigation* 34: 565.
Asarnow, R. A.; Steffy, D. J.; MacCrimmon, D. J.; and Cleghorn, J. M. 1977. An attentional assessment of foster children at risk for schizophrenia. *Journal of Abnormal Psychology* 86: 267–275.
Asmussen, E. Growth in muscular strength and power. 1973. In *Physical activity: human growth and development*, ed. G. L. Rarick, pp. 60–79. New York: Academic Press.
Atkinson, R. C. 1974. Teaching children to read using a computer. *American Psychologist* 29: 169–178.
Bajema, C. J. 1963. Estimation of the direction and intensity of selection in relation to human intelligence by means of the intrinsic rate of natural increase. *Eugenics Quarterly* 10: 175–187.
————. Relation of fertility to occupational status, IQ, educational attainment, and size of family of origin: a follow-up study of a male Kalamazoo public school population. *Eugenics Quarterly* 15: 198–203.
Bakan, D. 1966. *The duality of human existence*. Boston: Beacon Press.
Baker, J. R. 1974. *Race*. New York: Oxford University Press.
Baller, W. R.; Charles, D. C.; and Miller, E. L. 1967. Mid-life attainment of the mentally retarded: a longitudinal study. *Genetic Psychology Monographs* 75: 235–329.
Baltes, P. B., and Schaie, K. W., eds. 1973. *Life-span developmental psychology: personality and socialization*. New York: Academic Press.
Bandura, A. 1969. *Principles of behavior modification*. New York: Holt, Rinehart & Winston.
Banks, M. S.; Aslin, R. N.; and Letson, R. D. 1975. Sensitive period for the development of human binocular vision. *Science* 190: 675–677.
Bardwick, J. M. 1971. *Psychology of women*. New York: Harper & Row.

Barron, F. 1965. The psychology of creativity. *New directions in psychology*, pp. 1–134. New York: Holt, Rinehart & Winston.

_____. 1969. *Creative person and creative process.* New York: Holt, Rinehart & Winston.

Barry, H. III; Bacon, M. K.; and Child, I. L. 1957. A cross-cultural survey of some sex differences in socialization. *Journal of Abnormal Psychology* 55: 327–332.

Bayley, N. 1933. Mental growth during the first three years. *Genetic Psychology Monographs* 14: 1–92.

_____. 1965. Comparisons of mental and motor test scores for ages 1–15 months by sex, birth order, race, geographical location, and education of parents. *Child Development* 36: 379–411.

Bee, H. L.; Van Egeren, L. F.; Streissguth, A. P.; Nyman, B. A.; and Leckie, M. S. 1969. Social class differences in maternal teaching strategies and speech patterns. *Developmental Psychology* 1: 726–734.

Bell, A. G. 1918. *The duration of life and conditions associated with longevity: a study of the Hyde genealogy.* Washington, D.C.: Genealogical Records Office.

Bell, R. Q. 1968. A reinterpretation of the direction of effects in studies of socialization. *Psychological Review* 75: 81–95.

Bem, D. J., and Allen, A. 1974. On predicting some of the people some of the time: the search for cross-situational consistencies in behavior. *Psychological Review* 81: 506–520.

Bem, S. L. 1974. The measurement of psychological androgyny. *Journal of Consulting and Clinical Psychology* 42: 155–162.

_____. 1975. Sex role adaptability: one consequence of psychological androgyny. *Journal of Personality and Social Psychology* 31: 634–643.

_____. 1977. On the utility of alternative procedures for assessing psychological androgyny. *Journal of Consulting and Clinical Psychology* 45: 196–205.

Bennett, G. K.; Seashore, H. G.; and Wesman, A. G. 1966. *Manual for the differential aptitude tests.* New York: Psychological Corporation.

Bereiter, C., and Engelmann, S. 1966. *Teaching disadvantaged children in the preschool.* Englewood Cliffs, N.J.: Prentice-Hall.

Berman, J. L., and Ford, R. 1970. Intelligence quotients and intelligence loss in patients with phenylketonuria and some variant states. *Journal of Pediatrics* 77: 764–770.

Bernstein, B. Language and social class. 1960. *British Journal of Sociology* 11: 271–276.

Berry, J. W. 1966. Temne and Eskimo perceptual skills. *International Journal of Psychology* 1: 207–229.

Bertelsen, A.; Harvald, B.; and Hauge, M. 1977. A Danish twin study of manic-depressive disorders. *British Journal of Psychiatry,* 130: 330–351.

Bexton, W. H.; Heron, W.; and Scott, T. H. 1954. Effects of decreased variation in the sensory environment. *Canadian Journal of Psychology* 8: 70–76.

Bickel, H.; Gerrard, J.; and Hickmans, E. M. 1954. Influence of phenylalanine intake on the chemistry and behavior of a phenyl-ketonuric child. *Acta Paediatrica* 43: 64.

Bieri, J. 1955. Cognitive complexity-simplicity and predictive behavior. *Journal of Abnormal and Social Psychology* 51: 263–268.

Biller, H. B. 1971. *Father, child, and sex role.* Lexington, Mass.: Heath & Co.

Binet, A., and Simon, T. 1905. The development of intelligence in children. *L'Annee Psychologique* 11: 163–191. Reprinted in *Classics in psychology,* ed. T. Shapley, pp. 872–919. New York: Philosophical Library.

Birch, H. G. 1964. The problem of brain damage. In *Brain damage in children,* ed. H. G. Birch, pp. 3–12. Baltimore: Williams & Wilkins.

Birch, H. G., and Gussow, J. D. 1970. *Disadvantaged children: health, nutrition, and school failure.* New York: Harcourt, Brace & World.

Birch, H. G.; Richardson, S. A.; Baird, D.; Horobin, G.; and Illsley, R. 1970. *Mental subnormality in the community: a clinical and epidemiologic study.* Baltimore: Williams & Wilkins.

Birren, J. E. 1974. Translations in gerontology—from lab to life: psychophysiology and speed of response. *American Psychologist* 29: 808–815.

Birren, J. E., and Renner, V. J. 1977. Research on the psychology of aging. In *Handbook of the psychology of aging,* ed. J. E. Birren and K. W. Schaie, pp. 3–38. New York: Van Nostrand Reinhold.

Birren, J. E., and Schaie, K. W., eds. 1977. *Handbook of the psychology of aging.* New York: Van Nostrand Reinhold.

Bishop, D. V. M. 1977. The P scale and psychosis. *Journal of Abnormal Psychology* 86: 127–134.

Bleuler, E. 1950. *Dementia praecox or the group of schizophrenias.* New York: International Universities Press. German edition, 1911.

Blewett, D. 1954. An experimental study of the inheritance of intelligence. *Journal of Mental Science* 100: 922–933.

Block, J. 1971. *Lives through time.* Berkeley, Calif.: Bancroft Books.

Block, J. H. 1973. Conceptions of sex role. *American Psychologist* 28: 512–526.

Bloom, B. S. 1964. *Stability and change in human characteristics.* New York: Wiley.

———. 1976. *Human characteristics and school learning.* New York: McGraw-Hill.

Bodmer, W. F., and Cavalli-Sforza, L. L. 1976. *Genetics, evolution, and man.* San Francisco: W. H. Freeman and Company.

Bohman, M. 1978. Some genetic aspects of alcoholism and criminality. *Archives of General Psychiatry* 35: 269–276.

Bornstein, M. H. 1973. Color vision and color naming: a psychophysiological hypothesis of cultural difference. *Psychological Bulletin* 80: 257–285.

Botwinck, J. Intellectual abilities. 1977. In *Handbook of the psychology of aging,* ed. J. E. Birren and K. W. Schaie, pp. 580–605. New York: Van Nostrand Reinhold.

Botwinick, J., and Storandt, M. 1974. Memory related functions and age. Springfield, Ill.: Charles C Thomas.

Bowers, K. S. 1973. Situationism in psychology: an analysis and a critique. Psychological Review 80: 307–336.

Boyle, E., Jr.; Griffey, W. P., Jr.; Nichaman, M. Z.; and Talbert, C. R., Jr. 1967. An epidemiological study of hypertension among racial groups of Charleston County, South Carolina. The Charleston Heart Study, Phase II. In The epidemiology of hypertension, ed. J. Stamler, R. Stamler, and T. N. Pullman, pp. 193–203. New York: Grune & Stratton.

Bracht, G. H. 1969. Experimental factors related to aptitude-treatment interactions. Review of Educational Research 40: 627–645.

Breland, H. M. 1973. Birth order effects: a reply to Schooler. Psychological Bulletin 80: 210–212.

Brim, O. G., Jr. 1958. Family structure and sex role learning by children: a further analysis of Helen Koch's data. Sociometry 21: 1–16.

Broadbent, D. E. 1958. Perception and communication. London: Pergamon.

Broman, S. H.; Nichols, P. L.; and Kennedy, W. A. 1975. Preschool IQ: prenatal and early developmental correlates. Hillsdale, N.J.: Lawrence Erlbaum Associates.

Bronfenbrenner, U. 1974. Experimental human ecology. Paper presented at the meeting of the American Psychological Association, New Orleans.

Bronson, W. C. 1966. Central orientations: a study of behavior organization from childhood to adolescence. Child Development 37: 125–155.

Brophy, J. E. 1970. Mothers as teachers of their own preschool children: the influence of socioeconomic status and task structure on teaching specificity. Child Development 41: 79–94.

Broverman, M.; Klaiber, E. L.; Kobayashi, Y.; and Vogel, W. 1968. Roles of activation and inhibition in sex differences in cognitive abilities. Psychological Review 75: 23–50.

Brown, F. W. 1942. Heredity in the psychoneuroses. Proceedings of the Royal Society of Medicine 35: 785–790.

Bruner, J. 1973. Organization of early skilled action. Child Development 44: 1–11.

Burkhardt, R. 1958. The relation of intelligence to art ability. Journal of Aestbetics and Art Criticism 17: 230–241.

Burks, B. S. 1928. The relative influence of nature and nurture upon mental development: a comparative study of foster parent-foster child resemblance and true parent-true child resemblance. 27th Yearbook of the National Society for the Study of Education, pt. 1, pp. 219–316. Bloomington, Ind.: Public School Publishing Co.

Burks, B. S.; Jensen, D. W.; and Terman, L. M. 1930. The promise of youth. Genetic Studies of Genius, vol. III. Stanford, Calif.: Stanford University Press.

Burt, C. 1949. The structure of the mind: a review of the results of factor analysis. British Journal of Educational Psychology 19: 100–111, 176–199.

————. 1961. Intelligence and social mobility. *The British Journal of Statistical Psychology* 14: 3–24.

————. 1966. The genetic determination of differences in intelligence: a study of monozygotic twins reared together and apart. *British Journal of Psychology* 57: 137–153.

Burton, R. V. 1963. Generality of honesty reconsidered. *Psychological Review* 70: 481–499.

Buss, A. H., and Plomin, R. 1975. *A temperament theory of personality development*. New York: Wiley.

Byrne, B. M.; Willerman, L.; and Ashmore, L. L. 1974. Severe and moderate language impairment: evidence for distinctive etiologies. *Behavior Genetics* 4: 331–345.

Cadoret, R. J. 1976. Evidence for genetic inheritance of primary affective disorder in adoptees. Unpublished manuscript.

Cadoret, R. J.; Cunningham, L.; Loftus, R.; and Edwards, J. 1976. Studies of adoptees from psychiatrically disturbed biological parents, III: medical symptoms in childhood and adolescence. *American Journal of Psychiatry* 133: 1316–1318.

Cadoret, R. J., and Gath, A. 1976a. Inheritance of alcoholism in adoptees. Unpublished manuscript.

————. 1976. Biologic correlates of hyperactivity: evidence for a genetic factor. Paper presented at the meeting of the Society for Life History Research in Psychopathology, Fort Worth, Texas.

Cain, L. F.; Levine, S.; and Elzey, F. F. 1963. *Manual for the Cain-Levine Social Competency Scale*. Palo Alto, Calif.: Consulting Psychologists Press.

Campbell, D. P. 1969. *Strong Vocational Interest Blanks Manual* (1969 supplement). Stanford, Calif.: Stanford University Press.

Campbell, D. T., and Fiske, D. W. 1959. Convergent and discriminant validation by the multitrait-multimethod matrix. *Psychological Bulletin* 56: 81–105.

Campbell, D. T., and Stanley, J. C. 1963. *Experimental and quasi-experimental designs for research*. Chicago: Rand McNally.

Cannon, W. B. 1939. *The wisdom of the body*. Rev. ed. New York: Norton.

Cantwell, D. P. 1972. Psychiatric illness in the families of hyperactive children. *Archives of General Psychiatry* 27: 414–417.

Carlsmith, L. 1964. Effect of early father-absence on scholastic aptitude. *Harvard Educational Review* 34: 3–21.

Carlson, R. 1971. Sex differences in ego functioning. *Journal of Consulting and Clinical Psychology* 37: 267–277.

Carpenter, W. T., Jr.; Strauss, J. S.; and Bartko, J. J. 1973. Flexible system for the diagnosis of schizophrenia: report from the WHO International Pilot Study of Schizophrenia. *Science* 182: 1275–1278.

Carr, A. T. 1974. Compulsive neurosis: a review of the literature. *Psychological Bulletin* 81: 311–318.

Cattell, J. Mck. 1890. Mental tests and measurements. *Mind* 15: 373–380.

Cattell, R. B. 1941. Some theoretical issues in adult intelligence testing. *Psychological Bulletin* 38: 592.

_____. 1942. The concept of social status. *Journal of Social Psychology* 15: 293–308.

_____. 1951. The fate of national intelligence: test of thirteen year prediction. *Eugenics Review* 42: 136–148.

_____. 1960. The multiple abstract variance analysis equations and solutions. *Psychological Review* 67: 353–372.

_____. 1965. *The scientific analysis of personality.* Chicago: Aldine.

_____. 1971. *Abilities: their structure, growth, and action.* Boston: Houghton Mifflin.

Cattell, R. B., and Butcher, J. 1968. *The prediction of achievement and creativity.* Indianapolis: Bobbs-Merrill.

Cattell, R. B., and Nesselroade, J. R. 1967. Likeness and completeness theories examined by sixteen personality factor measures on stably and unstably married couples. *Journal of Personality and Social Psychology* 1: 351–361.

Cattell, R. B., and Warburton, F. W. 1967. *Objective personality and motivation tests.* Urbana, Ill.: University of Illinois Press.

Cavalli-Sforza, L. L., and Bodmer, W. F. 1971. *The genetics of human populations.* San Francisco: W. H. Freeman and Company.

Chapman, L. J., and Chapman, J. P. 1973. *Disordered thought in schizophrenia.* Englewood Cliffs, N.J.: Prentice-Hall.

Chase, W. G., and Simon, H. A. 1973. Perception in chess. *Cognitive Psychology* 4: 55–81.

Cheek, D. B. 1968. *Human growth: body composition, cell growth, energy, and intelligence.* Philadelphia: Lea & Febiger.

Child, I. L. 1965. Personality correlates of esthetic judgment in college students. *Journal of Personality* 33: 476–511.

Chomsky, N. 1972. *Language and mind.* New York: Harcourt Brace Jovanovich.

Christian, A. M., and Paterson, D. G. 1936. Growth of vocabulary in later maturity. *Journal of Psychology* 1: 167–169.

Chung, C. S., and Myrianthopoulos, N. C. 1968. Racial and prenatal factors in major congenital malformations. *American Journal of Human Genetics* 20: 44.

Claiborne, W. L. 1969. Expectancy effects in the classroom: failure to replicate. *Journal of Educational Psychology* 60: 377–383.

Claridge, G. 1973. A nervous typological analysis of personality variation in normal twins. In *Personality differences and biological variations,* ed. G. Claridge, S. Canter, and W. I. Hume, pp. 132–148. New York: Pergamon Press.

Clark, E. 1963. Sex-role preference in mentally retarded children. *American Journal of Mental Deficiency* 67: 606–610.

Clark, R. A. 1952. The projective measurement of experimentally induced levels of sexual motivation. *Journal of Experimental Psychology* 44: 391–399.

Clarke, A. M., and Clarke, A. D. B. 1976. *Early experience: myth and evidence.* New York: The Free Press.

Cleary, T. A.; Humphreys, L. G.; Kendrick, S. A.; and Wesman, A. 1975.

Educational uses of tests with disadvantaged students. *American Psychologist* 30: 15–41.

Cohen, D. B. 1973. Sex role orientation and dream recall. *Journal of Abnormal Psychology* 82: 246–252.

Cohen, D. J.; Dibble, E.; Grawe, J. M.; and Pollin, W. 1973. Separating identical from fraternal twins. *Archives of General Psychiatry* 29: 465–469.

Coleman, J. S. et al. 1966. *Equality and educational opportunity.* Washington, D.C.: U.S. Office of Education.

Collaborative Study of Children Treated for Phenylketonuria, Preliminary Report No. 8. 1975. Principle Investigator, R. Koch. Presented at the 11th General Medical Conference, Stateline, Nevada, February 1975.

Conn, L. K.; Edwards, C. N.; Rosenthal, R.; and Crowne, D. 1968. Perception of emotion and response to teachers' expectancy by elementary school children. *Psychological Reports* 22: 27–34.

Conry, R., and Plant, W. T. 1965. WAIS and group test predictions of an academic success criterion: high school and college. *Educational and Psychological Measurement* 25: 493–500.

Constantinople, A. 1973. Masculinity-femininity: an exception to a famous dictum? *Psychological Bulletin* 80:389–407.

Cooper, G. D.; York, M. W.; Daston, P. G.; and Adams, H. B. 1967. The Porteus Test and various measures of intelligence with Southern Negro adolescents. *American Journal of Mental Deficiency* 71: 787–792.

Coppen, A.; Cowie, V.; and Slater, E. 1965. Familial aspects of "neuroticism" and "extraversion." *British Journal of Psychiatry* 111: 70–83.

Corso, J. F. 1977. Auditory perception and communication. In *Handbook of the psychology of aging,* ed. J. E. Birren and K. W. Schaie, pp. 535–553. New York: Van Nostrand Reinhold.

Cortes, J. B., and Gatti, F. M. 1972. *Delinquency and crime: a biosocial approach.* New York: Seminar Press.

Cotzin, M., and Dallenbach, K. M. 1950. "Facial vision": the role of pitch and loudness in the perception of obstacles by the blind. *American Journal of Psychology* 63: 485–515.

Cox, C. M. 1926. *The early mental traits of three hundred geniuses.* Genetic Studies of Genius, vol. II. Stanford, Calif.: Stanford University Press.

Cronbach, L. J. 1957. The two disciplines of scientific psychology. *American Psychologist* 12: 671–684.

———. 1970. *Fundamentals of psychological testing.* New York: Harper & Row.

———. 1975. Beyond the two disciplines of scientific psychology. *American Psychologist* 30: 116–127.

Cronbach, L. J., and Gleser, G. C. 1965. *Psychological tests and personnel decisions.* 2d ed. Urbana: University of Illinois Press.

Cronbach, L. J., and Snow, R. E. 1969. *Individual differences in learning ability as a function of instructional variables: final report.* Stanford, Calif.: Stanford University School of Education.

Crossman, E. R. F. W., and Szafran, J. 1956. Changes with age in the speed of information intake and discrimination. *Experientia Supplementum* iv: 128–135.

Crow, J. F., and Kimura, M. 1970. *An introduction to population genetics theory.* New York: Harper & Row.

Crowe, R. R. 1972. The adopted offspring of women offenders. *Archives of General Psychiatry* 27: 600–603.

————. 1974. An adoption study of antisocial personality. *Archives of General Psychiatry* 31: 785–791.

Csikszentmihalyi, M., and Getzels, J. W. 1971. Discovery-oriented behavior and the originality of artistic products: a study of artists. *Journal of Personality and Social Psychology* 19: 47–52.

Cumming, E., and Henry, W. E. 1961. *Growing old.* New York: Basic Books.

Cunningham, L.; Cadoret, R. J.; Loftus, R.; and Edwards, J. E. 1975. Studies of adoptees from psychiatrically disturbed biological parents: psychiatric conditions in childhood and adolescence. *British Journal of Psychiatry* 126: 534–549.

Darwin, C. 1859. *The origin of the species by means of natural selection or the preservation of favoured races in the struggle for life.* London: John Murray. Reprint. New York: New American Library, 1958.

Datta, L. E. 1963. Test instructions and identification of creative scientific talent. *Psychological Reports* 13: 495–500.

Davis, D. J.; Cahan, S.; and Bashi, J. 1977. Birth order and intellectual development: the confluence model in the light of cross-cultural evidence. *Science* 196: 1470–1471.

DeFries, J. C. 1972. Quantitative aspects of genetics and environment in the determination of behavior. In *Genetics, environment, and behavior: implications for educational policy*, ed. L. Ehrman, G. S. Omenn, and E. Caspari, pp. 5–16. New York: Academic Press.

DeFries, J. C.; Vandenberg, S. G.; and McClearn, G. E. 1976. Genetics of specific cognitive abilities. *Annual Review of Genetics* 10: 179–207.

DeFries, J. C.; Vandenberg, S. G.; McClearn, G. E.; Kuse, A. R.; Wilson, J. R.; Ashton, G. C.; and Johnson, R. C. 1974. Near identity of cognitive structure in two ethnic groups. *Science* 183: 338–339.

Dennis, W. 1947. Does culture appreciably affect patterns of infant behavior? In *Readings in social psychology*, ed. T. Newcomb and E. Hartley, pp. 40–46. New York: Holt.

Dennis, W. and Najarian, P. 1957. Infant development under environmental handicap. *Psychological Monographs* 71: no. 7.

Devereaux, E. C.; Shouval, R.; Bronfenbrenner, U.; Rodgers, R. R.; Kav-Vanaki, S.; Kiely, E.; and Karson, E. 1974. Socialization practices of parents, teachers, and peers in Israel. *Child Development* 45: 269–281.

Dewey, W. J.; Barrai, I.; Morton, N. E.; and Mi, M. P. 1965. Recessive genes in severe mental defect. *American Journal of Human Genetics* 17: 237–256.

Diamond, S. 1957. *Personality and temperament.* New York: Harper & Brothers.

Doll, E. A. 1965. *Vineland Social Maturity Scale.* Minneapolis: American Guidance Service.

Domino, G. 1971. Interactive effects of achievement orientation and teaching style on academic achievement. *Journal of Educational Psychology* 62: 427–431.

Drillien, C. M. 1964. *The growth and development of the prematurely born infant.* Baltimore: Williams & Wilkins.

DuBois, P. H. 1970. *A history of psychological testing.* Boston: Allyn & Bacon.

Dugdale, R. L. 1877. *The Jukes.* New York: G. T. Putnam's Sons.

Duncan, A. D. W. 1969. Behavior rates of gifted and regular elementary school children. *Monograph, National Association for Gifted Children,* pp. 1–25.

Duncan, O. D.; Featherman, D. L.; and Duncan, B. 1972. *Socioeconomic background and achievement.* New York: Seminar Press.

Dunham, H. W.; Phillips, P.; and Srinivasan, B. 1966. A research note on diagnosed mental illness and social class. *American Sociological Review* 31: 223–227.

Ehrhardt, A. A., and Baker, S. W. 1974. Fetal androgens, human central nervous system differentiation, and behavior sex differences. In *Sex differences in behavior,* ed. R. C. Friedman, R. M. Richart, and R. L. Vande Wiele, pp. 33–51.

Ehrhardt, A. A.; Epstein, R.; and Money, J. 1968. Fetal androgens and female gender identity in the early-treated andrenogenital syndrome. *Johns Hopkins Medical Journal* 122: 160–167.

Ehrhardt, A. A., and Money, J. 1967. Progestin-induced hermaphroditism: IQ and psychosexual identity in a study of ten girls. *Journal of Sex Research* 3: 83–100.

Eichorn, D. H. 1970. Physiological development. In *Charmichael's manual of child psychology,* ed. P. H. Mussen, pp. 157–283. New York: Wiley.

Eitinger, L., and Strøm, A. 1973. *Mortality and morbidity after excessive stress.* New York: Humanities Press.

Endler, N. S., and Hunt, J. McV. 1966. Sources of behavioral variance as measured by the S-R inventory of anxiousness. *Psychological Bulletin* 65: 336–346.

Engen, T. 1977. Taste and smell. In *Handbook of the psychology of aging,* ed. J. E. Birren and K. W. Schaie, pp. 554–561. New York: Van Nostrand Reinhold.

Erikson, E. H. 1963. *Childhood and society.* 2d ed. New York: Norton.

Erlenmeyer-Kimling, L., and Jarvik, L. F. 1963. Genetics and intelligence: a review. *Science* 142: 1478–1479.

Erlenmeyer-Kimling, L., and Stern, S. E. 1973. Technical comment. *Science* 182: 1044–1045.

Estes, W. K. 1974. Learning theory and intelligence. *American Psychologist* 29: 740–749.

Evans, J. T., and Rosenthal, R. 1969. Interpersonal self-fulfilling prophecies: further extrapolations from the laboratory to the classroom. *Proceedings of the 77th Annual Convention of the American Psychological Association* 4: 371–372.

Eyferth, K. 1961. Leistungen verschiedener Gruppen von Besatzungskindern in Hamburg-Wechsler Intelligenztest fur Kinder (HAWIK). *Archiv fur die gesamte Psychologie* 113: 222–241.

Eysenck, H. J. 1947. *Dimensions of personality*. London: Routledge and Kegan Paul.

_____. 1967. *The biological basis of personality*. Springfield, Ill.: Charles C Thomas.

_____, ed. 1973. *Handbook of abnormal psychology*. 2d ed. San Diego: R. R. Knapp.

Falconer, D. S. 1960. *Introduction to quantitative genetics*. Edinburgh: Oliver & Boyd.

Farley, J.; Woodruff, R. A., Jr.; and Guze, S. B. 1968. The prevalence of hysteria and conversion symptoms. *British Journal of Psychiatry* 114: 1121–1125.

Fenigstein, A.; Scheier, M.; and Buss, A. H. 1975. Public and private self-consciousness: assessment and theory. *Journal of Consulting and Clinical Psychology* 43: 522–527.

Ferguson, L. R., and Maccoby, E. E. 1966. Interpersonal correlates of differential abilities. *Child development* 37: 549–571.

Fialkow, P. J. 1967. Thyroid antibodies, Down's syndrome, and maternal age. *Nature* 214: 1253–1254.

Fielder, W. R.; Cohen, R. D.; and Feeney, S. 1971. An attempt to replicate the teacher expectancy effect. *Psychological Reports* 29: 1223–1228.

Fishbein, M., and Ajzen, I. 1974. Attitudes towards objects as predictors of single and multiple behavioral criteria. *Psychological Review* 81: 59–74.

Fisher, J. 1959. The twisted pear and the prediction of behavior. *Journal of Consulting Psychology* 23: 400–405.

Fiske, D. W. 1971. *Measuring the concepts of personality*. Chicago: Aldine.

Fiske, D. W., and Butler, J. M. 1963. The experimental conditions for measuring individual differences. *Educational and Psychological Measurement* 23: 249–266.

Flanagan, J. C., and Cooley, W. W. 1966. Project TALENT one-year follow-up studies. Cooperative Research Project Number 2333. School of Education, University of Pittsburgh.

Flavell, J. H.; Beach, D. H.; and Chinsky, J. M. 1966. Spontaneous verbal rehearsal in a memory task as a function of age. *Child Development* 37: 283–299.

Fletcher, J. D., and Atkinson, R. C. 1972. Evaluation of the Stanford CAI program in initial reading. *Journal of Educational Psychology*, 63: 597–602.

Fling, S., and Manosevitz, M. 1972. Sex typing in nursery school children's play interests. *Developmental Psychology* 7: 146–152.

Flowers, C. E. 1966. Effects of an arbitrary accelerated group placement on the tested academic achievement of educationally disadvantaged students. *Dissertation Abstracts International* 27: 991-A.

Følling, A. 1934. Uber Ausscheidung von Phenylbrenztraubensaure in den Harn als Stoffwechselanomalie in Verbindung mit Imbezzillitat. *Atschrift for Physiol. Chem.* 227: 169–176. Quoted in Knox, W. E. 1972. Phenylketonuria. In *The metabolic basis of inherited disease.* ed. J. B. Stanbury, J. B. Wyngaarden, and D. S. Fredrickson, pp. 266–295. New York: McGraw-Hill.

Forrest, D. K. 1974. *Francis Galton: the life and work of a Victorian genius.* New York: Taplinger.

Foulds, G. A., and Raven, J. C. 1948. Neural changes in mental abilities of adults as age advances. *Journal of Mental Science* 94: 133–142.

Fozard, J. L.; Wolf, E.; Bell, B.; McFarland, R. A.; and Podolsky, S. 1977. Visual perception and communication. In *Handbook of the psychology of aging,* ed. J. E. Birren and K. W. Schaie, pp. 497–534. New York: Von Nostrand Reinhold.

Francois, J. 1961. *Heredity in opthalmology.* St. Louis: C. V. Mosby.

Fraser, G. R. 1965. The role of Mendelian inheritance in the causation of childhood deafness and blindness. In *Mutation in population (Proceedings of the Symposium on the mutational process),* ed. R. R. Honcariv. Prague: Academia.

———. 1971. Genetic approaches to the nosology of deafness. *Birth Defects: Original Article Series* 7: 52–63.

Freedman, D. G. 1965. An ethological approach to the genetic study of human behavior. In *Methods and goals in human behavior genetics,* ed. S. G. Vandenberg, pp. 141–161. New York: Academic Press.

———. 1974. *Human infancy: an evolutionary perspective.* Hillsdale, N.J.: Lawrence Erlbaum Associates.

Freedman, D. G., and Freedman, N. C. 1969. Behavioral differences between Chinese-American and European-American newborns. *Nature* 224: 1227.

Freire-Maia, A.; Freire-Maia, D. V.; and Morton, N. E. 1974. Sex effect on intelligence and mental retardation. *Behavior Genetics* 4: 269–272.

Fuller, J. L., and Thompson, W. R. 1960. *Behavior genetics.* New York: Wiley.

Furby, L. 1974. Attentional habituation and mental retardation. *Human Development* 17: 118–138.

Furneaux, W. D. 1961. Intellectual abilities and problem-solving behavior. In H. J. Eysenck (Ed.) *Handbook of abnormal psychology,* ed. H. J. Eysenck, pp. 167–192. New York: Basic Books.

Furth, H. G. 1964. Research with the deaf: implications for language and cognition. *Psychological Bulletin* 62: 145–164.

———. 1966. A comparison of reading test norms of deaf and hearing children. *American Annals of the Deaf* 111: 461–462.

———. 1971. Linguistic deficiency and thinking: research with deaf subjects, 1964–1969. *Psychological Bulletin* 76: 58–72.

———. 1973. *Deafness and learning.* Belmont, Calif.: Wadsworth.

Galton, F. 1869. *Hereditary genius: an inquiry into its laws and conse-*

quences. London: Macmillan Co. Reprinted. New York: World Publishing Co., 1962.

Garai, J. E., and Scheinfeld, A. 1968. Sex differences in mental and behavioral traits. *Genetic Psychology Monographs* 11: 169–299.

Gardner, R. W.; Holzman, P. S.; Klein, G. S.; Linton, H. B.; and Spence, D. P. 1959. Cognitive control: a study of individual consistencies in cognitive behavior. *Psychological Issues* 1: no. 4 (Monograph 4).

Garmezy, N., with the collaboration of Streitman, S. 1974. Children at risk: the search for the antecedents of schizophrenia, Part I: conceptual models and research methods. *Schizophrenia Bulletin* (Spring): 14–90.

Garrett, H. E. 1949. A review and interpretation of investigations of factors related to scholastic success in colleges of arts and sciences and teachers colleges. *Journal of Experimental Education* 18: 91–138.

Garrod, A. E. 1909. *Inborn errors of metabolism.* London: Oxford University Press.

Garron, D. C. 1972. Paper presented at the Annual Meeting of the American Psychological Association, Honolulu, Hawaii.

Gates, A. I. 1958. *Gates Basic Reading Tests Manual.* New York: Bureau of Publications, Teachers College, Columbia University.

Geber, M., and Dean, R. F. A. 1957. Gesell tests on African children. *Pediatrics* 20: 1055–1065.

Gentile, A., and DiFrancesca, S. 1969. *Academic achievement test performance of hearing impaired students.* Washington, D.C.: Gallaudet College Press.

Gerard, H. B., and Miller, N. Factors contributing to adjustment and achievement in racially desegregated public schools. University of California at Los Angeles, 1971.

Gesell, A. L., and Thompson, H. 1929. Learning and growth in identical infant twins. *Genetic Psychology Monographs* 6: 5–120.

Getzels, J. W., and Csikszentmihalyi, M. 1966. The study of creativity in future artists: the criterion problem. In *Experience, structure, and adaptability,* ed. O. J. Harvey, pp. 349–368. New York: Springer.

_____. 1968. On the roles, values, and performance of future artists: a conceptual and empirical exploration. *Sociological Quarterly* 9: 516–530.

_____. 1975. From problem solving to problem finding. In *Perspectives in creativity,* ed. I. A. Taylor and J. W. Getzels, pp. 90–116. Chicago: Aldine.

Getzels, J. W., and Jackson, P. W. 1962. *Creativity and intelligence: explorations with gifted students.* New York: Wiley.

Ghiselli, E. E. 1963. Moderating effects and differential reliability and validity. *Journal of Applied Psychology* 47: 81–86.

Gibson, J. B. 1970. Biological aspects of a high socio-economic group. *Journal of Biosocial Science* 2: 1–16.

Glueck, S., and Glueck, E. 1956. *Unraveling juvenile delinquency.* New York: Harper & Row.

Goddard, H. H. 1912. *The Kallikak family.* New York: Macmillan.

Goeffney, B.; Henderson, N. B.; and Butler, B. V. 1971. Negro-white male-female eight-month developmental scores compared with seven-year WISC and Bender test scores. *Child Development* 42: 595–604.

Goldberg, E. M., and Morrison, S. L. 1963. Schizophrenia and social class. *British Journal of Psychiatry* 109: 785–802.

Golding, S. L. 1975. Flies in the ointment: methodological problems in the analysis of the percentage of variance due to persons and situations. *Psychological Bulletin* 82: 278–288.

Goodwin, D. W.; Schulsinger, F.; Hermansen, L.; Guze, S. B.; and Winokur, G. 1973. Alcohol problems in adoptees raised apart from alcoholic biological parents. *Archives of General Psychiatry* 28: 238–243.

Goodwin, D. W.; Schulsinger, F.; Knop, J.; Mednick, S.; and Guze, S. B. 1977. Alcoholism and depression in adopted-out daughters of alcoholics. *Archives of General Psychiatry* 34: 751–755.

Gordon, E. 1967. *A three-year longitudinal predictive validity study of the Musical Aptitude Profile.* Studies in the Psychology of Music, vol. V. Iowa City: University of Iowa Press.

Gordon, H. 1923. Mental and scholastic tests among retarded children: an inquiry into the effects of schooling on the various tests. *Education Pamphlets*, no. 44. London Board of Education.

Gottesman, I. I. 1968. Biogenetics of race and class. In *Social class, race, and psychological development*, ed. M. Deutsch, I. Katz, and A. R. Jensen, pp. 11–51. New York: Holt, Rinehart & Winston.

Gottesman, I. I., and Shields, J. 1966. Schizophrenia in twins: 16 years, consecutive admissions to a psychiatric clinic. *British Journal of Psychiatry* 112: 809–818.

Gough, H. G. 1952. Identifying psychological femininity. *Educational and Psychological Measurement* 12: 427–439.

————. 1957. *Manual for the California Psychological Inventory.* Palo Alto, Calif.: Consulting Psychologists Press.

Goulet, L. R., and Baltes, P. B., eds. 1970. *Life-span developmental psychology: research and theory.* New York: Academic Press.

Green, D. R., ed. 1974. *The aptitude achievement distinction.* New York: McGraw-Hill.

Green, R. F. 1972. On the correlation between IQ and amount of "white" blood. *Proceedings, 80th Annual Convention of the American Psychological Association* 7: 285–286.

Greenough, W. T. 1975. Experiential modification of the developing brain. *American Scientist* 63: 37–46.

Griffith, J. D.; Cavanaugh, J.; Held, N. N.; and Oates, J. A. 1972. Dextroamphetamine: evaluation of psychotomimetic properties in man. *Archives of General Psychiatry* 26: 97–100.

Gross, M. 1967. *Learning readiness in two Jewish groups.* New York: Center for Urban Education.

Grossman, H., ed. 1973. *Manual on terminology and classification in mental retardation, 1973 revision.* Washington, D.C.: American Association on Mental Deficiency.

Guilford, J. P. 1954. *Psychometric methods.* 2d ed. New York: McGraw-Hill.

———. 1959. *Personality.* New York: McGraw-Hill.

———. 1967. *The nature of human intelligence.* New York: McGraw-Hill.

Guthrie, R., and Susi, A. 1963. A simple phenylketonuria screening method for newborn infants. *Pediatrics* 32: 338–343.

Gutmann, D. L. 1965. Women and the corruption of ego strength. *Merrill-Palmer Quarterly* 11: 229–240.

Haggard, E. A. 1958. *Intraclass correlation and the analysis of variance.* New York: Dryden Press.

Hall, C. S., and Lindzey, G. 1970. *Theories of personality.* New York: Wiley.

Haller, M. H. 1963. *Eugenics: hereditarian attitudes in American thought.* New Brunswick, N.J.: Rutgers University Press.

Hallgren, B. 1950. Specific dyslexia (congenital word blindness: a clinical and genetic study). *Acta Psychiatrica et Neurologica Supplement,* no. 65.

Halstead, W. C. 1947. *Brain and intelligence.* Chicago: University of Chicago Press.

Hamilton, C. H. 1964. The Negro leaves the South. 1: 273–295.

Hammermeister, F. K. 1971. Reading achievement in deaf adults. *American Annals of the Deaf* 116: 25–28.

Hanson, D. R., and Gottesman, I. I. 1976. The genetics, if any, of infantile autism and childhood schizophrenia. *Journal of Autism and Childhood Schizophrenia* 6: 209–234.

Harburg, E.; Schull, W. J.; Erfort, J. C.; and Schork, M. A. 1970. A family set method for estimating heredity and stress, I: a pilot survey of blood pressure among Negroes in high and low stress areas, Detroit, 1966–1967. *Journal of Chronic Diseases* 23: 69–81.

Hare, E. H., and Price, J. S. 1969. Birth order and family size: bias caused by changes in birth rate. *British Journal of Psychiatry* 115: 647–657.

Hare, R. D. 1965. Temporal gradient of fear arousal in psychopathy. *Journal of Abnormal Psychology* 70: 442–445.

———. In press. Electrodermal and cardiovascular correlates of psychopathy. In *Psychopathic behavior: approaches to research,* ed. R. D. Hare and D. Schalling. London: Wiley.

Harrington, D. M. 1975. Effects of explicit instructions to "be creative" on the psychological meaning of divergent thinking test scores. *Journal of Personality* 43: 434–454.

Harris, H. 1966. Enzyme polymorphisms in man. *Proceedings of the Royal Society* 164: 298–310.

Harter, S. 1965. Discrimination learning set in children as a function of IQ and MA. *Journal of Experimental Child Psychology* 2: 31–43.

———. 1967. Mental age, IQ, and motivational factors in the discrimination learning set performance of normal and retarded children. *Journal of Experimental Child Psychology* 5: 123–141.

Hartshorne, H.; and May, M. A. 1928. *Studies in the nature of character.* Vol. 1. New York: Macmillan.

Hartshorne, H.; May, M. A.; and Shuttleworth, F. K. 1930. *Studies in the nature of character.* Vol. 3. New York: Macmillan.

Hathaway, S. R., and McKinley, J. C. 1943. *The Minnesota Multiphasic Personality Inventory.* New York: Psychological Corporation.

Hathaway, S. R., and Monachesi, E. D. 1963. *Adolescent personality and behavior.* Minneapolis: University of Minnesota Press.

Haug, J. O. 1962. Pneumoencephalographic studies in mental disease. *Acta Psychiatric Neurologica Scandinavia Supplement* no. 38.

Hauser, S.; Delong, G.; and Rosman, N. 1975. Pneumographic findings in the infantile autism syndrome, a correlation with temporal lobe disease. *Brain* 98: 667–688.

Hayes, K. J. 1953. The backward curve: A method for the study of learning. *Psychological Review* 60: 269–275.

Hayes, S. P. 1941. *Contributions to the psychology of blindness.* New York: American Foundation for the Blind.

Hayflick, L. 1974. Cytogerontology. In *Theoretical aspects of aging,* ed. M. Rockstein, pp. 83–103. New York: Academic Press.

Hebb, D. O. 1949. *The organization of behavior.* New York: Wiley.

Heber, R. 1976. Sociocultural mental retardation—a longitudinal study. Paper presented at the Vermont Conference on the Primary Prevention of Psychopathology, June 1976.

Heber, R.; Dever, R.; and Conry, J. 1968. The influence of environmental and genetic variables on intellectual development. In *Behavioral research in mental retardation,* ed. H. J. Prehm, L. A. Hamerlynck, and J. E. Crosson, pp. 1–23. Eugene: University of Oregon Press.

Heber, R.; Garber, H.; Harrington, S.; Hoffman, C.; and Falender, C. 1972. *Rehabilitation of families at risk for mental retardation.* Progress report of the Rehabilitation Research and Training Center in Mental Retardation, University of Wisconsin at Madison, February 1972.

Helmreich, R. 1968. Birth order effects. *Naval Research Reviews.* pp. 1–6.

Hess, R., and Shipman, V. 1965. Early experience and the socialization of cognitive modes in children. *Child Development* 36: 869–886.

Heston, L. L. 1966. Psychiatric disorders in foster home reared children of schizophrenic mothers. *British Journal of Psychiatry* 112: 819–825.

————. 1970. The genetics of schizophrenic and schizoid disease. *Science* 167: 249–256.

Hetherington, E. M. 1965. A developmental study of the effects of sex of the dominant parent on sex-role preference, identification, and imitation in children. *Journal of Personality and Social Psychology* 2: 188–194.

————. 1972. Effects of father absence on personality development in adolescent daughters. *Developmental Psychology* 7: 313–326.

Higgins, J. V.; Reed, E. W.; and Reed, S. C. 1962. Intelligence and family size: a paradox resolved. *Eugenics Quarterly* 9: 84–90.

Hilgard, E. R., and Bower, G. H. 1966. *Theories of learning.* New York: Appleton-Century-Crofts.

Hilgard, J. R. 1933. The effect of early and delayed practice on memory and motor performance studied by the method of cotwin control. *Genetic Psychology Monographs* 14: 493–567.

Hodge, R. W.; Trieman, D. J.; and Rossi, P. H. 1966. A comparative study of occupational prestige. In *Class, status, and power*, ed. R. Bendix and S. M. Lipset, pp. 309–321. New York: The Free Press.

Holden, R. H., and Willerman, L. 1972. Neurological abnormality in infancy, intelligence, and social class. In *Readings on the exceptional child*, 2d ed., ed. E. P. Trapp and P. Himelstein, pp. 501–511. New York: Appleton-Century-Crofts.

Holley, W.; Rosenbaum, A.; and Churchill, J. 1969. Effects of rapid succession of pregnancy. In *Perinatal factors affecting human development*, pp. 41–44. Washington, D.C.: Pan American Health Organization Science Publications.

Hollingshead, A. B. 1950. Cultural factors in the selection of marriage mates. *American Sociological Review* 15: 619–627.

Hollingshead, A. B., and Redlich, F. C. 1958. *Social class and mental illness*. New York: Wiley.

Hollingsworth, L. S. 1942. *Children above the 180 IQ*. New York: Harcourt, Brace & World.

Hollister, L. E. 1962. Drug-induced psychoses and schizophrenic reactions: a critical comparison. *Annals, New York Academy of Sciences* 96: 80–88.

Honzik, M. P.; Macfarlane, J. W.; and Allen, L. 1948. The stability of mental test performance between two and eighteen years. *Journal of Experimental Education* 17: 309–334.

Hopkinson, G., and Ley, P. 1969. A genetic study of affective disorder. *British Journal of Psychiatry* 115: 917–922.

Horn, C. A., and Smith, L. F. 1945. The Horn Art Aptitude Inventory. *Journal of Applied Psychology* 29: 350–355.

Horn, J. L. 1967. Intelligence—why it grows, why it declines. *Transaction* (November): 23–31.

———. 1970. Organization of data on life-span development of human abilities. In *Life-span developmental psychology: research and theory*, ed. L. R. Goulet and P. B. Baltes, pp. 423–466. New York: Academic Press.

Horn, J. L., and Cattell, R. B. 1966. Age differences in primary mental ability factors. *Journal of Gerontology* 21: 210–220.

Horn, J. L., and Donaldson, G. 1976. On the myth of intellectual decline in adulthood. *American Psychologist* 31: 701–719.

Horn, J. L., and Knapp, J. R. 1973. On the subjective character of the empirical base of Guilford's structure of intellect model. *Psychological Bulletin* 80: 33–43.

Horn, J. M.; Green, M.; Carney, R.; and Erickson, M. T. 1975. Bias against genetic hypotheses in adoption studies. *Archives of General Psychiatry* 32: 1365–1367.

Horn, J. M.; Loehlin, J. C.; and Willerman, L. In preparation. The Texas adoption project.

Horn, J. M.; Plomin, R.; and Rosenman, R. 1976. Heritability of personality traits in adult male twins. *Behavior Genetics* 6: 17–30.

Horn, J. M., and Turner, R. G. 1974. Personality correlates of differential abilities in a sample of lower than average ability. *Psychological Reports* 35: 1211–1220.

Humphreys, L. G. 1957. Characteristics of type concepts with special reference to Sheldon's typology. *Psychological Bulletin* 54: 218–228.

Hunt, E., and Landsman, M. 1975. Cognitive theory applied to individual differences. In *Handbook of learning and cognitive processes*, ed. W. K. Estes, pp. 81–110. New York: Lawrence Erlbaum Associates.

Hunt, E.; Lunneborg, C.; and Lewis, J. 1975. What does it mean to be high verbal? *Cognitive psychology* 7: 194–227.

Hunt, J. McV. 1961. *Intelligence and experience*. New York: Ronald Press.

Husband, R. W. 1939. Intercorrelations among learning abilities: I. *Journal of Genetic Psychology* 55: 353–364.

———. 1941. Intercorrelations among learning abilities, III: the effects of length of tests upon intercorrelations. *Journal of Genetic Psychology* 58: 427–430.

Hutchings, B., and Mednick, S. A. 1974. Registered criminality in the adoptive and biological parents of registered male adoptees. In *Genetics, environment, and psychopathology*, ed. S. A. Mednick, F. Schulsinger, J. Higgins, and B. Bell, pp. 215–227. New York: Elsevier.

Imperato-McGinley, J.; Guerrero, L.; Gautier, T.; and Peterson, R. E. 1974. Steroid 5 alpha-reductase deficiency in man: an inherited form of male pseudohermaphroditism. *Science* 186: 1213–1215.

Ingham, J. G. 1966. Changes in MPI scores in neurotic patients: a three year follow-up. *British Journal of Psychiatry* 112: 931–939.

Inglis, J.; Ankus, M. N.; and Sykes, D. H. 1968. Age-related differences in learning and short term memory from childhood to the senium. *Human Development* 11: 42–52.

Izard, C. E. 1972. *Patterns of emotions: a new analysis of anxiety and depression*. New York: Academic Press.

Jaccard, J. J. 1974. Predicting social behavior from personality traits. *Journal of Research in Personality* 1: 358–367.

Jackson, D. N. 1967. *Personality Research Form Manual*. Goshen, N.Y.: Research Psychologists Press.

Jacobson, G., and Ryder, R. G. 1969. Parental loss and some characteristics of the early marriage relationship. *American Journal of Orthopsychiatry* 39: 779–787.

Jencks, C. 1973. The methodology of Inequality. *Sociology of Education* 46: 451–470.

Jencks, C.; Smith, M.; Acland, H.; Bane, M. J.; Cohen, D.; Gintis, H.; Heyns, B.; and Michelson, S. 1972. *Inequality*. New York: Basic Books.

Jensen, A. R. 1963. Learning abilities in retarded, average, and gifted children. *Merrill-Palmer Quarterly* 9: 123–140.

———. 1967. Estimation of the limits of heritability of traits by comparison of monozygotic and dizygotic twins. *Proceedings of the National Academy of Sciences* 58: 149–156.

———. 1969. How much can we boost IQ and scholastic achievement? *Harvard Educational Review*, 39: 1–123.

_____. 1970a. A theory of primary and secondary familial mental retardation. In *International review of research in mental retardation*, vol. 4, ed. N. R. Ellis, pp. 33–105. New York: Academic Press.

_____. 1970b. IQ's of identical twins reared apart. *Behavior Genetics* 1: 133–147.

_____. 1971a. Do schools cheat minority children? *Educational Research* 14: 3–28.

_____. 1971b. The race × ability × sex interaction. In *Intelligence: genetic and environmental influences*, ed. R. Cancro, pp. 107–161. New York: Grune & Stratton.

_____. 1971c. The role of verbal mediation in mental development. *Journal of Genetic Psychology* 118: 39–70.

_____. 1973a. *Educability and group differences*. New York: Harper & Row.

_____. 1973b. Let's understand Skodak and Skeels, finally. *Educational Psychologist* 10: 30–35.

_____. 1974a. Kinship correlations reported by Sir Cyril Burt. *Behavior Genetics* 4: 1–28.

_____. 1974b. Cumulative deficit: a testable hypothesis? *Developmental Psychology* 10: 996–1019.

_____. 1974c. How biased are culture-loaded tests? *Genetic Psychology Monographs* 90: 185–244.

_____. 1977. Cumulative deficit in IQ of blacks in the rural South. *Developmental Psychology* 13: 184–191.

_____. 1978. Genetic and behavioral effects of nonrandom mating. In *Human variation: biopsychology of age, race, and sex*, ed. R. T. Osborne, C. E. Noble, and N. Weyl, pp. 51–105. New York: Academic Press.

Jervis, G. A. 1939. The genetics of phenylpyruvic oligophrenia. *Journal of Mental Science* 85: 719.

_____. 1953. Phenylpyruvic oligophrenia: deficiency of phenylalanine oxidizing system. *Proceedings Society of Experimental Biology and Medicine* 82: 514.

Jewkes, J.; Sawers, D.; and Stillerman, R. 1969. *The sources of invention*. 2d ed. New York: Norton.

Jinks, J. L., and Fulker, D. W. 1970. A comparison of the biometrical genetical, MAVA and classical approaches to the analysis of human behavior. *Psychological Bulletin* 73: 311–349.

Johnson, J. T., Jr., and Olley, J. G. 1971. Behavioral comparisons of mongoloid and nonmongoloid retarded persons: a review. *American Journal of Mental Deficiency* 75: 546–559.

Johnston, R. F., and Selander, R. K. 1964. House sparrows: rapid evolution of races in North America. *Science* 144: 548–550.

Jones, H. E. 1949. *Motor performance and growth*. Berkeley: University of California Press.

_____. 1954. The environment and mental development. In *Manual of child psychology*, 2d ed., ed. L Carmichael, pp. 631–696. New York: Wiley.

Jones, M. B., and Fennell, R. S. 1965. Runway performance in two strains of rats. *Quarterly Journal of the Florida Academy of Sciences* 28: 289–296.

Jones, M. C. 1924. A laboratory study of fear: the case of Peter. *Pedagogical Seminary* 31: 308–315.

Jones, M. C.; Bayley, N.; Macfarlane, J. W.; and Honzik, M. P. 1971. *The course of human development.* Waltham, Mass.: Xerox College Publishing.

Jose, J., and Cody, J. 1971. Teacher-pupil interaction as it relates to attempted changes in teacher expectancy of academic ability and achievement. *American Educational Research Journal* 8: 39–49.

Juel-Nielsen, N. 1965. Individual and environment: a psychiatric-psychological investigation of monozygous twins reared apart. *Acta Psychiatrica Scandinavica Supplement,* no. 183.

Kagan, J. 1966a. Reflection-impulsivity: the generality and dynamics of conceptual tempo. *Journal of Abnormal Psychology* 71: 17–24.

———. 1966b. Developmental studies in reflection and analysis. In *Perceptual development in children,* ed. A. Kidd and J. Rivoire, pp. 487–522. New York: International Universities Press.

Kagan, J., and Klein, R. E. 1973. Cross-cultural perspectives on early development. *American Psychologist* 28: 947–961.

Kagan, J., and Kogan, N. 1970. Individual variation in cognitive processes. In *Manual of child psychology,* ed. P. Mussen, pp. 1273–1365. New York: Wiley.

Kagan, J., and Moss, H. A. 1962. *Birth to maturity: a study in psychological development.* New York: Wiley.

Kahl, J. A., and Davis, J. A. 1955. A comparison of indices of socioeconomic status. *American Sociological Review* 38: 766–776.

Kaij, L. 1960. *Alcoholism in twins: studies on the etiology and sequels of abuse of alcohol.* Stockholm: Almquist and Wiksell.

Kallmann, F. J. 1938. *The genetics of schizophrenia.* New York: J. J. Augustin.

Kallmann, F. J., and Jarvik, L. F. 1959. Individual differences in constitution and genetic background. In *Handbook of aging and the individual,* ed. J. E. Birren, pp. 216–263. Chicago: University of Chicago Press.

Kamin, L. J. 1973. Heredity, intelligence, politics, and psychology. Paper presented at the meeting of the Eastern Psychological Association, Washington, D.C.

———. 1974. *The science and politics of IQ.* Potomac, Md.: Lawrence Erlbaum Associates.

Kangas, J., and Bradway, K. 1971. Intelligence at middle-age: a thirty-eight-year follow-up. *Developmental Psychology* 5: 333–337.

Karlsson, J. L. 1966. *The biologic basis of schizophrenia.* Springfield, Ill.: Charles C Thomas.

Karnes, M. B. 1973. Evaluation and implications of research with young handicapped and low-income children. In *Compensatory education for children, ages 2 to 8,* ed. J. C. Stanley, pp. 109–144. Baltimore: Johns Hopkins University Press.

Kaufman, I. C., and Rosenblum, L. A. 1967. Depression in infant monkeys separated from their mothers. *Science* 155: 1030–1031.

Kausler, D. H. 1974. *Psychology of verbal learning and memory.* New York: Academic Press.

Keating, D. P. 1976. Precocious cognitive development at the level of formal operations. *Child Development* 46: 276–280.

Kelley, T. L. 1928. *Crossroads in the mind of man.* Stanford, Calif.: Stanford University Press.

Kelly, E. L. 1955. Consistency of the adult personality. *American Psychologist* 10: 659–681.

Kennedy, W. A. 1969. A follow-up normative study of Negro intelligence and achievement. *Monographs of the Society for Research in Child Development* 34, no. 126.

Kennedy, W. A.; Van De Riet, V.; and White, J. C., Jr. 1963. A normative sample of intelligence and achievement of Negro elementary school children in the Southeastern United States. *Monographs of the Society for Research in Child Development* 28, no. 90.

Kety, S. S.; Rosenthal, D.; Wender, P. H.; and Schulsinger, F. 1968. The types and prevalence of mental illness in the biological and adoptive families of adoptive schizophrenics. In *The transmission of schizophrenia,* ed. D. Rosenthal and S. S. Kety, pp. 345–362. London: Pergamon.

———. 1976. Studies based on a total sample of adopted individuals and their relatives: why they were necessary, what they demonstrated and failed to demonstrate. *Schizophrenia Bulletin* 2: 413–428.

Kinsbourne, M. 1973. Minimal brain dysfunction as a neurodevelopmental lag. *Annals of the New York Academy of Sciences* 205: 268–273.

Klatzky, R. L. 1975. *Human memory: structure and processes.* San Francisco: W. H. Freeman and Company.

Kleinmutz, B. 1967. *Personality measurement: an introduction.* Homewood, Ill.: Dorsey Press.

Klineberg, O. 1935. *Race differences.* New York: Harper & Row.

Klingler, D. E., and Saunders, D. R. 1975. A factor analysis of the items for nine subtests of the WAIS. *Multivariate Behavioral Research* 10: 131–154.

Knox, W. E. 1972. Phenylketonuria. In *The metabolic basis of inherited disease,* ed. J. B. Stanbury, J. B. Wyngaarden, and D. S. Frederickson, pp. 266–295. New York: McGraw-Hill.

Koch, H. L. 1956. Sissiness and tomboyishness in relation to sibling characteristics. *Journal of Genetic Psychology* 88: 231–244.

Kohlberg, L., and Zigler, E. 1967. The impact of cognitive maturity on the development of sex-role attitudes in the years 4 to 8. *Genetic Psychology Monographs* 75: 84–165.

Koluchová, J. 1972. Severe deprivation in twins: a case study. *Journal of Child Psychology and Psychiatry* 13: 107–114.

———. 1976. A report on the further development of twins after severe and prolonged deprivation. In *Early experience: myth and evidence,* ed. A. M. Clarke and A. D. B. Clarke, pp. 56–66. New York: The Free Press.

Kretschner, E. 1925. *Physique and character.* New York: Harcourt.

Landy, F.; Rosenberg, B. G.; and Sutton-Smith, B. 1969. The effect of limited father-absence on cognitive development. *Child Development* 40: 941–944.

Lange, J. 1931. *Crime as destiny.* London: Allen & Unwin.

Laycock, F., and Caylor, J. S. 1964. Physiques of gifted children and their less gifted siblings. *Child Development* 35: 63–74.

Leahy, A. M. 1935. Nature-nurture and intelligence. *Genetic Psychology Monographs* 17: 236–308.

Learned, W. S., and Wood, B. D. 1938. *The student and his knowledge.* New York: Carnegie Foundation for the Advancement of Teaching.

Lee, E. S. 1951. Negro intelligence and selective migration: a Philadelphia test of the Klineberg hypothesis. *American Sociological Review* 16: 227–233.

Leff, M.; Roatch, J.; and Bunney, W. 1970. Environmental factors preceding the onset of severe depressions. *Psychiatry* 33: 293–311.

Leiderman, P. H.; Babu, B.; Kagia, J.; Kraemer, H. C.; and Leiderman, G. F. 1973. African infant precocity and some social influences during the first year. *Nature* 242: 247–249.

Lerner, I. M. 1968. *Heredity, evolution, and society.* San Francisco: W. H. Freeman and Company.

Lesch, M., and Nyhan, W. L. 1964. A familial disorder of uric acid metabolism and central nervous system function. *American Journal of Medicine* 36: 561.

Lesser, G. S.; Fifer, G.; and Clark, D. H. 1965. Mental abilities of children from different social-class and cultural groups. *Monographs of the Society for Research in Child Development* 30, no. 4.

Levin, S. M.; Balistrieri, J.; and Schukit, M. 1972. The development of sexual discrimination in children. *Journal of Child Psychology and Psychiatry* 13: 47–53.

Levitt, E. E. 1972. A brief commentary on the "psychiatric breakthrough" with emphasis on the hematology of anxiety. In *Anxiety: current trends in theory and research*, vol. 1, ed. C. D. Spielberger, pp. 227–234. New York: Academic Press.

Lewis, E. D. 1929. *Report on an investigation into the evidence of mental deficiency in six areas, 1925–1927.* London: H. M. Stationery Office.

Lewis, M. 1975. The development of attention and perception in the infant and young child. In *Perceptual and learning disabilities in children*, vol. 2, ed. W. M. Cruickshank and D. P. Hallahan, pp. 137–162. Syracuse: Syracuse University Press.

Lewontin, R. C., and Hubby, J. L. 1966. A molecular approach to the study of genetic heterozygosity in natural populations, II: amount of variation and degree of heterozygosity in natural populations of *Drosophila Pseudoobscura. Genetics* 54: 595–609.

Lidz, T.; Fleck, S.; and Cornelison, A. R. 1965. *Schizophrenia and the family.* New York: International Universities Press.

Liem, J. H. 1974. Effects of verbal communications of parents and children: a comparison of normal and schizophrenic families. *Journal of Consulting and Clinical Psychology* 42: 438–450.

Lilienfeld, A. M., and Parkhurst, E. A. 1951. A study of the association of factors of pregnancy and parturition with the development of cerebral palsy: preliminary report. *American Journal of Hygiene* 53: 262–282.

Lindjsö, A. 1974. Down's syndrome in Sweden: an epidemiological study of a three-year material. *Acta Paediatrica Scandinavica* 63: 571–576.

Lindzey, G. 1967a. Behavior and morphological variation. In *Genetic diversity and human behavior*, ed. J. N. Spuhler, pp. 227–240. Chicago: Aldine.

_____. 1967b. Some remarks concerning incest, the incest taboo, and psychoanalytic theory. *American Psychologist* 22: 1051–1059.

Lodge, A., and Kleinfeld, P. B. 1973. *Early behavioral development in Down's syndrome.* London: North-Holland.

Loehlin, J. C.; Lindzey, G.; and Spuhler, J. N. 1975. *Race differences in intelligence.* San Francisco: W. H. Freeman and Company.

Loehlin, J. C., and Nichols, R. C. 1976. *Heredity, environment, and personality: a study of 850 sets of twins.* Austin: University of Texas Press.

Loehlin, J. C., and Vandenberg, S. G. 1968. Genetic and environmental components in the covariation of cognitive abilities: an additive model. In *Progress in human behavior genetics*, ed. S. G. Vandenberg, pp. 261–285. Baltimore: Johns Hopkins Press.

Loehlin, J. C.; Vandenberg, S. G.; and Osborne, R. T. 1973. Blood group genes and Negro-White ability differences. *Behavior Genetics* 3: 263–270.

Lorge, I. 1936. The influence of the test upon the nature of mental decline as a function of age. *Journal of Educational Psychology* 27: 100–110.

Lowenfeld, B. 1971. Psychological problems of children with impaired vision. In *Psychology of exceptional children and youth*, 3d ed., ed. W. M. Cruickshank, pp. 211–307. Englewood Cliffs, N.J.: Prentice-Hall.

Lunneborg, P. W. 1972. Dimensionality of MF. *Journal of Clinical Psychology* 28: 313–317.

Lykken, D. T. 1957. A study of anxiety in the sociopathic personality. *Journal of Abnormal and Social Psychology* 59: 6–10.

Lynn, D. B. 1974. *The father: his role in child development.* Monterey, Calif.: Brooks/Cole.

McCall, R. B. 1977. Childhood IQ's as predictors of adult educational and occupational status. *Science* 197: 482–483.

McCall, R. B.; Hogarty, P. S.; and Hurlburt, N. 1972. Transitions in infant sensorimotor development and the prediction of childhood IQ. *American Psychologist* 27: 728–746.

MacArthur, R. S. 1967. Sex differences in field dependence for the Eskimo: replication of Berry's findings. *International Journal of Psychology* 2: 139–140.

McCarthy, D.; Anthony, R. J.; and Domino, G. 1970. A comparison of the CPI, Franck, MMPI, and WAIS Masculinity-Femininity indexes. *Journal of Consulting and Clinical Psychology* 35: 414–416.

McCauley, C.; Kellas, G.; Dugas, J.; and DeVellis, R. F. 1976. Effects of serial rehearsal training on memory search. *Journal of Educational Psychology* 68: 474–481.

McClearn, G. E. 1963. The inheritance of behavior. In *Psychology in the making*, ed. L. J. Postman, pp. 144–252. New York: Knopf.

————. 1972. Genetics as a tool in alcohol research. *Annals of the New York Academy of Sciences* 197: 26–31.

McClearn, G. E., and DeFries, J. C. 1973. *Introduction to behavioral genetics*. San Francisco: W. H. Freeman and Company.

McClelland, D. C. 1973. Testing for competence rather than for "intelligence." *American Psychologist* 28: 1–14.

Maccoby, E. E., and Jacklin, C. N. 1974. *The psychology of sex differences*. Stanford, Calif.: Stanford University Press.

McFarland, R. A. 1968. The sensory and perceptual processes in aging. In *Theory and methods of research on aging*, ed. K. W. Schaie, pp. 9–52. Morgantown: West Virginia University.

McFarland, R. A.; Domey, R. G.; Warren, A. B.; and Ward, D. C. 1960. Dark adaptation as a function of age, I: a statistical analysis. *Journal of Gerontology* 15: 149–154.

McFarland, R. A. and Fisher, M. B. 1955. Alterations in dark adaptation as a function of age. *Journal of Gerontology* 10: 424–428.

McGuire, L. S.; Ryan, K. O.; and Omenn, G. S. 1975. Congenital adrenal hyperplasia, II: cognitive and behavioral studies. *Behavior Genetics* 5: 175–188.

MacKinnon, D. W. 1975. IPAR's contribution to the conceptualization and study of creativity. In *Perspectives in creativity*, ed. I. A. Taylor and J. W. Getzels, pp. 60–89. Chicago: Aldine.

McKusick, V. A. 1969. *Human genetics*. 2d ed. Englewood Cliffs, N.J.: Prentice-Hall.

McNeill, W. H. 1963. *The rise of the west*. Chicago: University of Chicago Press.

McNemar, Q. 1942. *The revision of the Stanford-Binet Scale*. Boston: Houghton Mifflin.

————. 1964. Lost: our intelligence? Why? *American Psychologist* 19: 871–882.

Madigan, F. C. 1957. Are sex mortality differentials biologically caused? *Milbank Memorial Fund Quarterly* 35: 202–223.

Makita, K. 1968. The rarity of reading disability in Japanese children. *American Journal of Orthopsychiatry* 38: 599–614.

Malina, R. M. 1973. Biological substrate. In *Comparative studies of blacks and whites in the United States*, ed. K. S. Miller and R. M. Dreger, pp. 53–123. New York: Seminar Press.

Marjoribanks, K. 1972. Ethnic and environmental influences on mental abilities. *American Journal of Sociology* 78: 323–337.

Matarazzo, J. D. 1972. *Wechsler's measurement and appraisal of adult intelligence*. 5th ed. Baltimore: Williams & Wilkins.

Mayeske, G. W. et al. 1972. *A study of our nation's schools*. DHEW Publication No. (OE) 72-131. Washington, D.C.: U.S. Government Printing Office.

Mayr, E. 1970. *Populations, species, and evolution.* Cambridge, Mass.: Belknap Press.

Mednick, S. A., and Mednick, M. 1967. *Remote Associates Test Manual.* New York: Psychological Corporation.

Mednick, S. A., and Schulsinger, F. 1968. Some premorbid characteristics related to breakdown in children with schizophrenic mothers. In *The transmission of schizophrenia,* ed. D. Rosenthal and S. S. Kety, pp. 267–291. London: Pergamon.

_____. 1974. Studies of children at high risk for schizophrenia. In *Genetics, environment, and psychopathology,* ed. S. A. Mednick, F. Schulsinger, J. Higgins, and B. Bell, pp. 103–116. New York: Elsevier.

Meehl, P. E. 1962. Schizotaxia, schizotypy, schizophrenia. *American Psychologist* 17: 827–838.

Meier, N. C. 1939. Factors in artistic aptitude: final summary of a ten-year study of a special ability. *Psychological Monographs* 51: 140–158, 871–882.

Mendel, G. J. 1866. Versuche uber Pflanzen-Hybriden. *Verhandlungen des Naturfor schunden Vereines in Bruenn* 4: 3–47. Translation in *The origin of genetics,* ed. C. Stern and E. R. Sherwood pp. 1–48. San Francisco: W. H. Freeman and Company.

Mendels, G. E., and Flanders, J. P. 1973. Teachers' expectations and pupil performance. *American Educational Research Journal* 10: 203–212.

Mendlewicz, J., and Rainer, J. D. 1977. Adoption study supporting genetic transmission in manic-depressive illness. *Nature* 268: 327–329.

Mercer, J. R. 1971. Pluralistic diagnosis in the evaluation of Black and Chicano children: a procedure for taking sociocultural variables into account in clinical assessment. Paper presented at the meeting of the American Psychological Association, Washington, D.C.

_____. 1973. *Labelling the mentally retarded.* Berkeley: University of California Press.

Merrell, D. J. 1962. *Evolution and genetics.* New York: Holt, Rinehart & Winston.

Merton, R. K. 1961. Singletons and multiples in scientific discovery. *Proceedings of the American Philosophical Society* 105: 470–486.

Messer, S. B. 1976. Reflection-impulsivity: a review. *Psychological Bulletin* 83: 1026–1052.

Metheny, E. 1941a. Breathing capacity and grip strength of preschool children. *University of Iowa Studies in Child Welfare* 11:207.

_____. 1941b. The present status of strength testing for children of elementary and preschool age. *Research Quarterly* 12: 115–130.

Metropolitan Life. 1975. *Statistical Bulletin* 56. New York.

Meyerson, L. A. 1963. a psychology of impaired hearing. In *Psychology of exceptional children and youth,* 2d ed., ed. W. Cruickshank. Englewood Cliffs, N.J.: Prentice-Hall.

Miles, C. C. 1954. Gifted children. In *Manual of child psychology,* ed. L. Carmichael, pp. 984–1063. New York: Wiley.

Miles, W. R. 1931. Measures of certain human abilities throughout the life span. *Proceedings of the National Academy of Sciences* 17: 627–633.

Miller, G. A. 1956. The magical number seven, plus or minus two: some limits on our capacity for processing information. *Psychological Review* 63: 81–97.

Miller, L. B., and Dyer, J. L. 1975. Four preschool programs: their dimensions and effects. *Monographs of the Society for Research in Child Development* 40, nos. 5 and 6.

Millichap, J. G. 1973. Drugs in the management of minimal brain dysfunction. *Annals of the New York Academy of Sciences* 205: 321–334.

Mills, N. 1973. *The great school bus controversy.* New York: Teachers College Press.

Milton, G. A. 1957. The effects of sex role identification upon problem solving skill. *Journal of Abnormal and Social Psychology* 55: 208–212.

Mischel, W. 1968. *Personality and Assessment.* New York: Wiley.

————. 1973. Toward a cognitive social learning reconceptualization of personality. *Psychological Review* 80: 252–283.

Mittler, P. 1971. *The study of twins.* Baltimore: Penguin Books.

Money, J. 1964. Cytogenetic and psychosexual incongruities with a note on space-form blindness. *American Journal of Psychiatry* 119: 820–827.

————. Ablatio penis: normal male infant sex-reassigned as a girl. *Archives of Sexual Behavior* 4: 65–72.

Money, J., and Ehrhardt, A. A. 1972. *Man and Woman, Boy and Girl.* Baltimore: Johns Hopkins Press.

Morrison, J. R., and Stewart, M. A. 1971. A family study of the hyperactive child syndrome. *Biological Psychiatry* 3: 189–195.

————. 1973. The psychiatric status of the legal families of adopted hyperactive children. *Archives of General Psychiatry* 28: 888–891.

Mosteller, F., and Moynihan, D. P., eds. 1972. *On equality of educational opportunity.* New York: Random House.

Munsinger, H. 1975. The adopted child's IQ: a critical review. *Psychological Bulletin* 82: 623–659.

Murray, H. A. 1938. *Explorations in personality.* New York: Oxford University Press.

Mussen, P. H. 1967. Early socialization: learning and identification. In *New Directions in Psychology III*, ed. G. Mandler, P. H. Mussen, N. Kogan, and M. A. Wallach, pp. 51–110. New York: Holt, Rinehart & Winston.

Mussen, P. H., and Distler, L. 1959. Masculinity, identification, and father-son relationship. *Journal of Abnormal and Social Psychology* 59: 350–356.

Mussen, P. H., and Rutherford, E. 1963. Parent-child relations and parental personality in relation to young children's sex-role preferences. *Child Development* 34: 589–607.

Myrianthopoulos, N. C., and Chung, C. S. 1974. Congenital malformations in singletons. *The National Foundation March of Dimes.* Miami: Symposia Specialists.

Myrianthopoulos, N. C.; Nichols, P. L.; Broman, S. H.; and Anderson, V. E. 1971. Intellectual development of a prospectively studied population of twins and comparison with singletons. *Human Genetics: Proceedings of the Fourth International Congress of Human Genetics,* pp. 244–257. Amsterdam: Excerpta Medica.

Nance, W. E., and McConnell, F. E. 1973. Status and prospects of research in hereditary deafness. In *Advances in human genetics,* vol. 4, ed. H. Harris and K. Hirschorn pp. 173–250. New York: Plenum Press.

Neel, J. V. 1955. On some pitfalls in developing an adequate genetic hypothesis. *American Journal of Human Genetics* 7: 1–14.

Neel, J. V.; Fajans, S. S.; Conn, J. W.; and Davidson, R. T. 1965. Diabetes mellitus. In *Genetics and epidemiology of chronic diseases,* ed. J. V. Neel, M. W. Shaw, and W. J. Schull, pp. 105–132. Public Health Service Publication No. 1163. Washington, D.C.: U.S. Government Printing Office.

Neilon, P. 1948. Shirley's babies after fifteen years: a personality study. *Journal of Genetic Psychology* 73: 175–186.

Neisser, U. 1967. *Cognitive psychology.* New York: Appleton-Century-Crofts.

Nesselroade, J. R., and Reese, H. W., eds. 1973. *Life-span developmental psychology: methodological issues.* New York: Academic Press.

Neugarten, B. L. 1973. Personality change in later life: a developmental perspective. In *The psychology of adult aging and development,* ed. C. Eisdorfer and M. P. Lawton, pp. 311–335. Washington, D.C.: American Psychological Association.

_____. 1977. Personality and aging. In *Handbook of the psychology of aging,* ed. J. E. Birren and K. W. Schaie, pp. 626–649. New York: Van Nostrand Reinhold.

Newman, H. H.; Freeman, F. N.; and Holzinger, K. J. 1937. *Twins: a study of heredity and environment.* Chicago: Chicago University Press.

Nichols, J. R. 1972. The children of addicts: what do they inherit? *Annals, New York Academy of Sciences* 197: 60–65.

Nichols, P. L. 1970. The effects of heredity and environment on intelligence test performance in 4 and 7 year white and Negro sibling pairs. Ph.D. dissertation, University of Minnesota. (Ann Arbor, Mich.: University Microfilms, 1970, no. 71-18, 874.)

Nichols, R. C. 1965. The National Merit Twin Study. In *Methods and goals in human behavior genetics,* ed. S. G. Vandenberg, pp. 231–243. New York: Academic Press.

_____. 1977. Black children adopted by white families. *American Psychologists* 32: 678–680.

Nichols, R. C., and Bilbro, W. C. 1966. The diagnosis of twin zygosity. *Acta Genetica* 16: 265–275.

Noll, A. M. 1966. Human or machine: a subjective comparison of Piet Mondrian's Composition With Lines (1917) and a computer-generated picture. *Psychological Record* 16: 1–10.

Norman, W. T. 1963. Toward an adequate taxonomy of personality attributes: replicated factor structure in peer nomination personality ratings. *Journal of Abnormal and Social Psychology* 66: 574–583.

Norris, A. H.; Shock, N. W.; and Wagman, I. H. 1953. Age changes in the maximum conduction velocity of motor fibers of human ulnar nerves. *Journal of Applied Psychology* 5: 589–593.

Nunnally, J. C. 1959. *Tests and measurements: assessment and prediction.* New York: McGraw-Hill.

———. 1967. *Psychometric theory.* New York: McGraw-Hill.

Nyhan, W. L. 1973. Disorder of nucleic acid metabolism. In *Biology of brain dysfunction,* ed. G. E. Gaull. New York: Plenum Press.

Oakley, K. P. 1972. Skill as a human possession. In *Perspectives on human evolution,* ed. S. Washburn and P. Dolhinow, pp. 14–50. New York: Holt, Rinehart & Winston.

Ogburn, W. F., and Thomas, D. 1922. Are inventions inevitable? *Political Science Quarterly* 37: 83–98.

Oki, T. 1967. A psychological study of early childhood neuroses. In *Clinical genetics in psychiatry,* ed. H. Mitsuda, pp. 344–359. Tokyo: Igaku Shoin.

Osler, S. F., and Weiss, S. R. 1962. Studies in concept attainment, III: effects of instructions at two levels of intelligence. *Journal of Experimental Psychology* 63: 528–533.

Owen, F. W.; Adams, P. A.; Forrest, T.; Stolz, L. M.; and Fisher, S. 1971. Learning disorders in children: sibling studies. *Monographs of the Society for Research in Child Development* 36, no. 144.

Owens, W. A. 1966. Age and mental abilities: a second follow-up. *Journal of Educational Psychology* 57: 311–325.

Paige, K. E. 1969. The effects of oral contraceptives on affective fluctuations associated with the menstrual cycle. Ph.D. dissertation, University of Michigan.

Parlee, M. B. 1972. Comments on D. M. Broverman, E. L. Klaiber, Y. Kobayashi, and W. Vogel: roles of activation and inhibition in sex differences in cognitive abilities. *Psychological Review* 79: 180–184.

———. 1973. The premenstrual syndrome. *Psychological Bulletin* 80: 454–465.

Partanen, J.; Bruun, K.; and Markkanen, T. 1966. *Inheritance of drinking behavior.* Helinski: Finnish Foundation for Alcohol Studies.

Pasamanick, B.; Knobloch, H.; and Lilienfeld, A. 1956. Socioeconomic status and some precursors of neuropsychiatric disorders. *American Journal of Orthopsychiatry* 26: 594–601.

Passini, F. T., and Norman, W. T. 1966. A universal conception of personality structure? *Journal of Personality and Social Psychology* 4: 44–49.

Pastore, N. 1949. *The nature-nurture controversy.* New York: Columbia University Press.

Paykel, E.; Myers, J.; Dienelt, M.; Klerman, G.; Lindenthal, J. J.; and Pepper, M. P. 1969. Life events and depression. *Archives of General Psychiatry* 21: 753–760.

Payne, R. W. 1973. Cognitive abnormalities. In *Handbook of abnormal psychology*, ed. H. J. Eysenck, pp. 420–483. San Diego: R. R. Knapp.

Pearson, K. 1914. *The life, letters, and labours of Francis Galton.* Cambridge: Cambridge University Press.

_____. 1930–1931. On the inheritance of mental disease. *Annals of Eugenics* 4: 362–380.

Pearson, K., and Jaederholm, C. A. 1913–1914. *On the continuity of mental defect.* Vol. 2. London: Dulau & Co.

Pederson, F. A., and Robson, K. S. 1969. Father participation in infancy. *American Journal of Orthopsychiatry* 39: 466–472.

Penrose, L. S. 1939. *A clinical and genetic study of 1280 cases of mental defect.* London: H. M. Stationery Office.

_____. 1963. *The biology of mental defect.* London: Sidgwick & Jackson.

_____. 1971. In *Genetik und Gesellschaft*, ed. G. G. Wendt. Stuttgart: Wiss. Verlagsges. Quoted in *Principles of human genetics*, by C. Stern. San Francisco: W. H. Freeman and Company, 1973.

Perris, C. 1966. A study of bipolar (manic-depressive) and unipolar recurrent depressive psychoses. *Acta Psychiatrica Scandinavica Supplement* 42, no. 194.

Person, E. S., and Ovesey, L. 1974. The psychodynamics of male transsexualism. In *Sex differences in behavior*, ed. R. C. Friedman, R. M. Richart, and R. L. Vande Wiele, pp. 315–325. New York: Wiley.

Pettigrew, T. F.; Useem, E. L.; Normand, C.; and Smith, M. S. 1973. Busing: a review of the evidence. *The Public Interest* 30: 88–118.

Pitt, C. C. V. 1956. An experimental study of the effects of teachers' knowledge or incorrect knowledge of pupil IQs in teachers' attitudes and practices and pupils' attitudes and achievements. *Dissertation Abstracts* 16: 2387–2388.

Plomin, R.; DeFries, J. C.; and Loehlin, J. C. 1977. Genotype-environment interaction and correlation in the analysis of human behavior. *Psychological Bulletin* 84: 309–322.

Plomin, R., and Willerman, L. 1975. A cotwin control and a twin study of reflection-impulsivity in children. *Journal of Educational Psychology* 67: 537–543.

Poincaré, H. 1952. Mathematical creation. In *The creative process*, ed. B. Ghiselin, pp. 33–42. Berkeley: University of California Press.

Pollack, M. 1967. Mental subnormality and "childhood schizophrenia." In *Psychopathology of mental development*, ed. J. Zubin and G. A. Jervis, pp. 460–471. New York: Grune & Stratton.

Posner, M. I.; Boies, S. J.; Eichelman, W. H.; and Taylor, R. L. 1969. Retention of visual and name codes of single letters. *Journal of Experimental Psychology* (monograph) 79: 1–16.

Pressey, S. L., and Jones, A. W. 1955. 1923–1953 and 20–60 age changes in moral codes, anxieties, and interests, as shown by the "x-o Tests." *Journal of Psychology* 79: 485–502.

Prytulak, L. S. 1975. Critique of S. S. Stevens' theory of measurement scale classification. *Perceptual and Motor Skills* 41: 3–28.

Pyles, M. K. 1932. Verbalization as a factor in learning. *Child Development* 3: 108–113.

Quay, L. C. 1971. Language dialect, reinforcement, and the intelligence-test performance of Negro children. *Child Development* 42: 5–15.

Rahe, R. H.; Floistad, I.; Bergan, T.; Ringdal, R.; Gerhardt, R.; Gunderson, E. K. E.; and Arthur, R. J. 1974. A model for life changes and illness research. *Archives of General Psychiatry* 31: 172–177.

Record, R. G.; McKeown, T.; and Edwards, J. H. 1970. An investigation of the difference in measured intelligence between twins and single births. *Annals of Human Genetics* 34: 11–20.

Reed, E. W., and Reed, S. C. 1965. *Mental retardation: a family study.* Philadelphia: W. B. Saunders.

Reed, T. E. 1969. Caucasian genes in American Negroes. *Science* 165: 762–768.

Rees, L. 1950. Body build, personality and neurosis in women. *Journal of Mental Science* 96: 426–434.

————. 1973. Constitutional factors and abnormal behavior. In *Handbook of abnormal psychology*, 2d ed., ed. H. J. Eysenck, pp. 487–539. San Diego: R. R. Knapp.

Rees, L., and Eysenck, H. J. 1945. A factorial study of some morphological and psychological aspects of human constitution. *Journal of Mental Science* 91: 8.

Reichard, S.; Livson, F.; and Peterson, P. G. 1962. *Aging and personality.* New York: Wiley.

Reitan, R. M. 1955. An investigation of the validity of Halstead's measures of biological intelligence. *Archives of Neurology and Psychiatry* 73: 28–35.

————. 1959. The effects of brain lesions on adaptive abilities in human beings. Mimeographed. Indianapolis: University of Indiana Medical School.

Reznikoff, M.; Domino, G.; Bridges, C.; and Honeyman, M. 1973. Creative abilities in identical and fraternal twins. *Behavior Genetics* 4: 365–377.

Riegel, K. F., and Riegel, R. M. 1972. Development, drop, and death. *Developmental Psychology* 6: 306–319.

Roberts, J. A. F. 1952. The genetics of mental deficiency. *Eugenics Review* 44: 71–83.

Robins, L. N. 1966. *Deviant children grown up.* Baltimore: Williams & Wilkins.

Robinson, N. M., and Robinson, H. B. (with the collaboration of Omenn, G. S., and Campione, J. C.). 1976. *The mentally retarded child.* 2d ed. New York: McGraw-Hill.

Rockstein, M., ed. 1974. *Theoretical aspects of aging.* New York: Academic Press.

Roe, A. 1945. Children of alcoholic parentage raised in foster homes. In *Alcohol, science, and society*, published by Quarterly Journal of Studies of Alcohol, pp. 115–127.

————. 1953. A psychological study of eminent psychologists and anthropologists, and a comparison with biological and physical scientists. *Psychological Monographs* 67: 1–55.

Rosenberg, C. M. 1967. Familial aspects of obsessional neuroses. *British Journal of Psychiatry* 113: 405–413.

Rosenblith, W. A., and Stevens, K. N. 1953. *Handbook of acoustic noise control.* Noise and Man, vol. 2. WADC Technical Report 52-204. Cambridge, Mass.: Bolt, Beranek, & Newman.

Rosenthal, D. 1961. Sex distribution and the severity of illness among samples of schizophrenic twins. *Journal of Psychiatric Research* 1: 26–36.

_____. 1970. *Genetic theory and abnormal behavior.* New York: McGraw-Hill.

_____. 1974. The concept of subschizophrenic disorders. In *Genetics, environment, and psychopathology,* ed. S. A. Mednick, F. Schulsinger, J. Higgins, and B. Bell, pp. 167–176. New York: Elsevier.

Rosenthal, D.; Wender, P. H.; Kety, S. S.; Schulsinger, F.; Welner, J.; and Ostergaard, L. 1968. Schizophrenics' offspring reared in adoptive homes. In *The transmission of schizophrenia,* ed. D. Rosenthal and S. S. Kety, pp. 377–391. London: Pergamon.

Rosenthal, D.; Wender, P. H.; Kety, S. S.; Welner, J.; and Schulsinger, F. 1971. The adopted-away offspring of schizophrenics. *American Journal of Psychiatry* 128: 307–311.

Rosenthal, R., and Jacobson, L. 1966. Teachers' expectancies: determinants of pupils' I.Q. gains. *Psychological Reports* 19: 115–118.

_____. 1968. *Pygmalion in the classroom.* New York: Holt, Rinehart & Winston.

Rossi, A. O. 1972. Genetics of learning disabilities. *Journal of Learning Disabilities* 5: 489–496.

Rozin, P.; Poritsky, S.; and Sotsky, R. 1971. American children with reading problems can easily learn to read English represented by Chinese characters. *Science* 171: 1264–1266.

Safer, D. J. 1973. A familial factor in minimal brain dysfunction. *Behavior Genetics* 3: 175–185.

St. John. N. H. 1975. *School desegregation outcomes for children.* New York: Wiley.

Sakai, T. 1967. Clinico-genetic study on obsessive-compulsive neurosis. In *Clinical genetics in psychiatry,* ed. H. Mitsuda, pp. 332–343. Tokyo: Igaku Shoin.

Salzinger, K. 1973. *Schizophrenia: behavioral aspects.* New York: Wiley.

Samelson, F. 1975. On the science and politics of the IQ. *Social Research* 42: 467–488.

Sarason, I. G. 1972. *Abnormal psychology.* New York: Appleton-Century-Crofts.

Scarr, S. 1966. Genetic factors in activity and motivation. *Child Development* 37: 663–673.

_____. Environmental bias in twin studies. In S. G. Vandenberg (Ed.) *Progress in human behavior genetics.* Baltimore: Johns Hopkins Press, 1968.

Scarr, S., and Barker, W. In preparation. The effects of family background: a study of cognitive differences among black and white twins.

Scarr, S., and Weinberg, R. A. 1976. IQ test performance of black children adopted by white families. *American Psychologist* 31: 726–739.

———. 1979. Intellectual similarities in adoptive and biologically-related families of adolescents. In *Readings about individual and group differences*, ed. L. Willerman and R. G. Turner. San Francisco: W. H. Freeman and Company.

Scarr-Salapatek. 1971. Race, social class, and IQ. *Science* 174: 1285–1295.

Schachter, S., and Latané, B. 1964. Crime, cognition, and the autonomic nervous system. *Nebraska Symposium on Motivation* 12: 221–275.

Schachter, S., and Singer, J. E. 1962. Cognitive, social, and physiological determinants of emotional state. *Psychological Review* 69: 379–399.

Schaefer, E. S. 1965. Does the sampling method produce the negative correlation of mean IQ with age reported by Kennedy, Van De Riet, and White? *Child Development* 36: 257–259.

Schaffer, H. R., and Emerson, P. E. 1964. Patterns of response to physical contact in early human development. *Journal of Child Psychology and Psychiatry* 5: 1–13.

Schaie, K. W. 1965. A general model for the study of developmental problems. *Psychological Bulletin* 64: 92–107.

Schaie, K. W., and Labouvie-Vief, G. 1974. Generational versus ontogenetic conpoments of change in adult cognitive behavior: a fourteen-year cross-sequential study. *Developmental Psychology* 10: 305–320.

Schaie, K. W.; Labouvie, G.; and Buech, B. U. 1973. Generational and cohort-specific differences in adult cognitive functioning: a fourteen-year study of independent samples. *Developmental Psychology* 9: 151–166.

Schaie, K. W., and Parnham, I. A. 1976. Stability of adult personality traits: fact or fable? *Journal of Personality and Social Psychology* 34: 146–158.

Schaie, K. W., and Strother, C. R. 1968. A cross-sequential study of age changes in cognitive behavior. *Psychological Bulletin* 70: 671–680.

Schaffer, H. R., and Emerson, P. E. 1964. Patterns of response to physical contact in early human development. *Journal of Child Psychology and Psychiatry* 5: 1–13.

Schapiro, S. 1968. Some physiological, biochemical, and behavioral consequences of neonatal hormone administration: cortisol and thyroxine. *General Comparative Endocrinology* 10: 214–228.

Scheerer, M.; Rothmann, E.; and Goldstein, K. 1945. A case of "Idiot Savant": an experimental study of personality organization. *Psychological Monographs* 58, no. 4.

Scheinfeld, A. 1939. *You and heredity*. Philadelphia: Lippincott.

Scheinfeld, A. 1965. *Your heredity and environment*. Philadelphia: Lippincott.

Schlesinger, I. M., and Guttman, L. 1969. Smallest space analysis of intelligence and achievement tests. *Psychological Bulletin* 71: 95–100.

Schonfield, D., and Robertson, B. 1966. Memory storage and aging. *Canadian Journal of Psychology* 20: 228–236.

Schonfield, D.; Trueman, V.; and Kline, D. 1972. Recognition tests of dichotic listening and the age variable. *Journal of Gerontology* 27: 487–493.

Schooler, C. 1972. Birth order effects: not here, not now! *Psychological Bulletin* 78: 161–175.

Schrank, W. R. 1968. The labeling effect of ability grouping. *The Journal of Educational Research* 62: 51–52.

_____. 1970. A further study of the labeling effect of ability grouping. *The Journal of Educational Research* 63: 358–360.

Schukit, M.; Goodwin, D. W.; and Winokur, G. 1972. A study of alcoholism in half-siblings. *American Journal of Psychiatry* 128: 1132–1136.

Schull, W. J., and Neel, J. V. 1965. *The effects of inbreeding on Japanese children.* New York: Harper & Row.

Schulsinger, F. 1972. Psychopathy: heredity and environment. *International Journal of Mental Health* 1: 190–206.

Searle, L. V. 1949. The organization of hereditary maze-brightness and maze-dullness. *Genetic Psychology Monographs* 39: 279–325.

Seashore, C. E. 1938. *Psychology of music.* New York: McGraw-Hill.

Seligman, M. E. P. 1975. *Helplessness: on depression, development, and death.* San Francisco: W. H. Freeman and Company.

Selye, H. 1956. *The stress of life.* New York: McGraw-Hill.

Senden, M. von. 1960. *Space and sight.* Glencoe, Ill.: The Free Press.

Sewell, W. H.; Hauser, R M.; and Featherman, D. L., eds. 1976. *Schooling and achievement in American society.* New York: Academic Press.

Shakow, D.; Dolkart, M. B.; and Goldman, R. 1941. The memory function in psychoses of the aged. *Diseases of the Nervous System* 2: 43–48.

Shaw, M. E. 1973. Changes in sociometric choices following forced integration of an elementary school. *Journal of Social Issues* 29: 143–157.

Sheldon, W. H. (with the collaboration of S. S. Stevens and W. B. Tucker) 1940. *The varieties of human physique: an introduction to constitutional psychology.* New York: Harper & Row.

Sherman, M., and Key, C. B. 1932. The intelligence of isolated mountain children. *Child Development* 3: 279–290.

Shields, J. 1962. *Monozygotic twins brought up apart and brought up together.* London: Oxford University Press.

_____. 1973. Heredity and psychological abnormality. In *Handbook of abnormal psychology,* ed. H. J. Eysenck, pp. 540–603. San Diego: R. R. Knapp.

Shields, J., and Gottesman, I. I. 1972. Cross-national diagnosis of schizophrenia in twins. *Archives of General Psychiatry* 27: 725–730.

Shirley, M. M. 1933. *Intellectual development.* The first two years: a study of twenty-five babies, vol. II. Minneapolis: University of Minnesota Press.

Shuey, A. M. 1966. *The testing of Negro intelligence.* 2d ed. New York: Social Science Press.

Shurrager, H. C., and Shurrager, P. S. 1964. *Haptic Intelligence Scale for Adult Blind.* Chicago: Psychology Research.

Shuter, R. 1968. *The psychology of musical ability.* London: Methuen.

Siceloff, M., and McAdory, M. 1933. *Validation and standardization of the McAdory Art Test.* New York: Teachers College Bureau of Publications.

Siegal, S. 1956. *Nonparametric statistics.* New York: McGraw-Hill.

Silvers, W. K., and Wachtel, S. S. 1977. H-Y antigen: behavior and function. *Science* 195: 956–960.

Simon, H. A. 1974. How big is a chunk? *Science* 183: 482–488.

Simonton, D. K. 1976. Biographical determinants of achieved eminence: a multivariate approach to the Cox data. *Journal of Personality and Social Psychology* 33: 218–226.

Sing, C. G.; Shreffler, D. C.; Neel, J. V.; and Napier, J. A. 1971. Studies on genetic selection in a completely ascertained population II. Family analyses of 11 blood groups systems. *The American Journal of Human Genetics* 23: 196–198.

Sitkei, E. G., and Meyers, C. E. 1969. Comparative structure of intellect in middle- and lower-class four-year olds of two ethnic groups. *Developmental Psychology* 1: 592–604.

Skager, R. W.; Schultz, C. B.; and Klein, S. P. 1966. The multidimensional scaling of a set of artistic drawings: perceived structure and scale correlates. *Multivariate Behavioral Research* 1: 425–436.

Skeels, H. M. 1966. Adult status of children with contrasting early life experiences. *Child Development Monographs* 31, no. 3.

Skeels, H. M., and Dye, H. B. 1939. A study of the effects of differential stimulation on mentally retarded children. *Proceedings of the American Association of Mental Deficiency* 44: 114–136.

Skodak, M., and Skeels, H. M. 1949. A final follow-up study of 100 adopted children. *Journal of Genetic Psychology* 75: 85–125.

Slater, E., and Cowie, V. 1971. *The genetics of mental disorders.* London: Oxford University Press.

Slater, E., and Shields, J. 1969. Genetical aspects of anxiety. In *Studies of anxiety*, ed. M. H. Lader, pp. 62–71. *British Journal of Psychiatry*, Special Publication No. 3. Ashford, Kent: Headley.

Smilansky, B. 1974. Paper presented at the meeting of the American Educational Research Association, Chicago.

Smith, M. E. 1963. Delayed recall of previously memorized material after fifty years. *Journal of Genetic Psychology* 102: 3–4.

Smith, M. S. 1972. Equality of educational opportunity: the basic findings reconsidered. In *On equality of educational opportunity*, ed. F. Mosteller and D. P. Moynihan, pp. 230–342. New York: Random House.

Snow, R. E. 1969. Unfinished Pygmalion. *Contemporary Psychology* 14: 197–199.

Snyder, S. H. 1974. *Madness and the brain.* New York: McGraw-Hill.

Solomon, R. L., and Wynne, L. C. 1954. Traumatic avoidance learning: the principles of anxiety conservation and partial irreversibility. *Psychological Review* 61: 353–385.

Spearman, C. 1927. *The abilities of man.* New York: Macmillan.

Spence, J. T.; Helmreich, R.; and Stapp, J. 1975. Ratings of self and peers on sex role attributes and their relation to self-esteem and conceptions of masculinity and femininity. *Journal of Personality and Social Psychology* 32: 29–39.

Spitz, H. H. 1973. The channel capacity of educable mental retardates. In *The experimental psychology of mental retardation,* ed. D. K. Routh, pp. 133–156. Chicago: Aldine.

Spuhler, J. N. 1968. Assortative mating with respect to physical characteristics. *Eugenics Quarterly* 15: 128–140.

Spuhler, J. N., and Lindzey, G. 1967. Racial differences in behavior. In *Behavior-genetic analysis,* ed. J. Hirsch, pp. 366–414. New York: McGraw-Hill.

Stafford, R. E. 1970. Estimation of the interaction between heredity and environment for musical aptitude of twins. *Human Heredity* 20: 356–360.

Stanley, J. C. 1971. Predicting college success of the educationally disadvantaged. *Science* 171: 640–647.

_____, ed. 1972. *Preschool programs for the disadvantaged.* Baltimore: Johns Hopkins University Press.

_____, ed. 1973. *Compensatory education for children ages 2 to 8.* Baltimore: Johns Hopkins University Press.

Stanley, J. C.; Keating, D. P.; and Fox, L. H. 1974. *Mathematical talent: discovery, description, and development.* Baltimore: Johns Hopkins University Press.

Stanton, H. 1935. Measurement of musical talent: the Eastman experiment. *University of Iowa Studies in the Psychology of Music* 2: 1–140.

Stein, Z.; Susser, M.; Saenger, G.; and Marolla, F. 1972. Nutrition and mental performance. *Science* 178: 708–713.

Steiner, J. 1972. A questionnaire study of risk-taking in psychiatric patients. *British Journal of Medical Psychology* 45: 365–374.

Stent, G. S. 1973. Prematurity and uniqueness in scientific discovery. *Scientific American* 228: 84–93.

_____. 1975. Limits to the scientific understanding of man. *Science* 187: 1052–1057.

Stern, C. 1973. *Principles of human genetics.* 3d ed. San Francisco: W. H. Freeman and Company.

Sternberg, R. J. 1977. Component processes in analogical reasoning. *Psychological Review* 84: 353–378.

Sternberg, S. 1966. High-speed scanning in human memory. *Science* 153: 652–654.

Stevens, S. S., ed. 1951. *Handbook of experimental psychology.* New York: Wiley.

Stewart, M. 1970. Hyperactive children. *Scientific American* 222: 94–98.

Stodolsky, S. S., and Lesser, G. S. 1967. Learning patterns in the disadvantaged. *Harvard Educational Review* 37: 546–593.

Storrs, E. E., and Williams, R. J. 1968. A study of monozygous quadruplet armadillos in relation to mammalian inheritance. *Proceedings of the National Academy of Sciences* 60: 910–914.

Strayer, L. C. 1930. The relative efficacy of early and deferred vocabulary training studied by the method of cotwin control. *Genetic Psychology Monographs* 8: 209–319.

Strong, E. K., Jr. 1943. *Vocational interests of men and women.* Stanford, Calif.: Stanford University Press.

———. 1951. Permanence of interest scores over 22 years. *Journal of Applied Psychology* 35: 89–91.

———. 1955. *Vocational interests 18 years after college.* Minneapolis: University of Minnesota Press.

Styczynski, L. 1975. Effects of facial attractiveness on the social, emotional, and intellectual development of early school age children. Dissertation prospectus, University of Texas at Austin.

Suppes, P. 1964. Modern learning theory and the elementary-school curriculum. *American Educational Research Journal* 1: 79–93.

Suppes, P., and Morningstar, M. 1969. Computer-assisted instruction. *Science* 166: 343–350.

Swenson, W. M.; Pearson, J. S.; and Osborne, D. 1973. *An MMPI source book: basic item, scale, and pattern data on 50,000 medical patients.* Minneapolis: University of Minnesota Press.

Tanner, J. M. 1970. Physical growth. In *Charmichael's Manual of Child Psychology,* ed. P. H. Mussen, pp. 77–155. New York: Wiley.

Taylor, H. C., and Russell, J. T. 1939. The relationship of validity coefficients to the practical effectiveness of tests in selection. *Journal of Applied Psychology* 23: 565–578.

Terman, L. M. 1917. The intelligence quotient of Francis Galton in childhood. *The American Journal of Psychology* 28: 208–215.

———. 1925. *Mental and physical traits of a thousand gifted children.* Genetic Studies of genius, vol. I. Stanford, Calif.: Stanford University Press.

Terman, L. M., and Merrill, M. A. 1937. *Measuring intelligence.* Boston: Houghton Mifflin.

Terman, L. M., and Miles, C. C. 1936. *Sex and personality: studies in masculinity and femininity.* New York: McGraw-Hill.

Terman, L. M., and Oden, M. 1947. *The gifted child grows up.* Genetic studies of genius, vol. III. Stanford, Calif.: Stanford University Press.

———. 1959. *The gifted group at mid-life.* Genetic studies of genius, vol. V. Stanford, Calif.: Stanford University Press.

Terman, L. M., and Tyler, L. E. 1954. Psychological sex differences. In *Manual of child psychology,* 2d ed., ed. L. Carmichael, pp. 1064–1114. New York: Wiley.

Thiessen, D. D. In press. Hormones and mammalian behavior. In *Personalized Psychology,* ed. W. H. Holtzman. New York: Harper & Row.

Thomas, A.; Chess, S.; and Birch, H. G. 1970. The origin of personality. *Scientific American* 223: 102–109.

Thompson, G. G., and Witryol, S. L. 1946. The relationship between intelligence and motor learning ability, as measured by a high relief finger maze. *Journal of Psychology* 22: 237–246.

Thompson, W. R., and Grusec, J. 1970. Studies of early experience. In *Charmichael's Manual of child psychology*, ed. P. H. Mussen, pp. 565–654. New York: Wiley.

Thomson, G. H. 1948. *The factorial analysis of human ability*. Boston: Houghton Mifflin.

Thorndike, E. L., et al. 1921. Intelligence and its measurement: a symposium. *Journal of Educational Psychology* 12: 123–147.

Thorndike, E. L.; Bregman, E. O.; Cobb, M. V.; and Woodyard, E. 1926. *The measurement of intelligence*. New York: Teachers College, Columbia University.

Thorndike, R. L. 1968. Review: Pygmalion in the classroom. *American Educational Research Journal* 5: 708–711.

Thorndike, R. L., and Hagen, E. *Ten thousand careers*. New York: Wiley.

Thurstone, L. L. 1926. The mental age concept. *Psychological Review* 33: 268–278.

_____. 1938. Primary mental abilities. *Psychometrika Monographs*, no. 1.

Tillman, M. H. 1967. The performance of blind and sighted children on the Wechsler Intelligence Scale for Children. *International Journal for the Education of the Blind* 16: 65–74.

Tilton, J. W. 1949. Intelligence test scores as indicative of ability to learn. *Educational and Psychological Measurement* 9: 291–296.

Tizard, B. 1974. IQ and race. *Nature* 247: 316.

Tizard, B., and Rees, J. 1974. A comparison of the effects of adoption, restoration to the natural mother, and continued institutionalization on the cognitive development of four-year-old children. *Child Development* 45: 92–99.

Toman, W. 1970. The duplication theorem of social relationships as tested in the general population. *Psychological Review* 78: 380–390.

Torrance, P. 1962. *Guiding creative talent*. Englewood Cliffs, N.J.: Prentice-Hall.

Trasler, G. 1973. Criminal behavior. In *Handbook of abnormal psychology*, ed. H. J. Eysenck, pp. 67–96. San Diego: R. R. Knapp.

Trivers, R. L. 1972. Parental investment and sexual selection. In *Sexual selection and the descent of man, 1871–1971*, ed. B. Campbell, pp. 136–179. Chicago: Aldine.

Trotman, F. K. 1977. Race, IQ, and the middle class. *Journal of Educational Psychology* 69: 266–273.

Tuddenham, R. D. 1959. The consistency of personality ratings over two decades. *Genetic Psychology Monographs* 60: 3–29.

_____. 1970. A "Piagetian" test of cognitive development. In *On intelligence*, ed. W. B. Dockrell, pp. 49–70. London: Methuen.

Tuddenham, R. D.; Blumenkrantz, J.; and Wilkin, W. R. 1968. Age changes on AGCT: a longitudinal study of average adults. *Journal of Clinical and Consulting Psychology* 32: 659–663.

Tuddenham, R. D., and Snyder, M. M. 1954. Physical growth of California boys and girls from birth to eighteen years. *University of California Publications in Child Development* 2: 183–364.

Turner, R. G. 1978. Consistency, self-consciousness, and the predictive validity of typical and maximal personality measures. *Journal of Research in Personality* 12: 117–132.

Turner, R. G., and Willerman, L. 1977. Sex differences in WAIS item performance. *Journal of Clinical Psychology* 33: 795–797.

Turner, R. G.; Willerman, L.; and Horn, J. M. 1976. Personality correlates of WAIS performance. *Journal of Clinical Psychology* 32: 349–354.

Tyler, L. E. 1965. *The psychology of human differences.* 3d ed. New York: Appleton-Century-Crofts.

Ullmann, L., and Krasner, L. 1969. *A psychological approach to abnormal behavior.* Englewood Cliffs, N.J.: Prentice-Hall.

Vale, J. R., and Vale, C. A. 1969. Individual differences and general laws in psychology. *American Psychologist* 24: 1093–1108.

Vandenberg, S. G. 1962. The hereditary abilities study: hereditary components in a psychological test battery. *American Journal of Human Genetics* 14: 220–237.

―――. 1965. Innate abilities, one or many? A new method and some results. *Acta Geneticae Medicae et Gemellologiae* 14: 41–47.

―――. 1967. Hereditary factors in normal personality traits (as measured by inventories). In *Recent advances in biological psychiatry,* vol. 9, ed. J. Wortis, pp. 65–104. New York: Plenum Press.

―――. 1968a. The nature and nurture of intelligence. In *Genetics,* ed. D. C. Glass, pp. 3–57. New York: Rockefeller University Press and The Russell Sage Foundation.

―――, ed. 1968b. *Progress in human behavior genetics.* Baltimore: Johns Hopkins University Press.

―――. 1969. A twin study of spatial ability. *Multivariate Behavioral Research* 4: 273–294.

―――. 1972. Assortative mating, or who marries whom? *Behavior Genetics* 2: 127–157.

Vernon, P. E. 1950. *The structure of human abilities.* New York: Wiley.

―――. 1972. The distinctiveness of field independence. *Journal of Personality* 40: 366–391.

Visher, S. S. 1947. *Scientists starred, 1903–1943, in American men of science.* Baltimore: Johns Hopkins Press.

Wachtel, P. 1973. Psychodynamics, behavior therapy, and the implacable experimenter: an inquiry into the consistency of personality. *Journal of Abnormal Psychology* 82: 324–334.

Walker, R. N. 1962. Body build and behavior in young children: body build and nursery school teacher's rating. *Child Development Monographs* 27, no. 84.

Wallace, J. 1966. An abilities conception of personality: some implications for personality measurement. *American Psychologist* 21: 132–138.

Wallach, M. A., and Wing, C. W., Jr. 1969. *The talented student.* New York: Holt, Rinehart & Winston.

Waller, J. H. 1971. Achievement and social mobility: relationships among IQ score, education and occupation in two generations. *Social Biology* 18: 252–259.

Walsh, D. A. 1976. Age differences in central perceptual processing: A dichoptic backward masking investigation. *Journal of Gerontology* 31: 178–185.

Wang, H. S. 1973. Cerebral correlates of intellectual function in senescence. In, *Intellectual functioning in adults*, ed. L. F. Jarvik, C. Eisdorfer, and J. E. Blum, pp. 95–106. New York: Springer.

Warren, N. 1972. African infant precocity. *Psychological Bulletin* 78: 353–367.

Watson, J. B. 1930. *Behaviorism*. New York: Norton.

Wechsler, D. 1939. *The measurement of adult intelligence*. Baltimore: Williams & Wilkins.

———. 1952. *Range of human capacities*. 2d ed. Baltimore: Williams & Wilkins.

———. 1958. *The measurement and appraisal of adult intelligence*. 4th ed. Baltimore: Williams & Wilkins.

———. 1975. Intelligence defined and undefined. *American Psychologist* 30: 135–139.

Weikart, D. P. 1972. Relationship of curriculum, teaching, and learning in preschool education. In *Preschool programs for the disadvantaged*, ed. J. C. Stanley, pp. 22–66. Baltimore: Johns Hopkins University Press.

Welford, A. T. 1958. *Aging and human skill*. London: Oxford University Press.

———. 1965. Performance, biological mechanisms and age: a theoretical sketch. In *Behavior, aging, and the nervous system*, ed. A. T. Welford and J. E. Birren, pp. 3–20. Springfield, Ill.: Charles C Thomas.

Wender, P. H. 1971. *Minimal brain dysfunction in children*. New York: Wiley.

Wender, P. H.; Rosenthal, D.; and Kety, S. S. 1968. A psychiatric assessment of the adoptive parents of schizophrenics. In *The transmission of schizophrenia*, ed. D. Rosenthal and S. S. Kety, pp. 235–250. London: Pergamon.

Wender, P. H.; Rosenthal, D.; Rainer, J. D.; Greenhill, L.; and Sarlin, M. B. 1977. Schizophrenics adopting parents. *Archives of General Psychiatry* 34: 777–784.

Wendt, H. 1972. *From ape to Adam*. Indianapolis: Bobbs-Merrill.

Werner, E.; Simonian, K.; Bierman, J. M.; and French, F. E. 1967. Cumulative effect of perinatal complications and deprived environment on physical, intellectual, and social development of preschool children. *Pediatrics* 39: 480–505.

Weyl, N. 1969. Some comparative performance indexes of American ethnic minorities. *The Mankind Quarterly* IX: 106–119.

Wiggins, J. S. 1973. *Personality and prediction*. Reading, Mass.: Addison-Wesley.

Wilkie, F. L., and Eisdorfer, C. 1973. Systemic disease and behavioral correlates. In *Intellectual functioning in adults*, ed. L. F. Jarvik, C. Eisdorfer, and J. C. Blum, pp. 83–93. New York: Springer.

Willerman, L. 1972. Biosocial influences on human development. *American Journal of Orthopsychiatry* 42: 452–462.

————. 1973. Activity level and hyperactivity in twins. *Child Development* 44: 288–293.

Willerman, L.; Broman, S. H.; and Fiedler, M. F. 1970. Infant development, preschool IQ, and social class. *Child Development* 41: 69–77.

Willerman, L., and Fiedler, M. F. 1974. Infant performance and intellectual precocity. *Child Development* 45: 483–486.

————. 1977. Intellectually precocious preschool children: early development and later intellectual accomplishments. *Journal of Genetic Psychology* 131: 13–20.

Willerman, L.; Horn, J. M.; and Loehlin, J. C. 1977. The aptitude-achievement test distinction: a study of unrelated children reared together. *Behavior Genetics* 7: 465–470.

Willerman, L.; Naylor, A. F.; and Myrianthopoulos, N. C. 1970. Intellectual development of children from interracial matings. *Science* 170: 1329–1331.

————. 1974. Intellectual development of children from interracial matings: performance in infancy and at four years. *Behavior Genetics* 4: 83–90.

Willerman, L.; Turner, R. G.; and Peterson, M. 1976. A comparison of the predictive validity of typical and maximal personality measures. *Journal of Research in Personality* 10: 482–492.

Wilson, E. O. 1975. *Sociobiology.* Cambridge, Mass.: Belknap Press.

Wilson, R. S. 1973. Technical comment. *Science* 182: 734–736.

Wilson, R. S.; Brown, A.; and Matheny, A. 1971. Emergence and persistence of behavioral differences in twins. *Child Development* 42: 1381–1398.

Winick, M.; Meyer, K. K.; and Harris, R. C. 1975. Malnutrition and environmental enrichment by early adoption. *Science* 190: 1173–1175.

Wissler, C. 1901. The correlation of mental and physical tests. *Psychological Review Monograph Supplement* 3, no. 16.

Witkin, H. A., and Berry, J. W. In press. Psychological differentiation in cross-cultural perspective. *Journal of Cross-Cultural Psychology.*

Witkin, H. A.; Birnbaum, J.; Lomonaco, S.; Lehr, S.; and Herman, J. L. 1968. Cognitive patterning in congenitally totally blind children. *Child Development* 39: 767–786.

Witkin, H. A.; Dyk, R. B.; Faterson, H. F.; Goodenough, D. R.; and Karp, S. A. 1962. *Psychological differentiation.* New York: Wiley.

Witkin, H. A., and Goodenough, D. R. 1977. Field dependence and interpersonal behavior. *Psychological Bulletin* 84: 661–689.

Witkin, H. A.; Goodenough, D. R.; and Karp, S. A. 1967. Stability of cognitive style from childhood to young adulthood. *Journal of Personality and Social Psychology* 7: 291–300.

Witkin, H. A.; Lewis, H. B.; Hertzman, M.; Machover, K.; Meissner, P. B.; and Wapner, S. 1954. *Personality through perception.* New York: Harper & Row.

Witkin, H. A.; Mednick, S. A.; et al. 1976. Criminality in XYY and XXY men. *Science* 193: 547–555.

Wolf, T. H. 1973. *Alfred Binet.* Chicago: University of Chicago Press.

Wolff, P. H. 1972. Ethnic differences in alcohol sensitivity. *Science* 175: 449–450.

———. 1973. Vasomotor sensitivity to alcohol in diverse Mongoloid populations. *American Journal of Human Genetics* 25: 193–199.

Wolfgang, M. E. 1958. *Patterns in criminal homicide*. Philadelphia: University of Pennsylvania Press.

Woodrow, H. 1946. The ability to learn. *Psychological Review* 53: 147–158.

Woodruff, D. S., and Birren, J. E. 1972. Age changes and cohort differences in personality. *Developmental Psychology* 6: 252–259.

Woolf, C. M., and Dukepoo, F. C. 1969. Hopi Indians, inbreeding and albinism. *Science* 164: 30–37.

Yalom, I. D.; Green, R.; and Fisk, N. 1973. Prenatal exposure to female hormones. *Archives of General Psychiatry* 28: 554–561.

Yarrow, M. R.; Campbell, J. D.; and Burton, R. V. 1970. Recollections of childhood: a study of the retrospective method. *Monographs of the Society for Research in Child Development* 35, no. 138.

Yerby, A. S. 1966. The disadvantaged and health care. *American Journal of Public Health* 56: 5–9.

Yerkes, R. M., ed. 1926. Psychological examining in the United States Army. *Memoirs of the National Academy of Sciences*, no. 15. Washington, D.C.: U.S. Government Printing Office.

Young, W. C.; Goy, R. W.; and Phoenix, C. H. 1965. Hormones and sexual behavior. In *Sex research: new developments*, ed. J. Money, pp. 176–196. New York: Holt, Rinehart & Winston.

Zajonc, R. B. 1976. Family configuration and intelligence. *Science* 192: 227–236.

Zajonc, R. B., and Markus, G. B. 1975. Birth order and intellectual development. *Psychological Review* 82: 74–88.

Zeaman, D. 1973. One programmatic approach to retardation. In *The experimental psychology of mental retardation*, ed. D. K. Routh, pp. 78–132. Chicago: Aldine.

Zeaman, D., and House, B. J. 1963. The role of attention in retardate discrimination learning. In *Handbook of mental deficiency*, ed. N. R. Ellis, pp. 155–223. New York: McGraw-Hill.

———. 1967. The relation of IQ and learning. In *Learning and individual differences*, ed. R. M. Gagne, pp. 192–212. Columbus, Ohio: Charles E. Merrill.

Zelniker, T., and Jeffrey, W. E. 1976. Reflective and impulsive children: strategies of information processing underlying differences in problem solving. *Monographs of the Society for Research in Child Development* 41, no. 5.

Zerbin-Rudin, E. 1967. Endogene Psychosen. In *Humangenetik: Ein kurzes Handbuch in funf Banden*, vol. 2, ed. P. E. Becker, pp. 446–577. Stuttgart: Georg Thieme Verlag. Cited by Rosenthal, D. *Genetic theory and abnormal behavior*. New York: McGraw-Hill, 1970.

Zigler, E. 1967. Familial mental retardation: a continuing dilemma. *Science* 155: 292–298.

_____. 1973. The retarded child as a whole person. In *The experimental psychology of mental retardation*, ed. D. K. Routh, pp. 231–322. Chicago: Aldine.

Zigler, E., and Butterfield, E. C. 1968. Motivational aspects of changes in IQ test performance of culturally deprived nursery school children. *Child Development* 39: 1–14.

Zubin, J. 1967. Classification of the behavior disorders. *Annual Review of Psychology* 18: 373–406. Palo Alto, Calif.: Annual Reviews.

Name Index

Subject Index